SERVANTS OF CORRUPTION

A REFERENCE OF FALSE TEACHERS, PREACHERS AND OTHER WOLVES IN SHEEP'S CLOTHING

"Servants of Corruption"
© 2020 M. Lea Saris

August, 2020

ISBN: 978-1-7351454-2-6

Published by:
The Old Paths Publications. Inc.
Cleveland, Ga 30528
www.theoldpathspublications.com
TOP@theoldpathspublications.com

Publisher's note: We have not reviewed this work in
detail or checked all the references, but we
presume the author's research is correct.

"Servants of Corruption"

This reference book is dedicated to our Lord and Saviour Jesus Christ, who without His sacrifice on the Cross of Calvary, I would not be a Christian.

I am also dedicating this book to my husband, with whom I would not have found our Lord many years ago.

"Servants of Corruption" is taken from II Peter 2:19:

"While they promise them liberty, they themselves are the servants of corruption: for of whom a man is overcome, of the same is he brought in bondage."

Unless otherwise indicated, Scripture quotations in this book are from the King James Version of the Bible. This author and editor cannot change other authors' Biblical versions, since they are directly from those authors' work product, hence they remain as found.

All websites and author's work product have been read by this editor, to ensure that the information is correct. Credit to the actual author has also been provided in the entirety of this book.

This author has corrected grammar, misspellings and punctuation. I have also italicized or underlined key words and terms that have been used by these deceivers and made scores of notes where necessary. I have italicized titles of conferences, books, movies and other references listed by the author of the article itself. Lastly, I have written the name of the person in bold for finding them easier.

Persons are listed in alphabetical order, with a list of names and page numbers in the Index.

May this be a blessing to all who read.

© 2020 M. Lea Saris

A:

- **Justin Paul & Rachel Abraham**: This couple originated from the "Emerge Wales" team, a group promoting <u>mystical</u> Christianity. Also an associate of **John Crowder** (Elijah List participant and <u>mystic</u>); Here in one of their podcasts...they state that Jesus used telepathy and we can too. Description of podcast: "We are <u>telepathic</u>! Surprised? Don't be! "Jesus is the Pattern of us, and he knew everyone's thoughts and feelings" (Rev 2:23 CEV).

"**Justin Paul** shares the Biblical basis and practical dynamics of telepathic communication." Extract from this <u>heretic</u> and blasphemous "Company of Burning Hearts" website: "Our message is that He is the Happy God. Heaven is fun. And we can experience it on Earth. In fact that's God's plan- that Earth would be flooded with Heaven." This statement sounds ever so similar to **Bill Johnson's** teaching from his book "When Heaven Invades earth." **Justin Abraham** is a close friend of the heretic **John Crowder**. https://wolvesinthepulpit.blogspot.com/2018/05/

- **Doug Addison**: <u>Metaphysics-contemplative spirituality; "soaking prayer":</u>

"<u>Soaking Prayer</u>" is nothing more than contemplative /centering /listening prayer and is used for <u>occult meditation</u>; soaking worship, spontaneous worship, saturating, prophetic worship; **Doug Addison** is a <u>prophetic</u> speaker, author, Life Coach and stand-up comedian" according to his online biography. He also claims to have the inside track to God.
This meme shows the level of **Doug's** extra-special superty-duperty knowledge. He is directing people to their own vain imaginations and to his website. He is NOT directing people to the true Word of God; instead, he is deliberately causing people to avoid it.

http://www.piratechristian.com/museum-of-idolatry/2016/12/

How do you know if you have "The Swiss Army Knife" anointing? **Doug Addison** says we'll all have "The Swiss Army Knife" anointing this season. (What season is he referring to? Halloween?). Remember folks, God can't equip you, unless you believe He is equipping you.

(But if you post a cheesy stock photo and make claims that don't exist in the Bible... well, you might be **Doug Addison.**)

What is "The Swiss Army Knife" anointing, you ask? How do you know if you have it? How do you know you have something that isn't even in the scripture?
Below are five signs you may have it: Lime green and yellow swag. Strong desire to be crammed into a drawer. Strong desire to be an unused corkscrew.
You fear being replaced by a discounted knock off of yourself. You think you're a three-inch saw capable of doing major lumberjack work. Like the corkscrew, is anyone really going to use the little saw to do major lumberjack work? Probably not. And this absurd list is just as absurd as creating an anointing that isn't even listed in Scripture.

Now you can learn the inside secrets to "Prophetic Tattoo and Piercing Interpretation" from **Doug Addison**. **Doug Addison's** online course gives you the training you need!

After years of development, **Doug Addison** is making this one-of-a-kind online training available to you, but only for a short while. You can receive everything you need to get started in this new cutting-edge outreach strategy!

What you will learn with the "Tattoo Interpretation Online "Training:

Why People Get Tattoos
Common Tattoo Designs and Their Meanings
How to Recognize Symbolic Messages in Tattoos
The Significance of Tattoo and Piercing Placement
How Negative Designs Can Have Positive Meanings
How to Develop Metaphoric Thinking
Tattoos in The Bible
Doing a Tattoo and Piercing Interpretation
Significance of The Interest With Zombies and Vampires
Outreach Ideas

Tattoos???

I find it a big enough stretch just to accept that some Christians nowadays feel it's ok to mark up their body which the Lord gave them but to find prophetic significance in it???? To my eyes (and I'm sure it's just me being from a different generation, trying to be charitable here) the tats look like diseases at best.   At worst they look demonic. If a brother or sister feels they must stick a green dot on their wrist to enhance their appearance, I'm all for freedom of choice, but--

a-- I'm a nurse and I've never forgotten the sight and sound of a tattoo removal using a wire wheel to grind off the upper and mid layers of skin on a patient's back in my training years.
b-- I'm a nurse and I don't trust tattoo artists to have clean ink, there are too many infections tracing back to the ink.
c-- I'm a nurse and I've seen skin cancers. At first glance that ink blob on someone's leg looks like a disease.
d- I've got eyes and I've seen some faded stretched out tattoos that aren't exactly what the person expected after life and some years distorted the pretty whatever it was.
e-- I remember reading SOMEWHERE in the O.T. that tats were forbidden as they had some connection with demon worship rituals etc. I know we have freedom, but that seems like a bit much.

But hey, I'm old. And I recall my mother telling me why it was wrong to get my ears pierced but I did, and I love wearing my earrings anyway. Plus I wear makeup, so maybe that is the same as a tattoo as body ornamentation, but in a more washable form. BUT again, and also HEY I can't see turning the tats into a prophetic message unless it's a message of warning.

http://www.piratechristian.com/museum-of-idolatry/2016/10

Doug Addison = Exhibit A: why "Elijah's List" is a joke--The fact he has been a guest on **Sid Roth 's** show is another red flag; there isn't a False <u>Prophet</u> or <u>Heretic</u> **Roth** won't allow on his show. **Doug Addison** does it ALL FOR MONEY and so he can FOREVER DECEIVE people in the Pentecostal and Charismatic Churches

https://dougaddison.store/product/2016-prophetic-forecast/.

There's less than a month left in 2016 and **Addison** is still trying to make a few more bucks off of his utterly useless book of predictions for 2016. He's gotta clear off space on his shelves before he publishes the "2017 Book of Worthless Christian Fortune Telling."

Instead of selling these idiotic books at a steep discount, why doesn't he tell everyone about all the stuff that came true since he published them 11 months ago?? He could sell a boatload of the 2017 Edition just by demonstrating all of the wonderful things that were accomplished since the 2016 edition was published and sold.

Doug Addison, what kind of God do you serve? You teach that this God is giving confusing and conflicting messages to his people, instead of the one and only Holy Bible that never changes. And we're supposed to believe that God gives special messages directly to you, and then you get to make money by charging people for it??
http://www.piratechristian.com/museum-of-idolatry/2016/2/

http://dougaddison.com/store/training/online-training/prophetic

- **Enoch Adeboye**: It is always a sad thing knowing someone is wrong in the most fundamental issues of life: Who God the Father is, Who Jesus Christ is, Who the Holy Spirit is, who the Devil is and who he himself, is.
It makes you sadder knowing the deceived person is involved in large-scale deception of others in the name of the God he does not know, even where he appears sincere. On the spiritual plane, sincerity is not enough. The Bible, containing the clear mind of God, has been written! We cannot say that loud enough to **Pastor Adeboye** and other <u>Word of Faith</u> and <u>Prosperity</u> preachers and their deceived and deceiving followers. Where do those annual prophecies pastor **Adeboye** and others pronounce on their followers, most of which never come to pass, come from?

Pastor Enoch Adeboye (same for everyone in Pentecostalism and Charismaticism) affirms his teachings originate from Azusa Street, Los Angeles. We published a few months ago, these clear, definitive materials on the beginning, history, beliefs and personalities associated with Azusa Street. It was demonstrated very clearly that the instigators and controllers of Azusa Street were <u>hypnotists, spiritist mediums, clairvoyants, diviners, wizards and black-magic men and women.</u>

In flagrant disobedience to clear commands of God in Deuteronomy 18:10-12, the ringing history of Azusa Street is that it was started by people who received open communications from the dead, in particular, demons posing as the dead.

4

To underscore **Pastor Adeboye's** similar connections to teachings from demons and the dead, we quote from his December 5, 2017 "Open Heavens" daily devotional:

"Not only are your sins never hidden from God, they are equally not hidden from the saints in Heaven. Someone who was privileged to visit Heaven and return to earth said that there is a curtain in Heaven that anyone there can pull and the fellow will be able to monitor the activities of anybody here on earth."

"Another brother who also had that same privilege spoke of how saints in Heaven gather together in a place like a stadium, where they watch earthly saints facing crucial trials of their faith. When a saint being watched compromises, they shout in disappointment, just like when your favourite football team concedes a goal."

In the highlighted quote above, two separate people, right from "heaven" had messages for members of **Pastor Adeboye's** church! Contrast this with the teaching of the Lord Jesus Christ in Luke 16:19-31 that God would never send anyone from among the dead to give any message about Him to the living. On this the Bible is very consistent: necromancers were forbidden in Deuteronomy 18:10-12, Isaiah 8:19; neither would God permit Apostle Paul (nor, Lazarus, John 11:39-45, or Dorcas, Acts 9:36-41) to reveal whatever he saw in his vision of the third heaven: II Cor 12:1-4.

Or, shall we consider the probability that **Pastor Adeboye** might be receiving communications from someone other than the Author of the Bible? The "heaven" these two travelers just returned from have no God and the Lord Jesus Christ in it. It is the 'heaven' made and maintained by fallen angels and demons. The communications **Pastor Adeboye** is retelling to his audience are from demons. The totality of the people hearing these statements, thinking they were receiving words from God were, in fact, being deceived by demons, I Kings 22:15-23.

What other rule of the Bible is **Pastor Adeboye** flouting here? The rule against adding to or deducting from the settled Bible, Rev 22:18-19. The specs of "curtains" and "stadium audiences" in heaven are additions to the Bible designed to entertain hearers and reinforce a fake plausibility. Listen to the self-adulation by **Pastor Enoch Adeboye** and his pandering to the vanities of men in the second video: "great men of God, great women of God!"

Do you know any true servant of God in the Bible who promoted his prowess this much or allowed anyone to address him with such accolades? The writings of Paul in II Corinthians 11:24-33 are sobering: labours, rods, stripes, stonings, imprisonments, perils of waters, perils of the wilderness, perils from fake brethren, being lowered over the city wall in a basket...

General Overseer of "Redeemed Christian Church of God," (RCCG) **Enoch Adeboye**, has revealed a short wooden staff that was blessed and handed over to him for miracles by founder of the church, the late **Rev. Joseph Akindayomi**. **Adeboye** showed the short wooden staff to RCCG congregants during the 65th annual convention of the church at the Redemption Camp, Lagos-Ibadan Expressway, Ogun State (Nigeria).

He said that God had instructed the late **Rev. Akindayomi** to make the short wooden staff to be blessed and to be handed over to him (**Adeboye**) for prayers and miracles.

Adeboye explained that the staff had been given to him years ago but God ordered that it should be used sparingly. He used it at the Convention for three special prayers, including a prayer for God to make a way where there is no way. The cleric raised it, mentioned a prayer point and the congregation prayed. The prayers done, he raised it up again to bless handkerchiefs which the congregation waved with shouts of "Halleluyah, Halleluyah!"

Speaking on the theme of the convention "Halleluyah," **Adeboye** said that Nigerians must stop complaining but praise God in the face of daunting life challenges. **Adeboye** said as long as Jesus lives, Nigerians should remain confident of a better tomorrow. He noted that praising God guarantees victory, success, dominion and abundant supply from heaven.
He said: "among every set of people, there are three subsets, comprising those who have lost battles in life, those still engaged in battles, and those who have won battles recently."
"For all three groups, there is a need to praise God continuously – the first set for hope and restoration; the second for God to fight their battles; and the third, who should not forget God and go partying because life is full of unending round of battles."

Also speaking, **Bishop David Oyedepo**, founder of "Living Faith Church Worldwide," also known as "Winners' Chapel," stressed the importance of praise. He listed the power of praise as including the invitation of God's presence and glory, which provides His favour, healing, access to revelation, breakthrough, and fresh oil.

What you have just read is not a special scoop from the 'hounds' at www.thetruechristianfaith.com It is from the revered **Pastor Adeboye** himself.

Do you yet doubt that pastor **Enoch Adeboye** has got nothing with the Lord Jesus Christ of the Bible? He says his powers come from a wooden stick. Do you believe him? You must or you are playing with your eternity. He receives his power from a totem. The Lord Jesus Christ is in heaven and does not deposit His power in a rod.

" They have not known nor understood: for he hath shut their eyes, that they cannot see; and their hearts, that they cannot understand. And none considers in his heart, neither is there knowledge nor understanding to say, I have burned part of it in the fire; yea, also I have baked bread upon the coals thereof; I have roasted flesh, and eaten it: and shall I make the residue thereof an abomination? Shall I fall down to the stock of a tree? He feeds on ashes: a deceived heart has turned him aside that he cannot deliver his soul, nor say, Is there not a lie in my right hand?" (Isa 44:18-20).

"My people ask counsel at their stocks, and their staff declares unto them: for the spirit of whoredoms has caused them to err, and they have gone a whoring from under their God" (Hos. 4:12). Are we happy **Pastor Enoch Adeboye** has confirmed publicly he is an occultist and a servant of the devil? No. We are sad, and we have been correct all along about his religion. We are sad about the uncountable millions of souls he is leading into hell on fake Christianity.

https://www.thetruechristianfaith.com/2017/08/20/

- **Ché Ahn:** He "anointed" **Todd Bentley** and "prophesied" about him; He is a NAR leader; **Ché Ahn** founded "Harvest International Ministries" (HIM) back in 1996);
Ché Ahn states that the Lord spoke to him, "through a word from respected prophet and author **Cindy Jacobs**, that he was to "father"a new movement –a "network of networks," meant to train and raise up others."

"**Ché** would have spiritual children in every continent who would reach the world." Notice the language of **Cindy Jacobs** in the day to **Ché Ahn**.   He was to father a new movement; was to "train and raise up others"; was to "have spiritual children." Nevertheless, **Ché** has been regarded as an "Apostle" by top NAR leaders like **Cindy Jacobs** and **C. Peter Wagner**. "Apostle" **Cindy Jacobs** released the following on her website in the year 2000: https://youtu.be/msDAmA6RUEk

https://www.biblebelievingtruthwatch.com/.

- **Randy Alcorn**: Another prolific writer, whose books are sometimes fanciful and questionable. Endorsed his best-selling book, "Heaven," in which he uses a lot of imagination, misapplies Biblical teachings and doctrine, questions the Millennium and whether Christians are going through or avoid the tribulation.

https://www.puritanboard.com/threads/ randy-alcorn.95786/

"He also quotes **Joni Eareckson Tada**..." (**NOTE: She is a false teacher, which puts him into a questionable light, as listed in the above link. There are other websites too numerous to list Ed.).

- **Noel Alexander** https://churchwatchcentral.com/2015/08/27/ guess-who-elijah-list-challenge-the-culprit-in-the-pulpit/

http://archive.openheaven.com/forums/ printer_friendly_posts.asp?TID=15314

https://www.facebook.com/ihopkc/photos/ noel-alexander-an-old-friend-of-mike-bickle-was-instrumental-in-starting-the-247/10157332036 713385/

Born in the Republic of South Africa. He has served for many years as a pastor in Kansas and Missouri. The passion of his heart is intercession for world-wide revival. He regularly ministers in conferences around the world concerning this theme.

Noel was given a mandate by the Lord to feed, clothe and shelter the poor of the earth through "Love Mercy." https://lovemercy.com/ about

(**NOTE: Sounds like he is doing a great work–except he is connected to IHOP and is a friend of **Mike Bickel**. Ed.).

- **Joni Ames-Fasekas** https://churchwatchcentral.com/2015/08/27/
guess-who-elijah-list-challenge-the-culprit-in-the-pulpit/

- **Sandy Armstrong:** Another false prophet; runs an organization called "Soldiers of Christ." Mixes Scripture with false teaching. Predicted several times when the return of Jesus Christ would happen, going as far back as 2010.

 https://www.raptureforums.com/forums/threads/
failed-2018-date-setting-predictions-i-e-false-prophets-on-yt-who-ignore-matthew-24-36.
134574/

https://www.youtube.com/ watch?v=cz9h9HLbu6M

https://www.youtube.com/ watch?v=4OwU4WQ51_I

- **Neil T. Anderson:** (**NOTE: So many things wrong with his teachings, it is best to read it for yourself. Ed.).

 https://www.equip.org/article/neil

https://www.apologeticsindex.org/a45.html

http://jbeard.users.rapidnet.com/bdm/exposes/anderson/demon.htm

https://ficm.org/about-us/steps-to-freedom-in-christ/

 (**NOTE: This one listed above is his actual "ministry" page. Ed.).

- **Steven Anderson:** (**NOTE: Another in a long line of false preachers, only this one screams his sermons! Ed.).

 https://pulpitandpen.org/2017/10/22/
my-visit-to-steven-andersons-faithful-word-baptist-church-and-the-surprises-i-found-there/

 https://www.creationliberty.com/articles/wolf-sanderson.php

https://biblicaltruthresources.wordpress.com/2018/09/05/
the-heresy-of-pastor-steven-anderson-exposed-beware-of-wolves-in-sheeps-clothing/
https://www.nowtheendbegins.com/
phony-baptist-pastor-jew-hating-false-teacher-steven-anderson-becomes-first-person-banned-from-country-of-ireland/

- **Ernest Angley:** Dozens of articles on the Web regarding this "prophet" and "preacher," who used his ability to deceive thousands of followers:

https://www.theblaze.com/news/2014/10/15/
this-man-is-a-monster-pastor-and-televangelist-faces-shocking-allegations-from-at-least-21-ex-c
hurch-members

https://www.wkyc.com/article/news/investigations/
exclusive-former-pastor-alleges-sexual-abuse-by-televangelist-ernest-angley/95-613097567

"...There is plenty of proof of his sexual atrocities with many men, and that he allowed the abuse of many youth in his cult congregation. He has preached for decades against the homosexual all while being one himself."

"... Untold multitudes of men have been forced to have a vasectomy. And hundreds of women have been strongly encouraged to abort their babies."

http://dustoffthebible.com/Blog-archive/2016/02/01/
inside-aging-ernest-angleys-grace-cathedral/

(**NOTE: This last one is from "the Amazing Randi's" website. Even though he is nationally known to expose frauds in the "unsaved, human being world," this particular expose' is spot on.

If a debunker such as Randi can see all the shams, then those who profess being a Christian should be able to recognize them as well. Ed.).

https://web.randi.org/swift/ disgraceful-revelations-about-faith-healer-ernest-angley

- **John Arnott/ Carol Arnott**: "Laughing Movement"; **Kenneth Hagin**, **Rodney Howard Browne**, the "Vineyard Church," the Toronto Church; NAR, Dominionism, Word of Faith);

http://www.deceptioninthechurch.com/TheTorontoDeception.htm

https://truthinreality.com/2012/09/16/the-toronto-blessing/

https://youtu.be/IIT3oaaed9U.

The Ecumenical Dominionist agendas have spread through the Church at such a rapid rate and this activity is the enemy's attempt to push people into accepting the one world order, where religion and politics unite. https://www.biblebelievingtruthwatch.com/

- **Jack & Kay Arthur:** https://bereanresearch.org/risky-business/.

This website is concerning **Kay**, as will the following blogspot:

http://themurkynewsblogspot.ca.

(**NOTE: This is not a hyperlink. You have to type in this information; it is someone's observation. Ed.).

"**Kay** is also very close to the **Grahams' (Billy** and **Franklin**), and has taught (preached???) at "The Cove" (BGM) many times. Ecumenism is embraced. This is all so very sad." Short statement from:
http://apprising.org/2012/11/16/ about-kay-arthur-of-precept-ministries-international/

Another article about **Kay Arthur**, which shows just how dangerous she is in her doctrine and teaching:
http://jbeard.users.rapidnet.com/bdm/exposes/arthur/general.htm.

Jack Arthur: Deceased; husband of **Kay Arthur**, part of her "ministry," according to the references listed above.

- **John Avanzini:** Is a "name-it-and-claim-it" mega-star used by TBN whenever they want to promote the "hundredfold blessing." **Avanzini** also promotes the heresy that God's reason for creating humanity is to duplicate himself; a prosperity wolf of the first rank.
http://defendchrist.org

John Avanzini : "Jesus had a nice house, a big house--big enough to have company stay the night with Him at the house.'
"Let me show you His house. Go over to John the first chapter and I'll show you His house. . . . Now, child of God, that's a house big enough to have company stay the night in. There's His house." ("Believer's Voice of Victory" program on TBN [20 January 1991].)

(**NOTE: The program "Believer's Voice of Victory" is **Kenneth Copeland's** program; note that the wolves stick together in their blasphemous teachings. Ed).

John Avanzini : "Jesus was handling big money because that treasurer He had was a thief. Now you can't tell me that a ministry with a treasurer that's a thief can operate on a few pennies. It took big money to operate that ministry because Judas was stealing out of that bag." ("Praise the Lord" program on TBN [15 September 1988].)

John Avanzini : "John 19 tells us that Jesus wore designer clothes. Well, what else you gonna call it? Designer clothes--that's blasphemy. No, that's what we call them today. I mean, you didn't get the stuff He wore off the rack." " It wasn't a one-size-fits-all deal. No, this was custom stuff." "It was the kind of a garment that kings and rich merchants wore. Kings and rich merchants wore that garment."
"Believer's Voice of Victory" program on TBN [20 January 1991].
http://www.banner.org.uk/wof/sayings.html

B:

- **Dionny Baez:** Located in Philadelphia, PA, he is aligned with the NAR; is considered a false prophet. https://www.marthamac.com/ false-teachers#list-of-false-teachers

Apostle **Guillermo Maldonado** and **Dionny Baez** show magician's illusion not miracles:

1. Maldonado holds the glass that changes clear water to pink.

This can be seen on YouTube in the following link--

Turns water into wine: "Nephtali1981." (2013 August 18). Counterfeit Fire: Gold Dust, **Guillermo Maldonado**, "Bethel," **Dionny Baez**, Miracle Gems & More.

Retrieved October 7, 2014 from YouTube: http://youtu.be/ ywfrfmgImEU?t=5m18s

 This video sequence by "Nephtali1981" (see his Facebook page https://www.facebook.com/ nephtali1981channel) has been edited from a number of video clips he has sourced on YouTube:
"Unfortunately I was not able to locate the original clip on "the water into wine illusion," although I did locate the clip on the gold dust which was included in his sequence. I agree with Nephtali1981 that **Baez** used a chemistry trick to change clear water in to pink water.

I agree for three reasons, firstly because these was liquid in the receiving glass, secondly because of the accompany performance of screaming and music, but my main reason is because this is a well known chemistry trick."

"See the YouTube video below that shows how this is done." About.com. (2012 November 2). How to turn water into wine.

Retrieved October 7, 2014 from YouTube: http://youtu.be/ ou0Jy9jmq5k {link failed}

http://bethelchurchresearch.blogspot.com/p/ deception.html

(**NOTE: The author of the above article stated that you could see the deception on You Tube, however the link failed, not because it is not available, but because you need to have a private access code to view it. Nevertheless, it is still proof as are other videos that show this is all a scam, magician's tricks and deceptive practices designed to fleece the flock. Ed.).

- **Heidi Baker:** (**NOTE: Dangerous false preacher of the WOF; brainwashes people into chanting "legacy" over and over again; "imparts" demons into people as evidenced in a YouTube video, listed below. Ed.):

 https://youtu.be/16H84rcaqyk https://truthinreality.com/2012/09/16/

"Iris Ministries" http://www.irisglobal.org

(**NOTE: This is her website so you can see for yourself how demonic she is. VERY dangerous woman insofar as her ability to summon demons. There are so many articles and You Tube videos that expose this charlatan, that it is impossible to list all of them. Also, notice that she calls it "Iris" ministries? Could that be the Illuminati "all seeing eye"? Ed.).

- **Jay Bakker** (son of **Jim & Tammy Bakker**): "Yes, I am definitely questioning the atonement and trying to discover how we can see it in a different way. We've got this image of God who needs some sort of flesh, some sort of blood, that needs some sort of vengeance to pay for sin. My experience of a loving God who's asked me to love my enemies – this isn't a God that demands something before you are accepted."

"I think Jesus died because Jesus was inclusive. God is inclusive. I think that the idea of God somehow being separated from us was more man's idea."

That's how **Pastor Jay Bakker** of "Revolution Church NYC " describes his views of the atonement, which to Christians has long been a non-negotiable doctrine of Christianity. The shedding of the blood of the lamb of God for the sins of the world is a rather big deal. You can't preach about repentance for sins and the hope of a risen Christ without that key element. The <u>LGBTQ-affirming</u> **Bakker** has released a new book in which he encourages Christians to doubt, question and re-examine their beliefs and the Bible in pursuit of the "unknown God of limitless grace."

In an interview with the "Christian Post," **Bakker**, son of **Jim and Tammy Faye**, explains how his book will cause even more Christians to doubt the fundamentals of their faith and be more inclusive and socially responsible. So much for teaching his followers about the one true message that really changes the world.

Here is the story and interview:

Pastor Jay Bakker of "Revolution Church NYC:" Son of televangelists **Jim Bakker** and the late **Tammy Faye Bakker Messner**, the 37-year-old self-described "evangelical punk preacher" believes the Christian Church has misrepresented God and contributed to the sufferings of many with its orthodox teachings on sin, salvation and eternity.

More inclined to be filed alongside the works of Peter Rollins, **Rob Bell, Brian D. McLaren** and other so-called emergent Christian leaders, "Faith, Doubt and Other Lines I've Crossed " is heavy on love and grace and selective in its assessment of Scripture – apparently a continuing theme from **Bakker's** previous work, "Fall to Grace: A Revolution of God, Self & Society" (2011).

Bakker's reflections on a faith that he feels needs to be reformed don't seem to rest on genuine biblical interpretation, as he chooses to ignore the more troublesome and demanding texts that test his own views. He claims Christians who believe the Bible is inerrant don't take that same Bible "seriously." Yet the New York City preacher leaves plenty of room in "Faith, Doubt and Other Lines I've Crossed" for others to make the same claim about him – and not because he disagrees with a God-inspired view of Scripture or believes that Scripture leaves room for homosexual relationships, <u>but rather because he separates the God of the Bible from much of what the Bible claims God has said and done.</u>

Although **Bakker's** theology may cause some readers to bristle, his demands for a more biblically literate, compassionate and socially-conscious Christian Church certainly hold merit.

As the preacher explained to "The Christian Post " this week, there is plenty that the Church has gotten right in terms of combating poverty and hunger, but he also insists Christians need to re-think the issues he believes much of the community has gotten wrong – especially when it comes to gays and lesbians.

Pastor Jay Bakker, who co-founded Revolution Church in Phoenix, Ariz. in 1994, leads "Revolution NYC" services every Sunday afternoon at Pete's Candy Store in the borough of Brooklyn. https://standupforthetruth.com http://www.maryellenmark.com/

- **Jim & Tammy Bakker** Were the owners of the now defunct "PTL and Heritage USA."
Tammy deceased; **Jim** now hawks survival/prepper foods. Convicted of $158M of fraud; 24 counts; a convicted felon; had an extramarital affair with Jessica Hahn, former porno star.
For $45, **Lance Wallnau** and **Jim Bakker** will sell you a Trump/Cyrus coin that you can use as a "point of contact" between you and God as you pray for Trump's re-election in 2020.

"False Teacher And Televangelist Fraud Jim Bakker Now Selling $45 Gold-Plated Trump Coin That Will Give You A 'Point Of Contact' With God."
Geoffrey Grider May 17, 2019 https://www.nowtheendbegins.com/

--Winnie Banov: preached at "Glory City Church" on July 7th, 2017 and it is patently clear from her behavior, words and whiteboard scribbles that she is in serious need of psychiatric care. But rather than get the help she needs, she was invited to spew her insane ramblings during the sermon time. Sadly, the people and leadership of "Glory City " didn't see it for what it is (the ravings of a mentally ill woman) but received this non-lucid nonsense as a "word from God."
The video below tells the story:

http://www.piratechristian.com/museum-of-idolatry/2017/7/
winnie-banov-has-lost-touch-with-sanity. (**NOTE: the video is on this website. Ed.).

--Georgian Banov: "Hi guys – feel I had to post my thoughts tonight as it's come to my attention that **Georgian Banov** will be in the UK at the end of the month (Oct. 2014)." "Of course the event(s) are being publicized now so that many attend...please please do your research before going to any of his meetings..."

"So far we know that: **Georgian** & his wife **Winnie**- minister together with **John & Lilly Crowder** in their mystical schools & **Crowders'** church in Santa Cruz...."

" **Crowder** –remember– believes in spiritual bi location –levitation –sucking from (lactating) from the breast of Jesus & smoking the Holy spirit..."

"Google: **Banov** & **Crowder**--they are on You Tube –**Georgian** clearly states the position of alignment between himself, **Crowde**r & Bethel... **Georgian** is a member of Revival Alliance –along with "**BJ**" & the **Arnott's** of "Toronto blessing" fame."

(**NOTE: "BJ" is **Bill Johnson** of Bethel Church fame. Ed.).

13

"**Georgian** regularly imparts – the supernatural to BSSM students at "Bethel." **"Georgian** preaches "quite well;" he has the ability to take scripture – teach it & make whatever he says incredibly plausible... there are many truths of the scriptures he communicates very effectively, however deception works by mixture-sounding good & right but having an undercurrent of falseness..."

https://rooftopsandrafters.wordpress.com/2014/10/17/ georgian-banov/

https://churchwatchcentral.com/2017/08/03/
amanda-wells-and-winnie-banov-drinking-from-the-same-polluted-source/

Enjoined to the NAR, "The Passion Translation" is used and promoted by "Bethel" Redding, (**Bill Johnson**) and by **Georgian and Winnie Banov**, and who knows how many others. It seems to be a favourite "translation" in the loosely organized but very broad and fast growing NAR. I encourage all Christians to do their research on this.

Winnie Banov in particular has another spirit within her: the spirit of the Kundalini. She goes through the same actions as **Beth Moore**—who is a close friend of theirs—as well as **Todd Bentley's** wives (current and past). **Winnie** and her husband **Georgian** are also close friends with **Heidi Baker**—another NAR demonically led "preacher."

Here are several screen shots from the **Banov's** Facebook page, where they repeatedly promote this heretical and blasphemous doctrine of equality with God (among other equally horrendous claims):

 (**NOTE: If you go to the website listed below, you will find the links to their Facebook page. Ed.).

This is from the official website for "The Passion Translation": "Encounter the heart of God. "The Passion Translation is a new, heart-level translation that expresses God's fiery heart of love to this generation using Hebrew, Greek, and Aramaic manuscripts, merging the emotion and life-changing truth of God's Word." "So why another translation? Many wonderful versions of our Bible now grace our bookshelves, bookstores, software programs, even apps on our phones. So why add one more?"

"The reason is simple: God longs to have his Word expressed in every language in a way that unlocks the passion of his heart."
"The goal of this work is to trigger inside every reader an overwhelming response to the truth of the Bible, revealing the deep mysteries of the Scriptures in the love language of God, the language of the heart."

"If you're hungry for God and want to know him on a deeper level, The Passion Translation will help you encounter God's heart and discover what he has for your life." (**Dr. Brian Simmons,** Author of the "Passion Translations" "Bible.").

Because, apparently no other translations have ever been quite good enough.

Notice the very obvious, <u>mystical </u>language, meant to appeal to the <u>emotion</u>, which is what the <u>NAR</u> is all about. (Experiences and encounters).

https://www.worthychristianforums.com/topic/ 223728-%E2%80%9Cthe-passion-translation%E2%80%9D-you-are-jesus-christ%E2%80%99s-equal /?page=2

- **Don Basham**: Deceased; https://www.latimes.com/archives/ la-xpm-1990-03-24-ca-667-story.html

https://ncmifringe.wordpress.com/tag/ don-basham/

- **Doug Batchelor**: <u>SDA</u> teaching: Prestigious defender of Seventh-Day Adventism, host of the popular "Amazing Facts" television program. Also hosts "Bible Answers Live" radio show. Many of his <u>prophecy</u> teachings are rejected by mainstream prophecy scholars and teachers.

He and other <u>Adventists</u> use "bait and switch" tactics at highly-publicized <u>prophecy seminars</u> (after many hours of <u>prophetic </u>teaching, participants are eventually told they will receive the "mark of the beast" if they don't convert to a <u>Seventh-Day Adventist</u>).
Many Christians are duped by this tactic <u>due to their lack of Bible prophecy knowledge.</u> These "Revelation Seminars" promote doctrines that are required knowledge for membership or baptism in the <u>SDA</u> Church.

 For example, popular teachings are the "great whore" of Babylon in Revelation 17 & 18 is the Catholic Church, and the "daughters of the whore" are Protestant Sunday-keeping churches of today. The origins of <u>SDA</u> doctrine are rooted in date setting, false prophecies and legalism. http://www.soundchristian.com/prophecy/who/

–**Mark Batterson:** Is the modern father of the practice of <u>prayer circles</u>. In his book, "The Circle Maker," **Batterson** <u>teaches an unbiblical form of prayer that mimics ancient witchcraft more than Christianity.</u> Based on an old Jewish Legend from the Talmud, **Batterson** teaches his readers to draw a circle on the ground, step inside the circle, and pray, and that by doing so, you will be able to access untold blessings from God.

 In his book, he also twists the Scriptures to teach a form of the prosperity gospel. He writes, "Your job is not to crunch numbers and make sure the will of God adds up. After all, the will of God is not a zero-sum game." " When God enters the equation, His output always exceeds your input. Your only job is to draw circles in the sand. And if you do the geometry, God will multiply the miracles in your life."

 "The Circle Maker," Chapter 3. The Scriptures, however, teach that we are to pray according to God's will (1 John 5:14).
 https://reformationcharlotte.org/2019/03/26/ false-teachers-evangelical-churches/

15

–Irwin Baxter: Popular radio Bible prophecy teacher, he has unique views of prophecy, says they are "his" theories, and thus has many good and bad ideas. He has a correct view on Israel's role in history, and correctly argues against preterism.

He does not believe the book of Revelation is chronological, which leads him to some fanciful interpretations. For example, he says we are now living in the midst of the sixth trumpet of Revelation 9, and we may soon witness (in 2016) the annihilation of 2 billion people.

The fifth trumpet he claims began in 1991 when Saddam Hussein ("Saddam" means "destroyer") set Kuwaiti oil fields on fire, and ended with his execution in December 2006. He thinks the 7-year tribulation period is yet future. He hosts the popular radio broadcast, "End of the Age" (formerly "Politics & Religion") and is founder & president of "Endtime Ministries" at www.endtime.com, where he also publishes "Endtime" Magazine.

 He does not accept the doctrine of the Trinity, and is affiliated with the United Pentecostal Church which claims its methods are the only true way to salvation. He also rejects a pre-tribulation rapture based on Revelation 20:4-6 which he claims is the "first resurrection."

He fails to follow the text which clearly describes this first resurrection as being for the martyrs of the tribulation period after Christ's Second Coming. He also believes the two witness of Revelation chapter 11 could possibly be here on earth now, and mistakenly thought they were to be revealed in Israel during the summer of 2011.
http://www.soundchristian.com/prophecy/who/

https://www.jesus-is-savior.com/Wolves/irvin_baxter.htm

-Mary K. Baxter: https://www.near-death.com/science/articles/critique-of-mary-baxters-nde.html

Miss Baxter is a false prophetess, who like **Ellen White** (1827-1915) claims to have received visions from God. In the Foreword, **Miss Baxter** states…" Unlike other books, I believe that the Holy Spirit has brought this writing into being for time and eternity."

"The experiences and the message are of utmost importance to the body of Christ."
SOURCE: **Mary K Baxter** "A Divine Revelation of Hell Heaven."

Just as with the self-proclaimed prophetess **Ellen G. White** of the Seventh Day Adventists, **Mary Katherine Baxter** is a false prophet. You don't need to wonder whether or not she is telling the truth--she is lying. Why would God need to give a "private" message to anyone, when God has openly told us MUCH about Hell already in the Scriptures?

In chapter 16, "The Center Of Hell," **Miss Baxter** states her alleged experience of being in Hell… "I heard the woman say, "Lord, I knew you would come someday. Please let me out of this place of torment." "She was dressed in the clothes of an ancient era, and she was very beautiful." "I knew that she had been here for many centuries but could not die. Her soul was in torment. She began to pull at the bars and cry."

Softly Jesus said, "Peace, be still." He spoke to her with sadness in His voice. "Woman, you know why you are here." "Yes," she said, "but I can change. I remember, when You let all those others out of paradise."

"I remember Your words of salvation. I will be good now," she cried, "and I will serve You." She clenched the bars of the cell in her tiny fists and began to scream, "Let me out! Let me out!" "At that, she began to change before our eyes. Her clothing began to burn. Her flesh fell off, and all that remained was a black skeleton with burned-out holes for eyes and a hollow shell of a soul. I watched in horror as the old woman fell to the floor. All her beauty had departed in a moment.
It staggered my imagination to think that she had been here since before Christ was born." Jesus said to her, "You knew on earth what your end would be. Moses gave you the law, and you heard it. But instead of obeying My law, you chose to be an instrument in the hands of Satan, a soothsayer and witch. You even taught the art of witchcraft."

"You loved darkness rather than light, and your deeds were evil. If you had repented with your heart, My Father would have forgiven you. But now, it is too late."
SOURCE: **Mary K Baxter** "A Divine Revelation of Hell Heaven."

Miss Baxter makes some serious theological blunders in her statements. She states that Jesus scolded the woman in Hell, for not "obeying my law." However, Jesus Himself said that law of God wasn't intended to be obeyed... "Wherefore the law was our schoolmaster to bring us unto Christ, that we might be justified by faith. But after that faith is come, we are no longer under a schoolmaster. For ye are all the children of God by faith in Christ Jesus" (Galatians 3:24-26). The purpose of the Old Testament Law was to be a measuring stick, to reveal our exceeding sinfulness, and show us our desperate need for a Savior.

Miss Baxter speaks a bunch of mumbo-jumbo, but never really presents a clear, concise, plan of salvation from the Scriptures. She mentions giving one's heart to the Lord, but that is not salvation. She mentions repenting from one's sins, but that is not salvation. Only though faith alone in the blood sacrifice of Jesus Christ can our sins be washed away (I Peter 1:18,19).

In her book, "A Divine Revelation Of Hell," **Mary Katherine Baxter** claims that God chose her to let the world know about the REALITIES of Hell...Hear the eyewitness testimony on the True Existence of Hell:
Mary Katherine Baxter was chosen by God to let the world know of the REALITY of Hell. Jesus Christ "appeared" to **Mary Baxter** on 40 consecutive nights and took **Mary** on a tour of Hell and Heaven. She walked, with Jesus, through the horrors of Hell and talked with many people. Jesus showed her what happens to souls when they die and what happens to the unbelievers and Servants of God who do not obey their calling.
SOURCE: **Mary K Baxter** "A Divine Revelation of Hell Heaven."

(**NOTE: This continues on, showing how she perverts and twists the Scriptures to fit her "prophecies" and lofty position in the website below. Ed.).

https://www.lovethetruth.com/wolves/false_visions.htm

https://cicministry.org/commentary/issue54.htm

- **Allen Beechick**: Holds to a Preterist viewpoint: those who believe Christ came already are called preterists. "Preterist" is Latin for "past." In contrast, futurists believe Christ's coming is yet future. Preterists criticize futurists for trying to predict the date of Christ's return, and rightly so, because He is coming at an hour when we think not, as we read above. But ironically preterists set their own date. They set that date at about a generation's time after Christ. According to them, Matthew 24 was fulfilled in 70 AD at the destruction of Jerusalem and the temple.

In setting a date, preterists diminish the urgent need for continual readiness. First generation Christians could delay getting ready until the close of the generation. And subsequent generations can ignore readiness verses that supposedly apply to first generation Christians. "Within the preterist view are shades of beliefs.

Full preterists place the resurrection of believers in the past, and partial preterists place the resurrection in the future. But all place the fulfillment of Matthew 24 in the past. So we will start with Matthew 24, and we will answer the preterist claims..."
(**NOTE: A very lengthy article on this website. Ed.):

https://www.preteristarchive.com/2004_beechick_promise-1/

- **Rob Bell:** Took a sabbatical with his family; starred in a movie called "The Heretic." Two of his statements in the movie are: "Jesus would be mortified that someone started a religion in His name," and "The Bible has caused so much damage." **Bell,** who made the cover of Time magazine, is an outlaw in the evangelical world. He was cast out of that kingdom in 2011 after he questioned the existence of hell in his New York Times best-selling book, "Love Wins." A very lengthy article on **Rob Bell** is found within this website:

https://theweeflea.com/2018/08/01/
sound-the-alarm-bell-a-review-of-rob-bells-premier-interview/

"...The same could not be said for "The Heretic," the new documentary about **Rob Bell's** journey from being a Michigan megachurch pastor to a surfing spiritual guru." Unsurprisingly given its title, "The Heretic" brandishes the label as a badge of honor, framing **Bell** as a rebel prophet and those who disavow him as stereotypical anti-gay, Trump-loving, bullhorn-brandishing fanatics. The film makes no effort to present critiques of **Bell.**
The voices it features are unanimous in their praise of the man behind "Love Wins."

Author Elizabeth Gilbert (" Eat, Pray, Love")is featured prominently, praising **Bell** as "the gangster of God," "a spiritual Jesse James," and someone "challenging a status quo that is profoundly invested in its conservative ideals."
Another featured voice is none other than **Carlton Pearson**, who calls **Bell** a "paradigm shifter and shaper" who is "way ahead of his time."

As the film follows **Bell** on his book tour for "What Is the Bible? " (read TGC's review), in places like Atlanta and Knoxville, we see people lining up to get books signed and hear spiritual vagaries about how "We are all of the same tribe" and how the religious and nonreligious are "all just expressions of the same thing."

Voices of dissent are seen only in cable news sound bites, as in **Franklin Graham** calling **Bell** a false teacher and a heretic. We later see **Graham** singing Trump's praises, advancing a connection the film really wants to make (that evangelicals who don't like **Bell** must also love Trump). Unfortunately, "The Heretic" comes across more as an extended PR reel for **Bell** than a documentary that engages all sides of his story and truly considers the implications of his beliefs.

The latter might have been interesting. The former is just boring. Ultimately the gospel of "inclusion" and "solidarity" that **Pearson** and **Bell** preach is powerless to give true hope to people in their sin. It demands no repentance and has no consequences.

https://www.thegospelcoalition.org/article/
come-sunday-heretic-sad-stories-rebel-pastors/

October 21, 2009: Shane Hipps, Teaches That All Religions Are Valid:

Shane Hipps, who is now **Rob Bell's** co-pastor at "Mars Hill Bible" church in Grand Rapids teaches that all religions are valid and that even Osama Bin Laden has the divine spark within him. NO KIDDING! This is a VERY serious and troubling heresy that Hipps promotes and we at the "Museum of Idolatry" believe that **Rob Bell** is not only fully aware of Hipps' teaching but that he agrees with it, otherwise Hipps would have never been called to be co-pastor at 'Mars Hill." https://crosebrough.typepad.com/ alittleleaven/false_gospels/

http://ichabodthegloryhasdeparted.blogspot.com/2010/11/
fuller-theological-seminary-alums-rob.html

- **Paul Begley:** https://www.paulbegleyprophecy.com/about
Pastor **Paul** caught the world's attention with the revelation of the "Hosea Prophecy" and "Texas Blood Lake;" which has been featured in Time magazine, CNN and many mainstream networks and magazines. As an evangelist, **Paul** holds revivals across America and internationally. **Paul** has held crusades as far away as Orissa, India.
http://americanloons.blogspot.com/2013/03/482-paul-begley.html

This is another site that exposes his teachings. It is September 24th, 2017. And lo and behold, the latest prophecy craze: the "September 23, 2017 – Revelation 12 Sign in the Heavens" prediction has failed. Numerous YouTube videos and blogs predicted either the Rapture, Great Tribulation or "something big!" would happen on September 23, 2017, all on the basis of observing celestial alignments of the constellations Virgo and Leo.

As "Beginning and End "detailed in our article: "The September 23, 2017 – Revelation 12 Sign Deception: False Prophecy Debunked," these prophecies were not only false, but based on the use of astrology, which is a sin in the Bible (Deut. 13:1-3).

God was well aware of false prophets who would attempt to dazzle believers with "signs and wonders."

Notice that some of these signs and wonders would even "come to pass" or actually happen. But that alone did not give the false prophet validity. The second part of the test was whether or not the teaching of that prophet was bringing one closer or farther away from God. "The September 23rd " false prophets very successfully lured many well-meaning believers to dabble in astrology – which is a sin in the Bible (Deut. 18:10-12). In each instance, the "September 23, 2017 " false prophets are breaking God's clear commands:

They looked to the stars, sun, moon and planets in order to determine or "divine" the future. The Lord called this an abomination (Isa. 47:13-14). To no surprise, there has been little repentance from the main purveyors of this astrological false doctrine. Robert Breaker, whose video on September 23, 2017 has over nine million views, has now disabled comments on the video and gone silent. The same can be said for **Steve Ciccoccanti** and **Paul Begley**.

In fact, **Begley** (who not only predicted the Great Tribulation but also the possibility of Nibiru/Planet X turning the Earth to ice) posted a video in the early hours of September 23rd to discuss the earthquake in Mexico as supposed evidence (on You Tube on this website).

Notice **Begley** is making his best attempt to stoke fear and alarm, almost hoping for catastrophe to justify his false prophecy. Pray that these false teachers repent and that those caught up in the latest prophecy craze will see it for what it is: astrology. Let the church turn back to the Bible and the prophecies contained within Scripture, not in the stars. Some have said that even if these prophecies fail there is a benefit because they are making people think about God. However, the Lord declared that it is His Word that will save souls, not constellations or pagan rituals. Preach the Gospel. Share the Bible with others and let the exciting prophecies of Scripture draw people, not astrology or "stargazing."

https://beginningandend.com/
the-september-23-2017-false-prophecies-fail-revelation-12-sign-officially-debunked/

-**Todd Bentley**: Recent controversies around the phenomenon of healer/evangelist **Todd Bentley** who has been so improbably kicking and hissing the Holy Spirit's power into the sick before audiences of thousands per night for months, is an interesting example of just how far many have gone beyond normal discernment in the area of beliefs. http://rollanscensoredissuesblog.blogspot.com.

Todd has also been allegedly committing the sins of sexual misconduct in Pakistan for several years. https://www.christianpost.com/news/
todd-bentley-sexual-misconduct-allegations-widen-to-pakistan.html

In spite of him "repenting" for his sins and seeking restoration, including confessing everything in his life, going back as far as age 10." https://rlorensandford.com/.
Married, divorced and remarried.
https://discernmentministriesinternational.wordpress.com/category /t-l-osborn/

https://www.christianpost.com/news/
fresh-fire-leader-todd-bentley-accused-of-perverse-sexual-addiction-preying-on-interns.html
https://www.youtube.com/watch?v=UDEsXVUQeLo

(**NOTE: There is ample proof of him and his demonic antics on You Tube. Also, since the web link says "**TL Osborn**," it is due to both of them being written about by the same author—as are several other "famous" names. A lot of them appear in this book. Ed.).

–John Bevere: **Bevere's** thesis is that submission to spiritual authority gives covering and protection. Conversely, to disobey spiritual authority is to place oneself in the arena of Satan with the clear implication that one who disobeys by failing to submit to spiritual authority is open to demonic attack. The same is true if the spiritual authority is challenged.

He says: "If those under authority take the yoke of judgment upon themselves as judges over their established leaders, they no longer are submitted to established authority, but have elevated themselves as judges over their leaders." " Their hearts are lifted up in pride above the ones God placed over them. They have exalted themselves over the ordinance and counsel of God." ("Under Cover," p. 116). **Bevere** makes many good, right and true points. We do not live in a spiritual democracy and authority is something with which we as twenty-first century Americans have great problems with.

"I have serious problems with **Bevere's** approach and his whole thesis on several different levels, some methodological, some exegetical, some theological. What follows are more or less disconnected observations and specific examples of problems and issues that jumped out at me as I read. These criticisms are by no means exhaustive, and the weightiest are at the end. Intended or not, and despite all the claims to humility, I sense an underlying arrogance."

Bevere invokes the voice of God throughout the book telling him in words that his teaching is the truth. These claims place an author above criticism, because to take issue with these claims is to reject divine revelation.
While I don't want to get sidetracked about prophecies and words of knowledge, I do want to mention that in I Thess. 5 Paul tells (or as **Bevere** might say: commands) his readers to: not treat prophecies with contempt. But examine all things; As an exegete and a theologian I have a tremendous problem with the way **Bevere** handles the text of Scripture. He nowhere builds a case with solid exegesis and theological thinking/reflection that his thesis is valid.

Instead he assumes from the first paragraph that he is right and mixes stories, proof texts and examples drawn out of context from the breadth of scripture and from his experiences. His proof texts are often pulled totally out of context and treated as timeless aphorisms rather than time-bound, culture-bound and context-bound statements that cannot simply be lifted out of their contexts without doing violence to their meaning.

Likewise, he regularly leverages one Biblical story against another and bridges them with anecdotes that tie the parts together artificially to make them serve his agenda. With reference to exegesis, he occasionally appeals to the meaning of Greek terms but employs sources that are out of date, and even these he uses improperly, building cases from lexical definitions and forcing those lexical definitions into contexts in which they do not fit. He seems to have little to no grasp of the universally understood hermeneutical principle that meaning is determined by context.

On other occasions he redefines terms to fit the point he is hammering, e.g. in James 2 he redefines works as "obedient actions" and quotes James 2:20-24, 26 substituting "obedient actions" for works throughout. ("Under Cover, p. 217). In his exposition of the verse "rebellion is as the sin of witchcraft" (I Sam 15:23), **Bevere** attempts to retranslate the verse as "rebellion is witchcraft" since the Hebrew text infers the "is ."

Again, he plays fast and loose with the meaning of the text as understood by the translators who are expert in Hebrew, to make points homiletically. He then continues to build a case that since rebellion is witchcraft those in rebellion fall under the curse placed upon those who practice witchcraft. In this context he takes Paul's rhetorical question to the Galatian churches, "O foolish Galatians, Who has bewitched you . . .?" He states:

"The bewitchment involved in disobeying God's word, not any curses that sorcerers conjured up, Why? Because rebellion is witchcraft! In essence the church in Galatia came under a witchcraft curse because of disobedience." (Ibid, p. 76).
While perhaps less problematic than some of the other weaknesses underlying the book, I find a strain of ethical absolutistism that denies that there are any gray areas in moral judgments. Every situation has a right and a wrong. I believe that this position, while on the surface is attractive it is not ultimately defensible. This feeds into his thesis that we must be under cover, submitted to our spiritual authorities so as not to sin and incur divine judgment.

 In the second section of "Under Cover, "God's Direct Covering," **Bevere** discusses the nature of sin claiming a definitive understanding from 1 John 3:4, "Sin is lawlessness."
This claim is utterly reductionistic. I hear in the background John Wesley's definition of sin as "a conscious act of willful disobedience (to a known law)." While this approach on the surface claims to treat sin seriously, in reality it utterly trivializes sin, reducing it to an act of the will, a choice. If sin were merely an act of the will all we would need is strong wills to defeat it. In reality sin goes to the depth of our being. There is no part of our existence that has not been touched by its tentacles.

More problematic yet is the framework in which **Bevere** builds his teaching. This framework is legal rather than relational. As I noted earlier, much of what **Bevere** has to say is true and right, but the framework in which something is presented has a profound effect on the way it is taken in. Merely having all the right pieces is not enough.

 My point here is that **Bevere** places his discussion within the framework of performance, the framework of slaves not sons and in so doing existentially compromises the transforming effect of the gospel in the life of the believer. **Bevere** quotes Romans 13:1ff as an absolute command, and then broadens it from the context of civil authorities/rulers to the sphere of spiritual authority. In its context judgment refers clearly to the police and court system. In the shift to spiritual authority **Bevere** turns this judgment into a direct spiritual judgment from God—something nowhere even suggested in the passage.

As I said earlier, much of what he says is good. But the framework he uses is one that is the cyanide in the Kool-Aid. While he may not go down this path himself, working out the implicit presuppositions of his teaching, I don't have to be a prophet to foresee that his followers will.

And when they do they will unleash a new torrent of spiritual abuse that effectively undermines the freedom produced by the Gospel and enslaves God's children in chains of bondage. In so doing they will come under the same curse that Paul pronounced upon those who were adding to the gospel Paul proclaimed to the Galatian church.

 https://credohouse.org/blog/ under-cover-authority-obedience-abuse

https://vimeo.com/35487644

(**NOTE: The above article was written by an author in the website link above. It is not mine. Ed.).

 - **Mike Bickle**: Founder of IHOP in 1999; heretical teaching; NAR;
Watch the emotionally manipulative video about the upcoming "One Thing" conference (2017) that IHOP holds every year, and notice the prominent teaching of Dominionism as well.

 In the video, **Mike Bickle** says: "God is raising up a church that is going to be prepared to be the vessels of His glory, to release His glory into the earth this very hour of intense darkness... He says "the beauty I possess I want to impart to you!" (Got a Bible verse to back that up, **Bickle**?).

Bickle, White, and many other NAR teachers have been pumping people up with this false teaching for decades now. How are they doing at "releasing His glory" and "imparting His beauty" and "becoming the Bible?" This is warmed-over Latter Rain Dominionism that excites people with a false belief in their own greatness (if they just go to enough conferences to learn the secret from the latest guru prancing around on stage).

http://www.piratechristian.com/museum-of-idolatry

C. Peter Wagner, in a "National School of the Prophets" conference on Friday May 12, 2000 11:00 am session, introduces **Bickle** saying, "God called **Mike Bickle** to turn over his church in Kansas City to Floyd McClung Jr., who you might know from YWAM (former International Executive Director), because he felt God calling him to start a prayer unit, a prayer house for the whole city of Kansas City, not just for one church, called "The International House of Prayer," which for short means the "Kansas City IHOP."
Bickle's books are a favorite read in YWAM.   **Bickle** claims that God is restoring contemplative prayer to the church, that this is a God ordained means of entering into the fullness of God.

http://mywordlikefire.com/2011/07/29/
mike-bickle-of-ihop-wants-book-about-catholic-mystics-to-be-manual-for-ihop-kc.

Bickle was formerly with the Kansas City Prophets who had **Paul Cain** as their senior prophet. They came into the Vineyard by invitation of **John Wimber** and brought the heretical Latter Rain teachings.

Bickle who is now heading up IHOP, has a teaching of "Bridal Intimacy " which is directly linked to Dominionism that was founded in the Latter Rain, the end time taking of the nations. Besides **Mike Bickle**, there are others to be concerned with: **Cindy Jacobs, Otis Jr., Dutch Sheets, Chuck Pierce** and **Bill Hamon**, all part of the NAR.

There are other connected people endorsed by **Bickle: George Otis, Jr.,** and **John Dawson** of YWAM. http://www.letusreason.org/ ecumen30.htm

(**NOTE: There are a lot of these wolves in this article, too numerous to link and write here. It is easier to go to the link listed above. Ed.).

- **Paul Billheimer**: Deceased; Dominionist teacher; "... For example, the impact of the teaching of **Paul Billheimer**, a Wesleyan holiness minister and author, still resonates within evangelical circles which include the Pentecostal and Charismatic movements."

His emphasis on "the authority of the believer" has been a captivating subject for so many Christians since the rapprochement of this individualizing devotional theme by the 19th and early 20th century Holiness movements out of which much of the Pentecostal movement sprang forth. But while there is much of **Billheimer's** teaching that provides solid, edifying thought, he tragically and sharply breaks with Christian doctrine about the nature of God in his popular book "Destined For The Throne " which is still widely read.

This departure from orthodox Christian thought is abrupt, unexpected and yet agonizingly unmistakable. Sounding more like a Mormon apostle or **Herbert W Armstrong** piously waxing eloquent in the technical language of biological genetics, **Billheimer** writes of the Christian that: "... we read in 1 Cor. 6:17, "He that is joined to the Lord is one spirit."

"The union goes beyond a mere formal functional or idealistic harmony or rapport. It is an organic unity, an organic relationship of personalities (Sauer). Through the new birth we become bona fide members of the original cosmic family (Eph. 3:15), actual generated sons of God (1 John 3:2), "partakers of the divine nature" (2 Pet. 1:4), begotten by Him, impregnated with his "genes," called the seed or "sperma" of God (1 John 5:1, 18 and 1 Pet. 1:3, 23), and bearing his heredity..."   "Thus, through the new birth - and I speak reverently - we become the "next of kin" to the Trinity, a kind of "extension" of the Godhead. ... a completely new, unique, and exclusive order of beings which may be called a "new species."   "God purposed to have a family circle of his very own, not only created but also generated by His own life, incorporating His own seed, "sperma," "genes," or heredity."

"... But for this plan, God's family relationship would have been forever confined to the Trinity. .. according to I John 3:2, that is just what they are, true genetic sons of God, and therefore, blood brothers of the Son." "Christ is the divine Prototype after which this new species is made.

They are to be exact copies of him, true genotypes, as utterly like Him as it is possible for the finite to be like the infinite."

"As sons of God begotten by Him, incorporating into their fundamental being and nature the very "genes" of God, they rank above all other created beings and are elevated to the most sublime height possible short of becoming members of the Trinity itself."
 Billheimer was one of the chief vanguards heralding the neo-gnostic belief that Christians are "extensions of the Godhead" but this didn't stop them from becoming a mainstay in the innumerable devotional magazines circulated in the mid 20th century.

He taught here that Christians are actual genetic "copies" of God Himself without pausing to realize that such a claim effectively removes any real distinction between Christians and Christ Himself. They are therefore a higher species than even other human beings, above all other creation due to its organically essential unity with the Godhead itself.
This teaching - by default - denies the unique nature, deity and Lordship of Christ altogether.

In what is surely an ironic twist, until his death in 1984, **Billheimer** and his wife worked closely with **Paul Crouch's** Trinity Broadcast Network, where his teaching so inspired **Crouch** that he authorized republication of **Billheimer's** books in special "TBN Partner Editions."
 http://www.spiritwatch.org/firefaith4.htm

 (**NOTE: This site above continues a quite lengthy expose' on **Paul Billheimer** that can be read by going to the site. Ed.).

- **Shawn Bolz:** NAR "prophet"; occultist; backs up **Patricia King**: **Shawn Bolz** is the founder and former senior pastor of Expression 58 Church and is now the CEO of Bolz Ministries.
Bolz is closely tied to Bethel Church in Redding California, a hyper-charismatic, New Apostolic Reformation church which is known for its music and its working of false signs and wonders.

According to **Bolz'** bio found on Bethel's website, he "has been a pioneer in ministry, including the prophetic movement, since he was in his teens," and "his focus is on intimacy with God, creativity through entertainment and social justice." **Bolz** is now a traveling speaker who visits different churches around the country to "prophesy" and give people "affirmation from God."

In the video, you can see **Bolz** giving what appears to be cold psychic readings much like those of the fraud **John Edward**.

 (**NOTE: the video is on the website. Ed.).

Bolz is also the author of a book titled "God Secrets," a book that promises to deepen your relationship with God through the pursuit of spiritual gifts, especially prophecy.
In the description of the book on **Bolz'** website, he says, "God loves to tell us specific information about people that we wouldn't naturally know on our own! God has been known to reveal birth dates, anniversaries, family nicknames, pet names, and even bank account numbers at times!

The sharing of these personal details help to develop trust and a strong connection to the Lord."

This, of course, is nonsense <u>and is no different than what fortune tellers do</u>—a practice starkly condemned in Scripture (Leviticus 19:31, Isaiah 8:19, Deuteronomy 18:10-12, etc.).   While **Bolz** claims to be drawing people closer to the Lord, in actuality, he is drawing people away from God by teaching for shameful gain things he ought not to teach (Titus 1:11).
Shawn Bolz is a false teacher, a fraud, and a wolf in sheep's clothing. What he practices is completely foreign to anything resembling Christianity. He should be marked and avoided. https://pulpitandpen.org/2017/06/06/

Shawn Bolz is a <u>false prophet</u>. In fact, he is a breathtakingly arrogant, <u>false prophet</u>. He not only pretends to hear from God but <u>he commits outright blasphemy against the Holy Spirit by pretending he can teach the gifts of the Spirit</u> when the Bible expressly says only the Holy Spirit gives the gifts as He sees fit.

Not only that <u>but he has the gall to charge people for pretending to teach them the gifts.</u> The Bible is replete with admonition after admonition against false prophets in our day. We are to mark them so we can know to avoid them. We are taught that they are the cause of division in the church. They lead people away from Christ and cost them a true chance at salvation. They are covered in the blood of the sheep that they slaughter. That is who **Shawn Bolz** is.
In many ways I do not blame him directly as he was taught this <u>heretical</u> nonsense by **Bill Johnson** and "Bethel Church." It is"Bethel" that operates a <u>school of the supernatural</u> where the gifts are taught.

Johnson routinely allows anyone to come up to the altar and "prophesy" during "prayer" services at Bethel.   It is no wonder that **Bolz**, who calls himself a <u>prophet</u>, would be so misinformed. So **Bolz** wrote a book called "Translating God." His premise is derived from the falseness at "Bethel." His opening salvo is that prophecy is a gift from God for every believer but we know from the Bible that is 100% false. Not every gift is for every person. That is absurd. Not content with the $15 he could make from the book, "Bethel" allowed him to translate this into an 8 week E-course on "Bethel TV " for $50.

Oh and for a measly $200 you can get the starter kit for "Translating God " from his online store. All for Jesus of course; wink wink. So apparently, **Mr. Bolz** received push back from this latest attempt to fleece the flock and he took to social media today to offer up the following defense which only further makes it obvious how false and poorly taught he is: "When it comes to my critics I am usually living in a bubble." "Sometimes I hear something that is so outlandish about myself I want to respond but it would sound defensive and is unnecessary." "It is shocking to me that immature Christians actually spend more time trying to expose or criticize other ministries more then they try and inspire people towards Christ.

 Maybe they think it's the same thing but how exhausting for them! I am praying for a lot of Saul's to come into their true identity!" "Some of these websites and Facebook groups that have thousands of followers that are all about what God isn't doing and they need an encounter with the love of God that leads them and others into true fruit of salvation!"

"I love the simple Gospel that causes us to have love that inspires faith and then we have to share it." "We tell the world who God is and what HE is doing, not what men are doing wrong or what the enemy is doing." "Can you imagine if they take a step back and see how much time they are spending that is not on God. Wow." -- **Shawn Bolz**

Let's reason together and go through this nonsense: I will try to stick to the larger points. First of all, it is interesting that **Bolz** thinks those who demand solid doctrine that lines up with the Bible are "immature."

This is in line with many of the false teachers and prophets of today. **Perry Noble** referred to such people as the "jackasses" in his congregation. Another mega-church pastor referred to them as the "excrement in the body of Christ." This is the purpose driven model (**Rick Warren**) at work. If anyone disagrees you "blessedly subtract" them.

It is clumsy here by **Bolz** and transparent. The second issue with this line however is the ridiculous disconnect. **Shawn Bolz** lives his life inspiring people away from Jesus Christ. The Bible says you are either gathering for Him or scattering away from Him.

When you preach a false gospel or say things on behalf of God that He has not said, you are not gathering to Him. When someone points out a false teaching or false prophet and leads people out from under deception, it is to lead them to Christ and His true Gospel. I cannot tell you the joy when I receive correspondence from someone who has come out from the darkness and into the light because they finally understood they were being lied to.
The second absurdity is the notion that anyone who suggests that he should not lie to people must be a "Saul"; which can only mean he is a persecuted Christian.

Yes poor persecuted **Shawn Bolz**. Makes a living off of lying about God and leading people away from Jesus Christ but in his own heart believes he is the victim. Then he starts to reveal how false he truly is. He reveals this sloppy agape love that drives his false ministries. That people who want the Bible need an "encounter."

No **Shawn**, you need to read the Bible because it says that only the Gospel has the power of God unto the salvation of man. Perhaps the most telling and dangerous absurdity however is this: "I love the simple Gospel that causes us to have love that inspires faith and then we have to share it." -- **Shawn Bolz**. What is missing from the equation **Shawn** has outlined for us? It is the same thing missing from the seeker friendly and purpose driven churches across this land. The answer is repentance. The true Gospel does not cause us to have love. It causes us to repent of our sins. Love is a fruit of the indwelt Holy Spirit. You do not get there without first repenting.
In the teaching sphere of **Shawn Bolz** however, love is a direct cause from hearing the Gospel and that could not be more wrong. There is a reason why **Shawn** views his Gospel as simple -- because it is.
He removed the difficult portions of it just like his pastor does. Singing about love and then hearing a message about love, and then hearing a false prophecy about love -- doesn't save anyone.

What **Shawn Bolz** is selling is experiential Christianity. He is convincing people to tap into their own wicked hearts and deceive themselves into thinking that emotional experiences are spiritual encounters. He does not tell the world who God is because he obviously does not know Him. If he knew God then he would fear God. He would think twice before lying about what God has and has not said. He would repent of charging people money to hear those lies and leading people away from the Cross.

In conclusion, Titus 1:9 commands ministers to openly rebuke those that are false. To do so is to be obedient to the Word. To do so is to spend time on God. **Shawn Bolz** however is content to make merchandise of the sheep of the Lord, deny the kingdom of heaven to those who are seeking, and grossly misspeak on the Lord's behalf. Normally he is content as he puts it -- to live in his bubble. Today he ventured out to give us a peek into the twisted and warped thinking of a false prophet so we could translate it using the written Word of God. Thanks for clarifying **Shawn.**

Rev. Anthony   http://www.828ministries.com/Diary/
Translating-the-Heresy-of-by-Anthony-Wade-Christianity_Faith_Prophet-170114-152.html.

Shawn Bolz is the founder and former senior pastor of Expression58 Church and is now the CEO of Bolz Ministries. **Bolz** is closely tied to Bethel Church in Redding California, a hyper-charismatic, New Apostolic Reformation church which is known for its music and its working of false signs and wonders. According to **Bolz'** bio found on Bethel's website, he "has been a pioneer in ministry, including the prophetic movement, since he was in his teens," and "his focus is on intimacy with God, creativity through entertainment and social justice."
Bolz is now a traveling speaker who visits different churches around the country to "prophesy" and give people "affirmation from God."

https://pulpitandpen.org/2017/06/06/ false-teacher-of-the-day-6-shawn-bolz/

- **Mel Bond**: (**NOTE: Questionable tactics in his approach to faith and healing. Not a lot of information about him on the Internet. The one listed below is from a Yahoo chat room—not a very solid site, but the answers are from every day people who know about him, so I have included it. Other websites say he is okay. I will let you decide, however keep in mind that he has also been on **Sid Roth's** "It's Supernatural" TV show, which may or may not factor into your decision. Ed.).
https://answers.yahoo.com/question/ index?qid=20170621094603AA9yvjc

- **Dietrich Bonhoeffer**: Deceased.   Adhered to the Neo-Orthodoxy beliefs:
Neo-Orthodoxy defines the Word of God as Jesus (John 1:1) and says that the Bible is simply man's interpretation of the Word's actions. Thus, the Bible is not inspired by God, and, being a human document, various parts of it may not be literally true. God spoke through "redemptive history," and He speaks now as people encounter Jesus, but the Bible itself is not objective truth. Neo-Orthodoxy teaches that the Bible is a medium of revelation, while orthodoxy believes it is revelation. That means that, to the neo-orthodox theologian, revelation depends on the experience (or personal interpretation) of each individual.

The Bible only "becomes" the Word of God when God uses its words to point someone to Christ. The details of the Bible are not as important as having a life-changing encounter with Jesus. Truth thus becomes a mystical experience and is not definitively stated in the Bible.

The neo-orthodox view of sin is that it is a rejection of our responsibility to treat our fellow man well. The result of sin is dehumanization, accompanied by unkindness, unforgiveness, loneliness, and a myriad of societal ills. Salvation comes to those who have a subjective encounter with Christ—no acceptance of a set of truths is necessary.
Neo-orthodoxy places an emphasis on social work and our ethical responsibility to love others. Neo-orthodoxy has influenced the less-conservative branches of Presbyterian and Lutheran churches in America, along with other denominations. While its original purpose, to provide a more biblical alternative to liberalism, is commendable, neo-orthodox teaching nevertheless carries some inherent dangers. Any time that truth is determined according to what is relevant to my experience, the possibility of relativism exists.

Any doctrine that sees the Bible as a wholly human document containing errors erodes the very foundation of biblical Christianity.

We cannot truly have a life-changing "encounter" with Jesus without also believing some facts as presented in the Bible. "Faith comes from hearing the message, and the message is heard through the word of Christ" (Romans 10:17). The content of our faith is the death and resurrection of Christ (1 Corinthians 15:3-4). The disciples had an "encounter" with Jesus in Luke 24. The disciples initially misinterpreted the event, however: "They were startled and frightened, thinking they saw a ghost" (verse 37).

It was not until Jesus informed them of the truth (that He had been bodily resurrected) that they grasped the reality of the situation. In other words, we need an encounter with Jesus, but we also need to have that encounter interpreted by the truth of God's Word. Otherwise, experience can lead us astray. Jude 1:3 tells us "to contend for the faith that was once for all entrusted to the saints." The faith was entrusted to us via the Bible, the written Word of God. We must not compromise the truth that God has spoken inerrantly and fully in His Word. https://www.gotquestions.org/neoorthodoxy.html

"Jesus answered, "It is written: Man does not live on bread alone, but on every word that comes from the mouth of God" (v. 4) Matthew 4:1-11. Early in the twentieth century, two European theologians mounted an assault on nineteenth-century liberalism.
The nineteenth-century liberals had tried to find the "historical Jesus" by discounting the testimony of the Bible and filtering the Biblical evidence through their own conceptions of what must have happened. They had used "literary science" to "prove" that the Bible is merely a collection of human opinions about God and not the Word of God at all.

The two theologians who attacked this idea, **Karl Barth** and **Emil Brunner**, were called "neo-orthodox" because they seemed to be affirming the orthodox Christian faith against the more liberal mind set. They maintained that the Bible was the Word of God and that God inspired it—but what they meant by these statements was radically different from true Christianity.

Barth and **Brunner** denied that the Bible was the Word of God in an objective sense. They said that the Bible was, at most, a collection of merely human documents.

But, they said, God uses these human documents to create an "encounter" with the reader, so that the Bible becomes the Word of God as we read it. Reading the Bible, which is full of factual error, sparks this "encounter."
 Orthodox Christianity, however, affirms that the Bible is objectively true in all respects while also insisting that we must have a personal relationship with God. There is no need to pit these two things against each other.
The Bible is true whether we accept it or not and whether we encounter Jesus Christ or not. The statements of the Bible are inherently revelatory and inherently true whether or not we respond to them. **Barth** was concerned throughout his life with the fact that human beings make mistakes. "To err is human" was one of his favorite maxims. **Barth** never seems to have realized that it is precisely because sinful human beings are prone to error—indeed prone to suppress God's truth with all their might—that it was necessary for God to superintend the writing of Scripture and insure that it be error free.

Coram Deo--Just because humans can err does not mean they must or will err in every situation. It is not a necessary part of the human condition. We can all pass spelling and simple math tests. If **Barth** were right, he would have to be wrong, as he too is human. Thank God for His error-free Word and for the mind He gave you.
https://www.ligonier.org/learn/devotionals/ (The neo-orthodox view).

Dietrich Bonhoeffer was executed on April 9, 1945.

(**NOTE: There is a very large biographical book of him, written by Eric Metaxas entitled, "Bonhoeffer: Pastor, Martyr, Prophet, Spy." (Thomas Nelson Publishers, © 2010; ISBN 978-1-59555-138-2, 978-1-59555-318-8). It is up to the reader to determine if he truly stood against Christianity and instead was a partaker of the "neo-orthodoxy" that the above links suggests. Ed.).

- **Reinhard Bonnke**: Deceased; German preacher who was heretical in his doctrine; was a Word of Faith heretic, decision theology, signs and wonders; also aligned with him is **Suzette Hetting, Reinhardt Bonnke's** "lead intercessor."
Suzette Hetting has also attempted to become an apostle by trying to fulfill a prophecy for Australia, rallying 10,000 warriors for an end-times revival back in 2007-8.

 https://pulpitandpen.org https://churchwatchcentral.com/2018/01/22/ (reinhard-bonnke-demonstrates-how-a-false-baptism-leads-people-to-confess-a-false-christ/.

Taking the supposed "mantle" and doing the same "works" as **Reinhard Bonnke**, is his young student, **Daniel Kolenda**, who promises and preaches the same false drivel as his mentor, **Reinhard**.

 (**NOTE: This article is very lengthy; it is easier to click on the link or paste it into the search box to read it. UPDATE: **Reinhard Bonnke** passed away on 12/7/19.

His successor, **Daniel Kolenda**, is taking over CFAN (Christ For All Nations. Ed.).

- **William Branham**: Old time preacher; left the truth for a "spirit" guide to help him; believes the "orbs" around him are God's angels, which in fact are demonic apparitions; (denied the Trinity) —founder of "Latter Day Rain" heresy; considered the greatest prophet of our times by several of the apostates; false teacher, false prophet, false signs and wonders.
HUGE cult following today--**William Branham** was a very knowledgeable study of these false prophets, and wanted to become like them.

For an unknown reason that he took to the grave, **Branham** modeled his doctrines, his teachings, and even his life after men that have been deemed a false prophet after their prophecy failed. One such study is that of **John Alexander Dowie** of Zion, Illinois;

Preaching in **Dowie's** commune-city, **Branham** promoted himself as the "Elisha" to **Dowie's** "Elijah." Both **Gordon Lindsay and F. F. Bosworth** were Zionists, followers of **Dowie.** Together, the two and **Branham** promoted **Dowie's** doctrines in the "Voice of Healing" magazine that **Branham** edited and sold. Both **Lindsay** and **Branham** were on the board of directors for the magazine. **Lindsay** went on to write books praising **Dowie** for his ministry of healing. Like **Dowie, Branham** was faced with a dreadful end, one that the real prophets of the Bible had prophesied about.

God does not stand for false teachings, and He takes false prophets out of our midst. So the elect are not led astray, God removes these false teachers from the face of the earth http://seekyethetruth.com).

In his later years **Branham** completely went off the deep end. Not only did he deny the doctrine of the Trinity, he taught a wacky doctrine called Serpent's Seed, which says that Eve had sex with a serpent which produced Cain. He thought he was Elijah. He also taught the false doctrines of the United Pentecostal Church regarding baptizing in Jesus' Name only, and various legalist positions.
In his earlier years of ministry however, **Branham** refused to teach or get entangled with doctrinal issues, stating that he was sent to preach Jesus, win the lost, and heal the sick.

It was only after he got himself into tax trouble and couldn't afford to hold crusades that he turned to the United Pentecostal churches for ministry opportunities, and ended up teaching these views.
What the critic didn't tell his listeners is that **William Branham** didn't begin teaching Unitarianism until the late 1950's (according to this website, **Branham's** teaching on the Trinity was all over the map, but there was a fundamental change in 1958 that eventually led to a complete rejection of Trinitarianism).

He was a preacher and ministered to the sick in the office of a prophet. He came under the influence of the United Pentecostal Church in the 50's, and as a result he began to teach some of their false doctrines. http://jewandgreek.com.

During the 1950's, **William Branham** led the revival in healing that would break the ground for such people as **Oral Roberts.** The Latter-Rain movement began in Canada from **William Branham** who laid hands on the leaders, which presumably included **Oral Roberts**.

The "Healing Revival" continued from 1947 to 1957, led by **Oral Roberts, T.L. Osborn, Jack Coe, A.A. Allen,** and **O.L. Jaggers,** and was popularized through **Gordon Lindsay's** "Voice of Healing" magazine. **Roberts** is the only one left alive of the original inner circle (along with **Paul Cain** who was discipled by **Branham**).

(**NOTE: Both of these men are deceased, but probably not when the author of the article wrote it. Ed.).

"Latter Rain" proponent **Franklin Hall** (who made famous the "fire baptism") wrote a book on fasting and prayer which was a major influence for the "Latter Rain" movement and in the ministry of **Oral Roberts**. Towards the end of his life he taught he was the reincarnated Elijah and the seventh angel of the Revelation as per Rev 10:7 and that the Trinity is a "demonic" doctrine. **Branham** was by any standards excessively in touch with angels, his own healer angel plus a variety of "ministering angels" who have subsequently been in touch with **Todd Bentley** and **John Crowder.**

Declining from mainstream beliefs about apocalypse (which are admittedly somewhat varied and disputed!) **Branham** taught a "Latter Rain" and "Manifest Sons of God " doctrine which meant that a last times generation would produce unprecedented miracles that would hasten Jesus' return to the world and cause an elite to come forth and be realized as semi-divine figures on earth.

In practice this means that new mystics tend to be Dominionists, seeking to intervene in secular laws and ready if need be to rant, rail and get weepy like **Lou Engle** at special rallies, assemblies, fasts, against the evils of modern society in order to make the world Christian, not least by law, in ways that will help institute the Millennium for Jesus. They are thus in some ways heavily political and close to the Christian Right.

Branham followers (none are exact) are effectively a loose cult group which have nonetheless sufficiently ignored or modified **Branham's** extremes to stay within the churches under the influence of especially the controversial **Bob Jones,** who was in touch with **Branham's** main disciple, **Paul Cain,** and the Kansas City Prophets.

Depending upon your view, **Bob Jones** is either someone who has prophetic gifts ... "of true biblical stature"..."when **Bob** comes to a church or city almost every person he encounters is left functioning on a higher spiritual level (**Rick Joyner**) --or he's the perfect fraud."

What's undisputed is that **Jones** was rejected by the Anaheim Vineyard church in the early nineties for "improprieties," most notably encouraging women to kit off in his office to receive prophecies from God in the nude– one gathers women have since been asking for protection against **Bob's** apparent tendency still to make unwanted appearances when they undress.

(Letter of Rev. Jesse Star of Texas reproduced at: http://eternalpath.com/lakeland.html).

William Branham picked up the Malachi 4:5 "Elijah" complex that many dangerous cult leaders who, for decades in the past, claimed to possess as well, including the murderous **Jim Jones.** https://pulpitandpen.org..
http://www.letusreason.org/ Latrain56.htm

–Barbie Breathitt: Author **Barbie Breathitt**, described as a "respected teacher of the supernatural manifestations of God," has just released a new book entitled "Dream Encounters," in which she claims Christians can have access to a secret dream language that God uses to reveal "hidden knowledge" to believers.

In this book **Breathitt** tells believers they will be enabled to use the "revelation" obtained from God through their dreams in order to unlock their "destinies" and live lives in which they are "productive, responsible, successful, prosperous, loved and fulfilled" (p. 138). According to **Breathitt**, this is done by decoding information that God has "embedded" into our dreams and through which he continues to communicate with us in personal, ongoing revelation.

But there are three significant problems with what **Breathitt** teaches, and I will attempt to develop why these issues are unsupported by Scripture.

The three problems are as follows:

1. **Breathitt's** teaching is more in alignment with a pagan and superstitious—even New Age—worldview than Christian;

2. **Breathitt** puts forth the idea that each believer has a "destiny" waiting to be unlocked, accessed, known and lived out, an idea that is contrary to the teaching of Scripture—that, as Christians, we have no "rights" to our lives.

3. **Breathitt's** teaching about ongoing, personal revelation from God goes against the clear teaching of Sola Scriptura, which is that God speaks to us through Scripture alone.

Dream Interpretation is New Age: To help explain how I can make the assertion that **Breathitt's** teaching on "dream interpretation" is much closer to being New Age (pagan) than Christian, let me back up for a moment.

I write this review not as a theologian but as a former New Ager who was saved by God's grace out of New Age Spirituality. My testimony is this: after rejecting the church as a teenager, I went wholeheartedly into New Age Spirituality. While in the New Age, I went down many different paths to seek enlightenment, truth, hidden knowledge and, yes, God.

I sampled from a buffet of religious practices and traditions, including psychological self-help, Hinduism, Buddhism, mysticism, paganism, shamanism, astrology, trance channeling, reiki, dream interpretation, yoga, astral projection, runes, numerology, chakra meditation, visualization, fortune telling, tarot cards, psychic readings and on and on.
But the problem with this freestyle way of attempting to approach God is that, at its core, it is pagan and therefore cannot give anyone access to God. However, this "freestyle approach" is also the chief allure of New Age Spirituality:

One is encouraged to choose any path or practice that "feels good" to them, that makes them feel closer to "God," and gives them a sense of purpose. What I know now is that without God's "special revelation" of Himself through His Word (the Bible) I never could have come to the saving knowledge of God. The Bible distinguishes between "general revelation" (found in nature) and "special revelation" (found only in God's Word) this way: "General revelation" is revelation of God found through observing nature and the surrounding world.

While "general revelation" gives enough revelation for people to know that there is a God to whom they are accountable, it does not give enough revelation for people to actually be saved. This was why God was so elusive to me while I was in the New Age. I was getting vague, shadowy glimpses of God through the many occult things I did but was unable to get a true understanding of his character, nature and what He required of me.

For this, I needed "special revelation," found only in the Bible, God's revelation of Himself, which teaches who He is and the way of salvation. New Age Spirituality, at its essence, is a pagan form of religion in that it can operate only within the realm of "general revelation." Even though plenty of biblical terminology and even scripture itself is used in the New Age, salvation is found only through faith in the atoning death of a Messiah who made propitiation, died and was resurrected—the correct view of Jesus that is clearly rejected by adherents of New Age teaching.

Before we go further, let me define paganism and explain how I can make the assertion that New Age is pagan at its core. Paganism is often thought of as sort of a nature religion, something practiced by primitive people groups who live in grass huts in remote areas and who carve idols and literally look to "signs" in nature in an attempt to know God. But in another sense, every religion that is not Christian can be considered to be pagan; there are simply different "flavors" of it. All false religions attempt to come up with ways to "reach" God, whether through yoga, meditation and fasting (Hinduism/Buddhism); mecca, prayers, Jihad (Islam); meditation, energy work, spells (Wicca).

Paganism, then, is the "default setting" of the natural mind when it is does not have the revelation of God's Word which only comes through the Bible ("special revelation"). As Pastor **John MacArthur** has said, "There are only two religions in the world...One is by works, the other is without works." Without benefit of God's "special revelation" given through his Word, pagans are forced to sift through the natural landscape, searching for clues about who God is and what he requires of them in the hopes of coming up with a system that makes sense of what they see.

 (**NOTE: **John MacArthur** himself is a heretic, but this is someone else's quote, so I will leave it here. See **John MacArthur** below in my booklet. Ed.).

So even though I identified myself at various times with specific religions when I was involved in New Age Spirituality, I was living and functioning as a pagan. In my view this kind of "functional paganism," is the main problem with **Breathitt's** book. Though she quotes plenty of Scripture in her book, she is continually pointing her readers back to the paganism of "divining" and interpreting omens and symbols in their dreams.

Breathitt seems to want to make a distinction between the kind of "Christianized divination" she is teaching and what she considers to be unbiblical, occultic divination, but the Bible makes no such distinction. Even though **Breathitt** specifically names psychics, mediums, witches, Wiccans and other New Age occultic means of divination as "counterfeits" (p 95), she is teaching her readers to do the same things that these occultic practitioners do.

The Bible, though, has very strong words for anyone who attempts to divine hidden or secret knowledge belonging only to the Lord (Deut 29:29):

"There shall not be found among you anyone who makes his son or his daughter pass through the fire, one who uses divination, one who practices witchcraft, or one who interprets omens, or a sorcerer, or one who casts a spell, or a medium, or a spiritist, or one who calls up the dead." "For whoever does these things is detestable to the LORD; and because of these detestable things the LORD your God will drive them out before you." Deut. 18:10-12, (my emphasis).

(**NOTE: This is the author's emphasis, not mine. Ed.).

This passage in Deuteronomy makes quite clear what the Lord considers to be occultic and wicked. Yet two of the above practices (divination and interpreting omens) are exactly what **Breathitt's** book is teaching! At least one third of **Breathitt's** book is devoted to teaching readers how to interpret symbols in their dreams such as colors, stones, numbers, sounds, types of clothing, types of buildings, modes of transportation, animals, weather, insects and others.

And incidentally, the type of dream interpretation as taught by **Breathitt** is virtually identical to the type of dream interpretation I was taught and practiced as a New Ager.
But these are pagan practices, and they are off-limits to Christians in that they are an attempt to usurp God's power and authority over our lives by discerning hidden knowledge. "A man will plan his course, but it is the Lord who determines his steps." (Prov 16:9).
In addition to the New Age practice of divination (which I have noted is an attempt to usurp power and authority that belongs only to God), another key teaching of the New Age is that people can direct their own destinies (which they do partly through divining the signs and omens in their life, dreams and in the world around them).

The main thrust of this teaching is that every person has a "right" to a life of good health, prosperity, transcendent happiness, wonderful relationships and exciting careers. This brings me to my second problem with **Breathitt's** book.
She teaches that God has a "divine plan for us to be successful" and that each believer has a "destiny"—a word she uses repeatedly—waiting to be unlocked, accessed, known, and lived out. This kind of man-centered, positive self-help sort of teaching has always been popular in America. Over the years it has latched itself to the culture and taken shape in many different forms ("Law of Attraction," "The Secret," "Possibility Thinking," "Word of Faith").
It has even taken on Christian terminology so as to become more palatable to confessing Christians who want a way to be "Christian" and still have control over their own lives and destinies.

Yet, this thinking is completely at odds with the crucified, yielded life that is described of New Testament believers.   The Bible teaches that it is God alone who reigns and rules sovereignly over our lives.   And while **Breathitt** makes mention occasionally that only God knows what the future holds for us, she also repeatedly puts forth the idea that once we are saved we are able to access this "hidden knowledge" about the "purpose" and "destiny" of our lives through dream interpretation and that our lives ought to be marked by happiness, success and prosperity.

 Breathitt asserts that it is the "right" of every Christian to access hidden knowledge through dream interpretation for the purpose of navigating their lives to "fulfilling destinies."
Indeed, **Breathitt** claims in her book that an astonishing array of blessings can and should be had by Christian believers if they will learn how to decode their dreams.

Some of these claims are that believers, through dream interpretation, will be able to:

- Unlock God's revelation
- Receive messages from God through angels
- Get answers to questions
- Steer clear of harmful events
- Fulfill their dreams and destinies
- Know the path to their future
- Be healthier, both physically and spiritually
- Achieve prosperity, success and increase
- Be more creative
- Live longer

But this teaching of physical blessing and prosperity flies in the face of the clear teaching of Scripture, which is that we have no "rights" to our lives, and that it is God alone who knows and determines our destinies.   In fact, a study of the Apostles does not give a sense of lives marked by "living longer," "steering clear of harmful events" or being "prosperous."

All but one of the Apostles were killed for the faith, most of them having suffered torturous deaths. Paul himself was shipwrecked, beaten, stoned, left for dead, imprisoned and ultimately martyred. Paul often referred to himself in his letters as a "slave to Christ," and it is this language that gives us a more biblical understanding of a Christian's "destiny," according to Paul.
Upon the moment of conversion, all "rights" to our lives are relinquished. We know that our lives are no longer our own; we have been bought for a price, and only God alone can know and direct our destiny. But oh, how this kind of language and teaching chafes today's Christians, especially American ones, who have been taught to esteem liberation and freedom, choice and autonomy. But is this the picture that Scripture paints for the life of a Christian? We do not have "rights" to our lives, nor do we have the power or ability to navigate our lives to "fulfilling destinies," as **Breathitt** claims.

If I make a plan for my life and God has a "destiny" in store for me other than the one I have mapped out, I must bend the knee in humble submission before God's greater plan for my life.

Just ask Stephen, who was stoned to death after rebuking the Sanhedrin for their sinful rejection of the prophets and Messiah himself. About Stephen, I wonder: did the "life of (his) dreams" include death by stoning? (Probably not, because in our flesh each of us is small, narcissistic, self-protective and vain.) But when submitted to the Lord, as Stephen was, and as we all must strive to be by God's grace, our lives have deeper meaning and serve eternal purposes that our finite minds cannot grasp.

But not according to **Barbie Breathitt**, in whose teaching I saw nothing of the crucified life, a life yielded to its Maker for His purposes. Rather, **Breathitt's** teaching seems designed more to tickle ears and pander to worldly and fleshly appetites for success, comfort, prestige and wealth, than to exhort true believers to lay down their lives in service of the Lord and to take up the cross and follow Christ, wherever that may lead. Christ never promised his followers that they would have successful, prosperous, fulfilled lives.

 In fact, one thing that He did tell them about their "destinies" was this: "If the world hates you, know that it has hated me before it hated you. If you were of the world, the world would love you as its own; but because you are not of the world, but I chose you out of the world, therefore the world hates you." "Remember the word that I said to you: 'A servant is not greater than his master.' If they persecuted me, they will also persecute you. If they kept my word, they will also keep yours." (John 15:18-20).
But to true Christians it doesn't matter. True believers don't come to Christ in the first place looking for "goodies" or worldly blessing; they come to Him because they know He and He alone offers forgiveness for sins and the way of salvation. True believers will follow Him anywhere, yielding their lives to Him, submitting their dreams, wants and desires to His perfect will (Mat 6:10), knowing that He alone knows what they need.

This is what the Bible teaches: a crucified self (Rom 6:6), a life yielded to its Maker.
Not a genie-in-a-bottle "God," or some hoop-jumping "God" or a "God" who is the outlet for us to "plug into" so we can get power for our dreams.

The Rejection of Sola Scriptura: "Long ago, at many times and in many ways, God spoke to our fathers by the prophets, but in these last days he has spoken to us by his Son, whom he appointed the heir of all things, through whom also he created the world." (Hebrews 1:1-2).

Which brings me to my third and final point:

According to **Breathitt**, believers will receive personal, ongoing revelation from God if they will learn how to "read" the "dream language" God supposedly gives them, which to her is the way He desires to communicate with believers. But this is a rebellion against and rejection of the means God has chosen by which to reveal Himself to us, which is through the Bible, a concept known as Sola Scriptura. "Sola Scriptura" teaches that we "hear" from God through the Bible alone.
In fact, this idea of personal, ongoing revelation from God is unbiblical, in that Hebrews 1:1-2 explains to us that God has spoken directly to prophets of His choosing in past ages, but that once His full revelation has been given, culminating in Jesus Christ, the final and greatest

Prophet, the canon is then closed and no further revelation will be given in the last days beyond what has been given in Scripture.

Let me point out that although **Breathitt** quotes a lot of Scripture in her book, it must be understood that the usage of Scripture does not necessarily mean that someone is teaching truth and that applying Scripture to wicked and forbidden practices does not somehow "cleanse" these practices of evil.

Let me repeat, the sprinkling of Scripture atop wicked practices will not sanctify them, nor will it imbue some kind of mystical protection over a Christian who innocently wanders into the occultic realm.

I can attest from my own experience that the occult is a very dangerous realm and nothing to meddle with. Even for Christians the occult is a dangerous realm. I often hear the argument that once a person is born again and sealed with the Holy Spirit they have a "supernatural protection" against deception. "Well, I hear what you're saying about things being occultic, but I would know if I were being deceived."

But isn't that the whole point of deception? After all, if we knew we were being deceived, isn't it rather self evident that we wouldn't actually be deceived? Deception's greatest trick is that it is evil masquerading as good. A "Christian" book by a "Christian" author teaching readers to do unbiblical things in the pursuit of forbidden, hidden knowledge is an example of this. A writer or teacher being loaded up on Christian terminology or Scripture doesn't necessarily mean that Biblical truth is being taught.

All Christians are exhorted by Scripture to test everything, to hold fast to what is true and to be like the Bereans, who were commended for their diligence in studying Scripture.

In short, Christians are not to blindly accept any and all teaching at face value. In fact, Paul exhorted believers not to believe even himself if he should come bearing a message that was different from the one handed down to the saints! Very strong words, and believers should take this as an exhortation to examine all teaching of Scripture to take care that it is being taught correctly and in context. As far as I can tell from reading **Breathitt's** book, the Bible functions as little more than a handbook of symbols for believers to search through for the purpose of decoding their dreams to "unlock" their destinies and live prosperous, successful lives.

Again, **Breathitt** seems to be deliberately pandering to sinful desires with this teaching. Pandering to the flesh and to the human desire for hidden knowledge is nothing new at all: "Now the serpent was more crafty than any of the wild animals the LORD God had made. He said to the woman, "Did God really say, 'You must not eat from any tree in the garden'?" " (Gen 3:1).

Isn't Satan himself insinuating to Eve that there is hidden knowledge being withheld from her? And lest we forget, it did not turn out well for Eve when she began to long for the fruit God had forbidden. And we must also remember that Satan will rarely present himself in all his awful glory. He delights in taking evil and presenting it as something good and alluring, such as a luscious piece of fruit that is "a delight to the eyes and good to taste."

In American culture, so rife with materialism and excess, the "forbidden fruit" that we seem to be continual lusting for is some form of worldly success or prosperity.

In closing, I believe **Breathitt** does her readers a grave disservice in her book by directing them away from the special revelation contained in the Bible and toward a "Christianized" kind of divination in which they will be reduced to living as functional pagans. While **Breathitt** does often quote Scripture, her references are heavily lopsided toward passages describing dream sequences, visions and the like. As far as **Breathitt's** teaching goes, the Bible seems only to be useful as a kind of "omens handbook."
This is amazingly bad theology coming from someone who professes to be a Christian, as **Breathitt** does. And contrary to **Breathitt's** teaching, Christians do not have some kind of "right" to access "hidden knowledge" once they are born again. They do not have the ability or power to navigate their own destinies toward prosperity, success and comfort.

And the pursuit of "hidden knowledge" for the purpose of such is sinful and condemned by God, as it is God alone who knows and directs the destinies of believers. I simply cannot recommend this book to Christians, as it will lead them not into a deeper understanding of the one true God as revealed in Scripture but rather into the shadowy world of pagan divination and a lust for hidden knowledge and worldly comfort. Buyer beware.

https://www.raptureforums.com/forums/threads/
christian-dream-interpretation-and-prophet-barbie-breathitt.83362/

Back to magic charms. A few posts back, I wrote about the growing popularity of magic charms and spells in the apostolic-prophetic movement, like a property cleansing kit that's supposed to rid your property of curses (still listed as a "top-selling product" on the "Elijah List"). Well, yesterday, the "Elijah List" sent another e-mail advertising another product that has more in common with the occult than Biblical Christianity:

Barbie Breathitt: "Dream Cards." That's right. For $10 a piece, you can buy cards that list the meanings of common dream symbols, like different types of animals, people and places (pictured above). If you buy all 12 cards, you can even get a discount: $96. Brought to you by **Barbie Breathitt**, of Breath of the Spirit Ministries, Inc.

Dream interpretation has never been easier. If the dream cards aren't bad enough, it gets worse. One of the cards has a chart that lists areas of the body along with colors and musical notes that are supposed to bring healing to those areas. What? Where is the Biblical basis for this practice? There isn't a Biblical basis. The "Elijah List' doesn't even try to give one in its ad.

But there is an occult and New Age basis. See, for example, this New York psychic's Web site where she lists colors and the areas of the body they heal. Or see the "Psychic Healing Room," which also talks about the healing power of colors and music.
Of course, we see throughout the Bible that God does give people dreams, and He gives His people the ability to interpret the meanings of those dreams. But where in the Bible do we see anything like dream cards? The people who interpret dreams in Scripture, like Daniel and Joseph, are given supernatural insight from God.

They certainly don't consult cards to find generic symbolic meanings.

Can you imagine Daniel saying, "Just one second, King Nebuchadnezzar. You said a statue? Well, according to this chart here, a statue represents …"? And we certainly don't see Daniel or Joseph creating cards with dream interpretations and selling them. This reminds me of Tarot cards.

What we do see is that both Daniel and Joseph make it clear that the source of their interpretations is God. (See Genesis 40:8, 41:16; Daniel 2:17-23, 27-28).   As far as healing colors and sounds: well, of course, music and colors can affect people's moods.

For example, music can be soothing, and a pastel-painted room (like a soft blue) might be a more relaxing environment than a brightly painted room (like red). But this is far different than claiming that a certain color or musical note can bring healing to a specific organ or body part.

It's not my goal to pick on professing Christians, but people like **Steve Shultz** — the founder and publisher of the "Elijah List" — need to be called to account for their shameful promotion of such products.

I believe true prophets of God (which **Shultz** claims to be) would be appalled by these dream cards. The "Elijah List" e-mails are so full of unbiblical (and often harmful) teachings that I've decided to add a separate category on my blog that will focus just on this ministry.

See the bar on the right side of my blog for the new category called "Elijah List."

http://www.spiritoferror.org/2006/11/dream-cards-and-occult-healing/36

https://www.honorofkings.org/false-prophet-listing/

(**NOTE: This is a listing of false prophets; although not exhaustive, it is for the most part naming the "giants" of the false prophets\false teachers that are on the circuit today. Ed.).

- **Rodney Howard Browne**: Originally from South Africa; Friend of the "Vineyard Church" and the "Toronto Revival," which consists of damnable heresies; Says he is the "Holy Ghost bartender," "so belly up to the bar;" teaches "tokin' the Ghost;" blasphemous; helped popularize the demonic "holy laughter," spurious manifestations; false prophet, pastor and teacher; another NAR-Emergent church proponent):

http://www.deceptioninthechurch.com/howard-browne.html

http://so4j.com/rodney-howard-browne-false-teacher

https://pulpitandpen.org/2017/11/21/

https://www.backtothebible.ca/articles/

https://billrandles.wordpress.com/2017/07/14/

https://www.equip.org/article/ (An evening with **RHB**–a reporter)

http://www.sermonindex.net/modules/newbb/view

https://www.lighthousetrailsresearch.com/blog/?p=23099

https://billrandles.wordpress.com/2017/07/14/
rodney-howard-browne-the-heretic-who-laid-hands-on-trump/

http://www.sermonindex.net/modules/newbb/ viewtopic.php?topic_id=6281&forum=35

https://www.rightwingwatch.org/post/
paula-white-the-white-house-is-holy-ground-because-where-i-stand-is-holy/

"...**Rodney Browne** began to make his appearance on TBN telling the audience about serving Joel's wine to the church and that they were to get drunk, so the church began to laugh hysterically, stuck to the floor for hours, lost the ability to speak as evil was increasing." The word "drunk" appears 3 times in the book of Revelation 17:2, 6;18:3.
It's not a good thing, it's spiritual fornication and the Bible tells us they kill the saints (who are not drunk).

Rodney Howard Browne was making everyone laugh while EVIL was increasing all around them which brought in self focus feelings. He told people not to pray but just accept what is happening to them as from God and they did. **Browne** convinced the church that in Acts 2, they must have been drunk on the new wine because the people (mockers, unbelievers) said they were drunk and filled with new wine.
 This was carried like a virus in the "Vineyard " churches under **John Wimber**, and broke loose in the "Toronto Airport Vineyard " under **John Arnott**. "Vineyard " churches already was prepared for these new unbiblical manifestations as **Jack Deere** and **Paul Cain**, **Mike Bickle** and **Bob Jones** were teaching of Joel's Army (one of the teachings of the Latter Rain), they look at it as a miracle working army of the church elite that invade places all over the earth.

The Bible teaches this takes place in the day of the LORD - the Tribulation; it's not a good thing. Others who called themselves Pentecostals and Charismatics got filled with the same spirit and the TV airwaves were filled with new spirit warriors that were an army marching through the land to remove demonic forces and evil that opposed God's kingdom. Every day a new revelation and prophesy was revealed on how the church would no longer be the tail but the head.
Rodney Howard-Browne at a **Kenneth Copeland** meeting was the red light flashing as they showed the church what they were both really about, as he prophesied the power that is coming to the church. "This is the day, this is the hour," saith the Lord "that I am moving in this earth." "This is the day that I'll cause you to step over into the realm of the supernatural. ... The drops of rain are beginning to fall to the glory of God.... For this is the day of the fire and the glory of God coming unto His Church."

 "Rise up this day.... To drink, to drink, to drink, to drink, to drink, to drink, to drink, to drink, to drink [tongues]." "We drink [tongues] [he laughs]." "O yea, yea, yea, yea, yea, we don't worry about what other people say." "No, it doesn't matter what they think. Ha, ha, ha, ho, oooh." Then he began to speak to **Copeland** in tongues who spoke back in tongues and they laughed at each others jokes spoken in tongues."

Kenneth Copeland then said to him, "Take a deep drink. Take a deep drink of the Holy Ghost." **Rodney** then laughed, and the man fell down to the floor. **Copeland** then spoke in tongues.

Rodney "prophesied" again and said, "My people after Calvary got nothing out of religion." "And the Holy Ghost came because they got nothing out of religion. Well, you silly thing." "Oh you silly goose. … Look, look, look, look, look, look, look, look saith the Lord. Cloven tongues. Look, look, look, cloven tongues like as of fire.   Look, look, look saith the Lord. It is happening right now." " When will Pentecost [come]?' It is happening right now."

"When will the outpouring come?" "It is happening right now. Feel, feel, feel, feel, feel the wind, the wind, the wind, the wind is blowing. Yes, yes, yes, cloven tongues like as of fire. Get up. Get up. See—see the glory."

"See the shekinah. You are in the midst of angels. You are in the midst of the shekinah cloud. You are in the midst of the fire. For the glory of the Lord has descended, and you are beholding, yes, yes, you are beholding my face." " You are seeing into the Spirit realm."

These men acted like they were spiritually insane, but the more meetings they acted this way the more acceptable it became. And so they introduced the new thing to a grateful audience, this is what we now know as the "Signs and Wonders movement." Which was a disguised revision of the Latter Rain that came from **William Branham** and the healing evangelists of the 40's. Each year more people watched them, they gave more money, more authority, more Biblical truth in exchange for what TBN and their 'special guests' were transferring.

 People falling down, shaking like they have Turret syndrome or another neurological disease. We entered an era of a new openness to the mystical, the "realm of the spirit." Their audience was being converted and didn't even know it. The participants in the Word Faith movement (also engaged in Latter Rain practices) were quick to jump in this newly formed river that eventually drowned people in the rapids as it ran swiftly to the waterfalls edge. http://www.letusreason.org/Pent64.htm

(**NOTE: There are a lot of You Tube videos showing how deceptive and dangerous **Rodney Howard Browne** really is. It is not too hard to compare his false preaching to the truth of the Bible. Ed.).

--**Matt Brown**: https://www.youtube.com/watch?v=PexaCBm0HIo
(**NOTE: Several YouTube videos about him. Search with his name, then the word "Enneagram" and several will come up. Your choice as to which one you want to watch—all a form of "personality testing," which is against the Scriptures and demonic in nature. Ed.).

https://tottministries.org/
the-enneagram-a-christian-perspective-by-richard-rohr-and-andreas-ebert/

https://www.gotquestions.org/Enneagram-of-Personality.html

https://sandalschurch.com/enneagram/ Their own church promoting it.

https://www.nowtheendbegins.com/
charismatic-emergent-churches-embracing-new-age-paganism-as-occultic-practice-of-enneagra
m-replaces-teaching-bible-doctrine/September 28, 2019.

(**NOTE: This so-called "preacher" uses an enneagram, a tool of the ancient pagan mystics, that can 'radically transform' your spirit life, according to the above article.   You have to paste the entire title in their search box. Ed.).

--**Michael Brown:** Since the inception of the "New Order of the Latter Rain" (NOLR) cult (which matured into the Charismatic movement and naturally morphed into the New Apostolic Reformation), people who are in these heretical sects have no problem denying their involvement in these movements. They do this only to usurp leadership of churches and denominations and convert people to NAR-ismaticism.

An example of someone doing exactly this is **Michael Brown**. He has been lying publicly that he is a Charismatic Pentecostal. For someone who parades the notion that he is a theological expert, this is duplicitous. The truth is, **Michael Brown** is **not** a Pentecostal. Back in 1949, Pentecostalism had both condemned, and later resisted, both the NOLR and its "offspring" movements such as the "Charismatic Renewal Movement" (CRM). Even worse, **Michael Brown** has been hiding behind the Charismatic title giving the impression that "Charismaticism" is distinguished from NAR theology.

This is deceitful when he has clearly demonstrated in his theology, language and practice that he knows his theology is in line with the NOLR heretical fathers and his "Apostle" friends in the New Apostolic Reformation (NAR).
For instance, in 1990 in his book, " What Happened to the Power of God ?" **Michael Brown** acknowledged where his heretical beliefs came from –the "New Order of the Latter Rain." Rather than point out why these teachings and leaders were dangerous because of their false Gospel, false Jesus, false spirit, false ecclesia and unbiblical faith, **Michael Brown** upholds these frauds and apostates: "From 1947-1958 there was a great outpouring of healing power, unprecedented in modern times. Until that time, healing anointings were rare. But in 1947 things changed."

" A new generation was being raised up, and suddenly the gifts were everywhere. There were hundreds of "healing evangelists" preaching through the United States and overseas, many of them with huge tents and even television ministries; It takes holy servants to be channels of the Spirit. He cannot be separated from His gifts. They are a manifestation of Him."
(**Dr. Michael Brown**, "What Happened to the Power of God?," Destiny Image, Revival Press, Published 1991, pg. 11-12.).

That "great outpouring of healing power" being referred to above was the NOLR. **Franklin Hall** and **William Branham** were the key figures that promoted and "raised up" a "new generation" of cultists promoting the "healing Gospel." These gifts came out of the "New Order of the Latter Rain" because they believed they could impart spiritual gifts/offices to others. That's how hundreds of healing evangelists emerged through the U.S. and overseas.

Michael Brown has the audacity to call them "holy servants" when they did not hesitate preaching the false "Power Gospel" or "Gospel of the Kingdom." This is a "Signs and Wonders Gospel" that convinces people that God is real to serve their needs, often espousing that healing was in the atonement (which later developed through **Oral Roberts** and the NOLR organization "Full Gospel Business Men's Fellowship International," that Jesus died to make people rich).

Michael Brown also teaches NOLR "Manifest Sons of God " heresy in his book, "What happened to the power of God?" (1990). These heretical teachings are littered throughout the "Brownsville Revival," a dangerous event that **Michael Brown** considers to be a genuine move of God. But why does **Michael Brown** endorse these heresies? The answer is simple: he believes in their heresies. Simply look at his statement of beliefs in his "FIRE" School and "FIRE" Church. **Brown** promotes the false NOLR demonic spirit and its false baptism that leads people to confess that Christ is NOT fully YHWH:

"We believe that Baptism in the Holy Spirit, primarily evidenced by speaking with other tongues as the Spirit gives utterance, is for all believers as promised by John the Baptist (Mat 3:11), Jesus (Acts 1:4, 5, 8), and Peter (Acts 2:38-41) and as witnessed by the early disciples of the Lord Jesus Christ (Acts 2:1-4; 10:44-46; 19:6)." Because of this spirit, **Brown** confesses the false NOLR healing gospel: "We believe that divine healing is also provided in the atonement (Isa 53:5)."

Because of this false spirit and false Gospel, **Brown** confesses a FALSE CHRIST: "[Jesus] was declared 'Son of God' with His resurrection, so He was born the Son of God, and then born again as the Son of God. You've got to listen to the whole teaching."

When **Dr. Brown** was asked about **Bill Johnson's** teaching on the born-again Jesus, **Dr. Brown** stated: "[**Johnson**] uses it in the Biblical sense, that He was declared 'Son of God' with His resurrection, so He was born the Son of God, and then born again as the Son of God. You've got to listen to the whole teaching." "[Jesus] always was fully God. But like many others teach, while He was on the earth, He did not use His divine prerogatives to heal, but heal by the Spirit." "Jesus Himself says that. 'I can only do what I see the Father doing.' 'The Spirit of the Lord is upon Me, because He has anointed Me to preach." "I drive out demons by the Spirit."

Once again, **Brown** did not refute this. "Yet Jesus told us that if we believed in Him, we could do the same works He did (John 14:12). Why, then, is there such a massive discrepancy between what He did by the Spirit and what we do by the Spirit?"
"I understand that Jesus was uniquely accredited by God with signs, wonders, and miracles (for example, Acts 2:22). But surely, if His words are true (and they are!), we should be seeing many more healings and miracles today." **Brown** promotes the false NOLR dooms-day cult model of "church":
"There is no church unless Jesus Christ holds it together, and neither is the church properly founded unless genuine, God-given apostles and prophets are in their rightful place according to the will of Jesus, the head (Eph 2:20-22; 4:11)."

These confessions put him outside of the Christian faith and lump him in with all the false prophets, apostles, healers and evangelists he endorses in the NOLR/VHM period between 1947-1960. In understanding **Michael Brown's** theological backdrop in endorsing the NOLR cults and their heretical leaders, this explains why **Michael Brown** was involved in, and gave his full support (while he was the "Principal of Brownsville Revival School of Ministry "), to NAR "Apostle" **Lou Engle** and NAR "Apostle" **Ché Ahn** for "The Call " rallies.

NAR "Apostle" **Lou Engle** with NAR "Apostle" **Bill Johnson** – friends of **Michael Brown** – all confess a different faith in a different spirit, different Christ and promote a doomsday cult model for believers to follow.

We do not know how long **Michael Brown** knew **Lou Engle**. However, if **Michael Brown** claims to be full of the Holy Spirit, theologically discerning and theologically careful who he chooses to fellowship with or support – **Lou Engle** is the last person **Michael Brown** should ever fellowship with.
 To claim **Michael Brown** was not part of the NAR is to remove those seven years from his life. https://churchwatchcentral.com.

While demons confess that Jesus Christ is Lord/YHWH, God and the son of the most high God, NAR "Prophets," NAR "Apostles," NAR leaders and others, like **Brown**, don't: "Ha! What do You want with us, Jesus of Nazareth? Have You come to destroy us? I know who You are, the Holy One of God!"– Luke 4:34. "What do you want with us, Son of God? … Have You come here to torture us before the proper time?" Matthew 8:29. The demons understood that Jesus is fully God and fully man.
But apparently not those who give only lip service to the hypostatic union (in order to convince others they hold to the belief that Jesus was fully God and fully man) – but go on to say that Jesus emptied, or put aside his divinity, so he could operate under the power of the Holy Spirit as a man.

Reverend Anthony Wade of "828 Ministries", an online discernment ministry, had a recent encounter with the less than discerning **Dr Michael Brown** on his "Line Of Fire" program: Anthony Wade: "I was on your show for twenty minutes today. You called me a liar, accused me of misrepresenting Scripture, said that people will condemn me to hell and that I am of a different spirit. In twenty minutes on the telephone." "But a man who fleeces the very flock of God for a living you see no reason to not call a brother in Christ." http://www.828ministries.com/articles/.

In the final minutes of the segment, **Dr. Brown** clearly demonstrates his own obvious lack of Biblical discernment with Pastor Anthony Wade (**NOTE: Video of this discussion is online. Ed.): https://churchwatchcentral.com.

We will focus on **Brown** leaving "Brownsville" and what that revealed about his involvement in the NAR and his NAR-postolic leadership.

If you are not convinced that "Brownsville" was part of the NAR, it is important to note the following:

NAR-postle **David Yonggi Cho** (real name **Paul Yonggi Cho**) prophesied this revival into existence (Previously **Cho** was convicted for fraud and served a suspended jail sentence. Now he's been investigated for an even larger fraud).

(The National Tax Service (NTS) is set to audit the Yoido Full Gospel Church (Assemblies of God), targeting pastor **David Yonggi Cho** who is suspected of embezzling 80 billion won ($67 million) of funds. The announcement came while the prosecutors' office is investigating **Cho's** aides over allegedly embezzling church funds.

He allegedly took 60 billion won of funds intended for overseas mission projects as well as an additional 20 billion won as severance pay without approval from the church.

The Seoul Central District Court sentenced the 80-year-old pastor to two and half years in jail with four years of suspension for inflicting 13.1 billion won of losses to the church and tax evasion worth 3.5 billion won by ordering church officials to buy stocks in his son's company with church funds at a rate more expensive than the market price. His son **Hee-joon** was arrested after being sentenced to three years in prison.

Critics say that the collapse of **Pastor Cho** illustrates how deeply corrupt Korea's megachurches are, after a rapid growth during the last few decades. (Korean Times 15 March 2016). Tax agency set to audit the biggest church in Korea over alleged embezzlement https://donaldelley.wordpress.com/2016).

NAR-postle **Benny Hinn** raised up NAR-postle **Rodney-Howard Browne** that birthed the "laughing revival" that spread to create the "Toronto Blessing" and revival in Holy Trinity Brompton (UK).

NAR-postle **Steve**, under NAR-postle **C. Peter Wagner**, worked with NAR-postle **Carlos Anacondia** in the Argentinian revivals, brought this 'spirit' of revival not just from Argentina but from Holy Trinity Brompton and the "Toronto Blessing "and triggered this "revival'" at "Brownsville."

John Kilpatrick was recognized by prophets as a NAR-postle. NAR prophet **Cindy Jacobs** was allowed to speak about **Wagner** and these global governing prophetic leaders at "Brownsville."

NAR-postles **David Yonggi Cho, Jentezen Franklin, Steve Hill, Carol Arnott** spoke at "Brownsville." These links should help make these issues very obvious: " Last Man Who Opposed **John Kilpatrick** is Dead;"

Why the "Brownsville Revival" was a demonic revival, run by Satan's servants. Even eyewitnesses confirm that the entire "Brownsville" "scam" was part of the New Apostolic Reformation. This witness observed the "dominion theology " and the signs and wonders NAR gospel espoused by **Michael Brown** and *Suzette Hetting** in the "Brownsville Revival School of Ministry" (BRSM): "The last class of the summer was called "Signs, Wonders and Divine Healing." Attendance was some 700 from all over the world, and those who came were not disappointed.

Suzette Hetting and **Dr. Michael Brown**, president of BRSM, taught the class...the Tuesday morning session began with an air of expectancy, and that gave way to worship as we began to sing praises to the King.
Suzette shared how her crusades are reaching the lost in areas of the world not often on evangelists' itineraries such as the stone age tribes in Indonesia. The first day was devoted to foundations. She talked about hindrances to the miraculous, especially head knowledge.

Pointing to her head, she said, "That's your unbelief box." She said if you are scared of making a mistake, you will never walk in the miraculous. She talked about God as the God of the miraculous. "Healing and the miraculous is like the food bell. Ring it and everybody runs to the table." "Pray in song – God inhabits that."

"**Dr. Brown** spent a lot of time showing us healing does continue today, in spite of what critics say. Divine healing is for today. "The healings of Jesus were closely related to His work of forgiving sins and were ultimately connected with His substitutionary death on the cross." Isaiah 53 says, "By His wounds, we are healed." This same witness recalls **Bill Suddeth** was "an usher at "Brownsville." But now he is recognized by **Wagner** and the ICAL as a NAR-postle." You can read the entire witness account of someone at "Brownsville" here:

http://www.theremnant.com/sept.html.

The fact that **Michael Brown** had no problem having his ministry associated with the NAR-postolic ministries of **Reinhardt Bonnke** and **Carlos Anacondia** shows how deeply embedded his theology, practices and positions are –placing him deeply in the pit of the NAR :

"The Wednesday night Revival crowd was huge with the overflows filled. A group from the Argentine Revival was there and they prayed with people as did." So **Michael Brown** was involved in: An NAR "Apostle" **Daniel Juster's** UMJC ministry from 1987-1994.

An NAR-driven "Brownsville Revival" and its "Brownsville Revival School of Ministry" from 1996-2000 and the NAR-driven "The Call'" rally from 2000-2001. And **Michael Brown** has repeatedly claimed he is NOT part of the NAR. There is ample evidence to demonstrate he was very much a part of it. His friends, networks, ministries and his own mouth prove that **Michael Brown** is a liar.

* (**Suzette Hetting** is the worship leader for **Rheinhard Bonnke**). https://pulpitandpen.org.

We encourage our audience to know different types of 'lies' to reveal how deceptive **Michael Brown** really is: In this article, we will create a time line to see how **Michael Brown** is involved in the "New Apostolic Reformation." This article documents evidence that appears to suggest **Michael Brown** has been lying about his apostleship from 2001 to this very day.

We focus on three major events (with other time-stamps that emphasize his connection to NAR apostolic relationships and networks), that demonstrate his involvement: 1987-1994: (Now "Tikkun International ," **Daniel Juster**); 1996-2000:"Brownsville Revival" and "Brownsville Revival School of Ministry" (BRSM) 2000-2001:" The Call" rallies.

It's important to note that **Wagner** identified unusual church phenomena through his lifetime but later in the 1990's coined the term "New Apostolic Reformation." **Wagner** was not the NAR-postle to observe this phenomena in decades past.

Bill Hamon, David Cartledge, Bob Jones and those that came out of the 1948 "Latter Rain" cult were all attempting to establish their end-time governing apostles across the visible Christian church. So NAR Apostles were already on the rise from 1948 onwards. **Michael Brown** states that he got saved in 1971. Chris Rosebrough did a sermon review of **Michael Brown** preaching about himself.

While speaking at "Jubilee Church" in 2016, **Michael Brown** does not name the church he was saved into or reveal the church he attended in the early 1980's. However, at one stage he informed his audience he was attending an Italian Pentecostal church. While possibly attending a Pentecostal church, **Brown** recalls that when he was asked to preach while his leaders and pastors were on a retreat back in Nov.1, 1982, the Holy Spirit fell.

Brown claimed he said in this sermon, "Put away your theology for a while! Let's go through the book of Acts." The result of this message was "altars were absolutely flooded" and people were being 'baptized' in the spirit. This is important to note as this reveals **Brown** was getting people 'spiritually baptized' in a Pentecostal church behind the leadership's back.

Michael Brown suggests he was exposed as causing division when his pastors weren't there. **Brown** was excommunicated from this church and his "best friends" turned against him. As a result, **Michael Brown** claimed God said to him in the spring of 2013, "You will be in the midst of a revival that will touch the whole world." If this was his Italian Pentecostal church – what was **Michael Brown** converting them to? Whatever the answer, **Brown** was showing the hallmark signs of his NAR-ismatic fruits – deceit, division and spiritual elitism.

Daniel C. Juster of "Union of Messianic Jewish Congregations" (UMJC) reports on **Michael Brown's** involvement with the "launching and establishment of what is now called "Tikkun International" from 1987-1994, a ministry that has many NAR teachings and has recognized apostles developing this movement. (https://www.narwatchisrael.info/blog/ fresh-foundations).

What attracted **Michael Brown** to this ministry? **Juster** records a conversation back in the fall of 1984, claiming Asher Intrater (https://reviveisrael.org/archive/language/english/2000/ 12-theology.htm) stated that their ministries needed to be "self-governing" and to have their "own apostolic flow."

(**NOTE: Notice the false preachers\prophets that are listed in his writing of the aforementioned link. That is very telling as to where this person stands. Ed.)

They wanted to "even have the beginning of [their] own five-fold leadership." **Juster** regarded this entire endeavor as a "formation of an apostolic network." These are NAR buzzwords and ideas. And these ideas among **Brown's** leaders, were thrust upon their organizations.

This may have been the first group of organizations that mixed Jewish Christian churches with influential NAR networks in America. Back in 1984, **Juster** not only rolled out his apostolic plans through UMJC, he then created a brochure (notice the language):

"After this meeting, I developed a brochure for the UMJC to explain that we accepted dual affiliation and wanted to welcome all Messianic Jews to take part in the UMJC."

The brochure noted that some would be members of new apostolic streams, as "God would raise up other apostles within our network." "My desire was to see the UMJC become more and more apostolic-led." This would happen as leaders were elected who had overseen large congregations and/or the multiplication of congregations. At this point, the UMJC was charismatic in expression.

"Thus, I was hopeful that the UMJC would come to share my convictions on five-fold ministry and leadership." In 1986, **Daniel Juster** was "designated the apostolic pastor"(UMJC). Although **Michael Brown** had been there since 1987, **Juster** stated, "Due to our increasing differences, **Mike** decided to leave us in 1994." "We still cooperate on many projects to this day and believe that **Mike** is having and will yet have a very significant contribution to Jewish ministry." https://pulpitandpen.org/

A revealing expose' concerning just what **Michael Brown** does believe:

https://bereanresearch.org/michael-brown-white-washed/

MICHAEL BROWN AGAIN PROMOTES FAKE RABBI AND FALSE PROPHET, **JONATHAN CAHN**
https://christianresearchnetwork.org/ ?s=jonathan+cahn&submit=Search

Or, how about this connection?: **JONATHAN CAHN** PARTNERS WITH ARCH HERETIC
KENNETH COPELAND https://christianresearchnetwork.org/
?s=jonathan+cahn&submit=Search

Objection: "According to the Law (Deuteronomy 13), Jesus was a false prophet because he taught us to follow other gods (namely, the Trinity, including the god Jesus), gods our fathers have never known or worshiped. This makes all his miracles utterly meaningless." by **Dr. Michael Brown**
Answer: "Have you ever read what Jesus and his followers taught? They emphasized, 'Love the LORD your God with all your heart, mind, soul, and strength. Follow him. Obey him!' Jesus pointed everyone to God his Heavenly Father — by his miracles, by his message, and by his life. He lived, died, and rose again for the glory of his Father.

Thus Jesus was a faithful and true prophet." (See "Answering Jewish Objections to Jesus," vol. 2, pp. 48-52.)
Dr. Michael L. Brown is founder and president of "ICN Ministries," devoted to taking the message of repentance and revival to **I**srael, the **C**hurch, and the **N**ations. He has preached throughout the United States and in numerous foreign countries, emphasizing radical discipleship,(an NAR buzzword-expression), holy living, and the visitation of the Spirit.

His books, articles, and messages have been translated into more than a dozen languages. In 1996, he became part of the ministry of the "Brownsville Revival," holding weekly sessions for leaders and heading up the revival's intensive two-year "School of Ministry."

Dr. Brown is now President of the "FIRE School of Ministry" located in Charlotte, NC. As a Jewish believer in Jesus, **Dr. Brown** is active in Jewish evangelism and has debated rabbis on radio, TV, and college campuses. He is also a published Old Testament and Semitic scholar, holding a Ph.D in Near Eastern Languages and Literatures from New York University.
In 1997, he was appointed Visiting Professor of Jewish Apologetics at Fuller Theological Seminary School of World Mission and has been affiliated with Regent University Divinity School as an Adjunct Professor of Old Testament and Jewish Studies.

https://sidroth.org/articles/ objection-according-law-jesus-was-false-prophet/

One major red flags about **Michael Brown** has to do with who and what he won't give a red flag. **Michael Brown** would never tell someone to avoid watching **Sid Roth's** "It's SuperNatural" because it's spiritually toxic and dangerous. **Sid Roth** is the Johnny Carson of the cuckoo, strange, weird, toxic and dangerous wing of charismania.
Once you're on his show, you gain a lot of credibility in charismania circles. Any Christian leader who presents as someone who stands for the truth, and as a shepherd of God's flock, shouldn't have to think twice about warning the sheep where to avoid. If there is a place that without question one of God's sheep should avoid, it's the toxic cesspool of **Sid Roth's** "It's SuperNatural."

The fact that **Michael Brown** would have hesitation, or might have to nuance and qualify his approach to **Sid Roth's** "It's SuperNatural" is all the proof you need to show how far in the charismania cesspool **Michael Brown** wades in.
Most episodes of "It's SuperNatural" are infomercials for the guest to pitch their products. The products usually teach the viewer some sort of spiritual trick to achieve breakthrough, healing, miracles, manifestations of God's presence, wealth, and you get the idea.
For a donation viewers are granted access to toxic and dangerous materials that do nothing but exploit them and sink their soul deeper into the cesspool of charismania.

(Video references): https://www.youtube.com/ watch?time_continue=169&v=tFssER9RE1I&feature=emb_logo

https://www.youtube.com/ watch?time_continue=104&v=9ymOjIQxcPQ&feature=emb_logo+

That's a small sample of the toxic cesspool. The videos above are not the exception to the rule for what's on **Sid's** show; rather they are the rule. **Roth** and **Brown** have been friends since 1984. **Michael Brown** is an articulate speaker for many values Christians affirm. There comes a point where even the most articulate speaker for the cause could end up leading someone in the wrong direction, resulting in them becoming twice as much a child of hell. Matthew 23:15.

His refusal to erect an unqualified red flag against the likes of **Sid Roth**, shows how dangerous **Michael Brown** is. With articulate lips he'll fill one's mind with some Christian moral values, but along the way he'll lead them in the direction of the flames of hell where **Sid's** wolves are waiting.

https://heterodoxresearchinitiative.wordpress.com/2019/05/29/ articulately-lead-to-the-cesspool-michael-browns-refusal-to-red-flag-sid-roth-proves-brown-is-dangerous/

--Mac Brunson: Basically protected his buddy **Darryl Gilyard** after sex offender charges. Is aligned with **Phil Waldrep**, another WOF preacher.
http://fbcjaxwatchdog.blogspot.com/2008/10/ come-someone-justify-this-greedy-double.html

http://fbcjaxwatchdog.blogspot.com/2008/10/ what-to-do-after-asking-for-1-million.html

--Ray Brubaker: Deceased; "Amillennial, preterist, and covenant and dominion theology 501c3 CEOs and teachers...**Ray Brubaker**..."

http://www.freeworldfilmworks.com/dov-10danger.htm

--Jamie Buckingham: Deceased; Once was **Kathryn Kuhlman's** "right hand man"; was her biographer, who wrote the book about Ms. **Kuhlman's** ministry titled, "Daughter of Destiny;" left the Charismatics and went to the NAR, WOF; Was the first minister to lay the foundation for the "Unity" movement.
Buckingham wrote: "I'm healed" in Charisma magazine; several months later he died of cancer. At the time Jamie was under a medical doctors care, "One day my wife ... suddenly spoke aloud [and] said, 'Your healing was purchased at the cross'..."Here is what I discovered. You have what you speak.
If you want to change something, you must believe it enough to speak it. ... If you say you're sick, you'll be (and remain) sick. It was not mine. It was the devil's. I didn't have cancer." "I had Jesus. The cancer was trying to have me, but the Word of God said I was healed through what Jesus did on Calvary. ... It was a Friday afternoon."

"The tape was an **Oral Roberts'** sermon ... I came up off the sofa, shouting, 'I'm healed!' My wife leaped out of her chair and shouted, 'Hallelujah!'" "For the next 30 minutes all we did was walk around the house shouting thanks to God and proclaiming my healing" (**Jamie Buckingham**, "My Summer of Miracles," Charisma, April 1991). Ten months after the publication of his article claiming he was healed, he died of cancer (Feb.17, 1992). This was a noticeable failure but the church turned a blind eye to these teachings and continued on, as if it never happened. http://www.letusreason.org

--Bob Buford: Deceased; One of the founders of the "Leadership Network," which is a cousin to the "Emergent Church," heretical teachings, however he was not the originator of the idea; that was **Peter Drucker**—deceased--who in turn was heavily influenced by the existential philosopher and mystic **Soren Kierkegaard**. (See **Peter Drucker** information below).

--Juanita Bynum: Is a prosperity preacher who considers herself to be a prophet, or "prophetess," which she defines not only as someone God reveals future events to, but also "empowered with a special gift to really change the hearts and minds and the direction of people by knowledge." Much of the time **Bynum** uses this 'gift' to try and get people to give her their money. Born in Chicago to a rug salesman and a school nutritionist, **Bynum**, who has four siblings, followed her parents, who both preached in their Pentecostal church, into ministry as a teen.

After graduating as valedictorian from Saints High, a school run by the Church of God in Christ in Memphis, Tenn., she worked as a beautician. A job as a Pan Am flight attendant brought her to New York almost two decades ago. In full-time ministry for the past 15 years, **Bynum** emerged from relative obscurity in the late 1990s when Dallas preacher Bishop **T.D. Jakes** asked her to address a singles conference. Her sermon, "No More Sheets," dealt with a slew of failed romances. Using four sheets borrowed from a hotel maid's cart, she demonstrated how every man she'd slept with who walked away left her in spiritual bondage.

Jackie Alnor, who produces the online church watchdog publication "The Christian Sentinel," criticizes **Bynum** for flawed teachings and aggressive fund-raising. "My biggest problem with her is that she's claiming she is a prophet." **Bynum's** pleas for money on her show amount to "spiritual extortion," Alnor says. "She focuses on the people struggling, living hand to mouth, and tells the poor to give to the rich. She's the opposite of Robin Hood." Alnor is also among those who criticize **Bynum's** 2002 televised wedding to Bishop Thomas W. Weeks III, pastor of the "Global Destiny Church " in Washington, D.C., at the Regent Wall Street Hotel in Manhattan.

Media reports said the ceremony featured a wedding party of 80, a gown with a bodice covered in crystals and a 7.76-carat diamond ring — a far cry from their private ceremony a year earlier at Las Vegas City Hall. **Bynum** had waited all her life to have a fairy-tale wedding, she says. "It started out with a $500,000 budget, and then it just started growing like the blob," she says, adding, "I didn't think it robbery to celebrate my day." She says she doesn't put much stock in what her critics say.

"It's just not important," she says, adding, "If you talk about me, and you don't talk to me, then that's too low for me. I can't come to that level." More than an expositor of the gospel, **Bynum** is also an industry. According to TBN, viewers around the world tune into her weekly "Weapons of Power" show. She's also an author and a Gospel singer, with her sermons, books and CDs for sale on her Web site. And she heads "Juanita Bynum Ministries Inc.," based in Waycross, GA.

Tonya Hall, her administrative assistant, declined to disclose either **Bynum's** or the ministry's income. "Her financials are something that we do not release," Hall says. (Although some religious institutions file financial disclosures, an Internal Revenue Service spokesman says **Bynum's** ministry has not.)

Source: "Evangelist with a big stick," NY Newsday, Oct. 23, 2004, Pat Burson, Staff Writer
http://www.apologeticsindex.org/595-juanita-bynum.

https://michellelesley.com/tag/juanita-bynum/ (**NOTE: These are quite lengthy. Go to the link to read them. Ed.).

C:

--**Jonathan Cahn** (Rabbi from Wayne, NJ; buddies with **Sid Roth**; another heretical preacher; author of "The Shemitah" blood moons which amounts to nothing supernatural; has also written several other books to back up his claims, all false predictions.

https://www.cicministry.org/commentary/issue129.htm

https://pulpitandpen.org/2017/10/26/
jonathan-cahn-sends-lamest-cease-and-desist-letter-ever-contends-he-never-gave-false-prophe
cy/

Or this website: https://christianresearchnetwork.org/ ?s=jonathan+cahn&submit=Search

Check out this site—Here we have **Jonathan Cahn** lighting a 9 stick Menorah; the Biblical Menorah is a 7 stick candle holder; the 9 stick is a false Menorah and reflects all paths leading to one God. For someone who is a Rabbi you would think he would know the difference between a Biblical Menorah and a Universal Menorah. But he does not, because he follows the Kabbalah that teaches all paths lead to one God (Lucifer).

https://www.discerningtheword.com/

His books, "The Mystery of the Shemitah" and "The Harbinger", are very interesting. So **Jonathan Cahn** knows the deep mysteries of God's Word that Christians don't know? And only **Jonathan Cahn** can reveal these mysteries to us? **Jonathan Cahn's** plan is also to restore the message that Jesus Christ preaches, to its original Jewish richness and power. So until **Jonathan Cahn** came along all born again believers for the last 2000+ years that have been reading the Scriptures were reading a Bible that had no value and no authority whatsoever. Isn't that nice, that **Jonathan Cahn** came to save the day?

Does he mean that we need to infuse the Bible with Kabbalah mysticism in order to understand it properly? There is a movement called the "Hebrew Roots Movement" where they believe that you cannot understand the Bible unless you go back to your Hebrew ways (become like the Jews) and read extra Biblical sources such as the Midrash, Zohar and the Talmud etc., to gain a higher "enlightenment" of the Scriptures.
It grieves my soul as I see humanity being led to the slaughter. When I first saw Mr. **Cahn** the Holy Spirit showed me that he was NOT of my "GOD". God's Holy Spirit also told me to stay away from all men/woman that are famous because they are all pawns of the Luciferian cult. When I say all I mean "ALL". Satan is the, "temporary", prince of this world. He has power over all kingdoms on earth.
Ephesians 6:12 KJV– "For we wrestle not against flesh and blood, but against principalities, against powers, against the rulers of the darkness of this world, against spiritual wickedness in high places."

People will NOT get TV shows, promote their books, become millionaires unless they sell out their soul to Satan. Tom "HORN" for example, claims that he used to be a pastor.

I found zero evidence. He is always throwing the devil hand signs and was allowed into the Vatican's telescope observatory at Mt. Graham called L.U.C.I.F.E.R.in Arizona.

Do you really believe the true-Christian haters, the Jesuits, would allow this ?? These men were trained to infiltrate the Protestant churches and eventually get people to not worship the Almighty. Be mad at these wolves that are devouring God's children.

Hos. 4:6– "My people are destroyed for lack of knowledge: because thou hast rejected knowledge, I will also reject thee, that thou shalt be no priest to me: seeing thou hast forgotten the law of thy God, I will also forget thy children."

(**NOTE: Writer "froggie" on the site listed below, with spelling corrections included. Ed.).

https://www.nowtheendbegins.com/ what-is-jonathan-cahn-doing-with-apostate-false-teacher-kenneth-copeland/

The menorah, a seven-branched candelabrum, is the oldest symbol of the Jewish religion, and a variation of it is used for the observance of Chanukah – the Festival of Lights. During Chanukah, the Festival of Lights, Jews worldwide will light the Chanukah, a modern-Hebrew word describing the candelabrum with nine branches that resembles a menorah and is used on this festival.
The original menorah stood in the First and Second Temples in Jerusalem. The priests would light it in the sanctuary each day, following detailed procedures as instructed in the Bible. Chanukah celebrates two miracles. First was the 2nd-century B.C.E. victory of a small band of Jewish fighters against the powerful Syrian-Greek army.

Second, upon the priests' return to the Holy Temple to light the menorah, a tiny amount of oil that should have lasted no more than a day in fact sufficed for eight days, thus enabling the Jews to produce more. The Talmud states that it is forbidden to use a seven-branched menorah outside of the Temple, which is why the modern-day Chanukah is slightly different.

(**NOTE: Writer "froggie" in the site listed above, with spelling corrections included. Ed.).

("Geoffrey Grider": NTEB is run by end times author and editor-in-chief Geoffrey Grider).

Geoffrey runs a successful web design company, and is a full-time minister of the gospel of the Lord Jesus Christ. In addition to running "NOW THE END BEGINS," he has a dynamic street preaching outreach and tract ministry team in Saint Augustine, FL.

"Nothing good ever happens within the "name it and claim it" crowd, it's all about money, private jets, huge mansions and more money. Televangelists are rightly disparaged because they reduce the entire Bible to nothing more than getting you to give them money.
And they tell any lie to get you to do that. They promise you 'miracle healings' if you will 'sow them your seed'.

Yet, when they themselves get sick, like **Rod Parsley** did last year, there are no miracle healings just old-fashioned doctor's visits and drugs. Liars one and all. Come on, **Jonathan**, you can do better than this. "Wherefore come out from among them, and be ye separate, saith the Lord, and touch not the unclean thing; and I will receive you," 2 Corinthians 6:17 (KJV).

Now let's look at a short bio, found here on **Cahn's** own web site: **Jonathan Cahn** is President of Hope of the World ministries, Senior Pastor and Messianic Rabbi of the Jerusalem Center/Beth Israel in Wayne, New Jersey. He is also the author of the best selling book "The Harbinger."
His teachings are broadcast daily over hundreds of radio stations throughout the United States and the world and on television. He ministers, as did the first Jewish messengers of the Gospel, sharing the message of Messiah to Jew and Gentile, Israel, and the nations.
 He has ministered before mass gatherings in India, Nigeria, Cuba, Mizoram, Honduras, Haiti, & throughout the world. His teachings are widely known for revealing the deep mysteries of God's word and for the restoring of the new covenant message to its original Biblically Jewish richness and power.

And another revealing bio, found here: **Jonathan Cahn** is President of Hope of the World ministries, Senior Pastor, and Rabbi of the "Beth Israel Worship Center" in Garfield, New Jersey. His teachings are broadcast daily over hundreds of radio stations throughout the United States and the world. He can also be seen weekly on television ("Something Different").

 Descended of the line of Aaron, he has been asked to sound the Jubilee trumpet [who "asked" him to do this, and what exactly does "sounding the Jubilee trumpet" mean?] and minister among the nations; "A PROPHETIC MINISTRY" [but true prophetic ministries do not exist today – only in the ungodly, heretical minds of New Apostolic Reformation "prophets" such as **Bill Johnson, Mick Bickle, John** and **Carol Arnott, Todd Bentley, Patricia King,** etc. etc.], of and to the Jew and the Gentile in the last days.

His teachings include "the revealing of ancient mysteries, the depth and wonders of God's Word, and the restoration of the Gospel message in its original Biblically Jewish context, richness, and power." [What exactly are the "ancient mysteries" **Cahn** is revealing?]
And what exactly does he mean by the "restoration" of the Gospel message? The Bible is sufficient in and of itself to tell us all we need, without having to be interpreted for us in new and revealing ways by a so-called "PROPHET" like **Cahn**.

Geoffrey Grider, David Kaus (another commenter on the same website):

"On the PTL 6:18 minute video, (**Bishop Clarence**) **McClendon** calls **Cahn** a PROPHET AND **CAHN** CALLS "THE HARBINGER" A PROPHETIC WARNING !!! The 38 second mark.........the 2:26 mark.............the 5:08 mark... http://apprising.org/2012/0

(**NOTE: The balance of the website information is missing, however if you type "apprising.org" you will see **Jonathan Cahn** and several other wolves' preaching dissected. Ed.). From the message: " Zohar Speaks." Well I guess **Cahn** really does use the Zohar. The Zo-har Speaks: Gulgalta - The Cosmic Skull. Zohar - Golgotha (1) -

YouTube Video for https://www.youtube.com/ watch?v=qAFtormiU_0... 3:08

https://www.youtube.com/wat... Apr 10, 2013 - Uploaded by Rabbi Kris Kringle...
THE RABBINIC MYSTERIES PART V, is a HERETICAL TEACHING ... to SUBSTANTIATE this claim type in ... https://www.youtube.com/wat...

https://pulpitandpen.org/2015/09/14/ jonathan-cahns-con-knowing-the-difference-between-shemitah-and-shinola/

CHRIS ROSEBROUGH SHORT CIRCUITS **JONATHAN CAHN** AND "THE HARBINGER" (**NOTE: Chris is a Christian Apologist. Ed.). https://christianresearchnetwork.org/ ?s=jonathan+cahn&submit=Search.
 Lastly, we have an excellent commentary on **Jonathan Cahn** from another source: Critical Issues Commentary:
 https://cicministry.org/commentary/issue129.htm

--**Paul Cain**: Deceased; Former associate of **William Branham**; exposed as a homosexual alcoholic, false prophet, proponent of today's New Apostolic Reformation.

"**Paul Cain**, a prophetic legend and a living bridge to **William Branham** and the "Latter Rain" of the 50's, has now been revealed to be an alcoholic and a practicing homosexual. Ironically, this disclosure came at the hands of his fellow prophets who had elevated him to a super prophet status and who themselves endeavored to attain the lofty prophetic mantle of **Cain** himself.
Bob Jones, a Kansas City prophet, himself discredited by sexual indiscretions in his prophetic practice, referred to **Cain's** prophetic ministry as: "the terror of the Lord" (Al Dager, "Vengeance is Ours," (Redmond, Washington: Sword Publishers), July, 1990, p.131).

In a special letter from **Rick Joyner's** website the following information was recently released: "In February 2004, we were made aware that **Paul** had become an alcoholic." "In April 2004, we confronted Paul with evidence that he had recently been involved in homosexual activity. **Paul** admitted to these sinful practices and was placed under discipline, agreeing to a process of restoration, which the three of us would oversee. However, **Paul** has resisted this process and has continued in his sin... With our deepest regrets and sincerity, **Rick Joyner, Jack Deere, Mike Bickle**."

http://www.morrnnsstrarministries.ore/ pages/ special~bulleu.ns/0ct_19.html

"**Paul's** mother, grandmother, and great grandmother had all been born with the gift of seeing. His great-grandmother would sometimes see things in broad daylight and ask her friend or family if they could see them too. If they said they could not, she would occasionally wave her hand upon them and they would immediately see the identical vision...
Paul now found he was "seeing" also and would know things that were going to happen to classmates at school or were happening to absent friends. He knew simple things like who would end up with a bloody nose or who would win a race...

By the age of nine "Little Brother" (as he was being affectionately referred to by adults, perhaps because it was the form of address used by the angel who spoke to him from time to time) began public preaching in a limited way...By the time **Paul** was about eighteen... he began traveling across America ministering as an evangelist and healer.

Those were the early days of the healing movement which swept through the Pentecostal churches during the forties and fifties under the leadership of evangelists like **William Branham, Oral Roberts, T.L Osborn, A.A. Allen, Jack Coe** and many others well known in those days...There was a special bond between **William Branham** and "Little Brother" in the early days of **Paul's** ministry...

Sometimes when **Branham** could not meet a commitment, he would send **Paul** in his place. The extent of their spiritual "light" was phenomenal. When they called each other by phone one would often say to the other in fun, "You're all right today. How am I?" and each would know the others state of health precisely.

On one occasion **Mike Bickle** had been complaining to his wife that he had "a bit of a sniffle" or a slight cold - something he rarely had - the phone rang, **Bickle** picked up the receiver and heard **Paul** on the line. He had heard about **Paul's** gift so he said by way of a joke, "Hi, **Paul**! You're all right today! How am I?" Immediately **Paul** answered him, "Why **Mike**, you've got a bit of a sniffle and you are all wet. Your hair is standing up on the left side of your head." (**Bickle** had just gotten out the shower). (David, Pytches pgs. 24,26,29,30; David Pytches "Some Say It Thundered," (Oliver-Nelson: Nashville, Th.), 1991, p.81.

http://www.deceptioninthechurch.com/orrel19.html

(**NOTE: This site is quite lengthy on its writing about **Paul Cain**. I have chosen just a few highlights from it. Ed.). Another site that gets into detail about his personal history:

http://www.letusreason.org/Latrain5.htm

--**Christine Caine** (Word of Faith teacher, Hillsong Leader). Six reasons not to follow Posted on January 3, 2016 " Six reasons why **Christine Caine** should be avoided." I'm sure there are more reasons:

1. **Christine Caine** engages in New Age practices condemned in the Bible, such as this "impartation" described in the link. (Acts 8:17-20, Matthew 6:9, Isaiah 57:8, Revelation 9:21). Simon the Magician tried to grab the power of the Spirit the wrong way and he was cursed for it. In addition, **Christine Caine** endorses practice of pagan/witchcraft as seen here in **Batterson's** "Circle Making" book blurb–

(**NOTE: You have to go to the link to read it. Ed.).

2. **Christine Caine** usurps male authority and rebels against the clear word of the Bible. She is an ordained pastor and functions in that capacity. Worse, she enjoys teaching young women to step into leadership roles that scripture forbids and is unashamed to say so. (1 Timothy 2:12; Revelation 2:20).

3. **Christine Caine** is part of the rise of the Feminine Church of Eden. (Revelation 2:20). But what we see with most of these women that are rising in popularity is what appears to be a female dominant role in their personal marriages. **Beth Moore** regularly travels to speaking and teaching engagements without her husband, as well as these others.
Christine Caine is an ordained pastor of her "church" in Australia, and also regularly speaks and travels without her husband. Husbands aren't overseeing their wives' writings and teachings, and any attention that they pay to their wives' work is not through the lens of Scripture.

4. **Christine Caine** partners with heretics, promotes them, and endorses them. (I Corinthians 15:33, 2 Corinthians 6:14; Romans 16:17-18,Ephesians 5:11). **Christine Caine** admits her spiritual roots were sprung from the bad fruit of heretics.

5. **Christine Caine** is a member-leader in a doctrinally heretical word-faith church. (I John 1:6-7). Or, as SBTS President Dr. Al Mohler put it, "a prosperity movement for millennials that minimizes the Gospel content and diffuses a presentation of 'spirituality' instead."

6. **Christine Caine** twists scripture. (II Peter 3:16). Here she is twisting a scripture that warns against false teachers, that is actually rebuking those who warn against false teachers – something the false teachers often do. Here is a Pastrix **Caine** sermon review: "What shall we do if we see a sister following these false teachers?" "Warn them, lovingly." "If needing to a second time, warn them lovingly again, seasoning your speech with salt.

If they persist despite the warnings and either don't have a husband to oversee them, have no proper oversight from a husband who has abdicated his duty, or who just are or are married to a discernment klutz, then various Scriptures say either to admonish them strongly a third time and/or to break fellowship."

"Breaking fellowship might seem a hard thing to do, but remember, if a sister persists in her sin or won't hear you after giving them the Scriptures, that means they have already broken fellowship with Jesus." "When we see a believing sister (or someone who at least professes Christ) who insists on following a false teacher despite the facts, like above, it's hard to know when to speak, when to remain silent, when to strongly exhort and when to be gentle."
" How many times does one snatch an undiscerning/uncaring sister from the fire and withstand their resulting tantrums that you didn't allow them to get burned?"

As for a person who stirs up division, after warning him once and then twice, have nothing more to do with him (Titus 3:10). And have mercy on those who doubt; save others by snatching them out of the fire; to others show mercy with fear, hating even the garment stained by the flesh (Jude 1:22-23). So do we warn, reject, have mercy, snatch from the fire, or fearfully hate the polluted flesh? Or all of them at different times? And when?

Here, Sinclair Ferguson gives excellent, EXCELLENT advice which for me, answers that question. The Proverb from chapter 26:4, "Answer not a fool according to his folly, lest you be like him yourself," is immediately followed in verse 5 thus: "Answer a fool as his folly deserves, That he not be wise in his own eyes." He said those two verses would seem to be at counter-productive odds, even contradicting each other. But they don't, and his teaching at a Ligonier Conference on when to answer and when not to answer is clear and helpful.

(**NOTE: The video spoken about is on You Tube. Ed.).

https://churchwatchcentral.com/2019/01/12/
looking-at-christine-caines-speech-at-passion-2019/

https://michellelesley.com/2016/03/04/ chhave-no-regard-for-the-offerings-of-caine/

https://www.christianpost.com/news/
beth-moore-christine-caine-march-around-dallas-hospital-in-prayer-during-priscilla-shirer-surgery.html

--**Stacy Campbell & Wesley Campbell**: False prophet & prophetess aligned with **John Wimber** in Toronto; she is known as the "shaking prophetess," since she shakes her head while supposedly giving a "prophecy;" very demonic in all her ways.

(**NOTE: Plenty of YouTube videos showing her demonstrating the demon that takes over her while she is on the platform. Ed.).

--**Ron Campbell**: https://kingdomchange.org/state-of-the-church/
prophets-that-i-know-about/

What does the Bible say about third millennium prophets? What's the difference between being a prophet and being prophetic ?

 In "The Prophetic Path," **Ron Campbell** guides emerging prophets along his own journey from South Africa to America and from the sanctuary to legislatures and boardrooms to reveal the prerequisites, principles, and perils of the office of the prophet.
 "You are to be commended for many fine gems of truth that sparkle throughout the book...I agree with your statement that the Church is weak because we are not founded on the basis of prophets and apostles, nor is the Nation." (**John Sandford** co-founder, Elijah House Ministries, Inc., author of "The Elijah Task.").

"The Prophetic Path" is a powerful discipleship resource, not only for emerging prophets but also for all who would be prophetic! "The Prophetic Path: A Practical Guide for New Testament Prophets."

(Sold on Amazon as both a book and an audiobook. Ed.).

--**Harold Camping**: Deceased; wrote several books on the end of the world–his predictions--which NONE of them came true...obviously!

(**NOTE: Several articles, even from secular newspapers and magazines all attest to him being a false prophet. It should not be hard to find them. Ed.).

--**Tony Campolo:** Is a popular "evangelical" speaker and author. He is professor emeritus of Sociology at Eastern University and an ordained minister in the liberal American Baptist Convention. According to Wikipedia, he currently serves as an associate pastor of the Mount Carmel Baptist Church in West Philadelphia, whereas his wife attends Central Baptist Church in Wayne, Pennsylvania. In an interview with me at the "New Baptist Covenant Celebration" in Atlanta in January 2008, he confirmed that he and his wife attend different churches.

Campolo is associated with the emerging church. For example, he co-authored "Adventures in Missing the Point" with **Brian McLaren**. **McLaren** also endorsed **Campolo's** book "Speaking My Mind: The Radical Evangelical Prophet Tackles the Tough Issues Christians Are Afraid to Face" (2004). **Campolo** is a master entertainer. No doubt about it. Of course, that is the kind of speaker who is popular in this confused, carnal hour. **Campolo** is dynamic, interesting, and personable. He appeals to the young and to the old.
He can make you laugh, and he can make you cry. He is full of zeal. He can move people.

But **Campolo** is a dangerous man because of his aberrant theology: A "GRADUAL" SALVATION EXPERIENCE--In "Letters to a Young Evangelical," **Campolo** described his own salvation experience in the following words:

"When I was a boy growing up in a lower-middle-class neighborhood in West Philadelphia, my mother, a convert to Evangelical Christianity from a Catholic Italian immigrant family, hoped I would have one of those dramatic 'born-again' experiences. That was the way she had come into a personal relationship with Christ. She took me to hear one evangelist after another, praying that I would go to the altar and come away 'converted.'
BUT IT NEVER WORKED FOR ME."
"I would go down the aisle as the people around me sang 'the invitation hymn,' but I just didn't feel as if anything happened to me. For a while I despaired, wondering if I would ever get 'saved.' It took me quite some time to realize that entering into a personal relationship with Christ DOES NOT ALWAYS HAPPEN THAT WAY..." "In my case INTIMACY WITH CHRIST WAS DEVELOPED GRADUALLY OVER THE YEARS, primarily through what Catholic mystics call 'centering prayer.'

Each morning, as soon as I wake up, I take time--sometimes as much as a half hour--to center myself on Jesus. I say his name over and over again to drive back the 101 things that begin to clutter up my mind the minute I open my eyes. Jesus is my mantra, as some would say..."
"I learned about this way of having a born-again experience from reading the Catholic mystics, especially "The Spiritual Exercises" of Ignatius of Loyola..."

"After the Reformation, we Protestants left behind much that was troubling about Roman Catholicism of the fifteenth century." "I am convinced that we left too much behind." " The methods of praying employed by the likes of Ignatius have become precious to me."

"With the help of some Catholic saints, my prayer life has deepened." ("Letters to a Young Evangelical," 2006, pp. 25, 26, 30, 31).

This is a very, very frightful testimony. **Campolo** does not have a Biblical testimony of salvation. He plainly admits that is not "born again" in the way that his mother was, through a dramatic Biblical-style conversion. Instead, he describes his "intimacy with Christ" as something that has developed gradually through the practice of Catholic mysticism. For one thing, this is to confuse salvation with spiritual growth. The conversions that are recorded in the New Testament are of the instantaneous, dramatic variety. The Lord Jesus Christ said that salvation is a birth (John 3:3). That is not a gradual thing that happens throughout one's life; it is an event!

Further, Catholic mysticism itself is unscriptural. Jesus forbade repetitious prayers (Mat. 6:7). He taught us to pray in a verbal, conscious manner, talking with God as with a Father, addressing God the Father external to us, not searching for a mystical oneness with God in the center of one's being through thoughtless meditation (Mat. 6:9-13).

Campolo's testimony is more akin to the Roman Catholicism that his mother was saved out of. It is repeating mantras and doing good works and progressing in spirituality. **Campolo** clearly attributes his "spirituality" to Catholic-style mysticism. He even speaks in terms of experiencing "oneness with God" and entering a "thin place" wherein God "is able to break through and envelop the soul."

"The constant repetition of his name clears my head of everything but the awareness of his presence. By driving back all other concerns, I am able to create what the ancient Celtic Christians called 'THE THIN PLACE.' The thin place is that spiritual condition wherein the separation between the self and God becomes so thin that God is able to break through and envelop the soul..."
Like most Catholic mystics, [Loyola] developed an intense desire to experience "A 'ONENESS' WITH GOD" ("Letters to a Young Evangelical," pp. 26, 30).

Roger Oakland observes: "This term 'thin place' originated with Celtic spirituality (i.e., contemplative) and is in line with panentheism... 'Thin places' imply that God is in all things, and the gap between God, evil, man, everything thins out and ultimately disappears in mediation" ("Faith Undone", pp. 114, 115). I suspect that **Campolo's** many heresies are largely the product of his unscriptural mystical practices which have brought him into intimate communion with something other than the Jesus Christ of the Bible.

After **Campolo** published the book "A Reasonable Faith," some evangelical leaders became concerned that he was teaching universalism. **Campolo** developed the idea that "Christ lives in all human beings, regardless of whether they are Christians." He asserted that the resurrected Jesus of history is "actually is present" in each person and said, "Jesus is the only Savior, but not everybody who is being saved by Him is aware that He is the one who is doing the saving." "Christianity Today" editor Kenneth Kantzer wrote that **Campolo** was entirely orthodox.

Campolo told "Christianity Today," "I'm worried that evangelical intellectuals will not say anything except the old phrases and the old worn out terminology ... The way evangelical Christianity is doing theology really bothers me."

"If everybody has to say only things that they know are safely orthodox, if we lose the capacity to be open and to share ideas that people may consider heretical, I think we will lose our creativity." This is a foolish statement, and for "Christianity Today" to leave it unchallenged is inexcusable. To call for a questioning of the "old worn out terminology," and for theological openness to new theology is the apostasy described in 2 Timothy 4:

"For the time will come when they will not endure sound doctrine; but after their own lusts shall they heap to themselves teachers, having itching ears; and they shall turn away their ears from the truth, and shall be turned unto fables." Today's evangelical leaders do not have the heart nor the spiritual discernment needed to protect the flock of God. They are blind guides and dumb dogs. Christianity Today's defense of **Campolo** does not demonstrate his orthodoxy, it demonstrates Christianity Today's confusion. **Campolo** complained that he was being persecuted, even though the theological watchdogs turned out to be pussycats.

On the authority of God's Word, we say that **Campolo** was a heretic in 1985 and since then he has proceeded from heresy to heresy, yet he is still accepted as an "evangelical theologian." When **Campolo** was examined by the evangelical leaders in 1985, they noted that "while he accepts an evolutionary view of the origin of man and the universe, he holds that this is consistent with Scripture that teaches only the fact (not the method) of Creation" (Christian News, Sept. 23, 1985).

Christianity Today did not see this as a serious problem because they allow room for all sorts of doctrinal error, but it is a very serious matter. It should be obvious even to a child that the Bible teaches not only the fact of creation, but the method, as well.

The Bible plainly teaches that the world was created by God in six days and six nights. There is no room for any sort of evolutionary thinking here, and to allow men such as **Campolo** to hold such views is folly. The doctrine of special creation is the only view that reveals the nature of man as distinct from the animals and that explains the literal fall of man in a literal Garden of Eden. If there were no literal creation and fall, the atonement of Christ on the cross is without meaning.

CAMPOLO DOESN'T BELIEVE THAT THE BIBLE IS INERRANTLY INSPIRED--In an interview with Shane Claiborne in 2005, **Campolo** was asked to define "evangelical." He replied: "An evangelical is someone who believes the doctrines of the Apostle's Creed. That outlines exactly what we believe in detail.

Secondly, an evangelical has a very high view of scripture THOUGH NOT NECESSARILY INERRANCY. And the third thing--we believe that salvation comes by being personally involved with a living resurrected Jesus. So I've defined evangelical in those three terms. There is a doctrinal statement, so that there is some content to what we believe. There is a source of truth, Scripture.

And there is a personal relationship with Jesus" ("On Evangelicals and Interfaith Cooperation," Crosscurrents, Spring 2005, http://findarticles.com/p/articles/ mi_m2096/is_1_55/ai_n13798048).

Campolo's doctrinal statement is not only exceedingly weak, shallow, vague, and confusing, but it is heretical as well! Further, defining salvation is "being personally involved with a living resurrected Jesus" allows for a world of heresy.

It allows for an Orthodox sacramental Gospel, a Roman Catholic mystical Gospel, a Church of Christ baptismal regeneration Gospel, you name it. In his book "Partly Right", **Campolo** said: "Abraham's knowledge of God fit no theological system. It complied with no dictates of knowledge..." [Kierkegaard] rejected the bibliolatry of those fundamentalists who would make the Scriptures the ultimate authority for faith." "Even though he would agree with those who hold to the doctrine of the inerrancy of Scriptures, he refused to put the Bible in a higher place of authority than the inward encounter with God" (p. 99).

Thus, **Campolo** holds to the heresy that the Bible is not the ultimate authority for faith and practice and exalts the liberal-mystical idea that an inward encounter with God is a higher authority than the Bible.

He does not explain how it is possible to test the genuineness of an "inward encounter with God" apart from the Bible and fails to acknowledge that "faith" is not a leap in the dark but that "faith cometh by hearing, and hearing by the Word of God" (Romans 10:17).

CAMPOLO IS AN ECUMENIST: I attended Missionsfest '92 in Vancouver, British Columbia, to hear **Campolo** speak. Though the participants represented a wide variety of belief and practice, most came under the evangelical label. There were Pentecostals, Baptists, Presbyterians, Mennonites, Anglicans, Lutherans, to name a few. I did not see any Catholic groups, though some of the people we talked to at the booths were strongly sympathetic toward Catholicism. **Campolo** spoke on Friday evening to a standing-room-only crowd, and he literally brought the people to their feet. The man is a very effective speaker, which of course makes him all the more dangerous.

He began his talk by noting how incredible and wonderful it was that so many different kinds of Christians had come together for the meeting. He mentioned Pentecostals, Baptists, Presbyterians, Anglicans, and Mennonites.

As **Campolo** stood before this mixed multitude, he did not have one word of warning about the false teaching represented by the various groups that were present. He did say, "If your theology is not right you will be messed up and not be able to follow Jesus adequately." But he did not explain what he meant, and of course he gave no examples of being "messed up theologically."

He appealed to the people to give themselves to world missions, and he made no exceptions for those who hold to false doctrine. Not only did **Campolo** approach this conference in a compromising ecumenical spirit, he did not even clarify the Gospel. He mentioned the Gospel; he referred to the Gospel. But he did not explain what the Gospel is. He did not preach the Gospel. He talked about "giving your life to Jesus Christ," but that is not the Gospel. He spoke of the necessity of winning people to Jesus Christ, and he said that "missions starts with the declaration that Jesus Christ must be the Lord of your life." But that is not the Gospel.

That kind of language is interpreted many different ways by the various denominations. **Campolo** said, "I believe in heaven, and I believe in hell." But that is not the Gospel. He mentioned the cross, but the cross must be explained. Especially is this true in this hour of doctrinal confusion. Even Rome mentions the cross, but Rome, of course, does not preach the Biblical Gospel. All of this is not surprising in light of the ecumenism of the conference.

If **Campolo** had preached a clear Gospel, he would have caused problems for some of the participants. He would have caused divisions. He could not preach against baptismal regeneration, because this was held by many of the Lutherans and Anglicans who were present. He could not preach against the heresy of losing your salvation, because this was held by many of the Pentecostals present. Ecumenists speak in generalities and inferences, not in plain doctrinal Bible language. They do not reprove and rebuke (2 Timothy 4:2).

Ecumenism has long been **Campolo's** methodology. His American Baptist Convention is the most liberal group of Baptists in the United States and is a member body of the **World Council of Churches.** Bible-believing Baptist churches long ago separated from this modernistic group. Any lip service **Campolo** gives to the importance of doctrinal correctness is negated by his constant fellowship with heretics.
In practice, the man has no concern for doctrinal purity. **Campolo** signed an article in the liberal "Sojourners" magazine in May 1981, which lambasted the United States and stated that Roman Catholicism was the one bright light in the dark situation in El Salvador.

Campolo was on the editorial board for the production of the film "Mother Teresa," which exalted the Roman Catholic nun and contained no warning about her false Gospel. **Campolo** often uses Mother Teresa as an example of Biblical Christianity, though she preached a false Gospel, believed that all men are children of God, worshiped the wafer of the mass, and prayed to Mary. **Campolo** has spoken at self-esteem guru **Robert Schuller's** "Institute for Church Growth." In 2001 he joined hands with Catholic priest Michael Moynihan at this Institute. **Campolo** referred positively to Seventh-day Adventism in his book "20 Hot Potatoes Christians Are Afraid to Touch" (chapter 3).

Campolo is exceedingly dangerous because he is an ecumenist who is willing to work with and fellowship with error. He refuses to obey Bible separation. He refuses to lift his voice against heresy. In fact, he often pokes fun at the fundamentalist position. This is wickedness. It is impossible to please God while preaching the kind of positive ecumenical message that **Campolo** preaches.
https://www.wayoflife.org/database/beware_of_tony_campolo.html

(**NOTE: Several more heretical teachings and beliefs are in this website, listed above. Ed.).

--**Charles Capps**: Deceased; "Word of Faith" cult false teacher). According to **Copeland** "the greatest living theologian;" **Capps**, like most of the Word of Faith teachers, preaches a different God. **Capps'** God is not omnipotent, and as God told **Capps**, He can only act as we allow: "You are under an attack of the evil one and I can't do anything about it. You have bound me by the words of your own mouth" (1).

What a pathetic God **Capps** worships. Thank the God of the Bible that He is in control and not subject to our wills. It is not surprising however that **Capps'** god is so impotent, for **Capps'** God created man equal to himself: "God duplicated Himself in kind!... Adam was an exact duplication of God's kind!" (2). Though heretical, this teaching is very prominent among the Word of Faith preachers.

64

However, Adam was not a duplication of God's kind. He was inferior and subordinate. While God is omnipotent, omniscient, and omnipresent, humans, including Adam, have always been limited in their knowledge and in their power, and limited to existing in only one place at one time.

Would **Capps** and friends ever teach that God is limited to existing in one place? Apparently they have no problem teaching that God is limited in knowledge and power. But if they wish to truly forward the idea that Adam was an exact duplicate of God, they would either have to limit God to a single place at any given time, or they would have to teach that Adam was omnipresent. **Capps** also has a different Jesus.

Like the other Word of Faith teachers, **Capps'** Jesus died spiritually and needed to be reborn: "Jesus was born again in the pit of hell. He was the firstborn, the first begotten, from the dead." " He started the Church of the firstborn in the gates of hell.... He went down to the gates and started His Church there....The Church started when Jesus was born again in the gates of hell" (3).

Capps could not make his thoughts more clear. However, the Bible in no way teaches this. Christ was not sinful man that He needed to be reborn. He did not need to go to hell. Firstborn from the dead clearly means that He was the first resurrected, not the first to die spiritually and be reborn. What a travesty that our sovereign Lord should be so maligned by **Capps.**

These are not teachings that Christians should sit still for but should stand very strongly against! **Charles Capps,** "The Tongue - A Creative Force," p. 67, emphasis in original.

Charles Capps, "Authority in Three Worlds" (Tulsa, OK: Harrison House, 1982), p. 16, emphasis in original. **Charles Capps**, "Authority in Three Worlds" (Tulsa OK: Harrison House, 1982), pp. 212-213, emphasis in original.

http://www.thebiblepage.org/ avoid/capps.shtml

The Birth of God the Son– According to **Charles Capps** & Word of Faith heretics– "At Christmas where we lower wattage Christians (i.e. non "Spirit-filled") lower our heads in humility while contemplating the incarnation of Jesus Christ, God the Son and Redeemer of the lost from sin, death and the grave." "Meanwhile, millions of other professing Christians see no mystery at all regarding the incarnation." "Quite the opposite, the birth of Jesus was simply a result of enacting the spiritual law that control the spiritual realm." " After all, the birth of Jesus was merely the end product of over a thousand years of positive confession."

The Word of Faith cult teaches that the prophets began to form Christ through their words over a thousand years ago.

They spoke about where He would be born (Micah 5:1-2); that He would be the Son of God (Ps. 2:7, Pro. 30:4); He would be anointed with the Holy Spirit (Isa. 11:2, 61:1, Ps. 45:7-8); He would serve as a Prophet (Deut. 18:15,18), a Priest (Ps. 110:4) and a King (Ps. 2:6).
In fact, there are a little over 300 Old Testament prophecies that Jesus fulfilled in His earthly ministry. All of these "faith-filled" words culminated in God being allowed to manifest what they said in the form of Jesus Christ, God the Son.
Let me go on to allow **Mr. Charles Capps** explain it for us in the following article:

"The exact process by which God the Son became flesh is not spelled out for us in the scriptures in any great detail. The most familiar passage of text regarding the incarnation is cited below":

Luke 1:35-38–"And the angel answered and said unto her, <u>The Holy Ghost shall come upon thee: and the power of the Highest shall overshadow thee: therefore also that holy thing which shall be born of thee shall be called the Son of God.</u>"

"And, behold, thy cousin Elisabeth, she hath also conceived a son in her old age: and this is the sixth month with her, who was called barren. For with God nothing shall be impossible. And Mary said, Behold the handmaid of the Lord"; (KJV bold type & underlining added for emphasis).

" All that we know from the Bible is that the conception and birth of Jesus Christ were miraculous from start to finish. We know that Mary was a virgin at this time (read Isa. 7:14) and that the Person of the Holy Spirit was the divine "agent" in bringing this miraculous conception about. After almost 2,000 years of theological silence on the actual mechanics on how this miracle occurred has been finally answered once and for all."

Even though the Bible itself is silent, God, through His chosen vessel, **Mr. Charles Capps**, has chosen to reveal to the Church exactly how this miraculous event transpired. As we shall see, it really was not so miraculous at all! **It was an act of the God-kind of faith that caused the miraculous conception**. It was the Word of God in her heart; then she went to Elisabeth's house and told her, "He hath done great things." (Luke 1:49). How did she know? Because the angel of the Lord had told her, and she receive that Word....She had conceived the Word of God in her spirit.

"Here is what the Spirit of God said to me about that situation: "**Mary conceived the Word sent to her by the angel (God's Word) and conceived it in the womb of her spirit, it manifested itself in her physical body. She received and conceived the Word of God in her spirit.**"

("Authority," **Charles Capps**, Harrison House, 1984, pp. 76-80, bold & italicized type added). All that took place was simply this: Mary used the "**God-kind of faith**" and through her use of this **spiritual law**, the law of faith, the miraculous conception took place.

According to <u>Faith</u> teachers, <u>there really was nothing so miraculous about the whole event</u>. Mary merely put into action certain <u>cosmic</u> <u>principles</u> and received the desired results, in this case, God being born as a man. Please do not skip over the importance of the claim **Mr. Capps** is setting forth in his statement. Note that it was the Holy Spirit Himself who revealed what happened to **Mr. Charles Capps** even places His words in italics so the reader knows when God is addressing him.

<u>Immediately</u> we all should clip out this statement and add it to the back of our Bibles. If God actually made these statements then they must be accepted as God-breathed by all the true Church. The Holy Spirit's revelation can be broken down into 3 simple steps:

1-Mary conceived (or received) the Word brought to her by the angel.
2-She conceived the Word in the womb of her spirit;
3-Nine months later it manifested in her physical body.

"As anyone can see, there is no big mystery as to how a virgin gave birth to God the Son....all that transpired was a simple application of the God-kind-of-faith or to state it another way—Mary used faith in the same way God uses it." **Capps** states "If she had said, 'Forget it, it won't work,' God would have had to find another woman" (pg. 82). "Mary was in control not God."
Never forget that the version of God the <u>Faith movement</u> presents is not the same God revealed in the Bible.

God does not use or need "faith." Only contingent beings need faith. God by definition knows everything, has all power and all wisdom to bring about whatsoever He has decreed.
What does God need to believe in or for? Absolutely nothing! (See our books on page 12 to learn more about the <u>Word of Faith</u> movement's leaders).
Capps continues to serve as a conduit for divine revelation: "The Lord said to me, 'My Word will get people healed and filled with the Holy Ghost the same way that the miraculous conception took place!   <u>Any believer can conceive My Word</u> concerning healing in their spirits, and healing will manifest in their physical bodies!"

"They can conceive My Word concerning <u>prosperity</u> of finances, and <u>prosperity</u> will manifest itself in their business affairs. If they will conceive My Word concerning the baptism of the Holy Spirit, it will manifest itself in their spirits (ibid. p. 83, italics added).
<u>In this astounding statement </u>we learn that "any believer can conceive My Word."

 So we like Mary, need only to apply the steps divinely revealed to **Mr. Capps** (similar concepts have also been revealed to **E.W. Kenyon, Ken Hagin, Copeland, Price, Cho**, and others) and we too can have our own miraculous conceptions. I must only wonder if what **Capps** says is true (remember to add this portion of text also to the back of your Bible, probably below the other portion, entitle it "First **Capps**") <u>then why isn't it working in the lives of those who subscribe to such beliefs</u>?

 E.W. Kenyon died of a tumor. **Buddy Harrison**, the son-in-law of **Ken Hagin** and the Publisher of **Charles's** book died of cancer in December of 1998. **T.L. Osborn's** wife, Daisy, died of cancer. **Capps** own wife, Peggy, had cancer and received medical treatment for it. **Betty Price, Fred Price's** wife also had cancer and was medically treated.

Joyce Meyer admitted she had breast cancer and only received medical treatment because her family urged her to! How come **Tammy-Faye Bakker Messner** didn't conceive/receive her divine healing from the cancer that untimely killed her? Why on earth did **Jan Crouch** even get cancer in the first place?   Why didn't these people simply conceive the promises of divine health & healing in the "womb" of their spirits and receive the miraculous fruit of divine health in their bodies? (Consider buying our message "The Sick Healers").
The answer is simple —**Mr. Capps** received no such revelation from God. It is a <u>false teaching</u> which does not produce the results **Capps** and others promise. <u>Their doctrine does not even</u>

work in their own lives. What is miraculous is that so many people willingly follow these "cunningly devised fables" and "doctrines of demons."

https://discernmentministriesinternational.wordpress.com/ 2010/02/11/
the-birth-of-god-the-son-according-to-charles-capps-word-of-faith-heretics/

--**Brian Carn:** According to the testimony of "Musician Minister" Pierre Whitlow and his wife, false prophet **Brian Carn** who hired Mr. Whitlow as the Music Director of KCC (Kingdom City Church) and relocated him and his family to Jacksonville, Florida had sex with minister Pierre Whitlow's wife while Pierre traveled home to get his children. **Brian Carn** called Pierre's wife and told her that he "felt her heavy in his spirit" and that he needed to stop by her apartment and pray with her immediately. She didn't suspect **Brian Carn** because he was paying for their apartment as a part of Pierre Whitlow's contract. **Brian Carn** arrived at Pierre Whitlow's apartment while their little daughter was asleep in an adjacent room, **Brian Carn's** "prayer" turned into groping and then sex.

 False prophet **Brian Carn** contacted Mrs. Whitlow daily for three weeks in an attempt to have another sex session until Mrs. Whitlow confessed everything to her husband. **Brian Carn** immediately fired Pierre Whitlow after being confronted by him, and ordered him and his family to move out of the apartment that he was paying for them. He attempted to serve Pierre a "cease and desist" letter to threaten him if he mentioned **Brian Carn's** actions. Listen to Pierre Whitlow's testimony...https://youtu.be/SVFrZ2OTT80.

(**NOTE: I listened to the first ten minutes and I have to say that this person's wife was indeed manipulated–his words–by this preacher, who when confronted, lied about what happened and used this person as his scapegoat because: do you believe the "prophet\preacher" or do you believe the person and his wife. Ed.).

Brian Carn is a mockery of anything considered to be holy. His filthy, despicable, vulgar, whorish behavior has continued far too long and "the church" has continued to tolerate it! **Brian Carn** is a menace to society, there are no woman (including young girls and children) safe in the church as long as **Carn** is mounting the pulpit. **Brian Carn** has displaced this family because he got caught sexually manipulating someone else's wife! I mean, LOOK AT HIM!

How could ANY WOMAN sleep with him while being sober? He's using witchcraft to put these women in a "trance" so that they will comply to have sex with him. I'm SURE that Pierre's wife can't believe that she had sex with this jerk. The kingdom of Christianity is certainly an evil force to be reckoned with.
A kingdom saturated with fornication, adultery, consulting sorcerers, drug use and sexual perversion IS NOT A KINGDOM OF GOD! It is a man-made kingdom that will be destroyed together with the world upon the return of Christ. Oh, we know what goes on "behind the scenes" **Brian Carn**, and so does Yah! What will it take for you people to stop following these false prophets?!
 https://babylon-today.com/2018/06/27/
false-prophet-brian-carn-cant-seem-to-keep-his-pants-up-again/

--**Morris Cerullo:** Deceased; <u>False prophet, false teacher</u>, <u>prosperity preacher</u>. Actually banned for life from television in Britain; convicted of unethical and fraudulent fund-raising techniques; also found guilty of tax evasion; made false and unsubstantiated claims of testimonials; http://www.deceptioninthechurch.com/cerullosuit.html

https://www.sandiegoreader.com/news/2013/nov/29/

In the early 1990s, **Cerullo** used $7 million in proceeds from donations to purchase a portion of disgraced televangelist **Jim Bakker's** PTL Ministry. Later that year, Britain's "Independent Television Commission" pulled the plug on **Cerullo's** "Victory with Morris Cerullo" for claiming to have special healing powers, a violation of the country's television program laws. More lawsuits followed, including one from a former executive for allegedly implementing "unethical and fraudulent fund-raising techniques." Then in 2005, **Cerullo**, whose supposed mission was to convert Jews to Christianity, was indicted on three counts of tax evasion after investigators said he filed false claims for three straight years, as reported by the Los Angeles Times.
According to a lawsuit, filed November 22 (2013) in San Diego Superior Court, **Cerullo** and his "Morris Cerullo World Evangelism, Inc.," says "World Religious Relief" took money intended for a new television contract to pay off a disputed debt, unbeknownst to **Cerullo** and his ministry. The conflict between the two sides dates back to 2011, when "World Religious Relief" said **Cerullo** and Co. failed to pay money owed for broadcasting their programming.
Cerullo disagreed, the conflict went unresolved, and the balance allegedly owed went unpaid. Then, in May of this year (2013), believing the issue was resolved, **Cerullo** entered into another contract with "World Religious Relief" to run his religious programs on the network at a cost of $2000 per broadcast for the span of one year, a total of $52,000.

Cerullo wrote "World Religious Relief" a check for $17,000 to begin running the "Victory Today" show. Instead, however, the network informed the evangelist that the money would be used to pay off his 2011 debt and that no new shows would air until the entire balance was paid. This preacher <u>sells elderships to his church by mail</u>.

http://www.bible.ca/tongues-TV-evangelist-IQ-test.htm

(NOTE: Several well known fraudsters appear on this website list above. Ed.).

--**Francis Chan:** Once was a good preacher; left the truth; currently his lies include: "It's gonna be the **unity** of the Church that's gonna get the world to believe;" "you're that temple." "And if anyone destroys God's temple, God will destroy him." "You wanna be on the right side of His protection;" "You better not criticize any <u>popular preachers</u> who claim to love me, or I might have to 'knock you off,' (if you catch my drift)..." "God told the Israelites not to speak or act against God's temple in the Old Testament, upon penalty of death." "In the New Testament, **people** are now the temple of God." "Therefore, we must never speak or act against God's temple-His people."

https://www.christianpost.com/news/
louie-giglio-reflects-on-changes-in-ministry-in-the-us-francis-chans-move-to-asia.html

"**Rick Warren, Mike Bickle**, and **Mark Driscoll** are men of God who should never be criticized, because **Francis Chan** knows them personally, and they have good hearts. "If you speak out against these "people of God," **Chan** wouldn't be surprised if God took your life, because that's what He promised in the Old Testament." (Also part of the IHOP movement). **Todd White** is happy to make large piles of money and live in a gigantic mansion; how does **Chan** feel about that? **Todd White** claims that he can "claim someone who doesn't believe and there's no way they can get out of it." How does **Francis Chan** feel about **Todd White** claiming to have the ability to sovereignly elect people?

 Francis Chan shows no sign of going to these events as a "missionary" in order to preach a true Gospel message to the people held captive by false teachers like **Mike Bickle** and **Todd White.** Instead, he appears to be endorsing a distinctly Charismatic understanding of the Christian faith. And by being a keynote speaker at this gigantic IHOP conference, he seems to be comfortable with the Dominionist, "Latter Rain/New Apostolic Reformation" type of teaching that IHOP and **Todd White** are known for. These are the words of a cult leader.

 How does **Francis Chan** feel about **Benny Hinn**? **Todd White** radically encountered the Holy Spirit at a **Benny Hinn** meeting, where he felt electricity "like he was plugged into a light socket," and the ushers on either side of **Todd White** were thrown "three feet in the air and about ten feet back." http://www.piratechristian.com

Chan is now a well-known conference speaker, regularly preaching alongside questionable at best, charismatics such as **Mike Bickle** of IHOPKC (International House of Prayer-Kansas City. Ed.) and many others. **Chan**, despite his solid theological educational background, is highly compromised in many ways, and not just because he regularly shares the stage with heretics. While that, in and of itself, is problematic, **Chan's** compromises are much deeper and stem from a serious lack of discernment. **Chan** aims to be a people-pleaser. It's understandable that a man in the flesh would desire the praise of other men, but God dislikes this attitude and the Apostle Paul warns against it (Galatians 1:10).

When **Chan** decided to leave his church several years ago to begin his charismatic crusade, he announced to his congregation "God was leading him elsewhere." Then, two years ago, while speaking at a gathering, speaking of his former church, he told the audience that they were all a "bunch of losers" who didn't exercise their spiritual gifts. **Francis Chan**, for several years, has been on the speaker circuit for several heretical crusades.
One of the most popular crusades he's frequented has been IHOPKC's annual "One Thing" conference alongside such heretics as **Todd White, Michael Brown, Joyce Meyer,** and Seventh Day Adventist, **Ben Carson**. This conference is not only heretical due to it's theological grounding steeped in New Apostolic Reformation ideology, it's also ecumenical, and holds a Catholic track. But **Chan** is no stranger to ecumenism.

 In 2003, Mike Gendron, a Christian apologist best known for his polemics and evangelistic resources for Catholics, was invited to speak at **Chan's** church. Gendron, a man who knows and loves Catholics enough to speak truthfully about the serious and damning theological errors they hold to, spoke to **Chan's** audience truthfully about the errors of purgatory, Mary, the

Eucharist, and the Biblical way of salvation. This prompted **Chan** to rebuke Mike Gendron in front of the entire gathering, stating that it "was a mistake" to host Gendron.

Chan's obvious discontent with Biblical truth shows that he is not only theologically inept and lacks serious discernment, but that he also seeks to not offend man, effectively offending God much worse. In his never-ending crusade to please the world, **Chan** continues to praise well-known, well-liked heretics while throwing solid men of God under the bus. **Chan** knows that men like Gendron are less popular with the world and the culture because they see the truth of Scripture as black and white — without compromise. At **Lou Engle's** 2019 "Send " Conference, **Chan** was noted praising arch-heretics, **Todd White** and **Daniel Kolenda**. **Todd White** is a fraudulent "faith-healer" who claims to have healed hundreds of people of various ailments without a shred of evidence.

Todd White holds to the Word of Faith heresy, "little God" theology, and is largely into the heretical New Apostolic Reformation movement that teaches that the office of Apostle —like the original 12 —has been reinstated and Apostles and Prophets exist today.

Besides the fact that every single "Apostle" and "Prophet" in this movement is morally compromised in some way, not a single one has ever prophesied the way the Biblical prophets have done. You can see **Chan** praising these men in the video below, toward the end.
Francis Chan, though he may occasionally speak things that sound right and Biblical, is a wolf in sheep's clothing to be avoided at all costs. Because of his associations with heretics and false teachers — and his considerable lack of discernment — **Chan** leads his people astray. He is not a shepherd to be followed, as he feeds his sheep directly to the wolves.

(**NOTE: Video can be seen on the link provided. Ed.):

https://reformationcharlotte.org/2019/02/24/ francis-chan-why-you-should-avoid-him/.

--Mahesh & Bonnie Chavda: "I have not personally encountered **Mrs. Chavda** in action. I have sat under her husband's ministry, even got slain in the spirit. (14) by **Mahesh** back in the early 1990's." As often is the case in public charismatic ministry you will find the wives either ministering equally with their husbands or leading them, such as **Joyce Meyer** who leads and her husband takes care of the off-stage work. **Gloria Copeland** preaches and teaches along her husband **Kenneth's** side (actually she is a better teacher than **Kenny**). Another famous example would be **Marilyn Hickey**, whose husband **Wally** is (was) an Assemblies of God pastor.
No charismatic can ever forget **Charles and Francis Hunter**, the "Happy Hunters" who tag-teamed preached and healed across the globe for forty plus years. Even so, we have the **Chavdas,** and who exactly are they? With over three miracle-packed decades of experience, **Mahesh and Bonnie Chavda** lead "Chavda Ministries international," a worldwide apostolic ministry.

The vision of CMI is "to proclaim Christ's kingdom with power, equip believers for ministry and usher in revival preparing for the return of the Lord." " Miracles are God's calling cards has been the clarion call of the prophetic movement for many years now." Folks, please get this if nothing else from this issue— miracles do not create faith.

Israel experienced DAILY miracles for forty years in the desert and DIED IN UNBELIEF. The premise that miracles are the method by which God draws and converts the lost is not shown in the Bible. It is a false premise. Thirty years of miracles? Ok, **Bonnie** where is the proof? This web site is not filled with x-rays, doctor's affidavits, independent witness testimony of miracles. At best we have anecdotal stories from either the **Chavdas** (let another man praise you Prov. 27:2) themselves or unidentifiable individual reports.

Next we read **Mahesh** and **Bonnie** are an "apostolic" team. "When were there any female apostles? Sorry dear sisters, there were not any. Also who called them to be apostles? Where is the fruit of their apostleship?" "Their job is to equip, i.e. impart spiritual gifts & power to believers so these empowered believers can go forth and become tools of God to usher in a global revival which MUST COME first."
After this preparatory work of Christianizing the world is done then Jesus Christ can return. This according to sign-gift theology is the role of today's restored apostle and prophet/prophetess. Jesus cannot return until the Church again embraces their ministries (apostolic/prophetic)." They base this belief on the following text (there are others too):

"Repent ye therefore, and be converted, that you sins may be blotted out when the times of refreshing shall come from the presence of the Lord."
"And he shall send Jesus Christ, which before was preached unto you: Whom the heaven must receive until the times of restitution of all things, which God hath spoken by the mouth of all his holy prophets since the world began. Acts 3:19-21." "Since their role is pivotal in the return of Jesus, it is only natural that they do all that is in their power to get the Church in agreement with them to hasten the return of Jesus."

This is where the prophetic movement gets very bizarre and possibly dangerous.

Let's allow God through **Bonnie** to warn the Church in a vision she received in 1995: "In the vision, I was standing on a land map of the USA." "The states stretched out from me in front and behind. I was facing west and above me, from horizon to horizon, was a ceiling of very thick, black, angry, clouds. Their appearance was that of an approaching terrible storm. In one place, there was an opening in the clouds. There, rays of very bright sunlight shone through." "Seeing this, I understood that a spiritual storm was imminent, and that in the wake of this storm, hope, peace, and joy, would shine from heaven. I heard a voice say, "This is the refreshing: IT WILL BE VERY VIOLENT."

"In 1995 **Bonnie** warned the Church and the world what the next great time of refreshing would be like. She profiled this during the height of the "Holy Laughter Revival " that a spiritual storm was imminent (uh, **Bonnie**, we're still waiting) and of all the oxymoronic language we are told that "this is the refreshing—it will be very violent." How refreshing is violence?"

Bonnie: "As I watched, a series of scenes from the movie adaptation of the American classic by L. Frank Baum, the "Wizard of Oz" passed before me. With each picture a voice described things that will take place as this coming "wind" moved over the land." "I understood that it will not be sinners, false religions, or even political institutions, including the media, that will most vehemently question and oppose the coming "wind." "It will be institutions of Christian tradition and influence, including those who claim the "fullness of the Spirit.""

(End). "Surprise of surprises it will not be the world that "hates" you (Jesus or the translators must have erred in John 15:8). False religions and polities will not be the forces questioning and opposing this latest move of God. Who will it be?" "It will be institutional Christianity (i.e. orthodox), Christian traditions and influence, and yup even some who claim to be filled with the Spirit (i.e. some Pentecostal types)."

"Please note the separation between Church institution/tradition and the Spirit-filled folk." "Never forget in the eyes of sign-gift enthusiasts you are a low-wattage, barely saved, spiritually weak and out of step with God. The entire movement, and sadly, much of the Church is driven with elitism, and it is always a stench." " **Bonnie**"...the Lord said, "There will be those who will call this wind "demonic" because of what it will make manifest. Demons will be stirred up, the flesh will be made obvious, things formerly hidden will be exposed and seen as they are in relation to My Spirit: BUT THIS WIND IS FROM ME." (?).

Over the years Tracy and I have sat and heard myriads of flakes come into meetings and spout stirring messages, many of which contained provisos to cover any question of the message or the messenger.
We see this tactic in **Bonnie's** drivel—"there will be those who..." those folks include anyone who does not swallow-and-follow the restored apostle and/or prophet." Please understand that these are not nice sweet folk theologically speaking. If they perceive you as a genuine threat they will decry you publicly, pray for your ruin, prophesy your downfall, pray the Lord to kill you. I have heard men and women do all of the above in the name of Jesus. What is more I and this portion of Christ's ministry has been a recipient of hate-filled ugly prophetic words because we left Charismania and because we cared enough to reveal the truth about what goes on behind closed "ministry" **SIN**istry doors.

Bonnie in her absurd vision, which has not taken place--so much for imminent--she takes the usual approach of denouncing those in the Church who cling to the Bible as their guide for faith and practice. All you have to do is go online and read some of her prophetic utterances and those of any so-called restored prophetic voice and you will read an eerie similarity when it comes to the historic Church and its role ("which is over by the way"). Obtained from: http://www.chavdaministries.org

https://discernmentministriesinternational.wordpress.com

- **Mark Chironna**: Television evangelist **Mark Chironna** is a frequent host of the Trinity Broadcasting Network's (TBN) "Praise the Lord" program and has his own show on TBN called "The Master's Touch." He's also the overseer of "The Master's Touch International Church" in Orlando, Florida. God Ceased to Exist?– Unfortunately, in his ministry, **Chironna** communicates a basic misunderstanding about many aspects of the Scriptures, starting with the nature of God.

He says "When He [Jesus] released Himself back into the hands of the loving and Almighty Father and He said 'It is finished,' literally...that moment when the immortal One died, rocks split apart, because that which held them for that brief moment was no longer in charge...and the whole earth went dark because that which held it together was expired for a moment."

How can the "Immortal One" expire? In reality, Jesus never ceased to exist, even for a moment, because it would have meant that God, who by definition is eternal, ceased to exist. In addition to the fact that the earth "went dark" starting at noon, not when Jesus died at 3:00 p.m., one might ask, if the rocks split because Jesus, the One who held them together, had died, then why didn't the rest of the universe, including everyone on earth, also split for a moment?

Preaching the Health and Wealth Gospel– **Chironna** teaches that to the poor the Good News of the Gospel is money. "So in Isaiah 61....The first thing He says is 'He has anointed me to bring good news to the poor." "What is good news to the poor? You don't have to be poor anymore. And if you don't believe me, even liberal scholars acknowledge that Christ is talking about economic compensation, payback, economic forgiveness....God wants to bring people out of places of poverty into places of abundance."
One would wonder why **Chironna,** who is supposed to be conservative, is quoting liberal scholars for support. To learn the context of this passage, **Chironna** would have done well to quote the rest of Isaiah 61:1, which continues, "He has sent me to bind up the brokenhearted, to proclaim freedom for the captives and release from darkness for the prisoners."

The passage in Isaiah that Jesus quotes describes what Jesus did in His ministry, and, in context, it is obvious that Jesus is presenting Good News for the poor in spirit, and for those oppressed by sin – the Good News being the forgiveness of sins. Likewise, in places like the Sermon on the Mount He talked about the poor in spirit, not the poor in pocket book. While Jesus did heal the blind and the lame, He didn't restore wealth to the physically poor, nor did He even give them a pep talk on how to escape physical poverty.

On the contrary, He warned people about the deceitfulness of wealth (Mark 10:24, 25).
 Giving God Permission to Act– **Chironna** tells followers to speak words of faith and give God permission to act. "How many of you know you're a new species of being?"
"If you really are, then what God did in the original creation you can now give Him permission to do again in the new creation....Now you have the mind of God on the inside....You realize the person of perfect health is already living inside your body even if you're sick right now."

"And what you and I need to understand is that God wants us to begin to think His thoughts after Him and once we think them, God the Son wants to then speak them on His behalf."

"That's what the word of faith is....And then once you hear something in the Spirit, speak it with your mouth. As the Father thinks, the Son speaks and then the Spirit takes what you say and begins to reorder your world to line up with your faith!"
If people need to give God permission to do anything then He is no longer sovereign!

Chironna teaches that Christians can speak things into existence. He states, "If I've been made in the image of God and I'm not like a giraffe or a monkey, the thing that makes me like God is I can talk. I can say 'Let there be' and there will be."
Imagine the chaos in the world if everyone could have exactly what they wanted, even if this ability applied only to Christians?

("Praise the Lord," Trinity Broadcasting Network, January-April 2003.
http://heresyhunter.blogspot.com/2009/10/ mark-chironna-man-of-god.html

Dr. Mark Chironna, who seems to be an open repository of false and non-Biblical claims, has done it once again. Listen for yourself as **Dr. Chironna** claims that Jesus was "spoken into existence" when God said "let there be light" in Genesis 1:11. This is truly unbelievable from anyone calling themselves a Christian. I mean I would expect to hear something like this from a Jehovah's Witness or even a Mormon, but certainly not a Christian. Which makes me wonder, does **Mark Chironna** claim to be a Christian minister?

https://youtu.be/hahgpvJbJ-M

Listen, for any **Mark Chironna** followers, or for those who think they have benefitted from **Dr. Chironna's** teaching, I take no joy in bringing these false doctrines and practices to light. I simply ask that his followers actually place the teaching of Scripture higher than the charisma of **Chironna**, ask him to repent, and help him to cease preaching non-Biblical doctrine.
The only way I know to get his attention towards this is by not sowing your money into assuming that it's blessed by God! The sad part to this is that it displays that neither the minister not the audience have any Biblical knowledge.
If Jesus was spoken into existence he could not and would not have been eternal as God. However he is eternal and he is God. Maybe We Should Examine What Jesus Didn't Do:

1- Jesus didn't simply switch hats in varying modes from the Father, to the Son to the Holy Ghost. That sort of teaching is called Sabellianism or modalism and is not a Scriptural concept of God nor the relationship between God the Father and God the Son and God the Holy Ghost. This is commonly known as "Jesus Only" teaching and what we find among Apostolic and "oneness" Pentecostals.   In other words Jesus has always been the Son and will always be the Son eternally and there is an ontological distinction between the Father and the Son.

 I'll do a post on this in the future, but our concept of who Jesus is in relationship to God the Father is vitally important and essential to communicating Biblical truth and accurately representing the message of Jesus to the world.

2- Jesus wasn't created by the Father and neither did he show up as an after-thought. Jesus being God was the personal power whereby the universe leapt into existence. The Scripture accord that all things that are made were made by him.
A Physicist will claim "big bang"...Well God, by Jesus, was greater than the supposed singularity, and who existed before time began was the author of everything that was created whether seen or unseen.

3- Jesus at no point ever had the role of an angel or any other angelic host. Jesus' role in heaven since the first of the heavenly creation were created was worshipped as God. Heaven ascribes nothing less than the highest praise to Jesus himself as HE is God. This theme is replete throughout Scripture especially throughout the NT narrative.

4- Jesus never claimed to BE the Father. Jesus claimed to be one with the Father. This indicates his oneness in nature or essence. However Jesus was never and has never been confused over the fact that he was not the Father. He spoke distinctly of himself in relationship terms with the Father even calling himself "Son".
Prior to Jesus, (and since) no Jewish teacher taught or teaches in personal relationship terms as Jesus did and does. Further, the Father is always the object and answerer of prayer to Jesus, further evidenced by Jesus himself often praying to the Father. As stated, the nature and essence of Jesus was that of God.

5- Jesus never claimed to BE the Holy Ghost. Throughout Scripture, Jesus spoke of the Holy Ghost in relational terms as well, claiming that the Holy Ghost would direct men to follow and remember his words and outlined his duties and operations among mankind and the church especially after Jesus would be taken away. Further, Peter understood that the Holy Ghost could be lied to (Ananias and Sapphira found this out) and Paul understood that the Holy Ghost could be grieved. In all cases there was a clear distinction in relationship and personality of Jesus and the Holy Ghost.

Conclusion--These are simply 5 of the most popular confusions on who Jesus is that I often hear. **Dr. Chironna** takes it to another level.

There are plenty other confusions of which I am aware including that of **Kenneth Copeland** who claimed that Jesus never said that he was God and that of **Creflo Dollar** who claimed that Jesus wasn't born God but became God over time. The false doctrine that **Dr. Chironna** spouts is another in the league of apostate teaching.
I thank God for each of you that present the God of the Bible, the true Gospel message that changes lives and saves souls and for those who never fail to lift up the true and living Lord for all men to see. Thank you and please be strong. We need you.

http://bethelburnett.blogspot.com/2010/03/ apostates-heretics-false-doctrines-ii.html

- **Paul and David Yonggi Cho**: The world's largest Pentecostal church; guilty of embezzling millions of dollars; located in South Korea; Word of Faith heretic;

(See article under **Dr. Michael Brown's** name. Ed.).

- **Deepak Chopra**: https://jesustruthdeliverance.com/ 2017/03/02/false-new-age-teacher-deepak-chopra/

https://www.theguardian.com/commentisfree/belief/ 2012/may/07/deepak-chopra-wealthy-knows-illusion

(**NOTE: These are quite lengthy. He is a New Age philosopher\teacher. Ed.).

- **Freddy Clark**: http://warren888.tripod.com/id174.html

(**NOTE: There is so much wrong with his teaching that unless you know the Bible, you won't spot it. I am including this link so you can read for yourself just how dangerous his doctrine is. I am also including a YouTube video so you can decide if he is real or not. Ed.).

https://www.youtube.com/ watch?v=A0fypG-0eBA

- **Randy Clark**: NAR false preacher. **Randy Clark** had been to the **Rodney Howard-Browne's** "laughter" meetings (1993) in Tulsa, Okla., at **Kenneth Hagin, Jr.'s** Rhema Bible Church (this is significant, as we see the same characters and concepts continually involved. **John Arnott** invited **Clark** to come to Toronto Airport Church, (Jan. 20, 1994) and that is when the "Toronto blessing" began. www.letusreason.org/Pent30.htm

Clark describes this fire they experienced being brought to Holy Trinity of Brompton (UK). They were laughing so hard. One guy had his eyes on the floor for about two hours and could not walk (**Randy Clark**, "Evidence Of This Present Move," Toronto Airport Vineyard, October 15, 1994). **Clark**: "I don't want you to quench the Holy Spirit, I don't want you to stop laughing, just please dial the decibels down a little bit."

(**Randy Clark**, "Let The Fire Fall Conference," Anaheim Vineyard, July 1994) .

CBN writes "He has been blessed to receive impartation from **Randy Clark, Bill Johnson, Roland** and **Heidi Baker** and **Benny Hinn**. What a strange brew this is!
 A little Latter Rain or a lot?" **Clark** then points him out (**Todd White**), as he is profusely antagonized with what most would consider palpitations and thinking he is having a heart attack and **Clark** says "you have been asking the Lord for a baptism of fire haven't you? And "boom" (his words) the Holy Spirit hits me and drops me between the seats and I'm screaming and think I'm gonna die..."its like I'm being electrocuted, it's the scariest thing" "I'm sitting there shaking and trembling" (**Todd White** speaking).

Randy Clark says, "you won't die--more Lord" ("The fire of God will Cost you, it's worth it" -video). And the same experience happened from the originator of this anointing, **Rodney Browne** from whom **Randy Clark** received it from.
Browne said "The anointing of God as wonderful as it is, is electricity" and describes it: "I was plugged into heaven's electric light supply and since then my desire has been to go and plug other people in." "My whole body was on fire from the top of my head to the soles of my feet." "The fire of God was coursing through my whole being and it didn't quit; because of that encounter with the Lord, my life was radically changed from that day on" (**Rodney Howard Browne**, "The Touch of God," pp. 73-74).
Where in the Bible does the baptism of the Spirit (which they say is the baptism of the fire) do this? And they are still plugging people into this false anointing. This is the common experience from Kundalini "fire" power. The Bible says the anointing is a Person, the Holy Spirit, who is God.   http://www.letusreason.org/Popteach85.htm http://www.stand4thelord.com).

- **Heather Clark**: From Canada; believes she is a <u>worship leader</u>, who claims that God has <u>anointed </u>her and all of us to practice what she is doing; was part of the "Lakeland Revival " in 2008; <u>heretical</u> teacher).

- **Ian Clayton:** A New Zealand <u>prophet</u> and father of four, is a man who found himself seemingly <u>chosen by the demonic realm </u>to become a great <u>occult</u> leader. Yet God had other plans, shifting the shadows of power aside to reveal Himself and lead **Ian** into an entirely different realm of grace. His story illustrates the powers of the <u>occult</u> as well as the ability of light to overcome the darkness in an individual's life, shifting them out of the shadows until they enter into authentic power and supernatural experiences initiated by the Holy Spirit.

Psychics claim that the ability to see and move in the supernatural is often inherited and can trace the lineage of relatives who moved in psychic power for generations past. In **Ian's** case, the generational lines seemed to offer two distinct destinies for **Ian's** spiritual gifts. On his mother's side of the family is a line of Jewish and Christian believers. One great grandfather was counted among the original Quakers in Africa. During the mid-1800s, another great grandfather experienced the Welsh revival. His father's side of the family was exactly the opposite.
 His father was the head of the spiritualist church in Africa. His family lineage included <u>Freemasons, Rosicrucians, and those with claims to other occult involvement. </u>It wasn't long before the two warring destinies manifested in **Ian's** life as power reached out and touched him at an early age. As a child, **Ian** would see visions of Jesus and angels.

 Eventually, his father took him to the <u>spiritualist</u> church and things began to change. The dark side aggressively pursued **Ian**, shifted him into the shadows, and lured him into the <u>occult</u>. At age 12, his growing awareness of God led him to the Bible and he started reading it from the beginning. Halfway through Deuteronomy he decided that it was full of rules and regulations and didn't want anything to do with it. Just as he shut the Bible he heard a voice say, "Put your hand on top of table and pick table up." **Ian** put his hand flat on the table top and it rose, sideways off the floor.

"It was an amazing power rush," **Ian** explained. "Suddenly, I walked in power." <u>Spirits started materializing at night and taught **Ian** how to do things such as astral travel and psychic healing, pendulum diagnosis, use of herbs in healing and in gaining power, and the power of demons in the spirit world. </u>

As the lessons continued, people grew frightened of **Ian's** power. Many would talk about the headaches they got after being around him—headaches **Ian** attributes to the <u>demonic resonance of the spirit force</u> around his life. Meanwhile, <u>signs and wonders </u>manifested in **Ian's** life much to his surprise and others' shock. "I would put my hand out and it would go into the wall—not up against it," he said.

By age 17, **Ian** was frightened of his own power and turned into an introvert attempting to shelter himself from others because of the phenomena that would occur. The power then transitioned him into deeper realms of a supernatural world. "<u>A generational sentinel appeared</u>

as a jaguar then became a man who taught me for a year about issues of sorcery and how to make and destroy things," **Ian** said.

"I thought I would use this power for the good of others without realizing the source was evil and would actually release demons into their lives. I didn't know this until I was born again."

According to **Ian**, the spirits taught him to become a psychic healer and he would lay hands on a body and take out the bits that were diseased. He could heal and he could kill with the same power that resided within him. "The moment I touched their flesh they submitted to the demon in my life."
"When I got angry at somebody I would release spirits and the people either were killed or became sick. At one point, my father got sick and my mother ended up in hospital because of my cursing them."

(**NOTE: This article continues on and on about his conversion to Jesus Christ. Ed.).
https://shiftingshadowsofpower.blogspot.com/2006/06/
from-sorcerer-to-prophet.html

https://spiritbodysoul.com/recognising-universalism/ :
Please contact us for more information regarding **Ian Clayton** and his "Order of Melchizedek" teachings as we have researched this extensively.

- **Kim Clement**: Deceased; was a false prophet, teacher, NAR; TBN darling; Made this statement about Salvation: "I do not believe that you must be born again to obtain salvation. I believe there is a distinction." "Prophet" **Kim Clement** was accepted into a home study Bible course through **Oral Roberts University.**
After explaining his situation of being rejected to the University and donating a few dollars in the envelope, a few weeks later boxes of books from **Oral Roberts** were delivered to his door. He read them over and over.   http://www.letusreason.org

- **Gerald Coates**: Not really very well known in the U.S., however his connections to the wolves in our country makes him noteworthy: "I was sent by Christian friends a copy of an audio tape of a talk which was given to **Gerald Coates** and workers in his "Pioneer Team" by Roger Ellis (Chichester).

To refresh minds **Gerald Coates** is one of three people who started the "Marches for Jesus."

He also fully endorsed the ministry of **Rodney Howard Browne** one of the 'key players' in the 'Toronto blessing' fiasco describing him as 'a breath of fresh air' and he referred to the heretical late Malcolm Muggeridge (for details of his heresies see 'News From The Front' December 1995) as a 'major prophet.'

On this tape Mr Ellis was urging people to go back and try and capture the 'Celtic Spirit':

As I listened to this very 'atmospheric' tape (on large segments a continuous drumbeat is heard and folk-type music is interspersed at intervals) I was highly alarmed by many of Mr Ellis' statements and noted many of them down planning to mention them in this article. However in the providence of God I was sent a copy of a little booklet called 'Modern Celtic Spirituality' by Paul Fahy and in the latter part of this booklet Mr Fahy gives a very good analysis of this very tape by Mr Ellis.

One of the expressions used by Mr Ellis which I noted with alarm was 'they (the Celts) <u>looked to release the divine spark in the people that they were evangelising</u>.'

Mr Fahy comments "What is meant by this spark is the image of God, but salvation is not <u>releasing</u> this image, it is a <u>radical</u> transformation by new life. This can be misinterpreted as the <u>doctrine of the mystics</u> currently much in vogue through New Age teachings...that is the <u>releasing of what is 'the divine in every man</u>."

This is completely anti-Christian...Man does not have a divine spark which only needs to be fanned into a flame. He is dead towards God and totally corrupt. "A corpse cannot help himself." There is no doubt that now that the excitement surrounding 'Toronto' has begun to subside it will be necessary for the leaders in (the extreme) charismatic circles to be on the look-out for some new 'spiritual plaything' to offer their followers and I just wonder if 'Celtic Spirituality' might be the next course on the menu. Much of the 'credit' for spreading this viral 'Blessing' in the UK was down to the 'ministry' of one **Rodney Howard Browne**. On video of a meeting that he held in England the supportive platform guests included **Gerald Coates**.

There are times when watching 'things Christian' on TV that I cringe and think to myself 'what must the unsaved think as they watch this'? Such an occasion occurred whilst watching 'Tonight' broadcast by ITV on 15th July 1999. For almost 15 minutes the latest 'charismatic craze' was exposed and examined in front of millions of viewers. The opening shots showed many people seated prayerfully with their hands clasped – not together but around their jaws. The prayer of the pastor at the front could be heard filling the auditorium – 'In the name of Jesus – fill teeth Lord – replace amalgam fillings with gold and with platinum'. Who were these people, what was the location and who was the pastor/prospector praying for an infilling, not of the Holy Spirit, but of precious metals?

We were in TORONTO – birthplace of the 1994 so-called 'BLESSING .' Same fellowship and same pastor – **John Arnott**. We were treated to **Mr Arnott** trying first to interview one laughing lady. Then he said to another man – "Let me see what God has done" and after inspecting the man's mouth [ably assisted by a torchbearer] he asked "How can God turn porcelain to gold"? And quick as a flash the man replied "My God can do anything." Next we had close ups of open mouths [lit up by torchbearers] belonging to some who believed they had received new or replacement gold fillings.

All this was to the accompaniment of excited squeals like those uttered by game show or lottery winners. The scene then shifted to England where similar 'miracles' were being claimed and once again we were re-tracing the 1994 TORONTO TRAIL. Now we were in the company of **Gerald Coates** and his Pioneer Church. According to a report by the "Back To The Bible " group based in The Netherlands [Newsletter 16] this 'tooth fairy' nonsense was also peddled in Holland by both **Mr Arnott** and Mr Escobar during visits there by them in May and June. (Mr. Escobar is a visiting preacher).

Pentecostal Preacher, Jacob Prasch, also made reference to these failed 'prophecies' when he published 'An Open Invitation to Gerald Coates'. Part of that 'Invitation' reads as follows –

Dear **Gerald Coates**,

"In 1990 you were perhaps chief among those who embraced the prophetic predictions which we have on video of **John Wimber, Paul Cain, Mike Bickel** and the Kansas City Prophets, that the greatest Revival in Britain's history would come to Britain in October of 1990. In the 5 years since, more Mosques have been built in Britain than Churches." "Who had the Revival **Mr Coates** – Mohammed?"
"There has never been a repentance by either yourself or those who falsely predicted revival in the name of the Lord." "You and they were dead wrong, and others misled by you." Whilst this particular publication by Jacob Prasch is not online there is a similar-themed article on his web site that can be accessed on

http://moriel.org/MorielArchive/index.php/
discernment/church-issues/nar/paul-cain-r-t-kendell-and-friends

http://www.takeheed.info/the-prophetic-poison-of-gerald-coates-in-songs-of-praise/

All of the names mentioned in that short extract from the 'Invitation' by Jacob Prasch are also mentioned VERY favourably by **Gerald Coates** in his book "An Intelligent Fire" that I quoted from earlier. In particular **Gerald Coates** gave prominence to supposed 'prophet' **Paul Cain** by devoting an 'Epilogue' in his book to '**Paul Cain's** Prophecy'.
This is the same **Paul Cain** that sadly had a very spectacular 'fall' and turned out to be an alcoholic homosexual as you can read on–

http://www.deceptioninthechurch.com/orrel19.html.

(**NOTE: This article is quite lengthy. I have provided highlights, since it names other "wolves". I did not add every paragraph. For that, you need to go to the website. Ed.):

http://www.takeheed.info/ the-prophetic-poison-of-gerald-coates-in-songs-of-praise/

and: http://www.e-n.org.uk/ 473-False-prophecy-today.htm

Paul Ellis – http://escapetoreality.org/2013/09/17/
12-ways-inclusionism-misleads/ and

http://escapetoreality.org/2013/09/27/ inclusionism-is-not-good-news/.

(Source: https://spiritbodysoul.com/recognising-universalism/)

- **Tasha Cobbs-Leonard**: While she may sing about the power in the name of Jesus, **Cobbs-Leonard** doesn't tend to preach the power of Christ, the truth of His Word, at all.

Like many of her **health- and wealth-preaching peers**, **Cobbs-Leonard's** m.o. is to quickly reference a passage of Scripture, manipulate its context then, for the next 40 minutes, somehow apply it to the hearers' breakthrough, purpose, destiny, dreams, goals or whatever else their itching ears desire to hear.

Meanwhile, the Lord is an after-thought. Yet, according to **Cobbs-Leonard**, she is a prophet of the Lord, and she tends to make numerous "prophetic" declarations in the midst of her sermons. "It's a governmental type of prophet that God's called me to be, that kings have to submit when I release a word," says **Cobbs-Leonard**."

Funny thing is God's Word says that He NO LONGER releases "a word" through men as He did through the prophets of old (Hebrews 1:1). Now that Christ has come, God speaks through His Son, Who is the culmination of all of the revelations God had previously made through the Law and the prophets (Hebrews 1:2; Luke 24:44; John 5:39,46).

In short, Jesus is the Word (John 1:1,14). As such, anyone making a true prophetic utterance in this day and age will speak ONLY that which directly aligns with the truth of Scripture (the FULL revelation thereof)!

Whatever they speak will be wholly verifiable and testable against what has already been said, and it will point the hearer to Jesus Christ. But let's hear **Cobbs-Leonard** out: During a sermon entitled "Sonship" **Cobbs-Leonard** shares that the Lord asked her to release a prophetic word from John 4:35, which she said was to tell the people that it is now harvest time!

But God didn't tell her that it was "harvest time" as it relates to our going into the world to reach the bountiful number of lost souls with the Gospel of Jesus Christ that they might repent and be saved, which is the meaning Jesus intended. Nope!

 Cobbs-Leonard says God told her to tell the congregants at the dRom Center Church of Atlanta that it is harvest time for their breakthrough, purpose, destiny, dreams, goals and whatever else their itching ears desired to hear. And the kicker?

She told them that to reap their harvest - which she'd just said was NOW ready, they had to "sow a seed" (give money). Now, I've just only started to dabble in gardening, but something about that order sounds off.

She went on to 'prophesy' a bit more, "I declare that some of the stuff that you didn't even work for is about to come into fruition in your life...You're going to live in houses that you did not build. You're going to drive cars that you don't have the money to drive. You're going to have land and property that you're not supposed to have!"

But in order to get these **free** material blessings, **Cobbs-Leonard** says"You're going to have to pay up." 'God' gave **Cobbs-Leonard** a similar 'prophetic' word to deliver during her sermon entitled "Who Gone Check Me Boo". In it, she references the story of Jesus healing the lame man at the pool of Bethesda, reading from John 5:1 through verse 12.

She goes on to 'prophesy', "I declare that the sons of the world will no longer break the line in front of the sons of God! I declare that the spirit of the thinker has just been released in this room!"

She continues, "I prophesy that the spirit of the innovator is taking over the "dReam Center Church" of Atlanta!"

Later she declares physical healing for those in the congregation who had documented illnesses and notes that there will be some who will heal their co-workers just by showing up to work that following week. She encouraged everyone to stop making excuses for not going after their dreams.

She declared a shift and a refreshing was taking place, then she spoke in tongues and cursed various spirits. The people shouted, some cried, the band crescendoed the music perfectly on cue for emotional effect. It was quite an experience! So much so, **Cobbs-Leonard** declared that Jesus was in the place that day. Which is odd because Jesus, who came to call men to repentance, let her teach a whole 40-minute sermon around breakthroughs, purposes, destinies, dreams, goals and whatever else their itching ears desired to hear, but never once compelled her to conclude the story of the newly healed man (John 5:14) - when Jesus told him to "STOP SINNING" (Repent!)!!!! https://www.lipstickalley.com

- **Nancy Coen** : (**NOTE: Other than a few You Tube videos, it is very hard to find written information about her, other than she is a believer in Universalism Ed.).

Here is one You Tube link: https://www.youtube.com/watch?v=gobikk2ZMkM

On this particular You Tube video, there is also another reference to her: https://www.youtube.com/ redirect?redir_token=Hj_l_5fdguvcGKRcKgDYD5rUl_58MTU3MjU3NTU1MUAxNTcyNDg5MTUx&q =http%3A%2F%2Fwww.moed-ministries.com%2Fshop-1&event=video_description&v=gobikk2 ZMkM (Ed.).

- **Chuck Colson**: Deceased. Evidence from **Colson's** own words that he is not a Christian at all, but is really an anti Christian ecumenical Romanist. Southern Baptist **Charles Colson** is the most effective propagandist for the Roman Catholic Church in America.

 Nearly seven years ago, in January and February 1994, "The Trinity Review " reviewed several of **Colson's** books—"Born Again," "Loving God," "The Body,'" Against the Night," "Who Speaks for God?" 'The God of Stones and Spiders," "Kingdoms in Conflict," "Life Sentence"– in the course of which we pointed out some of **Colson's** anti-Christian and Roman Catholic ideas:

1. **Colson** asserts that the Bible is paradoxical ("Loving God").
2. **Colson** praises the nun Teresa of Calcutta as one of the "contemporary giants of the faith" and as the "greatest saint in the world" (Loving God").
3. **Colson** asserts that faith is "not just belief, but belief lived out—practiced" ("Loving God," 37).
4. **Colson** advocates "mere Christianity," the doctrines on which "all Christians agree" ("The Body," 104, 108, 185).
5. **Colson** praises ecumenical discussions between Lutherans and Roman Catholics ("The Body," 271).

6. **Colson** favors making the sign of the cross ("The Body," 106).

7. **Colson** laments the lack of an ecclesiastical Magisterium among Protestantism ("The Body," 132).

8. **Colson** heatedly attacks "individualism," "lone rangers," and the "entrepreneurial spirit" ("The Body," 32, 134).

9. **Colson** advocates private communion ("The Body," 140).

10. **Colson** laments the lack of a monolithic church structure ("The Body," 199).

11. **Colson** laments the fact that Americans are free to choose the churches they will attend ("The Body," 199).

12. **Colson** believes that Roman "Catholics have better made visible the spiritual reality of worship" ("The Body," 73).

13. **Colson** constantly uses the title "Father" in referring to Roman and Orthodox priests.

14. **Colson** vigorously defends "Mother Teresa's Christian commitment" ("The Body," 87).

15. **Colson** endorses "natural law" ("The Body," 196).

16. **Colson** praises **Billy Graham** for including Roman Catholic priests in staffing his crusades ("The Body," 333).

17. **Colson** includes all denominations in Prison Fellowship ("The Body," "Life Sentence").

18. **Colson** endorses "Catholic evangelicals" ("The Body," 101) as "a great movement of the Holy Spirit among people completely committed to Christian living within the Catholic Church" ("Foreword to Evangelical Catholics").

19. **Colson** asserts that "the church is hierarchical and authoritarian and ultimately answerable only to God" ("The Body," 133).

20. **Colson** criticizes Protestants who opposed John Kennedy's election as President ("The Body," 169).

21. **Colson** implies that anti-abortion activism is more important than a correct understanding of the doctrine of justification ("The Body," 114).

22. **Colson** praises the Roman Church-State for "calling heretics to account" ("The Body," 132).

23. **Colson** recommends reading Roman Catholic authors ("The Body").

24. **Colson** asserts that Rome no longer offers indulgences ("The Body," 271).

25. **Colson** uses "inclusive language" in his own books while denouncing such inclusive language as "code words...of a feminist orthodoxy" which "represent subscription to the entire [feminist] agenda" ("The Body," 242).

26. **Colson** endorses a Roman Catholic monk as a "Christian"—a monk who teaches that obedience to God's commands is "not difficult" and "very simple" ("The Body," 320).

27. **Colson** asserts that "it is so crucial for the members of the Body to put aside their less significant differences and join forces around our integrated world-view" ("The Body," 199).

28. **Colson** endorses one world church: "It is about time for Christians who recite the creed and mean it to come together for fellowship and witness regardless of denominational identity" ("The Body," 99).

29. **Colson** attends mass with his Roman Catholic wife ("Life Sentence," 39, 93).

30. **Colson** asserts that "Christianity has been firmly established in Poland for a thousand years" ("Kingdoms in Conflict," 196).

31. **Colson** enthusiastically praises Roman Catholic masses in Poland and the worship of the Black Madonna ("Kingdoms in Conflict," 196).

32. **Colson** participated in mass in Northern Ireland ("Loving God" tapes).

33. **Colson** defends lying for pious purposes ("Kingdoms in Conflict," 286).

Here are 33 reasons to **Chuck Colson**, and now he has provided even more in his latest book, " How Now Shall We Live?" Since we reviewed those earlier **Colson** books, **Colson** has publicly attacked the Biblical doctrine of justification by faith alone in "Evangelicals and Catholics Together" and "The Gift of Salvation," and if their pattern holds, we can expect another such quasi-Romanist document from the Cardinal Cassidy **Colsonites** this year.

Colson's jihad against Biblical Christianity continues to open new theaters of conflict, and he and his Romanist and crypto-Romanist friends have already inflicted many casualties, including some within the Southern Baptist Convention and the Presbyterian Church in America.

Far from being a "champion of the faith," as CEO Joel Belz of "World " magazine described **Colson** in a shameless puff piece in his neo-evangelical magazine, **Colson** is an enemy of the Christian faith—one of the slickest that has yet emerged from the theological swamp of American neo-evangelicalism. http://www.trinityfoundation.org/journal.php?id=126

- **Ray Comfort**: Teaches the damnable heresy of Lordship Salvation along with **Kirk Cameron**, a former sitcom star.
https://www.thepathoftruth.com/false-teachers/ray-comfort.htm

https://www.jesus-is-savior.com/Wolves/comfort_and_cameron.htm

https://www.evangelicaloutreach.org/raycomfort.htm

http://www.jesusisprecious.org/
false_doctrine/lordship_salvation/ray_comfort-genius_the_movie.htm

- **Graham Cooke**: Says, "Grace is the empowering presence of God to make us feel good about ourselves as we are in the process of becoming more and more Christlike." Scarcely has a greater lie been told. A visitor at "The Path of Truth" wrote to us, asking about **Graham Cooke**: "I have listened to the teachings of **Graham Cooke** and it appears to me that he is saying that we are all mini gods when we accept Salvation and we no longer sin."

(**NOTE: You Tube videos that explain this false preacher. Ed.):
https://www.youtube.com/watch?v=w7MC69JuH54

https://www.youtube.com/watch?v=2jJda73aGSs

https://www.youtube.com/watch?v=hdMjfc7t8X0

Graham is more about magic and mysticism than the practical reality of the Spirit of God, beginning with his alleged conversion experience in the field with a being who didn't identify himself. **Graham** appears to be a "How to" or "Self-help" man, one whose boastful emphasis is on our innate power to realize God's Presence in our lives and for us to be "in tune" with Him and to "hear His Voice," the voice of the One Who, says **Graham**, wants to speak to us all the time, which is another lie of many. Which philosophy is ironic, because **Graham** does say that the initial salvation event is God's doing and that there's really nothing we can do to make it happen. But it seems we can pretty much make the rest of it happen by just "tapping in."

New Agers could easily cozy up to **Graham**, saying, "Wow! Isn't that really what WE believe? Only you put it in your own religious words." In all of his communication, there's not a word of sin or repentance – not one;

I haven't pursued the rest of his videos to examine everything, but a cup of the water from the well tells what the rest of it is like, doesn't it? **Graham** flatters God in men's ears, which may lead his hearers to wonder what can be possibly false about him if he speaks so well of God. Satan's ways are artful, subtle, and powerfully deceptive.

Graham goes on to say God's Voice is not judgmental. Isn't it? Where in Scripture do we ever find that lie? We don't. Saying God's Voice isn't judgmental is an argument that misrepresents God and His ways.

It's Satan savoring the things of men, things that please, appease and tease the flesh. **Graham** goes on to say in https://www.youtube.com/ watch?v=dUlLpmJeDh4   [no longer available],

"The voice of God that makes you feel the beloved, that would be Him. The voice of God that makes you feel good about yourself, even while you're in the process of changing, that would be Him... Listen to the voice that's kind cause it will NOT be the enemy.
The enemy will not be kind to you; he'd rather cut his tongue out than say anything kind to you...."

Lies, blatant anti-Biblical lies these are. So Satan DOESN'T come with kindness? What did Jesus say to Peter when Peter came rebuking the Lord, reasoning with Him "in kindness", telling Him He needn't fear such negative things as He was speaking. We are called to reprove and even rebuke sharply. Paul said he would come to the Corinthians with a rod if they continued in their ways. So God never speaks in stern manner? So Paul was wrong? He was in the flesh?

On the other hand, Satan is full of kindness, flattery and gentle persuasion... "Yea, has God said?" not, "He's a big fat liar!" And, "If You throw Yourself down from the pinnacle of the Temple, the angels will protect You. It says so in His Word!"

Doesn't Satan, contrary to what **Graham** claims, use kind, gentle, gracious, loving...generous words? Let's see what God says about that by His Word: "Again, the Devil took Him up into a very high mountain and showed Him all the kingdoms of the world and their glory. And he said to Him, All these things I will give You if You will fall down and worship me" (Matthew 4:8-9 MKJV). I'd say that would be very generous. On the other hand, God "covetously" and jealously requires our very lives: "Then Jesus said to His disciples, If anyone desires to come after Me, let him deny himself and take up his cross and follow Me. For whoever desires to save his life shall lose it, and whoever desires to lose his life for My sake shall find it" (Matthew 16:24-25 MKJV).

We can be rather certain that **Graham** speaks relatively little, if at all, about God's severity (Romans 11:22) – the apostle tells us to behold it along with God's goodness, but **Graham** certainly will have none of that.

https://www.thepathoftruth.com/false-teachers/graham-cooke.htm

Nowadays, however, my email is flooded with people asking me about another form of false prophet. These types of prophets are very hard to pin down because they are not so obvious. They are calm, cool and collect people who seem to have a real grasp of the Word and they use their particular Scriptural analysis to justify the hyper-spiritual and permissive behavior of their followers.

Because they seem so "sheepish" in nature, it's very tempting to want to give them a pass. I freely admit that when I get these emails asking about **Graham Cooke, Bill Johnson, Kris Vallotton** and **Rick Joyner**, I am initially faced with much fear and trepidation. How can you say that someone who seems to have his act together, and who is known for "many wonderful works," is a false prophet? How can your argument stand against the fruit of the ones who seem so "chill?"

You can't, unless you do a little digging. You dig, because the deception runs deep. False prophets are not always obvious; they are "hidden" in sheep's clothing. Because of this, you don't go looking for wolves...you look at the sheep and see who is displaying the behavior and worldview of a wolf. Then you start peeling back the layers. It's not an easy process, but that's how the hidden is made manifest.

Graham Cooke is great example of subtlety. In this series, I'm going to be using **Graham Cooke** as an example – not because he is better or worse than the others mentioned above, but because he seems to be the one that is asked about the most by my readers.

I have also found in him a great example of the subtlety in which this breed of false prophets operate. But don't hesitate to apply these principles to the rest of the not-so-funky bunch because, rest assured, it applies.

Unlike many of the "unusual" people in the prophetic movement, **Graham** does not attempt to prophesy over regions, encourage "fire tunnels" or "manifest the spirit" by moving and shaking like a piece of bacon on a frying pan.

In all truthfulness, he seems to be a fairly down-to-earth guy. Along with his endearing personality, **Graham Cooke** has dazzled multitudes over the years with his impressive and convincing speech that appeals to the emotions and the scriptural ignorance of the listener. When I worked for the Elijah List, I listened to several of his teachings and was quite impressed with his smooth tone and clever expressions. He genuinely appeared to be a warm and caring man with a deep knowledge of the Most High.

But looking back, in spite of **Graham's** impressive and convincing talk, in spite of his calm and gentle demeanor, I must still lump him in with the rest of the Elijah List false prophets, and here are a few of my reasons **Graham Cooke** fails the Deuteronomy 13 test:

Graham Cooke does not preach obedience to the commandments; he preaches a twisted and dispensational doctrine of grace, therefore he fails this test. The second (and admittedly less strong) reason **Graham Cooke** is a false prophet is that he keeps company with false prophets. The Word says: Proverbs 13:20 " He who walks with wise men will be wise, but the companion of fools will be destroyed."

Graham may not exhibit the foolish behavior of **Bentley, Crowder** and company, but he is seen in their circles. You are known by and take on the values of the company you keep. If **Graham** doesn't repent of these affiliations, he too will be destroyed in the end, and will take his followers with him.

But the aforementioned reasons are not what I want to bring your focus to, in this series. There is a more insidious tactic being used by the enemy to bring about your demise. Most people who come to the realization that false prophets exist and are deceiving people look for conspicuous behavioral patterns and blatantly false doctrines.

This type of analysis weeds out the obvious nut jobs. But as I mentioned above, we must understand that false prophets are disguised and not obvious. The most effective deception is never obvious – it is a work of subtlety.

It takes effort, a keen eye and knowledge of the Word to peel back the layers of wool to reveal the wolf inside. The well-known verse in Matthew says: Matthew 7:15 "Beware of false prophets, who come to you in sheep's clothing, but inwardly they are ravenous wolves." In some ways, the translation of this verse is a little misleading because it gives the impression that the disguise, as well as the infiltration into the flock, is intentional. Countless memes show a hungry, vicious wolf unzipping his sheep costume to target an unsuspecting sheep for his next meal. Only a few verses later, we find that these false prophets are completely caught off guard... amazed that everything they had ever done "in Jesus' name" was for naught. This strongly suggests that false prophets have no clue what they are doing.

They honestly think that they are doing the will of the Father when in fact, they "practice lawlessness." Matthew 7:15 says that they are "ravenous wolves" "inwardly" or "from within."

This means that there is something on the inside of a false prophet that is invisible to the casual observer... maybe even invisible to the false prophet himself/herself. It is a concern for "self" that supersedes the mandate to speak the Father's words.

A stronger, though very well concealed, reason I believe that **Graham Cooke** is a false prophet is that, as God's supposed spokesman/representative (a "prophet"), he completely misrepresents the character and nature of God. I cannot say whether **Graham** is doing this intentionally or not. What I can say is that the words coming out of his mouth reinforce the scriptural ignorance of his followers and further augment a false image of our Messiah. This distortion is very easy to swallow because it is cloaked in soft language that appeals to the emotions, having just enough tidbits of Scripture (carelessly taken out of context) to validate it in the ears of the uninformed listener.

Graham, as well as other, more "sedate" false prophets are VERY, VERY good at this. Now, take a step back and consider this. If you claim to be a prophet – a "spokesman" for the Most High – you are guilty of a very serious offense if you misrepresent His character and distort His words. The false prophets will be absolutely STUNNED in that day, because they were CONVINCED they were doing the right thing... "in Jesus name!"

This proves that intent has nothing to do with whether or not a prophet will be judged as "true" or "false." It is because they misrepresented Him and led others to do the same that their judgment will stand. This is why I can look at these calm, cool and collected false teachers/prophets and place them in the same category as the "obvious offenders," because they claim to speak "in the name of the Lord," and lead the masses down lawless paths by taking His words and twisting them, promoting a perverted version of His character.

(**NOTE: The balance of this article is very lengthy. It includes a number of Scriptures, so I am adding the link to finish reading it if you would like. Ed.):

https://www.honorofkings.org/ discerning-soft-core-false-prophet/

Here is one more piece of information, surprisingly written about a supposedly "Christian" women's fellowship organization. This is from a reader of the above article, who wrote about her concern for not only **Graham Cooke**, but the women's organization as well. It is worth noting because it also unintentionally includes a teaching from **C. Peter Wagner** himself—without realizing it:

"From the head, to the leaders, down to the local leaders, they are teaching his course called Game Changers." (She lists herself on her statement as "B").**C. Peter Wagner's** thrust is all about "game changers" or as a different title, "change agents." This is also from the above attached website. **Graham Cooke** is without doubt into New Age doctrine and advocates a departure from adhering to the Word of God for a journey into dreams where logic is abandoned and feelings are the new norm.
In addition, much of his teachings are in step with the New Apostolic Reformation (NAR) movement. I would strongly advise anyone who is looking into **Graham Cooke** as a possible Christian teacher source to look elsewhere.

https://bcooper.wordpress.com/2016/05/16/ apostasy-and-graham-cooke/

–**William "Todd" Coontz**: North Carolina televangelist **Todd Coontz** was found guilty of failing to pay taxes and filing false tax returns, including claiming luxury cars and a $1.5 million condo as tax expenses, by a federal jury on Thursday in Charlotte (4/6/18).
 Coontz, who has written several books on the topic of seed giving that he says can make people rich, was found to have claimed as business expenses his family's $1.5 million condo, along with several luxury cars, including a Ferrari and a Maserati. The United States Attorney's Office said in a statement that the televangelist's supposed business expenses included more than $200,000 for clothes and $140,000 for meals.

"**Coontz** has been released on bond. The failure to pay tax charge carries a maximum prison term of one year and a $100,000 fine, per count. The aiding and assisting in the filing of false tax returns charge carries a maximum prison term of three years and a $250,000 fine, per count," the U.S. Attorney's Office added.   **Coontz** served as minister of "Rock Wealth International Ministries " from 2010 to 2014.

WSOC-TV Channel 9 attempted to interview **Coontz** as he left the courthouse following the verdict, but he gave no comment when asked about the years of tax fraud he was found guilty of.

Coontz's legal team attempted to argue in court that the preacher, who also appeared on TV shows pushing his seed giving message, was not trying to deceive the government. "It wasn't intentional. It was due to a series of miscommunications and misunderstandings, and obviously the jury felt otherwise," defense attorney Mark Foster argued.

Jury foreman Kenneth Letts said that the evidence against **Coontz** was "overwhelming." When announcing the charges in June 2017, U.S. Attorney Jill Rose said: "This is a classic example of 'Do as I say, not as I do." Rose added: "As a minister, **Coontz** preached about receiving and managing wealth, yet he failed to keep his own finances in order."

Coontz will now receive a first-hand lesson in 'rendering unto Caesar' that which is due." Foster insisted back then that the preacher "has always endeavored to follow the law and to be a good citizen, father, and minister. He trusted others to manage his finances and taxes for him and was shocked to find out he was under criminal investigation by the IRS."

"Trinity Foundation," a group that monitors ecclesiastical fraud, told "The Christian Post" last year in relation to **Coontz's** case that "it's time the IRS started looking into these people that are raping the Christian community." "They are cheating the people of knowing the mystery of God,"
"Trinity Foundation" President Ole Anthony added. https://www.christianpost.com/news/televangelist-todd-coontz-found-guilty-buying-luxury-cars-house-clothes-tax-fraud.html

In his multiple roles as author, financial adviser and man of the cloth, **Todd Coontz** preached the benefits of "Biblical Economics:" how God bestows financial blessings, which **Coontz** could help his clients manage according to Scripture, his website says. But in building his network of businesses, including a television ministry that claimed to have reached 200 countries and 90 million homes, the former Charlotte-area evangelist sidestepped a key piece of New Testament advice: "Render to Caesar the things that are Caesar's; and to God the things that are God's." This week, Caesar got his. The preacher lived a life of luxury.

But the feds just indicted him on tax fraud. On Tuesday, **Coontz** was sentenced to five years in prison following his April conviction for tax fraud and evasion, shorthand for what federal prosecutors say were years of **Coontz'** efforts to hide some $1.7 million of income and assets from the government.
According to court documents in the case, **Coontz**, while living in Charlotte, tucked away many of the more visible trappings of his opulent lifestyle — from expensive real estate and jewelry to a boat and a fleet of sports cars — under the misleading umbrella of business expenses. **Coontz** also diverted tens of thousands of dollars in business reimbursements to his personal use, documents say.
His write-offs included more than $227,000 on clothes, another $140,000 on meals and entertainment expenses, including 400 separate charges at movie theaters. Rather than pay himself a salary, **Coontz** ignored his accountants' advice and took his living expenses out of his business accounts, including **Coontz'** "Rockwealth Ministries."

Coontz, according to his prosecutor, Assistant U.S. Attorney Jenny Sugar, "failed to practice what he preached."

In her sentencing recommendation, Sugar estimates **Coontz**, currently a resident of Fort Lauderdale, Fla., evaded more than $750,000 in taxes while also repeatedly ignoring IRS warnings about overdue tax payments on the income he did report.
"This case involves someone who has been delinquent on his taxes for more than fifteen years. Someone who regularly received mail from the IRS regarding his unpaid taxes. Someone who employed — and failed to follow the advice of — two different CPAs. ... Someone who treated every meal, piece of clothing and movie ticket as a business expense."

Coontz was the author of several financial self-help books, including "Please Don't Repo My Car." In real life, **Coontz** and his family parked in a different neighborhood.
They drove three BMWs, two Ferraris, a Maserati, a Land Rover along with an expensive boat. All were listed as business expenses. Arguing in vain for a lighter sentence for his client, defense attorney Mark Foster said prosecutors miscalculated the amount of **Coontz**' tax liability and falsely accused the minister of obstruction of justice.

The obstruction charge was tied to travel-and-expense-related emails that Foster said were destroyed by an employee without **Coontz**' knowledge. A significant prison sentence, Foster said, "would jeopardize and perhaps kill the ministry **Coontz** has worked these many years to develop and obviously kill his ability to fully repay his tax obligations," Foster wrote. According to his website, **Coontz** built his wealth-management philosophy on Old Testament principles. Some of them found are found in the Book of Deuteronomy in which Moses preaches some of his last sermons to the Israelites before they entered the Promised Land. "But remember the Lord your God, for it is he who gives you the ability to produce wealth, and so confirms his covenant," according to one verse cited on the website.

In reality, prosecutors say **Coontz** stole from fellow churches, billing them for the full cost of a first-class airline travel for his appearances when his actually paid far less for his tickets.
In her filings, Sugar argued that "a significant sentence" was required to punish and deter **Coontz**. Conrad gave her one. The judge also accepted the government's estimate of what **Coontz** owes in taxes and ordered $755,669 of restitution.

https://www.charlotteobserver.com/news/local/crime/ article225181225.html (JANUARY 29, 2019).

- **Kenneth/Gloria Copeland**: Proponents of the Word of Faith movement, if not THE biggest; uses Satanic hand signals; heretical preachers "Name it and Claim it"; wrote the "Kenneth Copeland Study Bible," filled with false teachings notes; has one of the largest false ministries and influences in America.

Copeland teaches that Adam was an exact duplicate of God. "God's reason for creating Adam was His desire to reproduce Himself. I mean a reproduction of Himself, and in the Garden of Eden He did just that. He was not a little like God. He was not almost like God. He was not subordinate to God even. . . . Adam is as much like God as you could get, just the same as Jesus. . . . Adam, in the Garden of Eden, was God manifested in the flesh."

("Following the Faith of Abraham I," Tape #01-3001 side 1.)
http://www.banner.org.uk/wof/sayings.html

Copeland teaches that Jesus became a demonic being when he was crucified and had to go to hell and be born again. The **Copeland's** attempt to specialize in word-faith teaching. **Copeland** calls God, the biggest loser in the Bible, and says Jesus was not God during his earthly life. https://www.truthprophecy.com

Kenneth Copeland: "Several people that I know had criticized and called that faith bunch out of Tulsa a cult. And some of 'em are dead right today in an early grave because of it, and there's more than one of them got cancer" ("Why All Are Not Healed," tape #01-4001).

http://www.banner.org.uk/wof/sayings.html

"The Spirit of God spoke to me and He said, 'Son, realize this. Now follow me in this and don't let your tradition trip you up.' He said, ... 'A born-again man defeated Satan, the firstborn of many brethren defeated him.' He said, 'You are the very image, the very copy of that one." ...

And I began to see what had gone on in there, and I said, 'Well now you don't mean, you couldn't dare mean, that I could have done the same thing?' He said, 'Oh yeah, if you'd had the knowledge of the Word of God that He did, you could have done the same thing, 'cause you're a reborn man too." ("Substitution and Identification," tape #00-0202, side 2).

Ken Copeland: Every Christian is a god ("Force of Love;" Tape #02-0028) ("Believer's Voice of Victory," broadcast July 9, 1987)
Ken Copeland: God and Adam looked exactly alike. ("The Authority of the Believer IV;" Tape #01-0304)
Ken Copeland: There is a god class of beings. ("Force of Love;" Tape #02-0028) ("Praise the Lord " broadcast (TBN), recorded 2/5/86)
Ken Copeland: All of God's attributes and abilities were invested in Adam. ("The Authority of the Believer IV;" Tape #01-0304)
Ken Copeland: Earth is a copy of the mother planet (Heaven). ("Following the Faith of Abraham," Tape #01-3001)
Ken Copeland: God is approximately 6'2" to 6'3" tall. ("Spirit, Soul, and Body;" Tape #01-0601)
Ken Copeland: God weighs approximately 200 lbs. ("Spirit, Soul, and Body;" Tape #01-0601)

Ken Copeland: Jesus death on the cross was not enough to save us. ("What Happened From the Cross to the Throne," Tape #00-0303) (Believer's Voice of Victory, September 1991) (Doctrinal Statement dated March 12, 1979)
Ken Copeland: "When His blood poured out, it did not atone" (letter written and signed by **Kenneth Copeland**, issued by his office on March 12th 1979).

Ken Copeland: The plan of redemption BEGAN when Jesus said "It is FINISHED". ("Classic Redemption," p.13)--"When Jesus cried, 'It is finished!' He was not speaking of the plan of redemption. There were still three days and nights to go through before He went to the throne...Jesus' death on the cross was only the beginning of the complete work of redemption. ("Jesus - Our Lord of Glory," "Believer's Voice of Victory Magazine" 10, 4; April 1982, p. 3); http://www.banner.org.uk/wof/sayings.html

Kenneth Copeland : "He [Jesus] is suffering all that there is to suffer. There is no suffering left apart from Him. His emaciated, poured out, little, wormy spirit is down in the bottom of that thing [hell]. And the Devil thinks he's got Him destroyed." ("Believer's Voice of Victory" program [21 April 1991].

(This message was originally delivered at the "Full Gospel Motorcycle Rally Association 1990 Rally " at Eagle Mountain Lake, Texas).

Ken Copeland: Jesus took on the nature of Satan when He was on the cross. (Jesus lost His divine nature). ("What Happened From the Cross to the Throne," Tape #00-0303) ("Classic Redemption," p.13);

Ken Copeland: Jesus was dragged down into the bowels of Hell where He was beaten and bruised by Satan and his demons until Jesus could finally fight His way out of Hell 3 days later. ("Believer's Voice of Victory," September 11, 1991) (Classic Redemption, p.13).

Kenneth Copeland (through whom Jesus allegedly delivered the following prophecy): "They crucified Me [Jesus] for claiming that I was God. But I didn't claim I was God; I just claimed I walked with Him [the Father] and that He was in Me." ("Take Time to Pray," "Believer's Voice of Victory 15, 2 [February 1987]:9.)

Ken Copeland: Jesus has a beginning and an end. ("What Happened From the Cross to the Throne," Tape #00-0303)

Ken Copeland: Jesus has not remained the same, he has changed. ("What Happened From the Cross to the Throne," Tape #00-0303).

Kenneth Copeland : "That Word of the living God went down into that pit of destruction and charged the spirit of Jesus with resurrection power! Suddenly His twisted, death-wracked spirit began to fill out and come back to life. He began to look like something the devil had never seen before." ("The Price of it All," "Believer's Voice of Victory" 19, 9 [September 1991]:4.)

Kenneth Copeland : "He [Jesus] was literally being reborn before the devil's very eyes. He began to flex His spiritual muscles. . . .Jesus was born again--the firstborn from the dead the Word calls Him--and He whipped the devil in his own backyard. He took everything he had away from him. He took his keys and his authority away from him." (Ibid., 4-6.)

Ken Copeland: Jesus was reborn in the pits of hell. ("What Happened From the Cross to the Throne," Tape #00-0303)

http://www.banner.org.uk/wof/sayings.html

In "The Force of Love," another sermon tape, **Kenneth Copeland** states, "You don't have a god in you, you are one."

In his book "Agony of Deceit," Michael Horton has documented **Kenneth Copeland** in a 19 July 1987 crusade as saying, "I say this and repeat it so it don't upset you too bad. When I read in the Bible where He (Jesus) says, I AM, I say, Yes, I am too!" (p. 268).

Speaking of 3 billionaires, **Copeland** stated "since I'm one of them it will only leave only 2 more"....but I'm not one of those three since I'm already am one, I've already appropriated and been walking in that a looong time... now don't tell them senators this,... that last time we totaled it up which been some time ago this ministry since its been in operation 41 years this month... there has been over a billion, three come into this ministry since it went into operation (applause).
He then says he is a billionaire not because of what came in but because the Lord said "I want you to confess the billion flow – as long as you were in the million flow you were winning millions you go into the billion flow you win billions." So I said yes sir, I believe and I receive it and its been number of years ago and I have confessed that I'm in the billion flow and that I am a billionaire In the kingdom of God" (audio on file).
This is what the church has made one of the worst false teachers in its history- a billionaire. He has convinced himself that God told him to confess it into reality. I don't think I need to go into the anti - Biblical teaching he is promoting as from God.

Copeland is one of the biggest offenders of the church and the Word; is someone who claims to teach the Word and its power, who is living glory that is **Kenneth Copeland**. He is one who said in prophecy at his "Victory "campaign in Dallas, Texas that Jesus did not say he was ever the son of God. Or God.

"Don't be disturbed when people accuse you of thinking you're God." "...Don't be disturbed when people put you down and speak harshly and roughly of you they spoke that way of Me." "Should they not speak that way of you?" "The more you get to be like me, the more they're going to think that way of you. They crucified Me for claiming that I was God."

But I didn't claim I was God; I just claimed I walked with Him and that He was in Me. Hallelujah" (Believer's Voice of Victory magazine, February 1987, "take time to pray," p. 9).

Later when he came under scrutiny for denying such an obvious false teaching he said "I didn't say Jesus wasn't God, I said He didn't claim to be God when He lived on the earth. Search the Gospels for yourself.   If you do, you'll find what I say is true.... He never made the assertion that He was the most High God.
   In fact, He told His disciples that the Father God was greater and mightier than He" (John 14:28). " Why didn't Jesus openly proclaim Himself as God during His 33 years on earth? For one simple reason. He hadn't come to earth as God, He's come as man" (Believer's Voice of Victory magazine, August 1988, p. 8).

The revealing point is in this so called prophecy is "I", this was supposed to be a prophecy which is God speaking to man (does God say "praise the Lord"?). Furthermore to say he came as man and NOT God is a lie that he attributes to God explaining his prophecy. The fact is that **Copeland** said we shouldn't be disturbed when people accuse you of thinking you're God.

And then says Jesus never claimed to be when He said he came from heaven as the Son of God (as if this was not implied in dozens of ways) is outrageous.

But the church was already becoming numb to truth and more responsive to the false teachers as their guides. "I want you to know something Adam in the Garden of Eden was God manifested in the flesh" ... "You see Adam was walking as a God, Adam walked in God's class"

(**Kenneth Copeland**, Following the Faith of Abraham I (Fort Worth, TX: **Kenneth Copeland Ministries**, 1989), tape #01-3001, side 1).

"Adam was just as much the Son of God as Jesus, Jesus just as much the Son of God as Adam" (**Kenneth Copeland**, Believer's Voice of Victory, January 29 2001).

So if Adam was God just like Jesus then so were his offspring. Then what's so special about Jesus? Once you digest this theosophy of **Copeland** everything else he says becomes clear. Then when **Kenneth Copeland** proclaims, "You don't have a god in you, you are one."

Kenneth Copeland, (The Force of Love audiotape #02-0028, side 1.)
You must understand the spirit that is exalting man and demoting Jesus. What person who believes in Christ's deity as the Bible teaches would ever say such a thing, as if the Bible actually says this?
The doctrine of antichrist has been promoted strongly on TBN for over 25 years by these people that have made into stars. http://www.letusreason.org/Pent64.htm

(**NOTE: This dialogue continues for a few more paragraphs. I have taken the liberty of writing the most disturbing. Ed.).

In John 8:58, I AM is a self proclamation of Jesus' own unique Deity from Exodus 3:14, 15. https://ucministries.wordpress.com/tag /dr-hobart-freeman/

(**NOTE: The link is related to not only **Dr. Hobart Freeman**, but several other "wolves" so I am including it. Ed.).

http://www.spiritwatch.org/ firefaith4.htm

- **Bob Coy**: Former strip club manager in 1981; addicted to porn; convicted of molesting a four year old, all the way until her teens. One of the founding members of "Calvary Chapel."

"Founder of Florida's Biggest Megachurch Accused of Molesting a 4-Year-Old" TIM ELFRINK | NOVEMBER 14, 2017--

The call came from California. A woman told Coral Springs Police she had recently learned something terrible: A South Florida man had molested her daughter for years. It began when the girl was just 4 years old. An officer noted the information and called the victim, who was then a teenager. She confirmed the story in stomach-churning detail. The man had forced her to perform oral sex, she said. He would regularly "finger and fondle her" genitals, make her touch his penis, and "dirty talk" to her. The abuse lasted until she was a teenager, she told the cop. She'd never even told her family about the crimes.

https://www.miaminewtimes.com/news/
bob-coy-founder-of-calvary-chapel-fort-lauderdale-accused-of-molesting-child-9827948

https://www.christianpost.com/news/
megachurch-founder-bob-coy-accused-of-molesting-4-y-o-sexually-abusing-her-into-her-teens.html

Bob Coy, founder of "Calvary Chapel " Fort Lauderdale in Florida who resigned as senior pastor over moral failings in 2014, has been accused of molesting a girl when she was 4 years old and into her teens.
According to an August 2015 report provided to "The Christian Post" by the Coral Springs Police Department, a mother living in Southern California reported that her then 17-year-old daughter came forward, saying she had been sexually abused by **Coy** for years. The accusations reveal in graphic detail that **Coy** forced the girl to perform oral sex on him, and that he "digitally penetrated her."

Police later spoke with the victim in September 2015, but she said she was not sure whether she wanted to go through with a criminal investigation or testify.

She also said that while she had not confronted **Coy** yet, **Coy** had been "confronted by pastoral staff in Tennessee and is likely aware of the allegations at this point." The following day, the victim told the police that she was not ready to proceed with a criminal investigation unless a second person came forward. The case was assigned to a detective and although police advised the victim that there does not seem to be a statute of limitations concerning the alleged crime, the girl reportedly did not cooperate in terms of pursuing the matter further. The case was thus closed and made "inactive" in October 2015 pending the victim's cooperation.

About half a year later, the victim visited the police department and said she had an "experience with God" and has found forgiveness for **Coy**. She subsequently said she does not want the abuse made public and even asked for the record to be destroyed, though she was informed that that would be against the law. The case was closed in 2016.
Coy resigned from "Calvary Chapel " Fort Lauderdale, which he founded in 1985 and grew to become one of the largest churches in the nation, in April 2014. According to a statement from the church at the time, he had confessed to a "moral failing." Then "Outreach" Pastor Chet Lowe specified to the congregation that **Coy** "committed adultery with more than one woman" and "committed sexual immorality, habitually, through pornography."

With the latest revelations on child molestation, "Calvary Chapel " Fort Lauderdale posted on Tuesday the following statement in response to the allegations:

"Our church was saddened to hear of the allegations made against **Bob Coy** years after his resignation and departure as senior pastor. We learned of this report after it was disclosed and reported to the appropriate authorities. "We take every allegation of abuse seriously and our prayers are with all those involved as they pursue redemption and healing. Because this is a personal matter, any further questions would be best addressed to **Bob Coy** himself."

- **Paul & Jan Crouch**: **Paul** and **Jan** are Deceased; started TBN; raked in BILLIONS; most of it went directly to them; responsible for the global export of heresy, paid off a homosexual to keep quiet; liar; WOF teacher; interviewed **Robert Schuller** and cleared him of the "false" charge that he promotes New Age concepts; he has openly stated his desire to kill Christian apologists who point out heresy preached on his stations.

 www.thebereancall.com;   https://www.truthprophecy.com.

The late Dr. Walter Martin details in "Agony Of Deceit" how he had the eye-opening privilege of sitting in **Crouch's** Santa Ana ministry offices "and once spent almost two hours attempting to convince me and three other ministers that we were 'little gods.'" Horton, ibid, p. 93. http://www.spiritwatch.org/firefaith4.htm

Paul Crouch: "That old rotten Sanhedrin crowd, twice dead, plucked up by the roots ... they're damned and on their way to hell and I don't think there's any redemption for them ... the hypocrites, the heresy hunters that want to find a little mote of illegal doctrine in some Christian's eyes ... when they've got a whole forest in their own lives." ... "I say, `To hell with you! Get out of my life! Get out of the way! Quit blockin' God's bridges! I'm tired of this! ... This is my spirit. Oh, hallelujah!' ...(TBN's "Praise-A-Thon," April 2, 1991).

Paul Crouch : "We gotten so caught up in theology and debating and discussing theology and nit picking on this, and the heretic hunters have smoke screened the whole thing." ("The Christian Channel Europe "Praise The Lord" 14/6/98). **Paul Crouch**: "....I want you all to listen carefully. This is a word - a prophetic word that came to me on September the 25th.... The ministry of TBN is about to explode..."

"It is time, once and for all, to take your sword in hand, the mighty sword of the Spirit, which is the Word of God. Speak it out. Proclaim defeat to the enemies of God." "Stand up, everybody. In the Name of Jesus, we proclaim defeat to the enemies of God..." "The enemies of God are defeated in the Name and by the blood of Jesus Christ." "They are under our feet by the victory of Jesus Christ when He said, "Behold, I am He Who was dead, but am alive forevermore, and have the keys of death and of hell." "We receive it in Jesus' Name. Take authority over the principalities and powers that dare to threaten this ministry."

"I have raised it up from infancy for My own purposes," saith the Lord. "Just as I commanded Ezekiel to prophesy life to dry bones, and they took on life, so I am commanding you to prophesy death to the threats, challenges, and bondages the enemy has placed on TBN."

"Command them to cease and desist, and you will see this dilemma die and disappear before your eyes." "God, we proclaim death to anything or anyone that will lift a hand against this network and this ministry that belongs to You, God.

It is Your work, it is Your idea, it is Your property, it is Your airwaves, it is Your world, and we proclaim death to anything that would stand in the way of God's great voice of proclamation to the whole world. In the Name of Jesus, and all the people said Amen!"
("Praise The Lord ," "Trinity Broadcasting Network" November 7, 1997).
http://www.banner.org.uk/wof/sayings.html

Paul Crouch, speaking to **Kenneth Copeland**, said : "Somebody said--I don't know who said it--but they claim that you Faith teachers declare that we are gods. You're a god. I'm a god. Small 'g' now, but we are the gods of this world. . . " "Well, are you a god--small 'g'?"
To this, **Jan Crouch**, referring to **Copeland**, enthusiastically exclaimed: "He's gonna say, 'Yes.' I love it." ("Praise the Lord" program on TBN [5 February 1986]).

Paul Crouch : "He [God] doesn't even draw a distinction between Himself and us. . . You know what else that's settled, then, tonight?
This hue and cry and controversy that has been spawned by the Devil to try and bring dissension within the body of Christ that we are gods."
"I am a little god! . . . I have His name. I'm one with Him. I'm in covenant relation. I am a little god! Critics, be gone!" ("Praise the Lord" program on TBN [7 July 1986].)
 http://www.banner.org.uk/wof/sayings.html

- **John Crowder**: People are now actually following the likes of **John Crowder** and **Benjamin Dunn** whose "tokin the Ghost" (pretending to smoke the Holy Spirit like grass) and rolling in "the drunken glory" of God, making holy chaos and sacred mess.

These are actually ministries, movements engaging healings and exorcisms actively promoted and eagerly sought after. Devotees are brought to heightened belief by "impartations" so that some claim they see (or commune and dance with!) Jesus and the angels in glory love fests and "Holy Ghost rave parties". It's all too good, or bad, to be true and some of it can seem little short of blasphemy of the Holy Spirit.

 Heresy was rarely so clownish and/or perverse as what some call the "post-modern" brand of "emergent" Christianity being peddled. **Crowder** claims to have been converted to Jesus in the course of an acid trip.

(**NOTE: Warning: **John Crowder** is VERY demonic. You can see how evil he is by watching a You Tube video of him with his "songs." Ed.).

http://rollanscensoredissuesblog.blogspot.com/

November 11, 2008 The Apostolic Birdie!?!

(Warning: This video is shocking, sad and EXTREMELY offensive.)

We are posting this here because it shows the true nature of the people promoting the Tokin' the Ghost heresy. (Remember we post this type of stuff because this is the Museum of

Idolatry). The man in the video is Brandon Barthrop and he has a "ministry" website called "Red Letter Ministries" that promotes getting high and whacked in the 'Holy Spirit'. Brandon has also made the rounds with **John Crowder** and **Benjamin Dunn** promoting the Tokin' heresy in churches.

This video exposes the true satanic nature of this heresy better than anything else we've witnessed. Do you think Jesus behaved in this manner or taught his disciples to do anything even closely resembling this? Of course not, yet there are people who call themselves Christians and churches that claim to be Christian that listen to and follow this man and his teaching. https://crosebrough.typepad.com/ alittleleaven/false_gospels/

D:

- **John Dawson**: YWAM; Dominionist teacher, "Elijah List." Daniel Kikawa and his book "Perpetuated In Righteousness", as well as the teaching of the "First Nations," YWAM (Youth With A Mission) and the New Apostolic Reformation (NAR) lay the basis for the ideas put forth by this movement.
Kikawa's book was endorsed by **John Dawson** of YWAM. YWAM is firmly a part of the NAR which is headed by **C. Peter Wagner, Chuck Pierce, Cindy Jacobs, Dutch Sheets, Bill Hamon, Tommy Tenney, Mike Bickle** and includes hundreds of other false apostles, false prophets and false teachers.

 If you want an in depth study of the NAR, read free articles here or go here to purchase the book and/or DVD/VHS series on the NAR. Richard Twiss and his ministry "Wiconi "are endorsed by the leadership of the NAR including **C. Peter Wagner, Francis Frangipane** and **Charles Kraft.**

This "First Nation's movement", for lack of a better term, is full of the false teachings of the Third Wave, New Apostolic Reformation, Word-Faith, Dominionism, Latter Rain and many other false theological systems. But it does have it's own distinctives that are driven by the works of Daniel Kikawa, Richard Twiss, and **John Dawson** in particular.

 Following are some of the things they have been doing and teaching all over the world. http://www.deceptioninthechurch.com/ acalltothenations.html

Our concerns lie with YWAM teachings and associations with which they participate. And there is lot to be concerned about! One must understand that YWAM presents itself as a missionary organization, but, sadly, it is also an ecumenical organization. And the most dangerous kind of ecumenism the church has ever seen is being promoted in YWAM by top leaders. An article titled "YWAM Builds Bridges to Catholics" (August 1993 issue of Charisma) makes it clear that YWAM) works with Catholics.

"Beginning in 1978, YWAM workers in Austria began to cooperate with Catholics there .... In 1984, YWAM adopted a policy allowing staff to work with Catholics ....1987 YWAM has installed a Catholic, Rob Clarke, as director of its discipleship training school in Dublin" .... Clarke has said: "We are trying to get away from the idea of simply 'converting' Catholics -- that is turning them into Protestants -- and towards a framework of ministry within the Catholic Church."

The "Sentinel Group" is led by **George Otis, Jr.**, an apostle in **Wagner/Pierces** NAR (New Apostolic Reformation). **Otis Jr.** promotes a latter rain message in his spiritual warfare videos, the same found in the teaching of the new prophetic and apostolic movements.
It is important to know what some of these men believe when it comes to the Gospel, Jesus Christ, and the last days. In **Otis' Jr.'s** book "The God They Never Knew," sin is a sickness false concept; he speaks against sin present in mankind as our nature.
"Thus we concur that though a sinful nature is present, it originates by choice."

So we make ourselves sinners. "The assertion that Jesus paid for our sins has caused immeasurable damage to the Body of Christ." (p. 93) "Jesus literally purchased our salvation with His blood, it not only portrays God as vindictive and bloodthirsty and totally incompatible with Biblical forgiveness" (p.109).

George Otis Jr. lectured on this, called "Moral Government Theology " at the Youth With A Mission base in Tacoma, Washington, 1981. **Otis Jr.** researched and published a book called "Strongholds of the 10/40 Window" through YWAM Publishing: "served as a guide for targeting prayers." "When we began we wondered if we might be able to help 1 million Christians to pray in one accord for the same nation on the same day during the month. However, when we finished, we found that 21 million had joined to fight the air war with powerful prayer!"("Praying Through The 10/40 Window IV: A Message from Peter Wagner"

http://www.ad2000.org/ ptw4wag.htm 07/21/99).

Now we find **George Otis Jr.** involved with the NAR of **Peter Wagner** who invented the New Apostolic Reformation, restoring prophets and apostles in the church.

There has been a long time symbiotic relationship between the apostolic/ prophet movement of **Wagner** and YWAM. And this is a major problem. **John Dawson** was formerly the International Director for "Urban Ministries of YWAM " (he later became president of YWAM).

His Gnostic "spiritual warfare" concepts were adopted in the New Apostolic program of **Peter Wagner**; "strategic-level spiritual warfare movement."
In his book "Taking Our Cities for God: How to Break Spiritual Strongholds" (Creation House:1989) and "Defeating Territorial Spirits" **Dawson** claims, "battles against evil spiritual forces controlling our cities can be waged and won." **Wagner** attributes his understanding of spiritual warfare to **Dawson**. In fact, they wrote a book together in 2012 "Territorial Spirits: Practical Strategies for How to Crush the Enemy through Spiritual Warfare."

Wagner has a long time relationship with **Dawson** since he taught at Fuller, "Fortunately, we now have a textbook on the subject, namely **John Dawson's** remarkable book, "Healing America's Wounds." "I require my students at Fuller Theological Seminary to read "Healing America's Wounds" and I invite **John Dawson** himself to come in and help me teach my classes." ("The Power to Heal the Past," **C. Peter Wagner**, http://www.pastornet.net.au/ renewal/journal8/8d-wagnr.html.

http://www.letusreason.org/ ecumen30.htm

(**NOTE: There are a lot of wolves listed in this website, too numerous to write. It is easier to go directly to the links listed above. Also under **George Otis, Jr.'s** name is further information about him and his teachings. Ed.).

- **William de Arteaga**: Wrote a book titled, "Past Life Visions," which defends **Agnes Sanford's** "visualization" and her belief in a pre-earth human existence. He suggests that "Christianity accommodate Hinduism's "karma/reincarnation," which he seems to accept as a result of having induced "past-life regressions in counselees."

(**NOTE: See "**Agnes Sanford**" below for a further description. Ed.).

- **Jack Deere**: "Charismaniac" currently serving as a pastor, former DTS (Dallas Theological Seminary); professor, false teacher). "Jack Deere's Doctrinal Demise" by Mr Alan Howe, 1997. "This Paper does not constitute a critique of **Dr. Deere's** book. Rather, it is the setting forth of the author's doctrinal demise, primarily in his own words."

http://op.50megs.com/ ditc/fprophets.html

- **Dr. M.R. De Haan**: Deceased; Member of the "Missions America Coalition." Wrote an excellent Christian medical book about the crucifixion of Jesus Christ, whom many feel is heretical and blasphemous. Founder of "Radio Bible Class" and "Our Daily Bread Ministries." He went to medical school - but that was about a hundred years ago now.
 Sure, he made a couple of old-fashioned medical blunders.
And I also know that he wrote that essay in very simple language, and oversimplified some things. But the basic message was right on target!

Yet **Dr. DeHaan's** little forty-page essay is greatly hated by so-called conservative "progressives" like **Dr. (John) MacArthur**. **DeHaan's** essay was written back in 1943, yet they regularly attack it as though it were a threat to them today! This is a strange reaction indeed. Most people have forgotten all about **Dr. DeHaan**. He died back in 1965. His books are largely forgotten.
The main thing that keeps his name alive is the "progressive's" reaction and condemnation of "The Chemistry of the Blood" (Zondervan, 1943). How does an all-but-forgotten, sixty-two-year-old essay harm them? How does it confuse people? Who does it hurt?

Yet men like **Dr. MacArthur** hurl fiery darts at it continually. I can only explain their reaction by quoting **Dr. DeHaan** himself: "Satan hates the blood and will do anything to get rid of that power of the blood of Christ!" (**M. R. DeHaan**, M.D., "The Chemistry of the Blood," Zondervan, 1981 reprint, p. 28). The overall message of "The Chemistry of the Blood "is perfectly sound, perfectly Scriptural, and really quite helpful. **Dr. DeHaan** had a wonderful way of taking complex subjects and making them simple and interesting. He was like a master Sunday School teacher.

That's why millions of people used to listen to him on the radio between 1930 and 1965. I heard him in person for five nights back in 1963 at the "Church of the Open Door," when **Dr. J. Vernon McGee** was pastor there. **DeHaan** was absolutely unique. I can still hear his rough, gravelly voice in my head. He was a wonderful old Bible teacher, and the basic message of "The Chemistry of the Blood" was exactly what we need to hear in this day of weak preaching and apostasy. https://www.rlhymersjr.com/Online_Sermons/2005/081405PM_DefenceOfDeHaanOnTheBlood.html

–**Nancy Leigh De Moss Wolgemuth**: Is another circle-maker, like **Batterson**, who started off well, but began to slide into this heretical teaching over the last few years. **De Moss**, like **Batterson**, mixes this pagan practice of drawing prayer circles with biblical Christianity.

De Moss is the leader of a popular women's prayer event called "Cry Out." At this event, she regularly turns to the prayer circle and attributes her teaching to an early 20th-century British Evangelist, Rodney (Gipsy) Smith. She writes, " Gipsy Smith was a nineteenth-century revivalist who did something unusual when he came to a new town. He'd stop on the outskirts and draw a circle in the dirt. Then he would stand inside that circle and say, "O God, please send a revival to this town, and let it begin inside this circle."

"Would you ask God to revive His people? Would you let the Holy Spirit draw a circle within your own heart? Then say, "Lord, I long for You to send a revival to my nation, my church, my marriage, and my children.
But Lord, would You first start a revival inside this circle? Let it begin in me." She's also a promoter of another well-known Emergent teacher and mystic, **Richard Foster**, one of the founders of spiritual formation — a movement whose central disciplines revolve around contemplative prayer and other forms of Eastern mysticism.

https://reformationcharlotte.org/2019/03/26/false-teachers-evangelical-churches/

- **Dr. James Dobson**: One of the most famous heretical "Christian" psychologists; his teachings are still on certain radio stations worldwide. You can listen for yourself and see how he mixes Christianity with a humanistic, godless slant on just about any Christian radio station.

- **Creflo/Taffy Dollar**: Another WOF preacher and Prosperity Gospel preacher; was once accused of assaulting his daughter; charges were dropped. Stated very plainly, " You are not a sinner saved by grace." "You are sons and daughters of the Most High God! You are gods!;" preached the Gospel of Greed.

https://www.828ministries.com/articles/When-False-Teachings-Colli-by-Anthony-Wade-God_Tithing_Truth-141111-886.html

(**NOTE: This is a two page article, too lengthy to post here. Ed.).

- **John Alexander Dowie**: Deceased; a preacher at Azusa in the early 1900's; believed in "spiritism." To his followers, **John Alexander Dowie** was the "Elijah" of Malachi 4, the end time messenger preparing the way for the coming Christ. Like **Branham, Dowie** claimed that he was visited by an angel, and was told that he would be the fore-runner of the second coming of Christ, just as John the Baptist was the fore-runner of the first coming.

As his fame spread, **Dowie** began to heavily promote himself as the "Elijah" and began speaking presumptuously in the name of the Lord. One such prophecy was a doomsday prophecy describing the end of America in 1954; **Dowie** had long since been deemed a false prophet, even by many of his own followers. In violent teachings against Islam, **Dowie** declared spiritual war in publications that quickly spread throughout Europe and America. In a publication in 1903, **Dowie** wrote, "If I am not a messenger of God on this earth, then no one is." The violent end came when **Dowie** accepted a challenge with a prophet of Islam.

While **Dowie** was standing on his own false words, the prophet of Islam was standing on his un-Christian religious beliefs. Without Christ on his side, **Dowie** was not under the protection of the Holy Spirit. **Dowie** was instantly paralyzed, completely unable to move. Once the great healer, **Dowie** lie helpless and unable to heal himself. When the followers began to question, they started digging deeply into everything.

Not only his teachings and false prophecies, but they investigated his personal life as well. It was found that **Dowie** had misappropriated over a million and a half dollars. It also appeared that he had given presents worth more than $300,000 to young girls in the town. Upon these findings, the leading follower of **Dowie** decided to depose **Dowie**. They sent him a telegram which said: "Unanimously the organization seriously objects to your expensive habits, hypocrisy, misstatements, exaggerations, and ill-temper. Therefore, you are hereby deposed from your office."
Dowie's following dropped from over a hundred-thousand to less than two-hundred. Though **Dowie's** false prophecy led him into a dreadful end, **Branham, Lindsay**, and **Bosworth** continued to promote him with both the "Voice of Healing" magazine and in **Branham's** sermons. **Branham** continued to visit Zion II to promote himself by promotion of **Dowie**.

http://seekyethetruth.com/blog

- **Roma Downey & Husband Mark Burnett**: Both are staunch Roman Catholics, both are New Age and both are considered to be involved in mysticism. **Ms. Downey** was once on the TV show "Touched By An Angel," in which she played the angel.
https://pulpitandpen.org/2016/08/09/
rick-warren-to-emcee-roman-catholic-mystic-roma-downeys-hollywood-award-ceremony/

https://www.lighthousetrailsresearch.com/ blog/?p=28991

http://www.truthkeepers.com/?p=525

http://christianresearchnetwork.org/ ?s=roma+downey&submit=Search

(**NOTE: This link, listed above has several other links to it that show exactly who **Roma Downey** and her husband **Mark Burnett** really are, which is that they are New Age Mystics. Ed.).

https://churchwatchcentral.com/2015/04/30/ who-is-roma-downey/

(**NOTE: Not to be outdone, both **Mark Burnett** and **Roma Downey**, his wife, recently released a confusing series movie on Netflix, called "The Messiah," in which the main character, who is supposed to be Jesus, never directly states that He is the Messiah, yet He is able to perform miracles. The audience is left wondering exactly what His message is and if He is a con artist. Typical of New Agers, who tell you that they have the way to God, but never open the Bible to lead you to Him, or twist and pervert the Word of God.. .Ed.).

https://www.nme.com/blogs/tv-blogs/ messiah-ending-explained-season-1-netflix-2592143

- **Mark Driscoll**: One of the founders of the Emergent Church; recently admitted his "straying ways;" left his church under pressure and humiliation. When discussing **Mark Driscoll** there is nothing left in the rumor mill. It is all proven fact. **Mark** may disagree about how people are reacting to it but he does not deny these are facts. He for example, thinks he was justified in taking the $200,000 + from tithes because his board approved it. "How is it loving to the former 12,000 congregants of Mars Hill Church in Seattle?"
 "How is it loving to embrace someone who bragged about running over his own sheep with the Mars Hill bus?"

"Secondly, how is it loving to **Mark**? He is going to answer for every careless word and deed as we all must." "If I ever found myself in a situation such as this, I would want people who love me to come alongside of me and tell me to repent. Not blindly support my new church plant when the bodies are still warm from my last." One last quote from **Pastor Idleman**: "We should consider the total portrait of one's life, character and ministry and evaluate on that basis. A few poorly chosen statements, angry outbursts or controlling decisions made over the course of many years shouldn't define a person." -- **Shane Idleman**.

Pastor Shane Idleman has tried vociferously to pretend that **Mark Driscoll's** offenses were just a handful of "oopsies" while defaming anyone who dared to stand up for what the Bible actually says regarding these offenses and the pastoral office. Perhaps to **Idleman**, referring to the sheep you have slaughtered as a pastor as a "pile of dead bodies" is just a "poorly chosen statement." Perhaps when he viciously attacked his own sheep and staff repeatedly for years, that was just "angry outbursts" to **Pastor Shane**.

 Perhaps stealing over $200,000 of tithe monies to cheat the NY Times Bestseller List was just a "controlling decision." I do not think I am out on a limb here to suggest that God does not see it that way. I do not think He sees it that way at all. **Mark** may disagree about how people are reacting to it but he does not deny these are facts. He for example, thinks he was justified in taking the $200,000 + from tithes because his board approved it.

Mark Driscoll Kicked Out Of His Own Organization by Sandy Simpson, 8/18/14

Driscoll was kicked out of the Acts 29 Network church planting group, his own organization, for his ungodly behavior. Seattle megachurch pastor **Mark Driscoll** has been removed from a church-planting network of more than 500 churches he helped found after a pattern of ungodly and disqualifying behavior. (Religion News Service, by Sarah Pulliam Balley, "Huffington Post," 8/9/14).   His behavior is not the only problem with this guy.
Check out his false teachings and behavior over the years.
http://op.50megs.com/ditc/fprophets.html

Controversial Megachurch **Pastor Mark Driscoll** Finds a New Flock at "Understand The Times," 2/27/16. There s a new church coming to Phoenix, Arizona. According to its website, the pastor, **Mark Driscoll,** is a "Jesus-following, mission-leading, church-serving, people-loving, Bible-preaching pastor...grateful to be a nobody trying to tell everybody about Somebody."
 Though there's no mention of it on "The Trinity Churches" shiny new website, **Driscoll** built and presided over Seattle s controversial "Mars Hill Church," and he is one of the most famous and disruptive figures in the history of the evangelical mega-church movement.

But as **Driscoll s** star rose, he was dogged by allegations from church members and pastors as well as from outsiders of bullying and spiritual abuse, misogyny and homophobia, plagiarism, and misuse of church funds, just to name a few. In 2014, after being asked to submit to a reconciliation plan proposed by the church board he organized, **Driscoll** quit.

On heels of **Mark Driscoll s** New Church Opening, "Seattle Times" Reports: "Racketeering suit claims **Mark Driscoll** misused "Mars Hill" donor dollars at Lighthouse Trails, 3/2/16."
Mark Driscoll Adheres to Calvinism.   May have moved on to a new city and a new church, but he faces the sharpest demand yet to account for his actions at "Mars Hill Church."

 On Monday, four former "Mars Hill" members filed a civil racketeering lawsuit against **Driscoll,** charging that the once swaggering pastor fraudulently used thousands if not millions of dollars raised by the church, which once boasted 15 branches in five states with 13,000 visitors on Sundays.   http://op.50megs.com/ ditc/fprophets.html

If you just say the words, "Emerging" or "Emergent Church," you are likely to be met with a whole host of attitudes and opinions. Many, like myself, have strong thoughts on the emerging church and many have no idea what the emerging/emergent church is. One of the most helpful articles I have read in recent years, regarding the emerging and emergent church, was written by **Mark Driscoll**. You can read that article here.

In this article, **Driscoll,** as many rightly do today, draw a distinction between emerging and emergent. I will not go into all the details here, as you can read all about it in **Driscoll's** article, but the bottom line is that there are a group of leaders in the emergent church who have clearly abandoned Biblical orthodoxy.

https://www.baptistmessenger.com/ is-it-unloving-to-call-someone-a-heretic/

"How can you tell if your church has adopted the "Leadership Network" paradigm?" The above question that a listener sent in to Mike LeMay and Amy Spreeman on "Stand Up For The Truth" a few years ago is a question that writer and speaker, Sarah Leslie, of "Discernment Research Group" and "Herescope" addressed near the end of their time together for this show. The main topic discussed is the shift that is taking place in many churches these days, maybe even in yours. It is a shift from Jesus Christ and Biblical truth, which is the foundation for the church, to an experiential based system where the pastor runs the church like a corporation and presents his own agenda to the people of the church.

Sadly, for those who do not stand with the pastor and his new vision for the church, they will either be pressured to conform, or they will be shoved under the bus as **Mark Driscoll** has said in the past to his congregation before the dismantling of his church finally took place due mainly because of his abusive behavior towards those in leadership positions at "Mars Hill Church " and those who also attended "Mars Hill Church."

When time allows, consider watching the above video, and keep these Scriptures in mind as you watch the video below:

https://www.youtube.com/watch? time_continue=81&v=M37cbXyd6LU&feature=emb_logo

John Piper has consistently supported and promoted the ministry of **Mark Driscoll**, the pastor of "Mars Hill Church" in Seattle. The false nature of **Driscoll's** ministry has been well documented, not least by a memo written by Cathy Mickels to the leaders of the "Gospel Coalition" in 2008.

But **Piper** has ignored all the justified criticism of **Driscoll's** ministry. Indeed, he claims to be mentoring the young **Mark Driscoll**, helping him not to use crude language. **Piper** even invited **Driscoll** to speak at the "Desiring God Conference:"
'Why did I venture to invite **Mark Driscoll** to come and address a conference on language and the use of words. Number one, I love **Mark Driscoll's** theology. That's bottom line for me, we stand together about glorious truths about God. That's huge to me...' [15] [see video]

https://www.youtube.com/ watch?time_continue=7&v=tILvXGp43Dc&feature=emb_logo

http://www.youtube.com/ watch?v=i38tv1AVnRY

(**NOTE: Plenty of information on **John Piper** on the internet. Decide for yourself if he is being truthful. Also See **John Piper** in this book. Ed.).

- **Peter Drucker**: Deceased; What the "Emergent Church," **Rick Warren** and **Bill Hybels** Have in Common: While the "Emergent Church" movement seems to be a reaction against the large, plastic, church growth phenomenon, both movements have in common a lineage that can be traced back to business management guru **Peter Drucker**. The genesis of Emergent can be traced back to an organization called "Leadership Network" This organization was introduced as a resource to help leaders of innovative postmodern churches to connect.

These efforts were aided by **Harold Myra** and **Paul Robbins** of "Christianity Today." In an article in the "Criswell Theological Review " written by formerly <u>Emergent</u> **Mark Driscoll**, co-founder and preaching pastor of "Mars Hill Church "in Seattle, **Mark** recalls the initiation of the "Emerging Church" movement which was launched by an organization called "Leadership Network:"

 "In the mid-1990's I was a young church planter trying to establish a church in the city of Seattle when I got a call to speak at my first conference. It was hosted by "Leadership Network" and focused on the subject of Generation X. . . .
Out of that conference a small team was formed to continue conversing about post-modernism.

"By this time "Leadership Network" hired **Doug Pagitt** to lead the team and organize the events. He began growing the team and it soon included **Brian McLaren**... **Pagitt, McLaren**, and others such as **Chris Seay, Tony Jones, Dan Kimball**, and **Andrew Jones** stayed together and continued speaking and writing together as friends..."
"**McLaren**, a very gifted writer, rose to team leader in part because he had an established family and church, which allowed him to devote a lot of time to the team.
That team eventually morphed into what is now known as "Emergent."[1]

Speaking of **Brian McLaren,** he was asked how this whole "Emerging Church" got started to which he offers the same story. He tells: "Well, back in the early 1990s there was an organization called "Leadership Network" funded by an individual in Texas, and "Leadership Network " was bringing together the leaders of megachurches around the country."
By the early and mid-'90s, they noticed, though, that the kinds of people that were coming to their events were getting a year older every year, and there wasn't a [group of] younger people filling in. They were one of the first major organizations to notice this.

"They started realizing that there was a sentence that was being said by church leaders of all denominations across the country, and that was, "You know, we don't have anybody between 18 and 35." . . .

"After a couple of years some of these young Gen X guys said, "You know, it's not really about a generation. <u>It's really about philosophy; it's really about a cultural shift</u>." "It's not just about a style of dress, a style of music, but that there's something going on in our culture. And those of us who are younger have to grapple with this and live with this." The term that they were using was the <u>shift</u> from modern to a postmodern culture.
 And so what began to happen — and as this thing had a life of its own, they said,
 "If it's not just about Gen X, then we have to make sure that we get some older people who aren't just in that age frame to talk about this."[2]

<u>"Leadership Network "</u> founder **Bob Buford** : Just who was this "individual in Texas" which **McLaren** spoke of who funded the "Leadership Network" organization? It is a man by the name of **Bob Buford**, an owner of a successful cable television company in Texas at the time. **Buford** happens to have a lot in common with influential megachurch pastors **Rick Warren** (Founder and Senior Pastor of "Saddleback Church") and **Bill Hybels** (Founder and Senior Pastor of "Willow Creek Community Church").

Some have referred to these three men as the "Druckerite" trinity for their relationships with business management guru **Peter Drucker**. Apologist and "Pirate Christian Radio" host **Chris Rosebrough** interviewed "Emergent" leader **Doug Pagitt** regarding the beginnings of the "Emergent Church." **Rosebrough** says that "without the "Druckerites " there may have never been an 'emerging church." He goes on to state that the "Druckerites" (**Bob Buford, Bill Hybels**, and **Rick Warren**) "formed, bankrolled and promoted the "Emerging Church" much the same way a music marketing company might form and promote a boy band like the "Backstreet Boys" or "N Sync."[3]

Who is Peter Drucker? **Peter Drucker** was born in 1909 in Austria and immigrated to America in 1937. He was a writer, management consultant, and self-described "social ecologist." **Drucker** had taught at California's "Claremont Graduate School " for more than 30 years, where the Management Center carries on his name. He published over thirty books in addition to articles for the Wall Street Journal, Harvard Business Review, and Forbes.
His books and popular scholarly articles explored how people are organized across the business, government and the nonprofit sectors of society.

Drucker's writings were characterized by a focus on relationships among people rather than number crunching. Before his death in 2005, he rose to a position of great esteem for his contributions to business and management.
In fact, he had a worldwide reputation as "the father of modern management." When it comes to management theory and practice, **Drucker** is one of the most widely influential thinkers and writers on the subject.
Drucker made time to consult with business leaders as well as government and nonprofit organizations. One feature on **Drucker** notes: "As the N.Y. Times noted (11/19/05), **Drucker** "devoted much of his energy to analyzing and advising" nonprofits, including church leaders, with a particular 'prescience about the growing role of megachurches in American society.'"
"Both **Drucker** and **Buford** recognized the potential of these churches to re-energize Christianity in this country and address societal issues that neither the public nor private sectors had been able to resolve.

Drucker was quoted in Forbes magazine as saying,'The pastoral megachurches that have been growing so very fast in the U.S. since 1980 are surely the most important social phenomenon in American society in the last 30 years.' Those leading the organizations of the "Emerging Church,' the "Purpose Driven Network" and the 'Willow Creek Association" also happen to be the most influential organizations in evangelical Christianity.

Time magazine named **Brian McLaren**, the "elder statesman" of the Emerging Church, **Bill Hybels**, senior pastor at "Willow Creek," and **Rick Warren**, the Purpose Driven pastor of Saddleback Church, as three of the most influential evangelicals in America.

Have these men become so influential within Evangelical Christianity because they are following the commandments of Jesus or because they are following best business management practices of **Peter Drucker**?

It is certainly peculiar that these movements have become so popular and well-received within Christendom when the Lord said to His disciples, "Woe unto you, when all men shall speak well of you! for so did their fathers to the false prophets" (Luke 6:26), and "ye shall be hated of all men for my name's sake" (Luke 21:17). How have these organizations become so prominent when "narrow is the way, which leadeth unto life, and few there be that find it" (Matthew 7:14)?

Though the organizations of "Leadership Network," the "Purpose Driven Network" and the "Willow Creek Association" are uniquely divided, they are intimately connected to one another. These three organizations are businesses that sell products to the target market of church leaders and pastors (based on **Peter Drucker's** business and management ideas). All of these organizations have designed products that appeal to their consumers (be it baby boomers or Generation X). It is no coincidence that these three successful and influential men in Christendom were all mentored by the late business management guru **Peter Drucker**.

Hybels & Drucker: Within the pages of "The Essential Drucker" by **Peter Drucker**, we read about how **Bill Hybels** utilized **Drucker's** business practices to design a "church" that catered to the "customers' needs." It says: "Willow Creek Community Church in South Barrington, Illinois, outside Chicago, has become the nation's largest church. . .

Bill Hybels, in his early twenties when he founded the church, chose the community because it had relatively few churchgoers, though the population was growing fast and churches were plentiful.

He went from door to door asking 'Why don't you go to church?' then he designed a church to answer the potential customers' needs: for instance it offers full services on Wednesday evenings because many working parents need Sunday to spend with their children." **Willow Creek Senior Pastor Bill Hybels**:

In **Bill Hybels'** book "Courageous Leadership," he cites his conversations with **Drucker** in regard to leadership. In his own words under a subsection entitled "Consulting Mentors About Performance Evaluations", **Hybels** referred to **Peter Drucker** as one of "the two men who have most shaped my thinking on this issue next to Jesus." **Hybels** crystalized his vision for 'Willow Creek" in the 1980's at a dinner conversation with **Drucker**.

"**Bill,** what is your unique contribution to Willow Creek?" **Drucker** asked. **Hybels** decided that one of his unique contributions to his church, aside from being the pastor, could be to create a resource for pastors who didn't have firsthand access to thinkers like **Drucker**.

This idea later turned into "Willow Creek's" business school called the "Global Leadership Summit.."

One reporter commented that "if evangelicalism does have a global power center, it would have to be "Willow Creek" thanks largely to its business school. At the "Willow Creek" campus in South Barrington, Illinois, pastors and laypeople are discipled in **Drucker's** leadership and management practices. Among the attendees were **Craig Groeschel** of "LifeChurch.tv" in Edmond, Oklahoma (27,000 weekly attendees); **Andy Stanley** of Atlanta's "North Point Community Church" (23,000); and **T.D. Jakes** of the "Potter's House" in Dallas (17,000).[1]

According to Leadership Network founder **Bob Buford**, who also plays a key role in the summit, "Willow Creek is the most influential Protestant church in the world — one might even say the most influential church in the world save for the Vatican."[11]
Author Gregory A. Pritchard wrote: "Willow Creek has so enthusiastically adopted and applied the principles of marketing that it has received growing attention from business schools and publications. Harvard Business School, for instance, selected Willow Creek as the subject of one of its famous case studies.

 Its author, who was eventually hired as the president of the Willow Creek Association, explains that the staff of Willow Creek 'attribute much of their success to the simple concept of knowing your customers and meeting their needs.' (emphasis added by author of the article.).

"Willow Creek's strategy has also been discussed in the pages of Fortune magazine and the Wall Street Journal. In the latter, **Peter Drucker** explains that Willow Creek and its imitators are employing simple marketing ideas: 'None of these marketing lessons are new. Anyone who has taken a marketing course these past 30 years or who has read a marketing text should know them.'"[12]
Buford & Drucker: Before Leadership Network began, its founder **Bob Buford** was consulting with business management guru **Peter Drucker**. **Bob Buford** is not only the founder of Leadership Network but also founded the Peter F. Drucker Foundation for Nonprofit Management.[13] **Buford** stated, "**Peter Drucker** who's **Bill [Hybels]'s** friend and mine, and I think one of the wisest men alive."[1] **Bob Buford** has often expressed his deep admiration for **Drucker**: "**Peter Drucker** is the 'intellectual father' of most all that guides my approach to philanthropy."

"I've long since ceased trying to determine what thoughts are mine and which come from **Peter**."[1]
Four years after beginning the Leadership Network, we read from **Bob Buford's** official website: "**Bob Buford** convinced **Peter Drucker** to lend his name, his great mind, and occasionally his presence to establish an operating foundation for the purpose of leading social sector organizations toward excellence in performance."[1]
In the aftermath of **Drucker's** death on November 11, 2005, Leadership Network had a press release reiterating this very information by their own admission.
This feature describes how **Drucker** was a close friend and mentor of **Bob Buford** and "**Drucker** was instrumental in the forming of Leadership Network and its development over the years." It goes as far as saying that the organization might not exist as all "were it not for **Peter Drucker**."[1]
The feature continues: "In 1997, Atlantic Monthly magazine editor Jack Beatty interviewed **Buford** for two hours for a book titled, "The World According to Peter Drucker."

 The entire volume contained only six words from **Buford**: 'He's the brains, I'm the legs' . . . "Their friendship grew over the years as they talked about management, the "Halftime" phenomenon of successful business people looking for significance in the second half of their lives, and other common interests-including the phenomenon of the large pastoral churches emerging in the United States since 1980."[1]

Buford based Leadership Network on business management principles that he learned from **Drucker**. Following **Drucker's** strategies, **Bob Buford** only recruited leaders from successful churches as the first customers, worked only with those who were receptive to his goals, and only worked on things that would make a great deal of impact if successful.

In 20 years of consultation with Leadership Network as a featured speaker and resource, **Drucker's** genius for business management caused the number of megachurches (over 2,000 attending) to grow tenfold. **Drucker's** influence was so remarkable on Leadership Network that **Buford** says the organization "belongs partly to him."[1]

It is significant that **Bob Buford** consulted with business guru **Peter Drucker** prior to the organizing of the Leadership Network which in turn gave birth the Emergent Church. **Buford** referred to **Drucker** as "my mentor",[2] "a great personal guide",[21] and "the man who formed my mind."[22]

Warren & Drucker: "Purpose Driven" Pastor **Rick Warren**: The **Drucker-Warren** relationship may surprise many, but it dates back over two decades, to when the young **Rick Warren** came to **Drucker** for advice. Under **Drucker's** tutelage, **Warren's** own success as from a "Purpose Driven" business entrepreneur to a large "Purpose Driven" company CEO has been considerable as his Saddleback church has grown to 20,000 members, one of the largest churches in America.

"The Purpose Driven Life" is this decade's best seller with over 30 million copies sold by 2007.[23]

At a 2005 Pew Forum on Religion gathering called "Myths of the Modern Mega-Church," **Rick Warren** stated: "I did a series of lectures for the faculty in the Kennedy School and also in the law school. I spoke to several groups of faculty and several groups of students and I started with this quote from **Peter Drucker**:

"The most significant sociological phenomenon of the first half of the 20th century was the rise of the corporation. The most significant sociological phenomenon of the second half of the 20th century has been the development of the large pastoral church – of the mega-church. It is the only organization that is actually working in our society."

"Now **Drucker** has said that at least six times. I happen to know because he's my mentor. I've spent 20 years under his tutelage learning about leadership from him, and he's written it in two or three books, and he says he think it's the only thing that really works in society."[2]

Warren also says that his staff at Saddleback reads and discusses **Drucker's** writings, using them to manage the church. In **Rick Warren's** office is a print signed by **Drucker** and given to **Warren** that reads: "What is our business? Who is our customer? What does the customer consider value?"[2] But what does God value?

This type of **Druckerian** language clearly reveals that Saddleback Church is a business with customers made to look like a church of Christians.

Drucker said, "The purpose of management for churches is not to make them more business-like, but to make them more church-like."[2]

However, the opposite has taken place. **Bob DeWaay** explains: "**Drucker** has helped **Warren** use cutting edge management ideas from the business world and implement them in his management of the local church. **Warren** has now taken those ideas and made a business system that can be implemented by church leaders all over the world to improve their own church management and bring their efforts and their budgets into alignment with **Warren's** Purpose Driven paradigm."[2]

Even **Warren** himself speaks of his Purpose Driven paradigm as a particular brand of product. The Purpose Driven franchise like any other successful business franchise such as McDonald's which enables ordinary people to replicate the substantial results of the new product and share the success of the innovator. Like any other business marketing model, **Warren's** Purpose Driven business church model is a brand name much like the brand names that come from Leadership Network or Willow Creek.

Warren describes how the Purpose Driven paradigm is a franchise system which any pastor can transfer to his church in order to replicate the same church growth results produced at **Warren's** Saddleback Church model. He says, "Well, one of our values is what I call "the good enough" principle."

"A person doesn't have to be perfect for God to use them. Because we want our church to be a model for other churches, we want average people doing average activities in order to get extraordinary results. Just like how the typical McDonalds is able to succeed while being staffed by high school students. Because the system works, it doesn't require unusual talent."[2]

Borrowing **Warren's** example, the **Druckerites Bob Buford, Bill Hybels** and **Rick Warren** are like the franchises Burger King, Wendy's and McDonalds. Just as all of those fast-food restaurants sell hamburgers, so the **Druckerites** all sell knowledge-based products to build churches. Though the different brands of hamburgers taste different and come with different toppings, they are all hamburgers.

In the same way, the **Druckerites** brand may vary, whether it be Leadership Network, Willow Creek or Purpose Driven, but they are all essentially the same in their implementation of best business practices for building the local church.

Druckerite Trinity: While these organizations have been built upon cutting edge business marketing and being relevant, whether it be to the unchurched or Gen X or baby boomers, no words can be more cutting in relevance and shaking to the core of these organizations than those of the Apostle Paul who said, "For do I now persuade men, or God? or do I seek to please men? for if I yet pleased men, I should not be the servant of Christ" (Galatians 1:10). Supposed conservatives like **Rick Warren** perceive the problems within the Emergent Church. **Rick Warren** initially criticized the Emerging Church:

"Let me talk specifically about what I think is most important—the Emerging Church's preoccupation with postmodernism. Postmodernism has never created anything. It is only destructive. It deconstructs. It cannot build anything, and so it will be dead in a matter of years. It cannot last. It is a fad.
But it is so like the church to jump on the bandwagon just as everyone is jumping off."
"Postmodernism is just a little, dinky, tiny sliver of young to middle-age, college-educated, affluent white people in America. . . ."

"Well, postmodernism is totally relativistic because they say there are no absolutes. And that's why it is incompatible with Christianity. It's just incompatible. You cannot say there are no absolutes. And that's why it is incompatible with Christianity. It's just incompatible. You cannot say that there are no absolutes."[2]

Though the influential "Purpose Driven " Pastor **Rick Warren** has distanced himself from the Emergent Church, he has been blatantly and unashamedly supporting the Emerging Church for years. On the one hand, **Warren** criticizes Emergent postmodernity for being incompatible with Christianity, but on the other hand he endorses the Emergent Church again and again.

Why? The only reason a supposedly conservative evangelical pastor like **Rick Warren** would associate himself with postmodern liberal Emergents like **Brian McLaren, Dan Kimball, Doug Pagitt,** and **Tony Jones** is because **Rick Warren** is a disciple of **Peter Drucker** and the Emergent Church is a product developed by **Druckerites.**

Dan Kimball's book "The Emerging Church" with forewords by **Rick Warren** and **Brian McLaren**. **Warren** helped launch the Emergent movement by writing the foreword **Dan Kimball's** book called "The Emerging Church."

Directly associating himself with other Emergents who endorsed this same book such as **Brian McLaren** (who wrote another foreword in the book), **Tony Jones, Chris Seay**, and **Spencer Burke, Warren** wrote: "This book is a wonderful, detailed example of what a purpose-driven church can look like in a postmodern world. My friend **Dan Kimball** writes passionately . . . While my book "The Purpose Driven Church" explained what the church is called to do, **Dan's** book explains how to do it with the cultural-creatives who think and feel in postmodern times. You need to pay attention to him because times are changing."[3]

Of course fellow-**Druckerite Bob Buford** endorsed the same book saying: "The future of the church in North America hinges on innovators like **Dan Kimball** and the ideas presented in this book.

Vintage Christianity can be applied to new and existing congregations to help reach the next generation."[31]

In **Rick Warren's** July 6, 2005 e-newsletter he featured an article he wrote entitled "Sharing Eternal Truth With an Ever-Emerging Culture." One of the recommended links in the issue was to Emergent leader **Spencer Burke's** organization "The Ooze."

Spencer Burke's "The Ooze" is described as a community that learns "from faith traditions outside the Christian fold" with "a Buddhist family in their church" with whom they "visited a Buddhist temple" and "participated in guided meditation with this family."[32]

Warren's "Ministry Toolbox" on his website Pastors.com features other articles favorably presenting the Emergent Church movement and its leaders such as **Brian McLaren, Doug Pagitt** and **Tony Jones.**[33] One featured article is called "Emerging Worship: Moving beyond only preaching and singing" by Emergent Church leader **Dan Kimball.**

As for mega-church pastor **Bill Hybels** and **Willow Creek's** role with Leadership Network, **Bob Buford** says:

"The first Foundation conference was held in Dallas and was the beginning of a partnership between **Bob and Linda**, "Leadership Network" and "Willow Creek Community Church." **Bob and Linda** provided the vision and willingness to underwrite any shortfall. **Bill Hybels** and the music and drama team from "Willow Creek " provided expertise in designing messages that hit the heart through a very high quality blend of the spoken work, music and drama."[3]

"Willow Creek" has repeatedly endorsed and yoked themselves with 'Emergents." In 2005, session three of the "Willow Creek " small groups conference was hosted by **Brian McLaren**.[3] In 2008, **McLaren** was invited back to "Willow Creek" to speak to youth ministers. **McLaren** told these young ministers that the emphasis Christians place on the doctrines of hell and the second coming of Jesus inhibits their ministry.[3]

In the "Willow Creek Association's" postmodern ministry resources, several books are recommended by "Emergent " authors including **Brian McLaren** and **Leonard Sweet**.

Emergent Church speaker and activist Brian McLaren:

Not only can the Purpose Driven movement and Emergent Church be traced back to the common ancestor and business guru **Peter Drucker**, but the individuals themselves are coming together to bring about a new Christianity. Considering how much these movements have in common, it is no surprise that Emergent Church father **Brian McLaren** attributes his becoming a pastor to **Rick Warren**.

He writes: "I first heard **Rick** share this material in 1985, when I was a college English professor." "As I heard **Rick** share the story of "Saddleback Valley Community Church," for the first time in my life I could envision a church that had authentic evangelism running through its veins, and for the first time I sensed that God might be inviting me to leave teaching to do this kind of church-based disciple-making.

I literally would not be doing what I am doing if not for **Rick's** impact on my life."[3]

At a recent national pastor's convention, Emergent Church father **Brian McLaren** was one of the workshop speakers and **Rick Warren** was a keynote speaker.[3]

The Druckerite Trinity is blatantly working together to bring about their reformation via knowledge-based **Druckerite** products. This synergy is clear when at **Bill Hybels** "Willow Creek Community Church," the Emergent Church leader **Brian McLaren** endorsed **Rick Warren's** "Purpose Driven P.E.A.C.E. Plan."

After boasting of U2 rock star Bono and Shane Claiborne, **McLaren** proceeds: "Many of you know **Rick Warren**, the well known pastor from southern California."

"I was so impressed, you know **Rick Warren** wrote a book called "The Purpose Driven Life," it broke all kinds of sales records. I don't know how many gazillion it sold, but it was an incredibly significant publication." "Now what would really be interesting when someone writes a book called "The Purpose Driven Life" and they suddenly get huge amounts of money and fame and influence coming their way, then it'll be interesting to watch: how does the author use all that fame, money and influence?"

"You'll really see what his purpose is at that point, not just what he writes about but how he lives. You know what **Rick** did with all of that fame and power and influence that came his way. He said we've got to get people concerned about global crisis.
He came up with a list of five. If you know **Rick**, you know it be in an acrostic P.E.A.C.E."[3]

Rick Warren also endorsed "Leadership Network " organizer **Bob Buford's** book "Halftime," calling **Buford** a "rare individual" and said "I want every man in my congregation to read this inspiring story."
 Bob Buford reciprocates admiration to **Rick Warren** saying on his official website: "**Expect to meet change makers.** In the early days of 'Leadership Network," it was **Bill Hybels** and **Rick Warren**. Now these two have enormous self-sufficient teaching ministries on their own."
[1]
Buford's Warren-endorsed book was dedicated to business management guru **Peter Drucker, Warren's** mentor and **Buford's** mind. Through "Leadership Network" and business management principles of **Peter Drucker**, the Purpose Driven Community, the "Willow Creek Association" and the "Emergent Church" **are working overtime together in order to market their new Christianity to the church of Jesus Christ.**

Druckerite Compromise

Inevitably, the leadership of the Emergent Church, Purpose Driven and Willow Creek organizations have made the highest compromise of the Gospel in seeking to serve two masters. Jesus said, "No servant can serve two masters: for either he will hate the one, and love the other; or else he will hold to the one, and despise the other" (Luke 16:13). Their pragmatism in catering to culture and pleasing of men rather than God can be demonstrated in several areas. Perhaps the most egregious abuses of their voices as Christian leaders has been in their endorsement of a Muslim document entitled "A Common Word between Us and You."

Dated October 13, 2007, "A Common Word between Us and You" is an open letter from leaders of the Muslim faith to leaders of the Christian faith. It calls to work for love for God and love for neighbor as common ground and understanding among both Christian and Muslim faiths. In the short time since its release, "A Common Word " has become the world's leading interfaith dialogue initiative between Christians and Muslims. [2]

A Christian response to the letter entitled "Loving God and Neighbor Together: A Christian Response to A Common Word Between Us and You" published in the New York Times. This response was endorsed by almost 300 Christian theologians and leaders, among whom are many personalities we have been discussing such as Emergent leader **Leith Anderson** (the President of the National Association of Evangelicals), mega-church pastor **Bill Hybels, Tony Jones** (National Coordinator of Emergent Village), **Brian McLaren**, and Purpose Driven Pastor **Rick Warren**. [3]

The problem is that the document contains statements that profess the false belief that Muslims and Christians worship the same God, that they "share the same Divine origin."

The document states: "It is hoped that this document will provide a common constitution for the many worthy organizations and individuals who are carrying out interfaith dialogue all over the world. Often these groups are unaware of each other, and duplicate each other's efforts." "Not only can "A Common Word Between Us" give them a starting point for cooperation and worldwide co-ordination, but it does so on the most solid theological ground possible: the teachings of the Qu'ran and the Prophet, and the commandments described by Jesus Christ in the Bible."

"Thus despite their differences, Islam and Christianity not only share the same Divine Origin and the same Abrahamic heritage, but the same two greatest commandments."

It is an atrocity that these professing Christian leaders would receive and endorse such a blasphemous document. Among many demonic doctrines of Islam, the Qur'an clearly denies the Deity of Christ and the crucifixion of Christ (Surah 4:157-158), which is in direct contrast to Christianity which declares that Jesus is both God and man (John 1:1,14; Colossians 2:9) and says there is no salvation apart from the cross (Matthew 26:28, 1 Corinthians 1:18).

In the summary of "A Common Word Between Us and You," it states, "The basis for this peace and understanding already exists. It is part of the very foundational principles of both faiths: love of the One God."

Both the letter and the Christian response refer to Muhammad as the "Prophet Muhammad" suggesting that he and Jesus both are prophets. However, according to the biblical standard, Muhammad has been proven to be a false prophet. And Jesus was not merely a prophet; He was the Son of God. Islam blasphemously teaches that the Messianic prophecy from Moses in Deuteronomy 18:15 that "God will raise up unto thee a Prophet" refers to Muhammad. How in the world could a Christian response be written and signed that doesn't even address these false teachings from the pit of the abyss?

Rather than "contending for the faith that was once delivered to the saints," the Christian response to the letter signed by the **Druckerites** further compromises in reference to God as the "All-Merciful One", a title given to Allah 57 times in the Qur'an. God is indeed merciful, but nowhere in the Bible is Jehovah referred to as the "All-Merciful One." This is a title reserved for the false god Allah.

The response states, "Before we 'shake your hand' in responding to your letter, we ask forgiveness of the All-Merciful One and of the Muslim community around the world." Though Christians may be in agreement with Muslims about finding common ground in not desiring strife, violence and war, it is on the basis of the Person of Jesus Christ that Christians do not kill. It is dishonest of the Christian response to selectively quote I John 4:10, "We love because he [God] first loved us" while excluding the second portion of the same verse which describes how God showed His love to the world in giving His Son Jesus Christ: "[God] sent his Son to be the propitiation for our sins."

The love of God is uniquely expressed in Christ dying for our sins upon the cross and rising again which Islam rejects.

The Bible is clear in that, "Whosoever denieth the Son, the same hath not the Father: (but) he that acknowledgeth the Son hath the Father also" (1 John 2:23). Muslims reject Jesus as the crucified and risen Son of God Savior of the world; therefore Muslims are rejecting God. Christians and Muslims **do not** stand together on a common ground or understanding of God or the love of God. "He that hath the Son hath life; and he that hath not the Son of God hath not life" (1 John 5:12).

According to the Bible, Islam is a lie and antichrist: "Who is a liar but he that denieth that Jesus is the Christ? He is antichrist, that denieth the Father and the Son" (1 John 2:22). **Brian McLaren** not only signed the response to "A Common Word " but he also validates Islam with Christianity suggesting that Muhammad had an encounter with God rather than a demon. **McLaren** writes: "And during his lifetime, Abraham—like Moses, Jesus, and Muhammad—had an encounter with God that distinguished him from his contemporaries and propelled him into a mission, introducing a new way of life that changed the world. . . . How appropriate that the three Abrahamic religions begin with a journey into the unknown." (emphasis added). Such statements and endorsement of the Islamic religion is rank heresy.

Implementing **Drucker's** secular business practices in the church will inevitably lead to destruction because the church is "built upon the foundation of the apostles and prophets, Jesus Christ himself being the chief corner stone" (Ephesians 2:20).
Drucker's business practices have acted like steroids being injected into the body causing unnatural monster growth from which the consequences will be severe and fatal. "Beware of false prophets, which come to you in sheep's clothing, but inwardly they are ravening wolves. Ye shall know them by their fruits. Do men gather grapes of thorns, or figs of thistles? Even so every good tree bringeth forth good fruit; but a corrupt tree bringeth forth evil fruit. A good tree cannot bring forth evil fruit, neither can a corrupt tree bring forth good fruit. Every tree that bringeth not forth good fruit is hewn down, and cast into the fire. Wherefore by their fruits ye shall know them" (Matthew 7:15-20).

Works Cited:

[1] **Driscoll, Mark**. "A Pastoral Perspective on the Emergent Church." pp.87-89. Available: http://bobfranquiz.typepad.com/bobfranquizcom/files/32

[2] Interview: **Brian McLaren**. "Religion and Ethics". PBS. July 15, 2005.
available: http://www.pbs.org/wnet/religionandethics/week846/

[3] Rosebrough, Chris. "The Druckerites Must Issue a Safety Recall For Their 'Emerging Church' Product Line."
Available: http://www.extremetheology.com/emergent-church/

"Peter Drucker." Wikipedia. available: available: http://en.wikipedia.org/wiki/Peter_Drucker

Leadership Network feature. November 14, 2005.
Available: http://www.pursuantgroup.com/leadnet/advance/nov05o.htm

"The 25 Most Influential Evangelicals in America." Time.

Available: http://www.time.com/time/covers/1101050207/photoessay/17.html

Drucker, Peter. "The Essential Drucker." Burlington, MA: Butterworth-Heinemann. 2007. p.31

Hybels, Bill. "Courageous Leadership." Grand Rapids, MI: Zondervan. 2002. pp.171,172

[1] Chu, Jeff. "How Willow Creek is Leading Evangelicals by Learning from the Business World." Fast Company. December 6, 2010. available: http://www.fastcompany.com/

[11] Ibid

[12] Pritchard, Gregory A. "Willow Creek Seeker Services." Grand Rapids, MI: Baker House Company. 1996. p.61

[13] Available: http://foundationcenter.org/

[1] "Willow Creek Community Church Creating A Volunteer Revolution Conference." Active Energy.net. October 28 & 29, 2004. available: http://activeenergy.net/

[1] "Drucker's Influence on Leadership Network" Leadership Network Advance, November 19, 2005.
Available: http://www.pursuantgroup.com/

[1] Available: http://www.activeenergy.net/

[1] Leadership Network feature. November 14, 2005. available: http://www.pursuantgroup.com/

[1] Ibid

[1] Ibid

[20] "Willow Creek Community Church Creating A Volunteer Revolution Conference." Active Energy.net. October 28 & 29, 2004. available: http://activeenergy.net/217047

[21] Leadership Network feature. November 14, 2005.
Available: http://www.pursuantgroup.com/leadnet/advance/nov05o.htm

[22] **Buford, Bob**. "Halftime." Grand Rapids, MI: Zondervan. 1994. dedication page

[23] Karlgaard, Rich. "Peter Drucker on Leadership." Forbes. November 11, 2004. Available: http://www.forbes.com/2004/11/19/cz_rk_1119drucker.html

[24] Available: http://pewforum.org/Christian/Evangelical-Protestant-Churches/

Leadership Network feature. November 14, 2005. available: http://www.pursuantgroup.com/leadnet/advance/nov05o.htm

[25] Ibid

[26] DeWaay, Bob. "Redefining Christianity: Understanding the Purpose Driven Movement." Springfield, MO: 21st Century Press. 2008. p.175

[27] Available: http://www.activeenergy.net/templates/cusactiveenergy/details

[28] Abanes, Richard. "Rick Warren and the Purpose That Drives Him." Eugene, OR: Harvest House Publishing. 2005. p.27

[30] Kimball, Dan. "The Emerging Church." Grand Rapids, MI: Zondervan. 2003. endorsement page

[31] Ibid

[32] Gibbs, Eddie and Bolger, Ryan K. "Emerging Churches: Creating Christian Community in Postmodern Cultures" Grand Rapids, MI:
Baker Academic of Baker Publishing Group. 2005. p.132

[33] Warner, Greg. "Brian McLaren: the story we find ourselves in." **Rick Warren's** Ministry Toolbox. Pastors.com. November 19, 2003. available: http://www.pastors.com/blogs/ministrytoolbox/archive/2003/03/28

Allen, Tom. "Younger pastors ask: Is preaching out of touch?" **Rick Warren's** Ministry Toolbox. Pastors.com. May 12, 2004.

Available: http://www.pastors.com/blogs/ministrytoolbox/archive/2004/03/03

[3] Available: http://www.activeenergy.org/templates/System/details.asp

[3] Available: http://www.willowcreek.com/events/ wca_resources.asp?linkRequest=smallgroups2005

[3] **Roach, David**. "Lessen focus on eternity, McLaren says at Willow Creek student ministries conference." Baptist Press. April 18, 2008.

Available: http://www.bpnews.net/bpnews.asp? id=27867&ref=BPNews-RSSFeed0418

[3] **McLaren, Brian**. "More Ready Than You Realize: Evangelism as Dance In The Postmodern Matrix." Grand Rapids, MI: Zondervan. 2002. p.186

[3] Available: http://www.zondervan.com/cultures/en-us/nationalconvention/

[3] Available: http://www.viddler.com/explore/xjm716/videos/12/

Buford, Bob. "Halftime.," Grand Rapids, MI: Zondervan. 1994. 2nd page of endorsements.
[1] available: http://www.activeenergy.net/templates/c
usactiveenergy/details.asp?id=29646&PID=207455

[2] "A Common Word Between Us and You." available:
http://en.wikipedia.org/wiki/A_Common_Word_Between_Us_and_You

[3] "Loving God and Neighbor Together: A Christian Response to A Common Word Between Us
and You." available: http://www.yale.edu/divinity/news/071118_news_nytimes.pdf

The Official Website of "A Common Word." available: http://www.acommonword.com/
Available: http://www.acommonword.com/index.php?lang=en&page=option1

"Loving God and Neighbor Together: A Christian Response to A Common Word Between Us and
You." Available: http://www.yale.edu/divinity/news/071118_news_nytimes.pdf

McLaren, Brian. "Finding Our Way Again." Nashville, TN: Thomas Nelson. 2008. pp.22,23.

(**NOTE: The above work is from a website, which is listed below; all emphasis mine. Ed.):
https://www.holybibleprophecy.org/2011/07/27/
druckers-discipleship-by-elliott-nesch/?doing_wp_cron=1555711769.9062271118164062500000

Who is Peter Drucker and who are the "Druckerites?"

Three key players are carrying forth **Peter Drucker's** legacy:
Rick Warren, Bob Buford and **Bill Hybels,** who all studied extensively under their friend,
Peter Drucker, and are considered the **Druckerite** "trinity." These three men more than any
others are responsible for innovating the church by purposely changing congregations from a
pastoral ministry model to a CEO / Innovative Change Agent leadership model.

What's more, all of these innovations were strategically crafted under the careful eye of **Peter
Drucker** himself. And all of these innovations were incubated, introduced and injected into the
church through the coordinated efforts of **Drucker's** disciples through their different but
intimately connected organizations: "Leadership Network," "The Purpose Driven Network" and
the "Willow Creek Association."
In a 1989 interview with **Peter Drucker** in this article titled, "Managing To Minister," **Drucker**
explains how he was influential in the successful reorganizing of major businesses like General
Motors and Sears as well as governmental agencies like the Department of Defense, before
turning his attention to what he called the "Third Sector:" nonprofit, human services
organizations and churches.

By 1994 **Drucker** was the main attraction at a special Summit on "The Futures of
Denominations." The groundbreaking event was part of the "Leadership Network" (birthed by
Bob Buford), which convened over 75 denominational leaders, senior ministers, consultants,

and others in Ontario, California.   The summit was a game changer for the Church as we now know it, as **Drucker's** telling comments reveal:

"Let us change the way we look at the Protestant church in America as a result of the meeting." "While acknowledging that there are still many unhealthy churches, there is a justified **"change in basic premises, basic attitudes, basic mind set... on the whole, we are on the march. We are not on the retreat."**

https://standupforthetruth.com/2014/04/peter-drucker-church/

(**NOTE: There are several related articles on this website worth reading. Ed.).

- **Ezekiel & Clare du Bois**: This couple has been in ministry for 30 years and run a local mission in New Mexico. The Lord has tasked them to prepare the "Bride of Christ". (That is, making all His believers ready for His coming). All their messages have to do with helping us to draw closer to God. They have an incredibly intimate walk with the Lord with very personal conversation which you may find odd...but once you get used to it it is beautiful.
The Lord posts a message through them almost daily at www.heartdwellers.org
http://endtimesready.com/media/prophets-and-apostles/

(**NOTE: Obviously this website listed above has no idea about this heresy, however I am listing it here to show how deceived a person can be if they follow blindly those that deceive. Ed.).

(Extra-Biblical, Mysticism, False Prophet, Faulty Biblical Exegesis) - EZEKIEL du BOIS
(Extra-Biblical, Mysticism, False Prophet, Faulty Biblical Exegesis) : http://so4j.com/heaven/
index.php?option=com_content&view=article&id=67&Itemid=171

- **Jesse Duplantis**: Another WOF and Prosperity preacher; ministry is riddled with errors. Presenting his messages with humor, **Duplantis** is a typical word-faith clone of **Kenneth Copeland,** often preaching from **Copeland's** pulpit ; flew **Oral Roberts** around for his preaching engagements.   https://www.truthprophecy.com).

E:

 Joni Eareckson-Tada : WOF and Prosperity proponent; "Daystar's" **Joni** proudly announced to a worldwide audience that **John Paul Jackson** was healed of cancer, when in fact he was not healed. He was also a WOF and NAR leader, and is now deceased;
She signed the Manhattan Declaration, which is a document pertaining to the One World government and One World Religion--and she endorsed "The Message," a blasphemous counterfeit Bible. http://watchmanforjesus.blogspot.com/2010/03

A small writing exposing her connection with the Catholic church and that all should be united into one "inter-denominational, inter-religious, ecumenical journal..."

https://excatholic4christ.wordpress.com/2015/10/08/

popular-evangelical-joni-eareckson-tada-endorses-ecumenical-first-things/ --

https://www.thebereancall.org/content/strange-fire-conference-spiritual-discernment-according-calvinism

"I have a 25-minute drive to work each morning and while I'm in my car I really enjoy download FT listening to a local Christian radio station." "Oh, it's a blessing to hear about the Lord at the start of every day! One of the scheduled messages broadcast each morning is a 5-minute clip from **Joni Eareckson Tada**. I'm sure many of you have heard of her." "**Joni**, a quadriplegic, provides daily messages of hope and encouragement for Christians who are struggling with challenges of all kinds." "Yesterday morning, my ears perked up when **Joni** cited "First Things" journal as an excellent publication and strongly encouraged her listeners to check it out. Well, "First Things" was started by influential Catholic priest, Richard John Neuhaus, in 1990."

 It's described as an "inter-denominational, inter-religious, ecumenical" journal featuring the writings of a broad spectrum of "Christians" (Catholic, Orthodox, and Protestant) and Jews. All of the declarations issued by **Chuck Colson's** and Neuhaus's ecumenical "Evangelicals and Catholics Together" project were initially published in "First Things."

The ecumenical spirit of "First Things" mirrors the teaching of Roman Catholicism which says all can be saved if they "seek the truth and do the will of God."
"Since Christ died for all, and since all men are in fact called to one and the same destiny, which is divine, we must hold that the Holy Spirit offers to all the possibility of being made partakers, in a way known to God, of the Paschal mystery."

 "Every man who is ignorant of the Gospel of Christ and of his Church, but seeks the truth and does the will of God in accordance with his understanding of it, can be saved." "It may be supposed that such persons would have desired Baptism explicitly if they had known its necessity." – Catechism of the Catholic Church, paragraph 1260.

The Catholic hierarchy once taught that only Catholics could be saved but, because they believe in salvation-by-merit, it was entirely predictable that they would eventually recognize all other works-righteousness religious systems – Judaism, Islam, Hinduism, Buddhism, etc. – as legitimate. Making their already-broad path even wider, **Pope Francis** has said EVEN ATHEISTS will be saved if they follow their consciences and pursue "righteousness." "Why do you call me good?" Jesus answered. "No one is good—except God alone." – Mark 10:18.

"But genuine believers are well aware that God's Word clearly proclaims that salvation is ONLY by God's grace through faith in Jesus Christ. There is NO other way. Bible verses which state salvation is only by accepting Jesus Christ as Savior can be found here [in the website].
The Gospel of Jesus Christ has nothing in common with the works-righteousness "Gospel" of Catholicism and the ecumenism of "First Things."

"So why would a high-profile Evangelical Christian, like **Joni Eareckson Tada**, irresponsibly recommend "First Things" and its ecumenical message to her listeners? What goes through her head? The postmodern <u>heresies</u> of <u>pluralism</u> and <u>relative truth</u> continue to spread like cancer and more and more Evangelicals ignore Biblical doctrine and succumb to accommodation, cooperation, and compromise."

(**NOTE: This article can be accessed using the websites listed at the beginning. There is a lot more to this, which makes it clear why she endorses it. Ed.).

- **John Eckhardt**: "I watched this video of **John** preaching at "Calvary Lighthouse" in 2014: https://www.youtube.com/watch?v=lSdE4VgDA0Q.

"This is spiritual vomit; it is blasphemous, presumptuous, demonic, nothing less or more. "This is a glory-seeking man who speaks in the Name of the Lord, out of the imagination of his own heart, powered by Satan, the dethroned prince of this world."

"**Eckhardt** is a <u>prophet</u> of Baal jumping up and down on his vile altar, supposing he'll move the crowd, if not God, to great works and manifestations, but to what end and for what cause? Here's what I wrote to a person whose Facebook account was promoting this "Lighthouse" video":

"We see you honoring a vile spewing of blasphemy out of the mouth of **John Eckhardt**. It is horrid, Mazel. It is not the Spirit of the Lord speaking but the spirit of a presumptuous exhibitionist. This man is devilish with false gifts of tongues and <u>prophecy</u> and carnal preaching. The man is a liar."
 "**John Eckhardt** and so many others like him are nothing less than prophets of Baal, the very kind against whom Elijah stood. John is jumping up and down on the altar, trying to impress God and man by demonstrating his zeal, but the Lord doesn't hear a word he says, much less speak through him. He will die the death of that Elijah slew."

"Frankly, the saints and angels in Heaven are indignant at these things done and spoken in His Name by such as **John Eckhardt**. His performance is revolting and nauseous to the sons and daughters of God." As of May 2017, **John Eckhardt's** website is infected with malware and not accessible. This article from "Charisma Magazine" presents an example of the treacherous ways and teachings of **John Eckhardt**. It begins:

"<u>Apostle</u> **John Eckhardt** believes that rejection is a bigger problem than most Christians realize. He calls rejection—the subject of his latest book—a 'major, undiagnosed, untreated problem in the body of Christ." If being rejected was the problem for the Body of Christ that **Eckhardt** proposes it is, then what about the Head of the Body, Who was rejected by all? The answer to dealing with rejection by men is to turn to the One we've all rejected, the One Who removes your sin and reconciles you to God and man.
Isn't that what **Eckhardt** is proposing?

No; he has written a long book presumably giving counsel from the Word of God, yet **Eckhardt** isn't directing people to the Lord, the Word made flesh. He is directing people to himself, the "<u>apostle</u>," and his own wisdom. That's why he accepts titles and the praise of men. That's why he <u>sells spiritual counsel</u>. That's why the article reports:

Concluding the event in prayer, he asked everyone to say out loud, 'I command these spirits to leave.' He also asked them to place a hand on their forehead, breaking the powers of hell over the mind so they could 'think clearly, think correctly' and so the mind would 'free and restored.'" **Eckhardt** gives lip service to the Lord Jesus Christ and Biblical principles, but he practices and promotes witchcraft, giving people the mistaken notion they can deliver themselves without holding himself or them to God's standards of walking in faith and repentance from sin.

John Eckhardt has it backwards. He focuses on receiving benefits from God rather than exercising responsibility towards God and man. He writes in his book: "An open door to rejection comes when we do not receive the love and acceptance of God."

That is Satan speaking, savoring the things of man in seeking to be loved rather than to love. The truth is, "An open door to rejection comes when we do not receive the loving correction of God." https://www.thepathoftruth.com/false-teachers/john-eckhardt.htm

http://www.828ministries.com/articles/

Personal-Clairvoyance--T-by-Anthony-Wade-Christianity_God_Prophet_Truth-170513-979.html

- **Mary Baker Eddy**: Deceased; Founder of Christian Science, which even today people like **Kenneth Hagin** practice. (**NOTE: Several websites and books regarding **Ms. Eddy** can be found anywhere. I am leaving the research up to the reader, so they can draw their own conclusions. Ed.).

- **Gene Edwards**: Is well known for a number of helpful books in the past. In fact, a number of his books are considered classics in certain circles. He wrote on the abuse of authority taking place in the "Shepherding Movement" that was popular in the 70's and 80's, "Tale of Three Kings" and also "Letters to a Devastated Christian."

But that was then and this is now. **Benny Hinn's** interview with **Gene Edwards** on "This Is Your Day'" program (4/27/04), proves that it does not matter if someone is close or far off in their Biblical teaching, as long as it tickles the ears of the listeners. This is not the first time **Gene Edwards** has been on **Hinn's** program.

However after hearing what he said, I and others became very concerned with the content and what he is teaching. Mysticism is "an immediate, direct, intuitive knowledge of God or of ultimate reality attained through personal religious experience" (Encarta Encyclopedia). "Thus, a mystic tries to find deeper meanings from the scripture that are unclear or not there. A belief in the existence of realities beyond perceptual or intellectual apprehension that are central to being and directly accessible by subjective experience" (Excerpted from American Heritage Dictionary by the author of this expose'. Ed.). There are numerous ways to be mystical.

"I began to do some research on **Edwards** and did not find so favorable comments on his writings as he once had years ago. Commenting on a tape by **Edwards**, the 11/96 "The Berean Call" states: "**Edwards** is obviously a mystic who applies his own esoteric meaning to words." After hearing what he said on **Hinn's** program and checking it by the Scripture, I can only come to the same conclusion.

Let's take a look at the statements he made on **Hinn's** program, in portions, to decipher what he saying and see if he is using a Biblical interpretation or has a Biblical position. "You will need patience to read this article as we unravel the <u>mystical views </u>of **Edwards**."

Benny Hinn introduces **Gene Edwards** and begins by saying **Suzanne** (**Hinn**) has talked to me about reading **Edwards'** incredible book, which surely touched her life.
 It's titled "The Day I Was Crucified " as Told by Jesus the Christ.

Benny Hinn then asks: "Why did you write this book?"
Gene Edwards: "Because almost no one knows the rest of the story. There is so much about what happened <u>on the cross that is not covered in the gospels, the epistles are filled with statements about what happened on the cross</u>."

"So I decided not to just tell about it but take these wonderful things, mostly spoken by Paul, and weave them into the story we are all so familiar with, Matthew, Luke and John the story of the crucifixion. And make those incredible statements, those unbelievable statements, incomprehensible statements and weave them in as though they were part of the story."

How can we not know the rest of the story? It's been written in the Bible for almost 2,000 years. Anyone can read the gospels and the epistles to know the rest of the story. **Edwards** is suggesting that only a small handful of people know the complete story of the cross. <u>The first clue of error comes from the beginning of this interview</u>.

Edwards implies that most have an inadequate Bible knowledge on what took place on the cross. Apparently, **Edwards** considers himself to be among that small handful of people of whom are able to grasp these (well known) facts, then write a book and share it with others. It certainly implies exclusivity and "corner-on-the-market" theology.
On **Edwards'** position, most respected theologians and scholars throughout the body of Christ would have to disagree, along with any student of the Word on his position. What Paul wrote is known as part of the story, and **Edwards** is not the first to put them together with the crucifixion. However, <u>he is the first to come to certain conclusions</u>.

The epistles are filled with statements about what happened on the cross; just not what **Edwards** says happened on the cross.
Hinn: "Would you share some of this?"
Edwards: "<u>Well, I was crucified that day and so was **Benny Hinn**</u>."

"So that's a part of the story...uh the world was crucified that day. So the world comes as part of the story and is crucified there on the cross with the Lord Jesus Christ. <u>The world is personified as a human being, as a person</u>, and is crucified with Christ and in Christ."

"<u>Sin comes as person and makes a incredible speech </u>and <u>becomes part of Christ </u>even as he's dying, and <u>then comes the death himself</u>, and they have quite an interaction between the two of them, the Lord and death, the <u>two great enemies that have never known defeat</u>."
"And then <u>the law is invited by the Lord commanded to come there and </u>he's part of the story."

"And the law is stern and unrelenting, and all of these rules and regulations, 613 of them to be exact that are in the law of Moses, and the law is crucified with Jesus Christ, so is creation itself, so is Adam's race and just as the Lord... and so is **Benny Hinn**."

"And just as the Lord is dying he takes them into his bosom and they die with him." "And you know brother **Benny** they really did die that day, in the eyes of God the world is gone. You and I are having a problem here on earth because we are fettered to time and space, but the Lord's not. He's already been there when it's all taken place."

"And He works from the viewpoint of the reality of all these things that have been crucified." You know it goes a little bit more than that. You and I can't be here on this earth, grasp how incredibly free he has made us, he has actually done away with these things."

Mystics make something sound profound when there is no Biblical basis.

 They then turn around to those who challenge the validity of their statements and say you are not spiritual enough to understand this. I hope that the people who follow **Hinn's** and **Edwards'** teachings will not be foolish and do this. What is incredible in this interview is how he, **Edwards,** spiritualizes plain, literal statements that have spiritual truths to denote something they do not.

Like a mystic, **Edwards** goes deeper into events than is in Scripture--extrapolating meanings that are foreign from the text. Taking literal events and spiritualizing them to mean another literal event is incorrect Bible interpretation. While there is a correct way to use a midrash interpretation (which seems to be what he is trying to accomplish), there is also an incorrect way, as we see here. Good teachers elaborate on Scripture all the time, but when the meaning is changed it is no longer good teaching. The Bible does use examples of personification (God's wisdom is personified; Prov. 8:22-23).

"Personify" means to give human or personal qualities to something that is not human.

What needs to be looked at more carefully is if **Edwards** is personifying things the way the Bible does. http://letusreason.org/b.hinn14.htm

 (**NOTE: This is very lengthy. The balance of this can be found on the website, listed above. Ed.).

http://www.angelfire.com/ ia/BereanInquirer/GeneEdwardsIntro.html

http://searchingtogether.org/geneedwards.htm

- **Lou Engle**:   Another NAR teacher\preacher; Has been an HIM Apostle and HIM member since **Ché Ahn** founded "Harvest International Ministries" (HIM) back in 1996. In the link, **Ché Ahn** states that the Lord spoke to him, "through a word from respected prophet and author, **Cindy Jacobs**, that he was to "father" a new movement – a "network of networks", meant to train and raise up others.   **Ché** would have spiritual children in every continent who would reach the world." https://pulpitandpen.org/

   Lou Engle revealing how **Franklin Hall's** work "Atomic Power with God" (Hall, 1946), influenced him and shaped the NOLR 'The Call' rallies: In 1996, God gave **Engle** a prophetic dream that spawned the movement now referred to as "The Call."
   In the dream, **Engle** was to pass on a letter to a young boy named Joel. **Engle** awakened with the thought that he had lost the letter that Joel was supposed to receive. "At that point, the Holy Spirit spoke to me, 'Don't drop Joel's letter!'" recalls **Lou**.
"I interpreted this to mean we shouldn't drop God's call, articulated in the second chapter of Joel, to pray and fast." The 'Joel' reference should already be sending alarm bells to Christians who are familiar with NOLR theology. But the 'pray and fast' mandate God called **Engle** to do should be the clincher. An iconic feature of the NOLR cult was its adherents' obsession in fasting and praying through the writings of heretic **Franklin Hall**.

Yet **Engle** in 1998 had no problem promoting in his book "Digging the Wells of Revival'," heretic **Franklin Hall**, his heretical teachings and the damnable practices of the NOLR.
In one of **Lou Engle's** articles below, he links people to this PDF where you can actually see for yourself how heretical **Franklin Hall's** writings actually are. 1946 – "Atomic Power With God" – **Franklin Hall**:

Lou Engle writes: "Just consider:

• This year, 1998, marks the 50th anniversary of the birth of the nation of Israel and the literal Jewish year of Jubilee.
• A massive reawakening of prayer and fasting is taking place – much like the great movement begun more than 50 years ago when **Franklin Hall** wrote "Atomic Power With God Through Prayer and Fasting" in 1946.
 • We are right in the middle of the "Jubilee year" commemorating the 1947-1949 worldwide outpouring of the Holy Spirit that gave rise to the healing revivals of the "Latter Day Rain," the campus revivals spearheaded by **Bill Bright**, and the release of great evangelists like **Billy Graham**. This is not just a once-off reference.

  Lou Engle seems to be dangerously obsessed with **Franklin Hall**, his heretical teachings, the NOLR revival and their abhorrent practices: "But tools of fasting and prayer are actually part of the nuclear arsenal of God." "Nuclear power ends wars."
Franklin Hall said, "Fasting literally becomes prayer to the praying Christian, prayer that is as different as an atomic bomb to an ordinary bomb." **Bill Bright** even explained the idea even more powerfully…"

 Source: **Lou Engle** & Dean Briggs, "The Jesus Fast " (MN: Baker Publishing Group, 2016.) Originally published in "Spread the Fire," December 1996, **Engle** wrote an article based off the title of **Franklin Hall's** notorious work titled "Atomic Power Through Fasting & Prayer."
  In this article we see that **Lou Engle** drew inspiration from **Franklin Hall**, the "New Order of the Latter Rain " (NOLR) cult and its heretical false teachers such as **Billy Graham, Bill Bright, William Branham, Oral Roberts and T.L. Osborn:**

"A great wave of fasting and prayer fervor swept America and the world in 1946-1947. A book, "Atomic Power With God Through Fasting and Prayer" by **Franklin Hall**, was the spark that inflamed thousands to go on extended fasts and to seek God for revival and the return of the gifts of the Spirit; Many went on 40-day fasts." Then in 1947-1952 the great healing revival broke out with men like **William Branham**, **Oral Roberts, and T.L. Osborn** who were used of God to perform extraordinary miracles. Most of the evangelists followed **Hall's** fasting methods.

(**NOTE: **William Branham** is a known heretic. See William Branham expose', above. Ed.).

In 1948 the "Latter Rain" outpouring hit North Battleford, Canada, and swept into the United States. The "Latter Rain" brethren wrote that the truth of fasting was a major catalyst to the revival. After reading "Atomic Power" they entered a season of the "grace of fasting" and continued for three months. Then the Spirit fell.
 In 1948 **Bill Bright** saw a vision of college campus awakenings, **Billy Graham's** ministry was released in 1949, and the "Asbury College Revival," along with many others, commenced in 1950.
 When in 1946 fasting prayer was trumpeted, from 47 to 52 massive revival tremors shook the earth. "Fifty years later, a jubilee call to fasting by **Bill Bright** in his book, "The Coming Revival," anticipated greater harvest and glory than we have ever seen." "In my own life, I have on several occasions gone on lengthy fasts, including a 40-day fast on juices and water in January 1996 after I read **Bright's** book." "Many of the people at our church in Pasadena, California, entered long fasts during that season."

 "Out of it was birthed a 24-hour, mostly continuous prayer meeting." "In fact, the renewal meetings in our city were birthed in a 21-day city-wide fast called by **Wesley Campbell** of Kelowna, B.C."

 "**Gordon Lindsey**, founder of "Christ for the Nations," and a Christian statesman, said during the healing revival that fasting prayer is the master key to the impossible. Let us turn that key in our generation." https://www.christianity.ca   https://churchwatchcentral.com.

Millions of young people around the world are being told that they can soon supernaturally receive the hovering mantle of evangelism from the late **Billy Graham**, and that this opportunity will be theirs on February 23.

 Please hear me Christian, there is no "mantle" from any person dead or alive that we are to activate or receive. Who is making these promises? **Lou Engle**, along with leaders in the YWAM organization, according to "Charisma News," in an article I will dissect here.

The article, titled "Major Charismatic Leaders Prophesy Billy Graham's Mantle Is About to Be Poured Out" was written by **Shawn Bolz**, whom I've warned about. **Bolz** is known widely as a "prophet" who can predict the future in a "thus sayeth the Lord" kind of way, like when **Bolz** took the stage at the heretical "Azusa Now" "revival" to do prophetic cold readings (parlor tricks) using his smart phone.

(**NOTE: I wouldn't intentionally send readers to what I know is a dangerous site as "Charisma News;" it is rife with false teaching from the "New Apostolic Reformation "(NAR) and Word of Faith teachers.
I have included a source link at the bottom of this article for those wishing to read the original. Ed.).

In December and again just a few days ago, the following was reported about a new movement called "The Send." The following paragraphs contain much of the vernacular you would hear in NAR churches: **Lou Engle** and key charismatic leaders believe that in 2019, God will ignite a movement in the next generation as never before.
Specifically, these leaders believe **Billy Graham's** mantle of evangelism will be poured out on the next generation—and they have called for a gathering to usher it in.

This event, called "The Send," will take place Feb. 23 (2019) at Camping World Stadium in Orlando, Florida.
Everyone involved says this isn't just a stadium event; it's a movement. In fact, **Engle** is so confident about this that he has ended his longtime ministry, "The Call," to pursue "The Send." "We believe that [**Graham's**] mantle is hovering, waiting for thousands to lay hold of it," **Engle** says. "It is a mantle that is a burden for evangelism—for a new era of Jesus the Evangelist—to manifest a new Jesus People movement harvest to take place."

"I believe "The Send "will be a flashpoint for the fulfillment of that word. I so believe in this shift that I have ended "The Call." **Lou Engle** has hosted his "The Call" stadium gatherings for almost 20 years, but in the past several years those events have gotten international attention. This year, **Engle** is telling the next generation of young Christians that he is mobilizing missions ministries, evangelism groups and churches across North America and even other continents, asking them to throw their weight behind one central theme: It's time to carry out the Great Commission and show the world Jesus the Evangelist.

I'm not sure who Jesus the Evangelist is, but we know that Jesus the Lord didn't give Himself such a title. Instead He has commissioned all of us to share the Gospel. That doesn't seem to be what this movement is about, however. Enter in the leaders of YWAM (Youth With A Mission), who heard an extra biblical word for **Engle,** telling him to start a new movement: Seven years ago, **Engle** says, YWAM leaders, led by Andy Byrd and Brian Brennt, came into his living room and prophesied a shift to "The Call." They shared prophetically how "The Call" was going to become a new movement: "The Send." Why "The Send?"

Byrd and Brennt prophesied that **Billy Graham's** mantle or ability to reach people would be released on many individuals and ministries, and that people would begin to adopt their neighborhoods, schools and cities with the same faith **Graham** had for winning souls. They also prophesied that stadiums would be filled by these believers with signs and wonders.

These conversations took place well before **Graham's** death in February 2018. These leaders had simply received revelation that just as Elisha received Elijah's mantle, so there was a generation that would receive **Graham's** mantle of evangelism.

(**NOTE: Here it is, the year 2020–and this heretical "mantle of evangelism" has not happened; nor will it, because it is not from God. Ed.).

When **Billy Graham** died last year, **Engle** got a new extra biblical revelation:...**Engle** was on a trip, seeking God, when he read 2 Kings 2, in which Elisha actually receives the mantle of Elijah. Elisha basically says, "I will not leave you, Elijah, until I get your spirit upon me."

As **Engle** read those words, the Holy Spirit gripped him, and he wrote in big letters in his Bible, "**BILLY GRAHAM** I WILL NOT LEAVE YOU UNTIL I GET A DOUBLE PORTION OF YOUR SPIRIT ON THE NEXT GENERATION!" He felt as though God was bringing him into a divine prophetic moment and that **Graham** was about ready to pass.
He sensed that the body of Christ was heading to a Jordan crossing, and it would release a double-portion Elisha movement of signs and wonders as sons and daughters would rise up and carry the mantle of **Billy Graham**.

(**NOTE: The Bible tells us that the last days, there will be those who seek signs and wonders; Jesus Himself said it in Matthew chapter 12, verse 39. Ed.).

On Feb. 16, **Engle** was flying from Hawaii while reading 2 Kings 2:20, where Elisha says, "Bring me a new bowl." "It was like a command shot right into my spirit, with the Lord saying, 'Bring me a new bowl!" **Engle** says.

(**NOTE: Elisha said, "bring me a new cruse, not a new "bowl," speaking to the widow woman in I K. 17: 1-16. They can't even get the Scriptures correct! Ed.).

"God went on to say: 'Whereas before you have seen stadiums filled with fasting and prayer, you are going to see bowls filled with the manifestation of the **scroll** of Jesus: "The Spirit of the Lord is upon me because the Lord has anointed me to bring good news to the afflicted.'"

(**NOTE: What is he talking about?? The "scroll of Jesus?" No such thing listed anywhere in the Scriptures except in Isa. 34:4 and in Revelation, where Jesus opens the scroll: Rev. 6:14. Neither of these Scriptures pertain to Jesus giving anyone a scroll! Ed.).

"Just a few days later, on Feb. 21, **Billy Graham** went home to glory—and I knew it was 'Game on!'" Next, **Engle** met with Andy Byrd of YWAM, **Daniel Kolenda** of "Christ for All Nations," Teofilo Hayashi of "Dunamis Brazil," Michael Koulianos of "Jesus Image," **Todd White** of "Lifestyle Christianity" and Brian Brennt of "Circuit Riders."

Many more partners have joined, including TBN, Bethel Church in Redding, One Voice, Every Home for Christ and Burn 24-7. The result: The new movement called "The Send."

Here is the website, promising every attendee will be "activated":
https://www.charismanews.com/us/74929-send-me

- **Werner Erhard**: Founder of EST; practice is of a 60-hr, two weekend course; also teaches "enlightenment". He and his teachings were popular in the mid 1970s through the mid 1980s.

- **Mike Evans**: Is another person in the Elijah List organization.

https://jewishisrael.com/profiles/blogs/
the-day-jimmy-carter-saved-the-jews-from-mike-evans-1
https://ecoxplorer.com/2014/05/ scam-alert-bogus-mideast-peace-charities/

http://watchmanforjesus.blogspot.com/2010/12/ list-of-false-christian-leaders-false.html

–**Tony Evans**: Is **Priscilla Shirer's** father. **Evans'** heresies include (but are not limited to) Pelagianism (the denial of original sin), Inclusivism (you don't have to be a Christian to be saved), and "Limited Theism" (the denial of God's omnipotence).

In an interview with Glenn Plumber at the NRB Convention in 2004, **Evans** affirms a Pelagian view of Christ's death and resurrection, stating, "But the thing that the death of Christ did was cover and overrule original sin so that no man is condemned because they are born in Adam, but men are condemned because they consciously reject salvation." **Evans** also holds to inclusivism, that is, you don't have to actually know Christ personally to be saved.
In this same interview, **Evans** says, "If a person believes somebody's up there that created this... I don't know who He is but I want to know Him... if that person were to have a heart attack at that moment, God could not condemn him and be just because God says he who seeks shall find, so since God makes that promise, if God doesn't give him the Gospel or give him a direct revelation then He has to judge him out of another dispensation."

Evans' works, like many of these other false teachers, as of the time of this writing, is still sold in LifeWay's book stores. (**NOTE: Most of the Lifeway bookstores have closed down. They are owned by the Southern Baptist Association. Ed.).

https://reformationcharlotte.org/2019/03/26/ false-teachers-evangelical-churches/

F:

- **Les Feldick**: Teaches his own heretical version of the Bible; **Les Feldick** is also questionable as he does not believe in repentance and considers the Gospels as irrelevant because they were mostly aimed at the Jews. He is definitely a believer in replacement theology.
http://watchmanforjesus.blogspot.com/2010/12/

http://www.teachingtheword.org/apps/articles/ ?articleid=72802&view=post&blogid=5446

- **Vince and Sean Finnegan**: **Vince** was a leader in "The Way International," who was under consideration to replace **Victor Paul Wierwille** as president after **Wierwille's** death.

Joel's link page: http://www.thehemphills.com/links.html recommends "For More On The Important Subject Of God".

At this site– http://www.21stcr.org/contributors/contributors.html

Notice **Anthony Buzzard, Dr. Joe Martin**, president of the anti-deity of Christ, anti-Trinitarian, anti-hell Atlanta Bible College, **Sean Finnegan**, and others who are associated with "The Church Of God General Conference."

(Not to be confused with the "Evangelical Pentecostal Church of God" headquartered in Cleveland, TN, or the "Church of God" headquartered in Anderson, IN).

http://watchmanforjesus.blogspot.com/2010/03

- **Don Finto**: Is another NAR-postle – recognized by the NAR ICA organization.

- **Richard Foster**: "Does **Richard Foster** Promote A Mantra Meditation Style Contemplative Prayer?" "Does **Richard Foster** endorse, promote and adhere to Eastern mystics, New Age gurus, universalists and false teachers?" We Believe He Does--

"[W]e must be willing to go down into the recreating silences, into the inner world of contemplation. In their writings, all of the masters of meditation strive to awaken us to the fact that the universe is much larger than we know, that there are vast unexplored inner regions that are just as real as the physical world we know so well. They tell us of exciting possibilities for new life and freedom. They call us to the adventure, to be pioneers in this frontier of the Spirit."
("Celebration of Discipline," 1980, p. 13.).

"**Richard Foster** advocates a prayer movement that indeed can be proven to have strong links to Eastern mysticism.
  And incidentally, this prayer method does not have its origins with the "Desert Fathers," as some believe, but rather dates back much further, probably as far back as the early days of mankind."—Ray Yungen from: "Richard Foster - Promoting Eastern Mysticism By Way of Proxy."

 Richard Foster, about **Agnes Sanford** "I had the privilege of being in **Agnes Sanford's** home and hearing her speak on numerous occasions, and I was always instructed by her good sense ... more than once I saw **Agnes Sanford** praying with great intensity and power one moment and laughing at a homespun joke the next ... such experiences freed me to be at home with God. I believe it will do the same for you." ("Spiritual Classics").

"Thomas Merton has 'priceless wisdom' for the spiritual life of the Christian." "Thomas Merton has perhaps done more than any other twentieth-century figure to make the life of prayer widely known and understood ... his interest in contemplation led him to investigate prayer forms in Eastern religion ...[he is] a gifted teacher ..." ("Spiritual Classics" - p.17).
Tilden Edwards (founder of "Shalem Prayer Institute")--On Edward's book, "Spiritual Friend," **Foster** says "an excellent book on spirituality."

In this book, Edwards says, "This mystical stream [contemplative prayer] is the Western bridge to Far Eastern spirituality" "The Cloud of Unknowing." "Why does this little prayer of one syllable pierce the heavens?" ("Spiritual Classics" -p.45). (Caution: Not a Christian site that they list).

Foster and "Out of Body Experiences"? Read His Own Words:

"[I]n your imagination allow your spiritual body, shining with light, to rise out of your physical body.

Look back so that you can see yourself lying in the grass and reassure your body that you will return momentarily ... Go deeper and deeper into outer space until there is nothing except the warm presence of the eternal Creator. Rest in His presence." **Richard Foster** in the 1978 edition of "Celebration of Discipline," pp. 26-27.

https://www.lighthousetrailsresearch.com/fosterlinks.htm

In the August 7, 2007 edition of Moody Bible Institute publication "Today in the Word," MBI professor Dr. Winfred O. Neely tells readers that "deep and prolonged thinking about the Lord's word, person, and work is Biblical." While he states that eastern style meditation is wrong and dangerous, he brings terrible confusion to the matter by also stating:

"For more in depth reading about the vital practice of biblical meditation, I suggest that you pick up **Richard Foster's** book, "The Celebration of Discipline." This is the book **Foster** said, "We should all without shame enroll in the school of contemplative prayer."
Foster is an advocate of mantra meditation and has promoted both directly and indirectly for decades.
 http://www.todayintheword.com/GenMoody/
default.asp?SectionID=8A64563A39F442418EB47C6F6CB3CD88&date=2007-08&submit=go.

(See:) http://www.todayintheword.org/
 itw_error.aspx?aspxerrorpath=/GenMoody/default.asp)

Once again, we beseech Moody Bible Institute to read "A Time of Departing " so professors and students alike will not be drawn into the deception of **Richard Foster's** spirituality. **Foster** has and continues to uplift and emulate the late monk Thomas Merton who said that God dwells in every human being. Merton knew that the silent state one goes into through contemplative would lead the practitioner into a view that God is in all.

 Is this really what MBI wants to convey to their students when they continue to include **Richard Foster**, Henri Nouwen, Larry Crabb, **Dallas Willard** in the lecture halls and publications of their institution? LTPC offer and challenge to MBI:

"Lighthouse Trails" is putting forth a challenge to MBI to have every professor there read "A Time of Departing" and "Faith Undone."
We believe the research in both books is so solid and well-documented that it will settle this very important case that cannot be refuted. With this challenge we offer to send a free copy of

each book to every professor there – no strings attached. This is a serious situation, and Lighthouse Trails would like help in any way possible.

We hope when those from MBI read this report, they will ask MBI president Dr. Easley to have someone contact Lighthouse Trails Publishing and request these books for the staff (503/873-9092).

Quotes by **Richard Foster**: "The wonderful thing about contemplative prayer is that it can be found everywhere, anywhere, anytime for anyone."-from the "Be Still" DVD.

"[W]e began experiencing that "sweet sinking into Deity" Madame Guyon speaks of. It, very honestly, had much the same "feel" and "smell" as the experiences I had been reading about in the "Devotional Masters" (from "Renovare Perspective." 01/ 1998).

"What an inviting picture of movement and work in harmony with the divine Center of the universe"("Inward Simplicity: The Divine Center"). "Can we live in virtually constant communion with the divine Center of the universe?"("Inward Simplicity: The Divine Center"). "Simplicity, then, is getting in touch with the divine center" ("Simplicity").

"Thomas Merton has perhaps done more than any other twentieth-century figure to make the life of prayer widely known and understood ... his interest in contemplation led him to investigate prayer forms in Eastern religion ... [he is] a gifted teacher ..." ("Spiritual Classics" – p.17).

"Dom John Main understood well the value of both silence and solitude ... Main rediscovered meditation while living in the Far East." ("Spiritual Classics" – p.155). https://www.lighthousetrailsresearch.com/blog/?p=2363

In February 2008, "Christianity Today " ran a glowing cover story about Evangelicalism's recent embrace of medieval Roman Catholic mysticism entitled "The Future lies in the Past."[1] The article traced the beginning of the movement as follows: "The movement seems to have exploded in a 24-month period in 1977-1978, which saw the publication of **Richard Foster's** best-selling "Celebration of Discipline: The Path to Spiritual Growth" and Robert Webber's "Common Roots: A Call to Evangelical Maturity."[2]

The article views **Foster** as one who continues to guide the movement: "From **Dallas Willard**, **Richard Foster**, and living practicing monks and nuns, they [those going back to Roman Catholic mysticism] must learn both the strengths and the limits of the historical ascetic disciplines."[3]

So **Foster** was instrumental in starting a movement that is still growing 30-plus years later. The irony about this particular CIC regarding **Foster's** 1978 book is that in 1978 I myself was living in a Christian community committed to practicing much of what he promotes in "Celebration of Discipline" (even though we had not learned it from him directly). So I am not criticizing a practice about which I know nothing (or one in which I have no experience).

I am criticizing a practice I foolishly allowed to deceive me for a significant portion of my early Christian life. When it comes to being deceived by mysticism, I have had abundant involvement.

The only way I escaped it was through discovering and adopting the Reformation principle of Sola Scriptura.

 In this article I will show that **Foster's** "journey inward" is unbiblical and dangerous. I will show that most of the spiritual disciplines that he calls "means of grace" are no means of grace at all—but a means of putting oneself under spiritual deception. The Bible nowhere describes an inward journey to explore the realm of the spirit. God chose to reveal the truth about spiritual reality through His ordained, Spirit-inspired, Biblical writers.
What is spiritual and not revealed by God is of the occult and, therefore, forbidden.

We have discussed this in many articles and have produced DVD seminars on the topic. But the concept of Sola Scriptura is totally lost on mystics such as **Richard Foster**. They, like the enthusiasts that Calvin and Luther warned against, believe they can gain valid and useful knowledge of spiritual things through direct, personal inspiration.

 Foster describes the idea of the disciplines that are the topic of his book: "The classical Disciplines of the spiritual life call us to move beyond surface living into the depths.
 They invite us to explore the inner caverns of the spiritual realm."4

So **Foster** has conceptually repudiated Sola Scriptura on page one to replace it with a journey inward to explore the realm of spirits. Something must have been seriously amiss in evangelicalism already in 1978 to render this book a bestseller! It ought to have been repudiated on the spot. In a footnote to that statement **Foster** writes, "In one form or another all of the devotional masters have affirmed the necessity of the Disciplines" (Foster: 1).
The devotional "masters," by the way, are mostly Roman Catholics who never were committed to the principle of Sola Scriptura. It is not surprising that they looked for spirituality through experimentation. But as an "inner light" Quaker, **Foster** never was committed to Sola Scriptura either.
 https://cicministry.org/commentary/issue112.htm

(Sola Scriptura means "the Bible Alone." Ed.).

- **Emmett Fox**: Calls himself one of the Unity founders; (Charles Fillmore's "spiritual children.").

- **Pope Francis**: And all other Popes before him and after him; all Jesuits, who hate Christianity and teach on One World Religion and that "Jesus failed," which was on the news.

- **Francis Frangipane**: "Latter Rain," Dominionist heretic.
https://discernmentministriesinternational.wordpress.com/ category/false-teaching/

(Keith) Gibson quotes prophetic movement leader **Francis Frangipane**: "We have instructed the church in nearly everything but becoming disciples of Jesus Christ."

"We have filled the people with doctrines instead of Deity; we have given them manuals instead of Emmanuel" (p. 122).   **Frangipane** and his cohorts have in fact done none of that. Gibson notes:

"**Frangipane** seems oblivious to the fact that teaching people to become disciples of Jesus Christ would necessitate doctrinal instruction if for no other reason than because to teach them who Jesus **is** necessitates a doctrinal discussion.

 Additionally, how else is the church to follow the words of Christ given in the great commission and 'teach them to observe all things whatsoever I have commanded you' without instruction in doctrine?" (p. 114).

Gibson's response is stunning in its simplicity, yet what is even more amazing is that so many are not thinking through what they are accepting. He adds, "It is simply neither possible nor profitable to attempt to bypass doctrinal instruction. Discipleship may certainly involve more than merely doctrinal instruction but it cannot involve less" (p. 114).

https://www.thebereancall.org/content/ they-claim-speak-god-part-one.

(**NOTE: Quoted from the book, "Wandering Stars: Contending for the Faith with the New Apostles and Prophets," by Keith Gibson. Ed.).

- **Jentezen Franklin**: Buddies with "Hillsongs" **Brian Houston**; another NAR preacher)
https://www.charismanews.com/opinion/
75139-jentezen-franklin-2019-is-the-year-of-a-thousand-times-more

There are many churches today participating in the current fad known as "The Daniel Fast." This is a man-made so-called spiritual activity that is supposed to automatically draw you closer to God by eating things that are on a list and not eating things that are not on a list. If you partake of this fast, other benefits mentioned on "The Daniel Fast" website are winning the battle over the flesh (hard to do when we are still flesh when the fast is done), losing weight and healings from diabetes, allergies, arthritis and cancer. Another benefit is said to be putting our spirit in charge of the other two parts of us, the soul and the body.

 It must be news to the Holy Spirit that we can put Him in charge of things.

Here is what others have experienced by fasting along with **Jentezen Franklin**: healed relationships, spiritual growth, physical healings, financial breakthroughs, and other blessings. Wow. "If that is the case, you have to wonder what blessings aren't being released, **Franklin** writes, what answers to prayer are not getting through...what bondages are not being broken...because we fail to fast."

The Word-Faith crowd always makes a point to say that we will lose out on something if we don't do it their way. This is an example. Fasting is a voluntary activity we engage in at the prompting of the Spirit or when we feel we need to humble ourselves in grief or repentance, or to focus on Jesus in a more pointed way. More on fasting in previous post.

Jentezen Franklin is the guru of fasting. He has written two books on it and is the one who championed "The Daniel Fast." His statements about why we fast include fasting to get a blessing, to earn God's favor, to get a public reward, to get our greatest breakthrough, to "release" a hundredfold return. So the lesson from "The Daniel Fast " and **Jentezen Franklin** is that we fast to get something. I do not believe we fast to get something, and I do not believe we should expect something and I do not believe we have the power to cause God to do something if we fast.

More on what fasting is all about in the previous post. Secondly, if we fast, **Franklin** says, it causes God to "release" these things into our lives. My understanding is that fasting is a private expression of a deeply felt spiritual need and a way to humble myself before Almighty God. All this elevates fasting to an importance the Bible does not give it nor did Jesus give it.

So who is this **Jentezen Franklin**? **Franklin** is pastor of a Holiness church in GA but he is also pastor of a Holiness church in CA. How does he do it? This article from "Charisma Magazine" explains:

"Every Sunday, **Franklin** arrives at "Free Chapel " in Gainesville (GA) by 5 a.m. for prayer, preaches two sermons and shakes hundreds of hands before boarding a private jet at 2 p.m. with his family and two staff members. They arrive at John Wayne Airport, located five minutes from "Free Chapel" Orange County (OC), and by 6 p.m. **Franklin** is in the pulpit. The next day is filled with Orange County staff meetings, and the group returns to Gainesville on Tuesday.

"This may sound like a crazy schedule, but it is actually exhilarating," **Franklin** says. …"My family comes first, and what shows me that this is of God is the way they can be with me more now than ever."

Franklin says. "The school systems have actually worked it out that my children can be off the two days so they can be with me." Is this a Biblical model of pastoring? Pastor means shepherd. How can he shepherd his flock if he has one pasture in Judah and one in Persia? He can't. It is not a Biblical model of shepherding. As for his family, is taking his children out of school for two days a week the best, most stable life for them? Is his ambition so great he plunks his children in the middle of his "crazy schedule" so he can enjoy the 'exhilaration'? And a private jet?? He had a choice to stay in GA. He chose the jet set lifestyle. Is this the proper Christian pastoring and fathering model we want to buy into?

It isn't for me, and I refuse to spend money buying his book. His friends tell us a lot about who **Franklin** is. This weekend he is preaching from the pulpit of false preacher **Joel Osteen's** stage at "Lakewood Church !" There is no worse false church in America than Lakewood. There is no worse false preacher than **Osteen! Osteen** denies the Gospel in favor of becoming a motivational guru to have "your best life now".

The only way you're having your best life now is if you're going to hell. (that was **John MacArthur's** wit). This **Jentezen Franklin** will be preaching from **Osteen's** stage for two days. That should tell us a lot.

FALSE PASTOR ALERT: If that is not enough, after this weekend **Franklin** will be hosting the "Praise the Lord" show with **Jan and Paul Crouch** on TBN. There is no deeper of a snake pit of false doctrine than "Praise the Lord " show on TBN and **Franklin** will be promoting it. **Franklin** should be excised from any Bible-believing church on these bases ALONE. But wait, there's more. As for his teachings, they are false doctrine too. He said in one sermon as he appealed for money, lots of it for over ten minutes, over sentimental music blared from loudspeakers, "I've never come to "Hillsong Conference" where I haven't sown at least a $1000 seed..."
Yet the Bible says, "So when you give to the needy, do not announce it with trumpets, as the hypocrites do in the synagogues and on the streets, to be honored by men. I tell you the truth, they have received their reward in full." Mt 6:2, and **Franklin** goes on, "$1000 seed...into this place, because if I sow now, the rain of now will fall on my life."

NAME IT CLAIM IT! Tithe big, you get big.

And what is "the rain of now" for heaven's sakes? His hands were fluttering down as rain, and the audience looked up as if expecting manna or Armani suits or money to fall from the sky right then. He is a <u>Word-Faith</u> preacher and we know those are false. The <u>Word-Faith</u> crowd is big on "if you do this, you get this." "If you do this it will cause God to move." They talk about '<u>releasing</u>' power into your life, but in fact the only thing we have the power to release is a fart after dinner. He elevates to us more power than we have and diminishes Jesus in the process.
"It is so easy to get caught up in the busyness of ministry," he says. "It's dangerous to have a growing ministry and a shrinking passion for God; something gets out of whack."

" When I find myself becoming mechanical in my preaching, even a one-day fast fine-tunes me and makes my heart sensitive. For me, fasting is the key." Fasting is not Jiffy Lube. It is the Word that fine-tunes you. Sigh.

But most telling, is the following:

He said, "<u>When I feel myself growing dry spiritually, when I don't sense that cutting-edge anointing, or when I need a fresh encounter with God, fasting is the secret key that unlocks heaven's door and slams shut the gates of hell. The discipline of fasting releases the anointing, the favor, and the blessing of God in the life of a Christian.</u>"

Don't gloss over this. It is the most abhorrent statement imaginable.

It is sacrilege. Jesus has the key to heaven and hell. Nothing we do unlocks it.
How sacrilegious to say that any activity we do unlocks heaven or shuts hell. This is wrong! On just that statement, he should be booted from every Bible-believing pulpit, our churches, and our bookshelves! And why is fasting characterized as a "secret"? It is not, at least not to

anyone who reads the Bible. And what is a 'cutting edge anointing'? Is it different from a regular anointing?

Franklin distinguished the "normal seed" from the "precious seed" in one 'name it claim it' sermon I'd listened to. I guess I am missing out on the "cutting edge" anointing and I just have to settle for the regular anointing we get when we're saved. (1 John 2:20).
See, that is the dangerous heresy in Word-Faith preachers like **Franklin**, they subtly elevate themselves and their teachings above what the Bible says, making everything else seem humdrum by comparison by using sexy words like "cutting edge," "fine-tune," "heart sensitive," "breakthroughs," "hundredfold return," "precious seeds".... it is all very exciting in **Franklin's** world, exhilarating, even.

By comparison, the staid old faith, prayer, service, obedience seems dry as yesterday's toast. The Word-Faith doctrine "puts confidence in the nature of faith rather then in the object of faith. It assumes that there's something inherent in believing that enacts [or "releases"] something when it isn't true at all. It is not the nature of faith that is effective, it is the object of faith. It is my faith in God that gets results not my faith in my faith." (Source: "A Biblical answer to the prosperity Gospel").

(**NOTE: The above quoted source is not mine, but the author of the article. Ed.).

Franklin Jentezen is a jet setting, TBN hosting, **Osteen** partnering Word-Faith prosperity preacher who has no business being in any Biblical church. He is a wolf. Avoid **Jentezen Franklin** and "The Daniel Fast." Rely on the Holy Spirit to direct your steps. Pray, fast when the Spirit prompts you, read your Bible so you will have the discernment to spot a false teaching when you come across one. Go have a good lunch, and don't forget to thank the Lord for it! http://the-end-time.blogspot.ca/2011/11/jentezen-franklin-and-his-false.html

https://thewordonthewordoffaithinfoblog.com/2014/12/20jentezen-franklin-and-his-false-teachings-on-fasting/

The seeker friendly industrial complex driven by the purpose driven church growth models employs a seemingly endless line of false teachers and prophets. Keeping up with the more brazen and public is the norm, which sometimes lends itself to missing several false teachers. For my ministry **Jentzen Franklin** is one such false teacher.
While I am sure I have referenced him in the past this may very well be the first devotional specifically about him. He is usually not this publicly sloppy so maybe this is a sign of things to come. Perhaps he is trying to expand his reach within the complex. Let us reason together through the above linked article and take a look at the theology of **Jentzen Franklin**:

"This coming year--2019--is going to be powerful. It's going to be the year of a thousand times more. Wouldn't you like to have a thousand times more of God's presence in your life and in the lives of your children and grandchildren? How about a thousand times more of God's favor in your church, your business and your home?" -- **Jentzen Franklin**.

A thousand times more? Why not just shoot for a million and get it over with? If you are pimping God out, why the hesitancy? This is a tell-tale sign of a false prophet, beloved. A "one size fits all prophecy" that cannot possibly be true but tickles the ears so much. How do we know it is not true? **Franklin** is claiming this is a word of God for His church. Everyone. So everyone gets a thousand times stuff? No one is in the valley? Can you imagine giving this absurd word to the underground church in China or the persecuted church in the Middle East?

Any word that falls apart when leaving our shores is false by definition.
Now let's watch how much **Franklin** respects Scripture in defending this mess: "I didn't pull that number out of thin air." "We find the Almighty God promising that very blessing in Deuteronomy 1:11: "May the Lord, the God of your fathers, make you a thousand times more numerous and bless you, just as He has promised you!" " That's what I'm believing for. And I'm believing it for your life. A thousand times more sounds pretty big, but our God is a big God." -- **Jentzen Franklin**.

Our God is a big God but that is no reason to butcher His word. The key verses today include Deuteronomy 1:11 as well as the immediate context. Is this God establishing some generational promise that we can all live by? Is He establishing an eternal principle of a thousand fold blessing? Hardly. What is happening here is that Moses is about to tell the tribes to pick leaders to serve as a buffer between him and the individual people in the tribes.

Quite simply, Israel had grown so much that Moses could no longer answer every single question, concern and complaint. He says as much in verse nine when he says I cannot bear you by myself. In verse ten he properly gives credit for this growth to Almighty God. In verse 11, the verse in question, Moses is merely reiterating the covenant God has made with Israel. He is reaffirming or praying if you will, that God will make the nation a thousand times more and bless them as He has promised. This is regarding Israel beloved, not the church.
After saying this sidebar prayer, Moses returns to the point in verse 12 -- how can I bear the burden and weight of your strife? Finally in verse 13 he instructs them to appoint leaders from their tribes.

So yes, **Jentzen Franklin** did not pull the notion out of thin air. Instead he ripped it out of context and pretended it somehow applies to today and us receiving a thousand times the goodies we want in 2019.
"At Free Chapel, we start out each new year with a 21-day fast. We do a "Daniel Fast," eating no meat, bread or sugar for 21 days. During this year's fast, we're going to be praying and seeking God's face for a thousand times more of Him than we've ever had in our lives." -- **Jentzen Franklin**. Uh-huh.

Let's start with this notion of a "Daniel fast," made popular by **Rick Warren** and the secular new age expert, Dr. Oz. In the first chapter we see the king want to give Daniel and his compatriots a portion of the meat the king ate and the wine he drank. The text clearly says that Daniel did not wish to defile himself so he cut a deal. He asked to be allowed to eat nothing but pulse, which was vegetables and seeds.

In ten days he presented himself to the king who saw he was no worse off and the king allowed them to continue to have only pulse for the duration of their training.

This lasted <u>years</u>, not 21 or 40 days but the issue was not fasting.   It was that the king's meat was not at the standard of clean for the Jewish boys and probably did not have the blood drained. The only other place where Daniel fasts is in the tenth chapter where he says that he is in mourning so he excludes delicacies, meat and wine for 21 days. The verse prior is where Daniel receives a great revelation that has caused him to mourn. The point being is there is a reason why Daniel chose to fast and <u>it certainly was not to seek God for a thousand times more stuff</u>. That said, fasting in general is a fine discipline to learn as a Christian.

The first rule however is everyone is different. Some people have diabetes. Others have low or high blood pressure. You cannot just call everyone to the fast you have decided. That is dangerous and unbiblical. The Bible says to fast in private and not let others know you are fasting. The object is to sacrifice something and during those times that you would usually enjoy what you are fasting from -- to draw closer to God. Not out of greed or silly prophecies of greed. Rather we draw close because He is God and we want to be closer to Him. For some their sacrifice might be no coffee. For others no sugar products. Can you imagine a vegan doing a Daniel fast? That is their diet!

I remember when I was on a regular fasting regimen I eventually had to expand it because what was a sacrifice at the start became less and less sacrificial. A "Daniel fast" may sound pious but it is not Biblical as designed and could jeopardize people's health.

It is yet another "look at me" trick with the narcissistic world of Charismania. "If we aren't careful, pride can cause us to pay a high price as well. That's why fasting is so important. When we fast, we humble ourselves before God."
"We are saying, "God, I need you right now just as much as I ever did. You've given me so much, but I know it's all through your power and not my own." "We must never get to the place where we feel we can do it on our own." "We must never feel our gifting, our talent, our education is enough." -- **Jentzen Franklin**.

While I agree that we should never rest in our own selves, his notion that fasting for a thousand times more things is somehow humble is laughable.
There is nothing humble about the fast he is undertaking.   First of all he is doing it in public and against Scripture. His entire premise was lifted from Deuteronomy without a care in the world about context. Then factor in the fact that his fast is essentially drawn from a desire for this thousand times stuff increase. That is the thing with false teachers. What God has already done is never enough.

Franklin concludes: "One of the greatest results of fasting is that we humble ourselves <u>so God can exalt us</u>." "When we ask for a thousand times more in 2019, we ask it humbly." "We ask it in the brokenness and humility of a fast."
" We ask it while recognizing that everything we are, everything we have, and everything we will ever accomplish is a gift from the hand of God." -- **Jentzen Franklin**.

Wow; what carnal thinking. First of all, there is no way to ask for a thousand times more in 2019 humbly. **Jentzen Franklin** seems to believe that the fasting will result in brokenness and thus when asking for the thousand times bonus it is from a place of brokenness.
No **Jentzen** it does not work that way.
 Fasting is not meant for us to go to God and say look -- I'm starving so give me what I want! All we need to know about the carnal theology of **Jentzen Franklin** can be highlighted in his assertion that we fast to humble ourselves because then God will <u>exalt us.</u>

The way **Franklin** states it here <u>we fast in order to be exalted!</u>
 Beloved do not fall for such fleshly desires. God is Lord and He deserves to be exalted. We are the created, not the Creator. Let 2019 be the year we draw closer to God for everything He has already given to us not for a faux humility that not only asks for more but asks for a thousand times more with an eye towards being exalted by God.

Rev. Anthony. http://www.828ministries.com/
Diary/Jentzen-Franklin--Calls-by-Anthony-Wade-God-190212-975.html

- **Dr. Hobart E. Freeman**: Deceased; Members of the cult, Faith Assembly (not affiliated with Faith Assembly of God), led by Hobart E. Freeman believed and practiced the following:

No doctors, dentists or medical care (pray to God for healing)
Belief that if no healing occurred, your faith was too weak (a sin)
No television
No holiday celebrations (not even Christmas or Easter)
No involvement in school sports or clubs ("Be ye not unequally yoked with unbelievers")
Frequent exorcisms as a common cure all remedy (especially for the mentally ill)
No voting in political elections
Home schooling of children highly recommended, but not mandatory
No dating from within the church, and especially not outside of it
Minimization of contact with the outside world, including cutting off contact with 'non-believing' family and friends

https://innertubes.wordpress.com/2010/01/19/
growing-up-in-faith-healing-cult-faith-assembly-led-by-hobart-e-freeman/

The name of **DR HOBART FREEMAN** will live on in infamy. He was <u>a Word of Faith</u> teacher & pastor of Faith Assembly – over 90 people died in his church following his teaching and then **Hobart** died due to a medically treatable disease. Many of those who came out of this experience have been emotionally traumatized...

THE EVENTUAL REALIZATION THAT WHAT THEY CONFESS THEY DON'T POSSESS!!! We have seen enough evidence to conclude that the <u>Word-Faith</u> message is a dangerous soul-destroying <u>heresy</u> that simply does not work. It is a body of presumptuous teachings that lacks the authority of the Word of God.

It is a system of thinking that has been generated by a group of men drawing from each others teachings with an amalgamation of Christian theology, mysticism and Gnosticism bound together by one of the most fanciful methods of Scripture interpretation ever devised. All of this is buttressed by a mutual admiration society among the most popular of the Word-Faith teachers that admonishes critics to "touch not the Lord's anointed," often under dire threats of divine displeasure.

"The Watchman Ministry" has coined this heresy very well, because it is SOUL DESTROYING. https://ucministries.wordpress.com/ tag/dr-hobart-freeman/

- **Daniel Fuller**: http://www.teachingtheword.org/apps/articles/ ?articleid=179316&view=post&blogid=5449

http://ichabodthegloryhasdeparted.blogspot.com/2010/11/ fuller-theological-seminary-alums-rob.html

- **Steven Furtick**: "Elevation Church"; calls true Christians "haters"; prosperity preacher; **Furtick** is charismatic in the pulpit, and he is eager to share his desire to reach the lost. But he seems to believe that once the lost are "found" his work is done. "If you know Jesus Christ, I'm sorry to break it to you, this church is not for you," **Furtick** says. This applies even if you've only known Christ for as little as a week.
 "Last week was the last week that "Elevation Church" existed for you," **Furtick** declares. **Furtick** forgets that Jesus says, "Feed my sheep." And we know the entire point of a pastor is to shepherd the flock under his care (John 21:17; 1 Peter 5:2-3). Even the "found" need to be faithfully fed and discipled in Christ.

Even Jesus, Himself, trained His disciples for three years during His earthly ministry. Yet, **Furtick** seems to be okay with letting his flock starve and mill about aimless and confused.
 Not only does he not teach the truth of God's Word, he doesn't encourage their study of it either. In his sermon entitled "Functional Faith," **Furtick** actually tells his congregation they "don't need all of this fancy, special knowledge" (knowledge of Scripture) to grow in their faith. He says all they need to know is a single Bible verse and, if they know how to apply it to their lives, they'll have "functional faith."
Though, "functional faith" doesn't seem to be very functional at all given that **Furtick** believes faith is synonymous with doubt. "The opposite of faith is not doubt. It's certainty," he declares. Meanwhile, Scripture is clear that faith is actually rooted in confidence.

 It is the "substance of things hoped for, and the evidence of things not seen" (Hebrews 11:1). How else could the just live and walk by it (Romans 1:17; Galatians 3:11)? "'Now the just shall live by faith;'" saith the Lord! "'But if anyone draws back, My soul has no pleasure in him.'" (Hebrews 10:38). Perhaps **Furtick** was operating in "functional faith" when he delivered his sermon "God Broke the Law for Love." According to **Furtick**, the Law was ineffective at redeeming mankind, **so God broke it to save us.** But not only did God NOT break the Law, the Law wasn't even abolished. And the Law, in itself, wasn't ineffective at anything. The Law is holy, just and good (Romans 7:12).

It is mankind's total depravity that renders us incapable of keeping the Law, God's righteous standard, on our own. This is why God, Who so loved the world, sent Jesus to FULFILL the Law!

The Law and the prophets hang from love, so it certainly was not broken for it (Matthew 22:40; Romans 13:10). The Law still stands, and Jesus says "Whoever therefore breaks one of the least of these commandments, and teaches men so, shall be called least in the kingdom of heaven..." (Matthew 5:17-20).

So to even claim that God, Himself, "broke the Law" would imply that God shall be called least in heaven. That's not only a false teaching. That's <u>heresy</u>!

Furtick speaks all manner of error from his pulpit, but this is easily among the most demonic. https://www.lipstickalley.com

G:

- **Joan Geison**: Worked with **Kathryn Kuhlman** for eight years as one of the "helpers," after **Ms. Kuhlman** passed away, she went to work for **Benny Hinn**; claims she has "healing powers"; Appeared on **Sid Roth's** "It's Supernatural" show.

-**Lou Giglio**: https://www.christianpost.com/news/ louie-giglio-on-winter-jam-2020-jesus-is-relevant-to-every-age-economic-status.html?uid=89fa9 f8477&utm_source=The+Christian+Post+List&utm_campaign=964b0d7dc3-EMAIL_CAMPAIGN _2019_12_02_08_27&utm_medium=email&utm_term=0_dce2601630-964b0d7dc3-2439333

"Passion City Church" Pastor **Louie Giglio** will be a guest speaker at "Winter Jam 2020" and says, like the popular tour, his mission is to share Jesus with all the world regardless of age, economic status or standing in the church. The "Winter Jam Tour Spectacular" is known for bringing Christian music's biggest names on tour together to inspire families all across the country. The popular first-quarter tour will kick off a new decade in 2020 with award-winning singer/songwriter (David) **Crowder** as the headliner.

Heading to 42 cities around the United States, "Winter Jam" known for it's "no ticket required"/$15 donation at the door, will have acclaimed pastor, author, speaker and "Passion Movement " founder **Louie Giglio** on selected dates. Also in the lineup is rapper Andy Mineo, pop group Building 429, the rock band RED, singer/songwriter Austin French and "Winter Jam" creators and tour hosts NewSong, among others.

("Others" include Hillsong's Young and Free, speakers Greg Steir, Zane Black; also appearing is the "Pre-Jam "party" with artists Riley Clemmons, Ballenger and Zaunfee. Ed.).

https://www.christianpost.com/news/ louie-giglio-reflects-on-changes-in-ministry-in-the-us-francis-chans-move-to-asia.html

Louie Giglio is a false teacher. For anyone with a modicum of theological acumen who also knows the kinds of things that **Giglio** teaches and practices, this is not up for debate. But for those who are unaware, for starters, **Giglio** promotes a <u>heresy</u> that is rampant in <u>Word of Faith</u> circles known as <u>little-god theology</u> — that essentially human beings are inherently divine.

144

Giglio is the pastor of "Passion City Church" in Atlanta and holds an annual conference that is popular with millennials and younger students and regularly hosts other false teachers such as **Francis Chan**, a charismatic Catholic sympathizer, and Hillsong's **Christine Caine, Judah Smith**, and **Carl Lentz**.

In short, as one blogger puts it, "Passion City Conference" is "an ecumenical affiliation of some of the worst heretics and false teachers who have ever been associated with the body of Christ." https://reformationcharlotte.org/2019/05/15/david-platt-promotes-false-teacher-louie-giglio/

- **Derek Gilbert**: Host of **Tom Horn's** Rapture Cult TV show "Skywatch TV" is teaching about "divine council", which is blasphemous and heretical in its content. He basically states that Israel is the Gentiles mediator, but that God turned them over to a "council" of angels. "The creation of the world is linked to a Babylonian myth..."

So says **Derek Gilbert** in his book, ("The Great Inception," page 110). Once was part of Calvary Chapel, who leader was **Chuck Smith**. Married to Anita Gilbert, committed adultery with Susan Lenox, background consists of rape, infidelity, violence and drug use.

His book, "Beyond Babylon" is a Gnostic teaching, which is yet another false Gospel. https://bereanresearch.org/

Has an excellent expose on **Derek Gilbert.** http://allpropastors.org/category/prophesy-history-discoveries/page/3/.
More of his drivel, only this time about ancient peoples named "Eridu," who he theorized that they were the first peoples of the world. He then goes on to try and support his "theories" which are partly speculation and partly imagination.
He states that when God led the people of Israel out of Egypt, there were other gods with Him ("The Great Inception," Derek Gilbert, page 115).

- **Darryl Gilyard**: Registered sex offender; buddies w**Paige Patterson** and **Mac Brunson**.

- **Anne Gimenez Ministries**: False teacher, promoting herself; wrote the book, "The Emerging Christian Woman" and others.

- **James Goll**: Another of the NAR doctrine teachers/leaders. https://churchwatchcentral.com/2015/08/27/guess-who-elijah-list-challenge-the-culprit-in-the-pulpit/

- **Marjoe Gortner**: Once a child preacher; parents used him to gain financial riches. His parents named him a combination of **Ma**ry and **Jo**seph; has a video out about his childhood preaching and how easy it was to fleece the gullible. There is also a book out called "Marjoe."

- **Lee Grady:** Editor of "Charisma " magazine. Has led many astray by the contents of the magazine, which are a combination of New Age doctrine, the WOF doctrine and the false belief of the NAR; secondary magazine is called "Destiny Image".

- **Dr. Billy Graham** https://carm.org/billy-graham https://pulpitandpen.org/2018/02/21/
http://truegospel.com/falsepreachers.html

http://www.providencemountainranch.com/

Although most people recognize him as one of the, if not the most famous preacher of all time, very few realize that his message also had statements that directly contradicted what God's Word says. The above links are a sampling of the exposed preaching of **Dr. Billy Graham.**
 Billy Graham is a member of the Family and has attended the "Prayer Breakfast" every year. He is close friends with a lot of the people involved.
Billy Graham was made a 33rd degree mason in 1966 at the House of the Temple, the headquarters of Scottish Rite Freemasonry, in Washington, D.C. Can't believe that? An examination of his crusades and things he has said will put him right in line with the ecumenical movement leading the way to the one world religion.

Sure he preaches a simple gospel message and many people have gotten saved, of course many people have heard about Jesus because of this man. But what is his crusades really doing for the kingdom? The truth is that a huge portion of the people that work on his crusades are not Christians but new agers. He works together and shares platforms with the Catholic church.
Mass numbers of people that get saved at the crusades are redirected to specific apostate denominations and even catholic churches, Jewish synagogues and Islamic mosques.
Billy is friends and a supporter of both **Robert Schuller** and **Norman Vincent Peale** 33rd degree freemasons. **Billy Graham** right before he was made a 33rd degree attended the World Council of Churches meeting in New Dehli in 1961.

Remember that organization? The one that all the old denominations ended up under, making way for a one world religion! He has attended the WCC meetings ever since and is an active member. The WCC and the ecumenical movement is endorsed by the new agers believing this to be setting up the one world religion for the new age Christ.
 Now we see how he was friends with the presidents because he was part of their secret society. Still don't believe he is a mason? His name appeared on a list of famous masons Genesee Lodge No. 174 in Michigan. After people started investigating the truth of this, days later his name was removed and the **Billy Graham** association denied any involvement.
When this news broke I myself decided to call this lodge and ask, saying I was researching famous masons for a project. I was redirected to the library of masons somewhere else where I was greeted by a lower level unsuspecting mason.

I asked him directly if the **Reverend Billy Graham** was a mason and he enthusiastically responded yes he was like he was proud of the fact. I guess this lower level mason didn't get the memo. There is another testimony of a man (named) Jim Shaw that was initiated into masonry and later got out and became a Christian. He testified that at his inauguration ceremony some 33rd degree masons were in attendance and one of those masons was **Billy Graham**. (Dr. James Wardner, p. 139. "Unholy Alliance").

Billy's son **Franklin Graham** is continuing in the same exact footprints as his father. If you need further proof on this here are a few articles:

http://www.rapidnet.com/~jbeard/bdm/exposes/graham/general.htm

There are many people who have done research on Graham and even written books.
http://www.youtube.com/watch?v=-HR4OZiNomQ

http://www.youtube.com/watch?v=axxlXy6bLH0

https://deceptionfree.wordpress.com/tag/ruth-heflin/

 (**NOTE: Yes, this says **Ruth Heflin,** because she is part of this article. This particular part concerns **Billy Graham**. Ed.).

- **Rev. Franklin Graham** (**Billy's** son, who took over his ministry):

http://www.atruechurch.info/franklingraham.html

https://www.pccmonroe.org/franklin-graham

https://www.wayoflife.org/database/franklin_grahams

Rev. Franklin Graham—Billy Graham's son—has taken the "mantle" so to speak, and has decided to preach like his father. Unfortunately, he follows the same deceptive path as **Dr. Billy Graham**, as seen in the above links.

- **W.V. Grant**: One of the early teachers\preachers of the healing movement, except with a distorted viewpoint; another proponent of "seed" blessings.

- **John Gray**: Mentored by **Joel Osteen**; appears on **Oprah's** show; current Pastor of "Redemption Church," SC; allegedly had a child through an extramarital affair; An associate pastor at Lakewood Church, **Gray** has served under **Joel Osteen's** leadership for more than five years. However, **Gray** recently announced that he will be relocating this year to take over as senior pastor of "Redemption Church" in Greenville, South Carolina.
(**NOTE: Update—**Gray's** lease has been terminated; he has been served with an eviction notice, so apparently this is not going to happen. Ed.).

https://www.christianpost.com/church-ministries/
john-grays-relentless-church-served-eviction-papers-ron-hope-carpenter-allegedly-want-church-back.html

Gray's personality is charming and unassuming. His preaching style is lively, often incorporating comedy, singing, dancing, and random references to popular secular music. He's so relevant and entertaining that, <u>if you're not careful, you won't even notice he's uttering all manner of doctrinal errors and theological confusion</u>.

Gray, who tends to preach around the truth, will make mention of Jesus by name, and he may even speak of our need for the Gospel, but he never quite gets around to actually teaching it. He also offers up a wealth of spiritual platitudes and often inserts misapplied Scriptures that his teaching actually sounds meaty to the undiscerning. But, ultimately, his speech is filled with empty words and his disturbingly odd (if not outright **demonic**) take on God's Word.

In his sermon "Breakthrough Worship" **Gray** explains that worship is the key to break free of the "guilt and condemnation of bad decisions". "For there is therefore now no condemnation for those who are in Christ Jesus," he exclaims, seamlessly mixing his error with the truth of Romans 8:1.

Indeed, there is now no condemnation for those in Christ Jesus. But in order for this to apply, the person has to actually BE in Christ Jesus -and that can't occur before repentance of sin. Someone in bondage to feelings of "guilt and condemnation" for their "bad decisions" must also desire to turn away from those "bad decisions" which I assume is **Osteen**-glish for "SINS".

They must repent of their SINS. They must also confess with their mouths that Jesus is Lord and believe in their hearts that God raised Him from the dead to be saved (Romans 10:9). Of course, **Gray** doesn't make any effort to clear up the confusion. Instead, he heaps on even more as he proceeds to make his case for "breakthrough worship" through a twisted application of Mark 5:1-20. In this passage, Jesus heals a man possessed by a legion of demons.

After a brief exchange with the demons, Jesus casts them out of the man into a nearby herd of pigs, which rush off into the sea and drown. The key takeaway from this passage is the POWER and AUTHORITY of Jesus Christ. Not only did He have the power and authority to command the demons out of the man, the demons trembled, knowing exactly Who He was and that He could destroy them.

But according to **Gray's** interpretation, this passage is about the power of the demon-possessed man! First, taking gross liberties with the passage, **Gray** says, "This man was stuck in a cemetery of his own bad decisions." " And every time he would try to break free, the Law would remind him that he couldn't get it right." **Gray** then claims the man began cutting himself because he was overcome by the burden of the Law.

*Of course we know the man was cutting himself because he was overcome by demons. But let's follow **Gray** down this rabbit hole for a moment.*
"But something about that man was so powerful that it took 2000 demons to hold him down, and they still couldn't stop him," **Gray** says. "Why would 2000 demons attack one man unless his worship was a threat to their kingdom?" *Again, it is Jesus who is a threat to Satan's kingdom. But, let's indulge **Gray** a little bit longer.* "And here's the trick. The man didn't know who Jesus was...The man didn't even know who he was worshiping. But guess who told him who it was?"
From this **Gray** suggests that because the demons inside the man knew who Jesus was, they confessed Christ for him, granting him the opportunity to be healed. "[The man] didn't even know who [Jesus] was... It was the devil that gave him the breakthrough," **Gray** exclaims. "The devil is going to have to free you and give you the answer to your miracle!"

Taaaa-daaaa! Blasphemy!!! Sadly this claim seemed to go over well with his audience. They even thanked him with a rousing applause ! **Gray** seemed pretty satisfied with his "revelation" as well.

Gray vain babbled his way through another sermon he delivered in 2016. The topic was also about worship, and it also included an interesting twist that took liberties with the truth of Scripture. In it **Gray** makes the bold claim that God created mankind from the dust and "all of this good stuff" that "fell off of Lucifer" after God cast him out of Heaven.

According to **Gray**, since Lucifer failed to worship God in Heaven, He needed to create mankind to worship Him on earth. As stated by **Gray**: "So God says, 'I've created all of these things. I spoke them. Now I need somebody to acknowledge me in the middle of it. So I need them to be able to have a worship relationship to me."

"But Lucifer was in charge of worship. His soul got tainted. But the thing I created on the inside can still be redeemed.'" **Gray** continues, "So God picks up dust and whatever else fell off of Lucifer, breathes into it, and then man was created.

And now we get to give God a sound that once belonged to angels exclusively. Which is why the enemy hates you so much."   "Because every time you open your mouth you remind him of what he used to be able to do." **Joel Osteen** trained him SOOOOOO well. And that's sad. https://www.lipstickalley.com

The mess down at "Relentless Church" is starting to smell pretty relentless. It is long past due to have a serious conversation about money and the office of pastor. One of the results of the purpose driven church model is the creation of cult of personality pastors who are such gifted speakers that they are soon in high demand.

This of course is not only because of their speech-craft but because they compromise the true Gospel of Jesus Christ. Do you think 50,000 people pack into Lakewood Church because **Joel Osteen** preaches the Gospel? Just the opposite. People flock to **Osteen** because he scratches their itching ears.

Paul Washer once quipped that **Osteen** was not a false teacher as much as he was God's wrath upon those willing to sit through his sermons. Such direct bluntness is sorely needed in these end times as many struggle to come out from under such bad teaching.

Speaking of **Osteen**, this week we are again dealing with his former Associate Pastor, **John Gray**. If the old expression is true that where there is smoke there is fire, then **John Gray's** world is ablaze with scandals and unforced errors that reveal the depravity in the heart of a hireling.

"The Holy Ghost said this to me so I'm going to speak it out, that there is severe weather coming to the region this spring because of all of the climate change and issues," **Gray** said.

"Whether you understand all the science behind it or not, or agree, I heard the Lord say, 'I want you to make sure the house is covered so that when storms come people can come in here and be covered."

"Just in case you were wondering where your money is going, it's going into these buildings." - **John Gray**.

Yeah **John,** did the Holy Ghost say anything about asking the sheep for $250,000 dollars when you are already living in a $1.8 million dollar home they provided for you for free? Did the Spirit of God point out how fake you look asking for nearly the exact amount of money you just spent on your wife's Lamborghini? I am not even going to get into the salacious stories of affairs, which **Gray** denies by saying they were "emotional not physical."

Apparently he never read where Jesus says that our adultery starts with how we look at someone. Despite these denials, the woman who claims to have been his mistress responded with voice mail recordings and in depth bedroom banter that I do not need to rehash because even without it **John Gray** is disqualified from being a pastor.

Let us deal with the topic of money in a pastorate position:

People love to selectively quote that the laborer deserves his wages but they ignore all of the surrounding context found in the first set of key verses. Who is this laborer that Paul is speaking to Timothy about? He is the one that "labors" in teaching and preaching as we see in the previous verse.
He is held to a higher standard of judgement in that the blood of his listeners is upon his head and because of that he is due double honor.
Let us not lose sight however that the laborer must labor in teaching and preaching the Gospel. **John Gray** does not preach nor teach the Gospel.
An adherent of **Osteen, Gray** preaches a prosperity and self-help Gospel devoid of sin and repentance and he routinely twists Scriptures by reading you into the Bible where you do not belong. So while the laborer is worth his wages, **John Gray** is not a laborer in teaching and preaching. He is a hireling and that explains why he has a hireling's mentality when questioned about such matters: "This year got on my nerves, and I'm so ready for 2018 to be gone. I'm so ready for 2018 to be out of here." -- **John Gray**.

"I have other streams of income, and I use that to bless my wife, not from (financial) sources the church provided," "First of it all, it wasn't a pastor that bought the car." "It was a husband that bought the car. Get that in your spirit, I'm a husband first -- don't confuse what I do with who I am."   "What I do is I pastor God's people. Who I am is a husband and a father, and I'll do anything to honor them and I won't ask permission from anybody to do it. No man should."—**John Gray** "I have created and been patient my whole life for this moment -- I'm 45." "I'm supposed to wait until I'm 70 to live my best life?

And my best life is seeing my wife happy."— **John Gray**.

Yes, 2018 that saw his affairs revealed, his Lamborghini purchase decried, and his status as a hireling exposed got on **John Gray's** nerves. I do not hear a whole lot of repentance in that statement. I hear a great deal of arrogance and victimhood but no sense that what he is doing is even mildly inappropriate as a pastor. Then we see the compartmentalization that most purpose driven pastors operate under.

Osteen defenders point to the fact that he draws no income from Lakewood but that is a gross distortion. Who do you think buys his books? Who buys **Gray's** books? Why does **John Gray** have a television show on **Oprah's** network? Everything **Gray** has is a direct result of the church. The shameless hireling admits that he is not a pastor first! We are not the ones confused **John**. You claim God called you but you treat the office you are in as a temp job for a staffing agency.

Beloved, the pastoral office is not something to be taken so cavalierly and haphazardly. It is not a regular 9-5 job. Do you take care of your family? Of course but the notion that the sheep of the Lord entrusted to you takes a back seat to anyone is simply not supported in Scripture.

The last quote here is a direct shout out to **Joel Osteen** and his mega hit book -- "Your Best Life Now!" Beloved if this is your best life then by definition, you are going to hell. Also the notion that your best life must involve $200,000 cars and two million dollar homes while asking the poor people in your church to fork over another 250K in addition to their tithes speaks to the mind of a true reprobate hireling.   A true man of God could not do that without being severely convicted by the Holy Spirit.

To further the unseemliness, **Gray** pretends God told him to ask for the $250K because "storms" are coming. Please.

What is truly sad is to read the comments attached to the secular article written about this incident, and there were plenty. People saying this is why they won't go to church.

Other's correctly discerning that he is lying about hearing from God. Beloved the witness for Christ is eviscerated by hirelings pretending to be pastors and we need to separate from them. He then topped it off with this: "The work must continue.   This is not a plea for money, it's a plea for partnership, so we can be what we're supposed to be."— **John Gray.**

No **John**, this is a plea for money. You can dress it up anyway you like but the world can see through this sham even if those in your church refuse to. So what do we have beloved.

A new senior pastor involved at a minimum in an "emotional" affair that led to so much internal condemnation he bought his wife a $200,000 luxury car to mend fences. This while living in a nearly two million dollar mansion paid for by the sheep.

 When asked anything about this he gets emotional, defensive, and angry. At this point does he seek the Lord's face? Does he fast and pray? Does he willingly submit to counseling or even a sabbatical? No.

He asks the congregation for an additional 250K to "partner" with him to fix the roof and lays the blame at God's feet:

"The Holy Ghost said this to me so I'm going to speak it out, that there is severe weather coming to the region this spring because of all of the climate change and issues," **Gray** said.

 "Whether you understand all the science behind it or not, or agree, I heard the Lord say, 'I want you to make sure the house is covered so that when storms come people can come in here and be covered.'"— **John Gray**

So we are supposed to believe that God audibly told **John Gray,** as he is dealing with the affair on his wife to not worry about the 7,247 square foot house worth $1.8 million dollars he lives in. God also said nothing apparently about the $200,000 Lamborghini hush payment made to his wife.

No, **Gray** wants us to believe that God told him to go beat the sheep until the money falls from their pockets so they can "partner" with him. Sorry **John** that was not God.

Just like it was not God when you invited the wife of the previous pastor to guest preach last week and she threatened a local newspaper for covering this story by warning them that she "cuts people and has a knife in her pocketbook." You simply cannot make this stuff up beloved.

The sad thing is the $1.8 million dollar home is more than 10 times the value of the median home value in Greenville County, yet the board voted to give it to this hireling because it "was needed to entice a pastor of **Gray's** caliber to relocate to Greenville." When using such carnal logic and enticements, you simply get what you pay for.

Rev. Anthony http://www.828ministries.com/
Diary/John-Gray--Mansions-Lam-by-Anthony-Wade-Christianity_God-190403-933.html

- **Bob Grey**: A Sodomite sympathizer; says they are "born that way"; buddies with **T.D. Jakes**.

- **Craig Groeshel**: Another Emerging, Seeker Sensitive; sometimes joins **Steve Furtick**.

H:

- **John Hagee**: DENIES Jesus Christ; believes that Christians have replaced Israel–replacement theology; deceives people into thinking he's all for Israel, when in fact he wants Israel to give up some of their land; believes Jews do not need Jesus; calls Covenant Theologians heretics, because they do not make a distinction between the church and Israel in the New Testament. Branding them as the "carriers of Hitler's anointing", **Hagee** divides the body of Christ on secondary issues.

http://www.defendchrist.org

What John Hagee Teaches: "I'm delighted to present my latest book, "In Defense of Israel." This book will expose the sins of the fathers in the vicious abuse of the Jewish people." "In Defense of Israel" will shake Christian theology. It Scripturally proves that the Jewish people, as a whole, did not reject Jesus as Messiah. It will also prove that Jesus did not come to Earth to be the Messiah.

It will prove that there was a Calvary conspiracy between Rome, the high priest and Herod to execute Jesus as an insurrectionist too dangerous to live. Since Jesus refused by word and deed to claim to be the Messiah, how can the Jews be blamed for rejecting what was never offered?...

For **John Hagee** to say Jesus refused by word and deed to claim to be the Messiah is antithetical to Bible truth, but that is his teaching! The Bible is explicitly clear in revealing **John Hagee's** deadly poisonous teachings. Part of the truth Jesus testified to was his own identity as Messiah, yet **John Hagee denies** this! Jesus also came to earth for multiple other important reasons too.
John Hagee says: "...how can the Jews be blamed for rejecting what was never offered?" "NOTE: The Lord's disciples believed they could be rightly blamed!" "You stiff-necked people,

152

with uncircumcised hearts and ears!" "You are just like your fathers: You always resist the Holy Spirit! Was there ever a prophet your fathers did not persecute?
They even killed those who predicted the coming of the Righteous One. And now you have betrayed and murdered him"—(Acts 7:51,52).

Then Paul and Barnabas answered them boldly: "We had to speak the word of God to you first. Since you reject it and do not consider yourselves worthy of eternal life, we now turn to the Gentiles" (Acts 13:46). Then know this, you and all the people of Israel: It is by the name of Jesus Christ of Nazareth, whom you crucified but whom God raised from the dead, that this man stands before you healed. He is "the stone you builders rejected, which has become the capstone" (Acts 4:10,11).

If **John Hagee** was trying to confuse the meaning of Messiah (or Christ) to only a future position when Jesus would take on the throne of David during the millennium, he is also disproved by Holy Writ. The following were written before Jesus' millennium reign: "Who is the liar? It is the man who denies that Jesus is the Christ. Such a man is the antichrist–he denies the Father and the Son" (I John 2:22); "Many deceivers, who do not acknowledge Jesus Christ as coming in the flesh, have gone out into the world. Any such person is the deceiver and the antichrist" (II John 1:7). "And we have seen and testify that the Father has sent his Son to be the Savior of the world" (I John 4:14).

Again, the context of those passages is before Jesus reigns on the throne of David. **John Hagee** is exposed as teaching falsely about Jesus' own personal claims about himself!

Shocking! Saints, BEWARE of **John Hagee** and warn others:

1 - HE PROMOTES the UNBIBLICAL PROSPERITY GOSPEL - i.e. Health and Wealth 24/7, that we should always be financially prosperous if we are obedient to God.
 John Hagee states in a TBN "Praise-a-thon" that: "poverty is caused by sin and disobeying the Word of God," and that "poverty is a curse" and much more.
 He believes that believers have the right to walk in perfect, divine health and prosper financially. This stems from the erroneous view that sickness was paid for by Christ's spiritual atonement in hell and that prosperity is a cosmic law ordained by God respectively.

2 - He sadly PROMOTES the UNBIBLICAL POSITIVE CONFESSIONS - The unbiblical belief that what is spoken can be brought into literal existence. He wrongly believes that Christians may simply "speak the things into existence" which they desire of God and that God is obligated to give it to them; hence the label "Name It and Claim It" Gospel.

If this sounds eerily like God's act of creation in Gen. 1 and 2, it is.

3 - SALVATION FOR THE JEWS WITHOUT CONVERSION TO CHRISTIANITY - **John Hagee** is recognized as a fierce foe of anti-Semitism. An outspoken supporter of the Jewish people, Judaism, and the nation Israel, he has been given the "Humanitarian of the Year" award by the San Antonio B'nai B'rith Council. **Hagee** has also been bestowed the "ZOA Israel Service Award" by the Zionist Organization in Dallas and honored with the "Henrietta Szold Award" by

the Texas Southern Region of Hadassah. While his bold stance against anti-Semitism is certainly praiseworthy, **Hagee**'s zealousness for the Jewish people and their cause has led him to commit a most serious doctrinal error — salvation for the Jews without conversion to Christianity.

One newspaper account puts it this way: Trying to convert Jews is a "waste of time," he [**John Hagee**] said. . . ."Everyone else, whether Buddhist or Baha'i, needs to believe in Jesus," he says. But not Jews. Jews already have a covenant with God that has never been replaced with Christianity, he says."The Jewish people have a relationship to God through the law of God as given through Moses," **John Hagee** said. "I believe that every Gentile person can only come to God through the cross of Christ." "I believe that every Jewish person who lives in the light of the Torah, which is the word of God, has a relationship with God and will come to redemption." "The law of Moses is sufficient enough to bring a person into the knowledge of God until God gives him a greater revelation, And God has not," said **John Hagee.**

"There are right now Jewish people on this earth who have a powerful and special relationship with God," declares **John Hagee** in one of his books. "They have been chosen by the 'election of grace' in which God does what he does without asking man to approve or understand it. "Let us put an end to the Christian chatter that "all the Jews are lost" and can't be in the will of God until they convert to Christianity! . . . there are a certain number of Jews in relationship with God right now through divine election." **Hagee** also affirms: "If God blinded the Jewish people to the identity of Jesus as Messiah, how could He send them to hell for not seeing what he had forbidden them to see?" He continues, "All people will gain entrance into heaven through Christ."

"The question is one of timing." Such rhetoric raises some thorny questions. When **Hagee** says "all people will gain entrance into heaven through Christ," he is either advocating universalism (literally all people — Jewish and Gentile — will be saved), or he believes that all Jews will be saved.
In either case, both positions are in serious error, but the latter is more consistent with his other statements. The "timing" of the salvation of the entire Jewish nation is actually irrelevant to **Hagee's** argument since he advocates that it is a waste of time attempting to convert them. At best then, **Hagee** implies that even if they are not currently saved, God will save all Jewish keepers of the Law — past, present, and future — at some future point...

To be saved, a person — whether Jew or Gentile — must turn to Christ (Gal 5:4-6; cf. John 14:6; Acts 4:12; Rom. 10:9-13) who is "the end of the law for righteousness for everyone who believes" (Rom. 10:4). In writing that the "message of the gospel was from Israel, not to Israel," **John Hagee** discourages Christians from sharing the Good News with unsaved Jews who, like everyone else, have need of the gospel if they are to spend eternity with God in heaven.
Salvation for the Jews without them having to "Repent and believe the Gospel of Jesus Christ" (Mark 1:15), and he also sadly promotes the False Teachings of the Word of Faith Prosperity Gospel.
Source: CRI--Christian Research Institute (**NOTE: Several articles about **John Hagee** are on their website; this is one of them. Ed.).

154

rense.com
John Hagee - False Prophet
By Harmony Grant
4-2-8

"Brothers and sisters, I have been wrong," **Hagee** said. Not even a cough was heard from the audience. "I have been wrong about Israel. The state I have spent so much of my life defending is actually indefensible. It persecutes Christians. It violates God's covenant demands for obedience. It was created in sinful brutality." "I led you astray into supporting an evil system that continues to crucify Christ in this world. I repent."

Yes, this is an imagined day. It's a confession of which we can only dream. San Antonio pastor and televangelist **John Hagee** speaks worldwide into 99 million homes. He forged an unprecedented alliance between Israel-loving Christians and Zionist Jews.
His organization, "Christians United for Israel," lobbies for the Jewish state and <u>opposes any land concessions for peace</u>. **Hagee** earns $1.25 million per year from speaking non-Biblical platitudes, urging aggressive foreign policy, and mis-teaching history.

http://www.washingtonspectator.com/._

He is an evangelical with clout. He was on Bush's "values team" during the presidential race in 2000. In 2002, one of his "Night to Honor Israel" events featured Republican majority leader **Tom De Lay**.
 (**NOTE: Here's an interesting excerpt from a website that gives you the affiliations of Mr. **Tom De Lay**, below. Ed.):

"The Committee on National Policy" is a vital link between multi-billion dollar defense contractors, Washington lobbyists like the convicted felon and Republican fundraiser, Jack Abramoff, and the Christian Right. It's at the heart of a new axis between right-wing military politics, support for the Pentagon war agenda globally and the neo-conservative political control of much of US foreign and defense policy.

 The CNP has been at the center of <u>Karl Rove's</u> carefully-constructed <u>Bush</u> political machine. **Tom Delay** and dozens of top <u>Bush Administration Republicans</u> are or have been members of the CNP. Few details about the organization are leaked to the public. As secretive as the Bilderberg Group if not more so, the CNP releases no press statements, meets in secret and never reveals names of its members willingly."
https://deceptionfree.wordpress.com/tag/ruth-heflin/.

 (**NOTE: On this link is dozens of names, not just **Tom De Lay** and **Ruth Heflin**, where the title came from. Ed.).

In 2006, **Hagee** met with Elliot Abrams, America's hotly Zionist deputy national security adviser--a neocon who helped push us to war. **Hagee** has boasted that his powerful

organization has more influence than the famous Jewish lobbying group AIPAC.
http://news.bbc.co.uk/2/hi/americas/5193092.stm

"When a congressman sees someone from AIPAC coming through the door, he knows he represents six million people. We represent 40 million people," the televangelist said. Christian groups like CUFI (Christians United For Israel) were defined by Walt and Mearsheimer as part of the "Israel lobby" in their infamous book. Without evangelical support (and money), the state of Israel would not exist in its present form."
Because of the power and effects of Christian Zionism, **Hagee's** teachings matter to us all. But they especially matter to Christians. As the race to the White House picks up, the pastors of the candidates have come under scrutiny. Obama has faced questions about his America-critical pastor.
Some wonder if McCain should distance himself from his "spiritual guides," **Hagee and Rod Parsley**. All have made their share of inflammatory statements. A bigger question brews here. Should average Christians disavow **Hagee or Parsley**? Should these men rake in millions as purveyors of our faith?

(**NOTE: Yes, that McCain! Ed.)

Hagee Gags the Gospel– John Hagee's 2007 book, "In Defense of Israel," is an easy-to-read and passionate guide to his convictions about the Jewish state. **Hagee** shares heartwarming moments as a child identifying with the birth of Israel. He recounts facing down opposition from both Jews and evangelicals to found "Christians United for Israel" and their "Night to Honor Israel." From the beginning, **Hagee** said, "I set forth an unbendable ground rule: members had to agree to set aside both theological and political agendas and focus on a single issue--support for Israel." "We agreed that all "Night to Honor Israel" events would be non-conversionary" (p 46).

So set aside all political agendas except undiluted support for a foreign nation. Set aside all theological agendas except one mandating Christians to silence the possible voice of the Holy Spirit or conscience (which might prompt them to share the gospel of hope). Bible-believing Christians should already be concerned. Silencing the gospel is the act of persecutors, not Christians.

The Book of Acts describes many times Jewish leaders commanded early Christians not to preach. Once Peter and John were ordered by powerful Jews to stop speaking about Jesus. They replied, "Judge for yourselves whether it is right in God's sight to obey you rather than God. For we cannot help speaking about what we have seen and heard" (Acts 4:19, 20). Early believers chose imprisonment and even death over silence.

John Hagee has forsaken a prime duty of Christians-to speak truth at God's leading--and shelved the Gospel in pursuit of political and social goals. He believes supporting the Zionist nation of Israel is "more important than seeking to save Jews' eternal souls."
There's a theological reason for this. **Hagee** isn't deeply concerned about Jewish repentance or obedience.

He holds a strongly Calvinist theology that teaches humanity's inescapable sinfulness and God's unconditional mercy. He writes of the Hebrew covenant with God—"These covenants are not based on man's faithfulness to God; they are based on God's faithfulness to man." (p. 54).

How does he back up this statement? With a relatively personal rationale: "If God broke covenant with the Jewish people, what scriptural justification do Christians have that he will not break covenant with us?" (p 54).
He inadvertently makes a good point. There isn't any Scriptural justification for believing God won't break covenant with us if we rebel!
Many Israel-first evangelicals are passionate about God's "faithfulness" to unrepentant Israel because it supports their belief that He will be "faithful" to them whether or not they sin. This is blasphemy.

The Scripture is interwoven and held together by God's insistence on human cooperation with His grace. Our Holy God honors His covenant when He withholds blessing from those who willfully and persistently rebel. Did **John Hagee** miss Deuteronomy— which threatens Israel that God will perpetually curse them in all aspects of their lives if they disobey Him? In my Bible, that's a pretty big section. But **Hagee** has every material incentive not to convert Jews. (I'm guessing the threat of eternal hell doesn't loom very big in his mind). His fat paycheck and cushy ministry would be cut off quickly if he criticized or sought to convert the "chosen people."
The New York Times recently ran a full-page ad from the "Worldwide Evangelical Alliance," signed by 44 Christian leaders. The ad defends evangelism of Jews and the ministries of "Jews for Jesus" and other messianic organizations seeking to "introduce individuals to the Messiah." The ad was promptly denounced and vilified by the powerful "Anti-Defamation League" of B'nai B'rith. Its head, Abe Foxman, didn't use merely political language to attack the ad.

He used Christian Zionist arguments– http://www.adl.org/PresRele/ChJew_31/5263_31.htm, claiming the ad is "offensive and insulting to the Jewish people and brazenly dismisses Jewish self-definition." Why?
Because it doesn't validate "God's irrevocable covenant with the Jewish people, and ongoing Jewish covenantal life, themes also found in their Scripture." This language comes straight from **John Hagee** and his ilk. His ideas are being used by Jewish antagonists to silence Christian evangelists. **John Hagee** will have a lot for which to answer, that's sure.

Stoning Stephen: Adding to Jewish Anti-Christianity: **Hagee** has made himself popular with some Jews by blaming Christians. http://www.jewsonfirst.org/08a/hagee_wise.html.

This interview from the evangelical-leery website "Jews on First" is mostly hostile to **Hagee**-- but appreciates that he at least accepts blame for anti-Semitism. "Jews on First" writer Robin Podolsky also appreciates **Hagee's** definition of Jesus as a "Reform rabbi." This is a frequent refrain. In his http://www.scoop.co.nz/stories/HL0803/S00365.htm

Easter sermon, while wearing a blue and white prayer shawl, **Hagee** boomed about Jesus, "You saw him leave personally as a Jewish rabbi. He's coming back as a Jewish rabbi." **Hagee** says Christianity could not exist without Judaism, yet Jews have had to suffer the intolerance of Christians for millennia.

Flatly, he states, "anti-Semitism has its origin and its complete root structure in Christianity, dating from the early days of the Christian church." "Until we come to terms with the true origins of anti-Semitism, we will not be able to correctly address this most egregious of sins" (17) (emphasis added).

Here, **Hagee** goes even farther than many Jews, who similarly deny any fault in Jewish actions but usually at least blame Gentiles in general for their irrational hatred.

Not **Hagee**. He blames Christianity for creating anti-Semitism in the beginning.

He also blames the church for Nazism. He attributes Hitler's ideas to Catholicism, writing that "Hitler, the most notable example of anti-Semitism in the twentieth century, simply enforced policies that had been approved by the church over the course of history and that remained the official policy of the church when the Nazi party came to power." **Hagee's** beliefs about earlier history are similarly unsympathetic to the faith he claims to hold.

He says the physical separation of Jews and Christians—when Christian Gentiles fled from Rome—formed the basis of antipathy.

"The physical separation of the two groups would prove to be permanent and would form the basis of the strained relationship between them" (19). He says the Gentiles fled because Jesus had warned them to flee to the mountains when they heard "wars and rumors of wars," and the Jews felt betrayed. That created animosity.

But hang on, **Hagee** attributes all the millennia of animosity to Christians and as coming from the Christians' side. It's hard to see how Jews' hurt feelings could have created a strain, since Jews share no blame for the "strained relationship." Modern anti-Semitism is, of course, a huge concern for the Texas pastor. He has publicly called for war with Iran and also raises Cain about "Christian anti-Semites"—meaning, believers who take seriously Christ's warnings to beware of the "synagogue of Satan."

Speaking of "replacement theologians" (with whom I also largely disagree) **Hagee** says, "Some pastors teach that Romans 9-11 refers to the church." **Hagee** writes, "that the church has become a "spiritual Israel" and has replaced the Jewish people. "This is an anti-Semitic theology that refuses to believe God still has a place in his heart for Israel and the Jewish people" (52).

"No Such Thing as a Palestinian": If that's anti-Semitic, what do you call **Hagee's** theology—which writes off a whole race of Semitic people?

Of the Promised Land's indigenous people, **Hagee** writes:

"The land of Israel never belonged to the Palestinians; there has never been a land called Palestine. There is no Palestinian language." "Before 1948, the people now called Palestinians lived in Egypt. They lived in Syria. They lived in Iraq." " They moved into the land of Israel when they were displaced by the war of 1948, which the Arab nations started, but Israel is not occupying territory these people now call home" (58).

What planet has **Hagee** been living on? The existence of at least 900,000 Palestinian Arabs in Palestine during the last century is an unquestioned fact of Mid-East history.

So is the fact that Israel's terror began with the Jewish massacre of 250 Arab men, women, and children at Deir Yassin in 1948 and drove more than 800,000 Palestinians out of Israel. This is what we call falsehood. Israel's "new historians"--themselves mostly Jewish!--exploded the Zionist/**Hagee** lie that there were no Palestinians before 1948.

Just this week the http://www.thejewishadvocate.com/ "Jewish Advocate" online published a column by Jewish writer Hannah Mermelstein calling for recognition of the catastrophe committed against the Palestinians. She writes that "more than 6 million Palestinian people remain refugees to this day all forbidden from returning to their homeland for one reason: they are not Jewish in name, and in the name of Jewish people throughout the world, an indigenous population was almost completely expelled." "Village names have been removed from the map, houses blown up." This is the truth, but—and as a Christian I find this hard to write—there seems to be more honest Jews than honest evangelicals.

Endnotes:

1. II Kings 18:4--Calvinism's false assurance was described by Jeremiah, when he spoke with God– "...Behold, the prophets say unto them, Ye shall not see the sword, neither shall ye have famine; but I will give you assured peace in this place." Then the Lord said unto me, "The prophets prophesy lies in my name. I sent them not, neither have I commanded them, neither spake unto them: they prophesy unto you a false vision and divination, and a thing of nought, and the deceit of their heart." Jeremiah 14:13-14.
The prophets of whom Jeremiah spoke were promising the Israelites peace in Canaan, even though they were in disobedience. Likewise, modern evangelists promise salvation, even without continuous trust and obedience to God. Such assurances are groundless and grievously destructive. "Hearken not to the words of the prophets that prophesy unto you: They make you vain: they speak a vision of their own heart, and not from the mouth of the LORD."

"They say still unto them that despise me, The LORD hath said, Ye shall have peace; And they say unto every one that walketh after the imagination of his own heart, No evil shall come upon you." Jeremiah 23:16-17.

These words were spoken by the Lord to his prophet Jeremiah thousands of years ago, yet they apply with deadly accuracy to modern evangelists who promise eternal security to all who once believed on Christ, including those now disobedient.

2. Far from an example of God's unconditional love, God's relationship with Israel actually proves His insistence on obedience. The Old Testament is riddled with demands for Hebrew obedience. Without obedience, the Jews cannot receive God's Words or spiritual blessing.

Please see: Ex. 15:26, 19:5; Lev. 26; Num. 32:15;

Deut. 4:29, 6:24-25, 7:9-15, 11:13-15, 11:26-28, 13:17-18, 15:4-5, 19:8-9, 28:1-68, 30:9-20, 31:16-17;
Josh. 24:19-20; I Sam. 2:30, 7:3, 12:14-15, 12:20-25;

I Kings 3:14, 6:12-13, 8:46-52, 9:4-9, 11:38; II Kings 18:11-12, 21:8;

I Chron. 28:9; II Chron. 7:17-22, 15:2, 30:9; Ezra 8:22; Neh. 1:8-9; Isa. 1:19-20, 1:28, 7:9, 58:9-14, 65:11;
Jer. 4:1-4, 7:5-7, 12:16-17, 13:22, 15:19, 17:24-25, 18:7-10, 22:4-5, 26:3-6, 38:17-18, 42:10-16;
Ezek. 18, 33:12-19; Hos. 5:4-5, 5:14, 7:13, 9:15-17, 10:13-15, 13:2-8;
Amos 4:1-2, 5:6, 9:10; Obad. 1:10; Micah 2:2-4, 3:4, 6:9-16; Nahum 1:2-8, Zech. 3:7, 7:11-14... (This list is not exhaustive).

Other references: https://rense.com/general81/haggee.htm

https://americanvision.org/12510/john-hagee

https://www.jesus-is-savior.com/False%20Doctrines/john_hagees
https://carm.org/john-hagee

Teaches blood moon prophecy and the leader of Christian Zionists.
http://www.youtube.com/watch?v=wzgmeO6mQio

http://www.youtube.com/watch?v=E3IKtguTYus

- **Ted Haggard**: "New Life Church;" involved in a sex scandal; was known to use "crystal meth"; his beliefs slant towards "gay tendencies;" He identifies as being bisexual; NAR.

- **Kenneth Hagin, Sr.**: Deceased; WOF; "seed of faith"; "positive confession movement"; "Redemption is not through the Blood of Jesus, but by Satan's torture of Christ three days and nights in hell." http://www.thebereancall.com);

Kenneth Hagin is well known for sharing about how God killed some folks who spoke against him. https://discernmentministriesinternational.wordpress.com/

Kenneth E. Hagin, (Jr.): " The believer is as much an incarnation of God as Jesus Christ ... If we ever wake up and realize who we are, we'll start doing the work that we're supposed to do. Because the church hasn't realized yet that they are Christ."

(**NOTE: The balance of this article can be found here. Ed.):

http://www.zedekiahlist.com/ cgi-bin/results.pl?&menuid=V&itemid=F

(**NOTE: There are a lot of You Tube videos showing how demonic he is. There is no one in the Bible that walks and "hisses" while doing so. He is a very dangerous person and should not be taken lightly. Ed.).

"We (the church) are Christ." **Kenneth Hagin**, "As Christ is — So are we," Tape #44H06). The Christian "is as much an incarnation as was Jesus of Nazareth." (**Kenneth Hagin**, "The Incarnation," THE WORD OF FAITH (Dec. 1980), 14.)

"Man is a spirit who possesses a soul and lives in a body...., He is in the same class with God. ...We know that God is a Spirit. And yet [He] took upon Himself a man's body....when God took upon Himself human form, He was no less God than when He didn't have a body. Man, at physical death, leaves his as he was when he had his body."

(**Kenneth Hagin**, "Man of Three Dimensions " [Tulsa: Faith Library, 1973]

"[Man] was created on terms of equality with God, and he could stand in God's presence without any consciousness of inferiority...God made us as much like Himself as possible...He made us the same class of being that He is Himself...Man lived in the realm of God. He lived on terms equal with God...[The] believer is called Christ...That's who we are; we're Christ."

Kenneth Hagin, "Zoe: The God-Kind of Life," 1989. pp. 35-36, 41).
https://ucministries.wordpress.com/ tag/dr-hobart-freeman/

(**NOTE: The link speaks of **Dr. Hobart Freeman**, but there are several other "wolves" in this link, hence my including it here. It also includes **Kenneth Hagin, Jr**. Ed.).

The Word of Faith movement grew out of the Pentecostal movement in the late 20th century. Its founder was **E. W. Kenyon**, who studied the metaphysical New Thought teachings of **Phineas Quimby**. Mind science (where "name it and claim it" originated) was combined with Pentecostalism, resulting in a peculiar mix of orthodox Christianity and mysticism.

Kenneth Hagin, in turn, studied under **E. W. Kenyon** and made the Word of Faith movement what it is today. Although individual teachings range from completely heretical to completely ridiculous, what follows is the basic theology most Word of Faith teachers align themselves with. At the heart of the Word of Faith movement is the belief in the "force of faith."

It is believed words can be used to manipulate the faith-force, and thus actually create what they believe Scripture promises (health and wealth). Laws supposedly governing the faith-force are said to operate independently of God's sovereign will and that God Himself is subject to these laws. This is nothing short of idolatry, turning our faith—and by extension ourselves—into god. From here, its theology just strays further and further from Scripture: it claims that God created human beings in His literal, physical image as little gods.

(**NOTE: Another famous Word of Faith heretical preacher who actually says we are all "little gods" is **Kenneth Copeland**. Please see my information on him, under his name. Ed.).

Before the fall, humans had the potential to call things into existence by using the faith-force. After the fall, humans took on Satan's nature and lost the ability to call things into existence. In order to correct this situation, Jesus Christ gave up His divinity and became a man, died spiritually, took Satan's nature upon Himself, went to hell, was born again, and rose from the dead with God's nature.
After this, Jesus sent the Holy Spirit to replicate the Incarnation in believers so they could become little gods as God had originally intended.

Following the natural progression of these teachings, as little gods we again have the ability to manipulate the faith-force and become prosperous in all areas of life. Illness, sin, and failure are the result of a lack of faith, and are remedied by confession—claiming God's promises for oneself into existence.
Simply put, the Word of Faith movement exalts man to god-status and reduces God to man-status. Needless to say, this is a false representation of what Christianity is all about. Obviously, Word of Faith teaching does not take into account what is found in Scripture. Personal revelation, not Scripture, is highly relied upon in order to come up with such absurd beliefs, which is just one more proof of its heretical nature. Countering Word of Faith teaching is a simple matter of reading the Bible.

God alone is the Sovereign Creator of the Universe (Genesis 1:3; 1 Timothy 6:15) and does not need faith—He is the object of faith (Mark 11:22; Hebrews 11:3).

God is spirit and does not have a physical body (John 4:24). Man was created in the image of God (Genesis 1:26, 27; 9:6), but this does not make him a little god or divine.

Only God has a divine nature (Galatians 4:8; Isaiah 1:6-11, 43:10, 44:6; Ezekiel 28:2; Psalm 8:6-8). Christ is Eternal, the Only Begotten Son, and the only incarnation of God (John 1:1, 2, 14, 15, 18; 3:16; 1 John 4:1).

In Him dwelt the fullness of the Godhead bodily (Colossians 2:9). By becoming a man, Jesus gave up the glory of heaven but not His divinity (Philippians 2:6-7), though He did choose to withhold His power while walking the earth as man.
https://www.gotquestions.org/Word-Faith.html

The Word of Faith movement is deceiving countless people, causing them to grasp after a way of life and faith that is not Biblical. At its core is the same lie Satan has been telling since the Garden: "You shall be as God" (Genesis 3:5).
Sadly, those who buy into the Word of Faith movement are still listening to him. Our hope is in the Lord, not in our own words, not even in our own faith (Psalm 33:20-22). Our faith comes from God in the first place (Ephesians 2:8; Hebrews 12:2) and is not something we create for ourselves. So, be wary of the Word of Faith movement and any church that aligns itself with Word of Faith teachings.
Kenneth Hagin must undoubtably be the father of the modern Word of Faith movement. His teachings form the foundation of what we now see as the movement. But where did he get his theology? In 1983, two students at **Oral Roberts University** alleged that the bulk of **Hagin's** theological teachings were lifted verbatim from the writings of other authors.

D.R. McConnell, who wrote his Master's thesis about the <u>Word of Faith</u> movement, alleged that **Hagin** had <u>plagiarized</u> the writings of evangelist **E.W. Kenyon**, teaching not only the ideas of **Kenyon** but also lifting text word-for-word from many of **Kenyon's** eighteen published works. You can examine the alleged plagiarism for yourself here:

http://www.intotruth.org/wof/ kenyon.html   (you be the judge).

https://urbantruthnetwork.wordpress.com/2014/11/29/ who-are-todays-cult-leaders/

- **Leslie Hale**: **Hale's** career as an independent evangelist began in 1961 when he resigned from his job as a clerk in a bakery, hired a tent and advertised his gospel services in a local newspaper. He was immediately memorable and distinctive with his American drawl, loose, informal and enthusiastic delivery, and his message. He preached the material benefits of salvation.
 Borrowing the theology wholesale from the Oklahoma evangelist **Oral Roberts, Hale** told his listeners that they could share the benefits of "seed faith."
In his religion, God's grace was translated into a slot machine. You put in so much, pulled the lever of prayer and God paid out tenfold. Nothing unique in that; all religions offer rewards in this life as well as the next, but Protestants' traditional conception of the rewards of religion involves notions of intangible improvements in one's personal and social life.

The **Roberts/Hale** "seed faith" gave a particularly concrete and financial color to all the Biblical propositions about casting one's bread upon the water. **Hale** gathered a Belfast congregation, a following in Moira, had a couple doing 'missionary work' in Dublin, and drew reasonable numbers for his Sunday evening meetings in Belfast's Ulster Hall.
 The media seemed willing to promote **Hale's** self-image as a dynamic evangelist.

Given the prominence which material rewards held in **Hale's** own preaching, it is not surprising that much media coverage focused on his own prosperous life style and the collections raised at his meetings. What is often missed though, was the willingness of the media to naively report **Hale's** own claims about his success. The desire for a good news story seems to have blunted any desire to investigate these claims.
 If **Hale's** rise was inadvertently, JJ assisted by a gullible media willing to represent the image **Hale** had of himself, his fall can also be put down to the media, although this time the influence was indirect. **Hale** was trying to repeat in Ulster what **Oral Roberts** (who now has, in addition to his prime time TV and radio shows, a large university and a hospital of his own) had pulled off in the States.

(**NOTE: Most people are aware that **Oral Roberts** University and hospital are long ago closed down, however the author of this article wrote it before that took place. Ed.).

Taking his product first, his message and style were all wrong for Ulster. The overt materialism of 'seed faith' may have big appeal in a healthy, thriving economy where people intuitively feel that hard work and ambition will produce the goods. America has a solid tradition of playing up the material benefits of the Christian faith, but in Ulster such preaching seems improper.
The style also jarred.

163

(**Ian**) **Paisley** has consistently played to the tradition of Ulster Presbyterianism. He is almost incapable of preaching for two minutes without mentioning **Knox, Calvin, Spurgeon** and **Cooke** (always leaving the audience to make the final link and identify **Paisley** as the heir to this rich tradition). His services follow classic Presbyterian lines and he wears the clerical garb of a nineteenth century minister. While **Paisley** has borrowed some elements of his religion from his fundamentalist friends in America, he is at pains to disguise such innovation. The claim he makes in what he says and in the symbols he uses is that he is simply the latest in an honorable and trusted tradition. In contrast **Hale** was a self-conscious innovator.

The hopping, hand-clapping, hugging your neighbor, praising the Lord, amening and allelujahing that **Hale** gave his people— a watered down version of the Black church service in the States—is offensive to the deeply conservative Protestants of Ulster and although it can be found in some of the very small Pentecostalist halls, it has not caught on in a culture in which almost everything is judged by how well it fits with, and supports, a tradition.

If in America you get bitten by a desire to become a preacher you raise somehow a small sum of money and buy a fifteen minute slot on your local radio station. If those who hear you like your style and appreciate your message then they will send in donations. You can raise a few extra bucks by selling your listeners religious gimmicks and knick-knacks, bringing in enough money for more air-time. Provided you have the talent and ambition, the openness of US radio and TV—the fact that almost anyone can buy time—allows you to reach vast audiences.

Hale, because he could not buy radio and TV to reach a mass audience, could only recruit those who were prepared to actually turn-up and see him, and this brings up his other problem. America has never had an established state church and there are few strong ties to any particular denomination. It is much more free enterprise. The believer is a consumer who checks out the available products. Although Ulster has a variety of denominations, the Presbyterian Church has numerical superiority and it has a parish system.
Although there may be some Sunday "commuting" to a favored church, many people simply attend their local parish church.

To continue with the soap powder imagery, **Hale** could not recruit a mass following because most of his potential market did not see themselves as free consumers, able to experiment with new brands; they were heavily loyal to their old traditional brand. Without access to the media, **Hale** needed bodies in the shop and his product was not sufficiently attractive to a large enough number of people in what is, after all, a very small and, compared to the United States, poor market. Opinions about the motivation of **Hale** will continue to be deeply divided.
For his dwindling band of followers he is still a man of God and he will lead them on to better days. For them his move to the States is a temporary fund-raising exercise.
To others **Hale** is perhaps. a charlatan who has got his just desserts. No matter.
The nature of the culture, the importance of traditional loyalties, and the closed nature of the media meant that a career pattern that is common in America could only have succeeded here if **Hale** had been supported by what he always claimed he had: Miracles! https://magill.ie/

-**Franklin Hall**: Deceased; NAR; Latter Rain proponent **Franklin Hall** (who made famous the " fire baptism") wrote a book on fasting and prayer which was a major influence for the Latter Rain movement and in the ministry of **Oral Roberts.**

Rev. Walter Frederick, former Assembly superintendent in Canada, sent **Brother Hall's** literature to every Pentecostal preacher in Canada...A few of the others (not too well-known then) ministers who had major fasting experiences by our writings in the 1946, 1947 to 1950 fasting era and who also became famous are:

Wm. Freeman, Gordon Lindsay, A.A. Allen, O.L. Jagger, Gayle Jackson, Oral Roberts, David Nunn, Wm. Branham, W.V. Grant, Wm. Hagen, Dale Hanson, [and] Tommy Hicks.

Franklin Hall: "Miracle Word" (Phoenix, AZ: "Hall Deliverance Foundation," Summer,1985, p.9);

Franklin Hall was one of the main people that influenced this heretical sect with his work "Atomic Power with God, Through Fasting and Prayer."
 In the online iHOP "Forerunner" bookstore, they state that **Franklin Hall's** book is, "highly recommended by **Todd White**."
From our research, **Franklin Hall** seemed to be the originator of this idea of the "manchild company," "Manifest Sons of God'," "Little gods" heresy' that will accompany the end-times church. https://churchwatchcentral.com.

- **Frank Hammond**: Believer\promoter in the Prophetic Movement, a.k.a. the "School of the Prophets".

- **Hank Hanegraaff**: and CRI (The "Bible Answer Man") doesn't really have the answers!; left the Evangelical teaching and went to the Eastern Orthodox church.

- **Bill Hamon:** False prophet, leader in the prophetic movement, false teacher, NAR, IHOP. Associated with most, if not all, of the "prophets" today.
(Plenty of information on him on the internet, including videos. Ed.).

- **Christian Harfouche**: Uses motivational speaking methods with Christian terms, concepts and scripture out of context to get people excited in their soul. One must check their Bible carefully to see the accuracy of what is being said.
Harfouche: Lay hands on yourself. Say, "I have within me through the indwelling of the Holy Spirit and the Word of God every provision necessary to fulfill my destiny in God. I am not afraid of transitional times. They are necessary to lead me to my destiny.
They are necessary to lead me to my miracle." (website).

 Lay hands on yourself? Really. Where's that in the Bible? Are you going to authorize yourself, energize yourself, or heal yourself? In our first article the news (KITV) interviewed him about his healing services where he stated "I believe the Lord has put in us as humans in our physical bodies the ability to heal ourselves." Man has the ability to heal oneself is a red flag to me and

it should be to anyone familiar with the Bible. **Harfouche** also teaches, "You now have both the Holy Spirit and the blood of Christ flowing within you."
(Course III GOD MAN- year one curriculum- IMI CORRESPONDENCE PROGRAM).

Excuse me ... the blood of Christ is in you? I have heard people pray for it to be applied but in you, like the Holy Spirit is in you? Bible verse—none. Sounds Catholic.
Harfouche has package wrapped word faith confession for possession, prophetic declarations, Latter Rain / Manifest Sons of God teachings and other fringe concepts that are not Biblical into his sermons, teachings and practices.
 Even when he speaks correctly on subjects, he expands them into unbiblical areas. "The power of the God kind of faith can never fail."

(** NOTE: **Haginism**. Ed.).

"Faith is a supernatural holy force. Faith is a spirit that is so holy and righteous.... When you have been gassed by God – then you come to life. You step to another level, because when the germination of the Almighty starts working on the inside of you there is no death, there is no sickness, there is no poverty, there is no power of sin or the enemy that can be active in your life." "Faith cannot be penetrated by an invading force, because faith is a Spirit."

Speaking of the God kind of faith, "have it and move, mountains, have it and have everything obey you..." I don't think this needs to be thoroughly explained. He used a Biblical concept and ends up in a very unbiblical interpretation. "God kind of faith;"
God does not have faith. Faith is putting trust in something greater than oneself, who would God trust? Is faith a spirit? Is faith a force? To tell people you become sinless, immune to the enemy. That "there is no death." Where is any of this promised in the Bible for today? Besides the statement of being "gassed" by God -- that certainly does not sound good.

Another case in point—his teaching on the Incarnation "He did not become a man to stay the only man that could do what he did when he was a man... he did not become human to stay the only one like himself." "He became (yelling) human to give us his ability to resemble him in one measure or another so that when people see us they'll say they have been with Jesus, (not by raising your voice like this, Jesus didn't.)

 "He became a man and walked around dependent upon the heavenly Father so that the anointing would work through him and when he did what no man could do, he didn't do it because of his divinity or his ability only,... he did it because of the anointing he was gaining in order to start something." "Jesus started something that he is calling you to help finish, thank you very much."

"...Somebody said well **Dr. Harfouche**, it is finished. Yes, Yes it is finished and he is sitting down waiting till all his enemies to be made his footstool."
What is he saying, implying, is that it is up to the church to take down his enemies. Jesus started it and we finish it. This is Manifest Sons of God teaching, and as a Dominionist and it is bleached through his sermons.

So Jesus needed the anointing to do what he did even though he was God? He takes this even further, "... The anointing can create something out of nothing. Even Jesus had to wait for the anointing. Jesus never did any miracles or confronted the enemy without the anointing." (Course V ANOINTING, IMI).

The anointing did not come and go with Jesus, it says the Spirit rested upon him (Jn.1:32-33); this theology **Harfouche** is presenting of Jesus needing the anointing to come to him (the Spirit) is incorrect. It presents Jesus as an ordinary human so that we too can do what he did, by the Spirit. **Harfouche** then goes into the book of Acts about receiving power.

Again, power for what? To do miracles, what else. The Bible says it is for being witnesses (martyrs): Acts 1:8 "But you shall receive power when the Holy Spirit has come upon you; and you shall be witnesses to Me in Jerusalem, and in all Judea and Samaria, and to the end of the earth."
The power is for us to speak boldly about the Gospel, to stand in the face of being a martyr. Jesus did not say here we were given power to do the exact same miracles he did (or greater). We are not duplicates. What he did say is signs and wonders would FOLLOW the preaching of the Word, but it did not occur all the time, even with the apostles. Jesus also warned about false prophets that will rise and show great signs and wonders to deceive the ELECT (Matt 24:24). So how does one know who is who? By their doctrine.

Harfouche: ".... As a matter of fact, Jesus says that we will do even greater work than He, because He goes to His Father on our behalf. Then he tells us that we have the authority to use His name." (Course V ANOINTING IMI). Greater works, not greater miracles, or greater signs and wonders.
No apostle did a greater miracle than Jesus, yet he tells them they can? The Apostles did not "feed the 5,000" or "still a storm" or "walk on water" or "appear and disappear at will." The Apostles who were personally trained by Jesus were unable to exhibit all the power Jesus did (Acts 27:9-44).
 No one should buy into the modern Latter Rain message that originated from **William Branham**, that they can do the same, or greater miracles than Jesus. It's not based on the proper interpretation of Scripture.

 http://www.letusreason.org/Popteach88.htm
 (**NOTE: This article is quite lengthy. Go on the website to read the balance. Ed.).

https://www.thepathoftruth.com/false-teachers/ christian-and-robin-harfouche.html

- **Jen Hatmaker**: There is no question that **Jen Hatmaker**, "evangelical wunderkind who is a one-woman columnist, book-writing machine, conference speaker and all-around mom of five kids and pastor's wife," is trying to change minds about what the Scriptures teach on many hot button social issues. As we've pointed out before, she follows the same basic playbook as "Progressive (Social Justice) "Christians" such as **Rob Bell**.

We've posted numerous articles to show you that **Jen** has both feet firmly planted in "Religious Left ideology." When she and husband, **Brandon**, came out in support of the LGBTQ+

community a few years ago, they were well aware that their statement would cause a big brouhaha in the evangelical community. Why? Because in so doing the couple chose to **deny** the Biblical teaching on marriage, sexuality and family. That was then. This is now.

Today **JD Hall** reports that "**Hatmaker** posted a long-winded status on Facebook that claims 'Jesus came to affirm the LGBT community, as well as to accomplish other leftist agenda items." Which Bible has the pastor's wife been reading? **Hall** has more on **Jen Hatmaker's** disturbing tweet over at Pulpit & Pen: When Pulpit & Pen first warned about **Jen Hatmaker**, she was still one of Lifeway's (bookstore) best-selling authors.

Eventually, she crossed the threshold into heresy such that not even Lifeway could tolerate (and that's saying something !). **Hatmaker**, a popular mommy-blogger and pseudo-Christian teacher came out in support of the sin of sodomy in 2016, and Lifeway subsequently stopped selling her anti-Biblical material.

Since then, **Hatmaker** has received even greater stardom and fame, being a constant figure on the leftist speaking circuit, propelling herself forward as a champion of "LGBT inclusivism" and speaking out against "patriarchy." Recently, **Hatmaker** tweeted that she wanted to be baptized an Episcopalian by a pro-gay bishop and her (still) good friend and compatriot, **Beth Moore**, 'liked' her tweet. Recently she accepted her daughter's "coming out."
Hatmaker's affirmation of sodomy came not long after "Obergfell vs Hodges," indicating that the dictates of the United States judiciary are what truly inform her moral resolve.
 She was immediately championed by the evangelical left for her bravery. Today, **Hatmaker** posted a long-winded status on Facebook that claims Jesus came to affirm the LGBT community, as well as to accomplish other leftist agenda items. "As a leader and author, pastor and teacher, let me just be positively clear where I stand on a few things."
" In the most outrageous twilight zone ever, these issues have now become "partisan" but to me, these are purely a matter of my faith which compels me." " I will always champion a working faith ethic that:"

"Condemns the pervasive, patriarchal power structures that keep women silenced, underpaid, under-represented, exploited, denigrated, shamed, and abused;" "Names, repents from, resists, and actively fights white supremacy in all its forms, structures, systems, language, and evil practices."

God set up a patriarchal power struggle, with an all-male leadership of Israel's tribes and an all-male roster of disciples, Apostles and elders. That aside, it's good to oppose "white supremacy" when and where it actually exists. One wonders who exactly she's talking about. It might also be worth asking if other kinds of supremacy are okay. "The thing is, this is the only way I understand the Gospel." "I cannot come to any other conclusion than this path laid out for us by Jesus." "Anything other than a radically inclusive faith that honors the dignity of every person makes no sense to me."

"I can't find any other road through my faith than one that condemns patriarchy, misogyny, sexism, racism, homophobia, ableism, abuse, and white supremacy. NOTHING ELSE MAKES SENSE. This is who Jesus is and what He came to do."

Affirming the "LGBT Community" is the only way **Jen Hatmaker** can understand the Gospel. Regardless of what else **Jen Hatmaker** may in fact understand, the Biblical Gospel is not on that list. You see, Christianity is not an "inclusive faith." It is an "exclusive faith," built upon the Doctrine of the Exclusivity of Christ.

God will one day exclude from His kingdom the sexually immoral, idolaters, adulterers, and those who practice homosexuality (I Corinthians 6:9-10). And while "misogyny, sexism, racism, ableism," and all kinds of racial supremacy are wrong and unloving to our neighbor, it is clear that **Hatmaker** doesn't understand the Gospel at all.
Of course the Law includes the Second Table (loving our neighbor), but it is not the Gospel.

And by the way, affirming people in their sin and thus facilitating their eternal perdition is not loving. It is extremely extremely hateful. https://pulpitandpen.org/2018
https://bereanresearch.org

It is worth noting that recently her own daughter came out as LGBTQ.

- **Jack Hayford**: Hyper-Charismatic; sometimes he works with **Jennifer LeClaire**, which is another proponent of NAR. He also works with **Kari Jobes**, a "worship leader" whose obvious popularity is from the NAR. https://www.charismanews.com/us/45585-jack-hayford-hands-israel-christian-nexus-baton-to-robert-stearns

(**NOTE: The article is about **Robert Stearns**, but also has information on **Jack Hayford**. Notice that this is derived from "Charisma News," a Charismatic New Age magazine. I am including it for your reference. Ed.).

- **Bob Hazlett**: Is described on his own website as "a proven prophetic voice. His teaching and prophetic ministry has been featured on GodTV, TBN, Daystar and Bethel TV.

Bob Hazlett is a friend to leaders and a sought-after speaker and author. "Strong healing and prophetic gifts follow his ministry." http://fitl.co.za/2018/06/21/the-acceleration-of-the-new-apostolic-reformations-influence-in-south-africa

- **Ruth Heflin**: Deceased; Promoter of the "gold dust" heresy, right along with her friend, **Benny Hinn**. Took part in the "Brownsville Revival;" You Tube has the following video available:
https://www.youtube.com/watch?v=C9BxERv4k0s

(**NOTE:..And many more, so you can see the false preacher for yourself and have your eyes opened to false preaching and false prophecies. Ed.).

Quite a few articles are on the Web regarding **Ms. Heflin**. These are two of many:
http://www.deceptioninthechurch.com/heflin.html

https://deceptionfree.wordpress.com/tag/ruth-heflin/

Known for her revival meetings marked by <u>gold dust</u>, **Heflin** underwent surgery April 25 but refused further treatment. **Ruth Ward Heflin,** considered by many to be a matriarch of Pentecostal faith, died at age 60 on Sept. 15, just a few months after she discovered she had cancer. During her nearly 40 years of ministry, **Heflin's** burden for Israel and for evangelism and discipleship took her around the world.

Heflin also was the founder and director of "Mount Zion Fellowship," an international prayer ministry in Jerusalem, where she lived for more than 25 years before returning to the United States. Her brother **Wallace Heflin, Jr.'s** death in 1997 prompted her return to the states to assume his job as director of Calvary Pentecostal Tabernacle (CPT), a church and campground in Ashland, Va., some 25 miles north of Richmond.

The camp, founded by parents **Wallace Heflin, Sr.** and **Edith Heflin** in the 1950s, continues to draw thousands of people to church services and conferences. Jane Lowder, who has served in **Heflin's** ministry for 25 years, has been named the new director at CPT. **Heflin** suffered a broken ankle in an automobile accident last year. In April doctors diagnosed her with breast cancer that already had spread into her bones. **Heflin** underwent a mastectomy on April 25, but refused chemotherapy or further cancer treatment because she said the Lord told her to refuse, according to Connie Wilson, her personal assistant.

Rumors that **Heflin's** beliefs influenced her decision not to seek treatment, and rumors that she refused treatment under pressure from critics within her ministry who allegedly oppose medical treatment, are completely unfounded, Lowder said.

"If she received criticism for her treatment, I have never heard it," Lowder said. "We were all standing in faith, believing for her healing, but we were all happy that she went to the doctor." "I have never heard Sister **Ruth** discourage anyone from going to the doctor."

A descendant of 18th-century revivalist Jonathan Edwards, **Heflin** recently has been a central figure in the so-called <u>gold dust revival.</u>

People who attended her camp meetings said they saw <u>gold dust </u>appear on their faces and hands, and some reported that God put gold fillings in their teeth. Some said they even saw diamonds, rubies or feathers appear.

Although she had expressed wishes that people not be informed about her cancer, many of her supporters had heard the news and were praying for her healing. Last July—just a little more than two months after her mastectomy—**Heflin** preached at the opening service of the annual camp meeting. "I wanted to preach on opening night to give the old devil a black eye," she said.

https://www.charismamag.com/site-archives/134-peopleevents/people-events/181-ruth-ward-heflin-revivalist-and-prayer-minister-dies-of-cancer-at-60.

(**NOTE: "Charisma" magazine has strayed far off course from the truth, promoting dozens of heretics, but this article is showing her obituary in their "Christian" circles. They also state that she is a direct descendent of Jonathan Edwards; that has never been proven. Ed.).

Ruth Ward Heflin Calvary Pentecostal Campground, Ashland, VA Died 15th September 2000. The Lord spoke to her audibly and said, that He is going to appear physically in one of our crusades in the next few months. Yeah, She... "I'm telling ya,.. she said, the Lord spoke to her audibly and said, tell **Benny [Hinn]** I'm going to appear..."

(**NOTE: the balance of this report is on this website. Ed.):
http://www.zedekiahlist.com/ cgi-bin/results.pl?&menuid=V&itemid=F

- **Joel Hemphill**: Denying the deity of Christ and the Holy Trinity at the following six anti-Deity of Christ sites: http://www.abc-coggc.org/books.html

 http://www.christianmonotheism.com **Joel Hemphill's** book "To God Be The Glory," is full of attacks on our Lord's Deity, and the Holy Trinity as you know.
 All one needs to do is read these attacks from his site at: http://www.trumpetcallbooks.com.

The Jesus of **Joel W. Hemphill**, gospel artist, eight time "Dove Award" winner, member of the "Southern Gospel Music Hall of Fame," is not the Jesus of Holy Scripture, the Early Church, nor the Christian Church today. His denial of the deity of Jesus Christ, and the Holy Trinity should be exposed for what it is: UNBIBLICAL AND UNORTHODOX
http://www.kingdomready.org/topics/god-old.php

This site has over one hundred tapes, videos, and pamphlets attacking the deity of Christ. His book "To God Be The Glory " is listed at:
http://www.kingdomready.org/blog/2010/01/13/.

Joel definitely says that Jesus is not equal with God and not God, just a Son of God.
http://watchmanforjesus.blogspot.com/2010/03/

- **Marilyn Hickey**: Was once not in the WOF heresy; now a WOF heretic, false teacher, "Prosperity"/gimmick queen; False Prophesies, "Holy Laughter," etc.

" **Marilyn Hickey** " by Rev. Robert S. Liichow, 1997—

"From her school (and these others) a new generation of Word of Faith ministries is being grown, with more and more error and heresy. Remember heresy does not get better, it does not improve with age, like a fine wine. It continues to drift further and further into darkness."
 "The only way heresy is stopped in the Church is by Godly people standing up for the truth and being willing to swim upstream against what is popular. I pray you will be some of these people."   http://op.50megs.com/ditc/fprophets

Televangelist **Marilyn Hickey** is a prominent Word-Faith teacher. Known for manipulative, deceptive fundraising tactics based on the so-called "Prosperity Gospel."

Sometimes referred to as "**Dr. Marilyn Hickey**," but according to Wikipedia, **Hickey** holds a Bachelor of Arts in Collective Foreign Languages from the University of Northern Colorado and an Honorary Doctorate of Divinity from **Oral Roberts University**.1

Marilyn Hickey Ministries is currently led by **Hickey** and her daughter, Sarah Bowling.
 Hickey's typical 'teachings' have included the following:

"What do you need? I need money. Start creating it. Start speaking about it. Start speaking it into being. Speak to your billfold. Say, "You big, thick billfold full of money." Speak to your checkbook. Say, "You, checkbook, you've never been so prosperous since I owned you. You're just jammed full of money." —Source: Audio tape #186, "Claim Your Miracles." Side 2.

Note: While researching various televangelist who promoted the prosperity scam I watched **Ms. Hickey** teach this very principle via a TV station in Southern California. Ten minutes later she told her viewers that if we didn't send money, her program would have to be dropped from the station. That meant **Ms. Hickey** did not believe her own teachings. If she did — and if the prosperity scam worked as she claimed — she would not have needed to ask her viewers for donations. Instead, in addition to promoting the prosperity scam she uses deceptive fundraising tactics:

Marilyn Hickey is selling anointed red rubber bands to wear on the wrist for seven days for only $10.00. In the past she has offered blessed pennies, miracle carrot seeds and magical healing cloths.
It is a travesty. – Source: G. Richard Fisher, "Can You Be Deceived ?," Personal Freedom Outreach, Vol. 20, no. 3, July-September 2000.

Faith teachers such as **Robert Tilton** and his female counterpart, **Marilyn Hickey**, have copied many of the scams pioneered by Pentecostal preachers such as **Oral Roberts** and **A. A. Allen**. In fact, **Tilton** and **Hickey** have managed to exceed even their predecessors' outrageous ploys. This is hard to believe when one considers what sort of schemes they had to outdo. […]

Marilyn Hickey, much like **Tilton**, employs a broad range of tactics to manipulate followers into sending her money. Among her many ploys are anointed prayer cloths, ceremonial breastplates, and ropes that can be used as points of contact.

In one of her appeal letters, **Hickey** promises she will slip into a ceremonial breastplate, "press your prayer request to my heart," and "place your requests on my shoulders" — all for a suggested donation. For the most part, **Hickey's** tricks and teachings are recycled from other prosperity peddlers like **Tilton, Hagin**, and **Copeland**. Her message is peppered with such "Faith" jargon as "the God-kind of faith," "confession brings possession," and "receiving follows giving."

– Source: **Hank Hanegraaff**, "What's wrong with the Word-Faith movement ?", Christian Research Journal, volume 15, number 3 (1993). PDF http://www.apologeticsindex.org/ 10258-marilyn-hickey

Marilyn Hickey, Wow, has she gotten off the path to righteousness. I am continually amazed at her tactics to raise money. She has now incorporated her daughter into the ministry and has her performing the same deceptive practices against the followers as her mother has done for years. I decided to send a prayer request to her ministry to see how they would respond and I have been inundated with one letter after the other asking for money.

Many of the letters come with some item or another like a piece of prayer cloth or a package of water or oil or something of that sort. Amazingly enough, the last item I received from her ministry had a letter telling me that she had set aside three days this summer for my personal "Supernatural Intervention". She claims God told her to do this and she set aside a set of days for this miracle.

 It amazes me <u>that people continue to believe that these people can decide for God when He is going to perform His miracles</u>.

They treat God like He is some kind of monkey on a organ, telling Him when to grind and when not to. It sickens me to death to see this kind of treatment towards our God. My reconciliation for the whole mess is I remind myself that "Vengeance is mine, sayeth the Lord". I can rest assured that God will deal with these types of people when their time comes to meet their Maker!
 In the meantime though, we are faced with a horrible situation. Millions of people around the world are following these people like they were God themselves.   They are being deceived and are in jeopardy of being led down the wide path which leads to destruction. We need to pray for these followers and for this Ministry itself that they would see the light and turn from their wickedness and follow the true God of the Bible and Jesus Christ and Him risen.

 Below is an article from Bill & Jackie Alnor which covers this ministry very well.
Please read this with an open mind and let the Holy Spirit direct you in your decisions about this ministry.

UPDATE: The last letter I received from **Marilyn Hickey Ministries** included a pair of "Chopsticks"! Can you believe it!

A pair of chopsticks that were supposed to bring me a blessing from God Himself.
I never did send any money back to the **Marilyn Hickey Ministry** but did send back some of the forms they requested which were supposed to be part of the miracle process.

 I have not heard back from their ministry in a while now so I have to assume that my special days of miracles and my healings from the chopsticks and the packet of oil are not going to work as there was no financial attachment involved. Sad isn't it?

"The Christian Sentinel " : **Marilyn Hickey**: Fairy Godmother of the <u>Word-faith</u> Movement?
February 1999 issue, Feature Article--
Why have some questioned the teachings of one of the most popular charismatic Bible teachers in the world? Why is she controversial? In this special report the "Christian Sentinel "focuses on her <u>Word-faith </u>teachings and her fund raising techniques.

By Bill & Jackie Alnor ©1999 " Christian Sentinel " —

If anyone personifies the fairy godmother of the <u>word-faith </u>movement it is **Marilyn Hickey**.
Although she claims to have a long track record of "decreeing things" into existence, and as she puts it, "calling those things that are not as though they are," her Biblical exegesis is often

faulty, and her fund-raising techniques are reprehensible. The result is that she is misleading thousands of Christians worldwide to follow a distorted message that adds greed to the Gospel.

These are facts that are easily supported. Yet nevertheless she has successfully marketed her formulas for success to an array of unsuspecting Christians around the world, as many see her as a wonderful role model for modern charismatic thinking women to follow. **Hickey's** television program, "Today With Marilyn" is seen regularly on the "Trinity Broadcasting Network" (TBN) 1,
on the "Black Entertainment Television" network, and on various local channels around the world. She also has a worldwide radio broadcast.
Besides her international ministry based near Denver, **Marilyn Hickey Ministries** has offices in England, South Africa and Australia. She is also the founder of the Word to the World College, (founded in 1981, it was formerly known as the "Marilyn Hickey Bible College"), she is also the only woman on Korean mega church **David (Paul) Yonggi Cho's** board of directors.

She is also the chairman of the Board of Regents of **Oral Roberts** University. One of the keys to **Hickey's** success is that she has frequently convinced her followers that she can hear from God better than they can. Throughout her writings over the years in her magazine she quotes "the voice of God" as if it speaks directly to her.
Though this is not unusual within many quarters of Christianity, it is typical of many of modern day false teachers and those she has identified as her heroes, such as **John G. Lake, Oral Roberts, David (Paul) Yonggi Cho**, and a host of others in the Word-faith camp.

Perhaps then it is no surprise that, according to an article in "Outpouring" magazine, the publication of her ministry, **Hickey** credits **William Branham** as the inspiration for receiving her call to ministry (see "God's Generals" review on page 13). **Branham**, who denied the historic doctrine of the Trinity, also laid hands on her in one of his tent meetings in 1958, **Hickey's** magazine recounts.

"Doctors had told **Marilyn** she would never have a child," according to the 1998 "special edition" issue, "but **Evangelist William Branham** told her that she was to go home, receive her healing, and have her baby."
This "miracle," however, was a long time in coming. Ten years later her daughter, Sarah, was born. That same article describes how **Hickey** made a commitment to Christ as a teenager, but during her college years she nearly turned her back on Christianity due to dissatisfaction with Pentecostals – particularly with her mother's brand of it. She "found it almost impossible to carry on a conversation with her mother because everything became an excuse for talking about the Holy Spirit," the article noted.
It wasn't long, however, before her mother got some unexpected help in guiding her daughter back to Pentecostalism when she met **Wallace Hickey**. So upon their pressure **Marilyn** responded to "an altar call to receive the baptism of the Holy Spirit." The two were married shortly thereafter.

(**Wallace Hickey** eventually became the founding pastor of their church, the "Orchard Road Christian Center," also known as the "happy church," in the Denver area.) It is apparent that the **Marilyn Hickey** empire is very well-funded by scores of followers. Her monthly mailings utilize many of the gimmicks and chicanery of well-known deceivers like **Peter Popoff** or **Robert Tilton** who have been repeatedly exposed by secular news broadcasts.

Many of the **Hickey** mailings the "Christian Sentinel " has received over the years are so <u>deceptive</u> that we are amazed that she can sleep at night.   For instance, in one mailing of the early 1990s, **Hickey** <u>donned an Old Testament priestly robe with special stones representing the 12 tribes of Israel. The idea was that **Hickey**, as a high priest, would make special intercession for her readers – if they would write back in a specially provided envelope (and presumably financially contribute to her).</u>

Hickey's Fund-Raising Methodology:

In analyzing these mailings <u>there are two tricks of the trade that she puts into practice consistently</u>:
1) send the people something that has to be returned in order to be affective; and
2) give a strict deadline for the readers to comply with.

 And of course, all of the gimmickry stands on the theory that **Hickey's** faith is more anointed and powerful than the readers' so they have the illusion they're tapping into a direct pipeline from **Hickey** to God. Almost every mailing promotes the false teaching called "<u>seed faith</u>" that has been popularized for years by the false teacher, **Oral Roberts**.
 Basically, the <u>seed faith concept </u>fits neatly within the <u>Word-faith</u> camp.
It states that if you want more riches, simply give to God's ministries financially, and these gifts become "seeds" that can grow into more wealth later for those who contribute.

Thus the motive behind giving to God, <u>in direct contradiction to Scripture</u>, becomes giving to God's ministries in order to get from God. **Hickey's** fundraising letters have this idea reduced to a science. <u>They repeatedly say that none of her formulas for miracles can work unless money is sent in to seal the deal with God</u>. After all, you can't reap unless you sow something first, they'll say.

A Leader in the "Holy Laughter " Movement:

Marilyn Hickey has been near the forefront in today's <u>holy laughter </u>movement, having participated in its bizarre manifestations that began in the early 1990s. 3
Charismatic leaders **Charles** and **Frances Hunter** credit **Hickey** as being the one that convinced them that **Rodney Howard-Browne**, a pioneer in the so-called <u>laughing revival</u>, was to be believed in spite of their initial reservations about him.

The **Hunters** were hesitant to attend the **Rodney Howard-Browne** meeting at Karl Strader's "Carpenter's Home Church " in Lakeland, Florida, after hearing reports of <u>strange signs and wonders </u>taking place there.
 But **Hickey** convinced them it was of God. "We have known **Marilyn** for many, many years and have always known her to walk in some of the greatest integrity of anyone in the Christian world," write the **Hunters** on page 36 in their book, "Holy Laughter." "Because of her sincerity and integrity... we decided to venture down and take a look at what was really going

on. We were skeptical, but if this was a <u>new move</u> of the Holy Spirit, we certainly didn't want to miss it."

1 TBN is the world's largest Christian network.
2 Numerous Word-faith teachers also emphasize the "poor widow woman."
3 See the "Christian Sentinel's previous works on the "holy laughter" movement available online at https://www.cultlink.com.

During some meetings participants have been known to act as if they were drunken, while others have demonstrated bizarre behavior such as barking like dogs, roaring like lions, while others have allegedly been "frozen" on the floor, unable to move for hours.
The Christian Sentinel staff is unanimous in considering this movement unscriptural and perhaps demonic. http://www.forgottenword.org/hickey.html

https://discernmentministriesinternational.wordpress.com/category/marilyn-hickey/

- **Roy Hicks, Sr**: **Oral Roberts** formed "Charismatic Bible Ministries" a few months after "Seduction" was published.

<u>CBM</u> leadership includes **Buckingham, Capps, Cerullo, Cho, Copeland, Crouch, Dortch, Giminez, the Hickeys, Roy Hicks, Sr., Hinn, the Hunters, Lea, MacNutt, Paulk, Price, Savelle, Strang, Lester Sumrall, Synan, Tilton, Treat, Tommy Tyson, Weiner** and **Ralph Wilkerson**.
Pledged not to correct one another's doctrine, their motto is "Love and Unity Through Signs and Wonders."
Their "4th Annual Conference" was held June 20-22, 1989 at **Oral Roberts** University in Tulsa.

https://www.thebereancall.org/ content/new-age-inroads-church

- **Steve Hill**: Deceased; Responsible for importing the "<u>signs and wonders</u>" non-revival from England to America; false <u>teacher/prophet;</u> taught <u>visualization communication with "spirit guides</u>" from the secular world;

Steve Hill's book "The God Mockers" and **Michael Brown's** book "Let No One Deceive You: Confronting Critics of Revival" used many invectives against the body of Christ: http://www.deceptioninthechurch.com/lies.html.

http://www.deceptioninthechurch.com/hill.html

It is also commonly assumed that <u>NAR</u> Apostle **Steve Hill** brought this same 'strange fire' from "Holy Trinity Brompton" in the U.K and released it at "Brownsville" on Father's Day in 1995. In that iconic Father's Day service, **Steve Hill** claimed that Baptists and even Catholics were receiving this unusual outpouring of the spirit. This is important to acknowledge because <u>The New Order of the Latter Rain</u> cult (NOLR) were keen to <u>unite</u> both Protestants and Catholics <u>through their spiritual outpouring in 1948</u> and did so when they birthed the Charismatic movement.

In 1967, the NAR claimed a revival was happening when many Catholics and Protestants came together and were 'baptized' in this false spirit. And it's important to note that just like the NOLR and the "Charismatic Renewal Movement" (CRM), the 1967 'revival' was not one that convicted sinners of their sins but was a 'revival' because the 'spirit was doing something new' and 'falling' on people to bring a 'unity'.

The 'laughing' revival and "Brownsville" revival were no different. It was at this Father's Day service that **Steve Hill** had the tenacity to then insist that Pentecostals get on board with what this 'spirit' was doing. https://pulpitandpen.org/

https://churchwatchcentral.com/2016/08/19/
the-sorcery-behind-the-pensacola-revival-rosebrough-exposes-dr-brown-steve-hill/

https://culteducation.com/group/853-brownsville-revival/
3356-secrets-inside-the-revivals.html

(**NOTE: If this false NAR teaching isn't enough, he has written a book, listed in the link below, with a forward written by **Perry Stone**, another heretical teacher, and he has appeared on **Sid Roth's** "It's Supernatural" TV show in 2013. Ed.).

https://www.bookdepository.com/Spiritual-Avalanche-Steve-Hill/9781621365327

-**John Hinkle**: 1994 was a key year. We find the Devil was hard at work introducing a lying false prophecy to the Church worldwide by a major "Christian" network, TBN. "**John Hinkle's prophecy** of June 9 1994 - the Lord will rip evil out"
Paul Crouch: "You know the Bible is very, very simple. There's one test of a true prophet - if his word comes to pass he's a prophet, if it doesn't, he's a false prophet."
"So in a very real sense you've stepped out and really put your whole ministry and name on the line haven't you **John**?"
John Hinkle: "Yes I have **Paul** because, well I haven't, I give my life to God, and all of a sudden I realize that he is using me now, that the Lord himself spoke - and when he speaks in that voice you simply cannot doubt it..."
Paul Crouch: "Alright..."
John: "it's just beyond that."
Paul Crouch: "For those who may have just tuned by, one more time before we get right into the heart of it now, what was the word of the Lord that came to you a few days ago?"
John: "A few weeks ago now..."
Paul Crouch: "Weeks ago."
John: "He said - it was about 2 o'clock in the morning, and this great loud voice like a trumpet, and it said, I heard it inside and out clearly, very clearly, and he said - "on Thursday, June the 9th, I will rip the evil out of this world."

Another interview:

John: "I was awakened and the Lord spoke to me in the most awesome voice, I heard it outside and inside, he didn't leave one speck of doubt."

Crouch: "Uh huh."

John: "And as I sat up, he said, "On Thursday, June the 9th, I will rip the evil out of this world."   And I turned the calendar to 1994 and there it was, Thursday, June the 9th, that he would rip the evil out of this world. And I knew then that the most cataclysmic experience that the world has ever known since the resurrection - I believe since the resurrection of the Lord - is going to happen."

Paul Crouch: "Remember, first of all, it was made clear to **John** this is not the second coming of Christ, this is..."

John: "Absolutely."

Paul Crouch: "...not the rapture of the church..."

John: "Nope."

Paul Crouch: "...of Jesus Christ, it's just something is going to happen on June the 9th."

John: "It will be the cleansing out of evil so that men can see Jesus really."

Another TBN interview:

John: "Well I don't know how many of you realize that we are on a countdown... days are getting fewer and fewer until a magnificent happening." "I believe it's ten days left now until June the 9th, I believe the climax of the greatest battle that history's ever known is about to come forth." " And that climax is a spiritual battle between good and evil, between the devil and his forces, and the power and the glory of God himself." "And aren't you fortunate to think, for one moment, that you're going to see the greatest event in all of history take place." "Yes I mean that. I believe it with all my heart, because on Thursday June the 9th the Lord will rip the evil out of this world."

In another program AFTER the date had come:

Host: " ...from Christchurch, **John Hinkle**." "And you remember it was Pastor **Hinkle** that got that tremendous word from the Lord about June the 9th? Okay."

"Dear **Paul** and **Jan**," - this is dated June 13th - "Praise the Lord for June the 9th, for the veil has been ripped and the good news is coming in to us from everywhere."
"People have been changed and their services filled with the new spirit and presence of the Lord." "Family relations are being healed, miracles of physical healings are taking place all over."
"At first I was disappointed in not seeing a greater manifestation of physical healings but the Lord said 'I have ripped the spiritual veil first so that men will not return to the world after they have been healed and filled with my spirit."
 "Thanks to you **Paul** and **Jan** for the world has received a new baptism of love from the message you dared to put out and the best is yet to come. I hope to talk to you in person before too long. God bless and love you always, lovingly **John Hinkle**, Pastor of Christchurch."

John Hinkle of "Christ Church " in Los Angeles made no apology for his this false revelation; in fact it solidified him in his deception. No apology was forthcoming from TBN, **Paul Crouch** (or **Pat Robertson** who joined in). None of it happened the way it was presented to the church.

This went out to the whole world. **Hinkle** then made it into a crinkle, saying, it was a "spiritual" removing of the evil! Evil has increased in the whole world just as the Bible said it would but **Hinkle's** prophecy that so many people accepted was just the beginning as the walls of discernment that were to protect were brought down.

The glory that he prophesied was leaving, not manifesting ; the Holy Spirit shows the truth to those who have ears to hear. **Crouch** said it correctly about a false prophet but ignored his own words. http://www.letusreason.org/Pent64.htm

- **Benny Hinn**: Claims to receive spiritual "power" from the gravesite of **Kathryn Kuhlman;** teaches WOF and the prosperity "Gospel;" heretic, false prophet/teacher/pastor, liar, fraud, adulterer. https://youtu.be/CkdaIF_H9JI https://www.biblebelievingtruthwatch.com/

Benny Hinn: "Those who put us down are a bunch of morons. ...You know, I've looked for one verse in the Bible, I just can't seem to find it. One verse that says, 'If you don't like 'em, kill 'em.' I really wish I could find it...Sometimes I wish God would give me a Holy Ghost machine gun — I blow your head off!" (**Benny Hinn** on TBN's "Praise-A-Thon," April 1990).

Benny Hinn: "Be careful! Your little ones may suffer because of your stupidity. Now I'm pointing my finger today, with the mighty power of God on me, and I speak...And your children will suffer."
"If you care for your kids, stop attacking **Benny Hinn**" (World Charismatic Conference, Aug. 7, 1992). http://www.banner.org.uk/wof/sayings.html

Benny Hinn: "I want to tell you why I believe people get sick...In II Chronicles 16, verse 10 - and I like to read this - verse 10 and 11 and 12, the Bible says sickness comes when individuals attack preachers..."

"And Asa in the thirty and ninth year of his reign was diseased in his feet, until his disease was exceeding great: yet in his disease he sought not to the LORD, but to the physicians."

"The reason this man was struck with sickness is because he had been persecuting God's servant and oppressing the people of God." " We see in the Word of God, God declares in His Word, "Touch not mine anointed and do my prophets no harm." "Now that was spoken concerning Israel, yet applies to the body of Christ today, and we must be so careful not to attack men of God even when these men of God are not living right."

(From "Praise The Lord," Trinity Broadcasting Network, June 8, 1998).
http://www.banner.org.uk/wof/sayings.html

Benny Hinn: "I place a curse on every man and every woman that would stretch his hand against this anointing; I curse that man who dares to speak a word against this ministry..."(Denver Crusade, September 17th 1999). (**NOTE: My emphasis. Ed.).

Benny Hinn: He raises about $12 million a year with the usual false promises of healing and prosperity in exchange for "seed faith" gifts --a condition for "miracles." "Give no less than

$100," he exhorts an audience, and promises to "lay hands on all the envelopes and ask God for financial miracles for the givers."
This comes from a man who just traded in his Mercedes for a Jaguar and recently moved from the exclusive Heathrow development to the even more exclusive Alaqua, where he now lives in a $685,000 home (**NOTE: Near Orlando, FL. Ed.).

His suits are tailored, his shoes are Italian leather, and his wrists and finger glitter with gold and diamonds ... what he considers a modest lifestyle, as if everyone lives like this. He wears his diamond Rolex, diamond rings, gold bracelet and custom suits for all to see..."
"What's the big deal, for goodness sake?" he says. "What am I supposed to do, drive a Honda? ..." That's not in the Bible. ...

I'm sick and tired about hearing about streets of gold [in heaven]. I don't need gold in heaven. I got to have it now."
(**NOTE: My emphasis. Ed.).

Benny Hinn: "Jesus at His death became one with Satan." (Benny Hinn broadcast, recorded 12/15/90). http://www.banner.org.uk/wof/sayings.html

I can't really believe that churches, even ones that I have attended still support **Benny Hinn**. Maybe in his beginnings he was legitimate but if you can't see he is way off his rocker you really lack spiritual discernment. He lives an over the top lavish lifestyle, has said so many things that are completely wacked out sometimes even apologizing later.
Here are some things **Benny** has said: http://www.cephasministry.com/benny_hinn.html

Scandals: http://www.pfo.org/scandals.htm

I'm sure there are many more on **Benny**. Do a search on **Benny Hinn** and Hypnotism and you will find many hits. Professional hypnotists have been hired to analyze **Benny Hinn** and they say that **Benny** is a real expert.
 When confronted in an interview **Benny Hinn** did not deny that he used hypnotism but rather said "Yes but the spirit was still there." I personally have attended two **Benny Hinn** meetings and I have to admit I did feel the power of hypnotism at work. The whole service was a gong show arranged to get people's money. He told a sad story of some poor orphans than jumped to an offering where he stated he needed money for a new top of the line jet.
He told people that they should sacrifice in their poverty for the Gospel so they could receive favor from God otherwise they would be cursed.

No word of a lie; I heard it with my own ears and to my astonishment right after that everybody was pulling out mad cash all around me, eager to give out of their poverty to **Benny Hinn's** wealthy empire so he could fly around in a new jet. On top of that I remember tons of people coming in on wheel chairs and leaving in wheel chairs. There were not any notable healings in either meeting.

Ruth Heflin told **Benny** that Jesus would appear in his meetings in bodily form because she stated the Lord told her... that never happened...From conversations with friends who still believe **Benny**, I have learned that God still uses people that have gone way off.
I touch more on this in the second half of the report. There are reports of genuine healings and salvations, but this is not the norm today. Maybe back in the day God was turning up, but also the counterfeit was turning up and today it appears **Benny** has got caught up in the counterfeit.
He is one of the people that I believe started out genuine and along the road got deceived by this counterfeit system. There are in fact counterfeit healings where people do get completely healed and there are also false manifestations and signs and wonders.

https://deceptionfree.wordpress.com/tag/ruth-heflin/

(**NOTE: Yes, this link has the name **Ruth Heflin** besides **Benny Hinn** and it also contains several other people in this deception. Ed.).

In an April 7,1991 sermon, **Hinn** revealed that he periodically visits **Kuhlman's** grave and that he is one of the few with a key to gain access to it. He also visits **Aimee's** grave. Where he says: "I felt a terrific anointing...I was shaking all over...trembling under the power of God...'Dear God, ' I said, 'I feel the anointing...I believe the anointing has lingered over **Aimee's** body." Obtained from http://www.deceptioninthechurch.com/ bhinn.html on 01-2007.
https://www.christianpost.com/news/
benny-hinns-nephew-calls-bethel-church-leader-kris-vallotton-false-prophet-who-deceives-peopl
e.html
(**NOTE: The above link is about a false preacher, but **Benny Hinn's** nephew also speaks about him as well, so I have included it. Ed.).

- **David Hogan**: Claims:
• He raises people from the dead;
• He is thrown supernaturally across rooms into walls;
• He multiplies food;
• He drives his vehicle underwater;
• Angels are assigned to him and have to go where he goes;
• He is miraculously transported from place to place without the aid of planes, trains or automobiles;
• He is invigorated when new demons are unleashed on him;
• A demon has tried to tear out the innards of his child;
• He has a little son who has a hanky that is so anointed he can make people fly just by shaking it at them;
• He has seen limbs grow on limbless people;
• He has seen the creation of new brains in a brainless baby;
• Jesus talks to his dog and horse;
• He has seen people fly around the room under the anointing of God.

The problem is nobody has actually ever seem him do these things! **Hogan** said: "I have a pretty serious imagination." To that I answer, yes **Mr Hogan** you seriously do. "I may be the most simple man you've ever met but you ain't never run into anybody in our generation that has touched as many dead men and let 'em get up as I have."

"How does that feel?" "I am ripped off of that bed and slammed into the wall. It was not a demon, it was the Holy Ghost."
"Revelation knowledge like I have never known in my life began to unfold in my mind. ... [I began] writing down pages and pages of revelation knowledge from heaven. ... This is the big one!"
 Anybody who is familiar with occultic practices, would know this is known as "automatic handwriting" What is automatic handwriting? "Automatic writing consists of producing written material by a medium who is not in control of his conscious self. The subject matter is said to be beyond any training, experience or knowledge of the medium.

("Handbook of Today's Religions").

Check out this next false claim:

"Now I'm fixing to tell you something that you're gonna have a hard time with."
He says there is no part of the human anatomy that he has not seen healed:

"New brains, new hearts, new livers, ... dead raising." He tells his audience of a baby whose head was split open when its head was dashed on a rock. They left the brains on the rock and brought the brainless baby to the church. After four hours of prayer, the baby came back to life and..."brains were still on the rock but he got some more now."

A Mexican man named Alvin LaVaughn Landry was a lifelong friend of **Hogan's** and served in **Hogan's** mission from 1983-1993. Few have been closer. Landry openly disclosed that: "**David's** problems go way back and he has been telling tall tales his whole life. I have caught him in so many lies that I have lost track." He was then asked if **Hogan** was a pathological liar. Alvin Landry said, "Yes." Landry says: "**David** picks up people to work for him that are insecure or with troubled backgrounds or in a crisis." " His main thing is control. He controls like a gang leader. ... He uses all kinds of profanity and covers it by saying that you should say all that is in your heart." "He has expressed very immoral and vulgar things about women using the rationale that if you say it out, you won't do it. ... He treats women like mules. ... His authority can't be challenged. ...
Somebody needs to stand up. ... He has serious mental problems." "No workers at Freedom Ranch have assets. He and his wife are the board and own everything. The board of reference is only on paper and knows little."
David has huge assets in his over 200-acre ranch. ... When you tell one lie after another like **David** does, you get hardened. **David** has no conscience and does not know where the beginning and end is of all the lies.
If one person, just one, were raised from the dead, it would be all over the Mexico newspapers. Most people in Mexico have never heard of **David Hogan**.

They only know of him in America and down there no one would believe any of the reports. Sooner or later, believe me, you will see buildings burning in Tempoal (Mexico), just like Waco. **David** is paranoid and anti-government and he sees his compound as an end time place of survival. With his personal slaves and hundreds of thousands of dollars in the bank he knows he will survive. He has huge investments." Alvin Landry was then asked if **David Hogan's** so called "Freedom Ranch" had any parallels to Jonestown, and if **David Hogan** had any similarities to Jim Jones, he said: "Most definitely."

https://testallthings.com/2007/03/19/ david-hogan/

https://www.christianissues.com/hogan.html

Today we look into a very popular person within the charismatic and "Bethel Church "(Redding, CA) movements. Self-proclaimed as an apostle and prophet, **David Hogan** knows how to put on a show and is an epic story teller. When I first came across **Hogan** on YouTube, he drew my interest because of his down-to-earth speaking style, brash personality (and without apology), and his claims of the miraculous healings. He tells many stories of raising the dead, miraculous healings, and very powerful spiritual encounters that he and his followers have supposedly experienced. Sure, he preached Jesus Christ but after watching him over time, some red flags came up:

(**NOTE: The author of this article wants you to watch a YouTube video, which I cannot find the link to, but if you go on the cited website, you can watch it. Ed.).

https://www.biblical-discernment.com/home/ false-teacher-series-david-hogan

- **Mike Hoggard**: Thinks the Nephilim are still around, the fallen angels had relations with women; does not believe in the Holy Ghost, speaking in tongues, or the gifts of the Spirit; he believes it is from the devil.
 Pastor **Mike Hoggard** of "Bethel Church" – A LIAR and FALSE PROPHET! "Christian Propaganda" March 10, 2013:

There has been a widespread and growing 'deadly cancer' in the Christian church as of late and that 'cancer' is the pulpits profusely proclaiming that anyone who wishes to do 'JUST AS' Jesus did and to walk in the same manner as Jesus did, those who choose this path have fallen out of grace and are claimed to have joined a cult. So is this true?
On March 5, 2013, **Mike Hoggard** vehemently shouted at the top of his lungs during his radio broadcast that the 4th Commandment of God was nailed to the cross.
 Now mind you, this is the ONE Commandment of God that contains the 'sign/mark" of His Covenant with all mankind that dates back to the seventh day of creation.

So could the Jesus that **Hoggard** preaches be the true Messiah that never spoke against or did anything in disobedience to God the Father? I would say without a doubt, NO, **Mike Hoggard** is not proclaiming the true Messiah that Moses and the Prophets wrote about but a different Messiah and a different Gospel and here is why:

Deut. 13:1; Exod. 31:13; Isa 56:1; Ezek. 20:11; Ezek. 20:23;

Mike Hoggard claims to be a watchman but teaches that His <u>seventh day Sabbath</u> is not for all mankind and those that claim it is are <u>heretics</u> and members of some cult. So what else do the Prophets have to say of His Sabbath as being valid for ALL mankind?
"So we see that it was NOT prophesied that the Sabbath would be nailed to anything, but rather it will be restored in all its glory as it was in the beginning." "So did Jesus of Nazareth speak to the continuation of the Father's perpetual and everlasting seventh day Sabbath for all mankind? Why yes, Jesus of Nazareth certainly did." Mat 24:4.

So as this false <u>prophet</u> **Mike Hoggard** claims that his Jesus nailed the 4th Commandment to the cross and that we no longer are bound by this burdensome law, but as we can see, the true Jesus of Nazareth of the King James Bible tells us just the opposite of what false <u>prophet</u> **Mike Hoggard** prophesies and that the true Jesus will be expecting us to keep and honor the 4th Commandment because as a disciple, one who imitates and emulates the Master, if one is a true disciple of Jesus, then one will joyfully do as Jesus did and not call ANY command of the Father burdensome. Mat 11:29; 1 Jn 5:1; Rom 10:5; Deut. 30:10.

Interestingly enough, **Hoggard** did quote from Paul about making void the Law of God, but then in the same breath he denied that which he just spoke while also ignoring the fact that Paul also taught us that we are to 'establish' the Law of God by doing it through faith just as Abraham 'established' the Law of God by doing it through faith.

Rom 3:31; Rom 6:1; 1 Jn 3:1. We are sons and daughters of God through the begotten Son of God and therefore, as He did, we are to do likewise so that through the Son, we also can be transformed into the likeness of the Father. II Cor. 3:18, "But we all, with open face beholding as in a glass the glory of the Lord, are changed into the same image from glory to glory, even as by the Spirit of the Lord."

Therefore, according to Scripture **Mike Hoggard** is a LIAR and a FALSE PROPHET !
https://churchwatchcentral.com/2015/08/27/
guess-who-elijah-list-challenge-the-culprit-in-the-pulpit/

Therefore, in denying that the WHOLE Word of God, from Genesis to Revelation is for ALL mankind, **Hoggard** is denying the very existence of the authority of God the Father and His only begotten Son and creating his own authority upon the earth with a <u>new Gospel</u> message of lawlessness towards God the Father that the only begotten Son of God never taught or preached.
https://constitutionallyspeaking.blog/2013/03/10/
pastor-mike-hoggard-of-bethel-church-a-liar-and-false-prophet/

Mike Hoggard - "Anti-apostasy Teacher or the Next **Harold Camping**?"

Lately a friend introduced me to the teachings of Pastor **Mike Hoggard**.
She had been listening to him, and was very impressed by the stand that he took against all the apostate things that are going on in the church.

To his credit, he believes that the KJV is the only accurate English translation of the Bible, which I have shown to be true in my article on the KJV Bible. (See http://bibleconundrumsandcontroversy.blogspot.com/2011/01/ king-james-version-only-controversy.html).

He teaches against contemplative prayer, which I have yet to address (I have now written that article) http://bibleconundrumsandcontroversy.blogspot.com/2012/07/ is-contemplative-prayer-scriptural-and.html,

but which I agree is a real danger to Christians. He teaches against rock music in the church

(See http://bibleconundrumsandcontroversy.blogspot.com/2011/01/ is-it-really-christian-music.html

(And a number of other things that have infiltrated, which I also agree are bad).

He also teaches a lot about the Masons and other occult teachings. It is good for people to be made aware of these things. In short, a great deal of what he teaches is good for people to know. He is attracting a bigger and bigger following, especially with people who are fed up with the apostasy in the church and are looking for some good old-fashioned Bible preaching.

So what is the problem? The problem is, in the midst of gathering a major audience of Christians who are looking for someone to lead them out of apostasy, and are following him because of the strong stand he takes against apostasy, he is slowly and subtly introducing to them teachings that are not Scriptural.

Because they are such little things within his sermons, nobody notices or gives it much thought, or they just let it pass like a blip on the screen, but when added up, it comes to a lot of things that are not correct. I also have concerns about the way he approaches his study of the Scripture, as well as the way he teaches it. I honestly see the beginnings of another **Harold Camping** in the making given enough time. For those of you who missed the **Harold Camping** hoopla, here is some info on that:

http://bibleconundrumsandcontroversy.blogspot.com/2011/03/ harold-camping-may-21-2011-rapture.html
and
http://bibleconundrumsandcontroversy.blogspot.com/2011/05/ harold-camping-failed-and-tries-again.html.)

I hope to show why I make that statement in the course of this article.
One of the first things I noticed was that he preaches about getting revelation (meaning special revealed knowledge of hidden things) from the Bible. Naturally studying the Bible is going to bring knowledge.

Knowledge about God, knowledge about Christ, knowledge about how we should walk and behave, etc. He is against using man's commentaries to learn what God teaches. I agree.

 I believe that we should allow God to teach us by studying God's Word verse by verse, chapter by chapter, book by book, comparing passages that speak to the same subject. Pastor **Hoggard** however seems to believe that God teaches you by "revelation."

By that I am gathering that he means that he'll look at a passage and have some sort of epiphany that shows him some secret piece of information, as what he teaches is not stuff that can be had from a simple literal reading of the Word. Concerning the subject of revelation **Hoggard** has made several statements that bother me. First he talks about the concept that the getting of "revelation" comes with a price.
He says, "There's a price [for having this stuff revealed to you]." He says that it "comes with a thorn."   In other words, if you go looking to study God's Word and have Him show you what His Word says, you had better be prepared to pay a steep price for it. His statements seemed aimed more at preventing people from studying God's Word rather than encouraging them.

He implies that you shouldn't do it unless you are willing to suffer some consequences. In fact he basically makes a threat against you if he finds out you are trying to study it. He says, "I pray for all of God's people who really have this thirst for knowledge and wisdom and they want these revelations from the Bible and they want to study more and they want to know more." "I'm going to pray that if necessary God will give you a massive thorn in your flesh." Not just a thorn but a massive one? How nice of him. This is supposedly to prevent people from getting arrogant.

So according to **Hoggard**, studying God's Word to learn what it says will make you arrogant. So does that mean basically you are better not studying?   And if you do and he finds out, he is going to pray against you to ask God to make you suffer for learning what God wants you to know? Why on earth would anybody do that? I desperately pray that people will pick up their Bibles and study them. And I certainly would not want them punished for it.

 I want them to learn as much as possible, so that they won't be deceived by people who are misusing and manipulating it to teach error. God says, "My people are destroyed for lack of knowledge: because thou hast rejected knowledge, I will also reject thee, that thou shalt be no priest to me: seeing thou hast forgotten the law of thy God, I will also forget thy children." Hosea 4:6.
God says if you don't study you will be destroyed for the lack of knowledge. That is because people will not pick up on the doctrines of demons they are being taught. He commands us to study as it is the only way to know what you are being taught is right or wrong.

II Timothy 2:15 " Study to shew thyself approved unto God, a workman that needeth not to be ashamed, rightly dividing the word of truth."
Those who do study will be blessed. Especially if they study Revelation which contains two blessings just for reading and heeding it. (Revelation 1:3, 22:7). Why should **Mike Hoggard** want to curse someone for doing what God has 1) commanded us to do and 2) said we will be

destroyed if we don't know what His Word says, due to lack of knowledge, and 3) will bless us for doing?

Hoggard believes that understanding God's Word comes from "revelation." He says that he preaches by "revelation." By "revelation" I have come to understand that he does not mean that you lay precept upon precept, but that you are reading along and BOOM, all of a sudden you will see something beyond the literal message given in the passage.

Pastor **Hoggard** does the same thing with numbers that he does with these "word" revelations. He draws conclusions about things by adding, or dividing, or doing other mathematical exercises with them, if required.

In fact he stated that when he studies the Bible, he keeps the Bible in one hand and a calculator in the other, as numbers are so important. Really? I have never had to sit with a calculator in hand tallying up numbers to understand the Word of God. There are times when I see parallels between numbers, such as the twelve tribes, and the twelve disciples, or forty year wandering in the desert and forty days of the temptation of Christ, but I don't see the need to add, subtract, multiply, or divide them to reveal some secret hidden message or code in God's Word. I'm not saying there might not be some interesting things to learn, but the obsessive way in which he uses numbers to show him what passages mean is where I start seeing a problem.

Harold Camping got off on this same tangent. Numbers became more important than simply reading what the Word said. Look where it led him. **Hoggard** seems to be taking this same route. In fact I question that he is using numbers in a proper way. A further concern is that he seems to spend an inordinate amount of time preaching about the occult, the Masons, and all Satanic things about the end times.

While a passing knowledge of these things is important for all Christians, it seems that everything he preaches comes back to this information. He seems as obsessed with this subject and everything related to Satan as he is about numbers. He takes occult legends and information and interprets the Bible from these sources rather than the other way around, even though he emphatically states that you should not bring anything to the Bible to interpret it other than the Bible itself.

Another of his teachings that he got from the Masons is about DNA. **Hoggard** has said, "I know pretty much what Albert Pike is trying to conceal in this book ("Morals and Dogma" – the Masonic bible). And how do I know it? Did I go to the meetings? No. Did I read the secret document? No." " I know that because the "revelation" came to me by the apostles and the prophets. That's how I know what is in here" (M & D).

"You want things revealed?" "Go right here (the Holy Bible)."

So **Hoggard** is using the Bible, or rather getting "revelations" from the Bible via clue words, numbers, etc. through the apostles and prophets that teach him what the Masonic book "Morals and Dogma" is hiding. Really? Instead of spending time studying the Bible, he's using the Bible as a codebreaker via "revelation" to figure out Albert Pike's big secret?

And this bothers nobody? It bothers me. And what is the big secret Albert Pike is hiding?

According to **Hoggard**, the secret is that the mark that the antichrist is going to make people take is a third DNA helix strand. **Hoggard** explains that in Genesis 6 the angels procreated with mankind creating hybrids, giants, men of renown.
According to **Hoggard** this gave man a third helix strand of DNA.

Now, I am not sure exactly how far he takes this, but he did reference the verse where Jesus calls the Pharisees a generation of serpents/vipers and says that Satan has a physical seed that these Jewish religious leaders had, as Jesus used both the word "generation" indicating that this was a bloodline, and "serpent" or "vipers" indicating that they were of Satan's seed.
Again, I have not heard him preach further on this idea of a seedline, so I do not know how far he takes it. As to the third helix strand, **Hoggard** teaches that this is the secret the <u>Masons</u> have been keeping. That the fallen angels or Nephilim are coming back, and that they want to turn us into them. And this is what the mark will be. That there will be hand held scanners (they are working on developing these for Homeland Security) that they will use on you to decide if you are one of them or one of us. This will be what allows you to buy and sell.

https://bibleconundrumsandcontroversy.blogspot.com/2012/03/
mike-hoggard-anti-apostasy-teacher-or.html

(**NOTE: There is a wealth of information on this website. Ed.).

http://www.rap-con.com/ forum/the-missing-piece-babylon-and-the-nwo

"Pastor **Mike Hoggard** and his wrong doctrine" by Helga Hickman:

Some two years ago, perhaps longer, since it is that as we get older time slips by without us noticing, in listening to Pastor **Mike** online I noted discrepancies in what he was stating. Innocently, I emailed him with a couple of questions. In response he stated that I asked too many questions. I responded, could he please just answer one! He never got back to me!
I posted on his Facebook wall: did he believe in the Dispensations? He never responded! I then asked a sister in Christ from England to pose the same question.

I believe I have a post somewhere here with his response to her, which I never forgot, to the effect: "Dispensationalism" was another "ism."
He had never cared to look into it! Now I had my response! Given his enormous intellect, his incredible savvy in exposing contemporary cults, the <u>occult</u>, etc.,

I am nothing but baffled that this man does not see that which is as plain as the nose on his face! I don't customarily listen to Pastor **Mike Hoggard**, whose day seems to be a whole lot longer than that of most, for the enormous wealth of videos he makes, thus it is only when someone refers me to a particular video that I do view it, but I found it particularly hard to listen to this! I know he is breaking the hearts of many who truly love him, and wish he would learn!

Some two weeks ago, Bryan Denlinger produced an incredibly sobering video on the erroneous teaching of **Mike Hoggard**! I prayed that **Mike Hoggard** would view it and come to

recognize the disservice he does to the word of God, and correct it! That is what we are to do when we learn that we are wrong! Last night I heard what can be said to be the very worst sermon ever by Pastor **Mike Hoggard**, in response to Bryan's video!
Right from the start, he entirely misrepresents the purpose of Bryan's video, and the reasons for him having made it! He even places us, the saved, on "judgment day!" He couldn't be more wrong! A sister in Christ has dubbed it a "foot in mouth" case!

I believe it to be so much worse: if not pride, it is the devil blinding him to the truth of God's word!
 As she said, she fears that Bryan's video would have those without a church scattering about! I replied, that is the Holy Spirit's problem!   Ours is to divulge the truth, and stick to it, regardless! Bryan was/is 100% correct! I have no doubt Bryan will make a video in response, perhaps after next Sunday's installment of Pastor **Mike's** continuation of yesterday's sermon, as he claimed there was more to come!
I truly like **Mike Hoggard**! I think him genuine, and am sure he is saved... yet confused!
 Small wonder, when it is he grew up never having heard about the Dispensations!
I wandered, in and out of churches for some 10 years, and never heard of them, either! Quite sad that such ignorance be so prevalent in the churches!

 http://rainhadocanto10-evangelicalchristian.blogspot.com
/2013/04/pastor-mike-hoggard-and-his-wrong.html

- **Joshua Holmes:** Self proclaimed that he is Jesus Christ; a false prophet; VERY demonic; copies **Benny Hinn** knocking down people by swinging his jacket.

- **Brian Houston**: Founder of "Hillsong," (one of the biggest deceivers in the world; has people convinced that his "gospel" is the truth, when none of it aligns with THE Gospel; his father was arrested for child molestation—and no one did a thing about it).
https://www.nowtheendbegins.com/
hillsong-church-alpha-conference-2020-mass-roman-catholic-priest-james-mallon-promote-one-world-religion-antichrist-chrislam/

- **Larry Huch/Tiz Huch**: Both are prosperity and "sowing seeds" preachers. Lives in a mansion, paid for by the believer's money; part of the NAR. (**NOTE: A few years ago they were still on TV;
I am not sure if they still are, but even so, there are plenty of YouTube videos about them and their "preaching." Ed.).

- **Charles & Frances Hunter** Known as the "Happy Hunter's; their daughter Joan also teaches the same New Age "charismania" that her parents did).

Teach Healing? by Rev. Robert S. Liichow, 1998—

"Got this in the mail a little while back and I thought it would be interesting for people to see that these folks at Toronto believe they can teach you how to heal the sick. This is nothing new, because the "Happy Hunters" have been holding "How to Heal the Sick" Seminars for

many, many years. In fact, my wife and I attended one in Ohio, and got to work directly with the **Hunters**.
Can't you see the Apostle Paul holding a healing seminar in Ephesus (I can't)?"

http://op.50megs.com/ditc/fprophets.html

- **Bill Hybels**: Another Emergent Church leader, NAR; Findings released from independent review of **Bill Hybels**, "Willow Creek." :

After six months of review, the "Independent Advisory Group" concluded that allegations of sexual misconduct against former pastor **Bill Hybels** are "credible."
Among the findings, the group said that **Hybels** initiated relationships with the female staff members and that there was "inappropriate language, sexual innuendo and lax use of alcohol" among staff, including **Hybels**. It also made a series of recommendations — including having a hotline to report misconduct and establishing standards on appropriate staff behavior — that would help "Willow Creek Community Church" and "Willow Creek Association" deal with such matters in the future.   newsletter@christianpost.com

http://www.cnn.com/2012/11/17/us/andy-stanley/index.html

(**NOTE: The above website mentions **Andy Stanley**, but **Bill Hybels** is on it as well. Ed.).

I:

- **Shane Idleman**: Is a regular contributor on "Charisma News" and this week has penned an opinion article defending **Mark Driscoll** by attacking those who do not support his return to ministry. As much as he tries to pretend he is neither criticizing not condoning, he makes it abundantly clear where he stands and it is not with the word of God.
 For while he does not come outright with his support for **Driscoll's** past, he is willing to minimize it for the sake of **his future**.
As for criticizing, **Idleman** makes is very clear that he is against anyone questioning pastors. Publicly preach that the people you have hurt in ministry are just a "pile of dead bodies?"; if you dare to say anything about the fact that a pastor with this horrific record is trying to start a new church just 16 months after ducking discipline from this debacle in Seattle then you are the one with the "critical spirit"; judgmental attitude"; or "sowing discord." What utter nonsense.

Let us reason together beloved and walk through the real judgment being made by **Idleman** here, one quote at a time:

An attitude of constant criticism toward Christian leaders often reveals an inner drive to exalt oneself" -- **Shane Idleman.**

There is a psychological term for this and it is called projection.
It is where you project your own issues onto others to deflect where the focus should be. What is important to note here is that there is a vast difference between criticism and discernment;

If I was to say that I think **Mark Driscoll** is disqualified from pastoral ministries based upon all Biblical qualifications provided in God's Word—that is not being critical; it is being accurate.

The truth here is that **Shane Idleman** is exalting the pastoral office far higher than God ever intended. He is paying lip service to the sins of **Driscoll** while beating any sheep who dares to raise their voice and say what God has actually said about what **Mark** has done.
"Biblical unity encourages us to go directly to the source when possible. Where are getting our information about a person, movement or ministry? Are we going directly to them and\ or reputable sources or are we looking to smear websites, gossipers and "heresy hunters" for the answers?"— **Shane Idleman**

The notion that anyone who has been correctly pointing out that **Driscoll** should not be in ministry should have gone directly to him is absurd and unbiblical. **Idleman** is trying to leverage Matthew 18 here but does so incorrectly. The verses in Matthew 18 deal specifically with personal sin: "If your brother sins against you, go and tell him his fault, between you and him alone. If he listens to you, you have gained your brother. - Matthew 18:15 (ESV).

So if I was one of the dead bodies behind the "Mars Hill " bus for example, I should follow Matthew 18 so I can forgive **Mark** for what he did. If I am however pointing out how unbiblical, mean spirited and unchristian the comments are, I do not need to seek **Driscoll** out. He has not sinned against me personally. I might add, he would never grant an audience to someone regarding this. But **Idleman** knows that and is just trying to muddy the water by blaming any criticism as a violation of Matthew 18 even though it is not. Furthermore, **Shane** tries to play the unity card but does so unbiblically.
 Unity is found only in doctrine, not singing "Kumbaya" with disgraced former pastors. The next thing to address is the red herrings of a "smear website," 'heresy hunters" and 'gossipers." **Idleman** is desperate to get the attention off of **Mark Driscoll**.

So he now conflates the notion of gossip, which is wrong, with truth telling, which is of course right. Gossip by definition is idle talk or rumor. When discussing **Mark Driscoll** there is nothing left in the rumor mill. It is all proven fact. **Mark** may disagree about how people are reacting to it but he does not deny these are facts; as for "heresy hunters," the Bible expressly instructs all ministers to not only preach sound doctrine but to rebuke those who do not.

A pastor who refuses to call out false teachings and teachers is actually being disobedient to Scripture. Heresy destroys real Christian unity. Heresy leads millions of people to hell. Why wouldn't any responsible pastor want to hunt it? Lastly, I do not personally know of any websites that are "smear websites."
I think **Idleman** is confusing telling the truth with 'smears" and "gossip." "Ask, "Do I have a critical spirit?" "This could translate into a cynical or negative attitude. This is one aspect of Jesus' words, "Judge not, that you not be judged." If you have a judgmental attitude, you've already turned a deaf ear to God's leading." "Ironically, I have noticed that those highly educated in Biblical doctrine can often be the most critical, cynical and negative."— **Shane Idleman**.

It sure sounds like **Pastor Idleman** has a critical spirit towards anyone who wishes to hold Christian leaders accountable. And yes a critical spirit could lead to a cynical or negative attitude if it is not firmly rooted in His Word. The more likely outcome of a Biblically motivated critical spirit however is the development of a Berean mind set where doctrine is more important than feelings. As if this were bad enough, **Idleman** then abuses the "judge not" verses from the Bible by referring to them wildly out of context:

"Judge not, that you be not judged. For with the judgment you pronounce you will be judged, and with the measure you use it will be measured to you. Why do you see the speck that is in your brother's eye, but do not notice the log that is in your own eye? Or how can you say to your brother, 'Let me take the speck out of your eye,' when there is the log in your own eye? You hypocrite, first take the log out of your own eye, and then you will see clearly to take the speck out of your brother's eye. - Matthew 7: 1-5 (ESV).

These verses are not about judging people. They are not even about judgment at all. They are about hypocrisy. Verse five gives that away clearly. If this were truly about "not judging" then why does Jesus instruct us to go back and help our brother with that speck in his eye? The truly sad portion of this excerpt from **Idleman** however is his silly attack upon people who strive for doctrinal knowledge.

This is a common attack within the <u>Seeker-Friendly Industrial Complex.</u> Educated and Biblically literate sheep are dangerous to false teachers because they eventually realize you are a liar and a <u>charlatan</u>. It is why **Perry Noble** referred to the people in his church who wish to go deeper in the word as "jackasses."

Another mega church pastor referred to them as "the excrement in the body of Christ." The reason why people highly educated in doctrine tend to call out falseness is they understand the Bible. They see the real damage being done by wolves and are fiercely protective of the flock instead of the wolves. It is clear that it is **Pastor Idleman** who has turned a deaf ear to God's leading. He did not like the criticisms coming out about **Mark Driscoll** opening a new church just 16 months after being disgraced in ministry. So he sat down to take pen to paper in protest and used the Bible to proof text his way to defend the indefensible. Rip "judge not" out of context? Mangle Matthew 18 along the way? Who cares?

"Ephesians 4: 31-32 states, "Let all bitterness, wrath, anger, outbursts, and blasphemies, with all malice, be taken away from you. And be kind to one another, tenderhearted, forgiving one another, just as God in Christ also forgave you." Simply stated, bitterness, negativity, and anger will lead you in the wrong direction."— **Shane Idleman**

The next set of verses to be misapplied are from Ephesians. Here we see the Apostle Paul speaking to the church at Ephesus about how we are to treat each other personally. What these verses are not however, is an instruction on how to treat wolves.

Where is **Pastor Idleman's** concern for the sheep of the Lord? Where is his concern for the sheep being robbed of over $200,000? Where is his concern for those who were hurt by **Pastor Mark** being mockingly referred to as a "pile of dead bodies." Where is his concern for the thievery involved with his plagiarism? By the way, it is the people who are calling for **Mark** to repent who are showing true Christian love for him. Not the people who write articles excusing his sin.

Mark Driscoll needs to repent for **Mark Driscoll's** sake first. Remember that he will answer for every dead body in his pile. The blood of his listeners will be upon his head.
 The key verses make that abundantly clear. No one is suggesting that **Mark Driscoll** should not have his walk restored. It is his ministry that is forfeited. That is not bitterness, anger, or malice. That is the Bible.

"I am deeply saddened by the spiritual condition of many Christians. We love to be arm chair quarterbacks and diss pastors and Christian leaders, yet we have no idea of the demands they encounter and the pain they feel. Our sinful tendency is to pull others down. We may think that somehow this makes us look better." " If we are truly concerned about the body of Christ, we will hold our tongue."— **Shane Idleman**.

<u>I am deeply saddened by the spiritual condition of many pastors today.</u> Who would think nothing of abusing the sheep of the Lord in order to defend someone in the good ole boys club.

Someone correctly pointing out that plagiarism is theft and theft is not allowed in the Bible is not an arm chair quarterback beloved. Someone who says that a pastor should not steal tithe money or try and cheat a Bestseller list is not "dissing a pastor." With all due respect, the difficulties of the job are irrelevant to this discussion.

Is **Shane** suggesting that we should water down what the Bible says because the job of pastor is difficult? I might add that **Mark Driscoll** lived in a million dollar mansion at the time everything became unraveled so spare me the "woe is me" angle. If **Pastor Idleman** wants to know the true sinful tendency, it is to cover up sin. It is as old as the Garden when Adam and Eve were hiding from God.   We see it with David and Bathsheba. We see it in this article by **Shane Idleman**.
In order to prop up his fellow pastor, **Idleman** is forced to tear down anyone who stands against him. "Strive to develop the type of love that protects and defends others."

 "For instance, why not believe that God is going to use **Mark's** past to help others?"— **Shane Idleman**. Glad you asked **Shane**. The answer is the Bible tells me not to believe that. What part of this is escaping you?
Mark Driscoll resigned in disgrace to avoid a deserved discipline that was coming 16 months ago. These are not trivial matters to be swept under the church rug.
If we cannot expect to hold someone like **Driscoll** to account for his behavior then we will hold no one responsible. He willfully and maliciously hurt the very people God called him to protect. Then he preached to everyone else not bloodied that these people were just a pile of dead bodies to him.
He stole their money. He cheated. He stole intellectual property and tried to pass it off as his own. He did all of this, has admitted to all of this, <u>and apologized for none of it.</u> He has repented of none of it.
Every time he has preached since leaving **Mars Hill** he has tried to paint himself as the victim. Yet despite all of this **Shane Idleman** thinks it is love to protect and defend this record. Not to protect and defend the sheep.

To have the hubris to actually ask why not believe God will use this unrepentant past to help others is staggering to me. I understand why **Shane Idleman** came to this point. It was not after careful prayer and Biblical Berean work.

It was his starting point. "Stop yourself when you're tempted to gossip or belittle others, and turn the conversation if someone is taking you in that direction." The Bible is clear: If you have not love, it profits you nothing (cf. 1Corinthians 13:3)— **Shane Idleman**
When your starting point was trying to prove a personal grudge instead of hearing what God might have to say you end up using the Bible. Leveraging it through proof-texting. The problem is that in order to get the Bible to say what you want instead of what God wants, you must wrest verses horribly out of context as we have already shown.

Idleman finishes the butchery with not understanding the famous love verses from I Corinthians. Beloved, what is love as Paul espouses for us here?
Is it to turn a blind eye to sin and offense to God? Is it love to beat the sheep of the Lord to protect your friend? No. Love here is true love as God requires both towards God and man. How do we love God again?

"If you love me, you will keep my commandments John 14: 15 (ESV). Not stealing is one of the actual first commandments.

Mark Driscoll not only stole the tithe monies but the plagiarism is also theft.
How do you think you have love, show love, or will profit from love by defending that against the Word of the Lord? How do we love each other then? "And you shall love the Lord your God with all your heart and with all your soul and with all your mind and with all your strength." "The second is this: 'You shall love your neighbor as yourself." 'There is no other commandment greater than these." - Mark 12: 30-31 (ESV).
Pastor Shane seems to be implying that it would be loving to pretend what **Mark Driscoll** did never happened. Just look the other way. There are two problems with that.

First off, it dismisses the real victims here. How is it loving to the former 12,000 congregants of "Mars Hill Church" in Seattle? How is it loving to embrace someone who bragged about running over his own sheep with the "Mars Hill" bus? Secondly, how is it loving to **Mark**? He is going to answer for every careless word and deed as we all must. If I ever found myself in a situation such as this I would want people who love me to come alongside of me and tell me to repent. Not blindly support my new church plant when the bodies are still warm from my last.

One last quote from **Pastor Idleman:** "We should consider the total portrait of one's life, character and ministry and evaluate on that basis. A few poorly chosen statements, angry outbursts or controlling decisions made over the course of many years shouldn't define a person."— **Shane Idleman.**

Pastor Shane Idleman has tried vociferously to pretend that **Mark Driscoll's** offenses were just a handful of "oopsies" while defaming anyone who dared to stand up for what the Bible actually says regarding these offenses and the pastoral office.

Perhaps to **Idleman**, referring to the sheep you have slaughtered as a pastor as a "pile of dead bodies" is just a "poorly chosen statement." Perhaps when he viciously attacked his own sheep and staff repeatedly for years, that was just "angry outbursts" to **Pastor Shane**.

 Perhaps stealing over $200,000 of tithe monies to cheat the NY Times Bestseller List was just a "controlling decision." I do not think I am out on a limb here to suggest that God does not see it that way. I do not think He sees it that way at all. www.828ministries.com

J:

- **John Paul Jackson** Deceased; claimed to have a "new" concept; also believed in the "law of attraction;" another false teacher of the NAR;
The man, **John Paul Jackson,** who I once took my dream interpretation training from has passed away (2015). The man was a proven false teacher and false prophet, and I am floored and grieved at this news. And unless he repented and found the truth, he stood before God in judgment, without Christ. Unfortunately, his work in deceiving masses will continue. Please be aware of who you follow and test everything through the perfect teaching of the Bible, which will never fail us. http://www.streamsministries.com/

https://mkayla.wordpress.com/2015/02/21/
death-of-a-false-prophet-john-paul-jackson-has-passed/

- **Cindy & Mike Jacobs**: False prophetess, started "Generals of Intercession" based on an "angelic" visit; totally demonic; aligned with the NAR. "Leaders" of the Emergent movement.

 Cindy Jacobs is known as a "spiritual warfare specialist," and a prophetess to the nations. She has written a book called "Possessing the Gates of the Enemy," a training manual for militant intercessors, the forward is written by **C. Peter Wagner**; (In it she states **Wagner** has been her mentor; actually she has had just as much influence on him that he has had on her.)
Numerous new concepts are introduced, for example, laughter in prayer means God's will is accomplished or the answer is on the way. I guess I missed the chapter and verse in the Bible on this one; can anyone help me find it? She uses prophetic intercession to pull down strongholds in the heavenlies that block evangelism.
Jacobs, along with others, hold to the "Latter Rain" teaching of the "overcomers."
That is, an endtime church will birth the manchild, which is a worldwide revival (the only Biblical precedent for this is in the tribulation, spoken of in Rev.7).

"The Generals of Intercession" are headed by **Cindy Jacobs,** who attends the "Vineyard " church with pastor **Dutch Sheets**, who wrote the book, "River of God", which was endorsed by prophet **Rick Joyner**. http://www.letusreason.org/ Latrain66.htm

(**NOTE: There are various articles and YouTube videos about **Ms. Jacobs** that I did not provide, since it may be easier to see for yourself. Ed.).

- **Sarah Jakes-Roberts**: Co-pastors "One Church LA," one of the fastest growing churches in Los Angeles, alongside her husband, **Touré Roberts**.

Much like her father, **T.D. Jakes, Jakes-Roberts** is a poised, articulate speaker who seems to possess a wealth of life wisdom.

She appears pensive, and she speaks in paced patterns that suggest she is sincerely delving into the Word of God with great care and divine guidance.

Yet, also like her father, she merely employs oratory techniques and leans a lot to her own understanding. An example of this is from her recent sermon "From Grace to Grit". During it **Jakes-Roberts** naively speaks on her desire to do more with the grace God has given her.

In fairness to her, it seems her point may have been to discuss one's need to be a faithful steward in life. Yet, her approach to this discussion proves she is not a faithful steward of God's Word. This is first evidenced by her decision to center her discussion around the concept of "God's grace", **which leads her to utter and teach damnable errors on the topic.**

"God, I don't want to just live in the space of grace," she says. "I want to live a life that requires more grace." Yet Scripture is clear that one living a life that requires "more grace" is one who is abusing God's grace by living in unrepentant sin.

As Paul writes: "Moreover the law entered that the offense might abound. But where sin abounded, grace abounded much more... What shall we say then? Shall we continue in sin that grace may abound?"

Certainly not! How shall we who died to sin live any longer in it?" (Romans 5:20, 6:1-2).

With this, **Jakes-Roberts** unwittingly encourages her congregants to remain in their sins and abuse the grace of God! Also, by noting that she wants to do more with God's grace, she implies that God's grace isn't sufficient, though He says it is (II Corinthians 12:9).

"When God gives us something freely, like grace, He does it because He expects something in return - and that's grit," she says. "Grit. It's when you put yourself in a position where you need grace again."

Ah! Somebody get her! It is painful to hear such statements uttered when you know the truth! There is nothing we can do to earn or repay God for His grace. "For by grace you have been saved through faith, and that not of yourselves; it is the gift of God, not of works, lest anyone should boast" (Ephesians 2:8-9).

And if she insists on taking actions to position herself to "need grace again" that means she's not under grace at all (Romans 11:6). Either we are saved by grace through faith, or we attempt to earn salvation through our own efforts (works or "grit") - which is what **Jakes-Roberts** naively encourages.

But the latter is futile. All we can do is be obedient to the guidance of the Holy Spirit. And by the grace of God, He helps us do that, too! "For it is God who works in you to will and to do for His good pleasure" (Philippians 2:13).

It is also clear that **Jakes-Roberts** is not faithful in studying God's word because later in the same sermon, she poorly exegetes the parable of the wheat and the tares (Matthew 13:24-30), which is hard to do because Jesus literally explains it a few verses later (Matthew 13:36-43).

After reading Matthew 13:24 through 30, **Jakes-Roberts** says, "As I was studying, I believe God gave me insight about an exchange taking place here.
The text says, 'You are good seed. You're still good seed.' And how do I know that you are good seed? Because you are still planted in this earth. As long as you are planted in this earth, you are still good."

Yet, this parable plainly states that both the wheat and the tares are planted in the earth. In fact, they are being allowed to grow up together, and they will both be harvested. Nevertheless, the wheat, which represents the righteous, will be redeemed for eternal life with Christ. But the tares, which represent the wicked, will be judged and cast into hell.
 Indeed, the "good seed" and tare seeds are out here --growing up together and even looking alike to the untrained eye.

But notice in the parable that even as the owner's servants were instructed not to uproot the tares, they could easily identify them by the crop they produced. This is consistent with what Jesus tells us about identifying false prophets/believers among us, "By their fruit, you will know them" (Matthew 7:20). "But when the grain had sprouted and produced a crop, then the tares also appeared. So the servants of the owner came and said to him, 'Sir, did you not sow good seed in your field? How then does it have tares?'

He said to them, 'An enemy has done this.' The servants said to him, 'Do you want us then to go and gather them up?' But he said, 'No, lest while you gather up the tares you also uproot the wheat with them" (Matthew 13:26-29). https://www.lipstickalley.com/

- **T.D. Jakes**: Once a Oneness Pentecostal; claimed to have switched; evidence is he is still a Oneness preacher, which is a heretical and blasphemous teaching from the 3rd c.; WOF false preacher. This one seems like it should be obvious, but sadly, it isn't. Up until recently, **T.D. Jakes** was sold in Southern Baptist LifeWay book stores around the country.

 Jakes is a Modalist — that is, he believes a damning heresy about the Biblical doctrine of the Trinity. The Modalist heresy teaches that the Trinity is not one God existing in three distinct persons simultaneously, as the orthodox creeds teach. It teaches that the Trinity takes on different modes (or personalities) at different times.
That God either exists as the Father, or the Son, or the Holy Spirit, but never all three simultaneously. Besides this blatant heresy, **Jakes** is also a prosperity Gospel teacher who essentially teaches that God is like a genie in a bottle and exists to provide us with whatever we desire, so long as we have enough faith.

https://reformationcharlotte.org/2019/03/26/ false-teachers-evangelical-churches/

-**Jeff Jansen**: Part of the New Apostolic Reformation, which in turn holds Dominion Theology

http://www.biblebelievingtruthwatch.com/ blog---dominionism beliefs, has written an article entitled The Power of Throne Room Decrees: The Rising Of The Daniel Company."

This article was featured at the "Elijah" list website http://www.elijahlist.com/words/ display_word.html?ID=16972 on November 17, 2016.

In this blog I will be sharing parts of the article and including comments and links in parentheses along the way. Here is a bio of him from the website:

Jeff Jansen is an internationally known conference speaker and crusade evangelist. He is also Founder of "Global Fire Ministries International," and Senior Leader of the "Global Fire Church and World Miracle Center" located in Murfreesboro, Tennessee. **Jeff's** burning desire is to see churches, cities, regions and whole nations ignited and transformed by the power of God.
He also teaches, trains and equips believers how to live and move in the supernatural Presence of God and emphasizes that communion and intimacy with the Holy Spirit is vital for transformation. "Global Fire Ministries" is an inter-denominational ministry aimed at equipping and igniting the Body of Christ for Global harvest. **Jeff**, his wife Jan and family live in the Nashville, Tennessee area. **Jeff** travels full-time hosting international crusades and ministering at conferences, churches and "Glory Gatherings" around the world.

(In this description we see several words and phrases which clue us into his dominionist thinking): For example, "churches, cities, regions and whole nations ignited and transformed"; "the supernatural Presence of God"; "vital for transformation"; "igniting the Body of Christ for Global harvest".
As explained in the link above about "Dominion Theology," the church is not to focus on transforming nations now, but is rather to preach the Gospel of salvation to individuals so they can be forgiven of their sins and spend eternity with Jesus.

The fact that this description of **Jansen's** ministry does not mention sin, repentance, forgiveness, cross, atonement, and so forth is a huge red flag). More red flags are found in this article: http://www.charismanews.com/opinion/watchman-on-the-wall/ 56395-jeff-jansen-sees-huge-gold-angel-at-azusa-now —

in which the following words by **Jansen** are related:

"As we were driving on Interstate 5 to the "Azusa Now" event on April 9, I saw a large gold angel standing over LA," **Jansen** says. "The Lord said, 'Just as the 1849 gold rush drew people to California ... So 4/9 2016 will mark a new gold rush of divine proportion that will once again draw the nations into revival."

(That **Jansen** even attended the "Azusa Now" event http://herescope.blogspot.co.uk/2016/05/ azusa-or-pentecost.html

and then his statement concerning "a large gold angel" alert us to his NAR beliefs, complete with a familiarity with false "signs and wonders").

Here are excerpts from **Jansen's** article:

"I think we can all agree that we have just witnessed a modern-day political miracle in America! It was nothing less than a David and Goliath victory. (While it is true that Donald Trump received 81% of the evangelical vote, it is equally true that Democrat voters did not simply coalesce around their candidate, with Hillary Clinton receiving six million less votes than Obama did in 2012). http://www.renewamerica.com/columns/news/161115).

"The odds were clearly stacked against us, and all the weight was clearly in favor of a "Goliath System" that would have brought our nation into deep darkness. Not only was the Church in America praying, but the corporate Body of Christ globally was standing in agreement for a miracle in our nation." "I firmly believe that it was not any one state in particular that swung this election, but rather it was the fervent prayer of the Church that charted the course of events that swung the vote for change."

"If My people, who are called by My Name, humble themselves, and pray and seek (crave, require as a necessity), My face and turn from their wicked ways, then I will hear [them] from heaven, and forgive their sin and heal their land. (II Chronicles 7:14" AMP).
(It is quite interesting to see how many preachers quote this scripture when it obviously does not apply to either America or to the church today. If the reader believes it does, I urge you to read this article:

https://michellelesleybooks.com/2016/11/10/
tbt-is-2-chronicles-714-gods-promise-to-american-christians-today-2/).

"Donald Trump was elected to be the 45th President of the United States in a time that is so critical to the soul of our nation. God purposed him as His servant, with a special set of skills, power and ability, to break the bars of iron and bronze and to restore hope, purity and purpose to our nation. ("Purity"?) **Jansen** must be joking.
 Just the news story at this link alone — https://www.washingtonpost.com/politics/
trump-recorded-having-extremely-lewd-conversation-about-women-in-2005/2016/10/07/3b9ce7
76-8cb4-11e6-bf8a-3d26847eeed4_story.html—

is enough to discredit that possibility. This would not have been possible if it weren't for the hidden "Daniel Company" who understood the times and the season and prayed fervently as they understood breakthrough was on the horizon.

It was Daniel who was reading the Word of the Lord in Jeremiah 29:10-11, that after 70 years the Jews would be released to go home to rebuild. "In the first year of his reign, I, Daniel, understood from the books the number of years which, according to the word of the Lord to Jeremiah the prophet, must pass before the desolations [which had been] pronounced on Jerusalem would end; and it was seventy years." "So I directed my attention to the Lord God to seek Him by prayer and supplications, with fasting, sackcloth and ashes." (Daniel 9:2-3 AMP).

(While this Scripture is historically correct, the jump that must be made in order to apply it to today is mind-boggling. Before the 70 years of captivity took place, Nebuchadnezzar and his armies conquered the nation of Judah, burned Jerusalem, destroyed the Temple, killed a

majority of the Jews, and marched the rest across 500 miles of desert to Babylon, where they would live out their lives as slaves).
Did anything close to these events happen to America? Obviously not.
   One cannot just cherry pick Scriptures and attempt to have them apply to this nation today).

It was the persistent prayers and prophetic decrees of the "Daniel Company " that swung the vote in America as they understood the severity of the times and season we were in. God heard and answered. "Just as justice and righteousness were restored to the nation of Israel as they were released from Babylonian captivity after 70 years, so we have been given the same opportunity here in America. We will look back to this amazing event in history as the time God single-handedly rescued our nation and brought saving grace back in the United States of America."
 (Saving grace has always been available to those who would repent and call on the Lord). But understand that it was the "Daniel Company "that stood in the gap and released powerful decrees and prayer" that brought about the change!

(Decreeing and declaring is part of the confession aspect of the Word of Faith false teaching which is explained quite well in this article—

https://thewordonthewordoffaithinfoblog.com/2013/02/10/
word-of-faith-positive-confession-is-really-occult-powers/thewordonthewordoffaithinfoblog.com/
2013/02/10/word-of-faith-positive-confession-is-really-occult-powers/

"I've personally witnessed the reality of becoming the voice piece of the Lord as I've traveled the nations.   I've watched the Lord move in union with my voice to bring about His personal directives for individuals, churches, cites and nations with amazing power.

 When the voice of the Lord speaks, I've seen, on numerous occasions, earthquakes, snowstorms, tornadoes, and hurricanes all dismantled through the power of the spoken decree."
 (That is a bunch of rubbish. We can pray for God's protection, but we are not the voice piece of the Lord to command storms). Another Word of Faith proponent is **Kenneth Copeland.**

In this audio clip - https://soundcloud.com/copeland-network/
hurricane-matthew-call-program—

we hear **Copeland** telling Hurricane Matthew to fold; to go to the bottom of the sea. "Go away now", he says. (Well, I happen to live in the southeastern United States and I, along with millions of people, can personally attest to the fact that **Kenneth Copeland** has no power to command storms, even if he says in the name of Jesus).

"We need to get ready for the new "Daniel Company." "These new oracle wonder workers will change cities, regions, and nations when they speak as the voice of God in the earth with the mighty word of power. They access and release realms of heavenly revelation with the unlimited anointing of power that comes from the presence of the Lord. Nothing will stand before them."

(More Dominionism talk).

"To date, we have seen many waves of revival hit the nations of the earth, but nothing like we are beginning to witness now."
"God is propelling the maturing Body of Christ into a new place on the planet. A "Daniel Company" is rising with the burning coals of Heaven on their lips."

"Like Moses, they will speak as "God-like ones," declaring and decreeing the very will of God through their words. "The multitudes will understand who God is as nations are shifted and multitudes come to Christ through demonstrations of power released through prophetic decree." "We've seen some pretty remarkable things in past revivals, including the "Welsh revival," "The Great Awakening," "Azusa Street," " Latter Rain," "The Voice of Healing of the 1940s and 1950s," and then later moves of God like the "Toronto Blessing"

http://www.biblebelievingtruthwatch.com/ toronto-blessing-error.html "Brownsville Revival" and others."

"Impressive as they were, they were merely "previews of the coming attraction." "They will all pale in comparison to the outpouring of this new season— the outpouring of the Spirit of Revival."
(All of these Scriptures speak of apostasy in the last days rather than huge revivals):

_Matthew 24:4-26; 2 Thessalonians 2:1-12; 1 Timothy 4: 1-3; 2 Timothy 3:1-9; 4:3, 4; 2 Peter 2:1-3:18; Jude 3-19; Revelation 3:14-16; 6:1-19:21). In the tribulation we do see multitudes saved as described in Rev. 7:9.

Here is an excellent article concerning the subject as well

http://taministries.net/wp-content/uploads/2010/11/
Will-there-be-a-World-Revival-v1.5.pdf

For anyone who is unaware of the tribulation period which will come upon this earth and the One World Order, comprised of the One World Religion and One World Government, which will be in effect during this time, I urge you to listen to the message at this link:

http://www.biblebelievingtruthwatch.com/ mystery-babylon.html.

It will describe how Jehovah Witnesses, Mormons, Muslims, New Age, Emergent Church, Occult, Word of Faith, Dominionists, Ecumenists, Mystics and all apostate Christianity, in all shapes, that are giving anyone another way of salvation apart from Jesus Christ and His death as the sacrifice for sin, plus nothing added to this, such as sacraments etc., are a part of the mystery Babylon system, culminating into the One World Order.

https://www.biblebelievingtruthwatch.net/ jeff-jansen-and-false-declarations.html.

- **Leroy Jenkins**: There was a time when everyone knew his name.

The Rev. **Leroy Jenkins** was famous in Delaware, where he started the "Healing Water Cathedral " in the 1970s. A televangelist and faith healer, **Jenkins**, 83, died from complications of pneumonia Wednesday morning in Florida, said his son, Danny Jenkins (June 21, 2017).

" He always had a big presence, and loved being around people, ' Danny Jenkins said. "He looked like Elvis, dressed like Liberace, ran for governor and said he had God-given powers," said Lee Yoakum, spokesman for the city of Delaware (Ohio) in an email. "Someone like that is going to leave a pretty colorful history — in any town — not just Delaware."
Jenkins would call strangers up to the stage from the audience and tell them all about themselves, then he would touch them and heal them if they were sick, said the Rev. Bob Frary, 73, **Jenkins'** assistant pastor for more than 40 years and a preacher in Grove City.

Jenkins was one of the area's first television evangelists. At one point, he claimed to be on at least 34 television stations across the country. **Jenkins** later switched to radio. "His ministry was based on doing something most pastors wish they could do," Frary said. "He didn't have a fake gift like some of these other crooks." "He had the real thing." **Jenkins** left Delaware for Arizona in the early 2000s, though he came back a few times to preach at the Ohio Theatre and over the years his name was the topic of many news articles.
Jenkins had legal troubles and he served time in prison on charges of conspiracy to commit arson and assault. He also filed for bankruptcy, was indicted for tax evasion and is accused of selling contaminated "miracle water." In May 2014, the building in Delaware that housed his chapel was condemned and demolished. It's currently vacant green space.

Born Feb. 19, 1934, **Jenkins** first started preaching in the 1960s after he badly injured his arm and then went to a tent revivalist. He pledged that if God healed his arm, he would serve Him for the rest of his life. "And he did," Danny Jenkins said.
Before his death, **Jenkins** lived near Orlando, Florida, where he moved two years before from Scottsdale, Arizona. "He wanted people to have hope that there is a God," Danny Jenkins said. "He preached faith, that was his biggest message." A private memorial service will be scheduled at a later date. More information can be found at Woodlawn Memorial Park and Funeral Home in Gotha, Florida.
https://www.dispatch.com/news/20170622/ televangelist-leroy-jenkins-dead-at-83

(**NOTE: The TV program, "Inside Edition," posted a video of **Leroy Jenkins**, exposing him as a fake healer in 2008. You can see it on You Tube. Ed.).

"This false prophet hits close to home with me because my father was greatly affected by him in the 1960's." "My grandmother used to tell me when I was a child how **Leroy** would pay people to perform for him during tent meetings." " My father worked with him and helped with his tent meetings during his early years." "My family is very familiar with this con-artist." "Like all faith healers, **Leroy** is a fraud who only cares about money." " It's sad that so many people are deceived by men like **Leroy Jenkins**." "These men can bring in thousands upon thousands of people per service by giving them false hopes and introducing them to a false Messiah."

"And yes, I am biased toward **Leroy Jenkins** because I have seen on a first-hand basis the power a false prophet has over those he influences. I praise God that He saved my father a few years ago by delivering him through the true Gospel of Jesus Christ, from the false Gospel **Leroy** gave him in the 1960's."

"Today, many of my family members are still caught up in the charismatic movement." " I pray for them (**Leroy** included) and long for the day the Lord delivers them the way He delivered my father." " I know this post is a bit personal, but I wanted to share it with my readers. I just wanted to use my father as an example of how the Lord can deliver us from the darkest of deceptions." (Matthew 19:25-26).
https://davidjosephhorn.wordpress.com/2010/05/25/ false-faith-healer-leroy-jenkins/

Leroy Jenkins jumped onto the traveling healing gig after allegedly being healed at an **A.A. Allen** meeting in 1960. **Jenkins** is probably one of the most controversial figures in the charismatic movement. **Leroy** is a convicted felon for his arson conviction of burning down a State trooper's home, he was sentenced to twelve years in prison in 1979. (3)
Leroy has also had issues with drugs and alcohol, like his mentor **A.A. Allen**.

"According to the "Dictionary of Pentecostal and Charismatic Movements," **Jenkins** was arrested on more than one occasion on drug and alcohol related charges while in the ministry, and divorced his wife." (4) More recently he married a handicapped elderly black woman in Las Vegas (who just happened to win a huge lottery prize):
The thrice married evangelist is said to 'combine a little bit of Jesus, and a little bit of Elvis.'

His Las Vegas controversial marriage last Jan 12 (later annulled) 16 days after his 71 year-old bride's husband died, drew charges from her family that **Jenkins** wanted her fortune of about $4 million (8/4 Huntsville Times). (5) I've seen Mr. **Jenkins** "perform" live on several occasions and I must admit he is every bit the showman that **Benny Hinn** is but on a much smaller platform.
Married three times, he and **Mr. Tilton** have that in common along with other noxious behaviors. https://discernmentministriesinternational.wordpress.com/ category/don-stewart/

- **Dr. David Jeremiah**: "Seed Sowing" heresy\Gospel of greed; associates with known RC New Age Mystics, **Roma Downey-Mark Burnett**; https://pulpitandpen.org/2015/10/06/.

Pastor **David Jeremiah** recently worked with "JesusCalling.com " to produce a podcast titled, "Keeping Hope In A Darkened World." In addition to promoting his new book, the pastor also promoted **Sarah Young**, the author of the "Jesus Calling" books, studies, devotionals, calendars, and coloring book.
The transcript of the interview regarding his admiration for the multi-million dollar "Jesus Calling" empire is as follows:
Narrator: "As a pastor and a teacher, **Dr. Jeremiah** advocates daily prayer and Scripture reading. He appreciates how **Sarah Young** has helped many with their prayer lives through the words of "Jesus Calling."

Excerpt from "Jesuscalling.com" – **Dr. Jeremiah**:

"When I read **Sarah's** work, it's pretty obvious to me why it's been so highly regarded and received. She makes prayer very personal." "Sometimes prayer isn't personal, sometimes prayer can be very cold and empty. Maybe that's why a lot of people have a hard time sustaining any kind of a prayer ministry."

" What **Sarah** has done has made it possible for people to say, "I talked to God today…I communicated with my Father." "That's what prayer is supposed to be and she has moved the ball down the field quite aggressively in that direction."

You may be asking yourself, "Is it a problem for fans of **Jeremiah** that he appears on the "Jesus Calling" site to promote his book? Isn't this just 'guilt by association?" Yes and no. Meaning, yes, it is a problem, and no, it's not a matter of "guilt by association."

You see, **Jeremiah** doesn't just accidentally appear on a stage with some of the most ferocious wolves and false teachers of the day. He actually teams up with them, telling his followers that these folks are perfectly fine to follow, listen to and/or read.

Jeremiah's daily radio program, "Turning Point Ministries," had a mission to "deliver the unchanging Word of God to an ever-changing world."
Unfortunately, **Sarah Young** has changed the Word of God into the musings of what Jesus "spoke" to her into a false narrative that is shipwrecking the faith of millions of sheep around the world. Her idea to write down what this "Jesus" was speaking to her actually came from two New Age, non-Christian authors of a book called "God Calling."
Young even says so in the intro to her "Jesus Calling" book, but in the revised new editions that reference to "God Calling" has been whitewashed by Thomas Nelson Publishing so that the sheep won't know.

If this were just one instance of affiliating with a false teacher, you could say that he ought to be talked to and warned. That's what happened a few years ago when **Jeremiah** joined hands with **Joel Osteen** and **Joyce Meyer**.

One red flag is enough to cause concern, but the many red flags of **Jeremiah's** ministry and affiliations, and you have to ask yourself if it's now time to mark and avoid.

Jeremiah regularly appears on Trinity Broadcasting Network (TBN), alongside a host of false teachers to preach and fund raise. He was also asked by the Catholic **Roma Downey/Mark Burnett** duo to write a companion book on Acts as a sequel to their miniseries titled "The Bible". Later he had them come to his church to promote the series.
Jeremiah, senior pastor, "Shadow Mountain Community Church," is also on President Donald Trump's Evangelical Advisory Committee.
http://www.piratechristian.com/berean-examiner/david-jeremiah

We share this out of concern for the hundreds of thousands who follow popular teacher **Dr. David Jeremiah**, who has reportedly has joined other prominent leaders (**Max Lucado, Mark Batterson, Lysa TerKeurst, Jennie Allen, Lee Strobel, Ann Voskamp, Sheila Walsh, Christine Caine, Roma Downey, Dr. Jack Graham**, etc.), in promoting and endorsing the "Jesus Calling" franchise, written by **Sarah Young.**

We want to share some other concerns we have about **Dr. Jeremiah**, for your consideration: **Jeremiah** regularly appears on Trinity Broadcasting Network (TBN), and was often alongside Word of Faith/prosperity teacher **Paul Crouch** (when he was alive). Last year, **Jeremiah** joined with Word of Faith heretics **Kenneth Copeland, Paula White,** and **Jan Crouch** in laying hands on and praying for Donald Trump.

Jeremiah hosted Catholic New Ager **Roma Downey** and **Mark Burnett** at his church to discuss and promote the new TV show "A.D." and **Jeremiah's** new companion book based on the Biblical book of Acts. **David Jeremiah** promoted New Age authors through his book, "Life Wide Open", in which he favorably quoted New Agers, Buddhist sympathizers, mystics and contemplatives.

The report also showed **Jeremiah's** affiliation with New Age sympathizer **Ken Blanchard** and "Lead Like Jesus." He cites contemplatives Brother Lawrence's "Practice of the Presence of God", and "When the heart Waits," by Sue Monk Kidd.

His book, "Captured by Grace," **Jeremiah** favorably points to mystical contemplative Catholic author, the late **Henri Nouwen**, (who said he was uncomfortable with those who say that Jesus is the only way of salvation and that he felt it was his calling to help people find their own path).
 In addition, inside the front of the book sits the name and endorsement of **Ken Blanchard.** It's a serious pattern of confusing the sheep. "Do not be unequally yoked with unbelievers.
 For what partnership has righteousness with lawlessness? Or what fellowship has light with darkness? 15 What accord has Christ with Belial? Or what portion does a believer share with an unbeliever? 16 What agreement has the temple of God with idols?" "For we are the temple of the living God; as God said, II Corinthians 6:14-18.
Additionally, it is dangerous to fellowship with false teachers because they can corrupt even sound theology.   https://bereanresearch.org/dr-david-jeremiah

- **Kari Jobes**: Is a popular musician being promoted in churches, especially to our youth. **Jobe,** out of seeker-sensitive NAR **Robert Morris'** "Gateway Church," is known for popular songs like "I Am Not Alone," and "Love Came Down."
 She is also under the leadership of "Gateway's NAR Apostle and elder, **Jack Hayford**, author of the song "Majesty," which teaches the heretical "Kingdom Now" theology. However, she is among those who "teach for shameful gain things she ought not to teach (Titus 1:11 Open in Logos Bible Software (if available)."

One of her most popular songs, "Forever," published by 'Bethel Music" (the same outfit that produced "Jesus Culture," contains some really aberrant theology. Besides the fact that she's a female pastor in a church, her theology alone should be enough to disqualify her as a teacher. Below is a sample of her lyrics:

One final breath He gave
As heaven looked away
The Son of God was laid in darkness
A battle in the grave

The war on death was waged
The power of hell forever broken

Then, in an interview about her song, "Forever," she said, "My favorite part of the whole thing is … we talk about the death on the cross and we talk about the resurrection, but that time in between was when Jesus was in hell <u>rendering hell</u>.   And <u>ransacking hell</u>.
 And defeating the enemy – taking those keys to death and hell and the grave to be victorious over that when He rose from the dead." Of course, we can pick apart almost any song, even some of the best traditional hymns.
But the serious error here is that she is teaching a <u>heresy</u> that strikes at the heart of Christian theology, which is the death, burial and resurrection of Jesus Christ. She gets a pass though, you know, because "artistic license and stuff."

<u>This idea that Jesus died and went to Hell to battle Satan stems from an old heresy that is prominent in Word of Faith circles that teach that Jesus died spiritually, and was "born again" after defeating Satan in Hell.</u>

 Popular teachers of this false teaching are **Joyce Meyer, Kenneth Copeland** and **Creflo Dollar**. **Joyce Meyer** writes in her book, "The Most Important Decision You'll Ever Make," the following: "Jesus paid on the cross and went to hell in my place. Then as God had promised, on the third day Jesus rose from the dead."

"The scene in the spirit realm went something like this: God rose up from his throne and said to <u>demon powers tormenting the sinless son of God, "let him go."</u> " Then the resurrection power of Almighty God <u>went through hell and filled Jesus."</u>

" On earth his grave where they had buried him was filled with light as the power of God filled his body. He was resurrected from the dead–the first born again man."

But if denying the power of the cross isn't enough to turn your head away from **Kari Jobe's** music, perhaps her treatment of Jesus would be enough to make your stomach turn.
Another popular song, "The More I Seek You," she treats Jesus more like a lover than a Savior:

The more I seek you,
The more I find you
The more I find you, the more I love you
I wanna sit at your feet
Drink from the cup in your hand.
Lay back against you and breathe, feel your heart beat
This love is so deep, it's more than I can stand.
I melt in your peace, it's overwhelming

Besides the theology in this song just being plain horrible, she displays a total lack of understanding of God's love for us. God's love for us is not an erotic (Greek: eros) love, but agape. "Agape" is a parental, sacrificial, unconditional love, whereas eros is a bodily, emotional kind of love. <u>The lyrics in this song pervert the nature of God's love.</u>

I don't see how anyone could worship our sovereign God to music like this, yet the eroticizing of God's love for us is gaining steam.

'Hillsong's "Forever Reign" is another popular song in evangelical churches that does this, while **Ann Voskamp**, a popular women's devotional writer, blogger, and author, promotes this same foolishness in her book, "1000 Gifts." **Voskamp** writes, "I fly to Paris and discover how to make love to God." One of the Hallmarks of NAR worship is to use repetitive phrases and rhythmic cadences to draw people into a trance-like state, believing that by doing so, you can have intimacy with God.
In reality, what it does is cause people to zone out, and not really think about what they are saying. Being under the influence of NAR Apostle, **Jack Hayford**, who has been instrumental in transforming the worship music scene, it comes as no surprise that her music incorporates this tactic.

Jack Hayford claims direct, divine revelation from God, and says that while driving by a Roman Catholic church, God directly told him not to judge them.

He says God directly said to him, " Why would I not be happy with a place [Catholic Church] where every morning the testimony of the blood of my Son is raised from the altar?"
Being that the Catholic Church worships a false Jesus, you can rest assured that **Hayford** did not hear that from God. Yet, this is a man influencing **Kari Jobes**, and many other modern worship music artists. All of this and more is what the evangelical church is feeding its sheep: Wolves, snake oil salesmen, bad theology...and nobody bats an eye.

Children are being sent off to church camps and "Christian" concerts to be fed goat's milk through worship. Sadly, many truly love Jesus, and desire to worship him rightly, but have no idea that their music is leading them down a path of destruction. Music is tearing down doctrinal lines and creating unholy alliances at a faster pace than once thought possible.

No longer do Evangelicals, Catholics, and other professing Christians have to stand against each other over "matters of secondary importance...like the Bible," we can now unite around our new idol of worship music.

"But I say, walk by the Spirit, and you will not gratify the desires of the flesh. For the desires of the flesh are against the Spirit, and the desires of the Spirit are against the flesh, for these are opposed to each other, to keep you from doing the things you want to do" (Gal. 5:16, 17).

https://reformationcharlotte.org/2019/02/23/
kari-jobes-sexualizing-of-gods-love-and-word-of-faith-heresy/

Their body "Gateway Church" is a very unbiblical seeker friendly mega sized and compromised religious body in various ways. They are NOT a true New Testament biblical body as modeled by the first century saints as these places put on shows of and for man. At "Gateway" they have on their website:

"Over the past 10 years, 'Gateway Worship" has evolved in their powerful expression of worship, as they passionately pursue a journey of discovery and understanding of the power of a unified response to God's presence and love for His people."

There is a video on the internet with **Kari** talking about how she grew up in prophetic ministry and how she hears "God's voice". See Rev 22. Hebrews 1 tells us: "In the past God spoke to our ancestors through the prophets at many times and in various ways, 2 but in these last days he has spoken to us by his Son, whom he appointed heir of all things, and through whom also he made the universe."
The Bible is what we should be following fully and obediently, not what we think is God's voice as we can be deceived easily. Jesus warned of much deception in the last days (See Matthew 24).

Yes we have a conscience and are now walking in the Spirit but these things she is speaking about is "false fire", false "signs and wonders." **Kari** is one of the performers at the "Lovely Woman's Conference" at **Bill Johnson's** 'Bethel " organization. **Johnson** has a demonic organization that is not modeling the true New Testament church Christ established. He has one of the most demon possessed churches out there! He is into extra biblical revelation, many signs and wonders, the dangerous NAR group.

They are a cult with strange manifestations going on there like "glory clouds," " gold dust" falling down, people convulsing and rolling on the ground which is NOT of God at all.

Kari is one of the participants at the "Women of Faith" conference in Houston, Texas with **Beth** "the heretic" **Moore** and others. **Beth Moore** has gone over to the mystic side and is teaching various unbiblical ways and linking herself to very questionable unbiblical groups of late, like Roman Catholics. **Moore** is also not obedient to God's Word in her dress. (1 Timothy 2 and 1 Corinthians 11).

 Kari performed at the "Passion" conference in 2013 originated by **Louie Giglio**, another heretic. **Lou** is a modern pastor at a large seeker body that is NOT Biblical and it is not modeled after the first century church Christ ordained.
He is into various strange associations like uniting with Roman Catholics and contemplative prayer.
Kari sings, writes and sells "instrumental emotional music" that is NOT part of God's plan for His true New Testament church. She is not obedient to God's Word in her dress (1 Timothy 2 and 1 Corinthians 11). She also (as we have shown) is united with many unbiblical people and error filled ways so we lovingly warn others to avoid her. https://eternalevangelism.com/kari-jobe-another-nar-heretic/

- **Bill Johnson**: Founder of IHOP; believes in "glory dust," "feathers" and "soaking worship"; one of the most influential leaders of the NAR; NAR Healing Rooms in Wales–"Bethel " Redding NAR invades Wales (through their "Sozo" healing rooms).

(**NOTE: "IHOP" stands for International House of Prayer. Ed.).

"Sozo" prayer is the brain child of husband and wife team **Bill** (self-proclaimed modern-day apostle) and **Beni** (New Age guru) **Johnson**, both of whom are pastors of the infamous 'Bethel Church" in Redding, CA. The word comes from the Greek "save" or "deliver." Allegedly "Sozo" is "a unique inner healing and deliverance ministry in which the main aim is to get to the root of those things hindering your personal connection with the Father, Son and Holy Spirit."

"The Berean Call" describes "Sozo" thusly: "Although claiming to be Biblical, "Sozo" is a problem-solving approach based upon discovering root issues that are blocking spiritual growth." "The issues supposedly reside in the subconscious memories of the individual and are identified as a person is regressed by the use of guided imagery and suggestion by the "Sozo" therapist."
 "Of course, the "Sozo" therapist is trained to believe that the guided visualization is superintended by the Holy Spirit.
This again is spiritualized psychotherapy, using techniques drawn from occult methodologies."
"Sozo" is decidedly unbiblical. And it is dangerous!
https://wolvesinthepulpit.blogspot.com/2018/04/.

(Below) is a link to a blogger who has first hand experience as being a trained "Sozo" healer and warns of the dangers of it:

https://mkayla.wordpress.com/2013/01/31/ inner-healing-christian-or-occult/

Bill Johnson and **Kris Vallotton** (and other "Bethel "pastors) put their own words above the Word of God. Listen to them talk and you'll hear very few actual Bible verses, but you will hear a lot of their own thoughts and ideas that they claim to have received directly from God.

This is not accidental. They believe they are a new and better type of Christian leader who can hear directly from God and get "downloads" of new information.   They believe the Bible is merely a good starting point that has useful information about God, but to really know Him you must go further than the Bible-you need to go "off the map."

"None of us has a full grasp of Scripture, but we all have the Holy Spirit. He is our common denominator who will always lead us into truth. But to follow Him, we must be willing to follow off the map—to go beyond what we know." — **Bill Johnson** "When Heaven Invades Earth-A Practical Guide to a Life of Miracles."

 1. "It's difficult to expect the same fruit of the early church when we value a book they didn't have more than the Holy Spirit they did have. It's not Father, Son and Holy Bible." — **Bill Johnson**, YouTube video: "Friendship With God"   https://youtu.be/P4RZ_ctiwlE

2. Go back to the previous point. Seriously, that is enough to end the discussion. If the Bible is only a starting point (because we need to get "new and better information") than this is not the historic Christian church. In fact, even the Roman Catholic Church believes that we can't have a bunch of different people running around claiming to speak for God; that's why they have only one Pope.

In the "Bethel" /NAR way of thinking, practically everyone is their own Pope! "Bethel " teaches that we must have a subjective and mystical connection to the Holy Spirit that allows us to receive more than the clear meaning of the Word of God, because the Word of God isn't enough.

3. Are you carefully considering how dangerous it is to degrade and devalue the Word of God the way **Bill Johnson, Kris Vallotton** and "Bethel " does? Are you really comfortable abandoning what the Christian Church has taught, confessed and believed since its very beginning? On top of that, are you really comfortable handing over the Christian Church and its doctrines to men like **Bill Johnson** and **Kris Vallotton**?
These men are getting rich off the sheep they claim to serve; they are constantly selling stuff and giving speeches for money. These men make no bones about it-they make a lot of money and they're happy to continue making more. Is that who we should trust with the future of the Christian faith? Please check out "A Biblical Guide to the Prosperity Gospel."

4. **Bill Johnson, Kris Vallotton** and "Bethel "twist the Bible to make it say what they want it to say. **Bill Johnson** will take the English word from the Bible and try to extract some special new meaning from it; but the original word was never in English!

Here's a really embarrassing example: "Renewing the mind begins with repentance..."Re" means to go back. "Pent" is like the penthouse, the top floor of the building. Repent, then, means to go back to God's perspective on reality." (**Bill Johnson**, "The Supernatural Power of a Transformed Mind," p. 44).

The word "repent" has nothing to do with penthouses-obviously! The original Greek word transliterated is "metanoia" and it means "I repent, change my mind, change the inner man (particularly with reference to acceptance of the will of God), repent," according to Strong's concordance. This is horrendous Bible twisting from a man who either has no idea what he's doing (and **Bill Johnson** has no training in the ancient languages that the Bible was written in), or he's so confident that he's hearing new messages from God that he doesn't care.

Here's another example from the same book: "For many years I misunderstood the Biblical concept of desire."

"Psalm 37:4 tells us: "Delight yourself in the Lord, and He shall give you the desires of your heart." "Like many pastors, I foolishly taught that if you delighted yourself in the Lord, He would change your desires by telling you what to desire." " But that's not at all what this means." "That verse literally means that God wants to be impacted by what you think and dream. God is after your desires." "The word desire is made up of the prefix 'de' meaning 'of,' and sire meaning 'father.' Desire is, by nature, of the Father." — **Bill Johnson**, "The Supernatural Power of a Transformed Mind," page 144.

Bill Johnson doesn't even bother to consult a concordance, which is a very simple way to learn the meaning of any word found in the Bible. Instead, he demonstrates that he is horribly incapable of teaching a Biblical passage.

The Hebrew word translated into English as desire is "mishalah." It simply means "request" or "petition," but **Bill Johnson** is telling people that "God is after their desires" because "de" and 'sire" means "of the father," according to him. This is a complete fabrication and a deliberate twisting of God's Word. Why would he do that? Who knows? Maybe it's because he's appealing to the selfish desires of his gullible audience. He is definitely tickling itching ears.

5. **Bill Johnson** didn't have enough sense to know that he was getting scammed by **Todd Bentley** at "The Charismatic Day of Infamy." All of the "Apostles" of the New Apostolic Reformation gathered together to commission **Todd Bentley** as the great new leader whose revival meetings (the "Lakeland Revival") were a big deal for a few months of "glory" in 2008.

But **Todd Bentley** was a fraud, adulterer and drunk, and none of those "Apostles" (**Bill Johnson** being a primary member) had enough discernment to figure it out. These are the men who claim to have all sorts of special insights directly from God, but they were utterly clueless.
Does that sound like the kind of guy whose direct "downloads" should be trusted to establish new doctrine? After **Todd Bentley** abandoned his wife and children,

Bill Johnson tried to restore him back to ministry—ignoring the fact that he was utterly disqualified by his despicable, sinful behavior. Even today, **Bill Johnson** supports and promotes the fraud **Todd Bentley**. Here's something he posted on his Facebook wall just recently: 2018-02-20.
 "So **Bill Johnson** openly supports and endorses his friend, the fraud **Todd Bentley**."
By the way, even that promo for **Bentley's** "revival" is fraudulent: that's an old photograph of a **Billy Graham** meeting in Los Angeles."

6. **Bill Johnson** and **Kris Vallotton** are both big fans of the creepy cult leader **William Branham** (1909-1965). **Branham** was so detached from Biblical Christianity that even Word of Faith founder **Kenneth Hagin** called him a false teacher and predicted he would die two years before it happened from a car accident in 1965. Although he died on Dec. 24, 1965, **Branham's** followers refused to bury his body since they believed he would rise from the dead.

They finally gave up and buried him on April 11th of the next year. **Branham** didn't believe in the Trinity. **Branham** believed he was the end-time "Elijah." **Branham** taught that Eve and the serpent had sexual intercourse and Cain was born, and that consequently every woman potentially carried the literal seed of the devil, so he always believed women to be inferior and untrustworthy. **Branham** was a pathological liar who told many variations of stories for decades with conflicting details. **Bill Johnson** and **Kris Vallotton** have stated that they want the "mantle" of **William Branham**.

7. "Bethel Church" claims to be special place where the "Presence" is tangible, and miracles happen every day, yet when a coven of witches went there to get prophetic words spoken over them, they were told nothing but positive things and were actually encouraged to continue in their witchcraft. Seriously. Read about it: "Bethel Church Tells Witch that She's "On the Right Path" and "God is So Proud of Her!'"

8. **Bill Johnson** has established new doctrines that are not taught anywhere in Scripture, and these new doctrines have become foundational beliefs that have caused a great deal of confusion. For example, a foundational belief at "Bethel " is that "we must create a culture that welcomes risk-taking." Once this belief is established, people feel free to make stuff up and do things that are weird, harmful and unbiblical.

Another foundational belief is that "we owe people an encounter with God." This "Encounter Gospel" teaches that people cannot believe in God unless we do some supernatural miracle for them, and it eliminates the need for a sinner to repent of their sins.

This idea adds a great deal of confusion and it conflicts with the Bible's teaching that the Holy Spirit works through the Word of God to convert people. On top of these new doctrines, **Bill Johnson & Co.** are always degrading the use of reason and elevating a mystical/gnostic approach to knowledge. This is a recipe for utter confusion, and it lays a foundation for people to abandon their Christian faith, which should be based on God's Word.

Check out these "Bethel " sayings and notice how murky, unbiblical and anti-intellectual the thinking is:

9. Although **Bill Johnson**, **Kris Vallotton** and other "Bethel " pastors will claim to be focusing on "nothing but Jesus" the truth is that they don't. Listen to these people "preach" and you'll hear lots of talking and stories, but the emphasis is never on the simple and finished Gospel message that Jesus Christ came and gave His life as an atoning sacrifice for our sins. The Apostle Paul said "I preach Christ and Him crucified," but the "Bethel" message is focused on what they're doing and what's going to happen next.

This is no accident. **Bill Johnson** has repeatedly said that he wants 'Bethel " to focus on only one thing: "revival." This is not what the Bible teaches—but it's what **Bill Johnson** teaches. Why? Because **Bill Johnson** had an experience at the "Toronto Blessing" that caused him to devote himself to this form of "revival."

The "Toronto Blessing " was so controversial that the founder of the 'Vineyard " movement, **John Wimber**, went to the "Toronto Airport Vineyard Church" and told them they were in serious error. **Wimber** then cut the church out of his "Vineyard " fellowship for being too far removed from Biblical Christianity.

Bill Johnson took over "Bethel Church " and steered it into the very controversial Toronto Blessing kind of teaching, and that caused the Assemblies of God to cut them off in a similar way. "Bethel Church " is so far on the fringe that it is creating its own new and unbiblical doctrines. http://www.piratechristian.com/messedupchurch/2018/2/10-reasons-why-bethel-redding-is-a-false-church

- **Jesus Culture**. Danger A "Bethel Church" (Redding California, head pastor **Bill Johnson**) youth ministry/worship band which promotes the revivalist teachings and practices of Bethel Church. **Cindy Jacobs** is a regular speaker at Jesus Culture events. http://www.cults.co.nz/j.php

- **Ian Johnson:** Is a false signs person who supports false signs of gold dust, feathers, and gem stones, and angelic appearances. He is based in Auckland and has toured New Zealand with false teachers such as **Ian Clayton** and **Kathie Walters**. http://www.cults.co.nz/j.php

- **Jenn Johnson**: Another false "prophet" of the Emergent church and the NAR.
She is as at fault as all of them, she is a teacher who claims to be a representative of God and His Word. She assumes that role when taking the place of a teacher in the house of God.

She is more dangerous than some of the other teachers because she is so idolized by many impressionable young people, some of the most innocent minds will be taken by this doctrine preached by her more than they would by someone that sounds a little more 'scientific'.
What she is teaching here is called "relative morality" or "relative truth."
 Literally she is calling on people to make judgment calls based on their thoughts, emotions, or their will (their soul) or by using the judgment of their heart. She leads them down a path of judging whether something is black or white,...which really is just another way of saying good or evil. She presents several items that are already judged by God in the Bible such as murder. God already says murder is evil in His Word (although she does not identify the Word of God as the source of that judgment), then she picks "loving everyone'.

Jesus already commands us to love our brother as our self, and to love our neighbor as our self, and to love our enemies (notice he didn't say your enemies were not enemies, He just said love them),...so we know loving people is good because it is the command of God according to the Word of God.
Also slander is identified as evil in the Word of God. Why would she present idolatry as the hinge point of good and evil(black and white)? Because this is where she has a total disconnect from God and His Word. Basically in her world ministry contains a lot of Idolatry.

Ministry figures in her world become idols and icons. Worship ministries, prophetic ministries, teaching ministries,...until people will go to an 'anointed one' instead of going to God.
Or they will go to an anointed one to get to God. They will soak in their icons music rather than enter into genuine worship, they will seek an icon's teaching rather that the Holy Spirit's revelation, and they will seek an icons prophetic word before spending hours in prayer to hear the voice of the Holy Spirit them selves.
 Their icons become their God and the revelation of their icons becomes more important to them than the Word of the living God,...this is why they don't talk about the Bible much.
http://www.zionfire.org/the-grey-scale-deception/

(**NOTE: There is a You Tube video of **Jenn Johnson** titled, "Black and White" that was held at a "Woman's " conference, in which she shows her deception in describing good and evil. Ed.).
Jenn Johnson: "The Lord Has A Reflector Mirror Under His Armpit" (This is normal in the world of "Bethel").
"**Jenn Johnson** Got More Cute By Believing What God Said About Her" (Yes, she really said this). http://www.piratechristian.com/messedupchurch/2018/2/
10-reasons-why-bethel-redding-is-a-false-church

- **Kim Jones-Pothier**: "Firstly, to address the elephant in the room, **Jones-Pothier** should NOT be shepherding her own church. As controversial as this is to say in our increasingly "progressive" society, the Lord modeled order in the church after His order for the family unit (Colossians 3:18-21; Ephesians 5:22-33). He is clear that He ordains the HUSBAND as the spiritual leader of the family.

As such, it is men who are the "HUSBAND of one wife, temperate, sober-minded, of good behavior, hospitable, able to teach..." who are qualified to shepherd the church - "for if a man does not know how to rule his own house, how will he take care of the church of God?" (I Timothy 3:2).

Second, even if **Jones-Pothier** only taught women, her teachings are not guided by the truth of Scripture. Her preaching, as passionate and dynamic as it sounds, is more **motivational new ageism** than it is rooted in sound Biblical theology and doctrine.

She gives you a 'feel good' message that will temporarily inspire you based on a generic, abstract idea of God. But if you want a WORD that is weighty, rooted in the transformative TRUTH and healing POWER of Jesus Christ, leave her teaching alone!

For example, **Jones-Pothier** recently tweeted a message encouraging those still haunted by pain from their past to "heal" themselves by making peace with their pasts and to heal their own toxic thoughts. First, truth is, if anyone is still struggling with mistakes and/or wounds from their past, they should look to Christ, not themselves. It is Christ who heals the brokenhearted and binds up our wounds (Psalm 147:3).

Second, if you have not and cannot overcome your past, it's a good indication you are still the same creature you were back then. But to be a new creature, Christ says you must be born again (John 3).   You must be transformed by the renewing of your mind (Romans 12:1-2), and that's only possible if you grow in the grace and knowledge of Christ by abiding in His word.

Third, we don't make peace with ourselves any more than we can save ourselves from our sin. We don't forgive ourselves any more than we can forgive our own sins. We make peace WITH GOD and are forgiven BY GOD through sincere repentance of sin and faith in Jesus Christ. God is good, and He gives us the encouraging reassurance that He is" FAITHFUL and JUST to forgive us our sins and cleanse us from all unrighteousness " if we confess them to Him (1 John 1:9).

Fourth, we must depend on Christ in all things, not ourselves. We have NO POWER outside of Christ, but we can do all things through Christ who strengthens us (John 15: 5; Philippians 4:13).   Being a Christian is not merely going to church and following popular Christian figures on Instagram and Twitter.

We must abide in Christ, and we abide in Him by abiding in His Word, which gives us the truth of God and the truth sets us FREE (John 8:31-32)!   Only God's word has POWER.

Not a tweet from **Jones-Pothier** (or anyone else), unless it aligns with the truth of God's Word. But regretfully, most things **Jones-Pothier** says don't meet that prerequisite. She seems to have a sincere passion for helping the broken. But she's not qualified to teach, and if she's not leading people to Christ with His truth, she's actually doing more harm than any good she intends."   https://www.lipstickalley.com

- **Robert (Bob) Jones**: Deceased; The unwanted visitations could represent gossip or hysteria but then one also reads his own associates have sometimes asked **Bob** after he has appeared in their dreams is he really doing that and **Bob** has admitted he does sometimes appear.

Whatever the truth it's clear both that **Bob** is one of the more heterosexual mystics (it was his "Emma angel" supposedly launched the Kansas Prophets' movement) and that he will go almost anywhere in the universe at the drop of a hat, even taking friends to the third heaven including **Bentley.** All they need to do is sit in a restaurant or wherever with him and he will take their hands so they will rise there – a procedure which recalls "rising on the planes" in occult circles.

(New Age visualization exercises have a lot to do with **Ms Todd** and **Ms King's** heavenly trips otherwise). When **Jones** was young he was an alcoholic bar room brawler and womanizer. Following a breakdown during which, he relates, Jesus improbably told him he would need to kill or forgive twelve people, Jesus also showed him heaven and hell and people dissolving into him. When **Jones** converted the devils that he said talked to him so often amid drink were exchanged for angels - some of them **Branham's.**

But were the devils still speaking under different guise? It's certainly peculiar that **Jones** claims to visit heaven, see Jesus daily and have prophecies galore yet has remained unhealed of kidney problems for which he's on dialysis.   God apparently told **Jones** (contrary to the rather strict Biblical standards in the area) it didn't matter if prophets got things wrong, prophets needed to be about 65 per cent right. It's a fact **Jones** is himself quite often right for which it seems people will forgive him almost anything. His forecast God had chosen a "burning Bush" to rule America was a gift to the religious right.

Bob Jones, who has been spiritual mentor to such as **Todd Bentley** and a guide, justification and "father" to many others – **Pat King** considers sitting at his feet next to doing the same before Jesus! All the following names who enjoy a certain respectability in charismatic circles they shouldn't have, show connections with **Bob Jones** and/or the Kansas City prophets or with **Patricia King** and **Todd Bentley**.

They include such iffy writers, preachers or campaigners (many promoted on **Steve Schultz's** "Elijah list" on the Net) as:

Mike Bickle (first and chief defender of **Bob Jones** in Kansas City), **Rick Joyner, John Crowder, David Herzog, Ryan Wyatt, Francis Frangipane, Bill Johnson, Chuck Pierce, James Goll, Stacey Campbell, Bobby Connor, Jill Austin, Lou Engel, Randy Clark, Shawn Bolz** (in touch with God's angelic minister and angels of finance), **C. Peter Wagner.**

Also **Kathie Walters**: "Angels" have let her ride a golden motorbike round the skies because God wants believers to have more fun), **Barbie Breathitt** of "Breath of the Spirit Ministries" (is there a name connection here?) who will sell you Tarot like cards to interpret your dreams and know why you have an illness...

John Paul Jackson: Chosen by an "angel" before birth and the wayward, **Paul Cain**, (periodically condemned and restored for a mixture of alcoholism and gay sex.
He absurdly considers **Branham** "the greatest prophet who ever lived").

Cain originally helped promote the ever smiling and filmstarrish **Matt Sorger** who takes two healing angels with him wherever he goes and invokes revival angels almost anywhere; occasionally connected with either **Jones** or **King** are **Bonnie and Mahesh Chavda** and sweet smiling **Jason Westerfield**. But **Jason** is another of the many-angels-to-help-him boys.

http://rollanscensoredissuesblog.blogspot.com
Was also a big NAR teacher; claims to have had a "revelation" concerning "green stones" or "green fire,"a New Age occult belief; sex offender).

- **Tony Jones**: Another Emergent church leader. The information in this article about **Tony Jones** (the US director of the Emergent Church and closely aligned with **Brian McLaren)** is bothersome, to think that **Tony Jones** may not be a true believer and yet is accepted by many in the church as though he were.
This is just an excerpt from a three part article on the Emergent Church by Richard Bennett.
We should pray that **Tony Jones** really meets Jesus and repents from promoting forms of Eastern mysticism and Roman Catholic heresies. I do not know if he is born again or not, I can only go by what he says, writes, and teaches. It is very important to carefully understand what a person teaches before we automatically assume that they are part of the body of Christ.

We need to test everything and test the teachings coming from the pulpits and books, even if the book is published by a "christian" publisher.
 "In neither of his two books, "Soul Shaper: Exploring Spirituality And Contemplative Practices In Youth Ministry " (2003) and "The Sacred Way: Spiritual Practices for Everyday Life " (2005), does **Jones** present the Gospel. Like so many leaders in the Emergent Church, his personal testimony is not of being a convicted sinner without hope before the all Holy God and in that conviction coming to Christ as the only Savior.

 Rather, in Chapter 1, "The Quest for God," **Jones**' testimony shows that in 2005 he is still fumbling in the darkness of unbelief. "[Some of us] have this nagging feeling that God is following us around, nudging us to live justly, and expecting us to talk to him every once in a while...Every time I leave God's side, as it were, it's not too long until I feel God tagging right along beside me, I can't seem to shake him."
"Yet having this sense of God's company doesn't necessarily translate to a meaningful spiritual life. I know this because despite my awareness of God's presence, I have spent most of my life trying to figure out what to do about it."

This sad testimony is of a man who is not "in Christ", and yet he is one of the leading lights of the Emergent Church movement in making and disseminating materials for youth pastors and youth groups. Of his growing up in a Protestant church, he says, "I'd say there was one word that summed up my religious life: obligation."
Predictably, he fell away from his pattern of obligatory prayer, Bible reading, and "quiet time", but felt guilt ridden about it.
His solution: "Something occurred to me: People have been trying to follow God for thousands of years...Maybe somewhere along the line some of them had come up with ways of connecting with God that could help people like me...I could think of no better way to spend it [his three

month sabbatical] than to travel and read about different <u>ancient ways of prayer and devotion.</u>"

His travels took him to round the clock prayer vigils and to Dublin, Ireland, to Catholic priest Alan McGuickian and the staff at the "Jesuit Communication Centre." He "voraciously read" Roman Catholic <u>mystics</u> and spoke with individuals who were Protestants, Roman Catholics, and Eastern Orthodox. Nowhere does he mention any in depth study of the Bible nor of searching after the great truths of Scripture.

In this way, his searching is reminiscent of Ignatius of Loyola and it is noteworthy that <u>he recommends the disciplines of the founder of the Jesuits to youth pastors and youths to learn and practice.</u>

What is clear from his statements is that "obligation" remains major in his understanding of what it means to be a Christian — but what becomes equally clear is that he has no dependable knowledge of God from God. That is, he has no knowledge of God through the Bible as revelation by His Spirit. Because **Jones** does not hold to the Bible alone as giving truthful knowledge of God, God Himself remains a truth undefined. Thus **Jones** is free to define his own god and to fulfill his obligation to this god of his own making.

Thus by making Roman Catholic and Greek tradition his current standard, he is able to fulfill what he sees as his obligation in a supposedly time-honored and acceptable way through these old, mostly Roman Catholic <u>mystical</u> exercises. Yet clearly before the All Holy God, he is still an alien and a stranger to saving grace in Christ Jesus.

Jones's definition of "Christian" needs careful attention. In "The Sacred Way," he states, "For years I'd been told that to be a Christian meant I had to do three things: (1) read the Bible, (2) pray, and (3) go to church." " But I had come to the realization that there must be something more." "And indeed there is. There is a long tradition of searching among the followers of Jesus — it's a quest, really, for ways to connect with God...The quest is to know Jesus better, to follow him more closely, to become — in some mysterious way — wrapped into his presence. And I thank God that some of these brilliant and spiritual persons wrote down what they learned". (pp. 16-17)

What is missing in **Jones's** definition of following Jesus more closely is any conviction of sin and therefore any need for a Savior. Without the conviction of sin one does not have life in Christ Jesus. The Lord declared that the Holy Spirit "will reprove the world of sin, and of righteousness, and of judgment." Conviction is the Spirit's work; He does it effectually, and none but He can open the mind and heart of a sinner to saving faith. **Jones** appears to be totally unaware of this, for he says nothing about the Lord Jesus Christ as Savior, or about the Holy Spirit's role of conviction.

"**Jones** is not a "follower of Jesus" in any Biblical sense since his god is not the All Holy God of the Bible. His "Jesus", therefore, is not the Lord Jesus Christ of the Bible."

http://thinkerup.blogspot.com/2006/06/ is-tony-jones-even-christian_25.html

Emerging church leader **Tony Jones'** March 2008 release, "The New Christians: Dispatches from the Emergent Frontier," may not come as a shock to those who have already read **Jones'** books, "An Emergent Manifesto of Hope" and "The Sacred Way."

But it does provide further insights into the true nature of the Emerging church.

In "The Sacred Way," **Jones** openly acknowledges his affinity with mysticism. With chapters on labyrinths, stations of the cross, the silence, centering (mantric) prayer, and more, **Jones'** leaves no doubt that he embraces eastern-style mystical prayer practices. In "An Emergent Manifesto of Hope," he takes it to the next level. The thesis of that book could be described as:
"The Kingdom of God is already here on earth, includes all people, all faiths, and in fact is in all people and all of creation and can be felt or realized through mysticism which connects everything together as ONE."
Those who have come to understand mantra meditation know that the usual outcome of going into altered states is a new spiritual consciousness that is open to both panentheism (God in all) and interspirituality (all religions lead to God).

In order to have this new spiritual outlook, one's view of "truth" must be adjusted - **Jones'** new book, "The New Christians," provides such an outline for this adjustment.
A theme of this book could go something like this:
Emergents say they believe in truth, but they define it as something that is always changing and being refined, can never be grasped, and enfolds all beliefs, except the ones that insist there is only one truth. It's not really any wonder that **Jones** says this - he credits **Brian McLaren** as "helping to birth this book" (p. 253). **McLaren's** view on truth resonates with the description above.

As is typical with many Emerging church books, "The New Christians" emphatically tries to convince readers that the "church is dead" (p. 4), at least church as we have known it.
"Emergent Manifesto of Hope " is the new release from "Emersion," a publishing partnership between Baker Books and Emergent Village.
The book, edited and compiled by Emergent leaders **Tony Jones** and **Doug Pagitt**, is a collection of essays by various emerging church leaders. **Pagitt** says the book "provides a rare glimpse inside the Emerging church."

This "rare glimpse" actually lays out the agenda of the movement, and in essence "Emergent Manifesto" is the Emerging church's coming out of the closet tribute.
The back cover of "Emergent Manifesto" describes it as a "front-row" look at this "influential international movement" and promises readers that they will come away with "a deeper understanding of the hopeful imagination that drives the Emerging church."

Readers are also told that they will "appreciate the beauty of a conversation that is continually being formed." However, the book fails to deliver any "beauty." A more accurate title for this book would be "Emergent Manifesto of False Hope," and a subtitle (albeit a lengthy one) that would describe it perfectly would go something like this:

The Kingdom of God is already here on earth, includes all people, all faiths, and in fact is in all people and all of creation and can be felt or realized through mysticism which connects everything together as ONE.

This new collective spirituality leads people into a socialistic community where rituals, practices, and social justice become a means of salvation, but not the salvation you think of in a personal sense of being born-again through Jesus Christ. This is a collective salvation that includes whole cultures and communities who follow the way of someone referred to as Jesus.

 (**NOTE: An excellent and continuing expose' of this Emergent Leader, **Tony Jones**, et al is on this website listed below for further reading. Ed.).

https://www.lighthousetrailsresearch.com/ tonyjones.htm

- **Bernard Jordan**: Another teacher of the "Prophetic Movement;" Prosperity Gospel.

- **Manasseh Jordan:** A self-proclaimed "prophet," who lives a lavish lifestyle in million dollar Florida homes, is telling his followers, including the faithful in Charlotte, that they will receive a "financial reward" - if they give him money. Truck driver Eric Elmore, who frequently drives through Charlotte, donated more than $3000 to **Manasseh Jordan Ministries** after receiving a robo-call. He thought the money would bring him blessings. "I just thought it would improve my quality of life and my current situation," said Elmore. "It did not."

Prophet **Yakim Manasseh Jordan** has engaged in what some call a "pay to pray scam." Robo-calls obtained by FOX 46, connected to **Jordan**, offer prayers from the non-existent "Saint Mary's Prayer Center" in exchange for money. Several churches with the name "Saint Mary" have had to issue alerts that they are not affiliated with the scheme.
Jordan, who has claimed to raise the dead, and heal the sick, promises riches and rewards to those who give him "seed" money.   "There has been some money that has been delayed," a robo-call recording on **Jordan's** behalf says. "In other words, you were supposed to receive it by now."

To receive God's "financial reward," people are urged to donate a "victory" or "releasing seed" to **Jordan**. "I want you to move quickly with a victory seed of $43, or $143, $243 seed," the robo-call says. "The $1,043 seed." The robo-calls, promising rewards and riches, are now preying on Charlotte's faith community. They are the same robo-calls that got **Jordan** in trouble with the Federal Communications Commission in 2016.
 In North Carolina, there have been 20 complaints filed against **Jordan** between 2013-2017 for robo-call violations, according to Attorney General Josh Stein's office.

"It was like all the things that were terrible in my life would come to an end," said one woman, who only wanted to give her first name, Debbie. Debbie also gave **Jordan** money - and then was hit up for more the next day. "The next day, yeah," she said. "Every day. Every day. Every day." **Jordan** says his "calling is to touch the people." He did not respond to "FOX 46's" multiple requests for comment over several weeks. He has been sued at least 20 times in federal court since 2013, according to court records.

One case accuses **Jordan's** robo-calls of calling one man 300 times. "It doesn't stop," said Andrew Notaro, a science teacher, who filed a complaint with the FCC. "It's no fun when I'm sitting there at work and I get a phone call and it's another number again. It changes every time that they call."

At Christ Church in Charlotte, Pastor Howard Brown preaches faith is free. "It makes me sad that people will continue to make faith a commodity that can be sold for personal benefit," said Brown. "It's part of a bigger problem, a kind of false belief that you have to earn God's favor. That God has to be paid something, or do a certain work, or certain good thing, in order for God to be good to you."

It is unclear how much money Prophet **Manasseh** is raking in. However, records show he lives a luxury lifestyle. He recently owned at least two waterfront properties in Florida worth over a million dollars each. As for Elmore, the only thing he was rewarded with was regret. After giving money to **Manasseh,** he was in an accident. Then he lost his job. "I do feel like I've been cheated," said Elmore. The money he gave, he now wishes he could get back. "The good Lord will judge him."

https://www.fox46charlotte.com/news/
pay-to-pray-a-self-proclaimed-prophet-preying-on-the-faithful

https://www.youtube.com/ watch?v=bSxEr5TXa1U

http://www.propheciesofrevelation.org/ false-teachers-prophets-5-elijah-list.html

- **T.B. Joshua: Temitope Balogun Joshua**, Arguably one of the most popular TV figures in Africa and Latin America, is set to hold two events at a Christian site in the city. Religious and political officials in Nazareth have demanded that the city cancel a planned visit next week by a Nigerian pastor and televangelist, and his plans to hold mass events at Mount Precipice. **Temitope Balogun Joshua**, also known as **T.B. Joshua**, is famous for performing exorcism rituals in his native country, and is set to hold two events at the Christian site in Nazareth.

His visit is supported by Nazareth Mayor Ali Sallam, but many in the city oppose it, some of them alleging that the pastor has ties to far-right Israelis. **Joshua** is the founder of "The Synagogue, Church of All Nations," a Christian organization that runs the "Emmanuel TV " television station from Lagos, which has a YouTube channel with 1.5 million subscribers.

Arguably one of the most popular figures on television across Africa and Latin America, **Joshua** has 3.5 million followers on Facebook. He has visited Israel in the past and written of forging a covenant with God to start his ministry, as well as hinting a couple of years ago of considering a relocation to Israel. Thousands participate in his prayer sessions and exorcism rituals. Many video clips have been released on social media in recent days announcing the "rock-star" pastor's visit.

The planned visit has drawn criticism in Nazareth across party and ethnic lines.

Church representatives have joined Islamic clerics in calls to cancel the events. Church officials meeting in Nazareth several days ago urged residents to boycott the event and clerics to avoid any mention of it in their sermons. "We beg you not to play in the hands of those organizing this type of festival which is an affront to the principles of Christianity, and our national identity, and deals a blow to the social fabric of a city like Nazareth," they wrote.

Church officials quoted text from the New Testament about how believers must be cautious about false messiahs who try to convince people they're performing miracles. Most of the churches in Nazareth have signed their support for the statement – all but the Roman Catholic Church, which has avoided taking a clear stand. In response to a query from Haaretz, Father Emil Shopany of the Catholic Church said there's no reason not to host such a visit and that he, as opposed to others, will support the mayor's position.
He said Nazareth is an open city and that you cannot stop a religious man from abroad who decides to visit from holding prayers like thousands of pilgrims do.
https://www.haaretz.com/israel-news/.
premium-nigerian-televangelist-t-b-joshua-is-coming-to-nazareth-and-locals-are-furious-1.73949
12

- **Stephan Joubert:** Teaches the "new positive" theology," Part of the "Confessionist" movement; also teaches the doctrines of the Emergent Church.

- **Rick Joyner**: "Morningstar" church Pastor–looks like a rock concert; not doctrinally sound; PROUD member of the Emergent Church teachings; NAR; One of the founders of the "Prophetic Movement" from 1985 and c.); not to mention, proud "Knights of Malta" member.

One of the pathetic movements' premier prophetic voices allegedly received a vision about the end times (naturally) and guess who was shown to be taken captive by demonic spirits, chained, and covered in feces—you guessed it, people like you and me; normal conservative, confessional Christians. Who was leading and winning the spiritual battle? Why the super-empowered apostles and prophets and those who embraced their restoration message of present day truths!   https://discernmentministriesinternational.wordpress.com

(**NOTE: There is an enormous amount of information on the internet regarding this wolf, including You Tube videos. Ed.).

- **Daniel Juster**: "Due to the connection with **John Wimber** and Steve Zaritt, Patty and I were invited by **Wimber** to attend the conference in Anaheim, California. We were given free registration. This was partly to comfort us after all we went through in connection to Patty's word at the UMJC conference." " Although we had already attended a **John Wimber** conference on healing in Baltimore, we had a sense we were supposed to be there at least for the relationships...We met with **John Wimber** for a significant appointment, and he came to the UMJC national conference in Los Angeles."

"Yet, the connection never got off the ground. In the coming years, new upheavals in the Vineyard would occupy **Wimber's** attention."   "It is fascinating to note that **Juster** reveals **Paul Cain** influenced the ministry of **John Wimber**."
Juster also reveals he was influenced by NAR Apostle/Prophet **Cindy Jacobs** and **John Dawson**. "These are big names who were pushing NOLR heresies and raising up the New Order of Apostles and Prophets across the face of the earth."

On June 14, 1998 – an unfortunate fire broke out near the **Juster's** family (of "Tikkun International "), their son losing his life shortly after the fire.

   Michael Brown alongside other NAR apostolic leaders and NAR apostolic ministries of NETWORKS either came to visit or joined in prayer "for a resurrection".
They later prayed " for a resurrection from the dead at the services". **Daniel Juster** records how "**Robert Stearns, Mike Brown, Don Finto, Rick Ridings**" and "**Susette Hetting**" prayed "for resurrection there and again at the site of burial".

"Asher Intrater called from Israel and told us that the prayer for Samuel in many towns in Israel was changing the atmosphere for believers in the nation." "We were to pray and believe to the full extent possible. We were able to hold off the doctors for 48 hours." "Samuel's heart continued to beat strong and steady." "Finally, I had to make the decision to disconnect Samuel from life support. We prayed for a resurrection."

 "After he was disconnected, his heart stopped. For one more hour, we prayed."
" We continued praying into the next day." " David and many others said that we should pray for a resurrection from the dead at the services." "Due to our friendship with Church leaders and our own network, over 1,400 attended his service."

 "**Robert Stearns, Mike Brown, Don Finto,** and **Rick Ridings** stood with us and many "Tikkun" leaders and congregation members in special commitment. We prayed for resurrection there and again at the site of burial." **Susette Hetting, Reinhard Bonnke's** lead intercessor, said "how appropriate it would be for this Messianic Jewish child to be raised from the dead." Yet, in the end, nothing happened." https://pulpitandpen.org

But as **Daniel Juster's** PDF reveals, this is not Jewish ministry but NAR ministry. The proof of this was found with the Apostles **Juster** worked with, and was influenced by. You may recognize their names:

-**Bill Hamon**: One who is involved in the NOLR and was an active NAR - Apostle/Prophet. Also recognized as an NAR Apostle in the 1990s.

-**Sid Roth**:   Host of NAR TV '"It's Supernatural'" (Good friend of **Michael Brown**),
NAR Apostle **Bob Weiner**,

-NAR Apostle and Prophet **Mike Bickle** who was instrumental in developing the NAR in the 1980s. Notorious NAR Prophet **Bob Jones** (sex offender). **Paul Cain** Apostle of the Latter Rain movement (homosexual),
-**John Wimber**: A highly recognized NAR Apostle, one of the pillars of NAR theology and its abhorrent practices.   It's worth noting how involved Apostle **Daniel Juster** was with **Wimber**.

It is fascinating to note that **Juster** reveals **Paul Cain** influenced the ministry of **John Wimber**. **Juster** also reveals he was influenced by NAR Apostle/Prophet **Cindy Jacobs** and

John Dawson. These are big names who were pushing <u>NOLR heresies</u> and raising up the <u>"New Order of Apostles and Prophets"</u> across the face of the earth.

(A comment from a former congregation member from **Daniel Juster's** church; her name is Jane Shulman; it has to do with how she was treated by him and his wife. Ed.):

"Thank you for this article. I attended Beth Messiah for some years while **Daniel** and **Patty Juster** "ruled." I was newly born-again-in-Messiah Yeshua and a 100 percent Jewish believer. Man-oh-man, did they ever give me my come-uppance for being an uppity newcomer to their cherished, exclusivistic scene."
"**Patty**, who is not even Jewish, and the very nominally Jewish **Daniel,** despised me because I had the heritage over them." "I was considered "proud." Huh? It was not ME -- it was THEM and others in their long-established order of favoritism."
 "I didn't know what I had gotten into and that it was all set up years before I came."

"**Patty** had absolutely no use for a woman in her 30's who was single and childless (as I was). She looked at me one day and said, "I wouldn't know what to do if I wasn't married. My husband is a very important man." What?? "Also, I once gave a lot of money to the "Tikkun" ministry. For my generosity (and I was not well off financially, I really wanted to make a difference), I was invited to a special dinner at a ritzy home somewhere in Washington, D.C."

"Apparently, **Daniel** was not pleased to see me, a NOBODY, there. Soon afterwards he preached from the pulpit disparagingly about "Those who want to think they are so great for supporting Tikkun." "Wow. These people are very weird." " They are only interested in furthering their own agendas, gaining fame, recognition, riches and a reputation in this world. Let them have it. I see other articles elsewhere proclaiming the humbleness of **Daniel Juster**. He does not know the meaning of the word."
(Ms. Shulman then quotes Scriptures: Matthew 7:13-14; Matthew 7:21-23, and Matthew 11:29; this was written about five months before January, 2018). https://pulpitandpen.org

K:

- **Morton Kelsey**: According to apologist Bob DeWaay and his 2004 article, "Contemporary Christian Divination," **Morton Kelsey** is "the most prolific writer among twentieth century Christian <u>mystics</u>."

Open to any religious practice that will aid one in his own unique "inner journey," **Kelsey** urges his followers to "guide others on their way and never impose our way upon them."[1]

"THE "KINGDOM WITHIN"--
The idea of a journey inward is an important one for **Kelsey**, as a common theme among his writings is that of the "kingdom within." **Agnes Sanford**, who was among the earliest to bring <u>mysticism</u> to twentieth century evangelicals, [2] had this to say in her book, "The Healing Light," published in 1947:

'The kingdom of God is within you,' said Jesus. And it is the indwelling light, the secret place of the consciousness of the Most High that is the kingdom of Heaven in its present manifestation on this earth.[3]

Interestingly, **Sanford** is quoted favorably multiple times in **Morton Kelsey's** book, "Healing and Christianity," the very book that is commended by the "Alpha Course" in the above audio as the "all time classic" book on the topic of healing. In fact, this idea of a "kingdom within" is found in **Kelsey's** book. He writes:

"The kingdom, as Jesus proclaimed it, may be viewed inwardly as well as eschatologically.
  It is true that Jesus and his followers undoubtedly looked for the immediate coming of the kingdom in history. However, the statements about it may also be seen as referring to the kingdom within, or the kingdom breaking through now in history." [4]

This "kingdom within" teaching stems largely from a misunderstanding of Luke 17:20, 21. Now having been questioned by the Pharisees as to when the kingdom of God was coming, He answered them and said, "The kingdom of God is not coming with signs to be observed; nor will they say, 'Look, here it is!' or 'There it is!' For behold, the kingdom of God is in your midst." (Luke 17:20—21, NASB).
 Here Jesus was teaching his listeners that the kingdom was among them in His very person, the person of Christ. He most certainly was not suggesting that man embark on a journey inward in order to discover this kingdom, for no man receives even the Holy Spirit unless he first repents and turns to Christ for salvation.

Yet, the teachings of **Kelsey** seem to indicate that he believed the Spirit of God to indwell all men, thus meaning that such an inward journey would not be in vain. Note the following quote from **Kelsey's** book, "Through Defeat to Victory," emphasis added:

 "Real listening is a kind of prayer, for as we listen, we penetrate through the human ego and hear the Spirit of God, which dwells in the heart of everyone. Real listening is a religious experience." " Often, when I have listened deeply to another, I have the same sense of awe as when I have entered into a holy place and communed with the heart of being itself." [5]
In such contemplations the danger of the erroneous, mystical teaching of the "kingdom within" becomes grossly evident.

MORTON KELSEY AND CARL JUNG:

Kelsey was greatly influenced by the notable psychologist Carl Jung, often combining various religious practices with Jung's teachings. In realizing the influence of Jung upon **Kelsey**, it is important to note, even if briefly, that Jung believed he had a spirit guide named Philemon.[6]

This cannot be ignored when considering Jung's teachings. The influence of Jung upon **Morton Kelsey** is quite evident in the book "Healing and Christianity," as he liberally and favorably appeals to Jung on multiple occasions. One primary area where Jung was of great influence on **Kelsey** is that of dream interpretation.   For **Kelsey**, dreams were a way in which the "Divine" would try to speak to men.   Jung believed that the "Other" could be found in the unconscious, which connects the individual to a spiritual reality.[7]

In the book so highly recommended by "Alpha," **Kelsey** states, "Thus Jung opened the door to the possibility of contact through the unconscious with an objective reality superior to human consciousness, which is able to order and vitalize human life when ego-consciousness is unable to do so." " If the human psyche can thus act as a bridge between the physical body and the power of a transcendental reality, then religion and religious experience, particularly healing experiences, become a real and most significant possibility." [8]

Unfortunately, the idea of seeking meaning or understanding from one's unconscious mind cannot be found in Scripture. Yet Christian mystics, and those who advocate their works, are striving nonetheless to mine these depths.

MORTON KELSEY, HEALING AND THE GOSPEL:

Morton Kelsey's book places great emphasis on the healing ministry of Jesus, making such statements as: " [Jesus] made clear that men in their present condition do not deserve or need judgment and punishment, which only drive them further into despair and defeat. Only twice did he make any point of speaking to the sick about their sins...[9]"
"Jesus thought not simply of 'saving souls,' to use a familiar Christian cliché. His redemptive concern necessarily encompassed the whole of man, including his body.[10]"

It is true, sickness is not always the direct result of one's sin. Jesus said so Himself in John 9:2-3. This does not mean, however, that a man's physical healing is of greater importance than his spiritual healing. Nor does it require a man to be physically healed in order to experience spiritual healing, i.e., salvation. In fact, the recordings of the Apostle John in the sixth chapter of his Gospel make evident that the miracles of Jesus often did not produce true or lasting faith in the recipient.

Rather, many people were following Christ solely for what they could gain from His miracles, but had little use for His message of salvation, ultimately rejecting it (John 6:66). One may well remember the story of the ten lepers that were healed as told in Luke 17:11—19. Jesus healed ten men from the terrible affliction of leprosy, then ordered them to show themselves to the priests. As the ten walked away, only one turned around and approached Jesus in thanksgiving, offering glory to God.

Kelsey also states that, "The most important reason that Jesus healed was that he cared about people and suffered when they did."[11]. Indeed, our Lord did experience compassion not only for the spiritually lost, but for the sick and ailing as well. This was not, however, His primary purpose in healing.
 Rather, Jesus healed men—made limbs to grow, eyes to see, dead men to breathe—so that men would know that He was the Christ, the Son of the Living God.
Even the blind man in John 9 recognized that he was healed by the power of God (John 9:31-33). Only Jesus Christ, the true Messiah, could offer full, complete healing of a person.

Thus are revealed some of the potentially dangerous teachings of **Morton Kelsey**, whose work comes so highly recommended by "The Alpha Course."

225

http://apprising.org/2012/12/02/
the-influence-of-christian-mystics-morton-kelsey-and-john-wimber-on-the-alpha-course/

- **E.W. Kenyon**: Famously known as the Father of the Word of Faith teachings from the early 1900's; all the WOF wolves received their "theology" from him.

One example is **Kenneth Hagin**, who copied (plagiarized) almost word for word **Kenyon's** teachings.

-**Kat Kerr**: Has prophesies that aren't 100 percent accurate 100 percent of the time (or are manipulated to come "true"); Points to any "Jesus" other than the Biblical one. Uses supernatural or occultist techniques in her prophecy;

Has a rebellious, unrepentant spirit; is in league with **Patricia King**; a 60-year-old woman living in Florida (and sporting pinkish hair dyed), she insists, 'in obedience' to God's command), has written a book entitled "Revealing Heaven: An Eyewitness Account."
 In it she reports on her direct encounters, her visits and conversations with 'the Father' in heaven's 'throne room'. **Kerr** is radically different from Paul (the Apostle) in that there is no hesitancy on her part; she freely talks about what she sees and hears.

It is apparent that her mission is to communicate what she has experienced in her visits to the 'throne room'. On one occasion the Father escorted her via time travel to the very occasion when Jesus was crucified; she says she was right there at the cross of Calvary.

Not only that, she was there at the resurrection. Not even the shamans have been as brazen as that!

Apology: As with the psychics and mediums of spiritism, she also 'visits' deceased loved ones, in order to bring back reports to the bereaved on their status. Always she reports that the departed are safe in heaven, much to the bereaved's comfort. In one instance, according to her testimony, a person who had lost a loved one was surprised to hear of the deceased person being in heaven at all!
She reports that every human being has at least one guardian angel from the moment of conception. These angels go with believers along the road of life and at death accompany them all the way to heaven. Sometimes however, Jesus personally does the work of escorting to heaven, at least for those who have been especially faithful.

She has learned that, if a person does bad things while on earth, the guardian angel is owed an apology upon arrival in heaven! **Kat Kerr** recounts her own conversion experience when aged four, then again aged five when she prayed 'the sinner's prayer' just to be sure.
She is of a Pentecostal persuasion and her rapidly growing audience is primarily among Charismatics and Pentecostals.

 It is not necessary to continue detailing the incredible things **Kerr** reports about her frequent visits to heaven; these can be garnered by visiting YouTube. One either accepts what she says is true or disagrees and objects. In the latter circumstance, it is tantamount to declaring her a false prophet. The Old Testament penalty for false prophecy was stoning, although the New Testament settles for rejecting the message.

Spiritism: There are further dangerous aspects to **Kat Kerr's** ministry:

First, acceptance of it opens the door to connection with spiritism and shamanism, for this is essentially what she is up to. We do not find mention in the New Testament of congregations developing such connections. The experiences of Paul and John were exceptional and were not in any way the same as **Kerr's**.

Second, there is a mind-bending process going on. People have to suspend scepticism in order to accept the often-bizarre nature of what she proclaims.

Third, **Kerr** reveals a not-so-subtle expectation that others could or should be doing what she herself is doing. You too can visit heaven and talk with the Father; and here's how — so why don't you? Christians will be moved along a slippery slope into the occult realm.

Fourth, those critical in their analysis are likely to be regarded as blaspheming the Spirit or rejecting what God is doing in 'these last days'.

Paul does not state that he spoke with any person within the Godhead in the third heaven; **Kat Kerr**, on the other hand, does. Her picture of the Father is akin to a description of conversation with a human friend. I think that this is exactly the relationship **Kerr** intends to convey — that she has such an exalted status that she is able to be in the very presence of God and talk directly with him just as Adam and Eve spoke with the Creator God in the Garden of Eden before the Fall.

But Paul speaks of God's utter transcendence: " He who is the blessed and only Sovereign, the King of kings and Lord of lords, who alone has immortality, who dwells in unapproachable light, whom no one has ever seen or can see" (1 Timothy 6:15-16).
It is true that the Spirit indwells all born-again Christians and, through Christ, they have access to the Father in prayer. The Scripture also affirms that we rest in the finished work of Christ and cease from our efforts of trying save ourselves. But that does not mean we treat God as just another friend or buddy.
Kerr ignores the historical Christian understanding of God's otherness and claims to have been repeatedly in his presence as though she were nearly his equal. This cannot be accepted or ignored. **Kat Kerr** is not the first to claim conscious contact with heavenly beings.
One thinks of **Mohammad, Joseph Smith, David Berg** (of the "Children of God," cult from the 1970's) **Sung Myung Moon** and countless others.

The claiming of special revelation is standard fare in the spiritual market-place. There are others too today currently claiming familiar heavenly conversations with the angels, Jesus and the Father. We must recognize that not everyone who claims spiritual experiences has to be accepted and believed.

In the last days there will be false signs and wonders performed through the power of Satan; and deceptive attacks and demonic tricks are often played out within the Christian community. We are to 'watch and pray', as Jesus told his disciples that last night in Gethsemane. 'Beloved, do not believe every spirit, but test the spirits, whether they are of God; because many false prophets have gone out into the world' (1 John 4:1). https://www.evangelical-times.org/

Has known the Lord since she was 4 years old. 15 years ago God asked her to reveal Heaven to the world. She has been there many times in spirit and reveals what it is like. God is taking the fear out of dying – Heaven is beautiful, real, and so close by!
In this video she talks about the new move God is bringing on this earth. While all these "end days" things are going to happen, the people of God are being equipped to walk in heavenly authority to usurp the power of darkness. This is a really great message.
She talks about a renewing of the earth...this WILL happen during the next millennium.

http://endtimesready.com/media/prophets-and-apostles/

(**NOTE: Obviously the person who posted this cannot see through her deceptive practices; I am including it so you can see how the blind can't see. Ed.).

- **John Kilpatrick**: Says he is not a prophet, he's just an average pastor— and always will be.

This is an intriguing statement, especially in light of the fact that he has stated countless times that he was prophesying; He says he has learned many hard lessons during the 2 ½ years of revival at his church, "Brownsville Assembly of God;" He says he can accept scrutiny and criticism;
"Brownsville" is FAMOUS for putting out books blasting anyone who disagrees with the "revival"; Subsequently, evangelist **Steve Hill** of "Brownsville AOG" visited the "Holy Trinity Brompton" church in England and received the "anointing" from Sandy Millar.
He then carried it back to his church, where the main pastor, **John Kilpatrick** was already into the movement and his wife had been "slain in the spirit" from a visit to the "Toronto Airport Christian Fellowship" church directly.
http://www.deceptioninthechurch.com/lies.html http://www.deceptioninthechurch.com

- **Dan Kimball**: "To start off this blog, I must say I am FURIOUS with **Dan Kimball** and other "Emerging" speakers of his ilk. As I described in a previous blog, the denomination I grew up in (the EFCI) will soon be having **Dan Kimball** as keynote speaker at their "Friends Youth Summit 2010 ". Following is my blog on this: https://davemosher.wordpress.com/2010/11/05/efci-friends-youth-summit-2010-promoting-emergents-and-occult-contemplative-spirituality-including-the-labyrinth/

It is theologically schizophrenic Emerging rascals like **Mr. Kimball** that are leading the EFCI youth down the road to Hell. Emerging Church leaders may be thinking they are helping our youth grow closer to Christ, but nothing could be further from the truth.

Dan Kimball is hard to pin down regarding what Christian doctrines he truly believes.

Also, he refuses to disassociate himself from false teachers – and it is difficult to pin him down on WHY he associates with them. Consider the following blog by Ingrid Schlueter at the "Crosstalk" blogsite. "I am copying and pasting the blog in its entirety.   NOTE – I have emphasized certain sections by bolding them."

To Ingrid Schlueter:

 Ingrid, it appears to me that **Dan Kimball** is showing the traits of a true "Bridger" (I like your use of the term – it seems very appropriate). **Kimball** is trying to make his teachings palatable to both sides of the church aisle – born again Christians as well as New Age seekers and worse. Thank, thank you, THANK YOU, for admonishing **Mr. Kimball** on behalf of the rest of us. This is what we need to see more of – erroneous individuals being addressed directly rather than being criticized behind their back. May God bless you and strengthen you on the front lines, Ingrid!
(Click on the link below to read Ingrid's original "Crosstalk " blog).

Additional comments have been posted at the blog since I copied and pasted it to here): "Phil Johnson on the Dearth of Conviction in the Emerging Church:"

Posted by Ingrid Schlueter in "Emergent Church, Featured Articles, Religion on November 21st, 2010."   In 2007, Phil Johnson wrote a very helpful piece on the Emerging church. In light of recent discussion of Emerging pastor **Dan Kimball**, what Johnson writes is important.

I've suggested recently that postmodernists always run in a straight line back to the notion that we should avoid making truth-claims with finality, clarity, or settled assurance. Everything (and of course I'm speaking in practical terms here, because absolute statements are deemed impolite in these postmodern times)—practically everything is supposed to remain perpetually on the table for debate and reconsideration.
 Here's the kind of thing I'm talking about: In a recent symposium on the Emerging Church movement (**Mark Driscoll** [et al.] "Listening to the Beliefs of the Emerging Churches" [Grand Rapids: Zondervan, 2007]).

 Dan Kimball says the only doctrines he is really sure about these days are a short list of credos generally agreed upon by Christians and spelled out in the Nicene and Apostles' Creeds. See if you don't think **Kimball's** perspective contains a classic echo of the kind of thinking I am suggesting colors the typical postmodern mind.
https://davemosher.wordpress.com/2010/11/21/
excerpts-from-crosstalk-readers-comments-slam-dan-kimball-for-not-disassociating-from-false-t
eachers/

 (**NOTE: The above "conversation" is from the blogger, whose website is listed above. It is not my words. Ed.).

https://www.worldviewweekend.com/news/article/
my-conversation-emergent-church-leader-dan-kimball

(**NOTE: The above listed website is another viewpoint of this <u>Emergent church leader</u>. Ed.).

-Deborah King: "<u>Master Healer;</u>" Through her subsequent journey of knowledge, she worked with <u>healers, sages</u>, and <u>shamans</u> from every corner of the globe. Ultimately, **Deborah** mastered these ancient techniques and now teaches them widely. **Deborah** firmly believes that Western cultures need the <u>energy medicine methods </u>of healing, transforming, and growing more than ever. Through her books, workshops, online events, and speaking engagements, she's helped thousands to find their truth and heal and transform their lives.

Deborah King is a New York Times best-selling author, <u>meditation teacher</u>, renowned <u>spiritual leader</u>, and a leading authority on <u>energy medicine</u>. A successful attorney in her 20s, **Deborah** masked childhood trauma and an abusive family life with drug and alcohol addictions while still managing to succeed in her professional life.   However, all of that radically changed when she was confronted with a cancer diagnosis in her early twenties.

Forced to evaluate her lifestyle, priorities, and unresolved issues from her past, **Deborah** saw her illness as a wake-up call that inspired huge shifts in her life. First steps included addressing her addictions, **learning to meditate**, and opening herself to <u>alternative possibilities</u>.

After receiving permission to delay the surgery from her physicians, **Deborah** worked with practitioners in the <u>energy medicine field</u>, and along with use of tools like <u>meditation</u> and journaling, she experienced a spontaneous remission of the cancer. After her recovery, she realized that ignoring unresolved emotions all her life had led her to the point of illness, addiction, and turmoil. The experience left **Deborah** determined to become a <u>thought leader</u> and speaker so that she could help others lead healthy, happy and harmonious lives.
https://deborahking.com/meet-deborah/

"Introducing The Most Spiritually Advanced Course In Mindvalley Academy":

Deborah King Unveils The Secret Magic Of <u>Sutras</u> — The Most Powerful Spiritual Tool For <u>Invoking Your Divinity From Within And Unlocking Your Psychic Gifts</u>.

<u>Get Initiated Into A Higher Level Of Spiritual Awareness, Soul Expression And Paranormal Powers... So You Can Finally Evolve into The Grandest Vision of Your Greatest Self</u>.

This course is for everyone who's looking to deepen the connection with their <u>divine self </u>and <u>unlock the spiritual gifts and psychic abilities </u>that they're meant to have.

Thousands of years ago, our ancestors had many spiritual abilities that we no longer have automatic access to, <u>including telepathy, aura reading, precognition</u>, and the ability to experience <u>Divinity </u>within their bodies.

However, even though we share the same DNA as our ancestors, we have long forgotten these abilities. Each week, **Deborah** will reveal more secrets along the path of <u>initiation</u>, providing you with practical exercises and <u>mystical tools </u>that allow you to clear and <u>balance your core energy </u>so the <u>sutras</u> <u>can be seeded in the fertile ground of your consciousness</u>..

"Sutras: The Key To Higher Consciousness And Spiritual Powers":

Like a seed that's buried in the ground, all it takes is exposure to sunlight and a little nourishment to nurse your spiritual gifts back to health. And that's where Sutras come in. With Sutras, it's easy for you to maintain a balanced energy field with no stress, stay in touch with your emotions, monitor your chakras and clear your blockages.

They are sacred threads that when woven together raise vibrations and open the doors to higher consciousness. They hold they key to supernatural powers such as telepathy, time travel, levitation and super-sensory perception. With the power of Sutras, anyone can re-activate their spiritual gifts.
https://www.mindvalley.com/modern-master/?utm_source=google

(**NOTE: Obviously all of this is Satanic. I included these articles, direct from her websites, to show how demonic all this is. Scriptures warn us of these "spiritual" practices. Imagine the destruction she—and countless others like her—are doing to unsuspecting people. Ed.).

- **Patricia King**: Another NAR teacher; believes and teaches the "law of attraction," regarding God, which is an occult teaching; Self appointed Extreme Prophet.
False teachings and New Age teachings. It is important to note where **Patricia King** met **Todd White** – at a "'glory school'." People need to be aware that in the NAR there is a secret mandate known as the 'Apostolic Mandate' which explains why they have many glory schools across the globe.
 NAR Apostles believe it is their job to raise up this New Breed for this final end-times chapter of the church.   https://churchwatchcentral.com

 Religious media figures in **King's** "eXtremeProphetic," a US TV programme you can watch streamed on the Net;   **Ms King**, founder of EP, **said to be a former witch** but whatever her past, now "crazy in love with Jesus", has traveled with angels in fiery chariots and reports making up lost hours in driving time getting teleported to conferences and so on.

She wants to raise the dead and her mentoring of **Bentley** may be responsible for his unsubstantiated claims to have resurrected 27 souls. Despite her extremes **Pat King**, like others in her line, has done apparently admirable down-to-earth work with street people.

Ms. King favours ecstatic trance dance worship which the likes of **Crowder** have developed big time and which at XP is in the hands of **Caleb Brundidge** an "ex gay" and if anything the least gay looking of some of **Ms King's** new mystic friends some of whom might be felt to give a rather gay/bi vibe though smilingly locked into their de rigueur marriages.

Caleb's style in dance events look like...well... much like any Saturday night at gay disco or perhaps we might think bisexual disco.... and "holy chaos" if done in the more drunk and druggy looking style of the buddies in "holy" ecstasy, **Crowder** and **Dunn**; Occasionally connected with either **Jones** or **King** are **Bonnie** and **Mahesh Chavda** and sweet smiling **Jason Westerfield**. But **Jason** is another of the many-angels-to-help-him boys.

http://rollanscensoredissuesblog.blogspot.com

- **Daniel Kolenda**: **Reinhard Bonnke's** assistant; constantly preaches about money; gives false hope of healings to citizens of African countries through his false preaching. Has taken over <u>CFAN</u> (Christ For The Nations) ministry started by the late **Reinhard Bonnke**; another <u>New Age</u> false <u>prophet</u>.

- **Kathryn Kuhlman**: Deceased; Had "spirits" guiding her; not Scriptural; also known as a "spiritualist;" Once was married to a man who divorced his wife for her, then divorced him. Cried to her "god" not to "take the "spirit" from me"; (NOT God's Spirit but a demonic spirit). Claims that "God" healed multiple thousands in her meetings, but had NO tangible medical proof; Her contemporary was **Aimee Semple McPherson**.
 It was with the coming of Methodism to America, women began to take on more active roles in these new frontier congregations. As Methodism took root in the US it developed offshoots, the main one being the Holiness movement and from them eventually came Pentecostalism.

 During the Great Depression **Aimee Semple McPherson** rose from obscurity within Pentecostalism and became America's first mega-church pastor and broadcast genius raking in millions of dollars. Sadly, she died with a tarnished reputation being caught as an adulteress and dying of a barbiturate overdose.
 Nonetheless, sister **Aimee** opened many formerly shut doors to other women to walk through including the charismatic mega-star **Kathryn Kuhlman** who almost single-handedly popularized the phenomena of being "slain in the spirit" by televising her healing crusades.

The fraud, liar, "SINister" and false <u>prophet</u> **Mr. Benny Hinn** cites **Kuhlman** as one of his main influences and <u>he visits both her grave and **McPherson's** to gain spiritual power </u>
(I kid you not.) (10). By the time **Kathryn** was on television (Believe In Miracles) in the late 60's and early 70's the floodgates for women's equality in ministry with men was a fait accompli within the charismatic movement and many of its sub-camps. (11)
Many of the movers-and-shakers (no pun intended) within charismania are women who are internationally recognized as <u>prophetesses</u> and they are having a huge impact on the lives of many of God's gullible. (12). For the remainder of this article I will be exposing some of the members in their high powered skulk. (13)

https://discernmentministriesinternational.wordpress.com

10. Visit my fellow truth-tellers at "Personal Freedom Outreach"   they have an excellent article on **Hinn's** necromancy at http://www.pfo.org/bhnecro.htm

11. By the late 60's early 70's within "charismania" we had pretty well established sub groups including: (1) <u>"The Discipleship </u>movement " with **Derek Prince, Ern Baxter** and others (2). <u>"The Word of Faith movement "</u> led by **Kenneth Hagin** initially soon to be cloned by sycophants like **Buddy Harrison, Copeland, Price**, and others. (3)
"The Jesus People movement " more or less dribbled into forms of discipleship. Against these stood classic Pentecostalism, the Assemblies of God, The Church of God in Christ, Pentecostal Assemblies of the World, etc.

12. I know there was no word "gullibles" until I scribed it. God's gullibles are Christian people who are doctrinally ignorant and thus prey to those pandering the rancid balm of false doctrine which infects and sickens the sheep.

13. A skulk is a group of foxes, and these women are sly to say the least.

https://discernmentministriesinternational.wordpress.com

Kathryn Kuhlman became obsessed with the sight of Roman Catholic priests attending her meetings and just a few years before her death she was invited to Rome and had a personal audience with the Pope. https://www.eaec.org/newsletters/2000/ NL2000feb.htm

- **Hank Kunneman**: https://www.charismanews.com/opinion/ 73043-september-prophecy-if-you-stand-with-me-i-will-put-my-words-in-your-mouth

https://reformationcharlotte.org/2019/09/04/ charismatic-prophet-says-abortion-gives-demons-the-blood-right-to-carry-out-mass-shootings/

https://christianresearchnetwork.org/2019/08/28/ watch-fake-tongues-on-jim-bakkers-program/

https://christianresearchnetwork.org/2019/08/28/ watch-fake-tongues-on-jim-bakkers-program/

https://www.patheos.com/blogs/dispatches/2020/01/18/ hank-kunneman-delivers-a-testable-prophecy/

(**NOTE: The above links should be sufficient for you to judge whether this person is of God or a false prophet\preacher. Ed.).

L:

- **Tim & Beverly LaHaye**: **Tim** is deceased; **Tim LaHaye** and **Beverly LaHaye** have from the beginning been supporters of **Sun Myung Moon** and have started organizations and have chaired organizations funded by **Sun Myung Moon.**

(**NOTE: Mr. Moon is deceased, however his wife still runs his "church." Ed.).

These organizations have some of the most prominent Christian names associated to it while meanwhile they support this New Age guru self proclaiming Christ paving the way for the one world religion. A few of these organizations are directly linked to the CFR, CIA and Masonry. **Moon** was arrested for tax evasions and **Tim La Haye** formed the CRF (Coalition for Religious Freedom) in order to get him out.

 Hal Lindsey and **Paul Crouch** (TBN) were also part of this. Besides supporting the "Moonies" and new agers **Tim LaHaye** is also guilty of starting the "Left Behind " series and the forerunner of the "Pre Trib" teaching on the rapture. It is scary that most churches now hold this view and teach this twisting of Scripture.

I'm not going to take a side on rapture theology but this view is based on pure speculation, fantasy and twisting of Scripture. I personally have done extensive research on this subject and above all I READ MY BIBLE! But this topic I will save for another paper.

The big cheese here is that this view is setting people up for massive deception and disappointment. Because it holds the view that Christians will be taken away before the big bad tribulation will happen when the rapture doesn't happen after the world goes to pot, people will doubt their faith in Jesus Christ. **Tim LaHaye** was responsible for gathering all the theologians together to make sure this was the view the church had. This view makes the church weak in the faith. http://www.pre-trib.org/ about.

I can go on for pages about this but here is a very shocking revealing fact about all of this. <u>All the significant production and release dates for "Left Behind" fall on Major Satanic Holidays</u>.

There are eight primary holidays in <u>witchcraft</u> and <u>Satanism</u>. There are four major and four minor ones:

1) Candlemas or Imbolg — Feb. 1,2- major
2) Ostara- March 21 (Spring Equinox) – minor
3) Beltane or Roodmas – May 1 (founding day for the Illuminati in 1776)- major
4) Litha– June 21 (summer solstice) – minor
5) Lughnasadh or Lammas- August 1 – major
6) Mabon- September 21 (autumnal equinox) – minor
7) Samhain or Hallowe'en- October 29-31 – major
8) Yule- December 21 (Winter solstice) – minor

<u>Luciferians</u> seek Satanic blessings by not only performing their jobs in their sacred locations where they believe there are vortexes of <u>occultic power</u> but also seek Satanic blessings by initiating their projects on their Satanic holy days.

On May 1, 2000, Beltane (major Satanic holiday) they began production on the movie "Left Behind'." 13 weeks later on August 1, Lughnasadh (major Satanic holiday) they released the 'making of "Left Behind"' for sale.

13 weeks later on October 31, Samhain (major Satanic holiday) they released the "Left Behind" movie for sale.
13 weeks from that date on Feb.2, 2001 Candlemas (major Satanic holiday) they released "Left Behind' into the theaters across the country.

The odds that Peter LaLonde hit those four <u>Occultic</u> days by chance with his production and release dates is 1 in 17,458,601,160. Or one in seventeen billion, four hundred fifty-eight million, six hundred and one thousand, one hundred sixty.
If you believe this is a coincidence then you probably believe it was a coincidence that Jesus died on Passover, was resurrected during Feast of Firstfruits and that the Holy Spirit fell and the church was born on the Feast of Pentecost.
https://deceptionfree.wordpress.com/tag/ruth-heflin/

(**NOTE: Yes, the link says **Ruth Heflin**, however this article is also on this link. It is obviously against Pre-Tribulation rapture teaching, which most studious Christians believe in. I have left it up to you to decide about all this. Ed.).

- **Dr. Alan Langstaff**: NAR promoter, **Langstaff** was key in helping spread the New Apostolic Reformation cult from America to New Zealand and Australia. He was instrumental in starting the "Temple Trust" and "Vision" Magazine.
(**NOTE: There is a lot more to this man than what is presented here, so the best suggestion is to go to the link below. Ed.):

https://churchwatchcentral.com/2016/08/21/ who-is-alan-langstaff-part-1/

- **Bob Larson**: This article first appeared in the "Christian Research Journal," volume 24, number 2 (2002). For further information or to subscribe to the "Christian Research Journal " go to: http://www.equip.org

Examples abound, but few exemplify the paradigm shift better than **Bob Larson**. **Larson's** newfound emphasis on spiritual warfare highlights his proclivity toward subjectivism, and his recent venture into performing live public exorcisms before capacity crowds further accentuates his sensationalistic approach to ministry.
While some of what **Bob Larson** teaches on demonology and spiritual warfare is theologically sound, what he gives with the right hand of sound Biblical exegesis is quickly snatched away with the left hand of alleged experiences with the supernatural.

Larson thus wavers between presenting balanced teaching grounded in Biblical truth and espousing dangerous ideas established by his alleged encounters with the supernatural.
 Unfortunately, even the Biblical aspects of **Larson's** theology end up overturned as a result of his supposed skirmishes with the demonic.
As **Larson's** focus on spiritual warfare intensifies, subjective experience reigns supreme. Throughout the millennia, the Christian church has faced myriad trials in the form of doctrinal controversies. While enduring these tests of faith, one constant temptation for believers has been to base their beliefs not on the objective written Word of God but rather on subjective experience.

 Movements such as Montanism and mysticism have enticed many away from objectivity grounded in Holy Scripture and into the realm of autonomous esoteric experience.
Not much has changed over the centuries.
 For years, the "Christian Research Institute" has been warning believers about a massive paradigm shift occurring within the contemporary church, as the faithful are being tempted to abandon Biblical exposition in favor of extra Biblical experiences. While any number of examples could be given to illustrate evangelicalism's growing obsession with subjectivity, few exemplify this paradigm shift better than Christian television and radio personality **Bob Larson**.

 Bob Larson uniquely embodies the church's perpetual struggle to subjugate personal experience to the inspired text of Holy Scripture. His evident desire to remain faithful to the Bible is tragically overridden time and again, and in the end most of what he teaches is based more on alleged encounters with the supernatural than on a careful exegesis of Scripture. https://www.equip.org/article/ an-examination-of-the-teachings-of-bob-larson/

(**NOTE: This article is quite lengthy. To continue reading, please refer to the website listed above. Ed.).

Sunday, March 26, 2006: "Exorcist casting the devil out of Tulsa"--

When Sherri roared like a bull, rolled her eyes into her skull, and lunged against the three men who were holding her, **Bob Larson** says he saw the devil. He should know. **Larson** is one of the leading practitioners of modern, Christian exorcisms, and here I was in a hotel conference room in Tulsa, Oklahoma, right across from **Oral Roberts University**, watching him wrestle with demons.
Larson performs his exorcisms in rooms full of people -- sometimes hundreds, sometimes thousands. One religious scholar says 600 Protestant churches have established what they call "Redemption Ministries " in recent years, which feature exorcisms or something like them.

At the heart of all this is a basic belief that demons are real and move among us, inhabiting people's bodies and driving them to all manner of bad behavior.
On this night, as **Larson** stood with his Bible in hand and called out demons, a half-dozen people howled, cried, and bellowed in strange voices, while he ordered their possessors back into the pit of hell. I am naturally skeptical of things that cannot be proven, so I had to ask: Is all this just a show?

Larson and the folks he confronted say absolutely not. **Larson** freely admits he has been called a charlatan, a flimflam man, and a snake-oil salesman. But he clearly has legions of followers -- people who believe exorcism can help them in the eternal battle between heaven and hell. Sherri says she feels a great weight was lifted from her through the experience. So what do you think: Are modern exorcisms a legitimate religious practice or spiritual vaudeville?

(Below are comments from their website. Ed.):

I think it's a psychological affliction that causes some people to think that 'demons' infest them and it requires an exorcism to save them. There is no medical evidence to support the brain being hijacked by anyone or anything else. Per physics the idea that it could occur is impossible--Newton said it most famously (and please allow me to paraphrase): If you interact with me, I can interact with you. Basically, if a demon could take over the physicality of the mind, then we could interact with said demon in the world of science. Over 400 years of accurate physics is proof positive that there are no demons, save the ones we create for ourselves. I think everyone involved honestly believes they are genuinely afflicted by a demon, but truthfully, it's an unconscious act by one person, and overt concern by the other.

It isn't real.

People possessed by demons are just another garden variety hypochondriac--they believe they really are stricken by demons, and so they show all the symptoms--regardless of the fact there is no cause, nor real demons in the night.

Posted By Anonymous Robert, Cary, NC.

In clinical psychological terms it's known as Dissociative Trance Disorder. "The research criteria for this diagnosis require the presence of either a trance state, or a possession trance state. A possession trance state is defined as the presence of a single or episodic altered state of consciousness, in which a person's customary identity is replaced by a new identity attributed to the influence of a spirit or deity (APA, 1994)"
Posted By Anonymous James J. Lisk (Binghamton, NY).

We live in a materialistic and self-serving age. To question whether spiritual forces are at work in the world today is to show that the wool is already over your eyes. We are entrenched in a society which continually wants to push God and the Bible, Heaven, Hell into the grey.
We would rather listen to i-pods than listen to the voice of the living God. We would rather be comfortable in this life of 80 or 90 years than think about living forever.

We would rather spend years being educated so that we may theorize we came from apes and ooze than spend five minutes reading the book of the ages which tells us we were made by a creator, we sinned against Him, we began to die, but He has made a way through His blood at Calvary so we may know Him truly. How great is our arrogance that we believe that our failing eyes see what is really real. Jesus said, you cannot see the wind, but you know it is real because you see its effects.
Is it such an outdated idea that we believe in God and pause from our endless toil to give some audience to His Word? Read the Bible and listen for Him to speak.

Posted By Anonymous Elijah 14607 NY

http://www.cnn.com/CNN/Programs/
anderson.cooper.360/blog/2006/03/exorcist-casting-devil-out-of-tulsa.html

--Greg Laurie: One world, one church, one apostasy. This is the inevitable result of mass marketing the gospel, targeted solely toward the young, with works of the flesh. As far as I know **Greg Laurie** is still preaching the Bible gospel message with his mouth.
But the unspoken message of a person's life does more real preaching than his/her words.
Laurie is up to his neck in partnering with Emerging church heretics and their false gospel of another Jesus.

"Pastor Believes We're Living in the 'Last Days.' And What He's About to Do Could Make History:"
Pastor **Greg Laurie** has toured the nation and world with his popular "Harvest Crusades " events — gatherings held over the past 25 years during which he has collectively shared the Christian gospel with millions and led hundreds of thousands to accept Jesus. Known for **Laurie's** compelling messages, the "Harvest Crusades" also include performances from

well-known Christian artists in an effort to encourage Bible believers to bring their friends along to learn more about the faith.

Laurie, 62, recently told "The Blaze" that he's taking what could be the "boldest step" ever since launching the "Harvest Crusades" in 1990 — a major event slated to be held on March 6, 2016, at AT&T Stadium in Arlington, Texas.

http://calltodiscernment.blogspot.com/

"We've taken bold steps of faith ... perhaps the boldest step we've taken of all is going to the AT&T stadium," he said of the event, titled, "Harvest America.." "[We thought], 'Why don't we try to stage what could be the largest evangelistic event in American history?'"
 http://www.theblaze.com/stories/2015/11/19/
pastor-believes-were-living-in-the-last-days-and-what-hes-about-to-do-could-make-history/

"Harvest America" is a free nationwide simulcast event on March 6, 2016, featuring music from **Chris Tomlin**, MercyMe, and Switchfoot, with a clear Gospel message by **Greg Laurie.**
We are blessed to announce that "Harvest America " and "Teen Challenge " (both USA and Global) are partnering to bring you "Harvest America" on Sunday, March 6, 2016, live from Dallas Cowboys' AT&T Stadium.

 http://harvestamerica.com/   August 25, 2012– **Greg Laurie's** "Harvest America: Royal Route To Heaven," **Rick Warren** & **The Message**.

As saddening as it may come to some, we are strongly encouraging our audience of readers to **not partake** or invite your friends to **Greg Laurie's** "Harvest America".
http://www.saidradio.net/2012/08/greg-laurie

Greg Laurie and the Emerging Church
http://www.lighthousetrailsresearch.com/blog/

GREG LAURIE : "Financing Contemplative Conferences" with **Leonard Sweet**
https://youtu.be/E5FvbDdx_x0

Greg Laurie - "Real Harvest or Bad Seeds" ?
https://youtu.be/3m4WQPMiXIo

"Lifest: A "Christian" Festival with Rock Music, Catholic Mass and **Greg Laurie**"
http://galatiansfour.blogspot.com/2011/07/

'Teen Challenge " Cult?
http://www.dailykos.com/story/2008/04/27/503961/

-Teen-Challenge-Coercive-groups-disguised-as-rehab
http://medicalwhistleblowernetwork.jigsy.com/teen-challenge

http://teenchallengecult.blogspot.com/

- **Ann Lee**: Was only the first of many women to impact the spiritual lives of the multitudes. Since her advent the Church has suffered through **Mary Baker Eddy**, founder of the Church of Christ Science (Christian Science) and first published her book "Science and Heath With Keys to the Scriptures" in 1875. Women have held no official role in the holy ministry, i.e. pastoral oversight of congregations for close to 1,600+ years across the denominational board.

There have been minor exceptions, obviously, but nothing really sanctioned until round the time of the **Wesley** brothers, **Charles and John** (started Methodist movement around the mid 1700's about the same time as **Ann Lee** was working in the USA).
Ann Lee is certainly the first restored neo-Montanist prophetess in America and she opened the floodgates for much of the extremism which is so rampant today.

Her organization, "The United Society of Believers in Christ's Second Appearing." a.k.a.
The Shakers were the first in America to
 (1) speak in other tongues; (2) experience so-called holy laughter; (3) spiritual drunkenness; (4) making animal sounds and expressions; (5) barking; (6) being slain in the spirit; (7) impart gifts by the laying on of hands; (8) led revival meetings and (9) giving verbal prophetic words from "God," along with other expressions of spiritual excess commonly seen and experienced by hundreds of thousands of professing believers today.

 6: Obtained from http://www.ccel.org/ccel/wace/biodict.toc.html?term=montanus
  underlining and highlights added for emphasis by the author;

 7: See http://en.wikipedia.org/wiki/Montanism; obtained on 06-06-11;

 8: Obtained from http://www.ccel.org/ccel/wace/biodict.toc.html?term=montanus

- **Jennifer Le Claire**: Another leader of the NAR; false prophetess; prosperity teacher.

https://www.thepathoftruth.com/false-teachers/ larry-tomczak.htm

 (**NOTE: **Ms. Le Claire** is mentioned in the article concerning **Larry Tomczak** on this website. Ed.).

- **Carl Lentz:** Lentz is not your papa's preacher. He's not a preacher of God's Word, either.
Lentz repeatedly compromises for the culture, often shrouding the truth in confusion and ambiguity to placate (lukewarm) Believers and non-believers alike.

To avoid stepping on toes with the truth, **Lentz** simply opts to tiptoe around it to remain in good graces with the cool kids. He is the "spiritual guide" to celebrities like **Justin Bieber, Kevin Durant, Carmelo Anthony** and more.
His approach to pastoring isn't to shepherd his flock per the requirements of 1 Timothy 3 or Titus 1 (especially Titus 1:9). Instead, **Lentz** is more of a well-groomed bro who will pray and take shots with you. Whenever asked his views on sin, **Lentz** is known to give a lukewarm

response, failing to answer the question head on and claiming that it isn't his job to call sin for what it is.

Rather, he says, his focus is more on getting to know people personally that he might deal with those matters on a case-by-case basis, behind closed doors. Abortion? **Lentz** says, "That's the kind of conversation we would have finding out your story, where you're from, what you believe." Homosexuality? **Lentz** says, "We have a lot of gay men and women in our church. I pray we always do." He adds, "When it comes to homosexuality, I refuse to let another human being or immediate moment dictate how we approach it."

But God's holy standards are objective and His truth is absolute. We can certainly approach such matters with gentleness and care as we minister to individuals, namely those who sincerely are lost. But we have to tell them the truth! Their eternal soul depends on it, and their blood is on our hands if we don't warn them (Ezekiel 3:18)! And when God grants us an opportunity to get the word out, we've gotta "O.T.M., bro! OWN THE MOMENT!,"

Or as, Scripture says, "Preach the word! Be ready in season and out of season. Convince, rebuke, exhort, with all longsuffering and teaching" (2 Timothy 4:2). Is abortion a sin? Short answer: Yes. For the Bible says: The Lord created mankind in His image, forms each of us in our mother's wombs and ordains our days even before He knits us together (Genesis 1:27; Job 31:15). We have free will, but we have no sovereign rights over our fellow man.

As such, we are not permitted to take a life - especially the life of an innocent, unborn baby - for reasons we, mere creations ourselves, have determined are justified (Exodus 20:13). Our God-given dominion is over the fish of the sea, the birds of the air, the beasts of the field, and every creeping thing that creepeth upon the earth (Genesis 1:26-28; Psalm 8:6-8).

But we DO NOT have dominion over one another. God, who rules over all creation, is especially mindful of mankind (Psalm 8:4; Matthew 10:30-31). If He cares for a sparrow that falls, of course He cares if an innocent human child is being dissolved, suctioned out of, or ripped apart in his own mother's womb, which should be a nurturing environment.

Is homosexuality a sin? Short answer: Yes. For the Bible says:

The Lord created mankind male and female, and He ordained marriage as the union between one man (an adult human biological male) and one woman (an adult human biological female) (Genesis 2:24; Matthew 19:4-6).
And since sex is reserved only for marriage, homosexual sex is an automatic affront to God. In fact, it is an abomination (Leviticus 18:22; Romans 1:26-27; Hebrews 13:4).

Can one be a homosexual Christian? Short answer: No.

For the Bible says: There is no such thing as a homosexual in Christ, because in Him we become a new creation (2 Corinthians 5:17). We put off our old sinful practices, and we are born again of the Holy Spirit, Who dwells in us and helps us live a holy life according to God's righteous standard (John 16:13; Galatians 5:25; Romans 8:26-27).

"Do not be deceived. Neither fornicators, nor idolaters, nor adulterers, nor homosexuals, nor sodomites, nor thieves, nor covetous, nor drunkards, nor revilers, nor extortioners will inherit the kingdom of God; And such WERE some of you."

" BUT YOU WERE WASHED, but you were sanctified, but you were justified in the name of the Lord Jesus and by the Spirit of our God" (I Corinthians 6:10-11). If homosexuality, or any other sin, feels natural, it's because it is a product of our sin nature. But one struggling with this sin, as with all other sins, can be delivered by the power of Jesus Christ, who makes all things new and is restoring creation back to God's "good" design (Acts 3:19-21).

Lentz is even tepid on matters that aren't political hot topics. When **Oprah** asked him if only Christians can have a relationship with God, **Lentz** replied, "No, I believe that when Jesus said that 'I am the way, the truth, and the life,' the way I read that, Jesus said that he is the road marker, he is the map, so I think that God loves people so much, that whether they accept or reject him, he's still gracious, and he's still moving, and he's still giving you massive red blinking lights, for chances to take a right turn when maybe you'd take a left, but I believe God loves people, and that's what this whole gospel is based on, it's love..."

For the record, that response was a very nasty, convoluted perversion of the Gospel. The Gospel is based on love, indeed. But that love holds up God's holy standards/commandments (Matthew 22:40; 1 John 5:3). If you love someone, you will tell them God's truth - and the truth is all mankind were born into sin and, apart from Christ, mankind stands subject to the wrath of God (John 3:18).

That's why we need to be SAVED and born AGAIN (John 3:3). "For the wages of sin is death, but the gift of God is eternal life in Christ Jesus our Lord" (Romans 6:23). "For God so loved the world that He gave His only begotten Son that WHOSOEVER believes on Him will not perish but have everlasting life" (John 3:16). There is no such thing as a Gospel based on love if that love isn't explicitly compelling others to repent of sin and turn to God through Jesus Christ.
https://www.lipstickalley.com

C.S. Lewis: Certainly not a preacher, but an author whose influence and writings have caused many unsuspecting Christians to adopt his _heretical_ writings as being Christian:

https://relevantmagazine.com/god/
6-heretics-should-be-banned-evangelicalism/

http://www.libertyadvocate.com/ C.S.%20Lewis.htm

C. S. Lewis, who believed in _purgatory, prayers for the dead_, and _baptismal salvation_, and denied the inerrancy of Scripture.

http://www.teachingtheword.org/apps/articles/ ?articleid=179316&view=post&blogid=5449

(**NOTE: The above statement and website concerns **John Piper**, however it also mentions others, including **C.S. Lewis**, which is why I am including it here. Ed.).

- **Roberts Liardon**: (1) "Roberts Liardon Leaves Ministry Over 'Moral Failure' by "Charisma News Service," Friday, December 21, 2001.

"Pastor and writer **Roberts Liardon** is stepping down from ministry after admitting to "moral failure."
He is taking a three-month leave of absence to seek "professional and church counseling related to a recent short-term homosexual relationship," according to a statement issued on behalf of his "Embassy Christian Center" in Irvine, Calif."

(2) "**Roberts Liardon** Back In The Pulpit Already?" by "Charisma News Service," Monday, March 11, 2002   "Unbelievable!"

(3) Regarding Colin Dye and **Roberts Liardon** by "Christian Witness Ministries," "Vanguard Magazine," Issue 6, 1999

The first false teacher who is championed and vaunted by Colin Dye is **Roberts Liardon**. Most of the information garnered on **Liardon** is taken from the following video:

"Are you really ready for the Promised Land?'," **Roberts Liardon** with Colin Dye (Kensington Temple/London City Church), Noel Richards and Band at the London Arena, December 12, 1993. Read Part 1 & Part 2.

http://www.deceptioninthechurch.com/ fprophets.html#rliardon

- **Gordon Lindsay**: Deceased; Connected with "Voice of Healing" ministries; Both **Gordon Lindsay** and **F. F. Bosworth** were Zionists, followers of **Dowie.**

 - **Eddie Long**: Deceased; prosperity preacher, accused of sexual behaviors with four young men. https://www.cnn.com

https://imspeakingtruth.wordpress.com/2009/01/15/ money-cometh-heresy/

- **Steve & Sandra Long**: "And Nadab and Abihu, the sons of Aaron, took either of them his censer, and put fire therein, and put incense thereon, and offered strange fire before the LORD, which he commanded them not." (Leviticus 10:1)).

"Strange fire." The meaning of the Hebrew word rendered here as "strange" is "unauthorized, foreign, profane." In some way, what these men did was totally improper, and utterly offensive to a holy God. It was an unacceptable action born of the flesh rather than of the spirit, and this episode continues to speak to us today about the rightness or otherwise of our actions and how our Creator views them.
And in modern times there can be few if any examples of "strange fire" more blatant and far-reaching in effect than what became known as the "Toronto Blessing," which was in reality a curse of gargantuan proportions, the toxic smouldering of which continues to chronically affect us to this day.

The unrestrained drunken revelry which characterized this supposed "revival" should have been ample proof that the phenomenon had nothing whatsoever to do with the Holy Spirit and everything to do with an alien one, but wisdom and discernment were the two spiritual gifts that hardly anyone seemed to have any interest in exercising. It was party time, and the only thing that was unacceptable to the writhing masses was anyone daring to rain on their parade by telling them the truth about their demonic delusion.

Which brings us to **Steve Long**, and his imminent visit to "City Church Cardiff " (which until June this year was known as "City Temple"). So who exactly is **Steve Long**? Well, he and wife **Sandra** have been pastors at the "Toronto Airport Christian Fellowship," now re-branded as 'Catch The Fire,' since 1994, when they arrived at **John Arnott's** church where the "Toronto Blessing's" "strange fire" had broken out in January of that year.

They were then commissioned by the **Arnott's** in 2006 as the Senior Pastors. **Mr. and Mrs. Long** also serve as Vice-Presidents of "Catch The Fire" (World) and Directors of "Catch The Fire" (Canada). It must be emphasized that **Steve Long** came to prominence precisely because of his deep participation in and global promotion of the "strange fire" of the "Toronto Blessing," for which he was rewarded by **John Arnott** personally by being given the leadership of his Toronto church when he stepped down from that position a decade ago.

Steve Long is absolutely inseparable from the so-called "Toronto Blessing," and this has to be clearly understood when evaluating his ministry.

The **Longs'** profile: http://catchthefire.com/media/profiles/ steve-sandra-long

informs us that they specialize in inner healing, deliverance and physical healing.

In this context, it will be more than relevant to here take a little look at a book that **Steve Long** has written on the subject of healing, entitled "'My Healing Belongs To Me'" with a foreword unsurprisingly penned by **John Arnott**.

Most tellingly, it is endorsed by some of the most well-known and utterly unsound ear-tickling "Christian" renegades on the planet, like **Bill Johnson, James Goll, Wesley** and **Stacey Campbell**, **Rolland** and **Heidi Baker**, and **Che' Ahn** amongst others - of whom we might particularly note two British individuals, namely David Campbell and Kevin Peat, who we'll return to shortly.
With so many false teachers and prophets on board to boost sales— you need to note the major New Apostolic Reformation connections!—it should really come as no shock to the system to find that the premise of **Long's** book is quite simply a lie.

The ear-tickling pitch is this: "GOD WANTS TO SEE EVERYONE, EVERYWHERE, BECOME HEALTHY." Source: http://www.catchthefirebooks.com/ myhealingbelongstome/

The very title of the book is itself an untruth! When **Long** asserts that "my healing belongs to me" he is simply regurgitating the old Word of Faith deception. Our healing DOES NOT belong to US - it very firmly belongs to GOD, and to Him alone! Period.

He is Sovereign, and it is He who decides on such matters, not us. He will grant, or NOT grant healing, as it pleases Him.

He alone has ownership of such things, and while we can meekly ask for a dispensation of a measure of His healing grace, the answer is far from guaranteed to be a "Yes!" Even the Apostle Paul met with a firm "No!" when he asked three times for his "thorn" to be removed. Hard as it may be for us to understand, illness and weakness can indeed form an integral part of God's plan and purpose for our lives. And like Trophimus, we too can be left sick (2 Tim. 4:20) or like Timothy have stomach trouble and frequent illnesses (1 Tim. 5:23).

Here is the Lord's answer to Paul's request and the Apostle's response to it, words that should really make us stop and think long and hard about these issues: (2 Corinthians 12:9-10). September 2016   http://watchman4wales.blogspot.com/2016/09/ steve-long-of-catch-fire-toronto-at.html

- **Max Lucado**: Teaches "contemplative prayer." He combines his beliefs with Panentheistic and Hasidism Jewish Mysticism; part of the "Covenant Church." Several books he has written show who his allegiance is to.

  http://www.828ministries.com/articles/ Max-Lucado-Say-it-Ain-t-S-by-Anthony-Wade-Faith-161219-30.html

  https://www.wayoflife.org/reports/ max-lucados-heresies-and-ecumenical-confusion.php

- **Keith and Sanna Luker**: Has a "ministry" called "Outpouring Ministries Revival and Prophetic Worship" ; false teachers, aligned with the New Age "prophets."

  http://www.propheciesofrevelation.org/ false-teachers-prophets-5-elijah-list.html

  http://www.piratechristian.com/berean-examiner/ pureflix-a-strategic-apostolic-alliance

  Keith Luker & Sanna Luker Soaking Prayer Music: https://simplicityinchrist.wordpress.com/ list-of-pretendersteachers/#l

M:

-**John MacArthur:** Denies the efficacy of Jesus' physical liquid blood. Also teaches the damnable heresy of Lordship Salvation; part of the Reformed Church, another false teaching and perversion of the Gospel). Promotes "another Gospel," as shown in this lengthy website:

  http://www.jesusisprecious.org/wolves/john_macarthur.htm

In October 2013, **John MacArthur** and "Grace Community Church" hosted a conference to address what he and the other speakers believe are major errors in the teachings and practices of the Charismatic and Pentecostal movements.

The conference introduction states: "Strange Fire, part of "Grace to You's Truth Matters" conference series, evaluates the doctrines, claims, and practices of the modern charismatic movement, and affirms the true Person and ministry of the Holy Spirit."

Seventeen messages were presented and two Q&A sessions offered. Besides **MacArthur**, the speakers were R. C. Sproul, Steve Lawson, Conrad Mbewe, Tom Pennington, Phil Johnson, Nathan Busenitz, **Justin Peters**, Todd Friel, and **Joni Eareckson-Tada**.
Prior to listening to all 19 of the presentations and carefully reviewing the transcripts of each talk, I hoped that the conference would add to the voices of discernment that have been addressing the false teachers of the Word/Faith, Healing and Prosperity, and the "Signs and Wonders" movements.   It's a huge problem worldwide and continues to grow.

 Nothing the speakers said was new to me or to the ministry of "The Berean Call," but it was good to hear these issues addressed before an audience who wasn't necessarily aware of the mostly "Trinity Broadcasting Network " (TBN) and "Charisma " cast of characters.

Nearly three decades ago, I had the privilege of helping Dave Hunt with "The Seduction of Christianity." That was a book in which we were heavily critical of the "Word/Faith" movement, "Prosperity gospel, " and "Signs and Wonders " teachings, which at the time made up most of what aired on so-called Christian television.
"Seduction" was published in 1985. Dave's 1987 follow-up book "Beyond Seduction" further explained the scriptural errors of the false teachers.

Similar books by other authors followed: "A Different Gospel," 1988, by D. R. McConnell; "The Agony of Deceit," 1990, Michael Horton, (Editor); "Charisma vs. Charismania," 1992, by **Chuck Smith**; "Charismatic Chaos," 1992, by **John MacArthur**; "Christianity in Crisis," 1993, by **Hank Hanegraaff**.   "Seduction" also motivated many of the apologetics ministries that focused on cults to address the cultic beliefs and practices that were influencing growing numbers of Charismatic, Pentecostal, and evangelical churches.

TBC has also continued to address such issues through our newsletter and website. The Internet has also given access to apologetics groups and individuals on websites, blogs, and via Facebook and Twitter, as many defend the faith.
Sadly, in spite of all that "contending for the faith," the number of false teachers, false teachings, and practices, along with their followers, continues to swell.

As I began listening to the "Strange Fire Conference" (SFC) presentations, it seemed odd to me that there was no reference to some of the long-established discernment ministries such as "Personal Freedom Outreach," " Herescope," "Christian Witness Ministries,'" Midwest Christian Outreach," "Watchman Fellowship" and many others that have addressed the conference's topic for years and no doubt supplied a good deal of the research for the content that was presented there.
At this point, something very disturbing became clear. The primary thrust of the conference subject matter was cessationism (the belief that some of the gifts of the Holy Spirit ceased for the church after the apostles died) and was presented by Calvinists and for Calvinists; this was the modus operandi of the entire program.

Reformed theology and Calvinism were set up as the screen through which the doctrines were evaluated.

Under the banner of Sola Scriptura ("the Bible alone"), the speakers claimed to have the antidote for restraining the exponential growth of false spiritual teachings: "Rightly dividing the Word of Truth," God's Word. No argument there. In fact, the good that came out of the conference took place when the Bible was, at times, "rightly divided."
Too often, however, the speakers deviated from the Scriptures to support the doctrines and practices of men. That was not good. Many of them turned to theological systems such as Calvinism and Reformed theology.

They leaned on fallible Calvinist icons as guardians of truth and were overtly biased against those outside the Reformed camp. The most damaging aspect was the confusion caused by the support of Calvinist cessationism. That's a double whammy error in my view: Calvinism "proving" cessationism.

In view of the stated objective of the conference, a launching platform for **MacArthur's** latest book "Strange Fire: The Danger of Offending the Holy Spirit with Counterfeit Worship," we agree that millions of professing and even true Christians have been duped by false teachers and spiritual con artists who prey upon those who are ignorant of what the Word of God teaches. Even a cursory glance at the activities surrounding the spiritual charlatans in the movement should reveal enough to ward off anyone with common sense.

The conference speakers had no shortage of outrageous examples of what transpires in the name of the Holy Spirit—things that are laughable to non-Christians and grievously blasphemous to true believers.
 Over the decades, many have addressed the erroneous teachings and the deceitful purveyors of what could be characterized as spiritual debauchery in a circus atmosphere, but very few have been rescued from the delusion in comparison to those who have been swept into it.

The chief reason, as was correctly communicated by some in the conference, is the preference in Christendom for subjective and experiential spirituality over a diligence in studying and obeying the objective Word of God, which is Sola Scriptura in actual practice.

Why are Christians so easily drawn into false teaching?

Perhaps they have an affinity for the temporal things of the world rather than the eternal; a desire for being spoon-fed the Scriptures rather than undertaking a disciplined reading of the Bible for themselves, and certainly the seductive power of the Adversary in drawing Christians away from God's Word comes into play.

In short, it's a combination of "the world, the flesh, and the devil" (1 John 2:15-17 ; Galatians 5:17; 1 Peter 5:8-9) in these days of increasing apostasy.
 Had the conference addressed those issues strictly from the Bible, there would have been much to agree with, but that was far from the case. To begin with, the speakers reflected an "us and them" mentality.

"Us" were all those in the Calvinist/Reformed cessationist camp. "Them" consisted of anyone who rejects the Calvinist/Reformed cessationist teaching (with the exception, of the "Charismatic Calvinists," who at least are among the elect).

Others were almost always marginalized by being indiscriminately thrown in with the obvious false leaders of the "Signs and Wonders " movement.
By direct teaching and/or implication, all the speakers adhered to the view that Calvinistic cessationism is the teaching of the Bible and is therefore the silver bullet for killing off the false doctrines and practices of the Pentecostal and Charismatic movements.

John MacArthur declared, "...read the Reformers, and read the Puritans, and follow the flow of the truth through history.... You're not going to go to an association of Reformed churches, those who believe the doctrines of the Reformation that take us back to the doctrines of the New Testament, and find false miracles...."

(All conference quotes are available at: www.gty.org/resources/sermon-series/325).

Steve Lawson said, "Those of us who are Reformed in our theology are enormously grateful for the revival of Reformed Theology that has swept through the body of Christ over these last years.... In fact, **Dr. MacArthur** has said, 'If you're not reformed right now, you are basically irrelevant.'" Lawson strengthened that statement, adding "If you're not reformed, you're wrong."

A litany of Calvinist icons were paraded before the audience to support the idea that Reformation theology is not only foundationally biblical, but it is also clearly cessationist.

None of the speakers made mention of some of the renowned men of the faith who were clearly non-cessationists such as John Wesley, D. L. Moody, H. A. Ironside, A. J, Gordon, George Müller, Andrew Murray, and A. W. Tozer, to name but a few.

Nevertheless, after presenting John Calvin's cessationist position, **MacArthur** says, "This is a time for the people who now stand on the shoulders of the Reformers in every area of their theology to be faithful to Reformation theology to its full rich intent."
"If we claim allegiance to the Reformers, then we ought to conduct ourselves with the same level of courage. Don't call yourself a "Charismatic Calvinist."

John Calvin would reject that. John Calvin did reject that. You'll have to drop the Calvinist part." Calvin wrote his "Institutes of the Christian Religion" at age 26, only two years after leaving the Catholic Church. That ought to give one pause, but it doesn't seem to prevent Calvinists from voicing their overwhelming praise of him for his knowledge and insights of the Bible.
Philip Schaff is quoted by Lawson: "Calvin was an exegetical genius of the first order." His commentaries are unsurpassed for originality, depth, perspicuity, soundness, and permanent value. Calvin was the king of the commentators."

Former Westminster Seminary president John Murray is also quoted regarding Calvin's proficiency: "Calvin was the exegete...of the Reformation and in the first rank of Biblical exegetes of all time." Lawson declares, "I do believe that Calvin towers over church history as the most substantial theologian that has been given to the church, its most powerful influence, and we would do well to hear from our older brother."

Of course, they are referring to John Calvin, aka "the Protestant pope of Geneva." Geneva, at that time, was a city of about 20,000 in which Calvin instigated the torturous persecution of hundreds, including more than 50 executions of residents, many of whom were drowned for simply disagreeing with his "Biblical" doctrine of infant baptism
(see Dave Hunt's "What Love Is This?").

Calvin, "the [church's] most substantial theologian" and foremost "exegete," interpreted Luke:14:23 to support his cruel and often lethal manner of "compelling." (See this issue's Q&A).

The SFC speakers also highly esteemed Augustine (Roman Catholicism's doctor of its major dogmas), John Chrysostom (who taught prayers for the dead), Martin Luther (who taught infant baptism, baptismal regeneration, and wrote a vicious anti-Semitic tract), Jonathan Edwards (who taught that God is the author of sin and evil),

B. B. Warfield (who taught theistic evolution and honored Darwin as "...one before whom we gladly doff our hats in true and admiring reverence"), as well as contemporary Reformed theologians J. I. Packer (a signer of "Evangelicals and Catholics Together " and R. C. Sproul (who teaches partial preterism).

Obviously, these Reformed models and their heroes are not superheroes of the faith except in the minds of the SFC speakers and the audience. They got some things right, but they also had some very significant doctrinal problems.
My point is that no matter what position one takes on a doctrinal issue, Sola Scriptura—not the views of fallible men (1 Corinthians 1:12-13), no matter what side they take—is the determiner of doctrinal truth.

Although the contributions to Christianity of Calvinism and Reformation theology
were declared throughout the SFC as bastions of Biblical truth compared to the abuses that have been fostered by non-Calvinist non-cessationists, none of the speakers mentioned that we can credit the Reformers and their inspirers and followers for many erroneous beliefs.
These include amillennialism, post millennialism, Theistic Evolution, Replacement Theology (which leads to anti-Semitism), pedobaptism (baptism of infants), preterism, Christian Reconstructionism, Theonomy, and Lordship Salvation, all of which are unbiblical.

Nevertheless, Lawson states, "If we are to see a new Reformation in this day, if we are to see this resurgence of reformed truth that has now begun in these last decades continue to expand...we must be exclusively committed to the written Word of God." To the former, no; to the latter, absolutely.
The SFC must be recognized in terms of its promotion of Calvinist cessationism as the antidote that will remedy all the ignorance and abuses of the gifts of the Holy Spirit.

That is at best a "Biblical" placebo that will do little to stop the current plague of the "Word/Faith, Healing, Prosperity," and "Signs and Wonders" false teachings and practices. For all of its continuous claims of Sola Scriptura, Reformed theology denies that sola in doctrine and practice. Its advocates, past and present, got some things right and others dreadfully wrong. Sola Scriptura is indeed the authority for every true believer, but it must be the full counsel of God.

The key address regarding cessationism was delivered by Tom Pennington.
He began by noting that non-cessationists point out that the New Testament nowhere directly states that the miraculous gifts will cease during the church age. His reply was that the New Testament doesn't directly say they will continue either. He continued with seven arguments as to why the miraculous gifts disappeared at the end of Apostolic age.
We appreciate his diligence in searching the Scriptures in order to come to the position he has. That's what we all need to do.
We have done this as well, but our understanding from the Scriptures is that the gifts of the Spirit (and of Christ—Ephesians:4:7-12) did not cease with the passing of the Apostles.

The Apostle Paul wrote quite a bit in his letters to the Corinthians addressing the subject of the gifts (given for the edification and building up of the church). What would be the point of his rather lengthy teachings if the gifts and the edification received from them were soon to cease? Obviously, cessationism and non-cessationism cannot both be correct.

Unlike the Gospel and other essentials of the faith that are objectively clear, the gifts of the Spirit are not essential for salvation and are more difficult to discern. Conclusions about them are developed in a more subjective process. Although what we believe about the gifts is not essential, it doesn't mean that our belief is unimportant. The gifts are given for the edification, strengthening, and enabling of the body of Christ—His church.

A wrong belief regarding the gifts of the Spirit will hinder the church's edification and fruitfulness. Scripture tells us that "the just shall live by [the] faith" (Habakkuk:2:4; Romans:1:17; Galatians:3:11; Hebrews:10:38).

Influential writers with opposing views may present their arguments and convince others, but in the end, we are all personally accountable for rightly dividing the Word of Truth (II Timothy:2:15) in determining what we believe and why we believe it. That must be both our declaration and our practice of Sola Scriptura.

https://www.thebereancall.org/ content/strange-fire-conference-spiritual-discernment-according-calvinism.
http://www.preachingjesuschrist.com/ why-lordship-salvation-is-not-biblical.html

- **James MacDonald:** His teaching is fear and intimidation; there are financial questions regarding the funds he has collected; He claimed that if his congregants were experiencing financial difficulties, it was because they were not obedient with tithing (never mind that tithing is not for the Christian). Isn't this like the claims of the Word of Faith heresy?

Participated in the"Code Orange Revival " in 2012.

This "revival" included a bevy of false teachers that no one with discernment should have joined with!   This article also points out other problems with **MacDonald,** including his endorsing false teachers like **Beth Moore**!
Then there was the "Elephant Room 2," where **MacDonald** defended **T.D. Jakes'** Word of Faith and anti-Trinitarian teachings, and thought he was an excellent teacher! Many sites exposed this situation, the "Cripplegate " being one of them, which had an excellent report of other issues with **MacDonald.**
 MacDonald helped heretic **T.D. Jakes** celebrate 35 years of heretical ministry.
He did this along with many other false teachers and celebrities such as **Oprah Winfrey**.
Does he really think God approved of this promotion of heresy?

MacDonald demonstrated his immaturity and need to be relevant by getting a tattoo, as well as buddying up with another "pastor" like himself, **Mark Driscoll.** (The comment string in the linked article is also quite enlightening as to **MacDonald's** ideology, below).
Well, all these things are just tips of the many icebergs at "Harvest Bible Chapel" under the leadership of **James MacDonald**. Some solid reporting from someone who attended HBC for many years can be found at Mary Dalke's blog. Her examinations are thorough, and should demonstrate conclusively why **James MacDonald** should not be trusted to teach the Word of God. (And you'll get to read about many of the false teachers promoted by **MacDonald** in some way or another!) http://watchmansbagpipes.blogspot.com/

https://bereanresearch.org/the-apostising-of-james-macdonald/

"I used to receive daily devotionals from **James MacDonald**. I have friends who have followed his ministry over the years and have been blessed by his teachings. He has long been considered a giant in the preaching business. The key verses remind us though that a pastor must guard two things. Doctrine is obviously important and we discuss that nearly every day regarding false teachers"
" Guarding your life though is just as important even if we tend to turn a blind eye to it more easily." "There is a reason why God lists many difficult qualifications for pastors and the bigger you get, the more Teflon you think you are as you begin to believe your own press."

Such appears to be the case with **James MacDonald.** "I have only written about him once, four months ago, when I said this":   "It details decades of financial malfeasance committed by **James MacDonald** to the tune of having his church once fall $70 million in debt while he was receiving a 40% pay increase to $350,000." "Tales of a **Mark Driscoll**-esque power grab where **MacDonald** expanded his board from 12 to 30 so they would have less individual power."
 "Publicly admitted gambling problems from **MacDonald** after railing against gambling from the pulpit. Accusing three such elders of being "satanic to the core" publicly because they had the temerity to ask for a line item budget of expenses." "I know this much beloved, when there is this much smoke there is usually a house on fire." -- Anthony Wade (November 2018).

The house that **James MacDonald** built burned to the ground today as he was fired from Harvest Bible Chapel. After years of trying to defend himself against accusations of moral failure in running the church, audio tapes have come to light where **MacDonald** was discussing putting child pornography on the computer of **Harold Smith**, the CEO of "Christianity Today."

Additionally there were other crude comments about reporters for "Christianity Today," whom **MacDonald** has had a long term issue with for their coverage of his previous problems. These comments are part of a 50 minute conversation with a radio personality that will be aired soon as a podcast. Beloved, the above link lists some of the rude and wildly inappropriate comments made by **MacDonald** during this interview. I will not repeat them. They are disgusting in general, let alone to come from the mouth of someone claiming to be a pastor.

This is just another sad outcome of believing the purpose driven lies of church growth and the false authority paradigms that come with it. The pastor is a shepherd of the flock, not the CEO of a business. He is to be fully accountable to the church not lord himself over it. The only cult of personality figure we need is Jesus. Too many people worship preachers to the point that they stand atop a pedestal so high that when they fall they will not survive when the bill comes due for not guarding their life and/or their doctrine.

That bill came due for **James MacDonald** today. Pray for the restoration of his walk -- not his ministry. Pray as well for the scattered and wounded sheep he leaves behind because they are the true victims.
Rev. Anthony www.828ministries.com/
Diary/The-Purpose-Driven-Lies-Cl-by-Anthony-Wade-Christianity-190213-725.html

"Harvest Bible Chapel " allegedly made **James MacDonald** a millionaire; ECFA terminates membership By Leonardo Blair, "Christian Post" Reporter, April 18, 2019.

Pastor **James MacDonald** founder of "Harvest Bible Chapel " in greater Chicago, who was recently fired under a cloud of financial abuse, was allegedly being paid nearly a million dollars per year in regular salary, had access to approximately a million more in discretionary spending, and is currently owed $2.6 million in deferred compensation by the debt-ridden church.
Independent journalist Julie Roys reported Wednesday that in 2018, HBC paid **MacDonald** $80,000 per month ($50,000 monthly in regular salary and $30,000 monthly in deferred compensation), which amounts to $960,000 annually.

"This number does not include additional money **MacDonald** may have received from his broadcast ministry, "Walk in the Word," "Harvest's" church planting network, "Vertical Church," its songwriting and worship ministry, "Vertical Worship," and books," Roys said. Roys reported that she confirmed the details **of MacDonald's** compensation arrangement with a senior leader at the church. "The Christian Post " reached out to HBC seeking comment on the report Thursday but officials authorized to speak on behalf of the church were not immediately available.

Citing Emmanuel "Manny" Bucur, a deacon and one-time volunteer bodyguard of **MacDonald's,** and Mark Banaszak, a "Harvest " member and captain of the church's Saturday night security team, as sources, Roys reported that HBC gave MacDonald between $800,000 to $1.2 million annually in discretionary funds. Half of the discretionary funds in general came from a senior pastor discretionary fund, and a similar amount came from a discretionary fund in "Walk in the Word."

Roys noted that the unnamed HBC leader she consulted with confirmed the discretionary funds were part of a hidden or "black budget." The news comes just over a month after HBC officials revealed they are struggling financially due to the hemorrhaging of members and donations in the fallout from **MacDonald's** Feb. 12 ouster from the megachurch.

In their message to members on March 10, officials reviewing finances at the church admitted that there was a "lack of financial control" over **MacDonald's** office but did not provide any details of how that lack of control manifested.
"As our Harvest 2020 team is charged with reviewing all finances within the church, we have found that there was a lack of financial control and oversight as well as questionable spending practices made by the senior pastor's office." "In addition, we have identified there was a separate budget for the senior pastor's office over which there was not sufficient controls and oversight," officials said.

According to Roys' report however, **MacDonald** was supposed to record any personal expenses charged to his discretionary funds and reimburse the church, but it is unclear if that happened. He reportedly counted having a bear stuffed and shipped from Alaska as a ministry expense. Church funds were also allegedly used to gift between six and eight Harley Davidson motorcycles to people inside and outside of the church.

The report also noted that HBC also handed over the "Walk in the Word " ministry to **MacDonald** even though the church pumped millions of dollars into it.
The Evangelical Council for Financial Accountability announced Wednesday that they had terminated HBC's membership based on further investigation into the megachurch's operation.
 "The Evangelical Council for Financial Accountability (ECFA) board voted today to update the membership status for "Harvest Bible Chapel " (Elgin, IL) from suspension to termination due to significant violations of four of ECFA's Seven Standards of Responsible Stewardship."

 Based on new information obtained by ECFA from the church while under suspension, ECFA determined that the church was not in compliance with Standards 2, 3, 4 and 6, which pertain to Governance, Financial Oversight, Use of Resources and Compliance with Laws, and Compensation-Setting and Related-Party Transactions," the organization said.
 "ECFA continues to champion integrity in God's Kingdom," Dan Busby, ECFA president said in the announcement. "We are committed to applying our standards rigorously and consistently."

MacDonald's ouster from HBC was triggered by "highly inappropriate recorded comments" he made on a radio program as well as "other conduct." He was recorded talking about planting child pornography on "Christianity Today" CEO Harold Smith's computer, and making crude remarks about independent journalist Julie Roys — including joking that she had an affair with

CT Editor-in-Chief Mark Galli — and a rude reference to Ed Stetzer, executive director of the Billy Graham Center at Wheaton College.

It was recently reported that **MacDonald** splurged thousands of dollars in church funds on a vintage car he gifted Stetzer. Stetzer said he had no idea **MacDonald** used money from church donations to pay for the gift. He reportedly reimbursed the ministry for the full value of the car, a just under $13,000 1971 VW Beetle, in March. https://www.christianpost.com/news/ harvest-bible-chapel-allegedly-made-james-macdonald-a-millionaire-ecfa-terminates-membership.html

---

"**James MacDonald** splurged thousands from church funds on vintage car gifted to Wheaton prof Ed Stetzer." By Leonardo Blair, Christian Post Reporter, April 09, 2019

Less than two months after "Harvest Bible Chapel ' in greater Chicago ousted founder **James MacDonald** for abuse of power and other sins, a new report says he splurged thousands of dollars on a vintage car he gifted Ed Stetzer, the "Billy Graham " chair of "Church, Mission, and Evangelism at Wheaton College" last spring.

Citing a tip published by Dee Parsons at "The Wartburg Watch," independent journalist Julie Roys, confirmed in a report Tuesday that **MacDonald** gifted Stetzer a just under $13,000 1971 VW Beetle last April.

Stetzer said he had no idea MacDonald used money from church donations to pay for the gift. "Long story short...**James** heard that my daughter and I were wanting to fix up an old VW bug as a father/daughter project."

" And, he surprised us with the gift of 1971 VW, which I assumed was from his personal funds," Stetzer told pastor and podcaster Joe Thorn in a message about the gift shortly after Parsons' post went public last Friday. Stetzer reportedly later checked with HBC after reading reports of the financial scandal at the church and discovered that the funds for the Beetle had come from **MacDonalds'** "Walk in the Word" broadcast ministry, a sub-ministry of the church. He reimbursed the ministry for the full value of the car in March.

Roys noted that Stetzer, who serves as contributing editor for "Christianity Today," and dean of the "School of Mission, Ministry, and Leadership at Wheaton College," and executive director of the "Billy Graham Center," might have improperly impacted the way in which CT reported on the HBC debacle as it unfolded in recent months.

"Stetzer's receipt of a large gift from a celebrity pastor like **MacDonald** raises conflict of interest issues, given Stetzer's position at Wheaton College and especially his role as an editor for "Christianity Today," Roys wrote.

As part of his paid journalistic relationship with CT, Stetzer manages one of eight special sections on CT's website called "The Exchange with Ed Stetzer."

Roys said Mark Galli, editor in chief for "Christianity Today," confirmed that Stetzer arranged a conversation (between **MacDonald** and CT Deputy Managing Editor Jeremy Weber) that led to the magazine publishing **MacDonald's** article defending his lawsuit against her and four other defendants, titled "Why Suing is Sometimes the Biblical Choice." Galli told CP that Stetzer was not instrumental in the publication of the op-ed.

The "Christian Post" reported last October that HBC slapped Roys and several former workers with a defamation lawsuit alleging the publication of false information about the church, its finances and governance that resulted in the loss of 2,000 members.
Roys and the former employees have since been vindicated in recent months.

In March, church officials admitted that there was a "lack of financial control" over **MacDonald's** office. "As our Harvest 2020 team is charged with reviewing all finances within the church, we have found that there was a lack of financial control and oversight as well as questionable spending practices made by the senior pastor's office."
"In addition, we have identified there was a separate budget for the senior pastor's office over which there was not sufficient controls and oversight," officials said.

Roys noted that in December, after her exposé on HBC was published in "WORLD,' "Christianity Today" published an article titled, "Harvest Bible Chapel Disputes World Investigation of James MacDonald." "CT's unusual coverage of the Harvest scandal doesn't necessarily show collusion between Stetzer, **MacDonald**, and CT."

But it certainly raises questions, especially in light of the gifted car. But it's not just Stetzer's position with CT that may present a conflict of interest," Roys argued. **MacDonald's** Feb. 12 ouster from "Harvest Bible Chapel " was triggered by "highly inappropriate recorded comments" he made on a radio program as well as "other conduct."

He was recorded talking about planting child pornography on "Christianity Today" CEO Harold Smith's computer, and making crude remarks about Roys — including joking that she had an affair with Galli — and a vulgar reference to Stetzer. https://www.christianpost.com/news/james-macdonald-splurged-thousands-church-funds-vintage-car-gifted-wheaton-prof-ed-stetzer.html

---

Tithes, offerings dip 40 percent, membership down by 3,500 after scandal at Harvest Bible Chapel   By Leonardo Blair, Christian Post Reporter, March 31, 2019

Officials at the multi campus "Harvest Bible Chapel " in greater Chicago urged faithful supporters to give to the ministry after reporting a drop in membership of 3,500 as well as a 40 percent dip in tithes and offering a month after the firing of founding Pastor **James MacDonald**. "If you call Harvest your church home, if this is where God is calling you to be, yet you have stopped giving your tithes, we are asking you to seek the Lord about restarting your giving," the Harvest 2020 team urged in a report to church members earlier this month.

MacDonald's Feb. 12 ouster from "Harvest Bible Chapel " was triggered by "highly inappropriate recorded comments" he made on a radio program as well as "other conduct."

(**NOTE: There is a video on this site where you can hear him planning the comments, unbeknownst to him that his mic was on. Ed.).

He was recorded talking about planting child pornography on "Christianity Today "
CEO's Harold Smith's computer, and making crude remarks about independent journalist Julie
Roys — including joking that she had an affair with CT Editor-in-Chief Mark Galli — and a vulgar
reference to Ed Stetzer, executive director of the "Billy Graham Center at Wheaton College."

He also exited the megachurch under a cloud of allegations of financial abuse. In their
message to members on March 10, church officials reviewing finances at the church admitted
that there was a "lack of financial control" over **MacDonald's** office.

"As our Harvest 2020 team is charged with reviewing all finances within the church, we have
found that there was a lack of financial control and oversight as well as questionable spending
practices made by the senior pastor's office.   "In addition, we have identified there was a
separate budget for the senior pastor's office over which there was not sufficient controls and
oversight," officials said.

Former HBC members like Scott and Marsha Thompson, who gave some $72,000 faithfully to
the church over several years, are so livid about the revelations they have demanded their
money back.

"All this is coming out that millions of dollars potentially has been mishandled," Scott told CBS.
He explained that he began questioning **MacDonald's** spending in 2006, when he saw his
home in Inverness featured in "Chicago" magazine.
 "We find out that the pastor is living in a $2 million house," said Scott, who walked away from
HBC in 2013.   "You drive over there, and sure enough there's the house that's in the picture
from the magazine article. Yep, that's the house on a private lake," he said.

MacDonald no longer owns the house and hasn't lived there in five years, CBS noted.
Church officials said they are doing a comprehensive review of HBC's finances and taking steps
to ensure better financial accountability. They noted that they would "Begin the process of
opening a new bank account to ensure every dollar of your tithes go toward existing ministry
expenses, banking obligations, and staff salaries."
 " All tithes will be isolated and treated solely for these purposes. Tithes will not be used toward
anything related to the Senior Pastor's office or his past budgets."

They also unveiled a plan to "reduce weekly operating expenses (not including mortgages) from
$409,000 to $308,000."   "If necessary, we will reduce our costs further to live within our
means," officials said. "We know trust is earned over time, and we are working diligently to
take actions and to communicate in ways that begin restoring trust." "We hope all that we have
shared above shows a step in that direction."
"We also face the reality of our expenses and declined giving. Above all else though, we are
trusting the Lord in all things," the officials said.
"This rebuilding of trust, unity, and health as a Christ-honoring church is hard."
 "We cannot do it alone. We need your prayers and your willingness to embrace this new
journey together," they added. https://www.christianpost.com/news/
tithes-offerings-dip-40-percent-membership-down-3500-scandal-harvest-bible-chapel.html

CHURCH & MINISTRIES, NOVEMBER 04, 2019:

"Harvest Bible Chapel " formally disqualifies former pastor **James MacDonald**, citing 1 Timothy 5. https://www.christianpost.com/news/ harvest-bible-church-formally-disqualifies-former-pastor-james-macdonald-citing-1-timothy-5.ht ml?uid=89fa9f8477

- **Francis MacNutt**: March 20, 2015

WHY AM I STILL ILL? THE PASTORAL RESPONSE OF **FRANCIS MACNUTT** AND **JOHN WIMBER** https://richardmoy.com/2015/03/20/ why-am-i-still-ill-the-pastoral-response-of-francis-macnutt-and-john-wimber/

(**NOTE: Very lengthy article. Please go to the link above. Ed.).

"Is There a Conflict Between Christianity and Psychology?" Would you recognize a false teaching if your pastor presented one next Sunday?
The evidence is that Christians everywhere are enthusiastically embracing false teachings in the church regarding success, health, and prosperity. 4.
  Should inner healing and inner guides be practiced in the church? Inner healing is a form of counseling which seeks to correct the harmful memories of the past by receiving them in the present through visualization and other techniques, often using Jesus as an "inner counselor" or "inner guide"
 It is a method based largely upon the theories of Freud and Jung, and often the practices of religious mysticism.

It has come into the Church through Jungian therapists and laymen such as **Agnes Sanford**, Episcopal priest **Morton Kelsey** (her pastor), **John Sanford** (her son), and **John** and **Paula Stanford, Dennis** and **Rite Bennett, Paul Yonggi Cho, Father Francis MacNutt**, and **Ruth Carter Stapleton**.
It has also entered the church through other Roman Catholic and Protestant charismatics and by some Christian psychologists and parapsychologists.
 The problem with most inner healing is that it is based upon an unproven assumption of an unconscious mind operating in a particular manner, in an alleged natural connection with, or as part of, God. The unconscious mind has become the means to meet Jesus and be sanctified.

Besides opening Christians to the occultic theories of Jung, inner healing may open them to the occult itself via inner guides who are really demons. Even the September 1986 "Charisma" magazine published an article on inner healing which warned, "According to some, Eastern mysticism and even necromancy are infiltrating the movement in some quarters.'

"I know this is going to offend some people," says Martin Lynch cautiously, 'but it has to be said. We're starting to see a deification of the unconscious. It's a major problem."
Lynch, who is Roman Catholic, says that certain people 'tend to be susceptible to the teachings of Carl Jung. But Jung is a nemesis. He's anti-Christian. He was a gnostic and a purveyor of Gnosticism.' The problem of "inner advisors" so often found in Jungian psychology, inner

healing, and in some <u>Christian psychotherapy is that it is often indistinguishable from the contacting of spirit guides in occultism.</u>

Inner "guides" may be either genuinely imaginative (as in dreams) or they may be <u>spiritistic.</u> Cultivating them may also progress from the purely imaginary to genuine <u>spiritism</u>. Thus, there is growing interest in what may be termed "<u>imagination spiritism</u>" where the imagination becomes the vehicle for <u>spirit contact</u>, whether deliberately sought or not (although often under another name).

Mary Watkins is <u>a psychotherapist </u>who uses Jungian "<u>active imagination</u>" and inner dialogue with "guides" in her patients' therapy. In her book, "Invisible Guests: the Development of Imaginal Dialogues," she sets forth her belief that <u>psychotherapy should encourage the emergence of "imaginal presence" and that the patient can benefit by deepening his relationship with them.</u>

She believes these psychic counselors are not spirits but, along with Jung, they are merely "indicative of the process of personification that occurs spontaneously in the unconscious." In other words, these are seen as Jungian archetypes; yet both Jung and she directly experienced that these are autonomous "<u>entities.</u>"

 Dr. Watkins admits, "<u>The imaginal other may have as much autonomy as the so-called real others I meet in consensual space.</u>"

In his autobiography Jung describes one of his archetypes, "Philemon," as being "quite real, as if he were a living personality" and compares his experience with Philemon to the ancient practice of contacting **a** god.   In fact, he admits both Philemon and another archetypal figure, "Ka," perfectly fit the category of <u>spirit guides</u>.

 In our opinion, when the church accepts Jungian and other dubious methods, it is treading on potentially dangerous ground. <u>What objects standards exist to discern imaginary inner guides from spirits who initially assume such a pose as a means of later contact or influence?</u>

(Such methods are, in fact, encouraged by the very spirit world which utilizes them <u>because they help mask spirit contact under the guise of psychotherapy</u>.) The question must be asked, "Are some portions of the church by innocence or naivete, at least in some cases, helping its own members to contact spirits?"

John Ankerberg & John Weldon   http://home.insightbb.com /~cathiadenham2/Facts%20on%20False%20Teaching%20In%20The%20Church/False%20Tea ching%20In%20The%20Church%20--%204.htm

- **Francis MacNutt**: is a Founding Director and Executive Committee member of CHM. https://www.christianhealingmin.org/ index.php?option=com_content&view=article&id =1056&catid=271&Itemid=101

- **C.J. Mahaney**: Covered up sex abuses within the SGM "Sovereign Grace Ministries" system:

Pam Palmer was at a barbecue when she heard the news. It was 2011, five years after her family had left "Covenant Life Church." But the Gaithersburg congregation and its founder, **C.J. Mahaney**, remained on her mind. Now one of her relatives was telling her that amid controversy **Mahaney** had surrendered the top post at the organization he had built into an international empire.

"Literally," Pam says, "that moment changed my life." Pam had been one of the church's early followers back in the 1980s. And she'd given 22 years of her life to the megachurch, in the all-in manner that many members embraced. Early on, her husband, Dominic Palmer, whom she'd met there, led one of the small fellowship groups that underscore church life, and she dutifully assisted him. When the couple had children, Pam home schooled them, as so many women in the church did. Every step of the way, a foundational principle of the church was reinforced—that Christian men knew best.

But in the years since the Palmers left "Covenant Life," Pam had come to see its culture as toxic. After the barbecue, she went online to find out more about the revolt inside "Sovereign Grace Ministries," the religious conglomerate that "Covenant Life" had grown into.
A few years earlier, a pair of disillusioned followers had launched a blog called "SGM Survivors." It was like a public square, and an increasingly crowded one at that, where former congregants of "Sovereign Grace" churches—there were roughly 90 at the time—gathered to vent.

Pam had visited the blog before. But this time, she encountered a whole new narrative. Parents were reporting that their children had been sexually abused by other church members. And they were sharing stories, saying they were mistreated by churches when they spoke up. Until that moment, Pam had no idea there were other families out there just like hers.
Mahaney, a shaggy-haired hippie from Takoma Park who was getting stoned when he was reborn as a Christian, had just joined the Jesus movement and wandered into a weeknight prayer meeting, full of raised hands and speaking in tongues. He struck up a friendship with one of its leaders, **Larry Tomczak**, and the men began to collaborate.

Wander into one of their services at "Christ Church" on Massachusetts Avenue, Northwest, in the 1970s and you could find nearly 2,000 people captivated by the music and their preaching. Barely in their twenties, the founders made a dynamic team. Before long, they were holding Sunday services, too, forming what would become "Covenant Life Church." By 1982, they'd launched their overarching ministry to "plant" new congregations, and they soon adopted what's now known as "Sovereign Grace Church" of Fairfax.

Over the years, the ministry expanded to Ashburn, Fredericksburg, and Germantown; Cleveland, Jacksonville, and Pasadena; and on to the Philippines, Mexico, and the UK, until it had some 28,000 adherents around the globe. SGM churches typically have a lead pastor and a staff of deputy pastors to oversee different spheres of church life.

The business has been a family affair. Over the years, many of **Mahaney's** friends and relatives have held the upper rungs of power. "People were the best of friends, the closest of friends," says Brent Detwiler, an early leader. "That continued for many, many years."

By 1997, **Tomczak** had left the movement. **Mahaney,** by contrast, was pinnacled upon a kingdom of his own making. He was also ensconced among the country's evangelical elite.

A college dropout with no formal training, he became an in-demand public speaker and author and befriended influential New Calvinist leaders—a group that included prominent Baptist minister **John Piper**, Albert Mohler, president of the powerful "Southern Baptist Theological Seminary;" and Mark Dever, leader of the "Capitol Hill Baptist Church," a go-to place of worship for evangelical Hill staffers...

https://www.washingtonian.com/2016/02/14/
the-sex-abuse-scandal-that-devastated-a-suburban-megachurch-sovereign-grace-ministries/
http://thewartburgwatch.com/2019/01/02/
do-you-remember-cj-mahaney-and-sovereign-grace-ministries-churches-the-media-does-and-ne
eds-your-help/
https://www.christianitytoday.com/news/2019/
april/sovereign-grace-churches-sgc-sgm-independent-investigation-.html

https://maranathaministriesrevisted.com/category/n the-nature-of-cult-leadership/

(**NOTE: Excellent articles; the Christianity Today web link–third one from the top in this discourse-- seems to show how intimidating a person can be, since one of the investigators seemed to have changed his mind. Ed).

- **Lord Maitreya** "Wherever I look today around the world, I see the shining points of Light of my people, those on whom I rely. These beacons of Light shall bring all men to me, and thus the Plan will unfold. May it be that you will gather yourselves around..."
" The crime of separation, of lawlessness must go from the world."   "All that hinders the manifestation of man's divinity must be driven from our planet. My law will take the place of separation."   http://www.zedekiahlist.com/ cgi-bin/results.pl?&menuid=V&itemid=F

- **Guillermo Maldonado**: Is associated with the New Apostolic Reformation, as he goes by the title, "Apostle" **Guillermo Maldonado**. He is a growing leader in the prosperity Gospel movement, especially among Latin Americans, as he proudly teaches that faith in God yields material wealth, health, and temporal blessings. Unfortunately, Guillermo is a false teacher who is leading many people astray.

The New Apostolic Reformation and the teaching of the restoration of modern day prophets and apostles are unbiblical, as these offices, along with the apostolic sign gifts of healing, tongues, and prophecy all ceased at the end of the apostolic age. Further, we do not get called by God through an audible voice that tells us "to bring God's supernatural power to this generation."
God has finally spoken to us through His Son, Jesus (Hebrews 1:1) who has called us not to bring "supernatural power," at least in the way it is presented by these false teachers, to this generation but to preach the gospel and make disciples (Matthew 28:19).

God's Word is the supernatural power to save (Romans 1:16), and we are to proclaim it to all nations. He has opened the door to even more serious error through his teachings while garnering financial wealth for himself at the expense of his followers. In the video below, **Maldonado** teaches the unbiblical concept of first-fruits seed-faith tithing.

He teaches that you can "activate" God's Word and the power of redemption by "honoring God" with your "first fruits" of your income. He promises that God will "redeem" the rest of your income for a year if you will set aside a month of giving your entire income to his church.

"The fasting of the first fruit has the power of multiplication...every time you honor [God] first...God will say that his money, his finances, is protected because he honored God first," **Maldonado** promises. This is not a teaching that can be found anywhere in Scripture. It is a false teaching that is designed to line the pockets of false teachers like **Guillermo Maldonado**. Sadly, this teaching has crept into many Evangelical churches today, even in a watered-down form, it's still dangerous.

(**NOTE: The video referred to in the above article can be found on the first web link listed below. Ed.).

https://pulpitandpen.org/2017/05/22/ false-teacher-of-the-day-5-guillermo-maldonado/

https://www.thegospelcoalition.org/article/ the-prosperity-gospel-in-latin-america/

http://bethelchurchresearch.blogspot.com/p/ deception.html

https://www.youtube.com/ watch?v=c21-lD8ZPEE&feature=youtu.be

(**NOTE: This YouTube video is **Paula White** preaching at **Guillermo Maldonado's** church. Ed.).

- **Brennan Manning**: Author of several books that claim to be inspired by God; they are demonically inspired). https://janetmefferd.com/2019/02/

- **Brian McClaren**: Another one of the founders of the Emerging Church; his influence is widespread. The "emerging church" movement follows the lead of the collapsing culture of the late 20th century, discarding invariable truths and precepts of God for the self-serving subjectivity of man. **Brian McLaren** is one of the movement's preeminent leaders, and we show how this "new" church movement is just another brand of false Christianity, supplanting faith with anti-Christ philosophy honoring false gods such as Allah and denying the Lord Jesus Christ.

McLaren writes: "The greatest threat to evangelicalism is evangelicals who tolerate hate and who promote hate camouflaged as piety.
"If that isn't a description of Islam – tolerating hate and promoting it as piety – I don't know what is. "No one can serve two masters. You can't serve God and greed, nor can you serve God and fear, nor God and hate."

McLaren is quite mistaken on the last point. There are many things God hates, and those who serve Him will hate them as well. He hates lies, for example, and there isn't a bigger lie than the Islamic religion, which falsely claims to originate with God, but hates Him.
 That, I assure you, He hates, as do we. Psalms 139:21-22.
 https://www.thepathoftruth.com/ false-teachers/brian-mclaren.htm

(**NOTE: A little lengthy, but good information can be found on the above link. Ed.).

Brian McLaren Calls Hell and the Cross "False Advertising for God;" Listen to Interview

"This is one of the huge problems with the traditional understanding of hell, because if the Cross is in line with Jesus' teaching, then I won't say the only and I certainly won't say ... or even the primary or a primary meaning of the Cross ... is that the Kingdom of God doesn't come like the kingdoms of this world by inflicting violence and coercing people."

"But that the kingdom of God comes thru suffering and willing voluntary sacrifice right? But in an ironic way the doctrine of hell basically says no, that's not really true. At the end God gets his way thru coercion and violence and intimidation and domination just like every other kingdom does. The Cross isn't the center then, the Cross is almost a distraction and false advertising for God."

Brian McLaren speaking, "From the Interview" :
 https://www.lighthousetrailsresearch.com/ brianmclaren.htm

(**NOTE: Also a little lengthy, but excellent information on this website. Ed.).

- **Josh McDowell**: "For example I trusted **Josh McDowell**, only to find that he occasionally teaches at "promise-keepers" events, which is wildly ecumenical.
 Who can we trust?" http://watchmanforjesus.blogspot.com/2010/03/

- **Aimee Semple McPherson:** Popular in the 30s; faked her kidnaping; false preacher.
Aimee Semple McPherson is unique among the healing hucksters in that she eventually founded her own denomination, the "Foursquare Gospel Church," which exists to this day. She was a good looking flamboyant woman preacher who flew in the face of the religious notions of her day. She was America's first mega-church pastor, was on the forefront of radio ministry and she set the pace for the women preachers who followed her.
 However, she had many moral problems. She was an adulteress, who faked her own kidnaping to be with her lover, these facts are all well documented in books, videos and on the internet.
"Sister" **Aimee** died in 1944 of a barbiturate overdose, some say it was accidental, but for one who proclaimed "Christ the Healer" why did she need any barbiturates to begin with?

 https://discernmentministriesinternational.wordpress.com/ category/ don-stewart/

(**NOTE: Several of the so-called "healers" are also listed on this website. Ed.).

- **Joyce Meyer**: WOF heretic, false teacher\preacher:

"There is no hope of anyone going to heaven unless they believe this truth I am presenting. You cannot go to heaven unless you believe with all your heart that Jesus took your place in hell" (p. 37). [The Most Important Decision You Will Ever Make, Booklet, 1991 edition].

http://www.banner.org.uk/wof/sayings.html

(**NOTE: One of many of her blasphemous quotes. Plenty of You Tube videos showing just how demonic her "teachings" are, as well as other websites. Ed.).

- **Jory Micah** Is a false teacher, and is teaching heretical doctrine and leading many women astray. Her hermeneutic of reading Scripture through the lens of feminism has led her to abandon sound doctrine and chase false doctrines; is a feminist "theologian" who has risen to promote egalitarianism and women in leadership.

Micah reads the Bible in light of her feminism and not the other way around. Such a reading of Scripture will not only lead to numerous heterodoxies but will cause someone to believe and teach heresy. This has happened many times with her theology.
A dissection of her Master's Thesis will show a few troubling doctrines. Besides a poor handling of God's Word and a few points that rely solely on creating confusion about the text of Scripture, one thing that stood out was in her introduction, when she said,

"While Jesus walked the earth as a male, there is no Biblical evidence that Jesus' glorified body is still male in Heaven." Either she is claiming that Jesus is a transgender or she is claiming that Jesus no longer has a human nature, the Eutychian heresy. Either way, that statement is a Christ-related (Christological) heresy.

God reveals Himself as a male. Every single pronoun used for any member of the Godhead is a masculine pronoun. However, **Jory Micah** says in her Master's Thesis, "God is just as much a Mother as He is a Father."
She has similarly said, "Our God is also a Mother – She births life and nurtures life." (Source). She makes the argument that the Hebrew word for spirit is a feminine noun, therefore the Holy Spirit must be female (By that same logic, sin is female, as the Hebrew word for sin is feminine). (Source).
God reveals Himself in the masculine, and that is because He is male. She has even claimed to get divine revelation, saying multiple times that God spoke to her and not referring to Scripture (Here and here, for example).

This claim of prophecy sets her supposed revelation as equal to Scripture, otherwise, it isn't Theopneustos – God-breathed – and God didn't really say it. If she is attributing something to God that God didn't say, then it is false prophecy. If she is to say this is Theopneustos, then she is saying that Scripture is either insufficient or incomplete (To say either is heresy) and she is embracing the Montanist heresy.
As John Owen said, "If private revelations agree with Scripture, they are unnecessary and if they disagree they are false." **Micah** has taken to defending the sin of immodesty. She wrote in one post on her site that "Modesty Rules" contribute to "Rape Culture".

She has made the argument on her Facebook against "modesty rules" as well. She made this argument based off of her own immodesty and how she felt when people corrected her, including that everyone else dressed that way so it should've been fine for her too.
She rightly points out that those whose eyes cause them to stumble are told it is better to gouge them out, but she ignores what Matthew 18:6 says.   https://pulpitandpen.org/2016/

(**NOTE: A few "sources" listed above, and the "here and here" notations are included in the website. Ed.).

- Joshua Mills:
Who oozes oil from his hands and (in something like an extension of America's prosperity gospel!) keeps receiving gold dust on his face or jewels from angelic realms and who, when his own ring was stolen, supposedly astral traveled to the thief's bedroom to regain it.
The Spirit has allegedly taught Josh how to play electric piano – it's remarkable how bland his "gift" sounds when demonstrated!
http://rollanscensoredissuesblog.blogspot.com

- Dr. José' Luis de Jesus Miranda: From Bogota, Columbia, this heretic says that "I am the Second Coming of Christ," meaning that he says that **HE** is Jesus Christ.

http://www.zedekiahlist.com/ cgi-bin/results.pl?&menuid=V&itemid=F

- Brenda Mitchell: Prophecy teacher; uses the non-canonical "Book of Jasher" to prophesy; She stated in this video that God came down to confuse the language at the tower of Babel, but He had a "divine council" with Him, since He says "let US go down..." He had to consult with them first. The website has topics that she taught, which are heretical:

https://christthecreativeword.net/messagesbybrendamitchell/

(**NOTE: A video of her is on You tube, speaking at the chapel in Akron, OH. Ed.).

- Beth Moore: Baptist "darling" who holds Women's Bible Studies; Heretical teacher; pseudo-biblical nonsense; She raises large amounts of money by soliciting funds for the SBC–Southern Baptist Convention; her meetings consist of mantras, imagination and visualizations, impartations, and other demonic practices; WOF preacher, friends with other women of NAR.

Why do people "hate" **Beth Moore**? What's the problem with **Beth Moore**?

SUMMARY: People with sound doctrine don't tend to support uniting with and promoting word of faith and prosperity gospel heretical teaching. You simply cannot trust the doctrine, theology, and teaching of someone who promotes and partners with heretical false teachers.

There are much better sources to get your teaching from than **Beth Moore**. You don't need to be a cessationist to have problems with **Beth Moore**. MAIN: Many in attempts to answer these questions end up getting bogged down in the continuist vs. cessationist debate.

I'm going to avoid that topic, and prove you don't need to be a <u>cessationist</u> to have concerns and problems with the teaching and ministry of **Beth Moore**. Continuists who believe tongues and prophecy are still active today can have real concerns with **Beth Moore**.

(By the way, this isn't about hating **Beth Moore**. (I chose the title for the search engines: Author of the article).

Beth Moore in 2016 joined <u>word of faith</u> teacher **Joyce Meyer** at her "Love Life Women's Conference." That is more than a simple friendship with someone.
https://reformationcharlotte.org/2019/01/02/
beth-moore-declares-spending-time-with-god-and-spending-time-with-the-bible-are-not-the-sa
me-thing/
https://www.nowtheendbegins.com/
false-teacher-beth-moore-crusade-to-tear-down-biblical-womanhood-throw-off-shackles-apostle
-paul-commands-new-testament-church/

https://www.christianpost.com/news/
beth-moore-christine-caine-march-around-dallas-hospital-in-prayer-during-priscilla-shirer-surger
y.html

-**Robert Morris**: Is right in that the lies he preaches about tithing will lure you into bondage with Satan. Absolutely. What he preaches is pure evil. That God does not want you to pay your bills or even buy food until **HE** gets His cut. **Morris** turns God into a bloodthirsty gangster who is waiting to whack you if you do not pay His protection money.

Perhaps worse than the gangsters of lore like Al Capone, the God **Morris** sells goes beyond merely not blessing you. No, **Robert Morris'** god will actually kneecap you too! Your money will actually be cursed by God if you do not pay up! I know loan sharks that are more forgiving.

The notion that God wants you to be so irresponsible with money that you end up sitting in the dark with no food as they come to evict you but at least you paid **Robert Morris** is absurd and spiritually criminal. He teaches here the dire importance of humility in your walk but has none for his own. In 2016 "Gateway Church" brought in over $127 million dollars.

I wonder how many foreclosures there were to reach those numbers? How many shattered faiths? Beloved God loves a cheerful giver and there is a universal principle of sowing and reaping which goes far beyond money. If you find a church that is truly preaching the Gospel of Jesus Christ then you will not find a better place to invest your money.
If you give to a snake oil salesman like **Robert Morris** however just remember that you are buying your way into bondage to Satan. That is what **Robert Morris** himself taught and ironically, he got that part right.
Rev. Anthony http://www.828ministries.com/
Diary/Robert-Morris-Gangster-Go-by-Anthony-Wade-Tithing-190401-623.html

- **Dayna Muldoon**: False <u>prophetess</u>; member of the <u>Emergent</u> church.

- **Mel Mullen**: False preacher; is in league with **Cindy Jacobs**, another false preacher\prophetess; NAR.

- **Bob Mumford**: "Charismatic Leaders Concede They Went Too Far" :
Movements: 'Shepherding' was often accused by outsiders and former members of being cultlike in requiring members to obey leaders in all aspects of their personal lives.

MARCH 24, 1990 FROM RELIGIOUS NEWS SERVICE--

NEW YORK — Several leaders of a movement in charismatic churches that often was criticized in the 1970s and 1980s for its authoritarian structure and rigid disciplinary requirements for members have acknowledged that they were guilty of excesses and non-biblical teachings. The movement, known as "shepherding," was often accused by outsiders and former members of being cultlike in requiring members to obey leaders in all aspects of their personal lives, including selection of marriage partners.

In response to what they saw as a lack of discipline within the tongues-speaking churches--similar to Pentecostalist churches--charismatic leaders **Bob Mumford, Charles Simpson, Derek Prince** and **Don Basham** joined together in 1970 to found an organization called "Christian Growth Ministries" in Ft. Lauderdale, Fla.
The movement began publishing the now-defunct "New Wine" magazine and holding leadership conferences around the country. At its peak in the mid-1970s, the movement had as many as 150,000 followers.

But several leaders have recently admitted to excesses, including **Mumford**, who said in a recent statement widely circulated among charismatics that there had been an "unhealthy submission resulting in perverse and unbiblical obedience to human leaders."
In an interview in "Christianity Today " magazine, **Mumford** said that "people took something that began in the spirit and attempted to perfect it in the flesh."
 "Ends began to justify means. The attitude became, 'I'm going to help you walk straight, even if I have to coerce you.' This is not the spirit of the Gospel."

The charismatic leader said that "part of the motivation behind my public apology is the realization that this wrong attitude is still present in hundreds of independent church groups who are answerable to no one." **Mumford** admitted that he had not listened to earlier warnings from the **Rev. Jack Hayford**, pastor of the "Church On the Way " in Van Nuys.
 It was after counseling from **Hayford** last year that **Mumford** released his public apology.
Hayford wrote in a recent article in "Ministries Today " magazine that "hundreds of pastors, like myself, have spent large amounts of time over the past 15 years picking up the pieces of broken lives that resulted from distortion of truth by extreme teachings and destructive applications on discipleship, authority and shepherding."
In addition, **Simpson** told "Charisma" magazine, "I have done things that I repent of and I do want forgiveness and I do want to see restoration." **Prince** left the movement in 1980 and is now an independent Bible teacher based in Ft. Lauderdale. **Basham** died in 1989.

In a related development, "Maranatha Christian Churches," an umbrella organization of about 70 congregations based in Gainesville, Fla., has dissolved as an international federation. It announced that its congregations will operate independently. In August, 1984, "Christianity Today" made public the report of an ad hoc committee of six cult-watching specialists who had been monitoring "Maranatha's" activities in response to complaints. The report said the organization's "authoritarian orientation" had "potentially negative consequences for members."

All the major personalities associated with the shepherding movement had addressed "Maranatha" gatherings, according to **Lee Grady**, managing editor of the "Maranatha" publication "The Forerunner" from 1981 until the organization disbanded.

The decision to disband as a federation was supported by "Maranatha's" president and founder, **Bob Weiner**, who made the formal proposal at the organization's annual conference in Texas. **Weiner** has been on a one-year sabbatical since last November. He said he doesn't have specific plans for his activities after his leave ends.

https://www.latimes.com/archives/ la-xpm-1990-03-24-ca-667-story.html

https://ncmifringe.wordpress.com/tag/ don-basham/

- **Myles Munroe**: Deceased; Another false teacher, WOF; aligned with "Destiny Image" **Steven Strang,** publishers of false preachers, teachers and prosperity believers.

- **Steve & Melodye Muncey**: WOF; https://www.fox32chicago.com/news/ family-of-nikki-smith-raise-new-questions-regarding-her-accidental-drowning

This is concerning a babysitter drowning in the pastor's pool and no one did anything to try and resuscitate her, nor did they call for an ambulance.

- **Mike Murdock**: VERY demonic "spiritual" leader; promotes all things false--False Prophesies, Prosperity Gospel, Name It-Claim It, WOF.

https://www.thepathoftruth.com/ false-teachers/mike-murdock.htm

- **Arnold Murray**: Deceased; Twisted teaching of the Bible; takes verses out of context, which makes it easy to twist their meaning; claims that Cain was actually the son of Eve and Satan—the "serpent seed" doctrine; says there will be no rapture; also teaches Modalism, a heretical doctrine that denies the Trinity--"Father," "Son," and "Spirit" are different titles that God uses at different times. As God takes on different jobs, He uses various names for Himself. Modalism was condemned as a heresy in the first few centuries of the Christian church.

It turns God into a deceiver, because in passages such as Matthew 3:16-17, they definitely describe the Father, Son, and Spirit interrelating to each other. "How can the Father speak in the presence of the Son and the Spirit descend on the Son without making it appear that the three of them are separate persons?"; Subscribed to the "Christian Identity Movement," which teaches the British are the real descendants of the ancient Israelites; his "church" was called the "Shepherd's Chapel." https://www.gotquestions.org/ Shepherds-Chapel.html

https://www.equip.org/article/ arnold-murray-and-the-shepherds-chapel/

https://ezekielcountdown.wordpress.com/2010/07/29/ arnold-murray-false-prophet-false-teacher/

N:

- **Watchman Nee**: To be fair, **Nee** has contributed some helpful material in areas of basic Christian doctrine such as authority and salvation. His most well-known book is "The Normal Christian Life," and there **Nee** writes: "Righteousness, the forgiveness of our sins, and peace with God are all ours by faith, and without faith in the finished work of Jesus Christ none can possess them." Obviously, **Nee** got the Gospel right. Yet his views on sanctification, the Holy Spirit, hermeneutics, baptism, the church and sin contain significant error.

 He had a flawed view of man, practiced an allegorical approach to interpreting Scripture, believed denominations were sinful, and frequently called others to join him in his perpetual quest for the deeper spiritual life—a quest that smacks of perfectionism.

Lack of clarity: Perhaps the best way to describe **Nee** is to label him a confused Christian mystic. Here's one lengthy but insightful example. I chose this example because it is indicative of his writing style, as well as an excellent example of his lack of clarity:

Some years ago I was ill. For six nights I had high fever and could find no sleep. Then at length God gave me from the Scripture a personal word of healing, and because of this I expected all symptoms of sickness to vanish at once. Instead of that, not a wink of sleep could I get, and I was not only sleepless but more restless than ever. My temperature rose higher, my pulse beat faster and my head ached more severely than before.
The enemy asked, 'Where is God's promise? Where is your faith? What about all your prayers?' So I was tempted to thrash the whole matter out in prayer again, but was rebuked, and this Scripture came to mind:

 "Thy word is truth" (John 17:17 Open in Logos Bible Software (if available)).

If God's Word is truth, I thought, then what are these symptoms? They must all be lies! So I declared to the enemy, 'This sleeplessness is a lie, this headache is a lie, this fever is a lie, this high pulse is a lie. In view of what God has said to me, all these symptoms of sickness are just your lies, and God's Word to me is truth.' In five minutes I was asleep, and I awoke the following morning perfectly well" ("The Normal Christian Life," 33-34).

 While **Nee** places heavy stock in personal "spiritual" experiences of that kind, the more significant danger prevalent throughout his books is his consistent lack of clarity.
 Nee does not come right out and say that faith can cure physical illness, nor does he claim outright that he receives direct revelation from the Lord.

He doesn't hold his experience up as an example to follow, but simply relates it as it happened, and then passes it along to us.

Several other authors have pointed out that when **Nee** was young, he was mentored by British missionary Margaret E. Barber, who held to Keswick theology.   It was the philosophy that claimed that the key to sanctification was to surrender your life to the power of Christ in you, and to cease from striving for sanctification.

 It put forward the idea of a "higher spiritual life" that some Christians obtained when they finally learned what it means to let go, and let Jesus live your Christian life for you. During **Nee's** life, that approach to sanctification was called quietism.

Simply put, it is the teaching that the best way to lead the Christian life was to have your earthly soul subsumed in the divine. It's a fundamentally flawed way of thinking about the Christian life and a dangerous approach to sanctification. And it appears to have been taught by **Nee** as well: https://thecripplegate.com/ beware-the-writings-of-the-watchman/

Many Christians uncritically accept the writings of **Watchman Nee** even though few know anything about his background. Many are impressed by the volume of his work and the dogmatism and feeling of deep spirituality that characterize his writings.
His ideas and books still influence charismatics, fundamentalists and people in between. But one need not be a theologian to discover that his teachings call for scrutiny and caution by Christians. Much can be learned about **Nee** from a cursory reading of some of his books and the writings of others who were around him. These show that his theology developed through encounters with four different people and it was from these that he "borrowed" ideas extensively.   Each new book seemed to develop from "discoveries" received from these teachers. http://www.apologeticsindex.org/ 2694-watching-out-for-watchman-nee

(**NOTE: There is a lot more information on this website and others similar to it. Decide for yourself if he was a Christian or not. Ed.).

- **Perry Noble** referred to the people in his church who wish to go deeper in the word as "jackasses." www.828ministries.com

"**Perry Noble** Threatens Pulpit & Pen With Legal Action"
PUBLISHED NOVEMBER 10, 2017 UPDATED MARCH 27, 2018–

Perry Noble: Is the (formerly?) drunken pastor who played "Highway to Hell" on Easter Sunday, cussed at his church members for wanting discipleship, was rebuked by his denomination for butchering the Ten Commandments, and who was released from his megachurch ministry position for unrepentance regarding alcohol and what appears to be marital indiscretions. Recently, we brought to you news of his divorce.

 Prior to that, we brought to you news that he was launching a ministry to help pastors grow their churches through what is essentially a business model. Yes, you may not have known it, but helping morally disqualified ministers remain in the pulpit is an actual profession.

Noble's PR guy is named **Hunter Frederick** and advertises himself as a "public relations and crisis manager." He bills himself as a well-meaning "servant" of Jesus. In fact, he's a sleazy opportunist who seeks to help fallen ministers be restored – not by churches who have gauged their repentance – but in the public eye, so they can continue to make money and stay on the job even though they've been biblically disciplined.

Frederick contacted "Pulpit & Pen" today, identified himself as **Noble's** "publicist," and told us to change our critical articles about the charlatan.

Because **Frederick** has provided his PR services to fallen ministers like **Tullian Tchividjian** (who had multiple extramarital affairs) and **Michael Gungor** (who angered his followers by denying the inerrancy of Scripture), his reputation preceded him.

The article he refers to is this one. He claims **Perry Noble** doesn't recall certain quotations ascribed to him (which makes sense, because he was likely drunk when he said them).

Before we give the rest of our interaction, a few things about **Hunter Frederick.**

"Berean Examiner," a polemicists' blog has done research into this spiritual crisis profiteer already.

It explains in its post, "Crisis Managed?," that **Frederick** needs "to know they are repentant before [he] will work with them." "Berean Examiner" writes, "I called **Frederick** yesterday to ask him about his newest client, **Tullian Tchividjian**. After losing his ministry job last week, the former pastor contacted the agency, and on Monday, **Frederick** took him under counsel."

According to the "Berean Examiner," **Frederick** is the one who calls discernment folks and polemicists on behalf of the ministry and asks them to retract or go soft (our paraphrase) on criticizing them. After all, he says they're repentant. "Berean Examiner" linked a post at the "Christian Newswire," which further explains **Frederick's** job...

With the constant news headlines of pastors and other Christian leaders falling away due to sexual immorality, misuse of church funds, denying certain Christian orthodoxy as well as others, the man that these Christian leaders turn to during a time of crisis believes he knows why our Christian leaders are failing...

Hunter Frederick, the owner of the entertainment and faith-based crisis management and public relations firm "Frederick & Associates" believes that a reason why we are seeing more and more Christian leaders fall is because of the celebrity status we give our Christian leaders. The article then explains what **Frederick** really thinks the problem is...those pesky discernment bloggers. **Frederick** also believes that the ongoing scrutiny from "ultra-conservative" Christian media outlets contribute to the celebrity status of those Christian leaders that they believe are preaching a false Gospel.

"While we need to communicate certain concern over false teachings, we need to be careful of the means in which we communicate these concerns." "A lot of these 'watchman ministries' believe it's their goal to 'call out' these leaders while at the same time evaluating their celebrity status and enable them to use said media attention to their advantage."

How dare we. Of course, if people were listening to us, they wouldn't have been listening to hucksters like **Perry Noble** and the rest of **Frederick's** clientele, to begin with. We responded with the following...

If you recall, **Tony Nolan** – the popular evangelist – had entered into a partnership with **Clayton Jennings** to help rebuild his ministry and restore him after multiple women came out to testify that he preyed upon them spiritually and sexually, and some had even been pressured with alcohol and to take the abortion pill. **Nolan** later explained that **Jennings** ended the restoration process because he had a team of "PR people" who would restore his ministry without making him take a time-out.

Whether or not that was **Hunter Frederick**, we do not know, but we do know that there will be a hot place of judgment for those with the vocational profession of circumventing Biblical church discipline for the sake of financial gain.

There are so many celebrity preachers falling into unrepentant sin that an entire industry of fake restoration has developed to help them rebuild their reputations. If you have any information about **Hunter Frederick** and know any of his other clients, please contact us at info@pulpitandpen.org. (**Frederick** also represented Lindsay Lohan).

(**NOTE: The "business model" is what **Peter Drucker** has proposed that all churches follow. Ed.).

https://pulpitandpen.org/2017/11/10/perry-noble-threatens-pulpit-pen-with-legal-action/

"Perry Noble Still Biblically Unfit to Preach," "NewSpring" Leaders Say MONDAY, JULY 24, 2017

Despite **Perry Noble's** return to preaching after successfully completing rehab, leaders of "NewSpring "— South Carolina's largest church — say their founder, who was fired from his job as senior pastor last July for alcohol abuse and other "unfortunate choices and decisions," is still not Biblically qualified to preach.

"We have been asked why **Perry** can preach at other churches but not at "NewSpring". We cannot speak for other churches and how they make decisions."
" For us, **Perry** currently does not meet the Biblical qualifications of a pastor, teacher, shepherd," "NewSpring " Teaching Pastor **Clayton King** told the megachurch in what was described as a family meeting last Friday. **Noble** returned to the pulpit in February with the blessing of his friend and confidante, **Steven Furtick**, just over seven months after he was fired by "NewSpring." He has continued to preach at other churches, including most recently at "Mission City Church" in Florida.

King explained that there had been questions in the congregation about whether it was wise to have fired **Noble** last year. There were also questions on why, now that he is back in the pulpit, he was being invited to preach at other churches and not "NewSpring."

"Our desire for tonight is to speak the truth in love and answer the questions you have asked us," said **King** whose team noted that giving was down since **Noble's** exit but the church now had more than $15 million in surplus in the bank after paying off debt.

"A little over a year ago we faced a situation that forced us to ask a question. Do we take the Bible seriously? Will we follow what the Bible teaches regarding the qualifications of a leader and the process of trying to lovingly confront sinful behavior that leads to restored relationships?" " Our founding pastor, our leaders and our governing documents took seriously the Scriptures that list the qualifications of a leader, shepherd," he said.

He then went on to highlight three Biblical Scriptures on leadership — Timothy 3:1-5, Titus 1:5b-9 and James 3:1 — and expounded on them briefly. "You may not like the standard laid out in Scripture, but would you ever entrust your life to the pilot of an airplane who could not meet the requirement to fly the aircraft you were sitting in?
"How much more important is it that we take seriously what the Bible says about those who lead us and care for our eternal souls. This does not, nor will ever mean that imperfect people aren't welcome at "NewSpring." The truth is none of us are perfect," he said.

With the support of "NewSpring's" new leadership team, **King** said they were following Matthew 18 when they made the decision to fire **Noble** last year. "As you can imagine, seeing your brother making choices that were hurting his ministry, his family and his personal walk with Jesus was very difficult. There is no doubt he was and is still loved by myself and the men standing with me tonight," **King** said.
 Leaders of "NewSpring Church" in South Carolina addressed the church at a meeting on Friday July 21, 2017. "We knew that to honor God's Word and to love **Perry** and his family well, we had to act."

There were numerous conversations and offers made to **Perry** so that he could receive the help he needed but he was unwilling to accept them." "This left the leadership of the church with only one option — a decision that no one wanted to make." "We believed that we had done all we could do to help **Perry** remain as our senior pastor. " So in July of last year, we released him from that position. This is when we brought the situation before you, the church, as outlined by Jesus in Matthew 18," he continued.
 "Some have questioned our decision to remove **Perry** especially in light of his return to preaching and speaking." "He's been vocal about how he feels, that we didn't reach out to him in the days following his release."
 " We understand how that has caused some to question whether we offered forgiveness and grace to our friend. The leaders on this stage have completely forgiven **Perry,**" he said to applause.
King said since **Noble's** firing, he and others from the church have been reaching out to **Noble** but said their efforts have been repeatedly rejected. "The truth is many people did reach out and we desired to spend time with him. In most instances, he declined. I have personally reached out to **Perry** consistently for 13 months and he has declined to meet with me," he said. He further noted that **Noble's** wife, Lucretia, desires to be reconciled with her husband but that is also yet to happen.

 "Many of us have walked with Lucretia over the past year and she is 100 percent committed to **Perry,** their marriage and desires reconciliation," **King** said. He told the church that since **Noble's** exit, God has given the church a new blueprint for team leadership "where Jesus Christ would be the senior pastor and chief shepherd of our church and one man would not have the entire weight and responsibility placed on him."

Lead pastors of the church are now: **Brad Cooper**, pastor of direction and culture; **Shane Duffey,** pastor of ministries; **Howard Frist,** pastor of campuses; and **Michael Mullikin,** pastor of operations. Along with **King,** teaching pastors were announced as: **Cooper,** as well as **Dan Lian** and **Lee McDerment**, who is also creative arts pastor.

The leadership structure is rounded out by campus pastors. "This will result in team leadership, team teaching and team ministry where everyone has a part to connecting people with Jesus and each other," **King** said.

In a series of posts in social media a day after "NewSpring's" meeting, **Noble** revealed that many people had reached out to him with support. "Oftentimes when we are under the weight of accusation and condemnation we forget about God's AMAZING grace, love and mercy!"

"Just because others are done with you - it does not mean God is done with you! Jesus pursued Peter when he denied, Thomas when he doubted and Paul when he flat out got it wrong!" (??) **Noble** wrote on Saturday. "And if He pursued them He will pursue us! So if you have screwed up - don't look down, look up - God is a God of second chances!"

Noble added: "Wanted to give a HUGE 'thank you' to everyone who has reached out to me over the past 24 hours with encouragement and questions about how I am doing. Honestly - I am doing great! Incredibly encouraged about the future and know greater things are on the horizon!" **Noble** recently marked one year since he entered rehab. He revealed last week that he has been sober for 319 days and noted that he does not blame anyone for his public firing.

https://www.christianpost.com/news/
perry-noble-still-biblically-unfit-to-preach-newspring-leaders-say.html

Too Soon for **Perry Noble's** "Second Chance" at Church?
"NewSpring" says its founder, who was fired last year, still isn't qualified to pastor.
AUGUST 09, 2017–

Pastor **Perry Noble's** former megachurch isn't ready to give him a second chance. So he's giving himself one. A year after firing **Noble** over his alcoholism, South Carolina multisite "NewSpring Church" continues to deem its founding pastor unfit to be restored to the pulpit. But that hasn't stopped the 46-year-old preacher from guest speaking at more than 10 other congregations—and recently filing paperwork to start his own.

Noble, who has been working as a church growth consultant and says he has been sober for nearly a year, registered "Second Chance Church" in South Carolina last month, watchdog blogger Warren Throckmorton reported. "I am able to confirm that the paperwork has indeed been filed for a new church in South Carolina—that is a matter of public record," **Noble's** assistant told CT ("Christianity Today."). "However, no timeline has been set for the church. **Perry** is dedicated to his clients at "The Growth Company," and serving them well."

Meanwhile, leaders at "NewSpring"—which spans across 15 locations in South Carolina—recently reiterated their concerns. They addressed his appearances at other churches, such as **Steven Furtick's** "Elevation Church" in neighboring North Carolina, at an event in late July. They declined to directly comment on **Noble's** new church venture.

"We have been asked why **Perry** can preach at other churches but not at "NewSpring," said teaching pastor **Clayton King**. "We cannot speak for other churches and how they make decisions. For us, **Perry** currently does not meet the Biblical qualifications of a pastor, teacher, shepherd." **King** listed 1 Timothy 3:1-5, Titus 1:5-9, and James 3:1 among their guidelines for the pastorate. He assured the congregation that the pastoral staff at "NewSpring" forgives **Noble**, though they won't be inviting him back.

Noble responded to the discussion in a Facebook live video, taking issue with what he saw as a misrepresentation of his 16-year ministry there. "There may be quite a few things I did wrong as senior pastor of "NewSpring Church;" however, I preached Jesus every Sunday that I had the privilege to serve at "NewSpring Church," he said. "They can continually talk about my sins."
"They can talk about how I'm seemingly unrepentant—although I would say in order to determine if someone is repentant, you have to have a relationship with them because it's hard to call out repentance from the cheap seats—but while I will allow those things to go on, I will not allow anyone to talk about my motives for ministry."

In recent years, plenty of popular pastors have had very public departures from their pulpits over moral issues—such as substance abuse, adultery, financial mismanagement, and toxic leadership. These fallen pastors have left their churches to decide when, if ever, they can be restored to leadership; whether to forgive and move on, or to disqualify them from public ministry. One pastor addressed this dilemma in a CT article, concluding:

"The fallen minister who confesses sin, seeks God's grace, and desires to remain in fellowship with the church of Christ, must be welcomed and received as any fallen Christian. He must be forgiven as Jesus commands (Matt. 18:22). But forgiveness and restoration to the fellowship of the church does not mean the former minister now meets the qualifications for holding the office of pastor/elder." "The church is not to punish the repenting man who has fallen." "But refusing to return him to the role of pastoral ministry is not punishment."

"To remove a fallen minister is to honor Christ's holy standards; it is to follow the wise counsel and pattern of leaders over the centuries; it is to protect the man himself and his family; and it is to guard the church body, loved so dearly by the Chief Shepherd." From the outset, **Noble** has not denied his missteps. He said "NewSpring" "made the right decision" to fire him.

"This was a spiritual and moral mistake on my part as I began to depend on alcohol for my refuge instead of Jesus and others," he wrote before spending a month in a rehab facility in Arizona last summer. Nearly 1 in 5 pastors has struggled with drug or alcohol addiction, according to a 2015 survey by Barna Group and Pepperdine University.
Those pastors were relatively split on whether being open about their own addiction would have a negative (46%) or positive (41%) impact on their ministry. **Noble** revealed just how low things got for him in a July 9 Facebook video entitled "The Day I Decided Not to Kill Myself:"

"After being fired and separating from his wife, he had planned his suicide while in rehab. He says a message from God convinced him not to take his own life. "It was the clearest I've ever heard his voice," **Noble** said. "He told me, 'I'm not finished with you yet.'" The South Carolina pastor and Waffle House regular has been active on social media for the past several months. He tracks his own progress in recovery, his 30-pound weight loss, and his work coaching and speaking at other churches.

Within six months of leaving "NewSpring," **Noble** faced criticism for returning to ministry too soon, saying, "If God has put something in your heart, don't sit around and wait for the approval of people who don't believe in you in the first place."
 Much of his recent messaging emphasizes his own imperfection and God's grace.   He thanked one church for "allowing this unqualified guy to preach there," as well as messages about how "in Christ my past does not have to define my future" and "we have not 'out-sinned' the price Jesus paid." **Noble** has not mentioned "Second Chance Church" on social media. He is keeping busy with his venture, "The Growth Company," and posted that he is booked with the exception of a handful of fall dates. His Twitter banner proclaims, "The best is yet to come."

"NewSpring" announced that rather than hire a senior pastor to replace **Noble**, the church will list Jesus Christ as its senior pastor and share leadership among multiple pastoral teams and campus pastors.   On Facebook, **Noble** confirmed that he has declined regular invites to meet with **King** over the past year, but it has been several months since he has heard from other staff members at "NewSpring." "CT" Pastors interviewed **King** last year, after he was appointed to an interim role following **Noble's** departure.

https://www.christianitytoday.com/news/2017/
august/fired-megachurch-pastor-perry-noble-second-chance-newspring.html

O:

- **Bianca Olthoff**: Not recommended. **Bianca** works as "Chief Storyteller" for the "A21 Campaign," false teacher **Christine Caine's** human trafficking organization.
A perusal of her calendar page shows her speaking at "Pray, Love, Lead" at "Saddleback" (**Rick Warren's** "church"), "IF Gathering," "Thrive" (**Lysa TerKeurst & Ann Voskamp**), "Bethel- Redding," " Elevation " (**Steven Furtick**), and numerous other conferences with false teachers and female "pastors," at least one of which is being held at a "church" pastored by a woman.   **Bianca** believes she receives extra-biblical revelation from God about people at her conferences needing healing. She also has several Sunday speaking engagements at churches, some of which, undoubtedly, will have her preaching to men.

(This video indicates she is preaching the Sunday sermon, which means she's preaching to men, and here she admits to teaching God's word to men. Ed.).

 https://michellelesley.com/2017/05/01/
the-mailbag-do-you-recommend-these-teachersauthors-volume-3/

- **T.L. Osborn**: Deceased. WOF preacher. www.mediaspotlight.org/pdfs/ Stigmata-IsLucyRael-ForReal.pdf. https://discernmentministriesinternational.wordpress.com/ category/t-l-osborn/

https://en.wikipedia.org/wiki/T._L._Osborn (**NOTE: Even though I have included a "wiki" page, the information contains his biography; it also lists several well known names, including he and his wife teaming up with **Marilyn Hickey**. Ed.).

- **Joel Osteen**: He does not consider himself to be a Christian, but rather a motivational speaker; however he is another WOF teacher; his wife Victoria's beliefs are heretical, as evidenced by videos of her speaking; he says "Even though you do not believe in Jesus, you can make it to Heaven."
Self Help Teacher, No Salvation Message, now into prosperity teachings.

(**NOTE: Plenty of articles about **Joel** are easy to find, as are his You Tube videos. Combined, they will all help you decide for yourself. Ed.).

- **George Otis Jr**: "Transformational" videos; https://www.bibleguidance.co.za/ Engarticles/Otisteachings.htm

http://www.deceptioninthechurch.com/ otis.html

(**NOTE: Both of these websites state the same thing. In order to verify an article showing the same thing written, I am including both. The proof lies in the duplication. Ed.).

(Of the 'Transformations' video fame) :

"The essence of Christ's Atonement existed in His obedience to the moral law on behalf of sinners. Christ obeyed during his life the moral law for us and that's really the essence of the Atonement." "Christ has not redeemed us by giving His life as a ransom for our sins in order that He might release us. God never kept man captive in sin. The truth is Christ paid no man's debt."

What **George Otis Jr** is teaching is called "christus victor" theology (i think it was first championed by liberal Scottish theologian George Macdonald. There's another guy, but I forgot his name). "Christus victor" theology says that the bloody sacrifice of God sacrificing His Son to atone for the sin of the world makes God into a monster.
 They believe that Christ made 'atonement' on the grounds that He defeated the devil (making the devil the instrument of atonement) and that He did not sin. They don't believe in substitutionary or penal atonement (do a wiki if you want to learn more about these terms).

Therefore, 'christus victor' was conceived from a totally wrong assumption to begin with, because there's nothing monstrous about God crucifying His Son, because the Son came to earth for the very purpose of bearing our sin on the cross, tasting death on our behalf, drinking the dreadful cup we should have drunk.

Bearing the penalty for my sins in His own body (penal substitution). He was wounded for OUR transgressions, bruised for OUR iniquity, He was chastised that WE could have peace, and by His stripes WE are healed. The Father laid on Him the sin of us all. (Isaiah 53) and was **satisfied** (vs. 11). He was fully in agreement and submitted to the cross, laying down His life, not murdered in the normal sense. How then can it be a monstrous thing, when the Son willingly agreed to take our penalty for us? It's amazing love that He would do that.

George Otis Jr has reached the top of charismania and he's spitting on Jesus.

https://ianvincent.wordpress.com/2008/09/20/ to-get-to-the-top-you-have-to-spit-on-jesus/

https://procinwarn.com/ george-otis-jr-mystical-warfare-kitsap-county/

"I want to begin this article by saying that we all need to pray more and praying has a lot to do with changing our heart just as much as it does others. God wants us in the correct attitude with Him to do His will. And we should be looking for opportunities to pray all the time.
 So, when a movement comes along that wants to incorporate more prayer in our lives; I'm sure you would agree in saying, "Great lets do it."
There is a video that is going through churches throughout the world that is making some very bold claims about the results in various countries, specifically four areas. It is called "Transformations."

The video is presented in these terms: "Imagine a community where 92 percent of the population is born-again; where city jails have been closed for lack of crime; where agricultural productivity has reached biblical proportions." "Imagine a town where local bars have been transformed into churches; where ancestral shrines have been destroyed; where entire family clans have come to faith in Christ. Don't imagine...BELIEVE!"

This video is endorsed by "Charisma Magazine," "CBA Marketplace," by the "National Prayer Committee."   Numerous ministries involved in prayer and evangelism are also distributing it on their web sites such as YWAM and "Americas National prayer committee"   under the section "Prayer Revival Videos," also "Campus Crusade," "Promise Keepers," and "Aglow "
(http://www1.gospelcom.net/npc/videos.html).

Endorsements have also come from **Jack W. Hayford**, Pastor of "The Church on the Way" and **Kenneth Hagin** ministries. They advertise it as:

 "We recommend the video to show churches and communities that God does indeed move when they pray. At a recent viewing during a "City Transformation Conference" in Woodbridge, Virginia, this June, when the credits started, the entire 500-plus audience leaped to their feet in praise--not for the video, but in genuine praise for what God has done. This applause lasted for more than five minutes."

"Transformations" video, has been viewed by some 35 million people so far.
(http://www.jesus.org.uk/ dawn/2000/dawn0039.html).

"Transformations" video has been aired on TV by CBS on August 26, 2000.

Its publicity by the various media associations has helped make it mainstream. I wonder how many people have checked out the claims to substantiate what is being told as fact in the video? It "is now available in 150 nations, and we know of almost 1,000 places in which Christians join in united prayer to experience what the video depicts"

(Source: **George Otis, Jr.**, "The Sentinel Group, USA"). Distribution of the video "has absolutely exploded," Petrie said. More than 80,000 copies,... and 40 international ministries use it. It is being translated into 25 languages, including Arabic, Mandarin, Chinese, and Hebrew. (http://www.joelnews.org/news-en/ jn323.htm).

The video is produced by "Global Net productions" copyrighted by the "Sentinel Group."

When one visits the site they find books and videos that are about the methodology of "Breaking Strongholds in your City" by **C. Peter Wagner**. However, the connection to **Wagner** and others shows what the true intent of the video is and the meaning of the key words said throughout it.

Wagner's philosophy of ministry is not Biblical but pragmatic as he states, "... we ought to see clearly that the end DOES justify the means. What else possible could justify the means? "If the method I am using accomplishes the goal I am aiming at, it is for that reason a good method." " If, on the other hand, my method is not accomplishing the goal, how can I be justified in continuing to use it?"

(**C. Peter Wagner**, "Your Church Can Grow - Seven Vital Signs Of A Healthy Church", 1976, p. 137 - emphasis in original). So if it works, no matter what it is, then it's fine by **Wagner**. It appears that many of the facts in the video are manipulated to make it look like it worked. They want it to work so they find whatever they can to promote it to suit their cause, in this case, prayer. There seems to be no proper investigation or substantial proof offered, which is normal for the Third Wave adherents, who often use unfounded unproven testimonies.

George Otis Jr. is president of "The Sentinel Group," a Christian research agency that produced the video, and co-coordinator of the "AD2000 United PrayerTrack.' **Wagner** has been the International coordinator of "United Prayer Track" and the "Spiritual Warfare Network" of the "AD2000 and Beyond" movement and founder of "Global Harvest" ministries. **George Otis Jr.** is on the board of the church in Cali, Colombia that is pastored by **Ruth Ruibal**, the wife of Julio (who was unfortunately gunned down) who is featured in the video. **Otis** has spoken in spiritual warfare seminars with many of the known names that traffic in spiritual warfare, the "Third Wave" and new revivals.

Several of his books are required reading in **C. Peter Wagner's** course on "Discerning Spiritual Strongholds." Among them are "Spiritual Mapping Field Research Manual," "The Last of the Giants" and "The Twilight Labyrinth."

In the "Transformation" video it does not speak of sin or repentance, nor is the Gospel clearly explained. When it is mentioned it is often connected to <u>signs and wonders</u>. There seems to be a reason for this. **George Otis Jr.'s** theology (if I may call it this) does not seem to allow for such views, at least in an orthodox way. He holds some different views that are contrary to Biblical evangelism, at least the way it was done by Spurgeon and the respected old timers. For more on the background of people involved check this web site:
[http://geocities.com/Heartland/Plains/ 4948/people.html]

Here are a few quotes from **Otis' Jr.'s** book "The God They Never Knew" (Chapter - sin is a sickness false concept 1):

"The thing that we ought to find most frightening of all, however, is the fact that more and more Christians are jumping on this bandwagon. One prominent Christian author refers to the 'sin infection,' contending that when Adam sinned 'that one sin infected the whole human race, still in his loins, with the sickness of sin and death." " Since then, all men are born sinners with the sentence of death upon them. It's a fatal disease with only one known cure."
"Where in Scripture is sin spoken of as a sickness or disease?" (p. 57 He is quoting Dr. Menninger favorably).
 He goes on in the next chapter to attribute to Augustine this grave mistake of formulating the doctrine of original sin.
http://www.letusreason.org/Latrain66.htm

(**NOTE: The above article is quite lengthy. If you wish to read the rest of this, please go to the website listed above. Ed.).

P:

- **Doug Pagitt:** <u>Emergent</u> church; yet another proponent of the <u>NAR</u>: "For the past few years "Apprising Ministries" has been a leading online apologetics and discernment work covering the now upgraded sinfully ecumenical neo-liberal cult of the <u>Emergent Church</u> aka the <u>Emerging Church</u>. The EC 2.0 has now cobbled together its own postmodern form of "Progressive Christian" theology."

"What we're actually dealing with here is a Liberalism 2.0, which these <u>apostates</u> will often refer to as "big tent" <u>Emergence Christianity</u>. Tragically, this theological poison is, right now, seeping into the veins of the mainstream evangelical camp—particularly within its younger sectors."

"In Biblical terms, it's leaven introduced into the lump of visible Christendom" (cf. Galatians 5:9) circa 2000 e.g. through <u>Living Spiritual Teacher</u> and EC guru **Brian McLaren**, <u>Universalist Emerging Church pastor</u> **Doug Pagitt**, and his friend **Dr. Tony Jones**, the <u>progressive</u> "theologian in residence" at Solomon's Porch."

"Such a loathsome legacy they're leaving. I've had the chance to talk with **Doug Pagitt** quite a few times through the years via phone and email. From what I can tell he seems like a nice guy who's sincere in his approach to what he wishes was Christianity; one that he's cobbled together down at the "Build-A-God Shop."

What **Pagitt** calls, "A Christianity Worth Believing" (ACWB);is the title of one of his books. However, what **Pagitt** et al are really doing is standing in the role of false prophets and God says: Do not listen to the words of the prophets who prophesy to you, filling you with vain hopes. They speak visions of their own minds, not from the mouth of the LORD. (Jeremiah 23:16).
http://apprising.org/2012/07/13/ doug-pagitt-emerging-false-prophets-original-sin/

(**NOTE: This article also includes screen shots of **Pagitt's** Facebook page that I cannot post here, however you can go to the above link and read the rest of the article and see the post **Pagitt** wrote. Ed.).

"One of those leaders is a pastor named **Doug Pagitt**. He is the pastor of "Solomon's Porch," a church that meets in Minneapolis, Minnesota. Over the years I have dialogued a little with **Doug** and it is simply clear that he and I do not see eye to eye on the core doctrines of the faith."
 "He has written several books that attempt to lay out his beliefs, however, after reading them, you might only grow more confused about what he actually does believe."
"Occasionally, I will check his blog just to see if anything new has developed and sometimes, I have taken the liberty to contribute to his discussions."

"A couple of weeks ago, **Doug** had a guest on his radio show that has been an open critic of **Doug's** theology. When you click on the link below, you can listen to the interview and follow the conversation through the posts that were published."
 "There is more I could say, but let me summarize by saying this: It is obvious from the Scripture that there is truth and error."
"We even see this from the mouth of the Lord Jesus Himself, when He rebuked those who were teaching false doctrine.   Of course, Paul also hammered on those who taught false doctrine as well." " Anyone who has ever read the Bible knows that false teachers were not lovingly spoken to. In fact, Jesus' harshest words were for those who taught and practiced wrong theology."
"As you will see in this discussion, the thrust of the debate is that **Doug** and others do not understand why people are so critical of him and his teaching. Some, as I do, call him a heretic because he is leading people away from the absolute truth of the Gospel."

"**Doug** openly denies original sin; the substitutionary, atoning work of Jesus on the Cross; he is an open theist that does not believe in a literal heaven or hell; and from what I can tell is a Universalist (although he will not clearly speak to that issue when asked)."
"From what I have read and heard from **Doug**, he is a false teacher that needs to be confronted. I do not think you should confront hatefully, but you should also not confront lightly either."
" He is teaching a false Gospel and that is something that should not be tolerated, no matter how unloving it may appear. As you will see, there are many posts in this discussion, many of which I myself do not agree with." "In fact, I do not even know any of the people in this

discussion." " All I would like you to do would be to listen to portions of the radio interview and then read the comments. Keep in mind, the Scripture never advocates tolerance for false doctrine and false teaching."

"The most unloving thing Christians can do is allow false doctrine to be spread. Here is the link to the discussion. Let me know what you think."
https://www.baptistmessenger.com/ is-it-unloving-to-call-someone-a-heretic/

(**NOTE: Found this article on the internet; seems to be on target with his writing of **Doug Pagitt**. Ed.).

https://christianresearchnetwork.org/ ?s=doug+pagitt&submit=Search

- **Luis Palau**: June 23, 2010– They Ought to Call It "Deathfest"
by Pastor Ralph Ovadal, Pilgrims Covenant Church, Monroe, Wisconsin

https://www.pccmonroe.org/ they-ought-to-call-it-deathfest.html

https://parousia.org/archives/8722

Luis Palau's Son (President of the Luis Palau Association) Teams Up With **Richard Foster's** Renovare November 25, 2017 by Lighthouse Trails Editors:
" **Richard Foster's** founding contemplative organization, "Renovare," has announced their upcoming (June 2018) celebration of the 40th anniversary of **Foster's** book "Celebration of Discipline." Kevin Palau, son of the world-wide known evangelist **Luis Palau** and president of the **Luis Palau** Association, is listed on the "Renovare" website as one of the speakers for the June 2018 ...
Posted in:
Conference Alerts, Contemplative Organizations, Contemplative Spirituality, Ecumenism, Interspirituality, New Evangelicalism, Road to Rome, The Emerging Church Tagged: **Billy Graham**, catholic church, contemplative prayer, Ecumenism, **Jim Wallis, Kevin Palau**, **Luis Palau**, panentheism, **Pope Francis,** Renovare, **Richard Foster**, Roman Catholicism.
https://www.lighthousetrailsresearch.com/blog/ ?tag=luis-palau

- **Rod Parsley**: WOF; NAR; False Prophesies; teaches prosperity message; is a word-faith preacher who specializes in whipping up his audiences into altered states of consciousness. His outlandish style is attractive to people who get emotionally carried away by repetitive music and mantras; https://truthprophecy.com.

https://www.jesus-is-savior.com/Wolves/rod_parsley.htm
(**NOTE: Multiple articles on this website regarding this false preacher. Ed.).

http://www.forgottenword.org/ parsley.html

http://www.bereanbiblechurch.org/ transcripts/matthew/som/7_15-20b.htm

https://churchwatchcentral.com/2016/09/04/
rod-parsley-preaches-nar-gospel-prophesies-narmageddon/

(**NOTE: There is enough on the internet that is also exposing this charlatan that you can see how twisted his "doctrine" is. Ed.).

- **Paige Patterson**: Another of the NAR "bible" titled "The Message"; scandalous report of spouse abuse. https://www.theatlantic.com/politics/archive/2018/05/ sbc-patterson/559532/

 https://religionnews.com/2019/11/21/
paige-pattersons-career-ended-after-she-came-forward-her-struggle-continues/

https://www.npr.org/2018/05/23/613636487/
southern-baptist-leader-removed-from-post-over-comments-on-domestic-abuse

- **Earl Paulk**: Deceased; Archbishop **Earl Paulk**, former pastor of "Chapel Hill Harvester Church" in Decatur, Georgia and presiding Bishop in the International Communion of Charismatic Churches* was a false preacher, teacher, self professed prophet and apostle and heretic. These are harsh words for someone who is supposed to be a representative of God and if I would be mistaken in my claims against him, surely God would not allow me to go unpunished. But as you will see, I am not the only one who makes these claims, and **Earl Paulk** proved himself to be all that I have said by what he has said and written.

I will present some of his false teachings here, some of which are indeed heretical.
I do this only as a last resort since I have contacted his Church four times without satisfaction, and because I was once a member of his congregation and may still have friends who attend there (although **Earl Paulk** passed away, March 29, 2009, his nephew/son, **Donnie Earl Paulk** continues to preach some of the false doctrines that were taught to him by his uncle/father, and has also adopted some new heresies).

The following links will take you through the different, false belief systems that **Earl Paulk** promoted.
 He is mentioned in many of them, although others who promote them are mentioned also. As you read about these different, complex belief systems, you should notice how they all seem to intertwine and relate to one another in some way.
 Even if you are not associated with **Earl Paulk**, your Church might be involved in some of the same beliefs and practices that he promotes. Bear in mind that there is some truth in these belief systems, but craftily, subtly, deception has crept in to confuse, and distort the truth according to God's Word.
Please go through the following links in succession if you can. The primary difficulties that exist with **Earl Paulk** and his Presbytery derive from this first and greatest heresy, "Kingdom Now Theology."

There are many components of "Kingdom Now " and some will be discussed in detail later on. Please understand that "Kingdom Now, Dominion, and Restoration Theology " are very similar, each borrowing components from the other.   Promoters of these movements don't necessarily agree with one another on every issue, but to a large extent, they do.

* **Earl Paulk** was forced to resign in October, 2006 as Archbishop of the "International Communion of Charismatic Churches" (ICCC) after a member of his local church—the 6,000-member "Cathedral at Chapel Hill " in Decatur, Georgia—
filed a lawsuit on August 31 charging him with using his position and spiritual role to manipulate women to have sex with himself, members of his family, and others, including visiting pastors, for many years. The ICCC partners with the Roman Catholic Church.

Update October 6, 2011--

My first concern about the legitimacy of this ministry began as **Earl Paulk** and the rest of his ministers repeatedly used the phrase, "...in covenant with God." After hearing that phrase over and over, I decided to do some study of my own about what it meant to be in covenant with God since I was hearing so much about it.

 My study took nearly a year, and what I found was that **Earl Paulk** and the leadership at CHHC were teaching a different covenant from that which Christ gave us according to the New Testament.

 What we were being taught resembled Old covenant principles mixed with something entirely new. I didn't realize it at the time, but it was all a part of "Kingdom Now Theology." To better understand what **Earl Paulk** meant about what it means to be in covenant with God, I have provided two versions of CHHC's New Member's Handbook.

The 1996 version is without notes and is slightly different than the 1998 version. The 1998 version shows my notes and what is highlighted are points with which I took issue.

"Earl Paulk is in a better place?" - By Bruce W. Robida

"The Gospel According to Paulk - A Critique of "Kingdom Theology" By Robert M. Bowman, Jr., with Craig S. Hawkins and Dan R. Schlesinger.

Review of the book: "That the World May Know," by **Earl Paulk**, (K. Dimension Publishers, 1987.) Reviewed - By Craig S. Hawkins.

"Sexual Misconduct Plagues Earl Paulk" - Articles and other resources related to the sexual misdeeds of **Earl Paulk**.

 "Kingdom Now" Theology--What is kingdom now teaching? " (in a nutshell) - by Got Questions? Ministries Word of Faith preacher; Word of Faith and the Charismatic Movement

Earl Paulk's Legacy - **Donnie Earl Paulk**; Videos featuring the teachings of **Earl Paulk**; Articles about **Earl Paulk**. "Article - 7 Characteristics of false Teachers' - By Thomas Brooks (1608-1680)
Paulk, Earl. "Satan Unmasked" (K Dimension, 1984), p. 97 and "Held In The Heavens Until" (K Dimension, 1985), p. 171.

Of all the ministers who've preached the view that they have a mandate to reign as gods in worlds of their own creation, perhaps it is **Paulk** and his brother **Don** who have most abominably taken this to heart in their public ministries and private lives.
 Their well-crafted public image of being two upright men of God on the cutting edge of progressive Pentecostal ministry has long ago been blown to bits by their inability to conceal their actual moral and spiritual degeneracy.

 Besides their autocratic relationship they established with others in their church staff in which they directed programs, liturgy and expenditure almost at whim, they also both sexually preyed upon women in their Atlanta area church as well.

 They sanctioned this by using a seduction approach in which they cited the need to manifest "God's love" through "Kingdom relationships" with them in twisted relationships as deviant as those of the cultic communal sexuality of the Children of God.
http://www.spiritwatch.org/firefaith4.htm

- **Donnie Earl Paulk** - Currently in transition to another ministry, "Church in the Now."
"Church in the Now " is under the leadership of bishop, **Jim Earl Swilley**, another
" Kingdom Now" preacher. It is possible that some of the preachers who are currently under the leadership of **DE Paulk**, will move with him.
 http://www.iamforsure.com/

Donnie Earl (D.E.) Paulk: Has finally teetered over the edge and has been given completely over to his reprobate mind...thanks to his Unc-Daddy **Earl** "The Abomination" **Paulk's** curse over the **Paulk** family. Of course, the Word of God has already foretold of this kind of demise: (Exodus 34:6-7).
In case you've been under a rock for the past few years, take a moment to be brought up to speed on the **Paulk** Family Disaster (courtesy of "Independent Conservative").

I have also documented **Donnie Earl's** slide into heresy since last spring – from his initial embrace of new-age teachings, to his embrace of **Carlton** "The Heretic" **Pearson** and the wicked "inclusion theology", culminating with the impending sale of **Earl's** (and **Donnie Earl's**) house of shame.
 Donnie Earl recently granted an interview to a gay newspaper here in Atlanta detailing his complete embrace of gay inclusion theology – and thus, his official departure from sound doctrine and his surrender to his reprobate mind.

(I am linking to the original article so that **D.E.'s** words are read in context. The website is pro-gay and overtly sexual, but it is important to leave it unedited so that you can truly see how **D.E.** has completely embraced a wicked and unrepentant culture; Author of article.):

" After scandal, pastor finds solace in preaching gay inclusion:"

As a series of scandals stripped away everything **Rev. D.E. Paulk** had — his church, his financial resources, even his father — he found the courage to speak his truth.

"I don't know how to say this, the scandal didn't make me inclusive, it took away my fear," **Paulk** says. "Before that I was saying that I'll preach about gay inclusion and just sort of mention it here or there."

"When you lose everything, you have nothing to lose. I looked at my wife one day and said all I have left is me, and what God is speaking to me." Clearly **Donnie Earl** is referring to either the god of this world (or Satan, specifically) because the God of Heaven would never evangelize to anyone about unrepentant inclusion and the acceptance of a gay lifestyle in concert with His Holiness.

But wait, there's more: Soon after **D.E. Paulk** took over as senior pastor, he faced what he now collectively calls "the scandal." A number of women came forward alleging **Earl Paulk** used his influence as bishop to coerce them into sexual relationships.

As part of the legal proceedings, **Earl Paulk** was forced to undergo a paternity test to see if he had fathered several children in the church.

The paternity test revealed that **Earl Paulk**, the man **D.E. Paulk** grew up believing was his uncle, was actually his biological father.

Yet it was as these scandals rocked the church that **D.E. Paulk** found the strength to say what was in his heart....thus the wicked "seed" that perpetuates the heresy and Godless allegiance that **Donnie Earl** finds himself in today. Unlike many of the lemmings who stay in abusive relationships with their pulpit pimps, **Donnie Earl's** congregation fled when Donnie's horns began to show:

"They stayed through the adultery allegations, the racketeering charges, there's been all sorts of things they've accused us of, some true, some not true, but the majority of the people stayed," he adds. "It wasn't really until I started teaching gay inclusion and other religious thought [that] people began to leave." Under fire from his congregation because of his teaching and marred by his family's legacy, **Paulk** considered leaving and starting over somewhere else.

So I guess that even though Unc-daddy **Earl's** money (and sex) pimping wasn't enough to close the Cathedral of Ill repute, but gay inclusion (non)theology was enough to pry the remnant from their pews.

So **Donnie Earl** took his new book to a gay bookstore for a signing party, and he seems right at home:

Paulk began to focus on his core principles and beliefs as he moved toward what he calls "radical inclusion" and away from Christianity. **Paulk** founded the organization 'Pro-Love " in 2004, which has sponsored inclusion marches every year since. He also began work on his new book, "I Don't Know … The Way of Knowing."

The book outlines his beliefs, a multi-national mixture of Hindu, Buddhist, Daoism and other religious thought combined with quotes from an array of historical and cultural figures. Throughout the book, **Paulk** admits he doesn't have the answers, and advocates the creation of groups of people all looking for the answers together.

"This is kind of playing my cards here; in several years we probably won't be called a church anymore, we'll just be called a community," **Paulk** says of his congregation, which now has about 1,000 members and is called Cathedral at Chapel Hill. "I think we'll just be a community of seekers."

Paulk is against the idea of defining God as a certain concept. <u>He refers to God as "The Christ" who takes many forms, including Jesus.</u> He told O'Bryan that he agreed with him and <u>says he doesn't believe in God and the devil, just God</u>.
So **Donnie Earl** thinks that his "club" will soon be referred to as a community?
Um...it already is...IT'S CALLED THE HOMOSEXUAL COMMUNITY.

Like every other <u>new-ager</u>, **Donnie Earl** completely eschews the Bible that he used to teach from and the Word of God that he (allegedly) used to believe in order to conform – make that ENDORSE – a wicked non-theological theory that "all good people will go to Heaven", and that Jesus Christ is NOT the propitiation of our sin debt and our only access to God the Father. And let me take a moment to further clarify, before the hate mail (and comments) start pouring in: homosexuality is a sin before God.
Rather than retyping, allow me to post a portion of an article I wrote when **Eddie Long** slowly began softening up about homosexuality (I wonder where **Eddie's** next book signing will be, by the way...):

"So, **Eddie** Doesn't Understand Homosexuality?"

Let me be CRYSTAL CLEAR – God loves us even in our mess – and in turn, our love for Him and His truth means we must leave our mess behind. We are filthy rags, deserving eternal damnation apart from the redeeming Blood of Jesus Christ and the turning away from our flesh. This is an uncompromisable point. We can't honestly serve a sinless Savior while holding onto the things that He hates! I am not a "gay basher," a homophobe, a "hater" or any other pejorative that will probably be hurled my way.
I'm not perfect, nor will I try to reason the varying degrees of "sin".

I understand that many have been hurt through sexual molestation, and confused regarding same-sex attraction, etc.
Homosexuality is a sin – and like every other unrepentant sin, it's consequence is eternal separation from the Father. I stand on the Word of God, specifically: Genesis 19:1-13; Leviticus 18:22; Romans 1:24-27; 1 Corinthians 6:9, and much more...

Is there deliverance from homosexuality? ABSOLUTELY – 1 Corinthians 6:11 and 2 Corinthians 5:17 specifically speaks of deliverance over ANY SIN through salvation and faith in Jesus Christ. Further, EVERY CHRISTIAN will struggle against sin – including sins of the flesh (Galatians 5:19-21). What separates us from the world, however, is that we always repent and turn back to God. You can't be "gay" and call yourself a true Christian if you continue in homosexual sin – remember, I Corinthians 6:11 Paul said "you were (fill in the blank)"...meaning before sanctification through the Blood of Jesus.

(**NOTE: The Author of the article is stating this, not me the Editor.).

That said, **Donnie Earl Paulk** has officially abandoned reason and has been handed over to the god of this world. Pray for his wife and children – that they align themselves with God through Jesus Christ and not the <u>witches, warlocks</u>, and homosexuals that **Donnie Earl** bows to. Oh, and rejoice for those who fled this <u>heresy</u> – both long ago and recently.

Yet more proof that God gives wisdom, and those that adhere to His wisdom are spared.

(**NOTE: A response to this article from someone who once was in this church is below. Ed.):

Donnie Earl never was much of a Bible preacher. He might break dance from the pulpit, or he might line up a bunch of the elders and deacons of the church and do a male interpretive swim team dance (if you think I'm joking, check it out, it's on YouTube), but **Donnie Earl** was never much on personal holiness, much like his Funcle **Earl**.

 Donnie Earl is usually about 10 years behind the times and now he is "reaching out" to the gay community because the **Paulks** are truly desperate for money. That is the only reason for his sudden interest in the gay community.

He sees them as a demographic of people who just might not have heard of the **Paulks** before and know to stay away from them. He just wants their cash. The **Paulks** are in the midst of losing the Cathedral they built in S. Dekalb (Georgia) and need another gig. This new turn of events shouldn't surprise anyone.

Donnie Earl and the rest of the **Paulks** have no moral compass and therefore nothing is too low for them to do for some quick cash. https://imspeakingtruth.wordpress.com

Earl Paulk of the "Harvester Church" in Atlanta, Georgia, in his work, "Satan Unmasked," explains it like this: "Adam and Eve were placed in the world as the seed and expression of God. Just as dogs have puppies and cats have kittens, so God has <u>little gods</u>; we have trouble comprehending this truth. Until we comprehend that we are <u>little gods</u>, we cannot manifest the kingdom of God" (p. 97). Cats and dogs may reproduce, but God did not copulate in order to create man.

Such foolishness is astounding. https://ucministries.wordpress.com/ tag/dr-hobart-freeman/

(**NOTE: Even though this link says "Hobart Freeman," the link also includes the **Paulks**. Ed.).

- **Norman Vincent Peale**: Deceased: "Power of Positive Thinking;" believed in "<u>positive confession</u>' which means that our faith will not save; found peace in a Shinto shrine; www.thebereancall.com).   (Also was **Donnie Earl Paulk's** mentor).

 https://imspeakingtruth.wordpress.com

Has had connections with **Rob Bell**:   https://www.thegospelcoalition.org/article/ come-sunday-heretic-sad-stories-rebel-pastors

- **Carlton Pearson**: Says that "Hell will NOT last for eternity; another <u>NAR</u> false teacher; has even been attacked by false teachers like **T.D. Jakes** for his support of the "doctrine of exclusion." This doctrine tries to reconcile Christianity and Islam, claiming the two religions are completely compatible; https://truthprophecy.com)

Netflix's "Come Sunday," about Pentecostal bishop **Carlton Pearson** and documentary "The Heretic," about **Rob Bell**, tell similar tales of prominent pastors who lost their congregations after they started "rethinking" hell and promoting messages of universalism. These films pitch their protagonists—**Pearson** and **Bell**—as brave rebels who challenged a rigid, bigoted, staid religious establishment in radical and costly ways. But if that's the case, why are these films so tedious and flat?

Perhaps it's because the supposedly groundbreaking "rethinking" these men advocate is nothing new—just boring old heresy in modern new clothes. Perhaps it's also because the "radical" message of inclusion they present—a Christ-less, cross-less, repentance-free Gospel of everything-affirming solidarity—is in no way subversive in today's world.
Rather, it's the bourgeois Gospel of **Oprah** and Disney movies and "Eat, Pray, Love."
Ho hum.

Based on a true story "Come Sunday" shows how **Carlton Pearson** went from being the celebrated pastor of one of Tulsa's largest churches ("Higher Dimensions Evangelistic Center") to being branded a heretic in the early 2000s.
After watching coverage of the Rwandan genocide on TV, the Pentecostal **Pearson**—a mentor of **Oral Roberts** became troubled with the idea of eternal torment for the scores of Africans who were dying without knowing Christ. He had previously accepted that some people went to hell, even members of his own family, because they had a choice, he tells his congregation in the film.

 "But when did these people in Africa separate from God? When did they make a choice? How do they get saved?" **Pearson** says he heard God's voice, "clear as my own" say: "They don't need to get saved. They're already saved. . . . They will all be with me in heaven.'" This doesn't go over well in **Pearson's** church. People walk out mid-sermon in droves.
Mentor **Oral Roberts** is disturbed. "That's heresy son," **Roberts** tells **Pearson** in the film. "Are you certain it was God's voice that you heard, and not the Devil?"

 Formed by an evangelical culture more driven by personality and novelty than ecclesial accountability and historical continuity, **Pearson** ignores **Roberts** (among other advisers, including a pastor played by Jason Segel) and doubles down on his newfound universalism. "God spoke to me and told me that all those people out there starving and dying in Africa without being saved, they're all going to heaven,"

Pearson says in one scene, offering his interpretation of I John 2:1–2 as proof: "It means Jesus died for everybody. That's the literal meaning. . . . Everyone is already saved. That is the finished work of the cross."

These unorthodox words rightly cause most of the congregation and its leaders to leave the church, shrinking "Higher Dimensions" from 5,000 to less than 1,000 and resulting in the building's foreclosure in 2006. Eventually **Pearson** lands at Tulsa's "All Souls Unitarian

Church," where he now serves as an "affiliate minister."
https://www.thegospelcoalition.org/article/
come-sunday-heretic-sad-stories-rebel-pastors/

- **Justin Peters**: http://www.bpnews.net/26217/ health-and-wealth-gospel-critiqued

(**NOTE: A very lengthy article that is well worth reading, listed above. Ed.).

https://www.youtube.com/
watch?time_continue=5&v=MJDmjFPFFJc&feature=emb_logo

https://slowtowrite.com/ seven-questions-with-justin-peters-part-1/

(**NOTE: Although his articles are spot on with regard to the Word of Faith movement, there are still some things that he believes and preaches that are off kilter. You decide for yourself. Ed.).

– **Eugene Peterson**: Deceased; **Peterson** was famous for his book, "The Message," which he referred to as a Bible translation.   "The Message," however, was not an accurate translation of the Scriptures by any means, it was a complete re-write and in many cases, changing the entire meaning of the text.   **Peterson** was an advocate of the Emergent Church and was known for building bridges between Emergent practices, such as contemplative prayer and mysticism, with mainstream and biblical Christianity.
Eugene Peterson also came out in support of gay marriage, but then partially retracted his support after "LifeWay " (Baptist bookstore) threatened to remove his materials from inventory, stating, "That's not something I would do out of respect to the congregation, the larger church body, and the historic Biblical Christian view and teaching on marriage."
" That said, I would still love such a couple as their pastor."
"They'd be welcome at my table, along with everybody else."
A pastor is someone who is set up to guard the sheep, and the fact that **Peterson** believed that he could still be a homosexual couple's pastor reveals that he believes that those living in rebellion to God could still be Christians.

https://reformationcharlotte.org/2019/03/26/ false-teachers-evangelical-churches/

- **Theresa Phillips**: (**NOTE: A personal testimony about the dangers of **Ms. Phillips** follows. Ed.).

Karen says– April 19, 2019 at 8:25 pm

My sister and her husband were going to a house church called Glory House, with pastor **Theresa Phillips** which you mention above. This was back in 2008. My sister and her husband were raised in a Biblically sound Bible church, but somehow veered off course and went to a supernatural-type seminar and started going to this house church afterwards.
They were very into seeing manifestations of "god" such as "gold dust appearing everywhere, and feathers or "manna" appearing in their Bibles. It was all so creepy. She said that when

Theresa would walk down the aisle, the whole floor would shake...and she's not a large woman.

It was a supernatural-type of shaking. So creepy.

Long story short, not long after they began attending this church, they both got caught up in hearing voices from "god" and then they thought God told them to up and leave for Hawaii, because the rapture was going to be coming in the next few weeks.

They were so demonically deceived. They left for Hawaii without telling anyone, and we were all trying to figure out where they went. They were gone for two months. When they returned, they were still messed up. That was 2009. It's now 2019, and they've both been to jail, and divorced, and my sister is now so mentally ill, I don't think I'll ever get to talk to my real sister again.

I'm not saying that the pastor did all this, but there certainly are familiar spirits involved in all of this pastor's angelic manifestations and what not. We are still dealing with the repercussion of my sister and her husband being sucked into believing in all these "signs and wonders" that they taught. Satan tore their family apart, and in turn, tore our whole family apart. Thankfully, the Lord is faithful, and is restoring each of our lives...but my sister is still messed up and in jail. Satan and his demons give these false prophets their visions, manifestations, miracles, etc.

There is no sign of the real God whatsoever in any of their teaching. Stay far away, unless you want your life to be in ruins like my sister and her ex-husband.

https://www.honorofkings.org/ false-prophet-listing/

- **Cal Pierce**: IAHR and the connection to **Bill Johnson** and "Bethel"- Redding
https://www.charismamag.com/site-archives/

"A network of healing rooms is spreading internationally, with several hundred being commissioned in India this week." "Launched in 1999, the "International Association of Healing Rooms " (IAHR) now oversees some 1,300 rooms in 52 nations. Roughly 400 are in India, and IAHR founder **Cal Pierce** is commissioning 600 more healing rooms there this week."

"A former real estate developer, **Pierce** embraced healing ministry after experiencing renewal at "Bethel Church" in Redding, Calif. He said he was dramatically changed in a meeting **Bill Johnson** called after he became pastor of the former Assemblies of God congregation. "**Bill** raised his hands to heaven and said, 'Come, Holy Spirit."

"And that was the last thing I could remember as the fire of God began to course through my being," **Pierce** said. "I wanted to run, laugh, shout, but I couldn't do anything but stand there and take it. After that encounter, I realized that my life was over so His life could take over."
https://wolvesinthepulpit.blogspot.com/2018/04/

https://bcooper.wordpress.com/2017/07/16/ healing-rooms-and-the-nar/

- **Chuck Pierce**: Chosen by **C. Peter Wagner** to be his successor. Prophet **Chuck Pierce**, author, president of "Global Spheres, Inc.," and president of "Glory of Zion International

Ministries." Though also getting along in years, **Pierce** made my list because he is an influential prophet and was chosen by **C. Peter Wagner** to be his successor and take over **Wagner's** "Global Harvest Ministries' (which **Pierce** renamed "Global Spheres, Inc.").

http://www.spiritoferror.org/2013/07/
the-changing-of-the-apostolic-guard-13-names-to-watch/3718

(**NOTE: The" list" that the Author is speaking of is their own list, not mine. Ed.).

- **Don Piper**: Another author in the "I went to Heaven" series–(false teaching). **Don Piper** is a Baptist, not known for Charismatic experiences. He was in an auto accident that supposedly killed him instantly.

90 minutes later, a pastor came upon the accident and felt that God wanted him to pray for **Piper,** who immediately came-to when this pastor prayed. During that 90 minutes, **Piper** claims to have visited Heaven, or at least the outskirts of Heaven, and met deceased friends and relatives.
He claimed in his book that he did not see God during his experience. Seven years later, he claimed that he looked up to the top of the highest hill and saw the brightest light, which was the Lord Almighty, high and lifted up. https://www.echozoe.com/ archives/3092

–**John Piper**: "I've been reading various blogs about **John Piper's** endorsement of **Rick Warren's** false Gospel this week. The one thing that stands out to me is that so many people are willing to accept **Rick Warren** as a "misunderstood" preacher of the gospel just because of **John Piper**." "This is a disturbing trend within those who should know better! They are quick to compromise the truth because they are in love with **Piper** instead of being in love with the Word."

"Years ago, when **Piper** endorsed the "cussing" pastor **Mark Driscoll**, this act should have sent red flags out to all who love sound doctrine, but instead of standing up for the truth, those who follow **Piper** just made excuses." "Now we fast forward to today and **Piper** has endorsed a false teacher as a teacher of the Gospel!
Rick Warren is a false teacher and **John Piper** has become a Judas goat." "When will the excuse making stop? When will people who love sound doctrine stand up for the truth and call out **John Piper** instead of compromising?"

"I simply do not see how people can defend **John Piper's** poor judgement in endorsing **Rick Warren**." "I just wag my head when I read other Reformed people defending **Piper** and **Warren**." "It's one thing to try to reach out to a person in error, but it's not right to endorse them as "sound in doctrine" when it's very clear there are problems." "I guess the old excuse of "No Perfect People" pardons **Piper** for failing to see the dangers **Rick Warren** presents to the body of Christ." – David J.

(**NOTE: The Author of the above article, whose website is listed below. Ed.).

https://davidjosephhorn.wordpress.com/2010/10/06/

this-is-a-disturbing-statement-from-john-piper/

"You invited **Rick Warren**; would you say he exemplifies "thinking"? "No, I don't think he exactly exemplifies what I'm after. But he is Biblical. He quoted 50 Scriptures from memory. Unbelievable, his mind is Vesuvius. So I asked him what impact reading Jonathan Edwards had on him." "What these authors like **Karl Barth** and Edwards do for him is give him a surge of theological energy that then comes through his wiring."

"What I wanted to do with **Rick** is force him to talk about thinking so pragmatists out there can say, "A lot of thinking goes into what he does."

https://www.christianitytoday.com/ct/2010/octoberweb-only/
50-11.0.html?sms_ss=blogger&at_xt=4caa2ac547df4008,0

"Is the ability to quote Scripture from memory a litmus test for determining if a person is Biblical? Does the fact that **Rick Warren** puts a lot of thinking into what he says and does make his actions and words Biblical?" "You received some negative feedback for inviting him." "It was real risky. I don't even know if I did the right thing.
If somebody said, "Are you sure you should have invited him?" "No." "I think the first thing I'd say—maybe the only thing—is I think he's been slandered." "I think we probably need to work harder at getting him right."
https://www.christianitytoday.com/ct/2010/octoberweb-only/
50-11.0.html?sms_ss=blogger&at_xt=4caa2ac547df4008,0

"Slandered?" " Ok, let's hear **Rick Warren** in his own words to see if he has been slandered by people who say he preaches a false gospel." https://youtu.be/mVth6gtHBNk

(**NOTE: This is where you hear him—a You Tube video, listed above. Ed.).

My friend and AM correspondent, Daniel Neades of"Better Than Sacrifice," has written "Enough!" Scripture twisting is not 'doctrinal and sound' concerning the message of **Rick Warren** at DG 2010; and today we were discussing the comments which I highlighted above. I told him I'd been reading again what **Dr. Piper** has said about **Warren**, as well as the alleged "slander" of **Rick Warren**.

The comment by **Dr. Piper**, "I think we probably need to work harder at getting him right," is a little vague. Some I've talked to thought **Dr. Piper** meant "we," whoever that is, need to make **Warren** "right" because his pragmatic Church Growth Movement techniques are "wrong." However, this would then be in contradiction with **Dr. John Piper's** view that **Rick Warren** "is Biblical."

Like I shared with Neades, I think that when **Dr. Piper** said, "we probably need to work harder at getting him right," most likely he means: Work harder to get people to understand **Warren** correctly like **Dr. Piper** apparently feels he does. And as far as the broad-brush charge of some slander by unnamed sources goes, the following cogent response from Daniel Neades is dead-on-target: "The major problem here is that **Rick Warren** refuses to engage his critics or defend his ideas. Unless he is willing to argue for, say, his handling of Scripture, there can be no development of the critics' understanding of his position."

"This is not the fault of the critics, who have shown themselves to be very willing to engage; but rather of **Warren**, who refuses to enter into the conversation." "Thus, the plea to 'work harder at getting him right' is misdirected if it is aimed at **Warren's** critics. Rather, it must be aimed at **Rick Warren** himself."

"If he is misunderstood, let him answer his critics and show that he is actually exegeting Scripture in a faithful way consistent with the historic orthodox Christian faith." I also pointed out that **Dr. Piper** seems to be making a distinction between "pragmatists" and **Rick Warren** (the King pragmatist) by saying, apparently unlike them, **Warren** does a lot of thinking. **Dr. Piper** says: "What I wanted to do with **Rick** is force him to talk about thinking so pragmatists out there can say, "A lot of thinking goes into what he does."

"The above reads to me as if **Dr. Piper** is actually coming to the defense of **Rick Warren** as opposed to whoever these pragmatists supposedly are.
That's why I believe these comments following from Daniel Neades are also helpful here as well as he brings out "And thus **Dr. John Piper** seems to be taking upon himself responsibility for **Warren's** errors." "That's not a position I'd want to assume."
Nor would I. https://davidjosephhorn.wordpress.com/2010/08/12/

(**NOTE: Same online source as above; same Author, David Joseph Horn. Ed.).

(Jeff Maples – Reformation Charlotte) **John Piper** used to be a reputable pastor. In <u>Reformed</u> circles, he was one that you could turn to for solid Biblical advice and theological teaching....
But his slide into theological disarray began with his reinterpretation of the historic Westminster Catechism quote, "Man's chief end is to glorify God, and enjoy him forever." **Piper** wrote his own version of this into to what now says, "God is most glorified when we are most satisfied in him."

This new interpretation is not a doctrine found anywhere in Scripture, yet, this subtle change changes the entire dynamics of one's theology.
John Piper, who has regularly attended **Louie Giglio's** Passion Conference for a number of years, has done so based on his own invention of this unbiblical doctrine. Of **Louie Giglio**, he writes in his book, "An All-Consuming Passion for Jesus"...

https://reformationcharlotte.org/2019/07/24/
john-piper-returns-to-passion-conference-in-2020-joins-host-of-false-teachers/

(**NOTE: The article listed above continues in the web link. Ed.).

His gross imposition on the doctrine of justification proves that he is a contemnor of the Gospel. He has historically tried to redefine significant doctrinal terms, and has put stipulations on salvation to make works a contributing factor. All of **Piper's** articles that mention "future" or "final" salvation is disturbing.

Piper argues that "our final salvation is made contingent upon the subsequent obedience which comes from faith." This is not the teachings of Christ. On the contrary, it is similar to Catholicism. Men are not acquitted because of their subsequent obedience, but by the gratuitous acquittal from God, and the attestation of righteousness that Christ imputes to those that He reconciled to the Father.

In his articles, it does not take an erudite to see that **Piper** relies on sophistry to redefine the meaning of "faith." Faith is not the cause, ground, or basis of our justification. The only grounds for justification is Christ's perfect righteousness—His alien perceptive and penal obedience—which God the Father reckons unto the account of sinners.
The instrument by which the righteousness of Christ is applied to sinners is through faith alone which unites the elect of God to their vicarious substitute and Savior. **Piper's** aversion to the doctrine of justification should not be surprising.

He was a pupil of **Daniel Fuller**, who affirmed justification by faith "and works." Therefore, he is just following in his footsteps. **Piper's** stance on justification is not that far off from Federal Vision. What is the Federal Vision (FV)?
FV is a detraction from Christian orthodoxy because it denies the imputation of Jesus' active obedience, and it distorts the Biblical teaching of justification by grace alone—by maintaining that faith and obedience are necessary for their final or future salvation.

Also FV teaches: baptismal regeneration, paedocommunion, incipient sacramentalism, and a contradicting position on election and the covenants. An objective observer should wonder if this is why **Piper** has defended **Doug Wilson**, a prominent FV heretic, by arguing that **Wilson** does not teach a false Gospel. There is a reason why **Piper** will not call out this wolf. That is because he is one also. Christians need to be warned about **Piper's** heresy.

Hirelings will not warn anyone. They will voluminously quote excerpts from his articles; post memes about him; and will call men "divisive," "unloving," and "prideful" for calling out **Piper**. Why is it a necessity that Christians are warned about this wolf? The doctrine of justification is the Gospel and it is not a secondary issue that Christians can agree to disagree on.

May God have mercy on these hirelings who are either ignorant or evil about **Piper's** stance on justification. And may God lead true Christians away from the heresy that is espoused by **John Piper** which trifles with the divine beneficence of Christ's meritorious work.

(**NOTE: The above article is quite lengthy. I have provided only a short presentation. The balance is on the website listed below. Ed.).

https://www.reformingamericaministries.com/ single-post
/2018/06/30/False-Teacher-John-Piper

John Piper Invites **Rick Warren** to speak at 2010 Desiring God Conference:
http://www.desiringgod.org/Blog/ 2323_more_details_about_our_national_conference/
(You will have to click on the video once on the page: Author of the article. Ed.).

http://www.trinityfoundation.org/ horror_show.php?id=47

Dr. John Piper maintains a large following in Evangelical, Fundamentalist, and <u>Reformed</u> churches and schools. But we can say on solid Biblical authority that his teachings are <u>damnable heresies.</u>
He is a man to be marked and avoided (Romans 16:17-18).
We frequently receive questions about the well-known writer and pastor, **Dr. John Piper**. I am frankly surprised and disturbed by the number of Bible-believing Christians and reputedly conservative churches and educational institutions that embrace **Dr. Piper**.
It must be said, without hesitation and on solid Biblical grounds, that **Dr. Piper** is a <u>heretic</u>. He preaches a false Gospel of justification by faith-plus-works, and a philosophy of so-called Christian living that is rooted in ungodly secular philosophy and denies the Biblical doctrine of the sanctification of the believer by the indwelling Spirit of God.

 http://www.teachingtheword.org/apps/articles/ ?articleid=179316&view=post&blogid=5449

http://www.trinityfoundation.org/ journal.php?id=113

http://www.trinityfoundation.org/PDF/
The%20Trinity%20Review%2000331%20345PiperonFinalJustificationbyWorks.pdf

http://www.newcalvinist.com/john-piper-2/

http://youtu.be/ZPol7k6Lpmc

https://reformedbaptistblog.com/2009/06/26/
disappointed-in-john-pipers-judgment-about-doug-wilson/

- **David Platt**: Founder "Radical Church;" <u>Calvinist</u>, preaches false Gospel; Says the"sinner's prayer" is an "incantation"; accepting Jesus into your heart is "superstitious" and "unbiblical"; uses Satanic hand signs in "Verve" 2012 conference.

(**NOTE: Several videos on YouTube. Ed.).

David Platt is a <u>New Calvinist</u> — that is, he affirms the five points of <u>Calvinism</u> but is not <u>Reformed</u>.
 <u>Calvinism</u> is not to be confused or equated with <u>Reformed Theology</u>. While those who are <u>Reformed</u> are <u>Calvinists</u>, not all <u>Calvinists</u> are <u>Reformed</u>.
Today's modern <u>New Calvinists</u> either reject or ignore many of the theological positions of the <u>Reformed</u> confessions. Among these, two that stand out are the <u>Regulative Principle of Worship and the cessation of the Apostolic sign gifts</u>.

David Platt, however, is intent on building bridges between those who reject sound doctrine in favor of experiential Christianity.

This is an interesting phenomenon, because listening to **Platt** teach and exposit the Scriptures, for the most part, would lead one to believe otherwise. **Platt** regularly teaches against heresies, false religions, and false Christian movements.
Yet, for some reason, **Platt** wants to promote **Louie Giglio** — one of the premier promulgators of false spirituality in the modern Church.

https://reformationcharlotte.org/2019/05/15/ david-platt-promotes-false-teacher-louie-giglio/

- **John Mark Poole**: https://www.christianforums.com/threads/
new-false-prophets-katrina.2074290/

http://www.deceptioninthechurch.com/ Ananatomyofafalseprophecy.html

Aligned with **Steve Shultz**, Author of The Elijah List, a veritable "Who's Who" of false preachers, prophets and teachers. **Steve** counts him as a true prophet of God.
Also can be seen on an old **Sid Roth** TV show http://www.sidroth.org/
tvbroadcasts.htm

- **Peter Popoff**: A big star once in the Charismatic\Pentecostal circles, until "The Amazing Randi" exposed his false prophecies. (He wore\wears an earpiece and his wife tells him what a person needs–from the "guest cards" that are filled out when a person goes to his meetings).

 Peter Popoff is back like a bad penny. Back in the late 1980's his alleged gifts of the "word of knowledge" and "word of wisdom" (1 Cor. 12:8) were exposed as being fraudulent by a former stage magician. His earlier claims were debunked in 1987 when noted skeptic James Randi and his assistant, Steve Shaw, researched **Popoff** by attending shows across the country for months.

They discovered that radio transmission were being sent by **Peter's** wife, Elizabeth Popoff, where she was reading information which she and her aides (Volmer Thrane, the brother of his manger Nancy Thrane, and Reeford Sherrill) had gathered from earlier conversations with members of the audience. **Popoff** would simply listen to these prompting with his in-ear receiver and repeat what he heard to the crowd.
After tapes of these transmissions were played on "The Tonight Show Starring Johnny Carson," **Popoff's** popularity and viewing audiences declined sharply, and his ministry declared bankruptcy later that year. (10)

The expose' on **Popoff** did not keep him off the pimping platform for very long. He can still be seen on early morning cable stations and still travels around the world fleecing the needy with false promises of healing and prosperity….laughing all the way to the bank. One way he gets his money is by sending out monthly "point-of-contact" items that when sent back to his SINistry with a donation will produce a host of blessings in the faithful devotee's life.

There are serious doubts that **Mr. Popoff** is saved (the Lord only knows). This much is certain, DMI prays he repents of his wickedness and is turned to Christ.
https://discernmentministriesinternational.wordpress.com/ category/don-stewart/

(**NOTE: The web link says "**Don Stewart**," but **Peter Popoff** and others are also on the link as well. Ed.).

- **Paul Pressler** http://thewartburgwatch.com/2017/12/13/
paul-pressler-accused-of-molestation-in-lawsuit/

- **Charles Pretlow**: No list of false prophets would be complete without **Charles Pretlow** of "Message of the Cross Chapel Fellowship" in Canyon City, CO.
Charles Pretlow passes himself off as being one who has the inside track on God's will, but if you scratch him, you will find a religious charlatan underneath.

When pressed for explanations of his theology, he first tries to baffle you with a labyrinthine tour of tangentially related Scriptures in a process that I refer to as "Rubik's Cube Theology". If that tactic doesn't succeed in deflecting the questioner, he becomes defensive.
 If the interlocutor presses further, **Charles Pretlow** will become angry and start yelling at the person who is coming to him for spiritual guidance.
He did this to me on numerous occasions. I suspect that his experience as a former US Marine leads him to see himself as something resembling a Christian version of a drill instructor; a perspective which wouldn't be objectionable if he were at least correct in his theology.

A favorite manipulation technique of his is to say "I'm going to hang up on you", followed by not hanging up on you and waiting to see if you are going to let yourself be cowed by him. It worked on me for several years starting in the mid 2000s when he was running his ministry out of his garage in Westcliffe, CO.
By the grace of God, I eventually broke out of his false ministry.

Part of why I was so easily drawn in is the fact that he can take general truths which anybody can discern for themselves, and expound upon them in near infinite detail in such a way that he sounds prophetic.
His presentation is so well polished that I now understand how people can be drawn into ridiculous cults like Scientology.

In essence, **Pretlow** is a wolf in sheep's clothing that claims to be fighting against the other wolves in sheep's clothing. **Pretlow** claims to be preparing people to meet the Lord in these last days by preparing them using the unique theology that the Lord has revealed to only him. Having been a past colleague of **John and Paula Sandford**, and holding out their teaching as a positive example (he keeps their book "The Transformation of the Inner Man" on his bookshelf as reference material and recommends it to counseling clients...like me), he teaches that the human spirit is fractured into multiple component parts which are disenfranchised from each other and yet which have all the aspects of personality.

 It is sort of like a sub-clinical version of multiple personality disorder. The idea is that by treating each of these "pieces" of you as lost individuals, they can be brought to a saving knowledge of Jesus Christ and then unified with your primary self. When this process conglomerates enough parts of "you" together into a single person, this new "you" becomes saved.

Part of **Pretlow's** success with this stems from the fact that this theory can explain some of the unanswered questions of Christianity while at the same time remaining safely unfalsifiable since Scripture does not challenge the theory directly and in some ways it actually does dovetail very well with Scripture. It is no surprise that he uses Scripture so much.

As the saying goes, a liar is never more dangerous than when he tells the truth. **Charles Pretlow** is hardly the first charlatan of this kind, and he will not be the last.

As a matter of personal witness I do swear before the Lord Jesus Christ and upon my very salvation that the following actually did happen to me:

Early on in my time with **Charles Pretlow's** ministry, his wife left him. Shortly after this, **Pretlow** asked me to pray in agreement with him that the Lord would end the life of his (now) ex-wife with the explanation that he had God's permission to do this (to the best of my knowledge she is still alive and well).

Pretlow also claimed that his wife had "spiritually attacked" him by way of one of her disenfranchised personality parts which Satan was able to establish control over and thus direct it (her?) against him, and that the attack was the reason that his voice failed causing him to speak with a distinct speech impediment.

He claims it was not a stroke.

On another occasion, without any solicitation on my part, **Charles Pretlow** shared intimate details of his ex-wife's sexual proclivities with me (as if I wanted to know).

He also badgered me by repeatedly asking the accusatory question "Are you a child molester?" I don't know if he does this with women too, but he did tell me that he always asks this to men. It didn't matter how many times I said "no."

He just kept repeating that question in successive counseling sessions.

Does a pastor with the gift of prophecy really need to interrogate somebody like that?

If anything, it seems like he should know the answer to that question before he even asks, especially since he and the Holy Spirit both consider it to be important. I pity anybody who has revealed personal information to **Pretlow** in a counseling session.

I should have learned from that early experience, but I didn't and I made that same mistake with him. I have no doubt that he has talked behind my back to other people just as he did with his ex-wife. I know I'm not supposed to expect angelic character qualities of church leaders, but does any of this really sound like the heart of a saved Christian much less a pastor?

I pity anybody who has ever trusted him as a confidant seeking prayer/deliverance.

I am deeply ashamed of myself for ever falling for this fraud. Every time I think of my time at **Pretlow's** "ministry" my chest sinks as I feel tears coming, and all I can do is give thanks to Lord Jesus for getting me out of there.

I warn everybody who will listen... **Charles Pretlow** is a used car salesman with a ThD degree. Don't trust him, only trust Scripture. If you do, you will find that Scripture will eventually lead you away from the **Pretlows** of the world ("Ye shall know the truth, and the truth shall set you free").

One last point. **Charles Pretlow** is also a prophetic earthquake predictor. His list of predictions for 2020 includes increases in earthquakes. Never mind the fact that the USGS says that same thing, or that he predicted an earthquake of the coast of Oregon back in 2011, and that the warning was taken down from his website after it didn't happen. It would seem that the Holy Spirit doesn't get it right every time.

 Oh well, the prophetically gifted **Charles "Chuck" Pretlow** will surely be right one of these years.

Here's his latest example of prophesying the obvious in case anybody's interested...
https://tinyurl.com/yx5nylkf (note the publication date, 08/29/2014).

(**NOTE: The above is a testimony of a commenter who had the unfortunate mishap of being in this wolves's congregation.
It is taken from the website listed below. Ed.).
https://www.honorofkings.org/false-prophet-listing/

- **Frederick K.C. Price**:   WOF teacher\preacher; Claims Jesus went to Hell, Prosperity Gospel;
 "The Bible says that He [Jesus] had a treasurer--a treasury (they called it "the bag"); that they had one man who was the treasurer, named Judas Iscariot; and the rascal was stealing out of the bag for three-and-a-half years and nobody knew that he was stealing. You know why? Because there was so much in it, He couldn't tell."

 "Nobody could tell that anything was missing. If He had three oranges in the bottom of the bag and he stole two of them, don't tell me He wouldn't know that some was missing." "
Beside that, if Jesus didn't have anything, what do you need a treasury for?"   "A treasury is for surplus. It's not for that which you're spending. It's only for surplus--to hold it until you need to spend it." "Therefore, He must have had a whole lot that needed to be held in advance that He wasn't spending. So He must have had more than He was living on."   ("Ever Increasing Faith" program on TBN 23 November 1990).

Fred Price: "Jesus and the disciples were rich, only rich people could take off for three and a half years." ("Ever Increasing Faith," recorded 11/23/90).

Fred Price: "The whole point is I'm trying to get you to see--to get you out of this malaise of thinking that Jesus and the disciples were poor and then relating that to you- thinking that you, as a child of God, have to follow Jesus." "The Bible says that He has left us an example that we should follow His steps."
 "That's the reason why I drive a Rolls Royce. I'm following Jesus' steps." ("Ever Increasing Faith" program on TBN (9 December 1990).

Fred Price: "God has displeasure in poverty." ("Ever Increasing Faith," recorded 11/16/90).
Frederick K.C. Price: "Do you think that the punishment for our sin was to die on a cross? If that were the case, the two thieves could have paid your price.

No, the punishment was to go into hell itself and to serve time in hell separated from God. . . ."
"Satan and all the demons of hell thought that they had Him bound."

"And they threw a net over Jesus and they dragged Him down to the very pit of hell itself to serve our sentence."

("Ever Increasing Faith Messenger" [June 1980], 7; quoted in D.R. McConnell, "A Different Gospel " [Peabody, MA: Hendrickson Publishers, 1988], 120.)
http://www.banner.org.uk/wof/sayings.html

- **Derek Prince**: Deceased; WOF, Universalist Unitarian; denies the Deity of Jesus Christ, among other false beliefs.
 https://www.latimes.com/archives/ la-xpm-1990-03-24-ca-667-story.html

http://thewartburgwatch.com/2011/01/28/ the-legacy-of-derek-prince/

Derek Prince has the dubious reputation as one of the founders of the unmitigated disaster known as the Shepherding Movement.
From 1970 the so called "Fort Lauderdale Five" (FL5) - **Derek Prince, Don Basham, Bob Mumford, Charles Simpson** and **Ern Baxter** (former Campaign Manager for proven false prophet and heretic **William Branham**) worked together in what they termed "covenant relationship."

The Shepherding Movement (also known as the Discipleship Movement) operated primarily in the United States, though the teachings were distributed worldwide through the Christian magazine 'New Wine'.

https://bewareofthewolves.blogspot.com/2014/11/ derek-prince-false-teacher-wolf-in.html

- **Joseph Prince** : False preacher; teaches "hyper-grace"; another of the WOF wolves; "Grace Only" preacher and turning to Prosperity Gospel; Word Faith teachers—Such as Xenonamandar Jegahusiee Singh better known as **Joseph Prince**--have never noticed Jesus' devastating prediction of damnation for people, who teach and act similar to them: Mat 7:21-23.
   https://www.evangelicaloutreach.org/
andrew-wommack-ministry-faith-healer-charis-bible-college-heresy.htm

(**NOTE: This website concerns another WOF teacher—**Andrew Wommack**—but it also references **Joseph Prince**, which is why it is listed here.   Ed.).

Q:

- **Phineas Quimby:**   Deceased; Although there are many opinions on who the actual founder of New Thought is, since the essence of the movement is rooted in the interpretation of **Quimby's** teachings, **Quimby** should be credited as the overall intellectual father of New Thought.   In 1838, **Quimby** began studying Mesmerism after attending a lecture by Doctor Collyer and soon began further experimentation with the help of Lucius Burkmar, who could fall into a trance and diagnose illnesses.

Quimby again saw the mental and placebo effect of the mind over the body when medicines prescribed by Burkmar, with no physical value, cured patients of diseases.

From the conclusions of these studies, **Phineas Quimby** developed theories of mentally aided healing and opened an office in Portland, Maine in 1859.

Among the students and patients who joined his studies and helped him to commit his teachings to writing were Warren Felt Evans, Annetta Seabury Dresser and Julious Dresser, the founders of New Thought as a named movement, and **Mary Baker Eddy**, the founder of the "Christian Science" movement. **Mary Baker Eddy** (formerly known as by the surname Patterson) developed a movement out of the ideas she derived from **Quimby's** teachings. Through the treatment for her poor health, **Eddy** came to be a student of **Phineas Quimby** and out of this came her own unique ideas about metaphysical healing.

In 1862, **Eddy** received treatment from **Quimby** and was cured quickly. Though her health tended to fluctuate, when she practiced the latter techniques her condition improved. Though the commonalities between their work are quite apparent, **Eddy** had to personally integrate her own Christian faith with **Quimby's** ideas since he tended to be critical of traditional religious practices. In 1879 practioners assembled the "Church of Christ, Scientist" and soon ordained **Eddy** as the pastor.

At this point the controversy that delineated the split between "New Thought" and "Christian Science" was characterized by the dispute between **Mary Baker Eddy** and Edward J. Arens, her former student, and Julius Dresser, who continued along with his wife and son to dispute **Eddy** over the origin of certain ideas.

However, "Christian Science" and **Mary Baker Eddy** weathered the storm of plagiarism accusations and the movement still survives today. Annetta and Julius Dresser continued their attack on **Eddy** throughout the rest of their lives. https://phineasquimby.wwwhubs.com/

R:

- **Dave Ramsey**: https://www.patheos.com/blogs/mercynotsacrifice/2011/07/25/why-dave-ramsey-is-the-problem/

https://churchsalt.com/2010/02/28/dave-has-a-problem/

http://bewareoffalse-unbiblicalteachers.blogspot.com/2019/03/dave-ramsey-tested-to-gods-word.html

https://www.youtube.com/ watch?time_continue=64&v=TsuSIwtKbj8&feature=emb_logo

http://www.piratechristian.com/messedupchurch/2017/2/dave-ramsey-gets-biblically-scrutinized

(**NOTE: There are those who are for **Dave Ramsey's** methods, and there are those that are against. For those that are against, it seems that the underlying rejection of his methods has to do with Biblical Christianity. For those of you who are for his methods, it seems to be acceptable within their understanding of Biblical principles. I have left this up to you the reader to judge for yourself. Ed.).

- **Rick Ridings**: Is an NARpostle – recognized in the NAR as a hyphenated apostle, involved in the "Apostolic Council of Prophetic Elders'.   He was also part of the initial leadership team that helped launch the Apostolic 'Antioch Network'. https://pulpitandpen.org

- **Oral Roberts**: In the 40s and 50s, good preacher; fell away from the true Gospel; appeared on TV and radio, asking for $8M or "God will kill me;" "seed faith" heresy; formed the Charismatic Bible Ministries;   He is deceased.

  Oral Roberts and son, **Richard Roberts** are both Word-Faith con-artists.
  Oral is the originator of the seed-faith doctrine. Have a need? Plant a seed. Large amounts of cash make the best seed for planting. Both men practice cultic doctrines of bringing their cohorts into altered states of consciousness; http://www.defendchrist.org

In 1947, **Oral Roberts** went through a time of extensive fasting and prayer. "The Voice of Healing" magazine, published in 1949, quoted **Branham** saying that **Roberts'** "commanding power over demons, over disease and over sin was the most amazing thing he had ever seen in the work of God." By 1950, **Roberts** was traveling the country with tent meetings that were simultaneous broadcast on TV stations, his healing ministry had begun.

 Among the many revelations **Oral Roberts** had, one was similar to **Branham.** He identified his healing ministry with John the Baptist. In the fall of 1948, according to **Roberts,** God "spoke to my heart and showed me that I would be the John the Baptist to my time in the sense that I would help prepare the way . . . for a great healing to come to the body of Christ."

 Roberts, as well as other revivalists, believed that the healing revival was a precursor to the second coming of Christ. Unlike **Branham, Roberts** never developed the idea that he was the forerunner to Christ's return.
 (See David E. Harrell, Jr., Oral Roberts: An American Life (Bloomington: Indiana University Press. http://www.letusreason.org)

- **Richard Roberts**: "Seed Faith" heresy; Made following statement: "I don't try to prove [that] multiplied thousands [are being healed]. I just say, "there's a person." "Let him tell you."
 [This is enough] to me and the person. . . I can't prove that any person who ever came to me was healed, that is I can't prove it to the satisfaction of everyone." ("The Faith Healers," p. 193).   http://www.letusreason.org)

-**Toure Roberts**: **Roberts** launched "One Church of LA" in 2002, but he recently joined it to "The Potter's House" brand in August 2017. Now officially linked to **T.D. Jakes'** business and theological influence, **Roberts** is contractually obligated to preach false doctrine for as long as he pastors his church.

This isn't to say **Roberts** wasn't already a purveyor of compromise and Biblical error in his own right, of course. In fact, **Roberts** made headlines -secular and faith-based -in 2013 when he called Michelle Williams and Kelly Rowland to the pulpit and repented to Destiny's Child on behalf of Body of Christ! "It's called 'identification repentance."

Where you stand in the gap of an individual, a community -it could be a race of people -that have wronged someone, and you repent on behalf of that people or that group," **Roberts** told his congregation. According to **Roberts,** he had the authority to repent in such a way because he's a pastor. Of course, "identification repentance" isn't Biblical. But it does pervert a Biblical truth.
Before Christ, under the Law, God ordained certain men high priests to "offer both gifts and sacrifices for sins" on behalf of the people and for themselves (Hebrews 5:1).

These men, being of a sin nature themselves, had compassion for those who were "ignorant and going astray" (Hebrews 5:2).
Yet their calling to stand in the gap was of God - not of their own accord; for matters pertaining to God -not matters pertaining to the world; and for sins committed against God -not for perceived offenses between mankind!

And their service was a foreshadow of Jesus Christ, who is NOW our High Priest - there is no other man serving in this role, nor is another needed, nor will there ever be another. When Jesus died for our sins on the cross, He was the final sacrifice for sins (Hebrews 10:12). And now He sits at the right hand of God and is the ONLY mediator between God and man (1 Timothy 2:5-6).

But back to **Roberts**, because he wasn't done repenting to celebrities on behalf of the Church. "I wish Bey was here. And in the spirit, she is...People accuse [Jay-Z] and accuse Kanye' of being anti-Church and anti-Jesus."

" But I'ma tell you something, the Church picked that fight."
Meanwhile, Jay-Z's rapping lines like "And Jesus can't save you, life starts when the church ends" and "God sent me to break the chain I'm the true and livin' God in the flesh, the rest of these [expletive] is vain".

Then Kanyés" changing his name to "Yeezus" (a portmanteau of his nickname "Yeezy" and the name of Jesus); publishing his own 'bible' and replacing every mention of "God" with "Yeezus"; and releasing a profanity-laced "Gospel" album.

Point is, these men are on record for blaspheming God on numerous occasions over the years, and it's a matter not to be taken lightly. But **Roberts** is defending THEM over US, his professed brethren?

"Woe to those who call evil good, and good evil; who put darkness for light, and light for darkness; who put bitter for sweet, and sweet for bitter!" (Isaiah 5:20).

But enough of pop culture, let's address an even deeper matter: **Roberts'** instructions to the saints in these last days–

In his sermon "It's Birthing Time" **Roberts** reads Romans 8:18 through verse 22 (for proper context, read through verse 25). Now, the text actually speaks to the sufferings of the present, fallen state of all of creation due to sin, yet the anticipated revealing of a new creation when Christ returns and redeems the Body of Christ.

Granted, this passage isn't as easy to exegete as the parable of the wheat and the tares, but if you understand the Gospel of Jesus Christ, you know that this passage is meant to encourage Believers to maintain our hope in Christ through sufferings (which are only going to get more intense).

Paul compares these sufferings to labor pains during childbirth, and Jesus elsewhere outlines what those specific sufferings/"labor pains" would be (Matthew 24; Mark 13; and Luke 21). Before a new life comes into the world, there is labor. So will it be with Jesus' return. Creation is in labor to usher in the return of Christ! (Praise God! Hallelujah! Come Lord Jesus! Come!). Yet, somehow, like most prosperity preachers, **Roberts** finds a way to make this passage about pursuing personal dreams and goals.
Let him tell it, the labor pains are a sign it's time to "turn up" and hurry to "be all God called us to be"!

"We're in labor," he says. "That's all that's happening...and I'm going to tell you what you're pregnant with: Yourself. You are pregnant with you!"
Argh!!!
But while **Roberts** is telling his congregation to pursue their destinies while they still have time, those of us who follow Jesus know He tells us to gird ourselves spiritually that we are strong enough to endure and love even in the midst of what's coming: severe persecution, hatred and lawlessness (Matthew 24:9-12; Mark 13:11-13; Luke 21:12-18).

All of this is because sin entered into the world through Adam, the first man in creation (Romans 5). But Christ, who died for our sins, was resurrected as the "First fruits" of a NEW creation (1 Corinthians 15:23). And if we confess with our mouths that Jesus Christ is Lord and believe in our hearts that God raised Him from the dead, we too will be raised to glory on the last day (Romans 10:9-10).

Paul is telling us to remain encouraged. Jesus is telling us to stay "woke" (Matthew 26:41)! But if you hang your hope on anything **Roberts** says, you'll be among those who are spiritually blind and unprepared -probably someplace repenting to celebrities - when Jesus returns."
https://www.lipstickalley.com

- **Pat Robertson, Gordon Robertson**: 700 Club founder; false prophesies, is a multi-billionaire who owns hundreds of thousands of acres of land in the U.S., now another false preacher in the NAR/ Dominionist movement. (**NOTE: Well documented online. Ed.).

- **James Robison**: Is an example of the ecumenical spirit that permeates the charismatic movement, and his case is a loud warning to those who are tempted to flirt with this movement. In the 1970s, he was a fiery Southern Baptist evangelist, preaching boldly against the theological liberalism that had permeated his denomination and urgently needed to be rooted out.

But during a spiritual crisis in 1982, and at the urging of his wife, he allowed a charismatic preacher named Milton Green to minister to him. Green said **Robison** was "the most demonized man I ever met," and **Robison** claims that his deliverance was like a giant claw being removed from his brain, but it appears that this was a matter of a misguided man misdiagnosing fleshly sins such as anger and lust, which is what **Robison** complained of, as "demons" (Gal. 5:16-23).

The solution to a situation in which a man trusts in Jesus Christ as His Lord and Saviour but struggles with the flesh is not to cast out demons but to deal with confession of sin and other aspects of how to walk in the Spirit. Instead, Green rebuked the devil and laid hands on **Robison**. I don't know, of course, what **James Robison's** actual spiritual problem was at that time, and I don't know what happened to him in that strange encounter, but I do know that as a consequence of his experience he turned away from reproving sin and false teaching and made a radical turn to the unscriptural Ecumenical philosophy.

His message began to focus on "non-judgmentalism" and "unity," and he started developing close relationships with the most heretical of charismatic preachers, such as **David Yonggi Cho, Paul Crouch**, and **Oral Roberts**.

In the Jan.-Feb. 1986, issue of his magazine, "Days of Restoration," **Robison** said: "There are going to be MIRACLES, SIGNS AND WONDERS surpassing anything seen even in New Testament times."

"Multitudes will begin to come to Christ, as the real Jesus is lifted up."
"EVERY TRUE DISCIPLE WILL BE DOING THE KIND OF WORKS JESUS DID." **Robison** even apologized for his part in the struggle between conservative Bible believers and theological liberals in the Southern Baptist Convention.

He visited liberal Baylor University and apologized in person to the leaders (when he should rather have rebuked them for giving the wicked doctrine of evolution and other heresies a home in this Baptist institution).

The new "undemonized" **James Robison** began to speak in sympathetic terms in regard to the Roman Catholic Church and to develop relationships with "evangelical" and "renewal" Catholics. At "New Orleans '87," which was attended by roughly twenty thousand Roman Catholics, **Robison** made this strange statement in his message on "Restoration":

"I tell you what, all the critical Protestants standing around knocking Catholics, you'd better watch it! God'll run right by you, pick up the whole Catholic movement, and wrap them up in

Jesus and just love them, and strip everything that is wrong there, and make them an expression to the whole earth."

"He may be doing it right now. I tell you what, one of the finest moral representatives of morality in this earth right now is the pope."
"People who know him really believe he is a born-again man."
I was sitting only a few feet away from **Robison** when he said this, and I transcribed it later directly from my own tape recording and published it in "O Timothy" magazine.
It was one of the first things **Robison** said in his sermon that day.

For a man to say that the pope, who devoted himself exclusively to Mary, is a fine example of morality and that he might be saved, and for a man to say that Bible believers should not judge the Roman Catholic Church is evidence of a great spiritual blindness and is plain and fearful disobedience to the Scriptures.

Robison participated in the "Washington for Jesus" rally on April 28, 1988. Wilson Ewin described this meeting in "The Spirit of Pentecostal-Charismatic Unity:" "It was a masterpiece of non-Catholic Pentecostal and Catholic Charismatic coordination."

"The bright stars of the electronic church such as **Pat Robertson** ("Christian Broadcasting Network ," **Rex Humbard** ("Cathedral of Tomorrow"), **Dr. Robert Schuller**, **James Robison** and **Jim Bakker** (P.T.L.), shared speaking time with Roman Catholic priests John Bertolucci, John Randall and Michael Scanlon."

Co-chairmen of the huge enterprise included Ben Armstrong (Executive Director, "National Religious Broadcasters"), **Pat Boone** (entertainer), Dr. Herbert Bowdoin ("United Methodist Hour"), **Nicky Cruz, David du Plessis** ("Mr. Pentecost "),
Dr. Edgar Johnson (General Secretary of the "Church of the Nazarene"), Dan Malachuk (Publisher, "Logos Journal") , **Demos Shakarian** (President F.G.B.M.F.I.), Dr. Thomas Zimmerman (General Superintendent, "Assemblies of God," and many others."

In 1988, **Benny Hinn** announced on Trinity Broadcasting Network (TBN) that **James Robison, Marilyn Hickey**, and **Paul** and **Jan Crouch** had all agreed to have an audition with the Pope (Bold Truth, October 10, 1988).

Hinn said: "Something is happening in the Catholic Church today that is really of God" ("Calvary Contender," Dec. 1, 1988). In his telecast on February 19, 1989, **Robison** used the woman of John chapter 4 to say it does not matter where (in which church) we worship. He said, "I can have fellowship with everybody!" ("Calvary Contender," March 1, 1989).

In his blog in May 2014, **Robison** called for unity with Roman Catholics based on Jesus' prayer in John 17. In July 2014, **James Robison** and his wife, Betty, joined seven other charismatics at the Vatican for an audience with **Pope Francis**.
Members of the party included **Kenneth Copeland** and **John** and **Carol Arnott**. **James** gave the pope a "high five" when he talked about the need for people to "have a personal relationship with Jesus."

Most recently, **Robison** recommended the movie "The Shack," which promotes a non-judgmental female God, universalism, and many other rank heresies.
https://www.wayoflife.org/reports/ the-downfall-of-james-robison.php

Beware: Any person who does not Love Jesus Christ enough to rise up violently and with divine truth smite the idea of the illegitimate pope, is also an antichrist.
Anyone, such as **James Robison, Kenneth Copeland, Rick Warren, Joel Osteen, Billy Graham,** etc., who facilitates and sells this antichrist system is also an antichrist.

Anything less than openly exposing this antichrist system that is damning the souls of over a billion people, reveals one to be against Christ for putting something, anything, or anyone in place of Christ (antichrist). Colossians 2:18-19. What do we not understand about Christ's declaration that "He that is not with me IS against me"? (Matthew 12:30).
When you truly know Jesus Christ because you've been born again, you know that He will share His blessed, divine glory with no mere sinful man and any man or system that deceitfully pretends to be a mediator between God and man will be destroyed (Isaiah 42:8; Acts 12:23, etc.).
If your so-called "pastor" or favorite teacher or leader is not coming out guns ablazing against this antichrist blasphemy of the pope, you have yoked yourself to a diabolical, self-serving antichrist. **James Robison** is a Catholic colluder.

James Robison is now a Catholic operative. Spread the word.
This man is an apostate wolf who must be marked according to apostolic mandate.

This is some of the sickest filth the true Christian will ever listen to.

In the video below you will see **Robison** spinelessly falling all over himself to admire, flatter, and endorse this robe-wearing, Roman Catholic pagan pharisee priest who teaches that "Jesus" is a piece of wheat. **James Robison** is an apostate (Jude).
He has departed from "THE faith." (1 Timothy 4:1-3).
This is the prophesied one world religion friends. "Evangelicals and Catholics together"? Total deceit! Now, modern evangelicalism is 99% apostate which proves they are not saved if they are yoking with this pagan religion (2 Cor. 6:14-18).

Well, the enemy's goal is to use his wolves to steal away sheep from the flock of God (Acts 20:29-31) and he does this through deceivers like **James Robison** who seeks to yoke Bible believers with pagans. Any student of Holy Scripture knows that God hates mixture (Col. 2:4, 8-10, etc.). **James Robison** is yet another wolf championing this evil cause to form a one world religion .... he joins vile devils like **Jack Van Impe, Pat Robertson, Billy Graham** and many others.

https://safeguardyoursoul.com/ james-robison-is-a-wolf-irrefutable-proof/

- **Hugh Ross**: Probably the world's leading Progressive Creationist.
In summary, **Dr Ross** accepts Astronomical Evolution (Big Bang and billions of years) and Geological Evolution (evolutionary geological time scale encompassing billions of years).

He does not accept Biological Evolution per se, but teaches that God created millions of creatures (species) in "batches" over billions of years (but using the basic evolutionary time scale and order of events), with death, struggle, extinction and disease occurring all along the way.

He does not accept the clear Biblical teaching of a global Flood, but instead teaches it was "universal" with respect to mankind (which **Ross** sometimes calls "worldwide"), which was living only in a limited geographical area in the Middle East.

He also advocates soulless hominids (who exhibited human characteristics of painting, burying dead, etc.) before Adam and Eve. When **Dr Ross** was first thrust to considerable prominence as a result of his books being published by NavPress and particularly his appearances on "Focus on the Family," (**Dr. James Dobson**), many Christian leaders embraced or endorsed his teachings.
 At first, **Dr Ross** appeared to be an answer to many an academic who wanted to maintain belief in billions of years, but did not want to be classed as an "evolutionist."

(Because of the phenomenal influence of the mainstream creation movement (e.g., AiG—Answers in Genesis, ICR), many in the church were aware of the inconsistency of positions such as Theistic Evolution —"God used evolution").

The teachings of **Dr Ross** seemingly allowed Christians to use the term "creationist," but still give them supposed academic respectability in the eyes of the world, by rejecting six literal days of creation and maintaining acceptance of billions of years.

However, AiG speakers and writers have spent considerable time alerting Christians to the fact that in reality, **Ross's** position still has the same basic compromise of evolutionary theory with Scripture as does Theistic Evolution, and ultimately undermines the authority of the Word of God and the Gospel of Jesus Christ.

Through such efforts, I have noticed in recent times that many who previously embraced **Ross's** teachings are now realizing how bankrupt they are—how much they undermine God's Holy Word—and how such teaching can lead people away from the Gospel. AiG staff researcher and writer, **Dr Terry Mortenson,** worked with Campus Crusade for twenty-six years. During that time, **Dr Mortenson** challenged (with gentleness but boldness) without success, the leaders of this commendable evangelistic organization to withdraw a major article by **Dr Ross** posted on one of CCC's Web sites.

Because of AiG's concern for those who have been publicly led astray by teaching that compromises God's Word, **Dr Mortenson** has written a detailed critique of this article. **Dr Mortenson's** article will not only help the readers to understand more about the compromise teachings of **Hugh Ross**, but will assist them to learn to be "Bereans" and thus to search the Scriptures to see if these teachings are true.

It will also help readers to see the importance of philosophical assumptions in science. This special feature article will equip and challenge—but most of all, what **Dr Mortenson** has written shows clearly AiG's position, that we must submit man's fallible ideas to the authority of God's infallible Word.

Ross gives the misleading and erroneous impression that he is an academic (by the use of the word "our'). "Academic" is a term generally used to refer to people who teach and research in an institution of higher learning, and this article appears in the Leadership U Web site, which is aimed at such an audience.
But the term does not describe **Ross**. He is also misleading in the impression that a noteworthy percentage of academics are now Young-Earth Creationists.
They are still very much in the minority on the college campus.

We would expect that in the next paragraph **Ross** is going to explain these "diametrically opposite" reasons why both some academics and a sizable segment of the evangelical community are embracing Young-Earth Creationism.
But in the next paragraph he instead talks about academic critics of Young-Earth Creationism.
He never does tell us what the diametrically opposite reasons are.

But it is wrong to think that the two groups of people have different reasons for holding to Young-Earth creationism. They have the same reasons: the Bible clearly teaches it and the scientific evidence confirms it. "Old-Earth Creationism" is dismissed by the evolutionists because they know full well that the Bible teaches Young-Earth Creationism.
They don't trust the "Old-Earth Creationists" handling of the Bible, so why should they respect their ('Old-Earthers') science? During the past 170 years or so most evangelicals, especially evangelical scholars, have been compromised by favoring one of the "Old-Earth" interpretations, such as "day-age," "gap" or "framework" theory, none of which is really Biblically or scientifically plausible, although with superficial examination they appear to be.

Only in the latter half of the 20th century has "Young-Earth Creationism" been revived and grown after being virtually extinct since about 1850. The growth has been primarily among lay people (including many well-trained scientists) and some pastors, but it still appears to be a minority view among Christians (except maybe in fundamentalist circles, where there are also many "Old-Earth Creationists").

Ross is being quite inconsistent here. In one quick stroke of the pen, he leads his reader to disregard the "when" of creation by stating that it has no bearing upon one's relationship with Christ. So, is one to superficially conclude that the "when" of creation is not important? The fact is that there is much chronological information in Genesis 1, as well as in chapters 5 and 11.
The "when" of creation is just as much revealed information, as "who", "what", "how" and "why," though we are hard pressed to find much in Genesis 1 to answer the "why" question.
And as we shall see, this "when" of creation is quite foundational to one's relationship to Christ.

They can reexamine the arguments used to support the young-earth position and acknowledge a strong case for an old-earth interpretation. But there are still many others who uphold the young-earth position as the front-line defense against modern (and postmodern) assaults on the Christian faith.

Reasons for this emotion-charged entrenchment are discussed in "Creation and Time," a book written by **Hugh**; we will attempt to summarize them here.

The source of resistance in all groups of "Young-Earth" proponents, however, seems the same: **fear**. Note: this is an attack on "Young-Earthers" character rather than their arguments.

By saying this is true of all groups of "Young-Earthers," he is also leading his readers to think that "Young-Earthers' are not resisting "Old-Earth" thinking for any exegetical or scientific reasons. The implication is that "Young-Earthers" are fearful simpletons.

The Bible gives us the real reason that these academics will not carefully consider the Gospel. It is not fear, but rebellion against their Creator.

They love the darkness of their unrighteousness rather than the light of the God's holy truth (John 3:19-20, Romans 1:18-23). In the Christians who remain adamantly committed to the "Young-Earth" view exists a deep-seated fear that someday, somewhere, somehow scientists will discover some fact that clearly and irrefutably contradicts a Scriptural statement. False.

"Young-Earth" creationists (at least well-informed ones) have no such fear, because we know that (1) the Bible is the inerrant Word of God; (2) it clearly teaches "Young-Earth Creationism," as careful exegesis and church history confirm; (3) the scientific "facts" that evolutionists claim as proof of evolution or millions of years are really interpretations of selected observations, and those interpretations have been made with anti-Biblical philosophical assumptions; and (4) history is littered with so-called "scientific facts" that supposedly proved the Bible wrong, but which years or decades later were shown to be not facts but erroneously interpreted observations (because of the anti-Biblical assumptions used).

And then where will we be? If we trust science, we'll lose our faith in that moment. But if Biblical truth stands above all else, above the so-called facts discovered through the work and thoughts of fallen men, our faith will remain intact. (That's how the reasoning goes.) Science, then, is entirely suspect and may be judged as hopelessly flawed.

It is not "science" that "Young-Earthers" think is entirely suspect and hopelessly flawed. Rather, evolutionary scientific theories, including "Old-Earth geological theory" and "Big Bang" old-universe astronomical theory " (both of which **Ross** accepts as fact) are hopelessly flawed because of the atheistic, anti-Biblical assumptions involved.

"YEC" are not opposed to science. Most of the leaders of the "YEC" organizations around the world, in fact, have PhDs in science. Nor are "YEC' opposed to scientific facts. We all have the same facts—the same living creatures, the same DNA molecules, the same fossils, the same rock layers, the same Grand Canyon, the same moon, the same planets, the same starlight from distant stars and galaxies, etc.

What are highly suspect are the evolutionary interpretations, which are misleadingly labeled as "facts" or "science." The cosmological "discoveries" are a mixture of a few facts and an enormous amount of philosophical assumptions and atheistic interpretations.

The actual evidence (whether seen with the naked eye or through the telescope) clearly shows that the universe is designed, not the product of an explosion and millions of years of time plus chance plus the laws of nature operating on primitive matter.

The "Big Bang" theory may point to the existence of a vaguely defined all-powerful "god" (though many evolutionists would deny this).

But if the theory is true, then it also shows that the Bible is in serious error, for the theory flatly contradicts the Genesis account of creation (which says, for starters, that the Earth was created before the sun, moon and stars, contrary to the "Big Bang" theory).

"Christians" faith is not built by wedding atheistic theories of history with the Bible. https://answersingenesis.org

(NOTE: Space does not permit the balance of this anti-God discourse; please go to the article itself by pasting in a search box the website address listed above. Ed.).

See also http://www.creationstudygroup.org for a quite lengthy discourse on Creation; another website to read is: http://www.trueorigin.org/hughross02.asp

- **Ian Ross**: NAR prophet; is friends with **Heidi Baker** and several others in the New Age preaching and teaching heresy. He is currently residing in Canada.

(**NOTE: While I could not find very much on this person, the link below has several of the "wolves" names, so you can see the connection between **Ian Ross** and those in the heretical teachings of the Vineyard and Bethel movements. Ed.).

https://www.fatherheartministry-ianross.com/references

- **Joel Rosenberg**: **Joel** is speaking at the ecumenical and emerging church conference "Break Forth 2010" (By the way, "Spring Harvest" is the UK's equivalent to "Break Forth"). This link from **Joel's** own site: http://joelrosenberg.com/spiritual.asp is a full description of **Joel's** spiritual journey to faith.

He spends most of the time talking about how his father came to faith, but skips over very quickly on how he turned to Jesus. Why spend so much time on his father's faith and not say how he came to faith (even though he was answering the question about his own salvation)? This other link from his site: http://joelrosenberg.com/ezekiel_q4.asp.

This is part of what he wrote:

"I believe the vast majority of evangelical Christians will maintain support of Israel to the bitter end." "Many Catholics and Christians from other denominations who are also passionate about their love for Jesus and their understanding of God's plan and purpose for the Jewish people will also stand with Israel."

"Indeed, true followers of Jesus Christ may be the only friends Israel and the Jewish people have left as this terrible war approaches." So he appears to be promoting Catholics as part of the church. Sounds ecumenical to me. Also, his reasoning for speaking at "Break Forth" is to try and get Christians to support Israel.

Why choose an event which is full of new-age, ecumenical, emerging churchers etc. to get the message to. The purpose of Emerging church is "Dominionism" or "Kingdom Now" where the church is the "new Israel" so what is to be achieved there, unless he is supportive of emerging church himself?   Yes, **Joel** may say some very good things and importantly he is supportive of Israel. However that could be because he (himself) is Jewish.
 Finally this link to his blog:

http://flashtrafficblog.wordpress.com/ gives another link entitled "would you like to know God personally" which takes you to "Campus Crusade For Christ" website:

 www.ccci.org/how-to-know-god/ would-you-like-to-know-god-personally/index.htm

(So **Joel** supports CCC which has become very ecumenical.) This site gives their version of how to be saved. I cannot say for sure but the wording sounds sort of "purpose driven" i.e. "God loves you and offers a wonderful plan for your life."

I assume this is also **Joel's** views. See what it says about repentance. It seems a bit weak. I may be wrong about **Joel**, but it does seem that he is ecumenical from this evidence based on the material. If anyone reading this has material (videos say) which prove that he is anti ecumenical please show me. Thanks. http://watchmanforjesus.blogspot.com/2010/03

- **Sid Roth**: host of NAR TV 'It's Supernatural' (Good friend of **Michael Brown**). **Sid Roth** is one Charismatic who offers the DVD and 3-CD "Personal Trainer for Tongues" for a $49 donation.
https://www.holybibleprophecy.org/2019/03/06/
holy-spirit-baptism-with-the-evidence-of-tongues/?doing_wp_cron=1555718405.889380931854
2480468750.

Sid Roth ("It's Supernatural")--Once you know that all Messianic ministries are false, it is clear about this show. He teaches "One New Man" is the Gentiles and the Khazarian Jews .. FALSE. Notice all those Kabbalah hexagrams covering the globe ... ? NWO?

Copyright © 2019 Olivet Journal:

Sid Roth, a former account executive for Merrill Lynch, was raised in a traditional Jewish home. Yet, religious tradition provided no answers when he hit rock bottom in 1972. With his life out of control and his marriage in shambles, **Sid** was set free from demonic oppression through a supernatural encounter with Jesus. Immediately, he began to boldly proclaim Jesus as the Jewish Messiah. In 1977 **Sid** started a ministry called "Messianic Vision" and a nationally syndicated radio broadcast by the same name.

But the "Messianic Vision" is more than a ministry or a program; it is a desire to reach out with the good news of the Messiah, "to the Jew first" (Romans 1:16).   This is not just God's historical order for spreading the gospel, but also His eternal spiritual order. When we follow this "law of evangelism," God opens a supernatural door to reach Gentiles as well. God's heart is to reach all people. His strategy is "to the Jew first."

"My name is **Sid Roth**. I am a Jew. Both of my parents were Jewish. I have Israeli and American citizenship. I attended a traditional synagogue where I was bar mitzvah."
"Like most American Jews, I found organized religion irrelevant to my life. I was proud of being Jewish, but bored with religion." " To be honest, my god was money. My goal was to be a millionaire by age 30. By 29, I had graduated college, was married, was the father of one daughter, and was an account executive for Merrill Lynch."

"Although I had a wonderful life and career, I felt I was a failure because I was not a millionaire." "I did something I am not proud of. I left my wife, daughter and Merrill Lynch and went searching for happiness. My search led me to Eastern meditation, the New Age." "During this search, I almost lost my mind. Life was too difficult."

"A Christian businessman challenged me that my Jewish Bible condemned my occult practices and told me that Jesus was the Jewish Messiah that my Orthodox Jewish upbringing had carefully hidden from me. I was stunned."
"So I began to read the Jewish Scriptures for myself and I got the shock of my life. What he had said might well be true. No sooner had that thought formed in my mind than the New Age spirit guide that I had surrendered to began to curse me from inside that same mind!"

" Previously, I thought I controlled this New Age spirit guide, but I now knew that was not true. I had a power, a strong power, and it was evil." "I went to sleep that night so full of fear, I wanted to die! In desperation I prayed, Jesus, help!" "I still did not know if Jesus was real, but I had nowhere else to turn."

" The next morning when I woke up, I knew immediately that the evil that had been inside of me was gone! Even my fear was gone! I knew it was that prayer I had prayed the night before!" "In place of fear and desperation, I had a tangible peace and feeling of love that I had never experienced before. And I knew that Jesus was real." "Not only did He reach down to save me and restore me to my right mind, but He also restored my marriage and gave me back my wonderful wife, Joy, and my precious daughter, Leigh."

"My entire immediate Jewish family, including my father, mother, sister and brother-in-law, came to know Jesus. And since 1972, I have devoted my life to telling Jewish people Jesus is our Messiah!" Read the full account of how **Sid** came to know Jesus as his Messiah in his autobiography, "There Must Be Something More!" **Sid** was featured as the cover story in the June 2015 issue of "Charisma" Magazine.

Sid Roth is a spiritual huckster who seeks out those making the most outrageous claims of works of God for his show, "It's Supernatural," in order to entertain people.
Now, we know that God does do miracles and marvelous acts, but how did Jesus approach such things? "**Sid Roth** is the main promoter of NAR [New Apostolic Reformation] celebrities. His internet show is called, "It's Supernatural'".

On this show he interviews and extols the wonders of all these miraculous signs and wonders and the people performing them. He's been doing this for 35 years.

"About 40 years ago he and I attended the same church, a Messianic synagogue in Rockville, Md, called Beth Messiah. While my wife and I attended that church, **Sid Roth** heard of our testimony of being delivered from the <u>occult</u> and having become born-again Christians."

"At that time he was doing a radio show where he interviewed people sharing their testimonies of how they became Christians. I think the show lasted 15 minutes."
"He normally interviewed guests for one show, allowing him to have five guests per week. He found our conversion story so interesting that he chose to have us on for the whole week. He split up the interview about half and half between my wife and myself, with me telling the story about how I was saved and my wife's story of coming out to rescue me from the Christians, and her subsequent salvation."

"Now I can't help but wonder if that interview planted the seed that led **Sid Roth** down the path of <u>embracing and promoting the infiltration of the occult into the Christian church today</u>."
"40 years ago our paths crossed, **Sid Roth** and myself. Since then we have gone in opposite directions. I briefly did a U-turn, and traveled his road."
"Thank God for exits. Somebody once said something about a fork in the road, and taking the one less traveled."

'Broad is the way that leads to destruction, and many be that go therein, but narrow is the way that leads to eternal life, and few there be that find it.'"

As a spiritual entrepreneur and opportunist, **Sid** was on the hunt for bigger and better things to catapult his spiritual sideshow into the limelight. It may be that the Lord delivered **Sid** from the <u>occult and demonic possession</u> and restored him to his right mind after he repented of leaving his wife and daughter to search for "happiness" (see http://sidroth.org/about/sids-story).

Just because the Lord gives good things to people, doesn't make them good. Many a person has been felled by their ambitions and desires because they never took up the cross to deny themselves and follow the Lord. They may appear as successes to some in the world, but the Lord says to them, "I never knew you."
https://www.thepathoftruth.com/false-teachers/sid-roth.htm

I was recently in a conversation with someone, about **Sid Roth** (Host of a TV show called 'It's Supernatural'). After having given more thought and prayer to the question of **Sid Roth** . . . here is my position: 2 Timothy 4:1-4.
I can only speculate as to why a man who is given a large audience, who claims to follow Jesus, who should know the word of God . . . why a man in such an advantageous position as his, to do great work for the LORD . . . would not obey Paul's charge. (Matthew 16:1-4).

The Western World today also, meets the definition of 'a wicked and adulterous generation'. As far as signs and wonders in our day, this is what the Bible warns: 2 Thessalonians 2:9), (Mark 13:22).

The signs that WILL happen during the end times, are said to be for the purpose of deceiving the elect (Christians)!! Now, with all that in mind, and the fact that these things ARE ALREADY HAPPENING–is it too much to expect that a true Christian, whom God has blessed with a means of reaching many people . . . that God would use such a person to EXPOSE the deception?

The fact that **Sid Roth** does NOT reprove or rebuke these false miracle workers, and (from what I saw) does not ask probing questions or hold their actions and beliefs up to the light of God's Word, leads me to believe that this man is a participant in the false signs and wonders that Jesus warned us about.

I can only guess at his heart–whether he is doing this knowingly, or in ignorance. However, the fact that he makes his living in this manner leads me to think that if he IS ignorant, it is willingly so.

It is said that **Sid Roth** has a powerful anointing himself. Not every anointing is from God. But it is possible that his is (2 Thessalonians 2:9-12). It is quite possible that God is using **Sid Roth** to help spread the Strong Delusion.

MAKE NO MISTAKE, this delusion will have an EXTREMELY powerful anointing . . . from God!! Only those who love the truth will be saved from it.

And where is truth? Is it in an experience? In spiritual manifestations? In powerful anointings? (As we have seen, there can purposely be a powerful anointing of God . . . ON DELUSION!).

Truth, my friends, is found in the Word of God–the Bible. Anything that does not conform to the doctrines that the Apostles outlined for the Church is not in alignment with the truth!

There are NO present day Apostles. There is no NEW revelation of truth from God!! There are no signs and wonders to win the lost. Everything that we need is right there in the King James Bible. As tempting as the fruit of the forbidden tree was to Adam and Eve–they had only ONE commandment to follow.

ONE boundary. Yet they chose instead to follow temptation and transgress that one boundary.

We, today, have ONE SOURCE for truth–the Bible. Will we accept the boundary of ONE that God has given to us, or will we yield to temptation and disobey Him? The stakes are as high for us, as they were for Adam and Eve. Those who transgress this boundary, who do not love the ONE source of truth that God has provided for us, who look for truth and understanding elsewhere . . . will end up believing the Great Delusion and being eternally damned!
 https://dontbefooled666.wordpress.com/2011/10/26/ is-sid-roth-a-deceiver/

SID ROTH has SOLD OUT! Babylon Today / June 16, 2019--

I never believed that **Sid Roth** OF ALL PEOPLE could ever-would ever promote the likes of renowned False prophets/Magicians/Occultists Alph Lukau, **TB Joshua**, Hakeem Collins and the despicable **Rich Vera**!

(**NOTE: You can see Alph Lukau, **T.B. Joshua** and **Rich Vera** on various You Tube videos. Decide for yourself if they are men of God or not. The short clip below should give you the impression of **Rich Vera**. Ed.).

https://www.youtube.com/watch?v=MJAfzdJkflU

I know that **Sid Roth** by his own admission is an ex-Satanist, an Occultist and a Psychic who once used Demonic Spirit Guides and practiced Astro-Projection. Perhaps he has decided to take a stroll back down memory lane by using his platform to introduce these pure, evil men as holy men of God! America is in trouble! Is **Sid Roth** under some type of demonic spell? Did he sell out for ratings, was he paid off or does **Sid Roth** have absolutely no spiritual insight at all?!

For **Sid Roth** to welcome these men who are undoubtedly the epitome of evil is causing great concern in the American Christian community. Why would **Sid Roth** welcome the images of these evil predators onto his platform? Why would he endorse these false prophets, witches and occultists who would do nothing but harm innocent men, women and children who will be led to them by his endorsement?
Sid Roth claims to be a "Bible believer," so perhaps he hasn't read Proverbs 4:14!
Do not set foot on the path of the wicked or walk in the way of evil men, or

Psalms 1:1 "Blessed is the man that walketh not in the counsel of the wicked, and standeth not in the way of sinners, and sitteth not in the seat of scorners."
MY GOD!!!! Many innocent people will be led straight to the camps of Satan himself thanks to false prophet **Rich Vera** and **Sid Roth's** platform.
Watch the video and see for yourself! https://videos.files.wordpress.com/ Fzqx870o/sid-roth-great-deception_dvd.mp4

https://babylon-today.com/2019/06/16/ sid-roth-has-sold-out/

- **Julio Cesar Ruibal**: Deceased; A false preacher who claims that after he was born again, the Spirit of God, through his "anointing" shook Bolivia, when actually it was NOT God's Spirit, but **Ruibal** who brought back a FALSE gospel to Bolivia, it spread like wild fire (because that is what false doctrines do, they spread very quickly) – the gospel truth on the other hand is hated). https://www.discerningtheworld.com.

S:

- **R. Loren Sandford**: (Anthony Wade – 8:28 Ministries).

It seems there is a civil war brewing within the apostate church.
For the sake of their master, I am sure they will remember how to sing Kumbaya but in the interim the irony is gratifying. **R. Loren Sandford** is a pastor in Colorado and apparently he thinks it is time the old guard goes off to that false prophet retirement ranch. What is delicious is he takes their own false prophet network language, weaponizes it and uses it against them.

Thus get ready get ready get ready because there is a <u>shift</u> coming in the <u>prophetic</u> atmosphere!

Let us reason together through above linked article:

"Something is about to <u>shift</u> in the prophetic world. A cleansing is imminent and already underway. As this purification of much that has been impure takes root, it will also include a changing of the guard."

"While faithful patriarchs such as **John Paul Jackson**, <u>Bishop</u> **Bill Hamon** and my own father, **John Sandford** (to name a few) have paved the way for <u>reliable prophetic</u> ministry, it seems clear that a fresh set of voices will now carry it forward."
"An older generation is passing away or simply fading from the spotlight while a fresh group of anointed prophets is just beginning to emerge." — **R. Loren Sandford**.

"Thanks for your contributions fellas! Don't let the door hit you on the way out now! There is a cleansing going on now! Do you know what needs cleansing beloved? Something that is dirty. Something that is filthy and disgusting." **Sandford** even goes as far as to call what has occurred before this moment:

"impure! Out with the old! In with the <u>new freshly anointed batch of false prophets</u>!"
"While I am not saying there was anything less than godly in those now fading from the spotlight, or in those now gone home to glory, and while I am certainly not in any way minimizing the contributions they made to the body of Christ, I am saying that the generation now <u>emerging</u> carries a fresh heart for a <u>new day</u>."

"These will speak more from humble intimacy with Jesus and from a pastoral spirit than from a concern for gifting." "Their words will flow more from the heart of the Father than from any felt need to prophesy, build a great ministry or stand on anyone's stage.

More than developing their gifts, they will seek <u>oneness with Jesus</u> and His nature. They will pursue rest in relationship with Him, more than being supernatural."
— **R. Loren Sandford**

http://www.828ministries.com/articles/
New-False-Prophets-to-the-by-Anthony-Wade-Christianity_God_Prophet-180823-113.html
(**NOTE: This is a lengthy article that can be accessed using the above referenced website. Ed.).

– **Agnes Sanford:** Founder of "inner healing;"–compared to **Mary Baker Eddy** of the "<u>Christian Science</u>" cult;

Agnes Sanford was an early founder of the "Manifest Sons" heresy; taught that "the Great Tribulation is past, we are now in the Millennium and Christians must "through science of the mind" techniques, take dominion over the earth, even removing the effects of the Fall (Adam & Eve)-<u>without the return of Christ</u>."

In her book "The Healing Light," she presents a false "God" who is the "life-force" in everyone and everything; it is a form of energy, like electricity;" "the original force that we call God...we are part of God...He's in nature and He is nature...

I was conscious of oneness with God and therefore with the **snake** that God has made." Her pantheism is very clear; She picked up many of her ideas, such as"God's love was blacked out from man by negative thought-vibrations."

(Jesus) lowered his thought vibrations to the thought vibrations of humanity" to accomplish "the at-one-ment"—which is a Unity term that **Charles Fillmore** called the "reconciliation of man's mind with divine Mind through the superconsciousness of Christ Mind;" **Agnes Sanford** commends the "prayers of Unity and other modern schools of prayer, which "project the power of God" for healing.

On a page in her book, she gives four steps for tapping into this "God-force," the second being "to turn it on...we can simply say, "Whoever you are—whatever you are—come into me now!;"

To support her "Science of Mind," she quotes a scientist:

"A vibration of very, very high intensity and an extremely fine wavelength, with tremendous healing power, caused by spiritual forces through the **mind of man**, is the next thing science expects to discover;" "The love-vibrations and the faith vibrations of God and His saints (she includes dead "saints"—" there is no death," enter through our thought vibrations of life and love.

In the same way, the destructive thought-vibrations of mankind, and of "Satan" (whoever or whatever Satan may be; her metaphysical system requires no personal devil) enter through our thoughts of illness, hate and death; "She then goes on to say that "everything is a matter of thought-vibrations."

"We can be made ill by our negative vibrations, can heal ourselves and others through positive vibrations and can even forgive the sins of others and turn them into Christians in this way."

"Project into the burglar's mind the love of God, by seeing him as a child of God and asking God to bless him." "A new age is being born...when love-power, projected, at the command of ministers and surveyors and children and everyone, is sufficient to change hearts...this is the beginning of a new order...the dawning of a new day!"

"As our prayers, our mental training and our acts of forgiveness fuse into a high consciousness of God's indwelling, we become more and more aware of an inner source of power that can be tapped at will."

Incredibly, **Agnes Sanford** is **defended** by church leaders. Her books sell well in Christian bookstores and at churches such as **John Wimber's** Vineyard fellowships."

"Inner healers" **John and Paula Sandford**, who were associated with **Agnes Sanford** for years, admit that **Agnes** was involved in "Unity," spiritualism, occultism.

John even declared that she had been unsaved and demon possessed at the time she wrote "The Healing Light" and founded the "Schools of Pastoral Care" where he taught with her—and that he led her to Christ and cast the demon out in 1964, yet he credits her-- while unsaved and demon possessed--with healing him of a back injury and leading the church into "the healing of memories."

All the while that **Steve Hill** was bringing "visualization communication" with spirit guides, **Agnes Sanford** took it into the church as part of "inner healing."
This most subtle and dangerous witchcraft practice is more than ever being promoted and defended by church leaders, and "Christian psychologists."

It is being used to contact "God," or "Jesus" in "dialogue with God," or what is known as "two-way prayer." Only a demon posing as "God" or "Christ" appears to those who follow this "relaxation/visualization" formula.
 (Excerpt taken from https://www.thebereancall.org)

--**Jerry Savelle**: WOF preacher, prosperity preacher--

"First Corinthians 2:9 (KJV) says, "But as it is written, Eye hath not seen, nor ear heard, neither have entered into the heart of man, the things which God hath prepared for them that love him." ... "What are the things which God hath prepared? It has to include the necessities of life. You can't live the good life if you are broke. God wants you blessed financially." ("Increased Activity of our Angels" online article 2002).
 "God plainly tells us that if we obey and serve him we shall - not may or might possibly but shall - spend our days in prosperity and our years in pleasures." ("Living In Divine Prosperity", Harrison House 1978);

http://www.sermonindex.net/modules/newbb/ viewtopic.php?topic_id=18960&forum=35

http://www.banner.org.uk/wof/sayings.html

https://www.9marks.org/article/ journalwhy-prosperity-gospel-attractive/

https://www.facebook.com/fpt.wordfaithtbn/posts/ 641201469341164:0

http://truthwatchers.com/ beware-new-prophets/

- **Francis Schaeffer**: When I first became a Christian, I was encouraged to read **Francis Schaeffer's** books. His view on abortion had a significant effect on my pro-life stance. In my mind, he was one of those super Christian celebrities who really "got" the Bible.
He believed that the Bible should influence society and culture. This influenced me to become involved in politics until the last decade or so when I realized that it wasn't my hill to die on.
But, **Schaeffer** was always high on my list of go to authors as a young Christian. Then, today, I learned that **Francis Schaeffer** abused his wife, **Edith**.
 He had a terrific temper and would hit her and throw things against walls. **Francis Schaeffer** allegedly physically abused his wife, **Edith**.

In 2013, Christianity Today published "Remembering Edith Schaeffer, the Evangelical in Pearls and Chanel No. 5."

Of course, **Edith** didn't really let us in on the secrets of the **Schaeffer** family; her son, **Frank**, did that later in his books "Crazy for God and Sex, Mom, and God," telling us of **Francis'** fits of abusive rage and apparent sex addiction, **Edith's** periods of manic activity and her obsession with maintaining the impression of her family's perfection, and his own drug use and sexual activity with the pretty hippie girls who dropped by L'Abri, all of which his parents knew about and carefully cloaked.

Even as I would've been helped in my early adulthood by knowing that she wasn't really that perfect, I had to sympathize with my dad's response to "Crazy for God:" "If for some reason you need to write a tell-all about me, could you please wait until I'm dead?"... **Edith** was from a different time; a time when people didn't air dirty laundry and where maintaining outward appearances was considered an important part of being a good "witness for Jesus."

I will not defend her self-abnegating vision of Christian womanhood (to the point that she seems to have tolerated abuse), nor the fact that she presented a picture of family bliss that was not, according to her children, at all accurate. Their children appeared to take second place to **Francis and Edith's** ministry.

"Christianity Today" published a two part series called "The Dissatisfaction of Francis Schaeffer," Part 1 and Part 2. These may have been the hardest years of marriage for the **Schaeffers,** both of whom were extraordinarily intense, work-centered personalities. **Edith** was by nature proud and competitive, and **Francis** had for a long time struggled with a plant-throwing, pot-smashing temper. Stormy sessions between them were not infrequent. **Francis and Edith Schaeffer** were Calvinist in their perspective.

According to their son, **Frank,** in "Sex, Mom & God" --
Frank indeed grew up in a strange world. Growing up the son of hardline Presbyterian missionaries in a missionary chalet and spiritual-seeker-haven in Switzerland would have to have been a very unique experience (though it must be added that many, many people count their visits and time at L'Abri as seminal moments in their own Christian journeys..."and I do wish I had been old enough to visit as well."
As **Francis** and **Edith** grew more popular, **Frank** was left alone for long periods of time as his parents went on their speaking tours. He witnessed a double-life in his parents as well that scarred him deeply. **Francis** had a terrible temper and would hit and throw objects at **Edith**.
 In 2014, their son **Frank** wrote "My Parents Stayed Married Because my Father Tearfully Apologized for Hitting Mom and then Worked to Curb his Violent Male Dominant (Calvinist-Fed) Temper."

 Eventually **Francis** apologized to **Edith** for hitting her (it took years) and worked on controlling his temper. Apparently this meant giving up on his idea that men were the head of the household, according to his son. "My parents gradually learned to ignore the Biblical teaching about men being the "head of the home" to our benefit".

Sure, his orthodox teachings were fine and he wanted to save the lost but he was a terror at home, raging and throwing things at the wall while smacking **Edith**. Is this a normal response of those who have the power of the Holy Spirit?

Did **Schaeffer's** theology, so admired by today's Calvinists, make a difference in the personal lives of these men?

'I have a theological dilemma, folks, and I need your help in figuring it out." How could **Schaeffer** abuse his wife while functioning under the power of the Holy Spirit? Since **Schaeffer** was a Calvinist, it is only fair that we view the Christian life through his lens to attempt to understand his actions– Calvinists believe that when God, via His Holy Spirit, calls His elect to come to Him, they must respond in the affirmative since he is part of the Godhead. This is "irresistible Grace," the letter "I" in the TULIP.

Irresistible Grace:

When God calls his elect into salvation, they cannot resist. God offers to all people the gospel message. This is called the external call. But to the elect, God extends an internal call and it cannot be resisted. This call is by the Holy Spirit who works in the hearts and minds of the elect to bring them to repentance and regeneration whereby they willingly and freely come to God.

Some of the verses used in support of this teaching are Romans 9:16 where it says that "it is not of him who wills nor of him who runs, but of God who has mercy"; Philippians 2:12-13 where God is said to be the one working salvation in the individual; John 6:28-29 where faith is declared to be the work of God; Acts 13:48 where God appoints people to believe; and John 1:12-13 where being born again is not by man's will, but by God's.

"All that the Father gives Me shall come to Me, and the one who comes to Me I will certainly not cast out," (John 6:37). Now, all Christians are given the Holy Spirit at the time of conversion. This is the same Holy Spirit that calls the elect to God.
 This is irresistible Holy Spirit now dwelling in the lives of the elect.
http://thewartburgwatch.com

- **Robert W. Schambach**: Deceased; Was an incredible con-artist used by CBN to raise money during their telethons. With scare tactics and false teaching, **Shambach** surgically convinces thousands to send their money to finance the heretical TBN;   https://truthprophecy.com
 Mighty preacher in the 40's to the early 90s; appeared on Daystar; promoted the WOF doctrine towards the end of his life. His mentor was **A.A. Allen**, who was a famous evangelist during the 1940s and 1950s.

 (**NOTE: There are a lot of You Tube videos of him to watch. Decide for yourself if he was a "con artist" as the above web link states. Ed.).

- **Robert Schuller**: Deceased; believed in "positive confession" meaning that our   faith will not save; promoted 'New Agers' concept and shamanism–the visualization of "spirit guides;" the occult technique–learned from demons posing as "Masters" of a "Temple of Wisdom" on the "astral plane' was brought into the business world by Napoleon Hill, whose teachings **Schuller** promoted in his "Possibilities" magazine;
believed and taught that "faith that will not save;" http://www.thebereancall.com;

Self Help Teacher, Claims HELL IS THE LOSS OF PRIDE--

Robert Schuller: Deceased; Attributes his concepts to **Norman Vincent Peale** as starting the positive thinking movement. **Peale** a 33rd degree mason denied just about all the core teachings of Christianity.   In fact **Schuller's** teaching on faith is really human potential in disguise, "Faith plus focus plus follow through equals achievement, and many people fail because they just don't have the faith in themselves" (Larry King Live on 1/28/94).
 "And I can feel the self-esteem rising all around me and within me, 'Rivers of living water shall flow from the inmost being of anyone who believes in me' (John 7:38). **Schuller** used to hold seminars for the Unity School of Christianity.

 I'll really feel good about myself" (**Robert Schuller**, "Self-Esteem: The New Reformation," p. 80). http://www.letusreason.org/latrain21.htm

- **John Scotland**: Aligned with **John** & **Carol Arnott**, NAR.
https://ucministries.wordpress.com/category/ john-scotland/

- **Gene Scott**: Deceased; NAR promoter;

https://www.latimes.com/archives/ la-xpm-2005-feb-23-me-scott23-story.html

http://www.youtube.com/ watch?v=BDU7rKleDFY

https://www.jesus-is-savior.com/Wolves/ gene_scott.htm

http://www.godsangryman.com/

(**NOTE: This last link has **Gene Scott** as a great preacher. You decide. Ed.).

- **Burton W. Seavey** (Wrote a book titled, "Christian Mediation: Doorway to the Spirit" (1988);

Twists defenders of the Gospel's words and meanings, but defends **Robert Schuller** and **David Yongghi Cho's** occult "fourth dimension" teachings; he also promotes the idea that God uses "faith", that we are "little gods," (a Word-Faith heretical teaching), the kingdom of God is 'man's spirit—a part of God placed within every infant birthed into this world." Dismisses fears of Eastern mysticism; says that Christianity is itself an "Eastern Mystical religion;" He teaches that unbelievers have access to the same God-powers as Christians—through meditation;

This involves entering the alpha level of altered consciousness, moving from left-into-right-brain, deprogramming the subconscious, and visualization.
His book has been endorsed by Harold N. Englund, C.E, director at **Robert Schuller's** Crystal Cathedral, who commends **Burton Seavey** for "unraveling some of the gross distortions in the work of Mr. Dave Hunt."

(Excerpt taken from https://www.thebereancall.org).

- **Michelle Seidler**: False <u>prophet</u>. Is aligned with **Shawn Bolz**; Websites state that she is a "<u>seer-prophet.</u>" https://www.youtube.com/ watch?v=_y5OYCBWU2E

https://www.eventbrite.com/e/ prophetic-equipping-conference-tickets-85640726719

(**NOTE: Not too much about her, other than her "prophetic" words. Please see Deut. 18: 10-22. Also Isa. 8:19, 20. God does not look favorably on those that say they are a "prophet," but He didn't send them. Ed.).

- **Demos Shakarian**: Large article containing information on **Oral Roberts, John Osteen, Franklin Hall, Jack Coe, Gordon Lindsay, R. W. Culpepper, William Branham**, and **Kenneth Hagin.**

Its founder, **Demos Shakarian**, rallied them to search for the "power of God "available to them for use in their business, to direct and guide them. If our lives are holy and consecrated to God, then we have boldness to come to Him and ask and receive the things He has intended that we should have. "Pentecostal businessmen would learn to invest spiritual meaning in the marketplace and cultivate religious pride in entrepreneurship." https://churchwatchcentral.com/2017/09/02/ further-connection-of-the-new-order-of-the-latter-rain-to-the-fgbmfi/

(**NOTE: Plenty of <u>Latter Rain</u> names are on the above website. Well worth reading how the FGBMFI started and by who. Ed.).

The <u>Prosperity Gospel</u>, or as it is also called "the Health and Wealth" Gospel, the "Word of Faith," "the Faith message," "<u>Positive Confession</u>," or the "<u>Name-It-Claim-It</u>" doctrine: is a false teaching that emerged out of Pentecostalism around 1951 through men like **Oral Roberts, Demos Shakarian**, and Full Gospel Business Men's Fellowship International (FGBMFI).[1]

Many, if not most Pentecostal and Charismatic pastors believe and teach this doctrine today. Although the Assemblies of God has an official "Position Paper" against it, that has hardly helped to curb the <u>heresy</u> from spreading.

The teaching of the <u>Prosperity Doctrine</u>, while falsely misquoting and misapplying Scriptures, is really based in <u>New Thought</u> or <u>New Age</u> thought:—specifically the sort of thinking taught by <u>Christian Science, Unity, "positive thinking," "mind over matter,"</u> and <u>other metaphysical cults</u> (see D. R. McConnell's "A Different Gospel").

[1] Vinson Synan, "In the Latter Days" (Fairfax, VA: Xulon Press, 2001), pp. 85-86. https://wesleygospel.com/2013/04/16/ the-prosperity-gospel-is-evil-john-boruff/

https://www.cbn.com/spirituallife/biblestudyandtheology/ discipleship/shakarian0212.aspx?mobile=false

The term "CHARISMATIC" came into usage in the 1950's when believers in Christ were baptized in the Holy Spirit outside regular Pentecostal churches.

This Pentecostal message was preached by healing evangelists like **William Branham, Oral Roberts, Gordon Lindsay** and **T.L. Osborn**. The movement really took off with the formation in 1951 of the Full Gospel Business Men's Fellowship International under the leadership of **Demos Shakarian**.

By 1965 the message had spread to thousands of Roman Catholics in the United States, and since the leadership of the Roman Catholic Church could not stop it, they embraced it and eventually hi-jacked the entire Charismatic movement.

Kathryn Kuhlman became obsessed with the sight of Roman Catholic priests attending her meetings and just a few years before her death she was invited to Rome and had a personal audience with the Pope.

The same thing happened to the Full Gospel Business Men. Their ranks were swelled by Catholics who then moved up into leadership positions. The teaching of doctrine changed and it was no longer necessary to be born again. People were prayed over, regardless if they were saved or not, just to be baptized in the Holy Spirit and many of them showed manifestations, like speaking in tongues.

As the CHARISMATIC MOVEMENT spread into Canada, Europe, Australia and all other areas of the world, Protestants, Episcopalians and Roman Catholics were mixed into one great "hodge-podge." In the late 1970's the movement had become mixed with the ECUMENICAL MOVEMENT and it was no longer a spiritual movement, but also a political movement set out to change the ORTHODOX CHRISTIAN DOCTRINE.

https://www.eaec.org/newsletters/2000/ NL2000feb.htm

http://www.cnview.com/on_line_resources/ the_charismatic_movement.htm

(**NOTE: This last website link shows the opposite of what **Demos Shakarian's** story means to those who do not believe in God directing Christians. Decide for yourself if the FGBMFI was directed by God or not. Ed.).

- **Charlie Shamp**: On **Steve Shultz'** " Elijah List". " I have heard of **Charlie Shamp**. The Elijah List promotes him quite regularly, which is a dead giveaway in my opinion. There's no way that the modern-day prophetic movement "prophets" will promote anyone who speaks of Torah."
(**NOTE: This comment is from the author of this website. Ed.).
https://www.honorofkings.org/false-prophet-listing/

–**Gwen Shaw**: Deceased "THE MORMON TEACHINGS OF GWEN SHAW;"
"THE GNOSTIC GOSPEL OF THE FALSE REVIVAL" https://watch-unto-prayer.org/eth-s.html

"We were taught that you receive the anointing when you fast and take the ETH (End Times Handmaidens) vows." The vows sound very impressive but require that you lay down your life, will, liberty. This is in fact a gnostic vow that denies the simplicity of the Gospel.

Through the fast you will become more pure and holy, separated unto God and elevated from other Christians. It is seen as an entry into the spiritual Levitical priesthood.'

Again and again the teaching from **Gwen** and others is that "we have to offer up to God our sacrifices" through fasting, praying and lots of other crazy stuff they do that is not Biblical. ETH has a gospel of works that invalidates the blood of Jesus and what he did for us on the cross.

"Although the group is called "End Time Handmaidens and Servants," it is predominantly women. My initial impression of **Gwen** was that she was a strong feminist." " Looking back I now see no difference between many of her teachings and the new age, occult, Wiccan feminist teachings." "These false teachings and beliefs wreck homes and families. Women are encouraged to put the "ministry" and the mission field above husbands and families." "It is seen as a badge of honor for a women to forsake her family to go to the mission field."
" In fact this was **Gwen's** experience as she describes it in her biography."

Rabbi Schneerson (false messiah and cabalistic occult leader of the Lubavitch movement). **Gwen** actually quoted him and lifted him up for his beliefs about women.

Considering that the Cabbala is nothing but satanic witchcraft, it was insulting to have her propagate Schneerson's beliefs as being Biblical. She then went on to compare the Zohar to the Bible by calling it a "Holy Book." This is blasphemy!!

I wrote to **Gwen** and held her accountable for these statements. My feeling is that she was building bridges with the orthodox community because of her house in Jerusalem.

ETH is part of the ecumenical, messianic, new world order. **Gwen's** teachings are based on the "Latter Rain, Manifest Sons of God" movement. **Gwen** is herself a false prophet and a false teacher. Every year they have a convention. Anything goes at these meetings and the wilder more off the wall it is, the better.

"End Time Handmaidens" pride themselves on being "way out there in the spirit realm." You go to the conventions to get more power. This is called "the anointing".

Dreams and Visions are encouraged and expected. Manifestations of psychic powers are called the Holy Spirit gifts in operation. Group mind control is practiced and people are manipulated through typical cultic techniques at the convention.

These include...sleep deprivation, the loss of time, music, dancing and singing for hours before each and every meeting to achieve altered states of consciences, group hypnosis and suggestions, demon deliverance, emotional manipulation, group travail, wailing and weeping.

People are conditioned to accept all the "new things" that God is doing.

The conventions are used to indoctrinate more people into the ETH cult and to raise money. I personally saw the children being neglected for hours at the conventions.

 Instead of leaving the meetings at a decent time and putting the kids to bed, they are left in a room typically until after midnight. This is a dangerous situation that I found quite alarming and abusive.

"It was at convention that I met **Ruth Heflin**. I'm not sure if she is a handmaiden, but she is one of the most popular speakers. Long before she was popular here in the United States, (through the "Brownsville" revival and the gold dust) she has been well know with the ETH for many years."

"**Ruth** is presented as a "Holy Woman of God" who is much more spiritually advanced than the rest of us." "So when **Ruth** started having her "glory gold dust" camp meetings, I went and was prepared to accept anything **Ruth** said."

"At that time I began to see this as a lying sign and wonder." "I saw how it did not line up with the Bible but actually was part of the end time apostasy. It was extremely Roman Catholic and very scary." (I won't go into that now, but if anyone is interested I can certainly elaborate on what I saw).

"**Gwen** had jumped on the fairy gold dust band wagon and was also shamelessly promoting this false glory.   That is when I woke up from a spiritual delusion concerning the ETH and cut all ties with them."

"I wrote to **Gwen** and told her why the gold dust was not a sign from God but a work of Satan. I warned her that if she did not repent of this blasphemy, her "End Time Handmaidens" were really becoming "Babylonian Harlots." January 1999 convention was held in Israel. The guest speakers (false prophet and prophetess) I want to mention were **Israel** and **Effrocine Auterbach** (not sure on the spelling of their last name)."

" This couple was very much promoted in the Messianic ETH family. He is an Israeli and she is Greek. They claim to own Samuel's mountain in Israel. There is so much mystical weirdness, confusion and a lot of crime with this couple. I believe she is a witch and he a Satanist.   I'm pointing out some things about this couple to show how anyone who claims to have a supernatural experience and visions is accepted in ETH."

"Friends of mine went on a tour of Israel with **Effrocine** and **Israel**. It was to be a "Hebrew Roots" experience while learning how to "flow in the spirit" and become a real Messianic (not an American imitation).   **Effrocine** is a control freak."

"This is where her witchcraft really comes out. **Israel** told my friends that if they did not do what **Effrocine** told them to they would be cursed with cancer. In the middle of the night, **Effrocine** and **Israel** stole the group touring van with luggage and personal belongings (I know because my coat was on the van!) and left my friends on their own in a foreign country." "These people had paid money to have the **Auterbachs** give them a tour of Israel.)

 Effrocine and **Israel** have infiltrated the ETH."
 "Myself and at least one other person I know tried to warn the leadership of ETH when it was announced that **Eff.** and **Is.** were to be guest speakers at the convention."
 "Because **Eff.** and **Is.** claim to be Messianic believers, ETH refuses to believe they are not what they appear to be. So many of **Gwen's** teachings are much more new age metaphysical than biblical. Here are a few of her doctrines from her books..."

Finding each other in the spirit. This is really psychic divination:

"ENDUED WITH LIGHT TO REIGN FOREVER" is one of her books on the Manifest Sons of God who are filled with the glory light from heaven and become as gods."
"Able to leap tall buildings at a single bound, faster than a speeding bullet, being translated, etc. She does quite a teaching on "Joel's Army.""

"REDEEMING THE LAND" This is one of her major doctrines that has now become very popular with the apostate crowd. When I first heard her teach this she said, "How can redeemed bodies be raptured out from unredeemed ground that belongs to Satan?"
This teaching opened the door to much of the spiritual warfare practices that are now so common with the apostolic prophetic revival.

"POUR OUT YOUR HEART" (That may not be the exact title of the book but I think it is). This book is all about travail and "birthing in the spirit." Again, a now very common practice and teaching in the apostate revival.
 Gwen was truly a spiritual mother and leader to prepare people to accept these false teachings."

"12 TRIBES" This is really wild. It is Gwen's version of astrology." "She does a Bible study on the tribes and their personalities. To which she adds her own translations, opinions and crazy conclusions to come up with formulas for people to figure out what their "spiritual tribe" is. It is very esoteric."

" Gwen oftentimes tells how she listens to the Holy Spirit and he tells her what to write. I now believe that she is listening to a familiar spirit who calls itself the holy spirit and she channels messages. Here is a quote from her newsletter that I received this evening..."
"I have been busy writing my book on Miriam all week. I have been in the libraries of Heaven, reading and studying and listening to the tales of yesterday so that I can give as accurate a report on Miriam as possible. Angels are always available to help when you need to do research (many of them lived in Egypt at the time of Moses and Miriam) and the Holy Spirit is a good instructor."

"Either Gwen is channeling or she is a liar! Whatever it is, she is selling her books."

(The above testimony was written by a former member of the "End-Time Handmaidens"). April 20, 2000. http://www.angelfire.com/journal2/watch-unto-prayer/eth.html

https://watch.pairsite.com/eth-gwenshaw.html

Excellent article that shows Gwen Shaw's Gnostic beliefs aligned with Helena Petrovna Blavatsky, the founder of Theosophy. Many of Gwen's practices came directly from this occult teachings.

"The membership of ETH (End Time Handmaidens) and Servants" includes:

Suzanne Hinn, the wife of Benny Hinn, who spoke at the 2001 World Convention; and Gwen Shaw occasionally appears on Benny Hinn's TV show, "This is Your Day."

Shaw also collaborates with **C. Peter Wagner,** President of the "United Prayer Track of AD 2000 and Beyond," as a leader in the Spiritual Warfare movement.

She is a member of **Wagner's** "Apostolic Council of Prophetic Elders," which includes **Mike Bickle, Paul Cain** (honorary member), **Stacey Campbell, Wesley Campbell, Chuck Pierce, Rick Ridings, John** and **Paula Sandford, Dutch Sheets, Tommy Tenney, Doris** and **Peter Wagner** and **Cindy Jacobs**, the President of "Generals of Intercession" who quotes **Gwen Shaw** as an authority on "spiritual warfare."

In the Charismatic world, one relatively unknown organization called the "End-Time Handmaidens and Servants" has, in large measure, managed to escape critical evaluation. The founder and president of the "End-Time Handmaidens and Servants," **Gwen Shaw**, is today a major player in the global "Signs and Wonders, Spiritual Warfare" and "Global Transformation" movements.

Each year ETH&S sponsors a World Convention, among its other conventions, whose featured speakers have included:

C. Peter Wagner, Cindy Jacobs, Benny Hinn, Mahesh and **Bonnie Chavda, Randy Clark, John** and **Carol Arnott, Chuck Pierce, Stacey Campbell, George Otis, Jr., Tommy Tenney, Derek Prince** and most recently, **Dutch Sheets**.

Another speaker was **Roberts Liardon**, a homosexual who claims he went to heaven, and alchemical gold-dust eaters, **Ruth Heflin** and **Robert Shattles**, who died of cancer in 2000 and 2001 respectively.

https://watch.pairsite.com/eth-gwenshaw.html

- **Bishop Fulton J Sheen**: Deceased; promoted the theory of the anti-Christ being a Catholic; also promoted the "Sacred Heart," which is pagan in its origin.

- **Dutch Sheets**: NAR; False prophet
http://www.deceptioninthechurch.com/ narfalseprophecies.html

http://www.828ministries.com/articles/
Dutch-Sheets-Displays-New-by-Anthony-Wade-Faith_God_Prophet-170429-510.html

I love supporting local Christian charities and missions. One I like transcribes the Bible into third world, lesser-known languages so people in remote areas can receive the Good News. The man who leads it (let's call him Bob) loves the Lord and he does a great job sending out newsletters letting his supporters know what the organization is doing around the world. I love getting his newsletters, but a recent one caught me by surprise and made me aware of a very real threat to Christianity happening today.

And, it's occurring right under our noses. Maybe this has happened to you: someone says something, or you come across something that doesn't quite sound right. It's odd enough that you do a double-take and ask, "Uh, what?" hoping for some clarity, but there isn't any. That's what happened when I read the latest newsletter. Evidently, Bob watched a video given by a man named **Dutch Sheets**. In the video, **Sheets** was promoting a practice of "releasing God to accomplish His will."

That "once we pray and release Him to have His way and work His will on earth, He is then able to move with power and accomplish His will." That "we have been given the responsibility and authority for what happens on earth."

In other words, if we don't release God through prayer to have His way in a situation, nothing will happen because He is waiting for us to release Him.
  What in the world was Bob trying to say? Why on earth (or anywhere else) would God need me to release Him to do anything? I mean, He's God! He doesn't need me to do a thing for Him. Isn't He all-powerful?

 Now, I'm not the kind of person to just walk away from something so strange.
I needed answers, so I started researching it. I did a quick Google search on **Dutch Sheets** and the results I got were incredible. Each website associated him with what one researcher called the fastest growing counter-Christian cult in the world today.

2 It's called the New Apostolic Reformation movement, or NAR, and it's sort of akin to Jehovah's Witnesses. First of all, the NAR is not an official Christian organization.
 It's a group of people with various religious affiliations who agree with a creed created by a man named **C. Peter Wagner** (1930–2016) back in the 1990s, though he claims it already existed.

Until his retirement, **Mr. Wagner** was the president of "Global Harvest Ministries" (a NAR organization), and he was a professor at Fuller Theological Seminary School of World Missions.
5 According to Cameron Buettel and Jeremiah Johnson at "Grace to You,"

 (**NOTE: John McArthur's** church. Ed.), two women "prophesied" to **Mr. Wagner** that he had been anointed to be an apostle.

Then in 1998, another supposed prophesy was given at some unusual ceremony that **Mr. Wagner** evidently thought was his official ordination to be a modern-day apostle.
 In 2001, **Mr. Wagner** claimed that the Holy Spirit revealed to him we have now entered a second apostolic age and so the NAR was born.

 His apostleship was then confirmed when he used his power to end mad cow disease in Germany, which by the way, still exists. 1

What **Mr. Wagner** fails to recognize is that the New Testament — indeed, God Himself — outlines the criteria to be an apostle.

All three conditions must be met:

A physical eyewitness of the resurrected Christ (Acts 1:22; 1 Corinthians 9:1; 15:7–8); Personally appointed by the Lord (Mark 3:14; Luke 6:13; Acts 1:2; 10:41; Galatians 1:1); Able to authenticate your apostleship with miraculous signs (Matthew 10:1; Acts 2:43; 5:12; 2 Corinthians 12:12; Hebrews 2:3, 4).

Now, unless **Mr. Wagner** has somehow traveled through time, I'm pretty sure he wasn't present the day they nailed our Savior to the cross nor anywhere nearby after His resurrection. And, somehow his name isn't mentioned as being among those in the upper room at Jesus' first post-resurrection appearance. By not meeting even the first requirement we know he is what the Bible calls a false teacher. His false claim of curing mad cow disease also confirms it. He's not an apostle.

 https://medium.com/@steppesoffaith/
the-fastest-growing-threat-to-christian-churches-you-never-heard-of-553ad821ea46

(**NOTE: There is a lot more to this article than what I have here. Please go to this web link listed above to continue reading. Ed.).

- **Dean Sherman:** Deceased; Dominionist preacher; NAR. Author of several books published by YWAM (Youth With A Mission), a major publisher of "Christian" books, but with a deceptive twist. http://www.letusreason.org/ Curren29.htm

(**NOTE: Several articles about YWAM on this web link, including the brief statement below. Ed.).

 YWAM: "The Facts About Their Headlong Dive Into Apostasy" by Sandy Simpson, 12/7/02. YWAM has been slipping into apostasy for years. I and many others have tried to help them back to orthodoxy, written letters to their leaders, all without success. It has been made plain to us and others that they have completely bought into every aspect of the New Apostolic Reformation and are now very visible and vocal proponents of the
C. Peter Wagner "gospel".

 http://www.deceptioninthechurch.com/ youthwithamission.html

https://www.bibleguidance.co.za/Engarticles/Sherman.htm

http://www.truegospel.co/articles/english/false-teaching/
142-sherman-also-teaches-dominionism

https://psuedocults.blogspot.com/2007/12/ dean-shermans-battle-with-irrational.html

- **Priscilla Shirer**: **Justin Peters** wrote an excellent review on **Shirer's** movie, "War Room," which basically sums up these false teachings as highly emotional and seductive to fallen human nature. **Priscilla Shirer** participated in a DVD on the contemplative prayer heresy called "Be Still."

She addresses her critics on her web page and though at first glance it may sound like she supports a Biblical view of prayer, looking deeper into what she is saying, it becomes clear that she doesn't understand what Biblical prayer and meditation are.

In her FAQ she says, "By participating in the "Be Still " project, we by no means meant to convey our agreement with the theological viewpoints and positions of other participants yet we did believe (and still do) in the over-arching theme of the resource and that is why I agreed to do it."

This is a contradictory statement. The theological viewpoints and positions of the participants are the over-arching theme of the DVD, and she says she supports it.
https://reformationcharlotte.org/2019/03/26/ false-teachers-evangelical-churches/

https://michellelesley.com/2019/09/27/
sheila-walsh/going-beyond-scripture-why-its-time-to-say-good-bye-to-priscilla-shirer-and-going-beyond-ministries/

(**NOTE: Although the web link above has the name "Sheila Walsh" in it, this particular link has a few dozen of false women authors, speakers and teachers. Ed.).

https://michellelesley.com/2015/09/18/

She is one of the many darlings of the Southern Baptist Convention, and a regular speaker on the "LifeWay" Women's speaking circuit. **Shirer**, daughter of Pelagian heretic, **Tony Evans**, is an advocate of mystical forms of prayer and contemplation that were born out of the Emergent movement.

- **Steve Shultz**: This is a sampling of false prophecies by many false prophets that have been distributed by " Elijah List." I have been collecting " Elijah List" newsletters for years. The following are but a tiny fraction of the false prophecies "Elijah List" has sent out. Prophecy, that is predictive, is to be judged not only on whether or not the prophecy came true, but on how it depicts the character and testimony of God, and whether or not it teaches what the Bible teaches.

If a Third Wave prophet happens to, on the very off chance, get a prediction right, his prophecy must still be judged as to whether or not it is consistent with the law and the testimony (Is. 8:20). If it is not, it is a lying prophecy, not from the Lord, but from either the delusions of his or her own mind (Jer. 14:14) or from evil (Jer. 23:10) which has it's origin from the evil one (Jas. 3:15, 1 Jn. 3:8).

Steve Shultz, head of "The Elijah List," states a very unbiblical premise for the prophecies he sends out to his mailing list of 100,000 plus.

"When we post any word at all on "The Elijah List" website-- ANY word some think it's from God and some think it's NOT from God."

"So, that's the way it's supposed to work. Over time, you will decide literally for yourself which words you feel are trustworthy for YOU and/or which prophets you feel have the least or best credibility."

(**Steve Shultz**: "DEBUGGING THE PROPHETIC--Questions and Answers with **Steve Shultz**," The "Elijah List," 12/4/07).

First of all, I want you to notice who the prophets listed below have claimed is speaking. They ALWAYS claim to be speaking what they heard from God. If the Lord has not spoken, as they claim, then why would there be a question as to their "trustworthiness," and why would "Elijah List" be sending these lying messages out?

The fact is that **Shultz**, the "Elijah List " and those who read it believe that ALL those who post prophecies are true prophets/prophetesses REGARDLESS of their telling the truth or spreading lies.
This idea that a prophet can be wrong when they are claiming to have heard from the Lord and still be considered a prophet of God is part of the theology of the " New Apostolic Reformation" or " Third Wave."

The alleged messages from God to these "ElijahList" prophets are often colored in blue to delineate them from the black color used for regular information.

This, I believe, is intended to be like the red letter text in some Bibles. It looks to me like this practice shows that they are putting prophecies on the same level as the written Word.
Another practice that is often repeated is to quote from the Old Testament, in particular from Israel taking the land of Canaan, and allegorically apply it to the Gentile Church. Promises and commands for Israel are teleported to modern times and turned into all kinds of mandates for the Church. This is what Gary Gilley of "Think On These Things" had called "fairy tale hermeneutics."

Most of the emails from "Elijah List" are full of the misapplication of Old Testament Scripture. I don't have time to detail all these instances but wanted to mention this aspect of the false prophecies in order to help the reader to understand that there are many dimensions to the false prophecies and false teachings I am detailing that are not fully covered by this article.
http://www.deceptioninthechurch.com/ elijahlist.htm

https://churchwatchcentral.com/2017/01/29/
rosebrough-exposes-the-elijah-lists-steve-shultz-as-a-false-prophet/

- **Edgardo Silvoso**: Is also involved behind the scenes; he wrote, "Taking our Cities for Christ." He believes that unity is essential for the world to believe.
Didn't the early church have unity? Was the world won to Christ then? Well that was then and this is now. We hear that God has revealed "new ways and methods" to achieve the results, so they say. **Silvoso** attributes the accelerated multiplication of churches within a radius of 100 miles of the city of Rosario because a prayer team broke the power of the spirit of Merigildo in 1985. **Silvoso** is one that also endorses the "Toronto Blessing/Holy laughter," drunkenness in the spirit.

http://www.talk2action.org/story/2010/10/29/1521/6485/
Front_Page/Quotes_From_Ed_Silvoso_and_Other_NAR_Apostles_About_Transformation

Ed Silvoso had developed what he calls a Biblical prototype to reach entire cities for Christ using "prayer evangelism" as the main tool. It has been implemented in 16 cities on three continents since 1994. With this background we know what this video is all about and where it is going. In an interview for 'Jesus Life' magazine **Ed Silvoso** was asked about revival and evangelism in Argentina: http://www.jesus.org.uk/ es.html

Cindy Jacobs has been involved in the spiritual warfare movement for a number of years, and was involved in the Argentinian revival with **Ed Silvoso** (who promoted spiritual mapping) that was a predecessor to the "Holy Laughter" movement by
Rodney Howard-Browne.
This subsequently became the "Toronto Blessing," transferred over to Pensacola and is now the "Brownsville revival." **Ed Silvoso** says, "Well, we find the "Toronto blessing' in every city we go to. I believe that it is a blessing indeed. ... the 'Toronto blessing" has to be kicked out of the church - kicked out of the church into the world!

If in each neighbourhood prayer house, there is a manifestation of Jesus, which I believe in its purest form that's what the "Toronto blessing " is, then the entire neighbourhood will flock to that house."   He should have stopped speaking at "kicked out of the church."
A manifestation of Jesus certainly needs to be defined considering what it means among today's revivals. Let me put it in another way: Is the "Toronto Blessing" a manifestation of Jesus in its purest form? Would you like to see everyone in your neighborhood acting like they do at "Toronto," completely out of control falling down and acting like animals?

- **Brian Simmons**: NAR teacher; originally from Long Island, NY. Founder of Stairway Ministries in Wichita, Kansas; **Simmons** is presently producing a new translation of the entire Bible aimed specifically at an NAR readership.   It has the potential to become the translation of choice for people participating in the NAR movement.

(**NOTE: This translation is already on the market. It is called "The Passion Bible").
http://www.spiritoferror.org/2013/07/

- **Chuck Smith**: Deceased; founder of Calvary Chapels; he never renounced his association (with **Kathryn Kuhlman**) and that of **Lonnie Frisbee**; the deception lives on. The false spirit of ecumenism and giving Catholicism a pass. https://www.discerningtheworld.com

- **Duncan & Kate Smith**: CBN.com (The Christian Broadcasting Network),
Are the Executive Directors of CTF Ministries. "Catch The Fire Ministries."

They joined the senior team at TACF in 2000 as Associate Pastors after careers in the UK. In their roles with CTF, **Duncan** and **Kate** travel internationally, taking revival and the love of the Father all over the globe, preaching the good news of Jesus Christ and ministering in the power of the Spirit.
They love to teach people how to do miracles, signs and wonders and have seen many blind, deaf and mute and those with serious illnesses healed by Jesus wherever they go.

Duncan was born to missionary parents spending his first 18 years in Nigeria, and consequently has a passionate heart for ministry in developing nations throughout the world. After 8 years in Toronto, **Duncan and Kate** have relocated to Raleigh, North Carolina. They are dedicating their time to strengthening and developing the US team and the national "Soaking Prayer Network.."
They are also leading the first "Catch the Fire" church, which is a part of a new church planting initiative that aims to raise up radical revival leaders and plant churches all around the world!

Duncan and Kate's passion is to impact leaders and pastors around the world with the supernatural reality of the Kingdom of God. They live in Raleigh with their three beautiful daughters Jessica, Abigail and Nathania. In 1994, the power of God fell on a little church at the end of a runway in Toronto.   "From Here To The Nations" tells the remarkable story of what would come to be called The "Toronto Blessing," and the incredible impact it has had on the church over the last 20 years.

Step inside the doors of "Catch The Fire," and read the full story from a close observer and participant. Let thankfulness arise as you hear the amazing stories of the Father's love, and let your spirit soar as you hear the prophecies for the next tsunami wave of revival!
 https://www.amazon.in/ Consumed-Love-Duncan-Smith/dp/1894310381

- **Pat Marvenko-Smith**:   www.revelationillustrated.com

(**NOTE: **Ms. Smith** is NOT a false preacher, prophet or teacher. She is an artist whose artwork depicts various Bible scenes and has them for sale. Beautiful illustrations that are worth looking at. Ed.).

- **Joseph Smith**: Founder of Jesus Christ of Latter Day Saints a.k.a. Mormons; taught that all of us are "gods" and an extensive amount of heretical doctrines; was a Freemason in 1842. (**NOTE: A simple search on the Internet can yield a few articles regarding the LDS. Ed.).

- **Torben Sondergaard**: Believes he has power to heal; speaks about the "electricity"radiating through him when he prays for people; has captivated   thousands of people with his false and dangerous "healings;" dangerous because it is a demonic spirit working through him; "trains" and teaches his followers to do the same.

"Does The Last Reformation Get Back to the Book of Acts? " by Elliot Nesch, 6/17/17.

Torben Sondergaard says, "It's time to get back to what we read in the Book of Acts." However, some of the Last Reformation movement's emphasized interpretations of baptism, speaking in tongues, signs and wonders, and casting out devils are at variance with the Book of Acts, rather than returning to the Book of Acts.

 Even more important than what they choose to promote within the movement is what The Last Reformation fails to mention or emphasize.   http://op.50megs.com/ditc/fprophets.html

–**David Spangler**: "The New Age is here now and the Christ is functioning within the inner realms of the earth, both in his ascended state from the depths of his past ministry and in his greater state of Aquarian Revelation."

"Lucifer works within each of us to bring us to wholeness, and as we move into a NEW AGE . . . each of us in some way is brought to that point which I term the LUCIFERIC INITIATION, the particular doorway through which the individual MUST..."   http://www.zedekiahlist.com/cgi-bin/results.pl?&menuid=V&itemid=F

--**Charles Stanley**: Was a fiery Pentecostal preacher–left to become a Baptist   preacher; "...psychologizer **Charles Stanley**; neo-evangelical theologian **John Sproule**; and **E. Brandt Gustavson**, then president of the National Religious Broadcasters (NRB).
 [**Kay Arthur** has also spoken at the "Billy Graham Training Center" in Asheville, North Carolina ("The Cove") every year since at least 1994.
 In 1/95, she also did a so-called Christian cruise with former SBC presidents and psychologizers **Charles Stanley, Jerry Vines, and Adrian Rogers.**]
 While this article is written about **Kay Arthur**, it is placed here to show her connection to **Charles Stanley** and other false teachers.
http://jbeard.users.rapidnet.com/bdm/exposes/arthur/general.htm

--**Andy Stanley**:   Followed in his father's footsteps: "North Point Community Church" Senior Pastor **Andy Stanley** has stated that Christians need to "unhitch" the Old Testament from their faith at "Forgotten Word Ministries," 5/12/18.
In the final part of a recent sermon series, **Stanley** explained that while he believes that the Old Testament is "divinely inspired," it should not be "the go-to source regarding any behavior in the church."

To justify this, **Stanley** preached last month about Acts 15, which described how the early church decided that Gentile converts did not need to strictly observe Jewish law to become Christians. "[First century] Church leaders unhitched the church from the worldview, value system, and regulations of the Jewish scriptures," said **Stanley**.

(ACTS Note: The apostles preached the Gospel using the Old Testament and the New Testament is a commentary on the Old. Though in the New Covenant Christians are freed from trying to be saved by the Law, nonetheless the law of Christ, which is love, is accomplished by the Holy Spirit writing the Law on our hearts. We then fulfill the law by being born again and loving the Lord and our neighbor as ourselves.)

Days before giving the third "Aftermath" sermon, **Stanley** preached at the "Orange Conference " held in Atlanta, Georgia, using Acts 15, as well as John 17, to argue that church unity was more important than "theological correctness."

(ACT Note: **Stanley** has obviously been reading the chorus of false teachers who value "experience" over "doctrine". But if your doctrine is not right, your experience won't be either.)
http://op.50megs.com/ditc/fprophets.html

It also mentions **Lou Giglio**, who is listed in this book with **Bill Hybels**.
It was, of course, inevitable that the Emergent Church would begin to have babies that were even more unbiblical than itself.

(**NOTE: This is another story that most people are not familiar with. The website may or may not be available, since several of the websites regarding **Andy Stanley** have been deleted, however there are others listed below to read. Ed.).

Andy Stanley is one of those spiritual offspring of a departure from Biblical faith and adoption by experiential religious deception.
 In 2016, he told a group of pastors at the Southern Baptist Convention that they needed to get the spotlight off the Bible. (August 2016 "Onward" conference).
Now his spiritual "children" are following suit.

https://www.lighthousetrailsresearch.com/ blog/?p=28876

https://www1.cbn.com/cbnnews/us/2018/september/
megachurch-pastor-in-hot-water-again-christians-are-not-required-to-obey-any-of-the-command
ments-from-the-ot

http://www.deliveredbygrace.com/ the-dangerous-false-teaching-of-andy-stanley/

http://www.piratechristian.com/messedupchurch/2016/2/
true-stories-from-the-messed-up-church-andy-stanleys-north-point-church

https://bereanresearch.org/ crisis-andy-stanleys-north-point-church/

https://churchwatchcentral.com/2016/02/13/
sacred-stanley-resigning-from-north-point-community-church/

- **Ruth Carter Stapleton**: Deceased; The smiling, carefully coiffed former beauty queen of a hundred newspaper photos is weak fiction next to the real thing: **Ruth Stapleton** is tough, impatient, curt with her staff, and generally wants things done her way. **Ruth Stapleton** is simply too busy to be nice.

Any interference with the rules that make it all work – her ministry, family, and followers, her corporation, her stiff schedule of speaking engagements – is just too much to bear. The latest demand on **Ruth Staple-ton's** energy is posed by Holovita ("whole life"), the elaborate religious retreat she is setting up on a 30-acre former working ranch just south of Denton.

The grand opening will come some time this summer, and with it the prospect of regular weekend retreats.   But for now, her volunteer staff of twenty or so, people from Denton, Bartonville, Argyle, Dallas and Fort Worth, are scurrying to lay out tomato plants, paint the kitchen, stock the library shelves, remodel the guest house.

 Ruth Stapleton has just arrived from Houston, and she likes what she sees.

"The whole thing is going to be an expression of my philosophy. You can't miss the message. See, everything is getting back to basics, to cotton and natural wood. Simplicity. People won't have to drive their cars here; they can walk." "And all the houses will be built for energy conservation."

She is animated as she talks, stroking the slipcover on the couch, gesturing toward the dark plank floors. Except for the small library, with its shelves of brightly colored inspirational texts, religious symbolism is oddly absent:

The sprouts growing in glass dishes on the kitchen counter say as much about **Stapleton's** hopes for Holovita as the single, modest cross in the living room.

"Too many people have a tendency to go off the deep end in religion and neglect all the other facets of life. They lose their sense of balance." "Well, the name of my programs will be 'A Design for Living.' I will probably be here almost every weekend. I'll do teaching myself about twice a month, and be here as a resource person the other times. I'll have people from all the different fields come in."

"I have one woman, her field is sexual repression. And then I have a doctor, with a drug center. And a man who is very much into proper healthy diet – not a fanatical diet, but eating the right foods." "Everyone can come – doctors, lawyers, journalists, housewives, people who have heard her speak and want to know more."
"They'll hear live evening concerts out on the lawn, eat meals prepared from Holovita's own garden, smell the flowers from its small greenhouse, just outside her own bedroom window"... Here, she implies, one can live life as it ought properly to be lived.

One bit of Holovita lore has it that **Ruth Stapleton** arrived at the decision to move the center of her ministry to Dallas after a long session of soul-searching, seated on the gnarled, low-lying trunk of "her tree," a natural landmark on the property. That may well be true, but when she discusses the move, soul-searching doesn't even come up.

She chose Dallas for some of the same reasons that many companies relocate here. Dallas is just so convenient. "The airport means everything to me. I live in airports. See, I have so many people flying from east to west. It's just so convenient to put into Dallas." " You see, I wasn't really thinking in terms of Texas as much as access.
But I wanted country." "I wanted water, trees and all. Now I think my work will probably center on Texas and the surrounding states – New Mexico, Arkansas, Oklahoma, Louisiana."

Later, a member of her staff says that Holovita's physical and spiritual refreshments will eventually include a "complete health and exercise center," with tennis, handball and racquetball courts, weight room, and sauna. The guests' fee for a weekend at this center of the Christian good life has not yet been established, but it will probably be substantial. Holovita is the latest and most elaborate fruit of **Ruth Stapleton's** personal ministry, which is called "Inner Healing."

A sort of Christian psychotherapy, one part each Full Gospel fundamentalism and Freudian psychology, "Inner Healing" is a controversial and original religious philosophy, and very much her own creation.

It has won her an impressive number of followers among charismatic Christians of all denominations over the past 20 years or so, and more recently, prominence in the secular world as well.
 If Full Gospel is the fastest growing sector of the Christian world, as some say, it is in part because of the excitement caused by **Ruth Carter Stapleton**.
In the early seventies, **Stapleton** established a corporate home for "Inner Healing – Behold, Inc.," a non-denominational, non-profit "healing corporation" in Fayetteville, North Carolina, where her family lives. "Behold " initially did little but mail out a free quarterly newsletter, "Behold and Be Whole," to anyone who requested it.

 Meanwhile, however, **Stapleton** was establishing herself on the evangelical lecture circuit, where religious celebrities are made. Her talks continue to be the backbone of her reputation: In March, she spoke in Texarkana, Pennsylvania, the Marin County Civic Center and Houston; over the next three months, her agent in Los Angeles has booked her for the New York Giants football stadium, a church in Caracas, Venezuela, and a tour of Israel.

Then there are her books: "The Gift of Inner Healing " and "The Experience of Inner Healing," both published by Word Inc. of Waco, TX.
According to Word's Russell Odell, "The Gift of Inner Healing " has sold just under a half million copies in 27 months; "The Experience of Inner Healing," about 70,000 copies in 10 months. "Neither of her books has been listed in the Publisher's Weekly or New York Times bestseller lists, even though they have outsold most that are listed," snorts Odell. "Those lists ignore the evangelical world, even though the Gallup Poll says that about 40 million people out there are evangelicals."

Stapleton has hit them, though; she cracked the National Religious Bestseller List in 1976 with "The Gift of Inner Healing." Additionally, **Stapleton** offers a small line of cassettes featuring an introduction to "Inner Healing," and her staff suggests that a line of video cassettes, for national distribution, is a possibility. **Ruth Stapleton**, it seems, is a bona fide religious celebrity, of the kind only fundamentalist Christianity can produce, sustain – and tolerate.
https://www.dmagazine.com/publications/d-magazine/1978/may/ the-new-jerusalem/

(**NOTE: I have included **Ruth Carter Stapleton**–the sister of former president Jimmy Carter–to show that in spite of all her "wonderful work," there is still that deception lying just below the surface. Ed.).

- **Robert Stearns**: Is an NAR-postle. https://forum.culteducation.com/
read.php?12,93025,98796

(**NOTE: The above is a forum of various commenters who have recognized the dangers of being involved with this organization If you read it, you will see just how devastating and

337

controlling this organization is, and the links below also attest to the dangers of being involved. Ed.).

https://www.scribd.com/doc/3894962/ Robert-Stearns-and-Eagles-Wings-Exposed

https://www.narwatchisrael.info/blog/ category/robert-stearns

https://www.charismanews.com/us/ 45585-jack-hayford-hands-israel-christian-nexus-baton-to-robert-stearns

https://thegoodnewsnewyork.com/ robert-stearns-flight-of-faith-mounting-up-and-soaring-with-eagles-wings-ministries-that-is/

https://pulpitandpen.org/2018

- **Don Stewart**: Says God touched him even before he was born. It was 1939, Prescott (Arizona). A 41-year-old pregnant woman was rushed from a country hovel to the county hospital in fierce labor pain. With the baby in breech, doctors and nurses were convinced the mother would die. Then a stranger walked into the room holding a prayer cloth. "Witnesses going down the hall said the room lit up when the man came in," **Stewart** says.
"The man . . . put the prayer cloth on my mother and said, 'You shall live and not die, and the child you shall have will be a chosen vessel.' "
Stewart presides today over a multimillion-dollar Phoenix ministry that reaches across the globe, although many Arizonans have never heard of him. The 69-year-old televangelist conducts energetic revivals across the country - he calls them "crusades" - that often feature rapid-fire faith-healing episodes.

Stewart oversees 85 churches in the Philippines, preaches to viewers through his "Power and Mercy" television show and conducts a direct-mail campaign that floods followers with requests to donate money.
Stewart also has built his ministry on charitable work and delivering aid to the world's poor and sick. But he has been dogged by controversy. Two decades ago, he was accused by another church of committing arson for an insurance payoff. A decade before that, church officials in his own ministry accused him of embezzlement.

And in 1997 the IRS accused **Stewart** of using his church for personal benefit and revoked the ministry's tax-exempt status.
 But **Stewart** has never been charged with a crime, and he dismisses the accusations as unproven, motivated by unscrupulous critics and disgruntled employees.
Stewart is not as flamboyantly recognizable as some televangelists. He does not have the extravagance of **Benny Hinn**, the audience of **Robert Tilton** or the mega-church of **Robert Schuller**.

 His ministry, the "Don Stewart Association," operates out of a nondescript warehouse in an industrial park near Interstate 17.

Stewart's calling also has brought him wealth. He lives in a $2.5 million Paradise Valley home owned by his church, and the church has paid his wife and his sons hundreds of thousands of dollars over the years. The church's charity also bought a Hummer, records show; it's unclear whether that was the same yellow Hummer driven by his wife, Brenda. **Stewart** calls this God's reward. It echoes the message he imparts to his followers: that God will reward the faithful with prosperity.

"I see the Bible through the lens of a young kid who didn't have a chance in life. No money, tattered and broken and heartbroken," **Stewart** says. "God says come and follow me and I will take care of all your needs. Not only will I do that, but I will give you the desires of your heart." **Stewart** did his growing up dirt poor in Clarkdale and Jerome (Arizona). His mother was a devout Christian, his father a bigamist who abandoned **Stewart's** mother and five siblings before he was born, **Stewart** says.

His father later returned to the family, repentant and religious. "He came back, and the dad I knew was a very distant man, a hard worker," **Stewart** says. "But he never told me he loved me or anything like that."
At 13, **Stewart** says he developed a bone disease. Four operations later, hips pinned, he could not walk without crutches. "I was in . . . a little Assembly of God church in Cottonwood," **Stewart** says. "Evangelists prayed for me. I threw my crutches away and ran around that building. I fell at the altar."

He describes the experience as an anointing, and like Saul on the road to Damascus, he heard God's voice. "How do I know it was God? Was it audible? Was it in my heart?"
"I can't tell you, but it was real to me. He said, 'Take my healing powers to the nations of the world.' "
Stewart's critics describe him as a huckster with a Bible. They say he takes his cues for coaxing money and emotions out of people from an old school of televangelists and Pentecostal preachers. "During his services, **Stewart** sings off key to people just before they are 'slain in the spirit' by his touch," Pastor G. Richard Fisher wrote in a 2002 article on **Stewart** in "New Quarterly " magazine.

"He warbles and croons songs (partially Scripture and partially positive affirmations) that sound like he is just making them up as they go along."
Fisher wrote that some ministries are "not only concerned with **Stewart's** lavish lifestyle . . . money-raising schemes, IRS problems . . . and overblown hype regarding his power," but also that "his published statements are replete with new-age buzz words."

Fisher is a senior researcher for "Personal Freedom Outreach," a non-denominational Christian watchdog group in Missouri that seeks to expose what it describes as false biblical teachings. The miracle engine of **Stewart's** empire is a green handkerchief called a "prosperity prayer cloth." **Stewart** says it's a touch point for God's blessing, not unlike the one the stranger carried into his mother's hospital room.
Stewart's promise: wealth and health in exchange for financial contributions. "Whatever you make happen for God's work, God will make happen for you," **Stewart** tells followers.

339

Stewart says he graduated 12th in a high-school class of 12. Instead of textbooks, he read the Bible and dialed in radio revivals.

One preacher in particular, a man named **A.A. Allen**, held him rapt with fiery sermons and vivid healings. "I had never heard anybody preach like that." One of the things **Allen** preached was how God wanted them to be <u>prosperous</u>.
"That struck a note of hope in me," **Stewart** says. "I found out that about over 20 percent of the Bible is made up of Scriptures that have something to do with money, gold, silver . . .I went through the Old Testament and I found that God's best friend was a millionaire; his name was Abraham." "He was blessed, he prospered."

The day that **Stewart** stepped into **Allen's** tent was the beginning of a 12-year friendship between the two men. **Asa Alonso Allen** was one of the forerunners of modern televangelism. At his most popular, **Allen** was broadcast on more than 50 daily radio stations and 40 television stations.

He also started a Bible college off Highway 92 south of Sierra Vista and west of Bisbee, a place called "Miracle Valley." **Allen** claimed he could heal the sick, turned sermons into prophecies and had a collection of bottles that he said held the evil spirits exorcized from his followers. **Stewar**t went from pounding tent stakes at **Allen's** revivals to driving a truck to preaching. He finally took over **Allen's** ministry.
Stewart calls **Allen** his spiritual father. And when **Allen** drank himself to death in 1970 at age 59, it was **Stewart** who attempted to clean up evidence of his mentor's alcoholic binge in a San Francisco hotel before the police arrived.

(**NOTE: This claim has been disputed since **A.A. Allen** passed away in 1970;
it has been accepted as truth. We will never know until we see Rev. Allen again in heaven...or not. At the end of my book, I have decided to include **A.A. Allen**. Ed.).

Stewart, who weeps when talking of **Allen**, says he wasn't trying to cover up anything. He says he was protecting one of God's chosen few. "The man changed my life, dear God," **Stewar**t says. "God takes human, frail beings and I don't understand how, but he anoints them. And anybody that will protect the anointed . . . will be blessed."
In the wake of **Allen's** death, **Stewart** was hit with allegations of embezzlement by **Allen's** brother-in-law, of pocketing offerings from the revivals.

Stewart denies embezzling money, saying the accusation was part of a power struggle that ended when **Allen's** brother-in-law got a restraining order against him that shut down operations for 24 hours. **Stewart** prevailed in court, and the restraining order was lifted. No theft was ever proved. The ministry's board of directors sided with **Stewart**, who renamed the ministry the "Don Stewart Evangelistic Association."
Later it became the "Don Stewart Association." At the age of 30, two months after **Allen's** death, **Stewart** says he was in a New York hotel when he had a vision about becoming the first faith healer to preach in the newly built Madison Square Garden.

"Suddenly, something came in my spirit and said, 'You are going to preach there.' "

Stewart says at that moment he "set a vision" to become the first minister of his type to preach in the Garden. And he did, filling the arena with followers.

Flush with success and a bigger audience than ever, **Stewart** moved his operation to Phoenix in the early 1970s.

Miracle Valley fell into disrepair and destruction. **Stewar**t leased the property to the Hispanic Assemblies of God for $1 a year.

But when a suspicious fire burned a key building to the ground in 1982 and **Stewart** opted for a cash insurance settlement rather than to rebuild, church officials accused him of arson. He denied having anything to do with the fire and was never charged. "They (Assemblies of God) felt I torched it so I could collect on the insurance,"

Stewart says, adding that a settlement was reached in which his ministry collected close to $1 million and the Assemblies of God got the property, "no strings attached."

A wane in the faith-healing revival era in the U.S. set the stage for **Stewart's** modern ministry. As the 1980s approached, **Stewart** says he tried to adjust and considered becoming a mainstream preacher and teacher.

"I believe there again God spoke to my spirit and told me to quit trying to adjust yourself to this society; go to a people that want what you have."

Stewart embarked on an international crusade, going to 86 countries and drawing audiences of half a million or more in the Philippines, Central America and South America. He says he initiated feeding programs through the church to address the horrific conditions and scenes of starvation that he witnessed. Charitable work became as much a part of the **Stewart** operation as the crusades.

His ministry found a loyal following among African-American audiences, a point of pride for **Stewart**, who was arrested in 1962 for refusing to segregate a South Carolina revival.

Stewart's crusades continue today. In hotel ballrooms, churches and auditoriums from Los Angeles to New York, he leads revivals that can last more than five hours. Anywhere from a few hundred to several thousand people attend.

A September revival in Secaucus, N.J., was no exception. "He's just wonderful," said Erica Boone of Newark, N.J., adding that **Stewart** inspires her and that the green handkerchief is always close at hand. "When I'm feeling down, I just put it up to my heart and I feel better." Beatrice Dicks of Patterson, N.J., said she has been following **Stewart** for years. "I believe he is a prophet of God, because everything he says to me, it is," she says. "If I had a million dollars, he'd have half of it."

Stewart acknowledges that the largest segment of his audience is made up of low-income individuals. He says he has no feelings of hypocrisy when asking them to contribute money to his ministry. He says giving is part of his faith, part of the lesson Jesus taught. But the suggestion draws a rare flash of ire toward critics. "Why weren't they criticizing me when I had to go around in telephone booths and try to find a quarter?

Why weren't they criticizing me when I'd go to the butcher and say, 'Do you have any dog bones?' Because if you ask for dog bones, they don't charge you," **Stewart** says. "Where were the critics then?"

http://archive.azcentral.com/arizonarepublic/news/articles/
2009/05/04/20090504charities-stewart0427.html#ixzz670srv3eh

http://archive.azcentral.com/arizonarepublic/news/articles/
2009/05/04/20090504charities-stewart0427.html#ixzz670rwX3Kq

http://archive.azcentral.com/arizonarepublic/news/articles/
2009/05/04/20090504charities-stewart0427.html#ixzz670rN45ak

http://archive.azcentral.com/arizonarepublic/news/articles/
2009/05/04/20090504charities-stewart0427.html#ixzz670nsOAqq

http://archive.azcentral.com/arizonarepublic/news/articles/
2009/05/04/20090504charities-stewart0427.html

https://phillyflash.wordpress.com/2007/05/02/ apostle-don-stewart/

https://discernmentministriesinternational.wordpress.com/ category/don-stewart/

- **John Stockwell:** One of the proponents of "G12 "; The G12 vision was started by pastor Cesar Castellanos at the International Charismatic Mission Church in Bogota, Columbia. He states God gave him a vision to build a church based on small groups of 12 that reflected the 12 tribes of Israel and 12 disciples of Jesus in order to better reach people for Christ, but uses heretical teaching.

-**Perry Stone**: His father is or was a Pentecostal preacher, as is **Perry,** as he claims; now he's on **Sid Roth**, etc. Sells "Communion" articles and other items at his bookstore;

"I found this on "Moriel Ministries" site. "I have been asked several times about **Perry Stone**, whether he is biblically 'sound' or not." "So I have decided to start a new thread on this specific subject. "I have to say I've not researched **Perry Stone** much – but I'm sure others here have."
"I do remember I read one of **Perry Stone's** prophecies before on the recommendation of another and was not only troubled by it, but concluded for the sake of my own personal understanding that he and the spirit he prophesied by was 'off'.

"And this was without my knowing about all the merchandising he does, or the 'judaising', or some of the people he hangs with such as the terrible pulpit pimps **Morris Cerullo** and **Paula White**, or his appearing on the even more terrible TBN."
"He has appeared on the **Paula White** Show; Headlined some conferences last year with **Morris Cerullo** (huge sign); Appears on TBN and the INSP network run by **David Cerullo** - **Morris Cerullo's** son (another huge sign as he is currently being investigated here in US for fraud and misuse of donor money);"

"Has issued many predictions (based on Jewish Feast days) which dates have come and gone, He had some thinking the rapture was going to occur on September 29, 2008 (again based on a Jewish Feast day) and then again possibly on September 29, 2009 (or thereabout) which has obviously come and gone."

"And much more than I care to list -although his financials seem to be in order for the most part--I can't seem to trust a man who fellowships and keeps company with the TBN crowd, and although Jesus kept company with the likes of many sinners - it was to teach them and save them - NOT to partake and join in their sinful activities."

"**Perry Stone's** teachings are mingled with some truth but there is a lot of dangerous heresy packaged in there. I also since discovered that **Perry Stone** sells a meal package on his "Voice of Evangelism" ministry website, calls it the Lord's Supper, and claims if you buy it from him and take it daily you'll be healed of any sickness or disease." "This is bad enough in and for itself, but there also seems to be some ideas more akin to Roman Catholicism within his teaching on 'communion' [e.g. of the Roman Catholic Eucharist, and the pagan idea of the actual "real presence" of Christ being manifest in the bread and wine and a mystical connotation that was never ever meant by what is meant to be a symbolic meal." "Breaking bread is also about communion with others, and is not to be done alone as then some of the main symbolism is lost!]"

"Look below how this idea is then ruthlessly pimped by **Paula White** and **Perry Stone**."

"This is despicable"--

Paula White: "I believe that as you take communion that there is protection through that blood. Then the bible declares that the blood not only saves us, not only protects us, but it also provides for us. You said there's a couple that we know very dear that had a financial need."
Perry Stone: "Yes!"
Paula White: "And their father, a great pastor, pastor Scott told them God gave him a revelation."
Perry Stone: "Yes."
Paula White: "To take communion once a day."
Perry Stone: "He said, 'Take it everyday and as you're praying thank God for blessing you financially. Thank Him that that's part of the provision. They needed $50,000 and they got an amazing, remarkable $50,000 miracle, this couple did!"
Paula White... "Call that toll free number! We want you to get the 'Meal That Heals!'"

(**Paula White** and **Perry Stone**, "**Paula White** Show," October 9, 2004).

Source: http://watchmanforjesus.blogspot.com/2010/03/

"I have further information about **Perry Stone**:"

"I listened to him on "God TV " last night. I was intrigued by what he was saying as it started off very well. He was talking on the latter and former rains in Israel. He mentioned a number of things about Israel that seemed accurate enough (as an introduction) but soon his message went weird." "He mentioned the cloud (seen by Elijah) coming over the Mediterranean the size of a man's hand. So far so good!"

343

"He then went off into mumbo jumbo land by talking about the five fingers on the hand and what it represented, that God was stating five principles."

" … Sorry I cannot remember what he said about those five fingers, but they were all to do with prosperity or success teaching. Like all false teachers they use Scriptures corruptively by going off on a tangent, bringing out of the Scriptures things not intended in the text."

"Where is there any indication (in the text)that God was showing Elijah the five laws or principles of success. God was simply telling Elijah that rain was on its way (after a long drought) - pure and simple physical RAIN."

" If God was showing Elijah a principle for success then you can be sure that Elijah would have clearly been told what it was and what he should do. Fact is, God did not say anything about the cloud. Actually, it is not recorded that God said anything at all to Elijah at that time. God had previously simply said "Go and present yourself to Ahab, and I will send rain on the land." "NOTHING ELSE!"

"Okay I accept that there may be a spiritual lesson to be learnt or implication behind what God was doing but "five fingers of success"??? Give me a break! That is surely just abusing the Word of God for financial gain."

http://watchmanforjesus.blogspot.com/2010/03

Perry and **Fred Stone** recall a visit by the ghost of Al Collins by Discern It, 1/17/12.
Perry Stone embraces Necromancy which the Bible forbids.
Why would God forbid it? Men are so easily deceived.
http://op.50megs.com/ditc/fprophets.html

- **Steven Strang**: Publisher of false teachings books; is the editor of "Charisma" magazine; promotes a false preacher's "ministry:" "Destiny Image" by the now deceased Don Nori; the publisher publishes books by such heretics as **James Goll, Bill Johnson, T.D. Jakes, Cindy Trimm, Myles Munroe, Sid Roth**, etc.
His publishing business is also known as "Strang Communications."

-**John Stott**: Deceased; Preached Lordship salvation, Reformed theology, among other heresies. http://www.christiandoctrine.com/ christian-doctrine/heresy-and-error/ 1280-john-stott-heretic

https://relevantmagazine.com/god/ 6-heretics-should-be-banned-evangelicalism/

http://www.teachingtheword.org/ apps/articles/web/articleid/75808/columnid/ 5449/default.asp

https://www.thegospelcoalition.org/blogs/evangelical-history/ 50-years-ago-today-the-split-between-john-stott-and-martyn-lloyd-jones/

- **Jimmy Swaggart**: Apparently he has come up with his own interpretation of the Scriptures. Unfortunately they are heretical. The last link listed should help you make your decision as to whether **Jimmy** is an honest Christian or not.

(**NOTE: It is up to you to decide what to believe or not, but keep in mind that the reporter(s) have nothing to gain by lying–except a libel charge against them. Ed).

http://www.libertyadvocate.com/ Swaggart's%20Perverted%20Gospel.htm

http://www.christiananswerman.com/ the-dangers-of-the-swaggart-bible/

https://www.theadvocate.com/baton_rouge/news/ article_23722ff9-9ab0-5d26-bd2f-ad7a27043a64.html

https://www.mikesiegel.com/news/ jimmy-swaggart-devil-not-angel/

- **Leonard Sweet:** False teacher\preacher; teaches the "Mandurah gods" of the New World Order;   **Sweet** calls for a "New Light movement of 'world-making' faith" that will "CREATE THE WORLD THAT IS TO, AND MAY YET BE"

 http://www.leonardsweet.com/ Quantum/quantum-ebook.pdf, p. 12.

He says the New Light was experienced by Mohammed, Moses, and Krishna.
Sweet says that some of the "New Light leaders" that have influenced his thinking are Matthew Fox, M. Scott Peck, Willis Harman, and Ken Wilber.
These are prominent New Agers who hold a pantheistic philosophy and believe in the divinity of man, as we have documented in the book "The New Age Tower of Babel."

 https://www.wayoflife.org/reports/ beware_leonard_sweet.html

(**NOTE: This is a very lengthy article. Please go to the above link for further reading. Ed.).

The Significance of Understanding Quantum Spirituality and **Leonard Sweet's** "More Magnificent Way" of Seeing Christ:

Over the past few decades, a number of New Age sympathizers have had a significant influence in the evangelical church. One of the chief is Methodist author, speaker, and teacher **Leonard Sweet**. **Sweet** openly calls the Father of the New Age Movement—the late Jesuit priest Teilhard de Chardin—"twentieth-century Christianity's major voice." **Sweet** also teaches the foundational New Age doctrine that God is "in" everyone and everything—that God is embedded in all creation.

Brought forward and popularized by **Rick Warren, Leonard Sweet** and his New Age sympathies have not been adequately addressed by today's pastors and church leaders.
A look on **Sweet's** website shows he has partnered with numerous popular figures such as **Brian McLaren, Mark Batterson** (Circle Maker), Erwin McManus, **Mark Driscoll**, Frank Viola, and Karen Swallow Prior (professor at Liberty University).
The following booklet by Warren Smith reveals the "New Age Christianity" that **Leonard Sweet** has helped to bring into the church. https://www.lighthousetrailsresearch.com/blog/ ?tag=leonard-sweet

345

(**NOTE: The booklet spoken about is on the website listed above. Ed.).

http://truthwatchers.com/ leonard-sweet-emergent-churchs-new-age-influence/

T:

- **Charles Templeton**: Deceased; former believer, but turned to being an <u>agnostic</u>; First professed faith in 1936 and became an evangelist that same year. In 1945 he met **Billy Graham** and the two became friends, rooming and ministering together during a 1946 YFC (Youth For Christ) evangelistic tour in Europe.

But by 1948 **Templeton's** life and worldview were beginning to go in a different direction than **Graham's.** Doubts about the Christian faith were solidifying as he planned to enter Princeton Theological Seminary.
Less than a decade later (1957), he would publicly declare that he had become an <u>agnostic</u>. In his 1996 memoir, "Farewell to God: My Reasons for Rejecting the Christian Faith," **Templeton** recounted a conversation with **Graham** in Montreat prior to entering seminary:

All our differences came to a head in a discussion which, better than anything I know, "explains" **Billy Graham** and his phenomenal success as an evangelist.
 In the course of our conversation I said, "But, **Billy**, it's simply not possible any longer to believe, for instance, the Biblical account of creation." "The world was not created over a period of days a few thousand years ago; it has evolved over millions of years. It's not a matter of speculation; it's a demonstrable fact."

"I don't accept that," **Billy** said. "And there are reputable scholars who don't."
"Who are these scholars?' I said. "Men in conservative Christian colleges?"
"Most of them, yes," he said. "But that is not the point. I believe the Genesis account of creation because it's in the Bible." "I've discovered something in my ministry:
"When I take the Bible literally, when I proclaim it as the word of God, my preaching has power. When I stand on the platform and say, 'God says,' or 'The Bible says,' the Holy Spirit uses me. There are results. Wiser men than you or I have been arguing questions like this for centuries."
 "I don't have the time or the intellect to examine all sides of the theological dispute, so I've decided once for all to stop questioning and accept the Bible as God's word."

"But **Billy**," I protested, "You cannot do that. You don't dare stop thinking about the most important question in life. Do it and you begin to die. It's intellectual suicide."
 "I don't know about anybody else," he said, "but I've decided that that's the path for me."
https://www.thegospelcoalition.org/blogs/

"The slippery slide to unbelief"– "A famous evangelist goes from hope to hopelessness"
by Ken Ham and Stacia Byers

But what could be the cause of such a slide into unbelief in a matter so vital and central to the Gospel, as the Resurrection? We suggest that one of the major reasons is that as people have compromised the book of Genesis with the idea of millions of years, and/or evolutionary concepts, increasing numbers have eventually consistently applied the same hermeneutics to the rest of the Bible. This has led to a mythologizing of the Word of God, an undermining of its absolute authority, and eventually often leads to a rejection of the orthodox Christian message.

'Progressive creationists' like **Dr Hugh Ross**, who insist on interpreting Genesis in the light of man's theories like the 'big bang', and the supposed 'proof' of an old earth (billions of years), insist that those who teach a young earth and literal Genesis 1–11 are the ones putting a stumbling block in the way of scientists and others accepting the Gospel message. However, time and time again, we have found that the opposite is true. Compromising Genesis with man's ideas from outside of Scripture opens the door to this 'slippery slide of unbelief'.

It becomes a major stumbling block to people being receptive to God's Word and the Gospel. Unbelievers are generally unimpressed when they see Christians clearly evading the obvious meaning of the beginning of their own book. Following is the sad account of the life of a once prominent and successful evangelist, his slide into unbelief and his rejection of Christianity:

In 1996, the book "Farewell to God " was published for all the world to see the author, **Charles Templeton**, claim: "I oppose the Christian Church because, for all the good it sometimes does, it presumes to speak in the name of God and to propound and advocate beliefs that are outdated, demonstrably untrue, and often, in their various manifestations, deleterious to individuals and to society."

As this story unfolds, you will see the devastating results of compromising man's theories with God's Word, beginning in Genesis.
Who is **Charles Templeton**? Fueled by concern about the spiritual state of post-Depression youth, mass evangelism exploded onto the American scene in the 1940s. Thousands of young servicemen and civilians streamed to arenas to see the programs, which included preaching, music, and various acts.
One of the leaders in this movement was a young man from Canada, **Charles Templeton**, born in 1915. He was generally acknowledged to be the most versatile of the new young evangelists. **Templeton** soon rose to prominence, even surpassing another dynamic young preacher, **Billy Graham**.

In 1946, he was listed among those best used of God by the National Association of Evangelicals. As the pastor of the rapidly growing Avenue Road Church in Toronto, which he had started with only his family and a few friends, **Templeton** also became one of three vice-presidents of the newly-formed Youth For Christ International organization in 1945.
He then nominated his good friend, **Billy Graham**, to be field evangelist for the new ministry. **Templeton, Graham**, and a few others regularly spoke to thousands, winning many to Christ both in America and in Europe. Newspapers and magazines carried reports of his meetings informing readers he was winning 150 converts a night.

In Evansville, Indiana, the total attendance over the two week campaign was 91,000 out of a population of 128,000. Church attendance went up 17%. However, despite his popularity and seeming success as an evangelist, all was not well with **Charles Templeton**.

The more he read, the more he found he was beginning to question the essentials of the Christian faith, because he could no longer believe God's Word beginning with Genesis. With this background of doubt about God's Word welling up inside, and lacking any type of formal education, he decided to pursue a degree in theology at Princeton Theological Seminary.

Resigning from the church he had pastored for several years, **Templeton** began, with special permission, his coursework at Princeton in 1948. Rather than assuage his doubts by providing sound theological answers for the questions he had concerning the authority of the Bible, the historical veracity of Genesis and the deity of Christ, Princeton only served to increase his qualms.

This is not surprising, considering the influences that had infiltrated Princeton through people like **Charles Hodge** and **B.B. Warfield** concerning one's approach to the Scripture in Genesis. For instance, **Hodge,** who accepted the millions of years and rejected literal creation-days, taught:

'It is of course admitted that, taking this account [Genesis] by itself, it would be most natural to understand the word [day] in its ordinary sense; but if that sense brings the Mosaic account into conflict with facts, [millions of years] and another sense avoids such conflict, then it is obligatory on us to adopt that other."

Warfield (1851–1921) went further and, unlike **Hodge,** even accepted Darwinism.

Templeton, like generations of others, was taught at Princeton to reject parts of Genesis in favour of man's beliefs concerning such things as billions of years.

After graduating from Princeton, **Templeton** accepted a position with the **National Council of Churches**, conducting preaching missions across the United States and Canada.

However, he faced increasing health problems, specifically frequent chest pains. He visited a specialist in Pennsylvania who encouraged him, after finding nothing wrong with his heart, to clear up the conflict in his life—namely the doubts he harbored about the authority of the Bible from which he so fervently preached to thousands each night.

This reminds of another who suffered illness because of a great conflict in his life regarding teaching that undermined God's Word.

Charles Darwin, who started out in training to be an Anglican minister, ended up rejecting Christianity the more he believed in evolution. It has been said that inner conflict, because of knowing that evolution would wipe the idea of God from the minds of millions, contributed greatly to Darwin's psychosomatic illness. **Templeton's** struggles affected others, too.

As **Templeton** wrestled with the 'demonstrable fact' of evolution which made it impossible for him to believe "the Biblical account of creation," he sought out his close friend, **Billy Graham**. This caused **Graham** as well to grapple with tough questions that shook the very roots of the faith he professed and preached daily—namely, 'was the Bible completely true?'

With 'science' pulling **Templeton** one way and the Bible seemingly pulling him in an altogether different direction, he resigned from his position with the **National Council of Churches** and took over the Department of Evangelism of the Presbyterian Church USA. At the same time, he hosted a CBS TV series, called "Look Up and Live."

Finally, however, the doubts about everything he stood for became too great and he decided to leave the ministry.

In his autobiography, "Farewell to God," **Charles Templeton** lists his 'reasons for rejecting the Christian faith'. Most of these relate to the origins issue and thus the accuracy of the book of beginnings—Genesis. [this Internet version of the Creation magazine article has hyperlinks added beneath each of **Templeton's** points, which link to answers on this website to his 'reasons."

https://creation.com/the-slippery-slide.

(**NOTE: The rest of this article in the above link has the footnotes and additional information about **Charles Templeton** as noted in the article. Ed.).

- **Tommy Tenney**: United Pentecostal preacher (Oneness).
https://midwestoutreach.org/2016/01/23/
chasing-what-god-examining-the-god-chasers-by-tommy-tenney/

http://www.deceptioninthechurch.com/ ttenney.html

http://www.deceptioninthechurch.com/ veil.html

https://discernmentministriesinternational.wordpress.com /tag/tommy-tenney/

(**NOTE: All the above web links are quite lengthy. Please go to them if you wish to learn about this heretic's teaching. Ed.).

- **Lysa TerKeurst**: Started the "Proverbs 31" organization; wrote 19+ books; has been on **Oprah**, and with **Beth Moore**; Member of **Steve Furtick's** Elevation Church; agrees with prosperity preachers, also has been with **Perry Noble**–who was with **Steve Furtick;** not doctrinally sound, promotes WOF; is a proponent of the listening\contemplative prayer; uses her own experiences and stories to produce her version of Scriptures and spiritual principles; believes in using imagination.

Lysa TerKeurst is a protégée of **Steven Furtick**, the loudmouth prosperity huckster out of Elevation Church in Charlotte, NC. **TerKeurst,** like her spiritual father **Furtick**, is a proponent of the prosperity gospel. In her latest book, "It's Not Supposed to Be This Way," she states, "We will be victorious because Jesus is victorious.

Victorious people were never meant to settle for normal." She also practices and promotes the contemplative prayer heresy, which teaches that you can receive direct, divine revelation from God if you "tune your frequency in" to his voice.

In a PDF she put out titled "How To Hear God's Voice," she writes, "God will never speak to us or tell us to do something that is contrary to His Word." But unless we know Scripture, we will not be able to discern whether what we are hearing is consistent or not with the Word."
https://reformationcharlotte.org/2019/03/26/ false-teachers-evangelical-churches/

https://michellelesley.com/2015/07/31/
leaving-lysa-why-you-shouldnt-be-following-lysa-terkeurst-or-proverbs-31-ministries/

- **R.B. Thieme, Jr**: Deceased; Denies the efficacy of Jesus' physical liquid blood.
https://internetmonk.com/archive/ whatever-happened-to-r-b-thieme

 https://forum.culteducation.com/ read.php?14,13233,71060

https://www.jesusisprecious.org/false_doctrine/ denying_blood/robert_thieme_jr.htm

- **Choo Thomas**: Deceased; https://annointing.wordpress.com/2011/02/05/
the-deceptions-of-the-book-heaven-is-so-real/

choothomasfalseprophet.blogspot.com/2013/10/choo-thomas-false-prophet_26.html

(**NOTE: Quite a heretic, **Ms. Thomas** was.   Read the web links to find out how anti-Biblical her teachings were. Ed.).

- **Harry Thomas**:   http://thewartburgwatch.com/2017/12/11/
well-known-pastor-harry-thomas-arrested-for-sexually-assaulting-4-children/

- **LeRoy Thompson**: Quotes from Leroy Thompson--

"You can't do nothing on $50,000 a month!" (Please excuse the poor grammar, I'm just repeating what they say: Author of article.).
 So according to **LeRoy Thompson**, you need more than $50,000 per month to be able to live properly. And this man calls himself a man of God!!?? It's heartbreaking to hear this kind of evil talk. There are millions of people all over the world who live on about $30 per month and are crying out for food. There are people dying every day because they haven't got enough food.

THERE ARE THOUSANDS OF CHILDREN, DYING EVERY DAY OF STARVATION!! And **LeRoy Thompson** goes and says something like that?! What an abomination that comes out of this mans mouth!   God detests what this man stands for and what he preaches. He loves the man, but HATES what he does, and so do I.

 "The Lord told me, this is the end time message."   "He is coming to look for His church without spot or wrinkle. But one of the biggest wrinkles the church has is being BROKE!" Actually **Mr. Thompson**, the biggest wrinkle the church has is SIN!
Take a look at the following from Ephesians which exposes what these prosperity gospel teachers preach.   (**LeRoy Thompson** said the above quote to **Kenneth Copeland** who agreed with him):

 Ephesians 5:3-7,27 ..."But fornication, and all uncleanness, or covetousness, let it not be once named among you, as becometh saints; Neither filthiness, nor foolish talking, nor jesting, which are not convenient: but rather giving of thanks." "For this ye know, that no whoremonger, nor

unclean person, nor covetous man, who is an idolater, hath any inheritance in the kingdom of Christ and of God."
"Let no man deceive you with vain words: for because of these things cometh the wrath of God upon the children of disobedience."   "Be not ye therefore partakers with them."
"That he might present it to himself a glorious church, not having spot, or wrinkle, or any such thing; but that it should be HOLY and without blemish."

Where does it say that not having money and possessions is the wrinkle? Nowhere! It is SIN that is the spot and wrinkle.
 According to the above verse, these prosperity gospel preachers, if they continue down the same path of coveting money, will NOT enter God's Kingdom, but will be thrown into hell fire.

Proverbs 13:7 ..."There is that maketh himself rich, yet hath nothing: there is that maketh himself poor, yet hath great riches." www.worshipinspiritandtruth.net/ page9.htm
https://imspeakingtruth.wordpress.com/2009/01/15/ money-cometh-heresy/

- **Steve Thompson**: A more orthodox belief held by mainline Charismatics (if there are any left) and Pentecostals is that if you have a prophetic word, it is generally better to state that it is indeed that. Some will disguise a word in prayer or by saying "I sense" in order to avoid having it judged.
Steve Thompson even criticizes this method of stealth-prophecy but acknowledges that the Toronto stream teaches this and he feels it is appropriate for renewal-type (i.e. soaking) meetings. (26)

Morningstar prophetic doctrine, as taught by **Rick Joyner, Bob Jones**, and **Steve Thompson** is based on the concept of "levels of revelation." **Joyner**, in his 1997 book "The Prophetic Ministry" outlines these levels to include Impressions, Visions, Open Visions, Dreams, Trances, Other Prophetic Experiences, the Lord's Audible Voice and Angelic Visitations. "Open Visions" for those who are not up to speed on such things, are when you continue to see the vision, like a movie, even as you go about everyday tasks such as driving. The root of this casual approach to prophecy comes directly from the Morningstar doctrines and practices.

 According to Bill Randles:

"**Bob Jones**, in the tape "Shepherds Rod " told us that God has revealed to him that the rhema (spoken word) would be two-thirds accurate in the days to come. In other words, up to two-thirds of the time the prophets would be "right on."
Why not 100% of the time? If you listen to **Bob Jones**, you would be glad for inaccurate prophets! Why ? God showed **Bob**, supposedly, that if enough power was released to give us 100% accuracy, we would have dead Annanias' and Sapphiras' all over the place.   (How's that for making people actually thankful for inaccurate prophets?).
 Jones says we shouldn't worry about inaccurate prophesies, for God told him that prophets are like guns and prophecies like bullets and inaccurate prophecies are like blanks.   And he also says that God told him, "I'm loading the guns, I'm putting the blanks in!" Incredible.
Jones would have us believe that God is responsible for inaccurate prophecies." (27)

351

Steve Thompson teaches on these levels in his book "You May All Prophesy".
He includes in his lists of ways to receive the following: <u>Impressions, Spiritual sight, Spiritual hearing, Spiritual smell, Spiritual touch, Spiritual taste, Dreams, Glimpses in the Spirit, Gentle Internal Visions, Strong Internal Visions, and Open Visions.</u>
Dreams may include <u>Literal Dreams, Symbolic Dreams</u> and <u>Dreams of Angels</u> or the Lord, which are not visitations but are <u>high-level revelations.</u>

According to this doctrine, <u>Impressions</u> are the "entry-level" revelations. Says **Thompson** "Many people who receive <u>impressions</u> like this may believe they are unstable because their emotions can change abruptly as they move from one situation to another. They do not understand that God is 'pulling the strings on their emotions' in order to speak to them." (28)

The highest levels of revelation, according to **Thompson** and others, are "<u>Trances</u>" and "<u>Caught up in the Spirit</u>". You may be more familiar with the terms "<u>Spirit Travel</u>", "<u>Astral Projection</u>" or "<u>Out of Body Experiences</u>". According to this teaching, being caught up in the Spirit is similar to a trance but the individual is actually transported somewhere.

26 Steve Thompson "You May All Prophesy".
27 Bill Randles, "Weight and Found Wanting" p. 64.
28 Steve Thompson "You May All Prophesy"

https://amos37.com/ dominionism-exposed-heresy/

- **Robert Tilton**: Well documented of opening mailed in prayer requests with   checks–and throwing the request away–and keeps the checks; News channel   caught his volunteers; <u>WOF</u>; False Prophesies, <u>Prosperity</u> Gospel & Deceiving Scam Artist.
https://www.dallasobserver.com/news/ the-robert-tilton-files-7117475

www.forgottenword.org/ tilton.html

- **Phyllis Tickle**: Deceased; One of the "<u>Contemplative prayer</u>" leaders; <u>Prosperity</u>, <u>WOF</u>; "Christian" feminist. https://www.holybibleprophecy.org/2015/09/23/ phyllis-tickle-modern-prophet-or-postmodern-apostate/

https://rootedinchrist.org/2010/11/30/the-great-emergence-or-a-great-deception

Posted on November 28, 2011 by reformednazarene--

Phyllis Tickle: Is one of the well known leaders in the <u>emergent church</u> movement.

She is particularly known for coining or popularizing the phrase "<u>Emergence Christianity</u>." She wrote a book called "The Great Emergence: How Christianity Is Changing And Why," in which her main point is that great changes always occur in the church every 500 years, and that we are in the midst of such a time again.
She compares this time to such other movements as the Protestant Reformation, among other movements in history.

According to **Tickle**, the Emerging church is now playing a pivotal role in yet again redefining the future of Christianity. Her premise is that a new and "more vital" form of Christianity is emerging. If this is true, we are in trouble. In chapter one of the book, she likens this supposed great new change to a rummage sale, where old things are cleaned out and discarded, and replaced with new fresh ideas and approaches to Christianity.

This is exactly what the Emergent church is all about. It's really the same concept that false teacher **Brian McLaren** promotes, that of a "New Kind Of Christianity", and as he states in the title of one of his books, "everything must change." And he really means it, and I'm sure **Phyllis Tickle** also agrees with him.

In his post "Who Is Phyllis Tickle ,?" Pastor Ken Silva of Apprising Ministries points out that she receives high praise for her Emergence concepts from false teacher and Emergent church leader **Doug Pagitt**, who promotes "Christian yoga," denies the concept of original sin, and seems to support a kind of "Christian universalism."
Pastor Silva also brings out another association: "...at her website we read the following endorsement from an apostate Episcopal "Bishop and Primate":

"**Phyllis Tickle** offers a creative and provocative overview of multiple social and cultural changes in our era, their relation to previous major paradigm shifts, and their particular impact on North American Christianity. This is an immensely important contribution to the current conversation about new and Emerging forms of Christianity in a post-modern environment—and a delight to read!"

—The Most Rev. Katharine Jefferts Schori,
Presiding Bishop and Primate, The Episcopal Church

Bishop Schori is clearly an apostate. She has stated in a message to the Episcopal General Conference that individual salvation is the greatest heresy in the church today, and that there is only a collective salvation.

(**Tickle**) is currently a Senior Fellow of Cathedral College of the Washington National Cathedral... A lay Eucharistic minister and lector in the Episcopal Church.

At the WNC website: "Washington National Cathedral is a church for national purposes called to embody God's love and to welcome people of all faiths and perspectives. A unique blend of the spiritual and the civic, this Episcopal Cathedral is a voice for generous-spirited Christianity and a catalyst for reconciliation and interfaith dialogue to promote respect and understanding. We invite all people to share in our commitment to create a more hopeful and just world."

Ken (Silva, Apprising Ministries), then points out that she is on the board of advisors of the **Mary Baker Eddy** Library. **Eddy** was the founder of the Christian Science cultic religion. As you dig deeper, the Cathedral promotes contemplative prayer, including centering prayer and practicing the silence.
I suggest you read the full post by Pastor Silva in order to get an even better look at the very dubious associations that **Tickle** has with apostate groups and false religions.

https://reformednazarene.wordpress.com/2011/11/28/ phylis-tickle-and-the-new-seminary-president/

(**NOTE: The above article by Ken Silva of Apprising Ministries, continues for a few more paragraphs, so it is best to go to that link to read it. Ed.).

- **Eckart Tolle**: https://www.eckharttollenow.com/ article/ Spirituality-And-The-Christian-Tradition

https://www.tikkun.org/tikkundaily/2012/07/07/ why-eckhart-tolles-evolutionary-activism-wont-save-us/

(**NOTE: This last link is not a Christian link, but it does show how demonic and deceptive this person is, so I decided to include it. Ed.).

- **Larry Tomczak**:   https://www.latimes.com/archives/ la-xpm-1990-03-24-ca-667-story.html

https://www.thepathoftruth.com/false-teachers/ larry-tomczak.htm.

https://www.washingtonian.com/2016/02/14/ the-sex-abuse-scandal-that-devastated-a-suburban-megachurch-sovereign-grace-ministries/

(**NOTE: **Larry Tomczak** is mentioned in the above website, which is why I am including it, since the thrust of the article is about **C.J. Mahaney**–another person in my book–who he mentored. Ed.).

https://www.thedailybeast.com/ pastor-accused-of-covering-up-abuse-returns-to-spotlight

(**NOTE: The above website is secular, but it also affirms the scandal and coverup, which is why I decided to include it. Ed.).

http://thewartburgwatch.com/2011/12/02/ tomczak-sets-the-record-straight/

http://www.828ministries.com/articles/ Larry-Tomczak--Butchering-by-Anthony-Wade-God_Religion_Spirit-170202-594.html

- **Chris Tomlin**: King of Worship Music: **Tomlin** holds the unscriptural ecumenical philosophy that is typical of the CCM crowd. **Tomlin** is a former staff member of Austin Stone Community Church in Texas, which holds the Emerging church philosophy.
 Tomlin has a close association with Roman Catholicism.

Chris Tomlin, "the king of worship music," is using his music to build the one-world "church," and nothing could be more unscriptural and spiritually dangerous.
http://www.wayoflife.org/index_files/

-**Casey Treat**: https://simplicityinchrist.wordpress.com/2007/01/13/ casey-treat/

www.federalwaymirror.com/news/
families-speak-out-as-federal-way-megachurch-faces-financial-sexual-abuse-suit/
https://www.seattleweekly.com/news/
federal-way-megachurch-slapped-with-another-sexual-exploitation-lawsuit/

- **Cindy Trimm**: Another proponent of the NAR; supposedly has a "healing" ministry.
 https://www.thepathoftruth.com/ false-teachers/cindy-trimm.htm

https://michellelesley.com/tag/ cindy-trimm/

- **Adam Tyson**: http://bewareoffalse-unbiblicalteachers.blogspot.com/2019/10/
adam-tyson-placarita-bible-church.html

https://bewareoffalse-unbiblicalteachers.blogspot.com/2019/11/
placerita-bible-church-adam-tyson.html

"For the following reasons; I would warn you to not take your teaching from them or associate
with them per Romans 16:17:

 1) They teach a false Galatians 1 accursed Calvinist gospel of once saved always saved. This
is a lie and see it exposed here": https://spiritandtruthdiscernment.blogspot.com/
search/label/Calvinism

See the Biblical Gospel here:https://www.dontperish.com/the-gospel.html

I guess it takes more than a Masters seminary educated pastor (**Adam Tyson**) for them to get
& know the BUILDING is NOT THE CHURCH per God's Word!

2) They are keeping the false feminized, paganized, worldly evangelical system of Sunday
religion NOT the true Holy NT body that Christ ordained.

See this 10 point test that exposed them: https://www.dontperish.com/ test-your-faith.html

Here is their PBC youth group claiming holiness; as they show off so much skin, we had to
block it out. *This is a worldly carnal unbiblical religious body (Godly obedient saints cover
their forms per God's Word). Even their other elder is of the world's ways via carnal sports
when they are to be holy (set apart) out of the world for God...

3) Their lead pastor is a carnal unbiblical Calvinist who has various SIN issues.

(*he attended college at and supports a heretic called **John MacArthur**.)

See **John M**. exposed here:
https://bewareoffalse-unbiblicalteachers.blogspot.com/2017/07/
john-macarthur-tested-to-gods-word.html

***Adam** has been counseling famous rap singer Kanye' West and has NOT told Kanye' he needs to repent and come out of that sinful fallen Hollywood music system. In fact; **Tyson** told West to… stay in it!

http://bewareoffalse-unbiblicalteachers.blogspot.com/2019/11/
placerita-bible-church-adam-tyson.html

- **Tommy Tyson**: Deceased; NAR, Renovare Church.
https://www.thebereancall.org/content/new-age-inroads-church

V:

- **Kris Vallotton**: NAR teacher. http://www.828ministries.com/articles/

Kris-Vallotton--Just-a-L-by-Anthony-Wade-God_Spirituality-190321-338.html

(**NOTE: Above is a three page article at the link provided. Ed.).

"Prophet" **Kris Vallotton**, author and senior associate pastor of "Bethel Church"
 in Redding, California. **Vallotton** is **Bill Johnson's** right-hand man and is the co-founder and senior overseer of "Bethel School of Supernatural Ministry."
Vallotton is attempting to mainstream the heterodox "Manifest Sons of God" teaching.

http://www.spiritoferror.org/2013/07/
the-changing-of-the-apostolic-guard-13-names-to-watch/3718

https://www.christianpost.com/news/
benny-hinns-nephew-calls-bethel-church-leader-kris-vallotton-false-prophet-who-deceives-peopl
e.html

- **Rich Vera**: Another prosperity WOF preacher aligned with **Sid Roth** and **Guillermo Maldonado**. (**NOTE: See articles on **Sid Roth** and **Guillermo Maldonado**.
It will help you to decide if this man is of God or not. Ed.).

- **Mark Virkler**: A believer in **Agnes Sanford's** apostate teaching; wrote a book titled, "Dialogue With God," which seduces Christians into contact with demons masquerading as "God" and "Christ." (See "Agnes Sanford" above).

https://www.thebereancall.org/content/new-age-inroads-church

- **Ann Voskamp**: Is a very popular author, poet, and blogger among the ladies. She writes in a tedious, melodramatic way that most people would find cumbersome.
 Yet, with a captivating charisma, she's attracted a massive following at her blog where she writes about the day-to-day happenings in her life that so many women can identify with.
However, **Voskamp** has stepped into the realm of Bible teacher and is also the author of many works that, while the theology is bad, are theological in nature.

Voskamp portrays God's love in a dangerous way, confusing his love for an "erotic" type of love. In her book, "100 Gifts," she writes of flying to Paris to "learn how to make love to God," and also, "I run my hand along the beams over my loft bed, wood hewn by a hand several hundred years ago." " I can hear Him. He's calling for a response; He's calling for <u>oneness.</u> <u>Communion</u>."

This view of God's love is antithetical to the Biblical view of God's love, which is agape. **Voskamp** teaches a relationship with God that is more like a relationship with a lover or a sex partner. https://reformationcharlotte.org/2019/03/26/false-teachers-evangelical-churches/

W:

-**David Wagner**: https://www.reddit.com/r/Christianity/comments/2rgusu/a_friend_is_pushing_me_to_see_this_david_wagner_a/

David Wagner Quotes--One Quote by: **David Wagner** of 'Father's Heart Ministries"—

"2012 is going to be known as year where true Hope is restored and healed. Hope will not disappoint in 2012! A harvest of four billion souls are about to come into the Kingdom of God over the next two years." Source here on the Internet. Dated: 1st January 2012.

(**NOTE: The above quote is taken from the website below. Ed.).

http://www.zedekiahlist.com/cgi-bin/ quotes.pl?&id=75482020

- **C. Peter Wagner**: Deceased; founder of a business model that he said would benefit the churches; mega-churches is his idea; **also believes that the older people in church need to leave if they won't adhere to his teachings**; also one of the founders of the <u>Emergent Church—Global Harvest Ministries;</u>

Advocated an assessment-based system of monitoring efficiency and effectiveness for charitable organizations, which included the concept of <u>merging State and Church (</u>including private charities) into faith-based endeavors.
A key facet of this results-based system was regulating "choices," which notably would include the concept of "vouchers."
These vouchers, while purportedly giving people "choice," <u>would actually function as a method</u> <u>of human control; in</u> **Drucker's** <u>model, human beings are referred to as "human capital" —</u> <u>their "value" is assessed in terms of how much they can contribute to the common good of</u> <u>Society."</u>

January 9, 2009–Herescope, as quoted in http://simplicityinchrist.wordpress.com

The **Wagner University** states the following: Our Foundation Founded in 1998 by **C. Peter Wagner,** <u>WU </u>reflects a new <u>paradigm</u> for unique training in practical ministry.

Unlike traditional seminaries, WU focuses on equipping 'in-service' leaders with a creative, revelatory style of teaching and learning, as well as impartation and activation, with opportunity for hands-on, practical application and ministry.

"Who We Are:" Inspired in 1998 by a prophetic word from **Cindy Jacobs**, **C. Peter Wagner**, built upon his legacy of developing world changers by creating Wagner Leadership Institute (WLI).

In 2010 **Dr. Wagner** appointed **Dr. Che' Ahn** as the International Chancellor and under his leadership WLI spread into numerous regional schools throughout the U.S. and into 11 nations. In 2017, WLI became Wagner University (WU).
Today, **Dr. Che' Ahn** continues to lead WLI into a new paradigm for unique training in practical ministry. Source: "About Us," Wagner University, http://wagner.university/about/, Accessed Nov 20 2017.

Occasionally she (**Cindy Jacobs**) spoke about **Wagner** and the council of prophets she was involved with to see what God was doing globally for his church. Yet this woman helped **Wagner** launch the WLI while the 'revival' was happening and also helped launch with **Wagner** the Apostolic Council of Prophetic Elders (ACPE) and International Coalition of Apostles (ICA).

In the JAN/FEB Edition of GI NEWS in the year 2000, **Cindy Jacobs** opens with this:

"We are stepping into this new millennium with a tremendous burden to bless the Jewish people. In December, God gave an urgent prayer mandate regarding Russian Jews to the "Council of Prophetic Elders," led apostolically by **Peter Wagner**."

"And in the January "Glory Fire" conference, after working closely with **Don Finto, Dan Juster,** and the "Towards Jerusalem 2 Council," we unveiled a proclamation of repentance **for the sins of Christian Americans towards the Jews**.

I really believe in God's promise that He will bless those who bless the seed of Abraham!" "It is also our great joy to participate in the million youth march that is being called "The Call." **Mike** and I will be in Washington, DC September 2, 2000 to support it along with our son, **Daniel**."
Who are the leading NAR Apostles leading "with a tremendous burden to bless the Jewish people"?
NAR-postle **C. Peter Wagner** and **Cindy Jacobs** with **"Don Finto**" and **"Dan Juster."**
Apostle **Dan Juster** of "Union of Messianic Jewish Congregations."

So he is regarded as an NAR Apostle and is working closely with NAR **C Peter Wagner**, NAR Apostle **Cindy Jacobs** and NAR Apostle **Don Finto**?
Wagner's "International Coalition of Apostles" recognized **Juster** straight away as an apostle when they formed in 1999. The ICA 2001 Apostles Directory confirms this as does **Wagner** in an interview in the archived GI link:

https://web.archive.org/web/20001209092200fw_/

http://www.generals.org:80/gi_news_2k.htm#gi%20news%20co-found

Wagner's "World Prayer Center," just one of the many groups that **Peter Wagner** has formed or is involved with the " Apostolic Council of Prophetic Elders." This group has become the internationally recognized authority on prayer and spiritual warfare.

"Apostolic Elders " include known people as, **Chuck Pierce, Dutch Sheets, Cindy Jacobs, Mike Bickle** and **Tommy Tenney**. The group's statement was released after they met in Colorado at the end of February 2000.
The council formed to provide a corporate forum for leaders with a recognized prophetic gift--was born out of a similar gathering at the prayer center in January. They say that it is necessary that every city have an Apostolic leadership over it.

Wagner also has released a new book "Apostles of the City: How to mobilize the territorial Apostles for city Transformation." **Peter Wagner** heads up the "Apostolic Council of Prophetic Elders." One of the prophecies of the council is "The church will be in key transition period between 2000-2003."
"During this period the youth in particular will be transitioning into revival. It is especially important for the apostolic government to be initially established and functioning in our cities by Oct. 2003 if we are to see the transformations that God wants to release."

In 1998, (George) **Otis'** "Sentinel Group," **Wagner's** "Global Harvest Ministries," and **Ted Haggard's** "Christian Information Network" plan to move into the high-tech "World Prayer Center" on the grounds of **Haggard's** "New Life Church" in Colorado Springs ("Christianity Today" May 20, 1996, p. 78).
This all comes together under **Wagner** who is the chief spiritual engineer.
He states, "Spiritual mapping will be central to the operation of this "electronic nerve center" to connect the intercessors and let each other know what they're hearing from the Holy Spirit" ("Christianity Today" Jan.12, 1998).
I guess this will be something like the CIA for those Christians involved in city and country warfare of spirit beings. It will immediately disseminate the information of what is taking place in the "spiritual realm" to others.

http://www.letusreason.org/ Latrain66.htm

- **Phil Waldrep**: Preaches WOF-Prosperity; uses **Rick Warren's** false Gospel; promotes "women's conferences" which teach that women are superior to men.

"I just ran across **Mac (Brunson)** being one the conference speakers at Pigeon Forge Oct 20-23 2008, in a conference held by **Phil Waldrep** Ministries." " Why haven't we heard about **Phil Waldrep** previously or have I just missed it? Has he ever spoken at FBC?" (**NOTE: The above comment is from the website listed below. Ed.).

http://fbcjaxwatchdog.blogspot.com/2008/10/ what-to-do-after-asking-for-1-million.html http://fbcjaxwatchdog.blogspot.com/2008/10/ come-someone-justify-this-greedy-double.html

https://celebstrendsnow.com/ phil-waldrep-net-worth/

- **Alice Walker**: Another New Age proponent; Possibly anti-Semite.

https://brandeiscenter.com/ alice-walker-got-what-she-deserves/

"**Walke**r, the Pulitzer prize-winning author of "The Color Purple," cited the controversial British writer David Icke's "And the Truth Shall Set You Free" when asked by the New York Times which books were on her night stand. "In Icke's books there is the whole of existence, on this planet and several others, to think about," said **Walker**. "A curious person's dream come true."

The paper came under fire for including the answer; Icke is a conspiracist who expounds the theory that the world is run by a cabal of giant, shape-shifting lizards, and is described as "essentially a hate preacher with a 21st-century spin on a very old antisemitic conspiracy theory" by the "Community Security Trust," a charity set up to protect the Jewish community.

"Tablet " magazine's Yair Rosenberg called the book highlighted by **Walker** "an unhinged antisemitic conspiracy tract written by one of Britain's most notorious anti-Semites".
https://www.theguardian.com/books/2018/dec/20/
weve-informed-you-new-york-times-defends-running-alice-walkers-david-icke-recommendation

(**NOTE: The link listed below is a person's abstract on **Ms. Walker's** questionable ideas about God. Quite interesting that **Ms. Walker** links together Christianity, Buddhism and Gnosticism. Ed.).
http://forumonpublicpolicy.com /wp-content/uploads/2017/10/ King-Walker.pdf

- **Jim Wallis**: False teacher, **Jim Wallis**, founder, and editor of the anti-gospel "Sojourners Magazine," has put out a video mocking the Biblical view of Complementarianism in the church. **Wallis** is well known for his Emergent style teachings and unbiblical promotion of mysticism, including contemplative prayer and Lectio Divina.. http://www.stand4thelord.com/2016/05/ biblical-response-to-false-teacher-jim.html

https://pulpitandpen.org/2016/05/06/
false-teacher-jim-wallis-puts-out-video-mocking-complementarianism/

https://bereanresearch.org/ progressive-christians-doctrines-devils/

- **Lance Wallnau**: NAR, promotes the "Seven Mountain Mandate"; Teacher **Lance Wallnau**, director of the Lance Learning Group, founder of 7M University, and member of Ken Blanchard's board. **Wallnau** has been described by People ForThe American Way as the hidden architect behind the NAR dominionist agenda known as the "Seven Mountain Mandate."
http://www.spiritoferror.org/2013/07/

- **Sheila Walsh**: http://readitorskipit.blogspot.com/2012/03/

sheila-walshs-incorrect-teachings.html

Sheila Is a women's Bible study and children's book author, speaker, and singer.
Formerly a co-host of The 700 Club for several years, she now co-hosts "Life Today" with
James Robison. "Life Today" routinely features false teachers as guests, including **Joel Osteen, Joyce Meyer, Paula White, T.D. Jakes,** Kim Walker-Smith (Jesus Culture), and
Beth Moore, among others.

Sheila habitually yokes in ministry and fraternizes with false and problematic teachers in other
venues as well. Space does not permit me to list every incidence of **Sheila** doing so, but the
following examples are representative:
 In 2014, **Sheila** joined **Beth Moore, Christine Caine, Priscilla Shirer, Victoria Osteen**,
and Lisa Harper for the Unwrap the Bible conference at **Joel Osteen**'s Lakewood "Church."
https://michellelesley.com/2019/09/27/ sheila-walsh/

- **Kathie Walters**: NAR ; wrote a book entitled, "Bright and Shining Revival," where she stated
that she rode a chariot from God in her living room, and other false claims.

"This is a life changing trip. It is not primarily a ministry trip or a mission trip - it's for YOU, to
chill out, relax and have some fun." "But I promise God will show up and you will never be the
same. You will get zapped and go in chariots and get delivered and set free!" "We stay in five
star hotels, go to Welsh revival places
 (Wales is called the Land of revival) go shopping, have cream teas, go sightseeing and visit the
local pubs (where the people are). There is not another tour like this."

(Source: http://www.kathiewaltersministry.com/ itinerary).

KATHY WALTERS AT FREEDOM CHURCH IN CWMBRAN (Wales)--

As the guests of Freedom Church, **Walters** & Co. were booked in for two days there, 11th. and
12th. October, for her to deliver a seminar entitled 'The Supernatural, Faith and Angels.' (Only
15 quid a head, inclusive of lunch and impartation!). **Ms. Walters**
 has a real "thing" about angels, as does Freedom Church as it happens, which boasts of itself:
"Freedom Church has an open Heaven and is packed full of angels."

Source: http://www.freedomchurchcwmbran.com/

Really? Trouble is, if Freedom Church is indeed packed with angels, they may just be of the
FALLEN kind! Pastor Robert King's appalling lack of discernment is evidenced by his opening
his church doors for a week-long **Todd Bentley** extravaganza in December 2011, and he was
even to have had him back there in 2012.

If the Home Office hadn't had infinitely more sense than **Mr.King** and banned him from
re-entering the UK! **Todd Bentley** at Two Locks Church in Cwmbran back in December,
2011. It re-branded itself as Freedom Church in 2013; new name, same deception...

If one might be tempted to excuse this deplorable neglect of his shepherding duty to protect the flock as a one-off aberration - and that would be quite an unjustified consideration given **Bentley's** planned return! - then such sympathies can be shown to be utterly misplaced by Robert King's hosting of **Kathie Walters**.

 Ms. Walters is one of the dearly beloved names on 'The Elijah List,' **Steve Shultz's** mega-distributor of the kind of fables referred to in the Scripture from II Timothy which headed this article, and which multitudes somehow manage to unquestioningly accept as actually being God-given prophetic words and visions!

WHILE FETED FALSE PROPHETS LIKE **KATHIE WALTERS** ARE BUSILY PROMISING CHARIOT RIDES AND FUN AND LAUGHTER, THE WORLD IS ABOUT TO CRASH AND BURN! HORRIBLY! THE PROPHETS PROPHESY OF WONDERFUL AND GLORIOUS TIMES AHEAD. BUT GOD'S HOLY AND INERRANT WORD WARNS OF A GREAT FALLING AWAY, PRIOR TO THE EMERGENCE OF THE ANTICHRIST AND THE MOST TERRIBLE TRIBULATION THAT THE WORLD HAS EVER KNOWN...   http://watchman4wales.blogspot.com/2014/10/ kathie-walters-rider-in-sky-lands-in.html

http://rollanscensoredissuesblog.blogspot.com /2008/09/new-mystics-fraud-and-spotting-false.html

https://www.honorofkings.org/ false-prophet-listing/

(**NOTE: The following link below is what **Kathie Walters** subscribes to on You Tube. "Ye shall know them by their fruits"—and associations. Ed.).

https://www.youtube.com/channel/ UCCBfkPh_AMAGKrvX3VpxGWg

- **George Warnock**: Mega church preacher; NAR, Latter Rain, Manifest Sons Of God.
 1949 **George Warnock** begins to teach on the "Restoration of all things" involved with Sharon Brethren.   1951 **George Warnock** publishes "Feast of Tabernacles" a manual for Latter Rain Doctrines & Practices.

 http://www.deceptioninthechurch.com/modern.htm

- **Rick Warren**: "In a communitarian worldview any truly private entity (family,   charity, church and small Christian school) poses a direct challenge to the "common good"). This is an interesting statement in light of **Rick Warren's** recent activities in   promulgating Communitarian agendas and ideals such as the "common good."

Peter Drucker was his mentor; **Rick Warren** is the most outspoken of the   "Emergent Church"; his P.E.A.C.E. Plan is to bring peace to the whole world   (globalism—an anti-Christ system); wrote the book "The Purpose Driven Life," a   mockery of the precepts and concepts of Christianity;

Believes in the metaphysical New Age "Gospel." (See **C. Peter Wagner** for further information); Seeker Friendly. His main goal is to usher in the Dominionist theory, to equip soldiers in his "march" towards taking over the Christian world.

(**NOTE: The articles below deals with his "emerging" theory of "change agent(s)," meaning that if you don't agree with this "new" teaching, they will make sure you are no longer a part of their "church" since you will not abide by their leadership. Ed.).
http://herescope.blogspot.com/2006/01/ change-agents-for-church.html

https://www.youtube.com/ watch?v=HCIgV2XCN3M&feature=emb_logo

- **Paul Washer**: Teaches the heresy of Lordship Salvation– "What is Lordship salvation and is it Biblical? " by Matt Slick

Though there are variations on what Lordship salvation really is, it is basically the view that in order to become a true Christian a person must receive Jesus as both Savior and Lord and that he must also cease from sin or be willing to cease from sin in order to be saved (i.e., repent).

The controversy deals with whether or not salvation is a one- or two-step process.
Is salvation by faith alone, and nothing beyond it is required (one step)?
Or, is faith to be accompanied by a submission to the Lordship of Christ and repentance (two steps)--both of which result in salvation?
Let's see if we can make sense of it. Related to this topic is what is called the Ordo Salutis, the order of salvation. As it relates to this discussion, we have to ask if regeneration precedes faith or does faith precede regeneration?

If regeneration precedes faith, then God is changing the person and enabling him to believe the Gospel and repent. Furthermore, this would mean that salvation and turning from sin are the result of God's regenerative work and would be, of course, a natural consequence of His making us new creatures (2 Corinthians 5:17).
 If, however, faith precedes regeneration, then a person's decision to believe in God and the Gospel would also require an attempt to turn from one's sinful behavior (Mark 1:15). It is in this second position that the controversy arises.

 If Lordship salvation is meant to say that a person must believe the Gospel and also repent of sin in order to be saved, then it is teaching that salvation is not by faith alone in Christ alone. Instead, it would be by faith and also the act of turning from sin as a person makes Jesus Lord of "all" of his life.
In other words, salvation is obtained by faith in God and turning from sin--which amounts to keeping the Law. This would be, of course, false. Now, we are not saying a person need not repent of his sins. Instead, repentance is the result of God's regenerative work in us.
 Let me explain:

The position of CARM is that regeneration precedes faith the way electricity precedes light in a light bulb. The order is logical--not temporal. Electricity must be present for light to occur in a lightbulb, but it's not true that light must be present in order for electricity to occur. We would

say that whenever electricity is present in a lightbulb, the automatic and natural result is light. The electricity is "logically" prior to the light--not temporally prior.
In other words, it is logically necessary that electricity precedes the light; and when electricity is present, light is also present.

With this analogy, I think it is easier to understand that it is God who regenerates us (2 Corinthians 5:17; 1 Peter 1:3; John 1:13), and that the necessary result of his regenerative work in us is our faith and repentance. God grants that we believe (Philippians 1:29) and grants that we repent (2 Timothy 2:25).
Therefore, our position is that repentance is a necessary result of God's work in us (yet it's also something that we do).

The issue of Lordship salvation incorrectly addresses the order of salvation by implying that faith leads to regeneration, which leads to repentance.
I believe this mistakenly puts the focus on man's ability instead of God's work, and this is where the error of Lordship salvation arises. The truth is that we are saved by grace alone, through faith alone, in Christ alone.

Repentance from sin is the result of salvation--not a contributing factor to it.
If it is God who grants us repentance (2 Timothy 2:25) and faith (Philippians 1:29), then there is no room for the Lordship salvation controversy. Instead, we understand that the Lordship of Christ and our repentance are both the natural result of the work of God--not the work of our faith and repentance.

https://carm.org/what-is-lordship-salvation-and-is-it-biblical

The main issue in the "Lordship Salvation" debate seems to focus on "MAN'S PART" in becoming a Christian, and the quality of his faith... as such, he seems to interject more into the matter than is absolutely necessary — which is simply responding to that work GOD is doing in our heart.

With that said, on the believer's part, it is simply a matter of...
    ~Acknowledging our sinfulness to Him
    ~Acknowledging our need of His forgiveness
    ~Acknowledging our need to have Christ in our life
    ~Acknowledging our desire to become His child

http://www.thetransformedsoul.com/
additional-studies/spiritual-life-studies/the-issue-of-lordship-salvation

(**NOTE: This is a very lengthy discourse on the subject. Please go to the site itself to read about it. Ed.).
http://www.christiandoctrine.com/
christian-doctrine/heresy-and-error/ 2068-lordship-salvation "Lordship Salvation"

(**NOTE: Another excellent article on this subject. Ed.)

http://www.preachingjesuschrist.com/
why-lordship-salvation-is-not-biblical.html

(**NOTE: And here is another excellent discourse on this subject; may be somewhat easier to understand than the others presented above. Ed.).

- **Beverley Watkins**: Another NAR teacher, heretic--

3 JUL 2018 "UNDERSTANDING THE GLORY OF GOD" BY BEVERLEY WATKINS--
Robert Winters Published on 21 May 2017

In this video message, entitled "Understanding the Glory of God", **Beverley Watkins** teaches on the various aspects of the glory of God. "In this hour it is crucial that the Body of Christ, as an "ekklesia", ascends in worship as "one new man" to become a corporate habitation of the glory of God."

Prepare the Way International Church www.preparethewayint.com

https://www.youtube.com/ watch?time_continue=4&v=M3sPw4KS8Go&feature=emb_logo

(**NOTE: Another mystical, heretical teacher\prophet. False claims to know how to intercede before God's throne for us; isn't that what Jesus does? Ed.).

- **Scott Webster**: https://visionarchitekt.com/ the-prophetic-function/

(**NOTE: Except these people say they are, but they are false prophets. Isa. 8:19, 20
Jer. 14: 14, 15; 23:30-32. KJV. Ed.).

- **Amanda Wells:** Australian "prophetess" who twists and perverts not only the Bible, but her own personal family's recollections of her compulsive lying, storytelling and embellishments of the family dynamic. One reference is from her own sibling—a sister named Kerri—who tries to get **Amanda** to stop lying and just tell the truth:

"I am the only sister of the false prophet, **Amanda Wells** (born Amanda Louise Ferguson 19th September 1955 in Sydney, Australia, a.k.a Mandy Ferguson, a.k.a. Aussie Amanda)..."
https://weedingoutwells.com/2016/

Ms. Wells is also part of the "Elijah's List" heresy, founded by **Steve Shultz**, who wholeheartedly endorses her "prophetic" gift.   **Ms. Wells'** constant, unrelenting and blatant lies—to anyone who will listen to her—which are engineered to place herself up on a higher scale than the average person, supposedly being used in a "prophetic" gift—is quite obvious once a person who can discern her motives and can see behind them:
https://weedingoutwells.com/

If that is not enough, here **Ms. Wells** is being called out for the sin of plagiarism–and the mockery of being called out in public, asking her to cease and desist; her response is very telling: https://churchwatchcentral.com/2016/11/20/

- **Jonathan Welton** : **Jonathan** is a product of men's religious systems.
He knows nothing at all of the Lord Jesus Christ, never having been taught of or by Him, despite his claim of being taught by the Holy Spirit.
 If there's any spirit involved, it's not God's. For credentials as a teacher, **Jonathan** says he has "two Master's degrees, one in Biblical studies and one in practical ministry."
Jonathan talks about being raised as a Pentecostal and mixing with Baptist friends, the former giving him "the power" and the latter "a love for the Word." He is completely deluded, as both of those are works of the flesh.

In this following passage, the apostle Paul highlights the differences between the faith of Christ and the religions of men: His teaching about the anti-Christ, for example, misses the essential truth that believers need to be delivered from the anti-Christ within, the man of sin spoken of in II Thessalonians 2.
 Since **Jonathan** hasn't experienced this deliverance himself, how can he lead others to the full salvation of Christ? And if he can't do that, what is he doing, except feeding people with knowledge and keeping them in bondage to Satan?

"I, **Jonathan Welton**, care more about truth than about money. My heart is to empower others and release the truth that sets people free."
Right off to the side of this announcement is a very visible "Donate" button, accompanied by all the credit cards **Jonathan** accepts.

 "Most men will proclaim every one his own goodness: but a faithful man who can find?" (Proverbs 20:6 KJV).

The one boasting about loving truth more than money, do you beg for money?
Jonathan denies the great miracle of our day –Behold, Israel and the Jew!– and appeals to the likes of Calvin and Spurgeon as "great church leaders."

Plenty of deadly error to poison the well. Read "The True Marks of a Cult and Diabolical Doctrines" for more thorough background on "What's wrong with this picture?" –not only applying to **Jonathan**, but to so many other false teachers who are spreading like Stage 4 cancer throughout the world.

 https://www.thepathoftruth.com/false-teachers/

Recently, a pastor I know received a provocative Christmas gift from a man in his church. It is a book titled "Normal Christianity," written by prophet **Jonathan Welton**–a leader in the New Apostolic Reformation (NAR) movement.
The message of **Welton's** book is that the "normal" Christian lifestyle should be characterized by the performance of miracles: walking on water, calming storms, and even raising the dead.

Yet–contrary to the book's title–**Welton's** version of Christianity is anything but normal. Beyond promoting the supernatural phenomena we see in Scripture, he also argues that every Christian should develop <u>magical powers</u> that historically have been practiced by <u>psychics</u>, <u>witches</u>, and <u>occultists</u>.

The end result is that "normal" Christianity turns out to be an unholy marriage between Christianity and the <u>occult</u>.

Gifts of the Spirit?

Welton claims that all Christians should be reclaiming the following practices from the <u>occult</u> as part of their normal Christian walk:

<u>Reading auras</u>: The ability to see invisible energy that surrounds a person and learning information about that person based on the color or form of his or her aura.

<u>Clairvoyance</u>: The ability to perceive extrasensory information about an object or event from the past, present, or future.

<u>Clairaudience</u>: The ability to hear sounds, music, and voices sent from the spirit realm.

<u>Clairsentience</u>: The ability to sense smells sent from the spirit realm, along with tastes and touches.

<u>The use of power objects</u>: Physical objects, such as <u>crystals</u> and <u>amulets</u>, that contain supernatural powers.

Welton's Misuse of Scripture–

Welton attempts to offer Biblical support for these practices. Yet, the few verses he cites do not support the practices. For example, to support <u>clairsentience</u>–that is, sensing smells from the spirit realm–he cites II Corinthians 2:14: "But thanks be to God, who always leads us in triumphal procession in Christ and through us spreads everywhere the fragrance of the knowledge of Him."

(**NOTE: in the KJV, the Scripture is: "Now thanks be unto God, which always causeth us to triumph in Christ, and maketh manifest the savour of his knowledge by us in every place." Quite a different meaning when you go to the true translation of the Bible from the original languages into English. Ed.).

It is painfully obvious that the apostle Paul is not speaking, in this verse, of a real fragrance. Rather, Paul uses the image of a fragrance to convey an idea: that idea being that God uses Christians to spread knowledge about Him wherever they go.
Yet **Welton** misuses this verse to defend his claim that a sweet scent like perfume–sent from heaven–<u>magically</u> appears in many of his meetings.

Well, maybe **Welton** has smelled something sweet in his meetings. But his interpretation of Scripture stinks. Shockingly Shameless--**Welton** doesn't see himself as introducing occult practices in the church. On the contrary, he sees himself as a "rogue theologian" who is reclaiming practices that New Agers and occultists stole from Christianity in the first place ("Normal Christianity," page 202).

Now that's brazen!

Welton's unabashed attempt to bring occult practices to the church reminds me of the man and woman who were openly practicing incest in the Corinthian church (I Corinthians 5:1-13). The apostle Paul was shocked that they would be so shameless--even boasting about--engaging in such a blatant form of sexual immorality.

Jonathan Welton is not only seeking to bring occult practices to the church, but he is also audacious enough to claim that these practices represent "normal" Christianity. And, unfortunately, his is not a lone voice. A growing number of NAR apostles and prophets have begun openly pushing occult practices.
The Big Lie--**Welton's** teachings may sound absurd. But that doesn't mean people won't believe them. Hitler had an infamous propaganda technique, known as the "Big Lie"--that is, if you tell a lie that is big enough then eventually people will believe it.

Why? Because no one will believe that you would actually make up something so crazy. And, sadly, **Welton's** message has already convinced people--which can be seen by the fact that my pastor friend received a copy of his book. So, what do you think the normal Christian life should look like?

September 28th, 2018: **Jonathan Welton** caught in a sexual scandal!

https://danlirette.ca/jonathan-welton-sexual-abuse-scandal/

http://www.spiritoferror.org/category/

Concerning **Dr. Jonathan Welton** of the Welton
Academy, Danny Silk writes:

To the Welton Academy students, River Credentialed Community & Leaders, and select leaders in relationship with either **Jonathan Welton** orWelton Academy,
I've been involved up close and person in a recent situation with **Jonathan Welton.** I've been working closely with a recently assembled advisory board comprised of people I respect and friends of the **Welton** family:

(Harold Eberle, **Bob Muncey**, Steve & Joy Hogan, Eric Gregson & **Doug Johnson**).
After many hours of conversation, investigation, and counsel, this advisory board recommends the following:

1. Accept **Jonathan Welton's** resignation from President of Welton Academy on September 10, 2018.

2. Jonathan will have no contact with the Welton Academy staff team moving forward.

3. The Welton Academy will be closed immediately and indefinitely.

4. Each staff member who was 'no longer needed' or terminated following their refusal to accept Jonathan's physical advances, or when confronting his selfish or bizarrely disrespectful actions or who quit because the work environment was beyond what they could endure, should be fully compensated for up to six months of their regular income.

5. Welton Academy will compensate staff members and former staff members who are in need of professional counseling

6. Welton Academy will refund all tuition that has been paid for the 2018-2019 academic year. **Jonathan** will refund the cost of the Summit ticket to anyone choosing to not attend.

7. Jonathan will seek psychiatric help and follow the advice and recommendations of said professional.

As you can see, these findings are severe. **Jon's** behavior is beyond hurtful and scary, he is now toxic to those who choose to be connected to him. A web of lies, created in a world that **Jon** controlled, is now revealing numerous victims of his extremely selfish, humiliating and habitual behavior. Upon first investigation, there are numerous confrontations from staff and members of his "Five-fold council" (that was disbanded by **Jon** upon these confrontations) in an effort to address an unsafe work environment.

Regular occurrences of physical advances, sexual innuendos, and highly inappropriate conversations became the culture **Jonathan** created around himself.

The staff, almost entirely younger women, were subject to this confusion and dishonor while attempting to help something and someone they held in high esteem. It grieves me to write this letter knowing the ramifications. This entire advisory board is friends with **Jonathan** and Karen. The staff at the Welton Academy, even those chased away, are rooting for his successful turnaround.

As of the writing of this letter, **Jon** is making slow if any progress. Repentance is not clear and thus the warning you hear in this letter. No repentance, no change. That reality creates an ongoing expectation of more of the same. **Jon** is not fit to be a leader, nor is he safe to have access to other people's vulnerability. After much discussion about the Welton Academy Summit, coming up in a month, the advisory board has decided to keep the event on the calendar.

The event will be shortened to the evening of Friday, October 26th through Saturday, October 27th. In honor of those who have given time to study "The Better Covenant" (which is still true), and for the numerous students who have already made plans to come to the event, we will provide a place of blessing, healing and possible clarity for you. Harold Eberle, **Bob Muncey** and myself will be among those leading the event this year. **Jonathan** will not be in attendance.

He is not yet able to convince anyone around him that he's broken over what he's done to so many and has absolutely no credibility when he speaks. This letter is written primarily to give clear information to people who are waiting to hear what is going on inside the Welton Academy. The authority of this letter is spiritual. There is no legal authority to this letter. The above list of recommendations are simply that, what we recommend happen moving forward.

Jonathan is the sole proprietor of the Welton Academy and can legally do whatever he chooses to do. There are numerous people victimized in this situation, none of them are named **Jonathan**. Up to now, he has spun all of his responsibility outward.

Will we see **Jon** own this enormous mess, change into a new man and reconcile with the many people who love and believe in him? Time will tell. I pray that God has mercy and grants repentance to my good friend, **Jonathan Welton**.

Peace, **Danny Silk**, MSW President of Loving On Purpose Senior Team, "Bethel Church" Redding, CA Senior Advisor, Jesus Culture Sacramento

https://danlirette.ca/jonathan-welton-sexual-abuse-scandal/

https://azusareport.com/ jonathan-welton-faithful/

https://weltonacademy.com/pages/2018-welton-academy-apostolic-summit

(**NOTE: This editor wrestled as to placing the above here in this book, since it is written from a "Bethel Church" member and member of the heretical "Jesus Culture" movement, however the information made sense to include it, since it is first-hand knowledge of the person in question, namely **Jonathan Welton**. The article also mentions another person in my book: **Bob Muncey**. I assume they all stick together. Ed.).

- **Bob Weiner**: NAR Apostle; https://maranathaministriesrevisted.com/category/the-nature-of-cult-leadership/

https://en.wikipedia.org/wiki/Maranatha_Campus_Ministries

(**NOTE: The "en.wikipedia" article is from a secular company, however it bolsters the claims from former MCM adherents as to how harmful it was, so I have made the decision to include it here. Ed.).

https://www.charismanews.com/opinion/heres-the-deal/69887-bob-jones-once-spoke-prophetically-that-something-significant-would-occur-after-5-key-leaders-died

(**NOTE: Reading the above website—although it promotes and condones the NAR and other questionable "Christian" groups--I have included it due to the fact that it names some heavy hitters in the "prophetic"\NAR practices, most of whom appear in my book. Ed.).
https://www.lighthousetrailsresearch.com/blog/ ?p=3295

http://thewartburgwatch.com/2017/08/09/
maranatha-ministries-revisited-a-relaunched-website-that-helps-us-learn-from-the-past/

https://www.latimes.com/archives/ la-xpm-1990-03-24-ca-667-story.html

- **Ronald Weinland**: The Church of God, Preparing for the Kingdom of God (COG-PKG) is an apocalypticist splinter sect of the Worldwide Church of God (WCG) that claims to provide "support, education and warning" to former members of the WCG.
[1]
 It is one of many groups that left the WCG after its sweeping doctrinal changes in the late 1980s, and forms a part of the seventh-day Sabbatarian Churches of God, following the teachings of the WCG 's founder, **Herbert W. Armstrong**.
 Headquartered in Cincinnati, Ohio, the COG-PKG is an international church which is mostly active on the Internet.
 It was founded in 1998 by **Ronald Weinland**, a former WCG minister and convicted tax evader [2] who has made a number of public end times predictions. [3]

 In November 2012, **Weinland** was sentenced to 42 months in prison for tax evasion;[4]. He began his prison term in February 2013,[5] though he continued to issue sermons and prophecies to his followers.

Pentecost predictions for 2019--

June 9th is the date prophesied by **Weinland** in his book "Prophecy Against the Nations" as the second coming of Jesus Christ, which would be preceded by several biblical events in conjunction with the start of World War III.[34]
During the time leading up to this date, **Weinland** began to express uncertainties in his prediction by issuing statements such as "not everything is going to pan out the way you thought" or "Is Christ About to Return?" on his website.[35][36]

 https://en.wikipedia.org/wiki/ Church_of_God_Preparing_for_the_Kingdom_of_God

(**NOTE: This "wikipedia" article continues on. If you are interested in more information, please go to that link, listed above. The numbers after each paragraph correspond to footnotes at the end of the article. Ed.).

https://fprw.wordpress.com/

Ronald Weinland has announced that he is God's final prophet before the end of this age, and one of the two witnesses of Revelation 11 (his wife is the other).

He has staked his claim to this high calling and office on the accuracy of the predictions he makes in the Name of God. One is that there will be a nuclear detonation in a major American city on or before July 16, 2008.

https://www.thepathoftruth.com/ false-teachers/ronald-weinland.htm

(**NOTE: The paragraph above is on the link listed above. Interesting that he is compared to the late **Herbert W. Armstrong**, another false prophet. Ed.).

https://www.youtube.com/ watch?v=bFvG5wwIs64

(**NOTE: You can see and hear for yourself his end time predictions on this link. Ed.).

- **Jason Westerfield**: "As for **Jason Westerfield**. I went with a friend recently to see **Jason Westerfield**. He is sweet, smiling young man. I believe people are being fooled by his tactics. He may be the next **Todd Bentley**. I just don't trust this guy."
"Some of the women that follow him around to his events act like they are seriously on drugs."

(**NOTE: In the rock music world, women like this are called "groupies," for following and idolizing the musicians, among other things. Is this a coincidence? Ed.).

"I understand people get moved in the spirit." " I am someone that loves Jesus with all my heart." "**Jason** and his young family are really cashing in as well. They live like "KINGS" in a mansion in Chester, CT. Something just feels not right about this guy."
"He seems to force people to be convinced they are healed and no longer need surgery. I do believe God does heal people. I am not saying that.
I have just seen him try to convince people they are healed and no longer need surgery etc. when it's not the case." " Beware of **Jason Westerfield** and Kingdom Reality."

http://rollanscensoredissuesblog.blogspot.com

(**NOTE: A responding post from "luv Jesus" on the forum listed above. What better testimony than that of a person who has first hand knowledge? Ed.).

- **Ellen G. White:** Founder of Seventh Day Adventist; taught Theosophy.

The Seventh-day Adventist doctrine of the investigative judgment and cleansing of the heavenly Sanctuary based upon Daniel 8:14 is indeed the central pillar of the Adventist faith. Some Adventists may disagree; however, it is.
Ellen White said, "The Scripture which above all others had been both the foundation and central pillar of the Advent faith was the declaration, 'Unto two thousand and three hundred days; then shall the sanctuary be cleansed."

There are many, perhaps the majority, of Adventist pastors and Bible teachers who want to run as far away from Daniel 8:14, 1844 and the investigative judgment, and the cleansing of the heavenly sanctuary as possible. Yet the church cannot dismiss this doctrine. This doctrine is not only the central pillar in name, it is the central pillar holding up the whole Adventist identity. Dr. Angel Rodriguez, professor of theology at the Adventist seminary and associate director of the Adventist Biblical Research Institute, stated forthrightly—

"Without 1844 and the doctrine of the Sanctuary ...there is no reason for us to exist. 1844 provided for us our identity and our mission. And if we are wrong, then we are simply wrong."
"I agree 100% with Dr. Rodriguez on this point."
If the Adventist church were to jettison this teaching, the organization would be morphed into something it is not. That is why the last two General Conference presidents have openly endorsed **Ellen White** and the sanctuary doctrine.
If they were to admit the errors of October 22, 1844, and the investigative judgment as the cleansing of the heavenly sanctuary as taught by **Ellen White**, then **Ellen White** would fall as "a continuing and authoritative source of truth."
If **Ellen White** is rejected, the doctrine of the remnant church would fall on the heap.
 If the remnant church doctrine goes, then the Sabbath as the seal of God for end time believers and Sunday as the mark of the beast crumbles into the dust.

 https://www.faithsocial.com/videos/v/ 4818104030

(**NOTE: The above excerpt is taken from the web link listed after the excerpt. There is a ten minute video of an ex-Adventist on this video, explaining how he came to the realization that **Ellen White** could not possibly be correct. Very good video worth watching. Ed.).

https://en.wikipedia.org/wiki/ Prophecy_in_the_Seventh-day_Adventist_Church

https://www.youtube.com/ playlist?list=PL5316CC6F66F24283.

https://www.youtube.com/ watch?time_continue=538&v=umBu2OvAZnk&feature=emb_logo

(**NOTE: Several videos concerning **Ellen G. White** are on You Tube. Ed.).

- **Paula White**: WOF, "seed faith," false teacher and "prophetess"; divorced; married for the third time in 2015 to Jonathan Cain, the lead singer of the rock group "Journey." It is his fourth marriage.   https://culteducation.com/group/853-brownsville-revival/
 3356-secrets-inside-the-revivals.html

https://www.rightwingwatch.org/post/
paula-white-the-white-house-is-holy-ground-because-where-i-stand-is-holy/

(**NOTE: The above video is her preaching at **Rodney Howard Browne's** church. Coincidence? Ed.).

(In this short YouTube video below, **Paula** states that she went to heaven and saw the face of God. Impossible, because even though Paul went there, he wasn't allowed to talk about it, yet she claims that God took her up to heaven? II Cor. 12:1-4. I will let you decide. Ed.).

https://www.youtube.com/ watch?time_continue=2&v=k2UHhKr5oPM&feature=emb_logo

https://www.youtube.com/watch?v=c21-ID8ZPEE&feature=youtu.be

(**NOTE: Here she is, preaching at **Guillermo Maldonado's** church in Miami. Ed.)

 (**NOTE: There is enough various You Tube videos to see that this person is not a "prophetess" or even a true teacher of the Bible. She is also on president Trump's "spiritual advisory council." Ed.).

- **Todd White**: "**Francis Chan** has been a very respected Evangelical pastor and author for over a decade now, but he has taken a very deliberate turn towards the "Signs and Wonders" New Apostolic Reformation- version of Christianity in recent years.

Chan does not teach the extreme Word of Faith doctrine at all; in fact, he's been really clear about wanting to stay away from man-centered false teaching altogether. He is to be commended for much of his Bible-based teaching, but that makes it even harder to understand his willingness to partner with IHOP and **Todd White**."

Todd White is happy to make large piles of money and live in a gigantic mansion; how does **Chan** feel about that? **Todd White** claims that he can "claim someone who doesn't believe and there's no way they can get out of it." How does **Francis Chan** feel about **Todd White** claiming to have the ability to sovereignly elect people?

Todd White says: "Christ coming out of us is His hope revealed!" So, Christ is not revealed in his Word, according to the egomaniac **Todd White**.
This man-centered teaching should come as no surprise, since **Todd White** is the guy who (literally) claims to "be the Bible."

Todd White claims that he is sinless just like Jesus. **Todd White** wants to raise $19 million to buy a gigantic mega-church, complete with auditorium, football field, Christian school and café. **Todd** portrays himself as a "street preacher" who demonstrates the "Power and Love of Jesus all day long," but he's really just another money-grubbing evangelist who has disguised the get-rich schemes of **Kenneth Copeland** and **Robert Morris** under his dreadlocks and blue jeans.

Todd wants to convince everyone to send him money because the "Smart Phone Prophet" **Shawn Bolz** got a direct revelation from God about this new land acquisition. For perpetuating this scheme, **Shawn** can be assured of a very profitable and ongoing speaking gig if this deal goes through. In the video, **Todd** says, "God has told me to multiply my heart." Hmm, I guess it would be too obvious if he said, "God told me to multiply my bank account and real estate holdings..."
When you give money to this "charity" you're largely putting money into **Todd White's** pocket; "Lifestyle Christianity" IS **Todd White**.

In 2015 "Lifestyle Christianity" had revenue of $1,521,776.00; so around 40% of all donations go directly to **Todd's** gigantic paycheck. It's interesting to note that total revenue was $496,407.00 in 2014, so **Todd** saw a million dollar increase from the year before-that's 300% growth. Who knows how much money he's raking in this year?
It would be much more honest if this was simply organized as a business.
Todd White is a professional speaker who gets paid very well to make speeches.

But **Todd White** is buying a gigantic $19 million church, and churches are not required to file a Form 990. Is **Todd White** trying to hide his future income? http://www.piratechristian.com/

An encounter with a Christian woman at a gym while waiting for her daughter, then another encounter with **Todd White** at a gym that she was at:

https://pulpitandpen.org/2017/03/08/

So let's look at some of the main statements he is teaching others on this--

In one video, "Lifestyle Christianity," **Todd** tells the people: "I didn't go to Bible school, didn't go to Bible college I just went to the Bible." (This will be refuted as we see what he teaches he has learned from others).
He says he lives his life by the Scripture: "you will hear so much Scripture come out of my mouth. My life is laced with so much Scripture because I live it... my days are saturated in my growing in whom God says I am." "I don't read the Bible so I can teach you-never read your Bible so you can teach people!" (and if you're a pastor or teacher what do you do?)...

"You read the Word--you get in there and you say 'God, this is who you say I am,
I need to become what this book says!" (Jesus said we can do nothing without him, he didn't just give us power to go on our own); "God places this inside of me, so that I can become a living epistle, known and read by men."
 I think it's more important to have a correct interpretation of Scripture, than bad applications which have you arrive at the wrong conclusions.

Todd is taking 2 Corinthians 3:2, <u>severing it from its context for the intention of esteeming the people to have power to do God's work</u>.

 II Cor. 3:1-3: "Do we begin again to commend ourselves? Or do we need, as some others, epistles of commendation to you or letters of commendation from you?"
" You are our epistle written in our hearts, known and read by all men; clearly you are an epistle of Christ, ministered by us, written not with ink but by the Spirit of the living God, not on tablets of stone but on tablets of flesh, that is, of the heart."

A "living epistle" to **Todd** means that we are to "become Scripture," for people to see Jesus. Paul is not at all telling people to "become the Bible." Paul was saying that the believers in Corinth were all like letters of recommendation because of their spiritual maturity. He is referring to their spiritual growth that God had done by his ministry through the Spirit.

(The early church wrote letters that recommended a member who was traveling that would validate the maturity of them as a teacher. I Cor.16:3).

Scripture is God's Holy Word, not us. Heb. 4:12 "For the word of God is living and powerful, and sharper than any two-edged sword, piercing even to the division of soul and spirit, and of joints and marrow, and is a discerner of the thoughts and intents of the heart."
After this **Todd** says, "God did NOT tell you to memorize Scripture, He told you to become it!"
First of all, God did tell us to memorize Scripture by example, "Thy word I have hid in my heart," said the King of Israel (David). Jesus, the Son of David cited the correct Scripture against the devil in his temptation in the wilderness, how? by memory.
Since we are to exhort in sound doctrine and refute those who contradict (Titus 1:9), this too involves knowing Scripture, the right Scripture in its correct interpretation.
 In fact when the Jewish scribes copied the word they memorized it. The average Jew in Israel memorized large portions of the Old Testament.
Maybe **Todd** looked and did not find the word "memorize" in Scripture but the words remember and keep are, and the intent is all through it.

So this claim to not memorize is wrong and to say you "become Scripture" is also wrong. This was something taught in the older Vineyard conferences under **John Wimber** and the prophets.

"YOU become that Word,' was part of the New Breed Latter Rain teaching.
 Since one of his teachers he is associated with (**Bill Johnson**), is repeating the errors of the Vineyard, I presume he heard it from him, because it is not found in the Bible.

I Chron. 10:13 Saul died for his unfaithfulness – "for he did not keep the word of the LORD, and also because he consulted a medium for guidance."

Where it all began for **Todd White**:
 Within the first year and a half of his Christian walk he was directed by **Jason Westerfield** to go to a conference with **Bill Johnson** and **Randy Clark**.
 He says it was called "Healing fusion," but he first instead said it was "The Voice of Healing" oops ... that is what **Gordon Lindsay's** magazine was called.

"The Voice of Healing" was about **William Branham's** ministry, of whom **Bill Johnson** of "Bethel" church recommends. This slip up tells me a lot of what he is learning." **Todd** thinks God answered the cry of his heart. And he wants other to have the same experience he had, that's dangerous. Overwhelmed with bodily sensations of utter discomfort, feeling like they are physically dying is not of God.
It does not matter if it is in Jesus' name.   http://www.stand4thelord.com)

A recent YouTube clip from **Todd White** on TBN has become popular. In this clip, he makes some staggeringly bad statements about the very core of Christian doctrine: the meaning and purpose of the cross of Christ (he made the exact same comments earlier in the year). Like many of the New Apostolic Reformation teachers, **Todd White** tells stories and invents analogies to replace the true teachings of the Bible.

For instance, **White** tells people that you wouldn't spend $150,000 for a $3,000 car, so if someone pays $150,000 for a car, it must really be worth that much. He then says that since God paid a very high price on the cross we must be very valuable, as opposed to being guilty as sinners. It could just as easily be said that Jesus had to die on the cross because of how bad our sin is; the "high price" of the cross shows us how terrible our situation was before Jesus paid our debt.

It only takes a little skepticism and a quick look at God's Word to see how demonic this teaching actually is. If we are so valuable, as **White** tells us, why did Jesus have to die on the cross? Why was Jesus punished in our place? **Todd White's** teaching is very confusing, but it really appeals to our selfish nature.

It makes no sense to die on the cross just to show people how valuable they are. There has to be a reason why Jesus was punished in our place. Otherwise, why didn't Jesus simply tell us how valuable we are and encourage us to continue doing all the wonderful things we were doing? He could've just sent us a fruit basket or given us a pat on the back, instead of dying a horrible death on the cross.

John the Baptist said (about Jesus): "Behold, the Lamb of God who takes away the sin of the world!" According to **Todd White**, John the Baptist should've said something like: "Behold, the Lamb of God who comes to tell you how valuable you are! You're doing great, now just remember your true identity!!"

The Bible says we are sinners who deserve God's wrath, but our sin is removed because of the atoning sacrifice of Jesus dying on the cross in our place. **Todd White** says we are really valuable, but the problem is, we just don't understand our value; we don't "know our true identity." So Jesus paid a really high price to convince us of our value.

Instead of focusing on God's gracious free gift of salvation, which was given in spite of our sin, **Todd White** flips the Gospel upside down and says that Jesus had to pay a high price to get us back, because we are so valuable.

Although **White** mentions our sin, it starts to sound as if we deserve God's salvation because we're so valuable. It almost seems as if **White** thinks we shouldn't be in awe of the amazing grace that God bestowed upon us, instead, we should puff ourselves up with the fact that God paid such a high price for us. This is a completely false Gospel. http://www.piratechristian.com/

And he was discovered to be this New Breed through the NAR Apostolic ministry of **Patricia King**:
"**Todd White** is part of "A New Breed" walking the earth with the Lord – full-on in God and full-on for God in all things at all times. This New Breed loves Jesus, loves people, and walks in the power of God that comes from His love and righteousness, and they are truly about the Father's business in the earth."
Todd White claims, "My God has found no fault in me because there is a place we can walk in purity and holiness and peace, and without, that no-one will see the Lord;"

"Back in 2008 when **Patricia King** came to a glory school and I met her for the first time and didn't know her." "I went through the glory school and it was very Biblical, just amazing." "Just precept upon precept, line upon line. I had no idea what it was.
It was awesome." " And she called me out and prophesied over me." " And when she did she prophesied these two words: New Breed. And it went right to my heart. Just knocked me down actually." "I was under the weight of that word in my heart. Just on the ground for while."

"... But what God's been stirring in me is that he's raising up a generation that will be the New Breed. A New Breed of Christianity. A New Breed, one that would walk in the love of God, that is so consumed by passionate love for him..."
" [...] When sonship is established, what we know is our dad. He's our dad."
"I'm a son. He's my dad." "And nothing gets in between here where there's a life of no compromise that's established." "Because compromise separates relationship... When this is established, when sonship is established, there's no compromise."

" Why would I want to join myself to another when I'm already joined to Him, unless it's in a marital status? This thing's amazing. It's totally different than anything I've ever even heard of, ever even dreamed of, because the Gospel is 100% supernatural."
"But there is such a place to be in God where sonship is established, where righteousness is the core of everything you are. Where He's the centre of everything you are. Where God is the focus of every day in everything. When we come to the realization that we can do absolutely nothing without Him."
"I can't go anywhere without Him because He's my dad and He loves me profusely...."

Source: **Patricia King**, 2014 – "A New Breed," XP Media, (014-a-new-breed/, Published 13/06/2017). https://churchwatchcentral.com

https://www.youtube.com/watch?v=oHyqUNODhV0

"The Ground Zero of the NAR is "Bethel Church" in Redding, California, with whom **Todd White** is strongly affiliated. **White** speaks at their conferences and is very tight with "Bethel Church's" commander-in-chief and senior pastor, **Bill Johnson**..."

"Some of the techniques used are: Getting kids "high" on the music, telling them it's the Holy Ghost moving, running the kids in lines through "fire tunnels" during intermission, laying hands on them and imparting the Kundalini Serpent Spirit..."

This is precisely what **Todd White** does, always "calling down fire" in the name of "Jesus," which is also precisely what we are warned will be one of the great deceptions of the Beast . . . calling down fire from heaven . . . a.k.a.: false signs and lying wonders (Revelation 13:13). Jesus Himself said it would be a deception so powerful, that if it were possible, "it would deceive even the very elect." https://www.worthychristianforums.com

- **Ralph Wilkerson**: Deceased; Reverend **Ralph Wilkerson** reportedly died on Wednesday, Dec. 12 (2018). With his wife Eileen, **Wilkerson** was the founder and pastor of the Melodyland Christian Center in Anaheim, California.

Wilkerson was best known for powerful teaching and healing miracles.

Melodyland, a former theater bought by **Wilkerson** in 1969, became one of the largest and most influential charismatic churches and was the site of great Holy Spirit outpouring in the 1970s. The campus eventually offered a drug rehabilitation program, charismatic clinics, a preschool and daycare center, Melodyland High School, the Melodyland School of Theology and the Anaheim Christian College. Several churches were birthed out of the move of God at Melodyland. The church campus was replaced in 2003 by the Anaheim Garden Walk.

Author Dr. Mark Rutland tweeted, "Just got the sad call that **Dr. Ralph Wilkerson** has passed away. I will miss him so much, as will many." "He led me into Spirit baptism in Dec. 1975, and he went to heaven, also in December, 43 years later. His impact on me was life-changing."
David Hall tweeted about **Wilkerson**: "Heaven has gained another hero! Pastor **Ralph Wilkerson**. I went with Dad when he preached at Melodyland in Anaheim in 1995." "He was so kind, he received an offering so we could go to Disneyland. Hero of the charismatic renewal in the 60s & 70s!"
On its YouTube channel, Encounter TV referred to **Wilkerson** as "a father in the faith" to many. In an interview, **Wilkerson** said, "The gifts of the Spirit are to be used every day, every day consumption. We can do this if we're full of the Holy Ghost."

Watch his full 2016 interview below:

(**NOTE: The above is from Charisma News. Because of that, you have to be a subscriber to their magazine in order to see the video they talk about, so since I am not a subscriber, I cannot post the video or the video link here. This is from You Tube.
 You may be able to find the above mentioned video on You Tube. Ed.).

(This is the friendship he had with **Benny Hinn**, one of the false preachers of our time.
It is from the **Benny Hinn** Ministries website, listed below. Ed.).

 https://www.youtube.com/ watch?v=qLvfSzhwgfM

- **Dallas Willard**: Deceased; https://www.youtube.com/ watch?time_continue=472&v=JxdvOLdG_34&feature=emb_logo

https://www.baptistboard.com/threads/ antichristian-mysticism-taught-by-dallas-willard.53424/

https://www.wayoflife.org/database/ dallas_willard.html

https://cicministry.org/commentary/ issue91.htm

(**NOTE: Apparently somewhere in this person's life he went off track and joined himself to a New Age discipline. Ed.).

- **Doug Wilson**: https://www.theaquilareport.com /a-question-for-doug-wilson-fans/

http://thewartburgwatch.com/2016/02/12/ what-is-the-problem-with-doug-wilson/

https://flockalert.wordpress.com/2009/10/28/ beware-of-douglas-wilson-part-1/

https://www.theamericanconservative.com/dreher/ scandal-in-moscow/

https://heidelblog.net/2019/07/
has-doug-wilson-really-changed-his-mind-about-the-federal-vision/

- **John Wimber** Deceased; Vineyard church, Toronto "outpouring;" a highly recognized NAR Apostle, one of the pillars of NAR theology and its abhorrent practices.
 https://pulpitandpen.org/2018

Signs & Wonders Movement, author of "Power Healing ":

Wimber claimed, "It's God's nature to heal, not to teach us through sickness. Sickness is generally not beneficial." (Benn and Burkill, p. 102 as cited by Paul G. Heibert in "Healing And The Kingdom").

 "I had what doctors later suspected were a series of coronary attacks." "When we returned home a series of medical tests confirmed my worst fears, I had a damaged heart, possibly seriously damaged." " Tests indicated that my heart was not functioning properly, a condition complicated and possibly caused by high blood pressure. These problems combined with my being overweight and overworked meant that I could die at any time."

John McArthur, "Does God Still Heal," Grace Community Church in Panorama City, California, transcribed from the tape, GC 90-60, titled "Charismatic Chaos" Part 9.

Wimber ultimately died from a hemorrhage as a result of a long battle with cancer. http://www.biblerays.com/false-preachers.html

SOAKING PRAYER: In 2000 Anne Hibbert was in Toronto having a break from her job as Prayer Development Officer for the Bible Reading Fellowship.

There was a conference at the Toronto Airport Christian Fellowship (TACF), a church Anne had heard much about as the centre of what has been called 'The Toronto Blessing.' The afternoon was free and Anne stayed in the main church building.
She lay on the church chairs while quiet music played on the sound system. Anne was not looking for anything particular, just relaxing in what felt like a good place. As she lay on the chairs Anne felt an overwhelming sense of God.

 "I was in my mother's womb, God was stroking my head and I was just feeling loved. This was the first time I really received Father God's love." This is a telling comment from someone whose whole job was to help people develop their praying. Anne Hibbert was doing what TACF calls "soaking prayer."
 Anne now leads the Well Christian Healing Centre in Leamington Spa (UK).

In the Pump Rooms every Wednesday afternoon there is <u>soaking prayer </u>open to anyone who wants to come. Quiet worship music is playing. After a five minute talk, people sit or lie quietly. "It's <u>chilling with God </u>to see what He wants to say or do," says Anne.

God's presence:

"<u>Soaking prayer</u>" is a modern form of <u>contemplative prayer</u>, described by Joyce Huggett in this magazine a few months ago. People put themselves in an attitude of stillness, focusing on Jesus and open to the Holy Spirit but with no requests or agenda. The aim is to be still in God's presence, "waste time with Jesus."
The Toronto church sees <u>soaking prayer </u>as one of the main ways in which they encourage people to be open to the Holy Spirit.

The more usual way is for people to stand and receive prayer ministry one to one with a member of their church, as is now common practice in many churches.
In the UK the most common model of prayer ministry is that taught by the American **John Wimber**. **John** was introduced to British Churches by David Watson, a leading Anglican Evangelical of the 1970s. **John** also founded the Vineyard association of churches, of which TACF was originally a part. The heart of the prayer ministry taught by **John Wimber** was to expect, invite, look for and welcome the Holy Spirit to come to individuals.

John taught that there are signs that the Holy Spirit is on a person.
"Some of these phenomena are obvious: weeping, cries, exuberant and prolonged expressions of praise, <u>shaking, trembling, calmness, bodily writhing and distortions, falling over (sometimes referred to as 'being slain in the Spirit'), laughter and jumping.</u>"
"Other phenomena are more subtle: slight trembling, fluttering of the eyelids, faint perspiring, a sheen on the face, ripples on the skin, deep breathing.."

Wimber <u>also said that people sometimes experience a sense of heaviness or tiredness, weeping or drunkenness. These symptoms that **Wimber** describes, along with the electric tingling and warm sensations described at TACF, are also the signs of what is called the Kundalini effect.</u>

Ray Yungen (deceased; a Christian apologetic) discusses this:

"Kundalini' is a Hindu term for the mystical power or force that underlies Hindu spirituality. In Hinduism it is commonly referred to as the serpent power."

St. Romain, a substance abuse counselor and devout Catholic lay minister, began his journey while practicing <u>contemplative prayer </u>or <u>"resting in the still point,</u>" as he called it.... Having rejected mental prayer as "unproductive," he embraced the prayer form that <u>switches off the mind,</u> <u>creating</u> what he described as a <u>mental passivity</u>.

What he encountered next underscores my concern with sobering clarity:

"Then came the lights! The gold swirls that I had noted on occasion began to intensify, forming themselves into patterns that both intrigued and captivated me." "... There were always four or five of these; as soon as one would fade, another would appear, even brighter and more intense ... They came through complete passivity and only after I had been in the silence for a while."

After this, St. Romain began to sense "wise sayings" coming into his mind and felt he was "receiving messages from another." He also had physical developments occur during his periods in the silence. He would feel "prickly sensations" on the top of his head and at times it would "fizzle with energy." This sensation would go on for days.

https://wolvesinthepulpit.blogspot.com/p/soaking-prayer-by-roger-harper-in-2000.html

The second book recommended by Alpha in the above audio is **John Wimber's** "Power Healing." (**NOTE: The Alpha Course is described below these articles. Ed.)

This book boasts an introduction by spiritual formation proponent **Richard Foster** in which **Foster** exclaims, "I thank God for "Power Healing." The website, "Healing and Revival," offers a thorough biography of **John Wimber**. There it is learned that **Wimber** experienced conversion in 1963 through his involvement in a Quaker Bible study.
Also noted is **Wimber's** close involvement with notable church growth expert **C. Peter Wagner**: In 1974 **Wimber** was offered a job by **Peter Wagner** to be the Founding Director of the Department of Church Growth at the "Fuller Institute of Evangelism and Church Growth." **Wimber** was traveling all over the world teaching on church growth. [12]

In 1977, **Wimber** and his wife, Carol, left their Quaker church to begin a church of their own. Prior to this time, it is claimed that Carol and a small group of people who were "seeking more of God" began to "experience the presence of the Holy Spirit," and that "God also spoke to Carol about the importance of intimate worship."[13].
It would not be long before **John Wimber** also allegedly was hearing from the Almighty. Due to Calvary Chapel's experience with the Holy Spirit in the Jesus Movement, **John** became connected with Calvary Chapel and established his church as Calvary Chapel of Yorba Linda in May 1977.

God began to speak to **Wimber** about healing the sick, and he began a church series on the subject. In March 1978, after ten months of preaching and praying without anyone healed, **Wimber** saw his first healing. The church grew rapidly and began to experience a greater outpouring of the Holy Spirit.
Unexpectedly God began to train **Wimber**, and the church, in deliverance.
This was a point of theological difference with Cavalry Chapel and they are (sic) asked to leave the denomination, but were recommended to associate with the Vineyard Church, another group in the area that was moving in similar directions. In 1982 **Wimber's** church became a Vineyard.[14].

JOHN WIMBER AND THE VINEYARD MOVEMENT:

In 1982, **John Wimber** also would become the head of the Vineyard churches.

According to the Vineyard USA website, "**John Wimber's** influence profoundly shaped the theology and practice of Vineyard churches from their earliest days until his death in November, 1997."[15] Throughout this time, **John Wimber** continued to teach at Fuller Theological Seminary. His course, "Signs and Wonders and Church Growth," became "the most popular, and the most controversial, at the school."[16]. The class was an interactive one and, in 1984, **Wimber** decided to take his lectures on the road.

Wimber began to train people all over the world about praying for the sick and "doing the works of ministry". His focus was on every-member ministry within the body. Healing and miracles occurred in these meetings.[17].
Preaching in 1991, **Dr. John MacArthur** spoke about the Vineyard Movement and it's moniker of "Third Wave," as coined by **C. Peter Wagner**:

"The main figure in what is known as the Third Wave is a man by the name of **John Wimber**, who is pastor of the Vineyard Christian Fellowship in Anaheim. He is the major figure in this movement that has come to be known as the Third Wave of the Holy Spirit. It is sometimes called the "Signs and Wonders Movement."
"And this latest Charismatic tide seems to have swept across the globe in the last decade. It is literally everywhere in the English-speaking parts of the world."

"The term the Third Wave was coined by **C. Peter Wagner** who is a missions professor at Fuller Seminary and the author of several books on church growth. He is really the leading proponent of the Third Wave philosophy and methodology. According to **Wagner**, he said, "The first wave was the Pentecostal movement, the second wave was the Charismatic movement, and now the third wave is joining them."

By that he means, an inundating wave of the power of the Holy Spirit manifesting itself in visible ways..."At its core, [the Third Wave] is an obsession with sensational experiences, a preoccupation with the Charismata, that is tongues, healings, prophecies, words of knowledge, visions and ecstatic experiences, and that is, of course, where we find the indisputable link between the Third Wave and the Charismatic and Pentecostal movements."
"In all three movements, there is a major absorption with these supernatural, sensational kind of power encounters or power displays as they like to call them."
"They de-emphasize what you and I would know as the traditional means of spiritual growth, prayer, Bible study, the teaching of the Word and the fellowship of other believers. They don't intend to do that and they wouldn't do that in statement or even in print, but because of the very surpassing emphasis on the sensational experiences, those matters tend to get pushed significantly, if not all together, into the background." [18]

Pastor Gary Gilley examined the Vineyard Movement and various aspects of its theology in a 1995 newsletter of "Think On These Things." He writes:

"The [Vineyard Movement] believes in "power evangelism" vs. "program evangelism."
"Program evangelism' is the presentation of the Gospel message to a lost sinner. While not

anti-program evangelism, the VM believes that it is an anemic way of bringing people to Christ, especially people in the Third World."

"What is needed is power evangelism, that is, signs and wonders. If, in conjunction with presenting the Gospel message, we also heal a person, raise the dead, cast out a demon, or speak a word of knowledge, our message will be with authority and power."

" The results of power evangelism, we are told, are far superior to program evangelism." "It is interesting, however, to examine the Scriptural record of the results of signs and wonders. It would appear that miracles seldom produced any true faith or lasting fruit. Even with Christ, we find people following Him in order to be healed or fed, yet rejecting his message" (e.g. John 6). [19].

Indeed, this line of thinking is quite similar to the teachings of **Morton Kelsey** as examined earlier. In 1989, **Wimber** became involved with **Mike Bickle** and the Kansas City Prophets. In the early 1990s, a movement known as the "Toronto Blessing" began to sweep through some churches. The primary church in this movement was a Vineyard church in Toronto, though according to "Healing and Revival," "**Wimber** did not agree with everything being taught in Toronto and eventually asked them to leave the association."[20]. In 1997, Todd Hunter, who reportedly "had been with **Wimber** since the beginning," assumed leadership of the Vineyard. [21] **Wimber** died in November of 1997.

JOHN WIMBER, NICKY GUMBEL AND THE ALPHA COURSE :

Aside from being a recommended author by "The Alpha Course," what additional impact might **John Wimber** have had upon Alpha and its longtime leader, Nicky Gumbel?

As noted above, Todd Hunter, who had been with **Wimber** from the beginning of his charismatic ministry, took over leadership of the Vineyard Movement not long before **Wimber's** death.
Later, Hunter would be asked by "Alpha USA " to come aboard as its new president.
In an interview with Hunter at that time, the great impact of **Wimber** upon Nicky Gumbel and, consequently upon "Alpha" is revealed:

Q: Nicky Gumbel says that **John Wimber** was the most influential person in his life?
A: Yes. Apparently, when Nicky was a young man he attended some of **John's** meetings and not only had his theological world, but also his experiential world rocked.

"During a clinic time, the Holy Spirit came powerfully on Nicky and **John** turned and said the Holy Spirit was going to use him to talk to the lost." [22].

Holy Trinity Brompton Church (HTB–England), where Gumbel currently serves as vicar, credits **John Wimber's** church growth strategies for building a desire for church planting into the fabric of HTB. [23].

This fact, along with **Wimber's** incredible influence upon Nicky Gumbel, leaves it as no surprise to know that **Wimber** was welcomed to speak at HTB on occasion. In his "Bible in One Year," devotional entries, Gumbel shares a bit more about **Wimber's** influence upon his life and ministry, stating that,

"Personally, I owe a huge debt to the ministry of **John Wimber**. We as a local church also owe him a huge debt." [24]. Gumbel also briefly shares an account of the first time that **Wimber** visited HTB :

"We often tell the story of when **John Wimber** first visited our church. We saw a remarkable outpouring of the Holy Spirit and several healings. One incident, which occurred on the second night, is indelibly printed in my memory." "One of our closest friends was eight months pregnant at the time. The Holy Spirit came upon her with great power. She started to whirl around at great speed. As she did so, she exclaimed over and over again, 'I feel so strong!'"

A few weeks later she gave birth to a son who from his earliest days showed not only spiritual and emotional strength but also extraordinary physical strength.
He became a superb athlete and rugby player. [25].
Accounts such as this further validate the reports that HTB was the center of the charismatic outpouring of the Holy Spirit in the UK.
 Similar to what was experienced in Toronto at the commencement of the Toronto Blessing , Nicky Gumbel and his HTB caused an outbreak of "holy laughter" in the city of London.

Time Magazine reported on this phenomenon in 1994:

"It's Sunday evening in London's fashionable Knightsbridge neighborhood. Though pathetically tiny flocks of Londoners attend many Anglican services, Holy Trinity Brompton has a standing-room-only turnout of 1500. After the usual Scripture readings, prayers and singing, the chairs are cleared away.
Curate Nicky Gumbel prays that the Holy Spirit will come upon the congregation. Soon a woman begins laughing. Others gradually join her with hearty belly laughs." "A young worshiper falls to the floor, hands twitching." " Another falls, then another and another."
"Within half an hour there are bodies everywhere as supplicants sob, shake, roar like lions, and strangest of all laugh uncontrollably. This frenzied display has become known as the 'laughing revival' or 'Toronto Blessing."

After first appearing at Holy Trinity only last May, laughing revivals have been reported in Anglican parishes from Manchester to York to Brighton. At London's Holy Trinity, schoolteacher Denise Williams says she 'came here a little skeptical' but soon was caught up in the fervor.
"There was a lovely feeling of warmth and peace." Lines outside Holy Trinity now start forming an hour and a half before services. [26]

It is evident that the teachings of **John Wimber** have had great influence not only upon Nicky Gumbel, but upon the life of HTB and also "The Alpha Course."
Wimber, in his traveling "Signs and Wonders" show, would identify those who needed to be healed allegedly by receiving "words of knowledge" from the Lord.

"The Alpha Course," as indicated by the audio clip which began this article, also believes that a healing ministry is of utmost importance. Writes Gumbel in his book, "How to Run The Alpha

Course :" "At this point we outline the model of healing prayer which we follow (Alpha—Questions of Life, Chapter 13)."

"We then explain that God sometimes gives words of knowledge (1 Cor. 12:8) which point out whom God wants us to pray for and which are also an aid to faith in this area." " We have found that people receive these words in various ways."
"Some may get a mental picture of the part of the body which God wants to heal."
 "Some will merely receive an impression, and others may sense that they hear or see words. We have found that one of the most common ways we receive words of knowledge is by what we call "a sympathy pain :" someone senses pain in their body, which they know is not really theirs." [27]

This description is nearly identical to what can be witnessed in videos of **John Wimber's** **"**1985 Signs and Wonders Conference."

CONCLUSION: "Alpha" does little to hide the fact that it places great emphasis upon what it teaches to be the ministry and power of the Holy Spirit. Nicky Gumbel details this in his own book, "How to Run The Alpha Course," referenced above, and numerous resources encouraging this emphasis are readily accessible at the official website of "The Alpha Course USA."

"Alpha" also does little to conceal the influence of mystics such as **Morton Kelsey** and **John Wimber** upon its ministry. After examining the teachings of these two men, who both come highly recommended by the leadership of "Alpha," concerns ought to be raised in the minds and hearts of Christians. The recommendation of these two authors did not come with a disclaimer, but rather with a hearty, almost urgent endorsement.
It has been demonstrated, however, that **Morton Kelsey** not only espoused an incorrect understanding of the relationship between Jesus' healing ministry and Gospel proclamation, but that he also was highly influenced by other mystics like **Agnes Sanford** and the psychologist Carl Jung.

This article also has revealed some of the erroneous teachings of the leader of the"Third Wave," **John Wimber**, and his profound effect upon "Alpha" leader Nicky Gumbel.
To be sure, this article has not examined every area of "The Alpha Course " that may be legitimately critiqued. Others have called into question its actual Gospel presentation. As already mentioned, CRN also has scrutinized the ecumenical nature of "The Alpha Course."
In spite of its errors, can God still use "Alpha" to save a person? Of course; after all, our God is sovereign! "But the fact that some people are saved despite being exposed to false teaching does not make that false teaching acceptable." [28]

When all of the information is taken into consideration, the Christian must test against Scripture what is being taught by "Alpha," as well as what is contained within the resources it recommends. It is after all, only the Word of God that will guide one into Truth, not the whims of men or the emotional rush of a so-called "outpouring of the Holy Spirit." Sanctify them in the truth; Your word is truth. (John 17:17, NASB)

FOOTNOTES:

(1)**Morton Kelsey,** "The Other Side of Silence," (Paulist Press: 1995), 75. Quoted in Bob DeWaay, "Contemporary Christian Divination," Critical Issues Commentary, no. 83, 2004.

(2) Bob DeWaay, "Contemporary Christian Divination," Critical Issues Commentary, no. 83, 2004.

(3) **Agnes Sanford**, "The Healing Light," (Charisma Books: 1972), 3. Quoted in Bob DeWaay, "Contemporary Christian Divination," Critical Issues Commentary, no. 83, 2004.

(4) **Morton Kelsey**, "Healing and Christianity," (Harper & Row Publishers: 1973), 53.

(5) http://www.inwardoutward.org/source/ through-defeat-victory, accessed 29 November 2012.

(6) Bob DeWaay, "Contemporary Christian Divination," Critical Issues Commentary, no. 83, 2004.

(7) Bob DeWaay, "Contemporary Christian Divination," Critical Issues Commentary, no. 83, 2004.

(8) **Morton Kelsey,** "Healing and Christianity," (Harper & Row Publishers: 1973), 289.

(9) **Morton Kelsey,** "Healing and Christianity," (Harper & Row Publishers: 1973), 65.

(10)**Morton Kelsey,** "Healing and Christianity," (Harper & Row Publishers: 1973), 362.

(11)**Morton Kelsey**, "Healing and Christianity," (Harper & Row Publishers: 1973), 88.

(12) http://healingandrevival.com/ BioJWimber.htm, accessed 28 November 2012.

(13) http://healingandrevival.com/ BioJWimber.htm, accessed 28 November 2012.

(14) http://healingandrevival.com/ BioJWimber.htm, accessed 28 November 2012.

(15) http://www.vineyardusa.org/ site/about/vineyard-history, accessed 28 November 2012.

(16) http://www.vineyardusa.org/ site/about/vineyard-history, accessed 28 November 2012.

(17) http://www.vineyardusa.org /site/about/vineyard-history, accessed 28 November 2012.

(18) **John MacArthur**, "The Third Wave," preached 25 August 1991.

(19) Gary Gilley, "The Vineyard Movement—Part 2," "Think On These Things" vol. 2, 1995.

(20) http://www.vineyardusa.org/site /about/vineyard-history, accessed 28 November 2012.

(21) http://www.vineyardusa.org/site /about/vineyard-history, accessed 28 November 2012.

(22) http://www.offthemap.com/ idealab/articles/idl0405-1-toddpres.html, accessed 28 November 2012.

(23) http://www.htb.org.uk/ about-htb/history, accessed 28 November 2012.

(24) http://www.htb.org.uk/ bible-in-one-year/more-trials-and-temptation, accessed 28 November 2012.

(25) http://www.htb.org.uk/ bible-in-one-year/holy-spirit-part-1, accessed 28 November 2012.

(26) Richard Ostling, "Laughing for the Lord," Time Magazine, 15 August 1994.

(27) Nicky Gumbel, "How to Run The Alpha Course," ("Alpha International:" 2004), 173.

(28) http://blog.betterthansacrifice.org/ 2010/07/15/a-closer-look-at-the-alpha-course-and-whether-it-is-permissible-to-judge-what-other-christians-teach/, accessed 28 November 2012.

(**NOTE: The above article is from: http://apprising.org/2012/12/02/ the-influence-of-christian-mystics-morton-kelsey-and-john-wimber-on-the-alpha-course/   Ed.).

- **Oprah Winfrey**: The biggest speaker about "spirit guides;" she has singlehandedly endorsed such anti-Christian beliefs as Yoga, inner healing through mind techniques and several other New Age teachings.

- **Bill Winston**: Prosperity, NAR, Word Faith preacher--

Bill Winston, the pastor of Living Word Christian Center in Forest Park (IL) is in the same circles that **Pastor Long** runs in. When the news of **Long's** problems hit the news, the reporter mentioned **Creflo Dollar** and **T.D. Jakes** as ministers with a similar profile as that of **Long**. Both pastors have spoken at Living Word many times.

I'm not implying that there is a hint of scandal at Living Word. As far as I know, **Bill Winston** is a man of integrity.
 But, as I've watched Living Word grow from just twelve members twenty years ago to 15,000 today, I've watched him consolidate power at the top of his organizations. Whenever I've called Living Word to get information for a story over the years, the person to whom I'm talking always has to check it out with **Pastor Winston**.

So identified is Living Word with **Bill Winston** that many of the programs there are referred to as coming from **Bill Winston Ministries** rather than from Living Word.
The advantage of that kind of authoritarian organizational structure is that it is efficient. Decisions get made and things get done.
The disadvantage is that when the leader stumbles, the whole organization falls and gets broken bones and bruises. I know several intelligent, competent, educated people who belong to Living Word. They trust their pastor completely. For their sake, I hope there continues to be no scandal at Living Word. My worry is that **Bill Winston** shares the same sinful human nature as I have, and I wouldn't trust myself with that much power.
October 1st, 2010 https://www.oakpark.com/Community/Blogs/10-1-2010/
The-danger-with-mega-churches-like-Living-Word-in-Forest-Park/

https://theoldblackchurch.blogspot.com/2013/02/ jesus-take-wheel-feds-shut-down.html

Posted 19th February 2013 by Ann Brock

"Jesus Take The Wheel: Feds Shut Down Megachurch **Bill Winston** Bank!"

Federal regulators late Friday shut down Covenant Bank on the West Side of Chicago which has been reported to have been losing money since its 2008 founding by megachurch pastor **Bill Winston**. What an unfortunate outcome for such a wonderful idea. I feel sorry for the church members who lost their money here.

From my reading and understanding, with the bank being closed by bank regulators that the sale will protect account holders, who are insured up to the $250,000 per-account maximum. But it will wipe out the bank's owners, including members of **Winston's** Living Word Christian Center in Forest Park who provided cash for the purchase.

388

"The Federal Deposit Insurance Corp. sold the bank's assets to Liberty Bank and Trust Co. of New Orleans. Article Here! So Sad!!"

(**NOTE: The first article and link are dated in 2013; the second one in 2010. Interesting that the first article was stating, "For their sake, I hope there continues to be no scandal at Living Word. My worry is that **Bill Winston** shares the same sinful human nature as I have, and I wouldn't trust myself with that much power" and then sure enough, it happened.
Just goes to show that a person with that much power cannot be trusted. Ed.).

- **Robert Wise**: A Jungian psychologist; he learned of "healing of the memories" from Rosalind Rinker, who in turn learned it from **Agnes Sanford**, of whom he praises and defends; claims he made contact with a "spirit being"; used visualization techniques to "see" Jesus, which began to act on its own (NOT the real Jesus); said "I was no longer creating the scene;" he wrote The Church Divided (1986):

 It had such contributors as **David Yonggi Cho, Dennis Bennett**, **Mark Virkler** (whose own book "Dialogue With God" seduces Christians into contact with demons masquerading as "God" and "Christ", and **William De Arteaga**, who considers **Agnes Sanford's** "The Healing Light" to be "among the first rank of Christian literature."

De Arteaga defends **Sanford's** visualization and her belief in a pre-earth human existence. He suggests that **Christianity accommodate Hinduism's "karma/reincarnation**," which he seems to accept as a result of having induced "past life regressions" in counselees. (Excerpt taken from https://www.thebereancall.org)

- **Steve Wohlberg:** SDA teacher. **Steve Wohlberg** is a Seventh-Day Adventist (SDA) minister--a sinister minister--who denies many clear teachings of the Bible, including:
The Pretribulation Rapture, The Tribulation Period, the person of the Antichrist, the restoration of Israel, and many other plain Bible teachings.

 In fact, **Mr. Wohlberg** is so hateful of Biblical truth that demonic Wiccan witches love and highly recommend **Steve Wohlberg's** books...

"We cannot recommend **Steve's** books strongly enough. The information and deceptions exposed in these books is something we all need to understand and share with others."
SOURCE: http://www.wiccawitchcraft.net/

Steve Wohlberg is a heretic, who teaches the lies of Seventh-Day Adventism, including the ridiculous and unbiblical theory of the Investigative Judgment (a far fetched doctrine fabricated by **Ellen G. White**).
 Occultist **Ellen G. White**, and others, officially founded SDA in 1963, which was spawned as a result of a failed prophecy by a heretic named William Miller. Miller predicted the Lord's return, and had set a date for October 22, 1844.
Followers of Miller sold their homes, quit their jobs, and gave away all worldly possessions. There were an estimated 10,000 followers of Miller, known as "Millerites." When Miller's prediction failed to come to fruition, people became suicidal.

To save face, a handful of Millerites scrambled to fabricate a cover for their blunder; thus, SDA was born.

This is the hilarious and yet tragic history upon which the SDA Church was founded. This alone should cause every SDA to leave their organization, and follow the Word of God instead! Jesus NEVER started a religion; BUT rather commanded us to... SEARCH THE SCRIPTURES (John 5:39). Just as with the damnable Catholic religion, SDAs have fabricated their own TRADITIONS which are completely unbiblical, and go 100% contrary to the plainest teachings of the Bible.
It is tragic that the pastor's of America's largest Independent Baptist Churches are more interested in writing books on finances, than on prophecy and the End times.

  The world is absolutely enamored with the subject of the end times; yet the church is fast asleep. **Steve Wohlberg** is delusional, and a false prophet. Seventh-day Adventism is a strange religion, that veers considerably from the plain teachings of the Scriptures. SDAs believe in "soul sleep," as do the Jehovah's Witnesses.
"Soul Sleep" is the false doctrine that a person is unconscious after death, and remains in such a state until a future resurrection.

 In sharp contrast, II Corinthians 5:8 states... "We are confident, I say, and willing rather to be absent from the body, and to be present with the Lord." Jesus told the thief on the cross... "Today shalt thou be with me in paradise" (Luke 23:43).
In Luke 16, Lazarus died and was carried by angels into Paradise (i.e., "Abraham's Bosom"). Such Biblical references are clear evidence against the false doctrine of Soul Sleep. There is no break in conscience at death, for the spirit cannot die physically.

Steve Wohlberg is a dangerous man, because he APPEARS to be a Christian; BUT, he is a wolf in sheep's clothing (Matthew 7:15). **Mr. Wohlberg's** books and teachings are in popular demand--a clear indicator of the apostasy of these last days.
For a man to deny so many fundamental teachings of the Scriptures, and still retain such a large following, is disturbing indeed.
Please do NOT be deceived--**Steve Wohlberg** is a Seventh-Day Adventist minister, who adheres to the damnable doctrine of the Investigative Judgment. He is NO Christian. Contrary to Walter Martin's claim, in his book "The Kingdom of the Cults," SDA is NOT a Christian cult! SDAs clearly adhere to a works-based salvation, which requires its members to endure 'til the end to be saved.

This is a lie of the Devil, as evidenced by Scriptures such as I Corinthians 3:15 and 5:5 which show that some believers live in horrible sin; YET still go to Heaven.
https://www.jesus-is-savior.com/ False%20Religions/Seventh-Day%20Adventist/wohlberg.htm

(**NOTE: The above listed web link is not exactly 100% correct, but for the most part it is, which is why I am including it. Ed.).

-**Andrew Wommack**: Fan of **Kenneth Hagin** and **Kenneth Copeland**. WOF; believes in a concept of having Brazilian slaves attend to him.

https://youtu.be/i4BARuTQ-nc

He relies on his subjective feelings which he believes are being directed by the Holy Spirit to make decisions about where in the Bible he is going to study.
 This removes the ability to utilize proper hermeneutics. When he does this, he can't have the broader context needed to harmonize Scripture with Scripture.
This mystical decision making process is abiblical. After picking the book of Numbers to study from, he skips the importance of the genealogies because he believes them to be tedious and boring.

I wonder if he knows what "theopneustos" means? (**NOTE: It means "God-breathed." Ed.).
At about 8 minutes and 16 seconds in he claims he makes it a habit to not teach things that are new for about a year, and that he sits on them, but of course he is going to break his own rule and teach a new teaching. What does the completely revealed finished word of God have to say about new teachings?
 At about the 15 minute mark **Andrew** starts doing what many other false teachers do, he gets a concordance out and makes a hash out of Hebrew to invent a false teaching that is not in Scripture and then impose it on his listeners.
 He uses it to claim that God does not afflict people. I wonder if he ever heard of Pharaoh, Jonah, Job, or for that matter the curse God inflicts all of Adam's progeny with? Just, wow!...
We all know from reading the same Scriptures that **Andrew** is twisting, that Moses is disgusted with the people and their selfish greed, and entitled feelings. Leading them was a great burden.
20 minute mark he starts on again about getting impressions from God and just knowing things in our hearts. This is no substitute for what God actually says in His word. How does one know if the idea that popped into their thoughts was not just of their own imagining, or even worse some demon speaking to them? I know, let's ask Muhammad, **Joseph Smith**, or **Ellen G. White**... NOT!

He keeps abusing I Corinthians 10:11-13. I wonder what he would tell the martyrs? Don't worry, the lions won't eat you, the flames won't be that hot... Come on... The intent of God in His word where He says, "God is faithful, and he will not let you be tempted beyond your ability" in context means that you can make it through any circumstance by God's grace. He provides a way out of sin, so that you won't have to sin while being beheaded, burned alive, cut off in traffic, being left behind by an adulterous spouse, the death of a child.
 You can go through these things, and by His grace choose to not sin. It doesn't mean bad things will never happen to you. This is insane. This idea that the men appointed to help Moses was not from God is just more nonsense. Did not Christ have Apostles? Are the Churches to not have more than one Elder?

Come on **Andrew**... Stop making such a hash out of Scripture. You twist it like it is free. One day you'll have to answer for all your twisting.
@ 26:50 he starts in again about suffering not being God's will, and he is placing a tremendous works righteousness burden on the people listening to him, that he himself doesn't even believe or perform.

He preaches a, "life enhancement Christianity" that is just not true. We don't have less suffering in our lives when we come to faith, matter of fact we suffer for our faith, unless you don't believe what God incarnate said in His own Word. I can't even begin to tell you how much it ticks me off to hear him talking about, "God's best."
How does he know what is God's best for you? We need to suffer. It is part of growing in faith. It is part of being sanctified.

Again, what would this clown tell Polycarp while he was being martyred? "Oh Polycarp, you just don't lay your burdens down on the Lord enough. You just aren't using the faith God gave you. You need to try harder to be more spiritual like me because I don't have any problems..."
Yeah, right! Pack it in and go home **Andrew** before you hurt anyone else!!!
@ 30:10 **Andy** says, "God doesn't put any negative things on us." Well, God says so in Isaiah 45:6,7.

Oh and say, let's not forget the flood, or Sodom and Gomorrah, or plagues and famines sent as discipline upon the people.
Andrew's theology is so anthropocentric it is no wonder his doctrines are so focused on life enhancement through the faith he invented. In Romans 1 we can see God's punishment in the form of people worshiping created things. This includes anthropocentric religion as well.

 Romans 1:21-25 "21 For even though they knew God, they did not honor Him as God or give thanks, but they became futile in their speculations, and their foolish heart was darkened. 22 Professing to be wise, they became fools, 23 and exchanged the glory of the incorruptible God for an image in the form of corruptible man and of birds and four-footed animals and crawling creatures."
24 Therefore God gave them over in the lusts of their hearts to impurity, so that their bodies would be dishonored among them. 25 For they exchanged the truth of God for a lie, and worshiped and served the creature rather than the Creator, who is blessed forever. Amen."

(**NOTE: Not KJV, but I am using someone else's opinion here. Ed.).

If your theology centers around man, you are an idolater.

@30:43 **Wommack's** god doesn't control any of the negative things that happen to us. His god isn't sovereign. So if 1 Corinthians 10 isn't about not suffering, what is it really about? I'm glad you asked. It is about being tempted to sin against the Lord in several different ways. It is focused on the glory of God, and obedience to Him as worship.
If you look at the verses in context you'll see that, not only did God allow suffering, He caused it as punishment and discipline on His people for giving in to sin. Let's take a look at the scripture in context. 1 Corinthians 10:1-13:

In verses 1-5 we see that the ones who persevered in faith in Christ, were the ones whom God was well pleased with. The rest God was putting under discipline. Verse 6 is pretty self-explanatory. Don't go after the sin that they went after, duh! The first group of sinners mentioned was the idolaters, then the immoral out of which God killed 23,000. Next were the ones who doubted and tried the Lord, He sent serpents to kill some of them.

Then there were the grumblers, the ones who complained about God's providence.
 God destroyed them with the destroyer, an angel sent to kill them in the desert. After reading all of this in addition to the verse that so often gets twisted, we can see that God is talking about sin here. In Christ, He has provided a way out for His elect.
We can choose to not sin, in any given temptation because we are no longer slaves to sin, but to Christ.
The Holy Spirit is in us, we are born again, made dead to sin and alive to Christ.

When temptation comes, fight against it with the promise of the Gospel, and a view of Christ's sufferings on the cross on behalf of you, because of your sins.
 If you do that, you won't want to add suffering to Christ so to speak, not that you could, but figuratively because as we know all of your sin, past, present, and future, was paid for over 2000 years ago by Jesus.
I watched the rest of the video and there was more and more about God telling you what to do in some mysterious way, via a word, or prompting. It was getting tedious and sickening to hear him keep burdening people with uncertainty, when the Bible is so clear.

People, IF YOU WANT TO KNOW WHAT GOD WANTS YOU TO DO, READ THE BIBLE!!!

@ 38:20 He talks about his skin cancer, and how he is committed to healing, so he won't go to the doctor over it. Now you know as well as I do, even though he told other people to do what they wanted in that regard, he made it sound like he was superior and the example, because he is committed to healing. Obviously if they decided to go to the doctor, they must not be. This is spiritual malpractice. He could be costing people their health with this pernicious nonsense.

He then goes on to tell people they have created their financial burdens themselves.
I agree that some people have, but what about medical hardships that cause financial hardships, oh wait... That's your fault to for not being committed to healing.
Silly me...
If this one lesson didn't offer enough health and prosperity false gospel for you, don't worry...
He has many more available on youtube for me and others like me to correct.
Please take care, and read your Bible. I agree with **Andrew** on that.
Read your Bible apart from his teachings. Systematically study it from beginning to end.
 If you do that, and still agree with **Wommack**, I pray the Holy Spirit will correct you.

 https://snyderssoapbox.com/2017/10/03/
false-teacher-andrew-wommack-whoa-mac-really-stop-stop-teaching-heresy/

(**NOTE: The following is a post on the same website listed above. He or she is lamenting being involved with **Andrew Wommack's** "ministry" as you can see. Ed.):

B. Cecile– (May 22, 2019).

Yes! Please stay away from **Andrew Wommack** and his Bible College–Charis Bible College.
They are now associating openly with the "New Apostolic Reformation"

(**Bill Johnson**- "Bethel Church" in Redding, CA).

My husband supported **Wommack** as a <u>Grace Partner</u> for a number of years and at retirement came up to the small mountain town in SO CO where his compound is located. He never made it past orientation.   Very cult-like and controlling. Unfortunately, we bought a house here and it will be another year before we can move.
 Wommack is definitely a presence in this small mountain town—sort of like <u>Scientology</u> in Clear Water Beach, FL!!

Bethel Church is becoming his favourite playground for spewing his heresy...

"God has already placed His healing power within us, and it is now under our authority. It isn't up to God to determine who receives healing; it's up to us!" "The Lord never told us to pray for the sick in the sense that we ask Him to heal them." " He told us to heal the sick."
Andrew Wommack believes in the "<u>Word of Faith</u>" theology that conceives of faith as a force conveyed by words that bring about reality. If you say, "I think I'm going to get a cold" you will actually create the cold (unless someone else counters your negative words by saying something positive). All of this takes place independently of God.

In his series titled "The Believer's Authority" **Andrew Wommack** tells the story of when his infant son kept waking up all through the night with symptoms of croup so severe that he could hardly breathe. This happened every half hour all night long.
Finally his mother said, "Admit it Andy, he's sick." **Andrew Wommack** said,
"Man I got right down in her face and stuck my finger in her face and I said, 'Satan in the name of Jesus I command you to shut up. ... And for two days she never said a word. We were on vacation. It was an awesome vacation – you can imagine."

Andrew Wommack teaches that God gave man all authority on earth, <u>so God Himself had no authority</u>. The reason Jesus had to come in human flesh was to gain that human authority. He teaches that God had limited His own authority by giving it to man such that God was unable to speak Jesus' body into existence.
And so God had to find men to do it on their authority. It took God 4000 years to find enough men with enough combined authority to create Jesus' body.

<u>Apart from the help of men God was unable to create a body for Jesus.</u>

Andrew Wommack utters this blasphemy:

"When (people) see that some sickness, disease, tragedy comes into their life, instead of taking their authority and rebuking the devil and commanding him to leave, instead <u>they go to God</u> ... and they beg God, 'Oh God please change this situation.
Oh God please get the devil off my back.' <u>And it's not within God's power and authority</u>. He gave us that power and authority."

2 Timothy 4:3-4 "3 For the time will come when they will not endure sound doctrine; but after their own lusts shall they heap to themselves teachers, having itching ears;

4 And they shall turn away their ears from the truth, and shall be turned unto fables."

https://www.discerningtheworld.com/2019/09/27/ andrew-wommack-false-teacher/

Though the Bible teaches a radical change when one passes from spiritual death to life and darkness to light (1 Cor. 6:11; Rom. 6:21; 1 Tim. 1:13; etc.), **Andrew Wommack** teaches a born again believer is still acting the same and yielding to those same old temptations!

Andrew Wommack: "Have you ever asked yourself what changed when you were "born again"? You look in the mirror and see the same reflection—your body hasn't changed. You find yourself acting the same and yielding to those same old temptations —that didn't seem to change either ("Spirit, Soul and Body," back cover).

That quote alone should set off spiritual loud red flashing warning bells, even if you are only semi-acquainted with the Bible! Where is the evidence of the power of the Gospel in **Wommack's** message?
The converts he produces are apparently still slaves to sin, which means they aren't real converts to Christianity at all! They remain unchanged evildoers.

Undoubtedly, the no-change salvation view alone reflects a serious spiritual problem. There certainly is something very WRONG. As we proceed, the evidence will become more and more clear. **Andrew Wommack's** teachings, which would have to extend beyond his books and over into his radio program, Charis Bible college and throughout his whole ministry, will be shown to be severely flawed and a detriment to SOULS.
Verbally you can hear that **Andrew Wommack** teaches, in essence, that Christians are powerless to live holy: "If you were truly born again you want to live for God."

"Now you might be doing a poor job of it because religion actually weakens you and strengthens sin. So there's many reasons why Christians don't live holy, but if you are truly born again you want to live for God." https://www.evangelicaloutreach.org/andrew-wommack-ministry-faith-healer-charis-bible-college-heresy.htm

- **George O. Wood**: Assembly of God Superintendent; questionable practices:
http://www.truthkeepers.com/ ?p=230

https://www.lighthousetrailsresearch.com/ blog/?p=23397

https://www.news-leader.com/story/news/2017/08/09/assemblies-god-elects-new-leader-after-wood-falling-short-votes-removes-himself-consideration/554112001/

https://bewareofthewolves.blogspot.com/2017/01 /george-o-wood-assemblies-of-god.html

http://www.truthkeepers.com/ ?p=225

(**NOTE: Some of what he has done or is doing is questionable; other things he is spot on. I am leaving it up to you the reader to decide. Ed.).

- **Maharesh Mahash Yogi**: Deceased; Hindu teacher; practiced <u>meditation</u> and <u>levitation</u>. "Lennon was right. The Giggling Guru was a shameless old fraud."

By DAVID JONES Last updated February 2008

To his millions of dream-eyed devotees, he was the ultimate spiritual leader; a <u>masterful guru whose meditation techniques could induce a state of euphoric bliss, and even teach them to defy gravity by "yogic flying"</u>.
To a sneering John Lennon, he was a money-grubbing, sex-obsessed fraud who cynically abused his influence over The Beatles and many other awed celebrities who worshipped, cross-legged, at his painted feet during the Flower Power era.

So which one was the real **Maharishi Mahesh Yogi**?
Was he the <u>enlightened saviour </u>he always proclaimed himself to be? Or the woolly bearded, flower-bedecked fraud portrayed in Lennon's acid lyrics? It's a debate that has lingered like the smell of burning incense for 40 years, ever since the Fab Four perplexed their fans by swopping flairs and kipper ties for flowing robes and love-beads.
And now that the Indian mystic's mortality has been proved with news of his death, at the approximate age of 91 (no one can be sure, for he dismissed birthdays as "an irrelevance"), it will doubtless resurface. However, as the last writer to have been granted an audience with the enigmatic **Maharishi** - and, indeed, the only journalist to have been invited inside the strange "<u>alternative nation</u>" where he lived his final years in seclusion - I know who I tend to believe.
My day with the man who probably did more than anyone else to make traditional Eastern beliefs fashionable in the West came in March 2006, when I visited the so- called Global Country of World Peace, in Vlodrop, southeastern Holland.

It must rank as the most bizarre day of my 30-year career. Before I take you behind the high walls of this closely-guarded community, however, it's worth remembering how an obscure Indian civil servant's son rose to control a vast spiritual fiefdom, with its own ministers and laws, and even its own currency, the Raam.
An empire, moreover, which became hugely lucrative thanks to the one quality the **Maharishi** never liked to publicize - his remarkable business acumen - aligned to an utterly shameless willingness to put aside his principles and embrace the detested "material world" when it suited his own ends.

He spent his early years in Jabalpur, where he was born, probably in 1917 or 1918.
Back then his name was plain **Mahesh Prasad Varma**, and, though his family were devout <u>Hindus</u>, there was nothing to suggest that he might become a world-renowned leader. A bright boy, he gained a maths and physics degree - a qualification he would use with great ingenuity later in life, when he impressed (and invariably baffled) his followers by "explaining" the ability of <u>meditation to change people's consciousness </u>in complex scientific terminology.

By all accounts, his life changed course radically in his late 20s, when he met his great mentor - a "swami" or Indian religious teacher, called **Guru Dev**. He joined the ageing holy man on a lengthy retreat in the Himalayas, where he was introduced to a new form of <u>meditation</u>. When he emerged, he called himself "**Maharishi**".

Unlike **Guru Dev,** who was content to wander, barefooted and in ragged clothes, from village to village and subsist on the simple charity of those he taught, his pupil developed more grandiose ideas.

Whether because he thought it his duty to spread his newfound enlightenment to as many people as possible, as he later claimed, or because he had an eye to the main chance, in 1958 he left India on his first "global tour." For obvious reasons, though, he based himself in Los Angeles. In those days, California was a Mecca for the Beat Generation, and among these forerunners of the hippies, a plausible, exotic young guru preaching love and peace - and offering a way of achieving a "natural high" without the need for drugs - quickly became a cult hero.

Soon his popularity spread among stressed business executives seeking an alternative to psychiatry, whose methods he scorned. "You must learn to take life less seriously and to laugh," he told them, chuckling as if he were privy to some sublime cosmic joke. "The highest state is laughter." Along with the adulation came money, of course.

At first, the **Maharishi** asked for nothing and, like his mentor **Guru Dev**, he lived off donations, albeit more substantial amounts than he would have received in India.

As his renown grew, however, he began to charge "tuition fees", realising his affluent audience could easily afford to pay for his words of wisdom. With a wink and a giggle, followers were also encouraged to contribute towards his "expenses": printing costs, transport rental, the hiring of halls and so on. In 1961, one rich woman blithely wrote him a cheque for $100,000: her contribution to a new ashram he wished to build in India. Another wealthy couple, accountant Roland Olson and his publicist wife Helen, gave him free use of a plush house in Hollywood.

The "Giggling Guru" appeared uninterested in these vast sums and never discussed or handled money himself, leaving it to his disciples. However, the burgeoning bank balance can hardly have escaped his all-seeing gaze. By the "beautiful summer" of 1967, when he famously came to the attention of The Beatles, the **Maharishi** boasted a considerable following, including celebrities such as Mike Love of the Beach Boys (who became a teacher of <u>Transcendental Meditation</u>), folk singer Donovan, Mia Farrow, and even the tough-guy actor Clint Eastwood.

Impressed after hearing him speak in London a few days earlier, on August 25, John, Paul, George and Ringo fatefully boarded a train from Paddington to Bangor, where they were to spend the Bank Holiday weekend on retreat with him (A British holiday).

Disaster struck midway through the seminar, when news came through that Brian Epstein, The Beatles' manager, had died from a drug overdose. The group, who relied on him to orchestrate every aspect of their lives, were devastated, but the **Maharishi** treated his death as a minor mishap.

"He was sort of saying, 'Look, forget it! Be happy!'" remarked Lennon later, adding caustically: "_____idiot." At the time The Beatles couldn't see through such insensitive behavior. It seemed only to confirm one of their new guru's favourite phrases (which became the title of a George Harrison LP): "All things must pass."

Desperate for an alternative to the increasingly crazy, pressure-cooker world they inhabited, and seeking a new guiding spirit with Epstein's passing, they became deeply immersed in the **Maharishi's** teaching. So, the following February, 1968, the four beaming, flower-garlanded band-members flew to India, where they were to spend several months deepening their knowledge of Transcendental Meditation at his ashram in Rishikesh.
They were accompanied by their respective partners and joined by a veritable array of mantra-chanting stars, including Farrow and her sister, Prudence.
 For the first few weeks, this intended spiritual awakening went well enough, but Ringo was first to depart - he hated Indian food and his wife, Maureen, couldn't bear the insects.   After five weeks, amid mounting mutterings that the **Maharishi** was a publicity-seeker with an unhealthy interest in meditating in close proximity to the Farrow sisters, Paul McCartney followed the drummer back to London.

That left John and George, always the most receptive (or gullible?) among the guru's pupils. In an episode now etched in Beatle folklore, however, they too packed their bags in disgust after Mia Farrow fled the **Maharishi's** cave in tears, claiming that the supposedly celibate swami had grabbed her in his hairy arms and tried to make advances towards her.   "Boys! Boys! What's wrong? Why are you leaving?" the **Maharishi** is said to have shouted after them. "If you're so "_____"cosmic, you'll know," came Lennon's withering reply. Thus ended The Beatles' brief dalliance with the **Maharish**i. Or, at least, so it was widely believed.
The **Maharishi** always disputed this highly unedifying version of events. In his one public pronouncement on the matter, he insisted that they were "too unstable and weren't prepared to end their Beatledom". This stand-off rumbled on for almost four decades, casting a huge question-mark over the **Maharishi's** credibility and the entire TM movement.
But then, two years ago, the guru's story appeared to be given credence by the self-help guru **Deepak Chopra** (one of the **Maharishi's** former disciples).
The **Maharishi** had actually ordered The Beatles to leave the ashram, **Chopra** said, because they refused to stop taking drugs. **Chopra** had just made his pronouncement when, quite unexpectedly, I was given the opportunity to hear the truth from the horse's mouth.
The **Maharishi** had not granted an interview since 1992, but after days of negotiations with his moony-eyed media chief, Bob Roth, I was summoned to the Global Country of World Peace.
No passport was required as I "left Holland" and drove to the Giggling Guru's kingdom, but it really was like entering another state; or rather, a parallel universe. Inside the spacious compound, all the men (I saw no women) wore identical fawn- coloured suits and disconcerting, far-away smiles. They were polite enough, but the place seemed utterly devoid of warmth.

However, Roth, a reconstructed San Francisco hippie in his 50s, repeatedly assured me that, for all manner of reasons, my karma was "just perfect for this interview".
But all this transparent schmoozing came with a warning. Questions about His Holiness's personal life were strictly off limits. Oh, and The Beatles were an absolute taboo.

This didn't seem to leave much room for discussion, but there were more surprises in store. For the historic interview I was ushered into the so-called brahmastan, a sort of giant pagoda-style wooden palace. I was flanked by two stern faced, light-suited "ministers", who introduced me, to the untold thousands of disciples watching this bizarre charade via the live global video-link by which the **Maharishi** communicated his edicts, as a "distinguished international journalist" - which was certainly a first for me.

Then, just as I was expecting him to make his entrance, a giant screen flickered to life and I was greeted not by a real live guru but by a sort of hologram with a cotton-wool beard and a shiny, teak-brown pate.Only then did I realise that the **Maharishi** would be addressing me only via closed-circuit TV from his chamber, presumably somewhere upstairs. "His Holiness never meets anyone because his doctor is concerned that he might catch germs," Roth whispered. "He hasn't been outside for years."

In truth, it was more a monologue than an interview. The **Maharishi** spouted incomprehensible mumbo jumbo for several minutes-then launched into a diatribe against Britain - a terrible country which believes in "divide and rule" and was responsible for much of the misery besetting the world.

This, he said, was why he had decided to "excommunicate" this country, meaning that his disciples were banned from teaching TM here (a state of affairs which, I regret to report, he later reversed).
My one small victory was that I managed to ask him - ever so politely - about The Beatles. Given all the bad blood, did he regret his involvement with the band who made him a household name? Suddenly, all that serenity evaporated and the mystic came over all mortal. "Forget about it!" he spluttered furiously. "If at all, (The) Beatles became substantial by my contact." "I did not become great by association of The Beatles! Beatles make **Maharishi** great? Pah! It is a waste of thought."

Perhaps so, but there's no denying that this trivial "waste of thought" is one good reason why the **Maharishi** leaves behind in trust an estate conservatively said to be worth some £600 million.   A few weeks ago, with extraordinary prescience perhaps, the mystic handed control of the TM movement to his anointed successor, a little-known Lebanese former research scientist named **Maharaja** Nader Ram (formerly Dr Tony Nader).

But his peaceful passing, I am assured, will have little noticeable effect on the empire he created, with its hefty bank balance and estates, including a huge campus university in Iowa. Meanwhile, with the charge for a three-day TM induction course now running at £1,280, the Giggling Guru's well-heeled "ministers" will doubtless go on living in the material world. All they need is love, maybe. But money - that's what they want.

https://www.dailymail.co.uk/tvshowbiz/article-512747/
Lennon-right-The-Giggling-Guru-shameless-old-fraud.html

Ref. Encyclopedia of New Age Beliefs "Eastern gurus constitute a large class of Hindu occultists who have come to the West to spread the teachings of the false religion Hinduism."

"The New Age Movement, with a collective following in the tens of millions, has also been powerfully influenced by Hinduism. In many respects, the philosophy
of the New Age movement parallels that of Hinduism. Gurus teach practices such as altered states of consciousness, meditation, and yoga, disciples are told they will achieve a form of spiritual 'enlightenment.'
Most, if not, all gurus claim to represent, or incarnate, God and to offer higher forms of spirituality."

Despite their claims to represent God or Jesus, the gurus' teaching and practices are implicitly hostile to Biblical theology and instruction. The Hindu gurus typically redefine Jesus Christ after their own likeness. Jesus becomes a teacher of Hinduism, a guru of the past who has been greatly misunderstood by Christians. The only Jesus the gurus praise is a Hindu Jesus.
The Biblical Jesus is either ignored or ridiculed or even condemned as a false Christ.
Jesus taught He was the promised Jewish Messiah and the only incarnation of God, the one and only Son of God. Jesus claimed He was God (John 14:7;9) and He proved it by resurrecting from the dead. In all of history, no Hindu guru has ever resurrected from the dead."
https://en.m.wikipedia.org/wiki/ Category:Gods_by_culture

https://en.m.wikipedia.org/wiki/ Category:Goddesses_by_culture
https://jesustruthdeliverance.com/2017/04/10/ hindueastern-gurus/

(**NOTE: My reason for including the "**Maharishi**" in this book is because of the demonic practices he taught to those who followed him. His teachings are equally as demonic—if not worse—than that of the other wolves I have listed here. I wanted to show where all these "meditative" and "enlightenment" teachings originated from.
He was not the first, nor will he be the last. Ed.).

- **Ed Young Jr.:** https://pulpitandpen.org/2016/09/08/
ed-young-rightfully-divides-and-exposits-a-yo-yo-performance/

https://www.charismanews.com/us/
44293-megachurch-pastor-ed-young-promises-to-refund-tithe-if-god-doesn-t-open-the-windows
-of-heaven

http://fbcjaxwatchdog.blogspot.com/2012/07/ ed-youngs-8000-sf-mansion-on-market-in.html

(**NOTE: This man is a professional motivational speaker; he is not a preacher according to the Bible. Ed.).

- **William P Young**: "The Shack" author: book and movie; "**William Paul Young** is a Heretic, Part One" Apr 20, 2017.

Let me say at the outset that there are two things I quite dislike. I very much dislike having to shell out my hard-earned money on really lousy books. And I also dislike the habit of some who accuse everyone who happens to disagree with them of being a heretic. Let me unpack that.

Sometimes I have to purchase a book I very strongly differ with, but I need to have it in order to write a review of it.

Thus I have had to pay good money for really bad books like "The God Delusion" by Richard Dawkins or "The Secret "by Rhonda Byrne. And I have warned in the past about how we can far too easily throw the term "heretic" around. One must be sparing and cautious in using this word.

But having just finished reading the new book by "The Shack author," I can say with complete conviction and certainty that **William Paul Young** is indeed a heretic – and I wish I did not have to pay for his lousy book. The reason **Young** is so much in the news right now is because the film based on his 2008 novel 'The Shack " is now in theaters. Sadly plenty of Christians are gushing over the movie just as they did the book. When the book first came out I did a two-part review of it.

At the time I really tried to be even-handed and fair with the book – perhaps too much. I must say, if I did the review again today I would be even firmer on its dangerous points, and less generous on its possible good points.

Here is that review:

billmuehlenberg.com/2008/04/11/a-review-of-the-shack-by-william-young-part-one/
billmuehlenberg.com/2008/04/11/ a-review-of-the-shack-by-william-young-part-two/

But now he has his brand new book out: "Lies We Believe about God " (Simon & Schuster, 2017). When I first read about this book, and saw some quotes from it, I realized I had indeed been far too soft on the guy. And now that I actually have the new book in my hands, I can see just how bad he really is theologically speaking.

To put it bluntly, <u>many theologically dangerous and damaging things are said in this book which directly contradict the clear teachings of Scripture.</u>

Plenty of reprehensible teachings are being pushed here: <u>pantheism, universalism, a rejection of the sovereignty of God, a rejection of the idea of sin and our sinful condition, a rejection of the very heart of Christianity: the atonement</u>, and so on.

If you are at all conversant with theological trends and ecclesiastical fads and fashions, you will see the errant foolishness of the <u>emerging church</u> movement written all over this book. In brief these folks stress the fact that we are all on a journey and we cannot really have any sort of certainty, including theological certainty.

Truth is as much what we discover and create as anything, making this movement a <u>spiritual version of postmodernism</u>. All the emphasis is placed on relationship, with all talk of rules, laws and boundaries seen as taboo.

All that matters is 'loving relationships' (whatever that means), and doctrine is downplayed and eschewed. Doubt is praised while firm theological convictions are seen as harmful and unwelcome.

In other words they pretty much mangle all vital Biblical truth claims, and push in their place a mushy, emotive, sentimental bit of pap which sounds really neat to trendy hipsters and hip cats in the West, <u>but has nothing to do with biblical Christianity</u>.

Young, like all the other <u>emergents,</u> is very proud of all this. In his intro he tells us of how he was raised in a "Western Evangelical Protestant tradition" and that in his younger years he used to present himself "as a person of intelligence and rationality".

But now he proudly has rejected all that, and rejoices in what can only be called irrationality, emotionalism, and subjectivity. Thus he even says, "Thankfully, I have changed a great deal." Yeah, he sure has. There is nothing here at all that is recognizable to the Evangelical Protestant tradition, which in turn is based on the historic Christian creedal affirmations such as the Apostles' Creed, the Nicene Creed, and so on.

As a proud and paid-up member of the <u>emerging church</u> faddists, he pushes the dangerous and unbiblical line that objective truth claims are now replaced by subjective opinions, and <u>he makes it clear that one of the worst things any believer can do is claim he has any theological certainty and objectivity.</u>

Everything we used to believe as Christians is now up for grabs, and the worst thing we can do is seek to be dogmatic about anything found in the Bible. All of which is really quite bizarre given that he has just penned a 250-page book telling us (in rather certain terms) that we have all been fed a bunch of lies, and now we must begin afresh with <u>our own</u> personal tastes, preferences and opinions on our spiritual journey.

That is somehow liberating he thinks.

No, that is nothing but the dead end of relativism, scepticism and subjectivism.

Truth is ultimately beyond all of us, so all we are left with is our own personal convictions which may or may not be right. But who cares? The main thing is that we are on a journey together and we can have a nifty conversation.

Hmm, somehow I just can't imagine how the prophets, Jesus, the disciples, and millions of martyrs over the past few millennia have all died horrible deaths by just having 'conversations' and tentative feelings about everything.

They seemed to be dead-set certain about what they believed, and they were willing to die for their beliefs. And millions did.

But with the <u>emergent relativism</u> and theological cotton candy of people like **Young,** there would never be any such thing as martyrs, because there never would be anyone with strong enough convictions about Biblical absolutes (or anything else for that matter) to be willing to die for them.

https://billmuehlenberg.com/2017/04/20/ william-paul-young-heretic-part-one/

(**NOTE: The journalist above continues to offer proof about the heretical teachings and beliefs of the author of the book itself. There is a lot more to this journalist's story, which I am not including. Instead, please go to the website listed above. Ed.).

Now, with the publication of his first non-fiction work, "Lies We Believe About God," **Young** gives a more propositional, concrete expression of his beliefs. Although this book casts itself as tentative and conversational (20–21), it definitely advocates theological positions, often quite energetically.

Its 28 chapters are each devoted to exposing a "lie" we believe about God, and expounding the corresponding opposite truth. Unfortunately, the theology espoused in this book represents a wide and unambiguous deviation from orthodox Christian views. I mean no personal animus to the author in saying this, nor do I question his intentions.

But the reason categories like "orthodoxy" and "heresy" arose in church history is because Christians have maintained there are right and wrong ways to think about God, and that pointing out the difference matters. When a book departs from historic, mainstream Christianity, it's important to make the differences clear.

While I cannot be exhaustive, I will focus on three troublesome aspects of the book's teaching (regarding the Gospel, humanity, and God), then one overarching concern about its method, then a concluding appeal. No one reading and embracing "Lies We Believe About God " will feel a need to repent of his or her sins and trust in Christ for salvation. That is because **Young denies we need to do so**:

"The Good News is not that Jesus has opened up the possibility of salvation and you have been invited to receive Jesus into your life. The Gospel is that Jesus has already included you into his life, into his relationship with God the Father, and into his anointing in the Holy Spirit. The Good News is that Jesus did this without your vote, and whether you believe it or not won't make it any less or more true. (117–18)."

Anticipating the charge of universalism, **Young** lays his cards on the table: "Are you suggesting that everyone is saved? That you believe in universal salvation? That is exactly what I am saying!" (118).
Later he is equally explicit: "Every human being you meet . . . is a child of God" (206). Thus, hell isn't separation from God, but simply the pain of resisting the salvation we have and can't escape (137); and death doesn't result in final judgment but simply introduces "a restorative process intended to free us to run into the arms of Love" (187).
"**Young** doesn't really provide argumentation for universalism, or even an organized account of what it entails (I'm curious whether he would, with Origen, affirm the salvation of all demons). But from piecing together various statements, it appears his universalism is grounded in a particular Christological vision.

One expression of it is found in C. Baxter Kruger's foreword, which **Young** endorses as "the foundation of what I propose as Truth" (20). Here Kruger, in an italicized abstract, basically sums up the Gospel as the good news that the triune God and humanity have been united in the incarnate work of Jesus Christ. For this reason, he explains, "Paul and I regard the widespread notion that human beings are separated from God as the fundamental lie, one that denies Jesus's very identity" (11).

This particular species of Christological universalism—in which "the fundamental lie" is that human beings are separated from God—may fairly be regarded as the greatest theme of the book. It comes up repeatedly—in the foreword (11), the acknowledgments (251), the concluding catena of verses (241–48), the abstract from **Bonhoeffer** (249–50), and throughout "lies" such as "you need to get saved" (ch. 13), "not everyone is a child of God" (ch. 24), and "sin separates us from God" (ch. 27).

What is at stake here isn't merely universalism, but a particular vision of the Gospel. For instance, when **Young** claims "Jesus did not come to build a bridge back to God or to offer the possibility of getting unseparated," he grounds this assertion in his understanding of Christ's work in which "there is 'nothing' outside of God . . . Jesus is actually and historically God fully joining us in our humanity" (232).

But in the Bible, human beings aren't universally and unconditionally included within the scope of Christ's saving work, but rather urgently called to appropriate that work through faith and repentance. The Bible does not say, "Jesus came to save us—you can't avoid it," but rather, "Jesus came to save us—repent and believe" (cf. Acts 3:19).

Regrettably, **Young** doesn't really engage the Biblical teaching that has led most Christians to reject universalism. One thinks, for example, of Jesus's recurrent warnings about hell as a place of "weeping and gnashing of teeth" (Matt. 8:12; 13:42; 13:50; 22:13; 24:51; 25:30; and so on). In fact, the undiscerning reader of **Young's** book may not even glean that universalism is a historically controversial issue, condemned (for instance) by the church in its Origenist formulation at the Fifth Ecumenical Council in Constantinople in AD 553.

https://www.thegospelcoalition.org/reviews/ lies-we-believe-god-william-paul-young/

(**NOTE: There is more on this website listed above, and while I don't necessarily recommend this site due to some conflicting statements on other subjects, this article is being recommended by me due to the author of said article critiquing the book. Ed.).

https://pulpitandpen.org/2017/02/27/
the-evangelical-endcap-little-debbies-the-shack-and-thom-rainer/

- **Sarah Young** ("Jesus Calling" book, which promotes another "Jesus;"   blasphemous boldly claims that her book contains the very words of Jesus).

This also seems like another obvious one, but again, sadly, it isn't. **Sarah Young's** books and studies are still widely sold in Christian bookstores, including LifeWay of the Southern Baptist Convention. In her book, "Jesus Calling," **Sarah Young** portrays herself as a recipient of divine revelation, who, like the Apostles, was tasked with writing down God's specific words. She claims to have personally heard from God himself, and her book is the written record of this new revelation. Of course, this is complete heresy. The canon of Scripture is closed and God does not speak directly and specifically in this way today. Further, much of what **Young** writes in her book is contradictory to what is already written in Scripture and has been edited several times when these contradictions were brought to light. https://reformationcharlotte.org/2019/03/26/ false-teachers-evangelical-churches/

- **Ravi Zacharias** https://www.jesusisprecious.org/wolves/ ravi_zacharias.htm https://reformationcharlotte.org/2019/03/28/ ravi-zacharias-jesus-body-dysphoria-transgender/

https://bereanresearch.org/ on-discerning-ravi-zacharias-its-time-to-say-what-needs-to-be-said/

- **Zig Ziglar**: Deceased; Christians have always had to be careful about deceptive teaching, and today the "gospel of success", by way of motivational authors and speakers such as **Zig Ziglar**, has spread into business settings where we might not expect it. Proponents of this "different Gospel" (Galatians 1:6) often quote Scripture passages, whose interpretation is subtly altered to suit their hidden agendas.
And during the last few years especially, these teachings have infiltrated various marketing seminars.

So let's look briefly at the origins and goals of **Ziglar's** philosophies:

In **Ziglar's** recent book, "Over the Top," he states (p. 273), "Many men qualify under one word or the other, but 'world renowned' and 'humble' are seldom used to describe one man. Godly, gentle, modest, generous, compassionate, dignified, and respectable all describe the character of the late **Dr. Norman Vincent Peale**.
 "I know this to be true, first, because as I mentioned earlier, I studied and applied his philosophies to my life with great success, and second, because I had the privilege of knowing him personally. Many times **Dr. Peale** and I shared the platform. I knew the public and the private man. He truly was what he appeared to be —and then some. His enormous success and popularity never turned his head or caused him to lose his sense of awe and gratitude."

The people he inspired and took over the top by way of his books, cassette recordings, and publications such as 'Guideposts' number in the millions. ... It is safe to say that **Dr. Peale** finished well."

The editor of "Freemasonry, A Celebration of the Craft " states that **Norman Vincent Peale** "is the best known champion of Freemasonry in America today".
 Peale wrote, in the Introduction, "There is, as I see it, nothing like Masonry."

"It is unique in its fellowship which spreads over much of the earth, in addition to our own country." " Moreover, this in-depth fellowship spans the years, even the centuries, running back into antiquity. To me it means a personal relationship with great historical personalities and, taken by and large, also with about the finest body of men whom it is possible to assemble anywhere".

So **Ziglar** is clearly a disciple of the late **Norman Vincent Peale**, the "best known champion of Freemasonry in America."
Now let's briefly see what Freemason authors write about their beliefs:

Manly Hall, 33rd degree Mason, in" Lost Keys of Freemasonry," wrote, "When the Mason learns that the key to the warrior on the block is the proper application of the dynamo of living power, he has learned the Mystery of his Craft." "The seething energies of Lucifer are in his hands" (page 48).

Albert Pike, 33rd degree Mason, Grand Commander, and author of "Morals and Dogma of the Ancient and Accepted Scottish Rite of Freemasonry," in his "Instructions to the 23 Supreme Councils of the World on July 14, 1889," reportedly stated that "Lucifer is God, and unfortunately Adonay is also God. ... Lucifer, God of Light and God of Good is struggling for humanity against Adonay, the God of Darkness and Evil". *

These statements clearly show the evil nature of Masonry. God says that Lucifer is "fallen from heaven" and assigns him "to the recesses of the pit" (Isaiah 14:12-15). But Adonai is our Lord: "The Lord Jehovah" in Ezekiel 2:4 is "Adonai Jehovah" (see Darby translation footnote), and we read of "the ark of Adonai Jehovah" in 1 Kings 2:26.
He is the One of whom we read: "God is light, and in him is no darkness at all" (1 John 1:5). Masonic teaching really calls evil good, and good evil; and puts darkness for light, and light for darkness. In Isaiah 5:20, God pronounces "Woe" on those who do this.
I would add that James Taylor, in "Ministry by J. Taylor, New Series," volume 45, page 176, perceptively links Masonry with Shinar (see Genesis 11:1-9) and notes that secret organizations including Masons "are inimical to the truth" (The word "inimical" means hostile).

Let us now consider some of the authors whom **Ziglar** espouses:

"In See you at the Top," he recommends books by **Norman Vincent Peale, Robert Schuller**, and Napoleon Hill in the "Further Reading" section.

In "Secrets of Closing the Sale," he states, "The following books have been very meaningful to me and I believe you will glean some useful ideas and inspiration from them".
The book list includes "The Power of Positive Thinking ," by **Norman Vincent Peale**, "Tough Times Never Last, but Tough People Do," by **Robert Schuller**, and "Success Through a Positive Mental Attitude," by Napoleon Hill and W. Clement Stone.

In their well-researched book "The Seduction of Christianity," Dave Hunt and T. McMahon write: "Ernest Holmes founded the Church of Religious Science, also known as Science of the Mind, upon the 'Supreme Secret' that the 'Masters of Wisdom' revealed to Napoleon Hill.
It is closely related to the "Positive Thinking " of **Norman Vincent Peale** and the "Possibility Thinking" of **Robert Schuller**... In 1958 Holmes prophesied, 'We have launched a Movement which, in the next 100 years, will be the great new religious impulse of modern times ... [destined] to envelop the world ... .'" (page 23).

Let's briefly see what these men teach:

The late **Norman Vincent Peale**, a 33rd degree Mason, confessed his indebtedness to "Science of Mind" founder Ernest Holmes, writing on the back cover of "Ernest Holmes: His Life and Times:" "Only those who knew me as a boy can fully appreciate what Ernest Holmes did for me. Why, he made me a positive thinker."
In 1980, during his keynote address at Mormon president Spencer Kimball's 85th birthday party, **Peale** called Mormon leaders men of God who are doing God's work and praised Kimball as a true prophet of Jesus Christ. To which god was **Peale** alluding?

Well, **Peale** was a Mason, Mormon church founder **Joseph Smith** was a Mason, Mormon leader Brigham Young plainly declared in "Journal of Discourses " (v. 5, p. 331) that the Christian God is "the Mormon's Devil", and the third Mormon president John Taylor stated in "Journal of Discourses " (v. 6, p. 167) that Christianity was "hatched in hell".
We have already noted that Lucifer is the god of the Masons. These things are very sobering to consider, especially for those who espouse the writings of **Peale** or his disciple, **Zig Ziglar.**

Robert Schuller, in "Time " magazine, March 18, 1985, stated, "I don't think anything has been done in the name of Christ and under the banner of Christianity that has proven more destructive to human personality and, hence, counterproductive to the evangelism enterprise than the often crude, uncouth, and unchristian strategy of attempting to make people aware of their lost and sinful condition."

https://www.plymouthbrethren.com/ success.htm

Frequent guest on "Focus on the Family." **Zig Ziglar** has been the "head liner" for the "Get Motivated" seminars (8/2004). He has been closely associated with **James Dobson** and "Focus on the Family" for years. One of **Ziglar's** famous books is "See You At The Top." On the back of the 1982 edition of the book is a photo of **Zig Ziglar** shaking hands with the 33rd degree Freemason, the late **Norman Vincent Peale**, who is endorsing the book. **Peale** was famous for promoting "Positive Thinking". https://procinwarn.com/counterfeit-christianity/

A Few of the Many (Matt 24:11-13)– Please pray for those under their influence.

(Lastly, I want to address the preaching of Rev. **A.A. Allen**, well known evangelist of the 1940s forward. Several sites have him being found with alcohol bottles in the hotel room he was staying in before a Gospel meeting; others have–under attestation–written a refutation, disputing the claim. I am including a few websites here and leaving it up to you, the reader to decide for yourself. Ed.).

https://www.tripline.net/trip/ A.A._Allen-0564347332151014909EDB1DED8799CD

https://www.asrmartins.com/ the-powerful-ministry-of-aa-allen/

https://www.eaec.org/ TruthAboutAAAllen.htm

http://www.deceptioninthechurch.com/ healthyself.html

https://www.jonasclark.com/ a-a-allen-they-called-him-the-miracle-man/

(This is a PDF file. You will have to type in what is listed here. It is six pages. Ed.).
http://www.eaec.org/bibleanswers/ Paul-Cunningham-Testimony.pdf

https://www.youtube.com/ watch?v=jMI8yMtzwjM

https://www.youtube.com/watch?v=jMI8yMtzwjM

(**NOTE: As an addendum, I am including brief information about other unchristian teachings that are prevalent since Christianity started. A few of them are from other authors, that I have included their websites. Ed.).

OTHER IMPORTANT FACTS TO KNOW:

The Church of Jesus Christ of Latter Day Saints (Mormons)– Known for following a **Joseph Smith**, who was "visited" by an angel called Moroni, supposedly in 1842.

They have a secretive organization, they believe in polygamy, they are not allowed to discuss their secret handshakes and passwords, they must attend the "Temple Endowment Session," in which they are taught the tenets of the faith; almost all of their false doctrine is borrowed from the Freemasons; most leaders belong to a Masonic Temple; they add to the Bible (extra biblical) teachings.

Manifest Sons of God\Joel's Army –**Patricia King** states, "... There is a new breed of believer arising. Men and women who know they are sons and daughters because they know their Heavenly Father. This new breed of believer gives God everything because they understand all that He gave for them. They live powerful lives of complete abandonment to the Lord, completely consumed by the reality of His Kingdom.

Todd White is a forerunner of this new breed. In this CD set he shares revelation, insight, and testimonies that illustrate what it is to be a part of this champion company that flows effortlessly in the power and presence of God." Source: **Patricia King**, "THE NEW BREED 2 CD TEACHING" BY **TODD WHITE,** XP Media,

 https://store.xpministries.com/
products/the-new-breed-2-cd-teaching-by-todd-white?variant=851952761, Published 13/06/2017.

"The 'champion company' is important language to recognize. Back in 1948, the Latter Rain (who gave us the NARismatic movement), called this heresy the 'manchild company'. And it's important we bring up the Latter Rain cult again."

Franklin Hall was one of the main people that influenced this heretical sect with his work "Atomic Power with God, Through Fasting and Prayer'." In the online iHOP Forerunner bookstore, they state that **Franklin Hall's** book is, "highly recommended by **Todd White.**"

From our research, **Franklin Hall** seemed to be the originator of this idea of the 'manchild company'/'manifest sons of god'/'little gods' heresy that will accompany the end-times church.

Modern Apostasy Exposed:

This website of Cephas Ministry contains lots of valuable information on the false doctrines in the Mormon Church, Jehovah Witnesses, the RCC, and other anti Christian organizations. In addition, the website exposes the unbiblical teachings of:

T.D. Jakes, Paul Crouch, Benny Hinn, Kenneth Copeland, Kenneth Hagin, E.V. Hill, Peter Popoff, Creflo Dollar, Bob Larson, and many other wolves in sheep's clothing. In the wake of **Joshua Harris'** apostasy — the Purity Culture pastor who divorced his wife, denounced Christianity, and embraced homosexuality — many people are wondering just exactly what went wrong. The apostasy follows a string of **The Gospel Coalition** contributors who have either been disqualified or have completely turned from their faith altogether.

From **Tullian Tjividjian** and **Mark Driscoll** to **James MacDonald** and **C.J. Mahaney**, many men that had been warned about by those "pesky discernment blogs" ultimately showed their true colors and were caught up in scams ranging from sex abuse cover-ups to bullying their staff at church. The entire paradigm exemplifying **The Gospel Coalition** gave rise to a new breed of professing Christian—New Calvinism.

While some, like Kevin De Young, ponder the reasoning behind the rampant apostasy at **The Gospel Coalition**, speculating that it is because they are too quick to "elevate gifted men," I suspect the problem is much deeper than that.

De Young writes, "What is worth exploring in this instance [**Harris'** apostasy]—and, we can tell you, has already for years generated a great deal of soul searching—is why a number of young men who were at one time closely associated with **The Gospel Coalition** have been forced to leave the ministry."

"Our primary takeaway is that in years past our tribe was too quick to elevate gifted men who may not have had enough time to prove themselves faithful for the long haul." "But even here, we would note that the public crises always get more attention than scores of young men who have quietly continued to serve the Lord with growing maturity." "The problem, you see, isn't being "too quick" to "elevate gifted men."

"The problem is elevating men who have a primary cause that fits the theme and narrative of **The Gospel Coalition**." "The problem is **The Gospel Coalition** isn't really about the Gospel — it's about other things, like social justice, egalitarianism, LGBTQ activism, open borders and mass illegal immigration, theological liberalism, self-advancement, etc."

The Gospel Coalition merely cloaks these causes in Christian-themed language, slaps the phrase "Gospel-centered" on it, and brings aboard anyone who is willing to advance their cause — or at least act as a cloak for the gospel while **The Gospel Coalition** advances their own cause. And the problem isn't that just a few men have been officially disqualified — **The Gospel Coalition** continues to be wrought with unqualified, disqualified, and outright dangerous men and women.

At **The Gospel Coalition,** the bad far outweigh the good. **The Gospel Coalition** still employs a massive number of homosexuals and LGBTQ activists, social justice warriors, and egalitarians.
The Gospel Coalition employs people who are funded by leftist billionaires like George Soros, James Riady, and Zack Exley. The problem is **The Gospel Coalition** isn't guided by the Gospel, the Scriptures, or even basic Christian principles.

It is guided by a leftist agenda whose primary purpose is to turn the Evangelical Church to the left politically and theologically. **Mark Driscoll** wasn't the problem. **Tullian Tjividjian** wasn't the problem. **C.J. Mahaney** wasn't the problem. **James MacDonald** wasn't the problem. And no, **Joshua Harris** wasn't the problem. All of these fallen men are merely symptoms of the problem.

The problem is that **The Gospel Coalition** — and the (very few) good men who may be left — continue to give a platform to leftists, use complicit men like these to disguise their agenda, and allow the leftists at the organization to promote their agenda unfettered. It's time to kiss **The Gospel Coalition** goodbye."

https://reformationcharlotte.org/2019/08/07/
time-to-kiss-the-gospel-coalition-goodbye/

NAR (NEW APOSTOLIC REFORMATION):

There is no greater present-day evidence of this than the NAR (New Apostolic Reformation). The Ground Zero of the NAR is "Bethel Church " in Redding, California, with whom **Todd White** is strongly affiliated.
White speaks at their conferences and is very tight with "Bethel Church's" commander-in-chief and senior pastor, **Bill Johnson**, whose "School of Supernatural Ministry" offers courses on doing precisely what **Todd White** does, as well as "teach" people to be ordained as "Prophets" and "Apostles" (if you are willing to pay their hefty tuition).
Upon completion of the courses, **Bill Johnson** himself "Knights" graduates. "Bethel" (and the NAR at large) inducts youth through the emotionalism of repetitive, hypnotic "worship" music, which has since morphed into the "Jesus Culture Movement,"
a rapidly rising youth movement spreading the NAR agenda like wildfire across the globe.
Some of the techniques used are: Getting kids "high" on the music, telling them it's the Holy Ghost moving, running the kids in lines through "fire tunnels" during intermission, laying hands on them and imparting the **Kundalini Serpent Spirit** . . . where they often fall down, twitch, convulse, oftentimes as if burning in agony, all in the name of "Jesus," calling it "Holy Ghost Fire," yelling commands to the Holy Ghost such as, "MORE! MORE! MORE, LORD!!! . . . DOUBLE IT!! DOUBLE IT!!", etc.

Todd White: This is precisely what **Todd White** does, always "calling down fire" in the name of "Jesus," which is also precisely what we are warned will be one of the great deceptions of the Beast . . . **calling down fire from heaven** . . . aka: false signs and lying wonders (Revelation 13:13).

Jesus Himself said it would be a deception so powerful, that if it were possible, it would deceive even the very elect.

In "Bethel's" best-selling book (co-authored by **Bill Johnson**), "The Physics of Heaven" (sold in their campus bookstore alongside a plethora of "Jesus Culture " CDs and a multitude of NAR authors), it states that Christians are "taking back truths" from the New Age that really belong to citizens of the Kingdom of God.

One of the "Bethel's" own "prophets" trained by their "Supernatural School "
unknowingly prophesied to a real practicing witch, telling her "[God] is pleased with you!" and "implored [her] to keep doing what [she] was doing."

http://www.patheos.com/blogs/agora/2015/07/
born-again-witch-witches-at-a-pentecostal-church-healings-and-prophecies/)

There are multiple videos and photos evidencing "Bethel" students on campus field trips, who take classes on "Grave Soaking/Sucking", as well as the **Johnson's** (**Bill** and wife **Benni**) traveling to grave sites to **"suck" or "soak" the anointing of the dead from faith healers like William Branham, the very godfather of the NAR, whom they worship like a god and who has multiple, easily verifiable, failed, false prophesies.**

This practice is an act the Word of God calls "Necromancy" (contacting the dead), condemning it as an abomination to God (Deuteronomy 18:11).

Another stunning fact is that **Todd White** received his **Kundalini** "anointing" from **Benny Hinn**. When **Hinn** laid hands on **Todd White, Todd** fell back, and **Hinn** repeatedly and creepily told him he was going to be part of a "great youth movement."
This is verifiable on video. (**NOTE: You can find this video on You Tube. Ed.).

What Christians may find difficult to believe is that Satan himself can indeed heal in the name of "Jesus," but it's "another Jesus" (2 Corinthians 11:4).
To verify this, **Johanna Michaelsen's** book or video testimony "The Beautiful Side of Evil," is highly recommended.   Her books was the catalyst that delivered author/speaker Warren B. Smith out of the New Age.
 Both he and **Michaelsen** are early pioneers of exposing New Age mysticism's creeping into modern Christianity, largely and sadly unaware by most.

As an ex-New Ager myself, I can attest that psychics, Yogi's, Reiki masters, and witches employ the exact same techniques as the NAR, by tapping into the demonic realm of unclean spirits, who supply very personal, intimate information (such as certain ailments or sickness they may have) about the individuals they approach (sort of like an invisible phone line direct to the demonic spirit realm).

These "mediums" also employ flattery, telling people how "amazing" they are and how much "Jesus loves them." This immediately impresses the recipients, who the mediums then asks if they can lay hands on them to heal them through the power of the "Holy Ghost," while doing it in the name of "Jesus" (another "Jesus" . . . a.k.a. Satan).

The recipients often feel "heat" or "electricity" (common sensations associated with the New Age practice of Reiki).

The recipient are told it is "Holy Ghost Fire" and that they just felt the power or even just received the Holy Ghost. Generally, not one word about sin, repentance, or even the Gospel is used. Jesus Christ said in the end times, many false prophets would come as wolves in sheep's clothing and that we would know them by their fruits.

And the greatest evidence of these falsehoods is that there is always "another Gospel" preached, void of the vital messages that save souls, which Jesus Christ Himself preached:

Repentance from sin, judgment, hell, fear of God vs. the NAR "Holy Ghost" which is all about an obsession with healing via "signs and wonders," power, seducing people through the emotionalism of music and the flattery of telling people how amazing they are with no conviction of sin and no contriteness or brokenness of spirit before a holy God, even though Jesus told us the ministry of the Holy Spirit of truth is to "reprove [convict] the world of sin, and of righteousness, and of judgment (John 16:8); a message absent from these mouths of these "faith healers.'"

A false prophet is not always known by what he does preach but often by what he doesn't preach. There is "another Gospel," "another Spirt," and "another Jesus."
In the warning of the Bible, it describing precisely the "Jesus" being promoted by **Todd White** and the rest of the NAR.

"Many will say to me in that day, Lord, Lord, have we not prophesied in thy name? and in thy name have cast out devils? and in thy name done many wonderful works? And then will I profess unto them, I never knew you: depart from me, ye that work iniquity"—Matthew 7:22-23 https://www.worthychristianforums.com

https://www.piratechristian.com/
messedupchurch?offset=1462219069201&category=False+Teachers

(**NOTE: Excellent website exposing these wolves of modern times is listed above; it is too lengthy to post here. Ed.).

"Here are some that I believe need to be added to the list: Russell and Kitty Walden, Bill and Marsha Burns, Raul and Ryan Reis, Levi Lusko, Brian Broderson, Mike MacIntosh, Barry Stagner, Barbara Gaines, Deborah Waldron Fry, **Kay Arthur**, Wade and Connie Urban, JoEllen Stevens. Some of these are prophets, some are teachers who associate with the Word of Faith movement and the NAR."

https://www.honorofkings.org/false-prophet-listing/

(**NOTE: The paragraph above the link is from a commenter on that website. Space does not permit me to research and list the names included. Ed.).

"Here are the full lists of all the heretical ecumenical organizations (within the "evangelical" umbrella) and its individual leading associates (as they stand at the moment on 18 Jan 2011) as follows. The lists are still a work in progress and will be added to or edited, as and when I have more details:"

Groups

Latter Rain
Manifest Sons Of God
Fullers Theological Seminary
Word of Faith
Shepherding Movement
Restoration and House Church Movement
New Frontiers
Spring Harvest
New Breed
Joel's Army and New Apostolic Reformation (NAR)
Third Wave Movement
Vineyard
Toronto Blessing, Pensacola and Lakeland Revivals
Alpha
Kingsway International Church (KICC)
TBN
Seeker Friendly
Purpose Driven (Rick Warren)
Emerging Church
HillSong
Promise-Keepers
Renovaré
Elijah List (list of prophetic Ministries)
Manhattan Declaration
Westminster 2010 Declaration
THE MESSAGE endorsers
Jerusalem Prayer Team
Lausanne Movement (founded By **Billy Graham**)
International Apostolic Council (IAC)
International Coalition of Apostles (ICA)
Mission America Coalition (MAC)
American Society for Church Growth (ASCG)
Evangelicals and Catholics Together 1994

(**NOTE: The list above is from the websites listed here. They are a product of the Author who wrote them. Ed.). http://watchmanforjesus.blogspot.com/

Chronological Emergence Of The Apostate Church Over Last 100 Years—
http://watchmanforjesus.blogspot.com/2011/01/ chronological-emergence-of-apostate.html

Leaders

Before you look at the list of leaders table (alphabetical order) please familiarize yourselves with a few pointers. Note "Emerging Church Links" is based on a list found on: http://www.buzzardhut.net/index/htm/

entitled "CENTERING PRAYER, CHURCH GROWTH, CONTEMPLATIVE SPIRITUALITY, EMERGING CHURCH, LABYRINTH, MYSTICISM, PURPOSE DRIVEN":

Abbreviated Category (Alphabetical order) Represents:

ASCG: American Society for Church Growth

ECT: Evangelicals and Catholics Together 1994 (Signed Ecumenical Document)

FL5 and SM: Fort Lauderdale 5 and Shepherding Movement

Fullers Graduated or Faculty (Lectured) at Fullers Theological Seminary

IAC: International Apostolic Council

ICA: International Coalition of Apostles (Council Membership)

JPT: Jerusalem Prayer Team

LM: Lausanne Movement

MAC: Missions America Coalition

MD: Signed the Ecumenical Manhattan Declaration

Message Endorsed: "The Message" Counterfeit Bible

NAR: New Apostolic Reformation

PK: Endorsed/speaker of Promise Keepers

SH: Spring Harvest

TB: Toronto Blessing

WD: Signed Ecumenical Westminster Declaration

WPC World Prayer Centre Leader

TEACHER, PROPHET, LEADER (Listed by Surname in alphabetical order);

GROUPS THEY ARE MOST COMMONLY LINKED WITH, i.e. WHO THEY LEAD, WORK FOR, ENDORSE, SUPPORT, OR ASSOCIATE WITH:

Dave Adams– New Frontiers

Julian Adams– New Frontiers

Miriam Adeney– LM

Doug Addison– Elijah List

Che' Ahn– ICA, Elijah List, MD

Daniel Akin- MD

Randy Alcorn– MD

Joe Aldrich– MAC member

Rory and Wendy Alec– God TV, Elijah List

Michael Nazir Ali– WD

Lon Allison– MAC vice chairman

Beth Alves– Elijah List

Joni Ames-Fasekas– Elijah List

David Anderson– MD

Julie Anderson– WD

Leith Anderson– Fullers (graduated), Message, LM, MD, MAC Board

Alan Andrews– MAC Board

Ian Andrews– Elijah List

Ernest Angley– Word Faith

Gleason Archer– Fullers (Faculty)

Don Argue– MAC member

Charles Arn– ASCG Past President

Carol Arnott– Latter Rain, NAR, TB, Elijah List

John Arnott– Latter Rain, NAR, TB, Alpha Supporter, Elijah List

Steven Arterburn–New Age Psychology http://www.atruechurch.info/newlifeministries.html

Kay Arthur– MD

Matthew Ashimolowo– Word Faith. KICC

Yemisi Ashimolowo– Word Faith. KICC

Paul Ashton– WD

David Augsburger– Fullers (Faculty)

Liz Babbs– Emerging Church Links

Mark L. Bailey– MD

George Bakalov– ICA

Heidi Baker– Elijah List, Word Faith, NAR

Jim and Lori Bakker– Elijah List

Colin Baron– New Frontiers

Karl Barth– Emerging Church

Ruth Haley Barton– Emerging Church Links

Don Basham– FL5 and SM

Gary Bauer– MD

Ern Baxter– FL5, SM, NAR

Bob Beckett– Latter Rain, Joel's Army

Rob Bell– Fullers (Graduated), Emerging Church, NAR, Word Faith

John Belt– Elijah List

Todd Bentley– Joel's Army, New Breed, NAR, Dominionism

John Bevere– Word Faith, Hillsong Speaker

Mike Bickle– Latter Rain, New Breed, NAR, TB, Alpha Supporter, Elijah List, Emerging Church Links

Adrian Birks– New Frontiers

Markus Bishop– Word Faith

Tim Blaber– New Frontiers

Paul and Cheryl Black– Elijah List

Henry Blackaby– PK Leader

Bishop Charles E. Blake– JPT

William Blake– Emerging Church

Ken Blanchard– Emerging Church Links

Ron Blue– PK Speaker

Ken Boa– MD

Ryan Bolger– Fullers (Faculty), Emerging Church

Shawn Bolz– Elijah List, NAR

Dietrich Bonhoeffer– Emerging Church, Neo-Orthodoxy

Reinhard Bonnke– Word Faith, MAC member

Wellington Boone– PK Leader, Message

Marcus Borg– Emerging Church

David Bosch– Emerging Church

Cynthia Bourgeault– Emerging Church

Lyndon Bowring– Elim, WD

Gregory Boyd– Emerging Church

Steve Brady– WD

William Branham– Latter Rain Founder, Manifest Sons Of God

Randy & Sarah Brannon– MD

Barbie Breathitt– Elijah List

James Brenneman– Fullers (Graduated)

Bill Bright– Fullers (Graduated), PK Speaker, JPT, ECT

Mrs. Vonette Bright– MAC member

Stuart and Jill Briscoe– Message

Troy Bronsink– Emerging Church Links

Peter Brooks– New Frontiers

Colin Brown– Fullers (Faculty)

Warren S. Brown– Fullers (Faculty)

Walter Brueggemann– Emerging Church

Jamie Buckingham– Renovare Board

Frederick Buechner– Message

Bob Buford– Emerging Church Links, NAR

Isak Burger– LM

Edward Buria– New Frontiers

Spencer Burke– Emerging Church

Jim Burns– Message

Glenn Burris, Jr– MAC Board

Luis Bush– MAC member

Nick Butterworth– Restoration

Dave Butts– MAC Board

Roger Bye– New Frontiers

Juanita Bynum– Word Faith, Prosperity

Christine Caine– Hillsong Speaker, Word Faith, Prosperity, NAR

Paul Cain– Latter Rain, Manifest Sons Of God, NAR

Clive Calver– SH, MAC member

Wes and Stacey Campbell– Elijah List, NAR, Word Faith

Tony Campolo– Emerging Church, SH, TB, Alpha Supporter, Renovare Board, Message

Peggy Campolo–Emerging Church, SH, TB, Alpha Supporter, Renovare Board, Message

Peter J. Cannon– MAC member

Michael Card– Message

George Carey– Alpha Supporter, WD

G. Raymond Carlson– Renovare Board

Edward John Carnell– Fullers (Faculty)

Michael Cassidy– LM

Paul Cedar– MAC Chairman

Morris Cerullo– Word Faith

Steve Chalke– Emerging Church, SH

Willie Champion– MAC Board

Bryan Chapell– LM, MD

Gary Chapman– Message

Pierre Teilhard de Chardin– Emerging Church

Martin Charlesworth– New Frontiers

Nick Chatrath– New Frontiers

Mahesh & Bonnie Chavda– Elijah List

Michel & Natalie Chevalier– Elijah List

Mark Chironna– ICA

Tapiwa Chizana– New Frontiers

James Chosa– ICA

Shane Claiborne– Emerging Church

Patsy Clairmont– Message

Heather Clark– Elijah List

Nolan Clark– Latter Rain, Joel's Army, Elijah List

Randy Clark– Latter Rain, NAR, Word Faith, Elijah List

Stephen Clark– Catholic renewalists joined Fort Lauderdale 5

Gary Clarke– Hillsong Speaker

Philip Clayton– Fullers (Graduated)

Kim Clement– Word Faith, Elijah List

Anita Cleverly– WD

Steve Clifford– WD

Denny and Ann Cline– Vineyard, Elijah List

Timothy Clinton– MD

Gerald Coates– Restoration, Pioneer Network Leader, TB, Alpha Supporter, WD

Chris Cole– WD

Edward Cole– PK Leader

Bob Coleman– MAC Board

Jim Collins– Emerging Church Links

Chuck Colson– PK Speaker, MD, MAC member, ECT (Co-Signer)

Bobby Conner– Elijah List

Gordon-Conwell– PK Speaker

Graham Cooke– Elijah List

Barney Coombs– Restoration, Salt and Light Leader

Kenneth Copeland– Word Faith, Message, JPT, NAR

John Corts– MAC member

Ron Cottle– ICA

Paul and Donna Cox– Elijah List

Larry Crabb– PK Speaker, Emerging Church Links

Denny Cramer– Elijah List

Andy Crouch– Emerging Church

Jan Crouch– TBN, NAR and Word Faith sympathizer

Paul Crouch– (deceased) TBN, NAR and Word Faith sympathizer

John Crowder– Latter Rain, NAR

Loren Cunningham– LM, MAC member

Jim Daly– LM, MD

Kimberly Daniels– Elijah List

Paul Keith Davis– New Breed, Elijah List

John Dawson– Latter Rain, Joel's Army, NAR, PK Speaker

Joy Dawson– Latter Rain, NAR

Pierre Teilhard de Chardin– Emerging Church

Jack Deere– Latter Rain, NAR

Eric Delve– SH

Martin DeHaan (Dr.) Deceased– MAC member

Danny de León– MAC Board

Mark DeMoss– PK Leader

Karl Dennis– KICC

Jacques Derrida– Emerging Church

David Devenish– New Frontiers

James Dobson (Dr.)– PK, MD, MAC member, Word Faith

Shirley Dobson– MAC member

Creflo Dollar– Word Faith, Prosperity

Steve Douglass– LM, MAC Board

Naomi Dowdy– ICA

James T. Draper– JPT

Dave Dravecky– Message

Mark Driscoll– Emerging Church Links, New Frontiers, NAR

Phil Driscoll– Message

Malcolm Duncan– SH

Maxie D Dunnam– MAC member

Martyn Dunsford– New Frontiers

Jesse Duplantis– Word Faith, Prosperity

Colin Dye– Elim links with Latter Rain and Word Faith

Joni Eareckson Tada– Message endorser, MD signer

John Eckhardt– ICA, Elijah List

Meister Eckhart– Emerging Church Links

Joel Edwards– New Frontiers, SH, EA, Alpha Supporter

Tilden Edwards– Emerging Church

Garris Elkins– Elijah List

Ray Ellis– ASCG Past President

Gordon England– PK Leader

Lou Engle– Elijah List

Ted W. Engstrom– Renovare Board, MAC member

Aaron Evans– Elijah List

Louis Evans– MAC member

Mike Evans– Elijah List

Tony Evans– PK Speaker

Jerry Falwell (deceased)– PK Speaker, JPT

Jeff Farmer– MAC Board

Gary Fawver– Renovare Board

Gordon Fee– Message

Richard Felix– Renovare Board

Ana Mendez-Ferrell– Elijah List

Emerson Mendez-Ferrell– Elijah List

Dave Fickett– Message

Edward L Foggs– MAC member

Ken Fong– LM

Leighton Ford– TB, Alpha Supporter, Message, LM, MAC member

Theresa Forkins-Phillips– Elijah List

Faith Forster– Restoration, Renovare Board

Roger Forster– Restoration, Ichthus Leader, TB, Alpha Supporter, Renovare Board

Richard Foster– Fullers (Faculty), Emerging Church, Renovare Founder, Message,

George Fox– Emerging Church Links

Matthew Fox– Emerging Church

Pat Francis– ICA

Francis Frangipane– Latter Rain, Joel's Army, NAR, Elijah List

Jentezen Franklin– Hillsong Speaker, NAR

William C. Frey– Renovare Board

Millard Fuller– Renovare Board, MAC member

Bill and Gloria Gaither– Message

Henry Gariepy– Renovare Board

Joseph Garlington– PK Leader, Elijah List

Carl F. George– ASCG Past President

Timothy George– LM

Eddie Gibbs– Fullers (Faculty), Emerging Church, ASCG Past President

Livy Gibbs– New Frontiers

Ken Gire– Emerging Church Links

John Glass– Elim, Links with New Age, WD

Martin Goldsmith– WD

James & Michel Ann Goll– Elijah List

Dr. Goodwill Shana– New Frontiers

Richard Gorsuch– Fullers (Faculty)

Ken Gott– TB, Alpha Supporter

Billy Graham (deceased)– Fullers (Trustees Board), PK Speaker (taped messages at events), LM (Founder), Message, MAC member

Franklin Graham– PK Speaker

Jack Graham– JPT, MD

Amy Grant– Message

Robert Grant– Fullers (Graduated)

Joel B. Green– Fullers (Faculty)

Lynn Green– WD

Phillip Greenslade– New Frontiers

Pete Greig– Emerging Church Links

Emilie Griffin– Emerging Church Links

Vernon Grounds– Message

John Groves– New Frontiers

Wayne Grudem– New Frontiers

John Guest– MAC member

Os Guinness– LM

Kenn Gulliksen– Vineyard

Nicky Gumbel– Alpha Leader, TB, Hillsong Speaker

Madam Guyon– Emerging Church

Ted Haggard– Latter Rain, Joels Army, NAR

Kenneth E Hagin, Sr. (Deceased) –Word Faith (father of movement; followed E.W. Kenyon's Word-Faith teaching)

Kenneth W Hagin Jr.– Word Faith

Bill Hamon– Latter Rain, NAR, ICA, Elijah List

Jane Hansen– MAC member

Michael Harper– Renovare Board

Greg Haslam– New Frontiers

Matt Hatch– New Frontiers

Gary Haugen– LM

Jack W. Hayford– TB, Alpha Supporter, PK Regular Speaker, Renovare Speaker, Message, JPT, LM, MAC member

David Hazard– Emerging Church Links

Keith Hazell– New Frontiers

Jack and Cynthia Heald– Message

Larry Helyer– Fullers (Graduated)

Ken Hemphill– MAC Board

Howard Hendricks– PK Speaker

James B Henry– MAC member

Les Henson– Fullers (Graduated)

Roberta Hestenes– Renovare Board

Marilyn Hickey– Word Faith, Prosperity

Andy Hickford– SH

Robert Hicks– PK Speaker

Scott Hicks– Elijah List

Alec Hill– MD, MAC member

Clifford and Monica Hill– WD

E.V. Hill– PK Speaker

Steve Hill– Latter Rain, NAR, Pensacola

Benny Hinn– New Breed, Word Faith, Message, Prosperity

Dean Hirsch– LM

C B Hogue– MAC member

Tom Hohstadt– Emerging Church

David Holden– New Frontiers

Liz Holden– New Frontiers

Simon Holley– New Frontiers

Adrian Holloway– New Frontiers

David Hope– Alpha Supporter

John Hosier– New Frontiers

Matt Hosier– New Frontiers

Sue Hosier– New Frontiers

Judith Hougen– Emerging Church Links

Bobbie Houston– Hillsong Speaker

Brian Houston– Hillsong Founder and Speaker, Prosperity, Emerging Church Links

Rodney Howard-Browne– Latter Rain, Word Faith, TB, Elijah List, NAR, Prosperity

David Hubbard– Fullers (Faculty)

Larry & Tiz Huch– Word Faith, NAR, Prosperity

John A Huffman Jr– MAC member

Ray Hughes– Elijah List

Hannah Hunard– Emerging Church Links

George Hunter III– ASCG Past President

Kent R Hunter– ASCG Past President

Theresa Hurlbert– Elijah List

Sterling Huston– MAC Board

Bill Hybels– Seeker Friendly, TB, Alpha Supporter, PK Speaker, Emerging Church Links, Message, NAR, Dominionism, Prosperity

Bill Jackson– Vineyard

John Paul Jackson (deceased) – Latter Rain, NAR, Dominionism

Harry Jackson Jr– Elijah List

Cindy Jacobs– Latter Rain, Joels Army, NAR, Elijah List, Word Faith, Prosperity

T.D. Jakes– (Author), Word Faith, Hillsong Speaker, JPT, Prosperity

Jerry Jenkins– Message

Willie Jennings– Fullers (Graduated)

Paul Jewett– Fullers (Faculty)

Kate and Paul Jinadu– WD

Bill Johnson– Latter Rain, NAR, Elijah List, New Age, Emerging Church Links, Prosperity

Jan Johnson– Emerging Church Links

Andy Johnston– New Frontiers

Alan Jones– Emerging Church Links

Bob Jones (deceased) – Latter Rain, NAR, Elijah List

Bonnie Jones– Elijah List

Bryn Jones– Restoration

Laurie Beth Jones– Emerging Church Links

Tony Jones– Fullers (Graduated), Emerging Church

Rick Joyner– Latter Rain, NAR. New Breed, Elijah List, Knight of Malta, Word Faith, Prosperity

Carl Jung– Emerging Church

Dan Juster– ICA

Stephen Kaberia– New Frontiers (Kenya)

Walter Kaiser Jr– Message

Veli-Matti Kärkkäinen– Fullers (Faculty)

Reese R. Kauffman– MAC member

Malcolm Kayes– New Frontiers

Thomas Keating– Emerging Church

Tim Keller– LM

Gerard Kelly– SH

John P Kelly– ICA (2010 Presiding Apostle), IAC

Morton Kelsey– Emerging Church Links
R.T. Kendall– Alpha Supporter

Billy and Caroline Kennedy– Restoration Link, National Churches Forum UK (Leader)

Ron Kenoly– Message

Carol Kent– Message

Keri Wyatt Kent– Emerging Church Links

E.W. Kenyon– Originator of Word Faith Teachings (leading to Kenneth E Hagin's becoming "father" of that movement)

Jay Kesler– Message

Lawrence Khong– IAC

Sue Monk Kidd– Emerging Church Links

Søren Kierkegaard– Emerging Church

John Kilpatrick– Latter Rain, NAR

Billy Kim– PK Speaker

Joon Gon Kim– Fullers (Graduated)

Dan Kimball– Emerging Church

Tim Kimmel– Message

Patricia King– Latter Rain, NAR, Elijah List, Word Faith

Dennis Kinlaw– MAC member

Immanuel Kinoti– New Frontiers(Kenya)

Kiogora– New Frontiers (Kenya)

Jerry R. Kirk– Renovare Board

Denny Kline– Latter Rain, Joel's Army

Mark Knoll– ECT

Stephen Gitonga Kobia– New Frontiers (Kenya)

Clarence A. Kopp, Sr.– Renovare Board

Alex Kpikpi– New Frontiers

John Kpikpi– New Frontiers

Charles H. Kraft– Fullers (Faculty), Third Wave

George Eldon Ladd– Fullers (Faculty)

Tim and Beverly LaHaye– JPT, MAC members,

Anne Lamont– Emerging Church

Richard Land– ECT

Beverley Landreth-Smith- New Frontiers

Curt Landry– Elijah List

Paul Larsen– MAC member

Greg Laurie– PK Speaker, Emerging Church Links, NAR

William Law– Emerging Church Links

Vinton Lee– PK Leader

Anderson Lekesike– New Frontiers(Kenya)

Madeleine L'Engle– Message

Robert Lenguliai– New Frontiers (Kenya)

David LeShana– Renovare Board

C.S. Lewis (Author)– Emerging Church

Larry Lewis– MAC Board, ECT

David Lillie– Restoration

Bishop Nathaniel Linsey– MAC member

Stef Liston– New Frontiers

Duane Litfin– LM

Lex Loizides– New Frontiers

H. B. London, Jr– PK Leader, Renovare

Bishop Eddie L. Long– Word Faith, Prosperity

Tremper Longman III– Message

Peter Lord– Renovare Board

Ray Lowe– New Frontiers

T.L. Lowery– JPT

Max Lucado– PK Speaker, Message, MAC member, New Age

Martha Lucia– Elijah List

Keith and Sanna Luker– Elijah List

Carl H. Lundquist– Renovare Board

Peter Lyne– Restoration

Gordon MacDonald– Message

Hugh McClellan– LM

Nancy Magiera– Elijah List

Peter Maiden– SH, WD

Al Maingi– New Frontiers(Kenya)

David & Karen Mains– Renovare Board

Mbonisi Malaba– New Frontiers

Alan Mann– Emerging Church

Judy Littler Manners– WD

Brennan Manning (author and speaker)– Emerging Church

David Mansell– Restoration

Jonathan Maracle– Elijah List

Scott Marques– New Frontiers

Ralph Martin– Catholic Renewalists, joined Fort Lauderdale 5

Martin Marty– Renovare Board

Yaqub Masih– WD

James Earl Massey– MAC member

John Mathison– MAC member

Joseph Mattera– ICA

David Matthew– Restoration

John Maxwell– Fullers (Graduated), Hillsong Speaker, Message, MAC member

Gerald May– Emerging Church Links

John Mbui– New Frontiers (Kenya)

Campbell McAlpine– Restoration

Bill McCartney– PK Top Leader, Vineyard, MAC member

Clarence McClendon– Word Faith

Floyd McClung– SH

Ian McCulloch– Restoration

Gordon MacDonald– Message

Josh McDowell– PK Speaker, MD, MAC member

Ken McGeorge– PK Leader

Cindy McGill– Elijah List

Alistair McGrath– Alpha Supporter

Gary L. McIntosh– ASCG Past President

Paul McKaughan– MAC member

David L. McKenna– Renovare Board

Brian McLaren– Emerging Church, SH, NAR, Word Faith, Prosperity

John McLaughlan– Restoration

Hugh Maclellan– LM

Alan McMahan– ASCG Past President

Erwin McManus– Emerging Church

Reeni Mederos– Elijah List

Ana Mendez-Ferrell– Elijah List

Emerson Mendez-Ferrell– Elijah List

Thomas Merton– Emerging Church, Dominionism, NAR

Joyce Meyer– Word Faith, Message, NAR, Emerging Church Links. Prosperity

Sandy Millar– Alpha Leader, TB

Calvin Miller– Renovare Board, Emerging Church Links

Donald Miller– Emerging Church

Guy Miller– New Frontiers

Keith Miller– Elijah List, Message

Joshua and Janet Mills– Elijah List

Jesse Miranda– LM, ECT

Don Moen– Message

R. Albert Mohler, Jr– MD

Jürgen Moltmann– Emerging Church

James Montgomery– MAC member

Beth Moore– Emerging Church, NAR, Word Faith, Prosperity

Derek Morphew– Vineyard

Robert Morris– Word Faith, Latter Rain, Prosperity, Emerging Church Links

Tony Morton– Restoration

Richard Mouw– Fullers (Faculty - Current President), LM, ECT

David Mugambi– New Frontiers (Kenya)

Mel Mullen– ICA

Richard Muller– Fullers (Faculty)

Wayne Muller– Emerging Church Links

Bob Mumford– FL5 and SM, NAR, Word Faith, Emerging Church Links

Eleanor Mumford– TB, Vineyard, Alpha Supporter

John Mumford– Vineyard

Robert "Bob" Mumford--

Myles Munroe– Word Faith, Elijah List

Steve & Melody Munsey– Word Faith

Mike Murdock– Word Faith, NAR, Prosperity

Ayub Murithi– New Frontiers (Kenya)

Nancy Murphy– Fullers (Faculty)

Michael Mutea– New Frontiers(Kenya)

Sammy Mutiria
New Frontiers(Kenya)

David J. Muyskens– Emerging Church Links

Harold L. Myra– MAC member

Michael Nazir-Ali– WD

Alex Ndombi– New Frontiers (Kenya)

David Neff– LM

Richard John Neuhaus– ECT Catholic Co-Signer

Joseph Njagi– New Frontiers (Kenya)

John Noble– Restoration

Perry Noble – Emerging Church Links, Prosperity, NAR, Latter Rain

Henri Nouwen– Emerging Church, Renovare Board

Nims Obunge– KICC

Peter Ochs– LM

Rt. Hon. Raila Odinga– KICC

Lloyd John Ogilvie– Renovare Board, MAC member

Gary Oliver– PK Speaker

Steve Oliver– New Frontiers

Jonathan Oloyede– WD

Dipo Oluyomi– KICC

Amos Onyango– New Frontiers(Kenya)

J. Edwin Orr– Fuller (Faculty)

John Ortberg– Fullers (Graduated), Emerging Church Links

Juan Carlos Ortiz– PK Speaker

T L Osborn– Latter Rain, Word Faith, Prosperity

Joel Osteen– Word Faith, Hillsong Speaker, Prosperity, motivational speaker

George Otis Jr– Latter Rain, Joel's Army, NAR

Jane Overstreet– LM

J.I. Packer– Alpha Supporter, Renovare Board, Message, MD, ECT

Doug Pagitt– Emerging Church, Latter Rain, NAR, Prosperity, Word Faith

Luis Palau– Alpha Supporter, PK Speaker, LM, MAC member

Tom Panich– Elijah List

William Pannell– Renovare Board

Joy Parrott– Elijah List

Les Parrott– Fullers (Graduated)

Roger Parrott– MAC Board

Rod Parsley– Word Faith, Message, NAR, Latter Rain, Prosperity

Richard Peace– Fullers (Faculty)

Dennis Peacock– ICA, IAC

M. Scott Peck– Emerging Church

Kathy Peel– Message

Basil Pennington– Emerging Church Links

John Perkins– LM, MAC member

Graham Perrins– Restoration

Ben Peters– Elijah List

Eugene H. Peterson– Renovare Board, Emerging Church Links, Author "The Message"

Mark Pfeifer– ICA

Randy Phillip– PK Leader

Jason Phillips– Elijah List

Theresa Forkins-Phillips– Elijah List

Tom Phillips– MAC Board

Chuck Pierce– Latter Rain, NAR, ICA, IAC, Elijah List, WPC Leader

Michael Pierce– Latter Rain, Joels Army

John Piper– Fullers (Graduated), LM, NAR links

Becky Pippert– LM

Sam Poe– New Frontiers

Bill Pollard– LM

John Poole– FL5 and SM

Peter Popoff– Word Faith, Prosperity

Philip Porter– PK Leader

Simon Ponsonby– Vineyard

Don Potter– Elijah List

Fred Price– Word Faith, Emerging Church Links, Latter Rain

Paula Price– Elijah List

Derek Prince (deceased)– FL5 and SM, Word Faith, Unitarian Universalist

Joseph Prince– Hillsong Speaker, Hyper-Grace, Word Faith, Prosperity

Mary Pytches– Vineyard

Dennis Rainey– PK Speaker

Rollin Ramsaran– Fullers (Graduated)

Larry Randolph– Elijah List

R. Daniel Reeves– ASCG Past President

Gustave Reininger– Emerging Church Links

Tricia Rhodes– Emerging Church Links

Robert Ricciardelli– Elijah List

Wayne Rice– Message

D. John Richard– MAC member

Rick Ridings– Elijah List

Alberto Rivera– (not Chick Pubs. Alberto), Elijah List

Kimberly Rivera– Elijah List (not Chick Pubs. Alberto)

John D. Robb– Fullers (Graduated)

Duffy Robbins– Message, Emerging Church Links

Maggie Robbins– Emerging Church Links

Cecil Mel Robeck– Fullers (Faculty)

Oral Roberts– Word Faith, JPT, Prosperity

Pat Robertson– (assumed Word Faith because of his strong links to those who are), MAC member, ECT

Haddon Robinson– PK Speaker

Ras Robinson– Elijah List

Tri Robinson– Vineyard

James Robison– PK Speaker

Rick Rogan– Fullers (Graduated)

Adrian Rogers (deceased)– MAC member

Richard Rohr– Emerging Church Links

Richard Rolle– Emerging Church Links

Rob Rufus– New Frontiers

Ruth Ruibal– Latter Rain, Joel's Army

Julio Ruibal– Latter Rain, Joel's Army

Rick Ryan– PK Speaker

Thomas Ryan– Emerging Church Links

James Ryle– Vineyard, PK Founder (Spoke 1994)

Rebecca St. James– Message

Philip St. Romain– Emerging Church Links

Will Sampson– Emerging Church Links

John & Paula Sandford– Elijah List, NAR, Latter Rain

Jerry Savelle– Message, NAR

Mark Scandrette– Emerging Church Links

Michael Scanlan– Renovare Board

Pete Scazzero– Emerging Church Links

Dale Schlafer– PK Leader

David M. Scholer– Fullers (Faculty)

Robert A Schuller Jr. – Fullers (Graduated), Seeker Friendly

Robert H Schuller Sr. (deceased) – Seeker Friendly, JPT, Emerging Church Links

Chris Seay– Emerging Church

Samir Selmanovic– Emerging Church Links

Peter Senge– Emerging Church Links

Dr. Cory SerVaas– JPT

R.W. Shambach– Word Faith, Prosperity

Dr. Goodwill Shana– New Frontiers

David LeShana– Renovare Board

Nick Sharp– New Frontiers

Luci Shaw– Message

Tom Shaw– New Frontiers

Dutch Sheets– Latter Rain, Joel's Army, NAR, Elijah List

Greg Shepherd– New Frontiers

Priscilla Shirer– Hillsong Speaker, Latter Rain, NAR, Emerging Church Links

David Shosanya– WD

Steve Shultz– Leader of Elijah List

Sibs Sibanda– New Frontiers

Ronald J. Sider– Renovare Board

Ed Silvoso– Latter Rain, Joel's Army, NAR, ICA, IAC

Brian Simmons– Elijah List

Arthur Simon– Renovare Board

Jeremy Simpkins– New Frontiers

Charles Simpson– FL 5 and SM

Kent Simpson– Elijah List

Mary Lance Sisk– MAC Board

Steve Sjogren– Vineyard

Donna Smallenberg– Elijah List

Gary Smalley– PK Speaker, Message

Lewis B. Smedes– Fullers (Faculty), Renovare Board

Chuck Smith Sr.? – PK Speaker (Spoke 1994), Latter Rain

Chuck Smith Jr. – Emerging Church Links, Latter Rain

David Smith– New Frontiers

Don Smith– New Frontiers

Judah Smith– Hillsong Speaker, Latter Rain, Emerging Church Links, Prosperity

Maurice Smith– Restoration

Michael W. Smith– Message

Rolland Smith– MAC member

Jim Smoke– PK Speaker

Ashleigh and PJ Smyth– New Frontiers

Olave Snelling– WD

Howard A. Snyder– Renovare Board

Matt Sorger– Latter Rain, Joel's Army, Elijah List

Peter Spencer– Elijah List

Russell P. Spittler– Fullers (Faculty), Renovare Board

Wess Stafford– LM

Glen Stassen– Fullers (Faculty)

Richard E. Stearns– MAC member

Dave Steel– SH

John Robert Stevens– Latter Rain, NAR, 'The Walk"

Don Stewart– Word Faith, Prosperity

Mark Stibbe– TB, Alpha Supporter, WD

John Stott– LM

Joseph Stowell– PK Speaker

Karl Strader– Word Faith

David Stroud– New Frontiers, Vineyard, WD

B. V. Subbamma– Fullers (Graduated)

Bill Sullivan– ASCG Past President

Dan and Tim Sutherland– Fullers (Graduated)

Jay Swallow– Elijah List

Leonard Sweet– Emerging Church, Latter Rain, Word Faith, Prosperity

Chuck Swindoll– PK Speaker, Message, MD

Joni Eareckson Tada– Message, MD, Word Faith, Prosperity

John Michael Talbot– Emerging Church Links

Thomas Talbott– Fullers (Faculty)

George Tarleton– Restoration (later became new ager)

Chad Taylor– Latter Rain, NAR

Mick Taylor– New Frontiers

Wade Taylor– Elijah List

Tommy Tenney– Latter Rain, NAR, Emerging Church Links

Brock and Bodie Thoene– Message

Gary Thomas– Emerging Church Links

Hugh Thompson– Restoration

Marianne Meye Thompson– Fullers (Faculty)

Tony Thompson– New Frontiers

Tite Tienou– LM

Phyllis Tickle– (deceased) Word Faith, Emerging Church, Prosperity, Mystical teacher

Robert Tilton– Word Faith, Prosperity

Mike Timmis– PK Speaker, a Roman Catholic and PK board member

Paul Tokunaga– LM

Elmer Towns– ASCG Past President

Patricia Treece– Emerging Church Links

Mike Treneer– LM

John Trent– PK Speaker

Ingrid Trobisch– Renovare Board

Richard Twiss– Latter Rain, NAR, Elijah List

Tommy Tyson– Renovare Board

Evelyn Underhill– Emerging Church Links

Jason Upton– Latter Rain, Joel's Army, Elijah List

Kris Vallotton– Elijah List, NAR, Prosperity, Word Faith

Charles VanEngen– ASCG Past President

Stephen Van Rhyn– New Frontiers

William Vaswig– Renovare Founder

John Vaughan– ASCG Past President

Alexander Venter– Vineyard

Joel Virgo– New Frontiers

Terry and Wendy Virgo
Restoration, New Frontiers Leaders

Miroslav Volf– Fullers (Faculty), Emerging Church

Berten A. Waggoner– Vineyard

C. Peter Wagner– Fullers (Faculty), Latter Rain, Joel's Army, New Breed, NAR, ICA (Ex Presiding Apostle), IAC, TB, Alpha Supporter, Renovare Board, Elijah List, WPC Leader, MAC Member, ASCG Founding President, New Age "business" model

Doris Wagner– ICA

E Glenn Wagner– PK Leader

Todd Wagner– MD

Simon Walker– New Frontiers

Jim Wallace– SH

Arthur Wallis– Restoration

Lance Wallnau– ICA

Brian Walsh– Emerging Church

David and Kathie Walters– Elijah List, Word Faith, mystic teachers

Thomas Wang– Renovare Board, MAC member

Walter Wangerin– Message

Karen Ward– Emerging Church Links

Sandy Warner– Elijah List

George Warnock– Latter Rain, Manifest Sons Of God

Mike Warnock– Latter Rain, NAR, Word Faith, Prosperity

Neil Clark Warren– Fullers (Faculty)

Rick Warren– Fullers (Graduated), New Breed, Seeker Friendly, Emerging Church Links, Message, LM, MAC member, promoter of One World Religion\Peace

Raleigh Washington– PK Leader

Robert Webber– Emerging Church, Renovare Board

Barbara Wentroble– Elijah List

John Wesley-White– PK Speaker

James White– Fullers (Graduated; Not the author)

John White– ECT

Paula White– Word Faith, New Age, NAR, Latter Rain, Prosperity

Mel White– Fullers (Faculty)

Paula White– Word Faith, Prosperity, New Age, NAR,

Luder Whitlock Jr.– MAC member

Warren Wiersbe– Message, New Age

Richard B. Wilke– Renovare Board

David Wilkerson– (deceased) JPT

Bruce Wilkinson– PK Speaker, MAC member

Dallas Willard– Emerging Church, Renovare

Andrea Williams– WD

Don Williams– Vineyard

Pat Williams– Message

Rowan Williams– Emerging Church

Andrew Wilson– New Frontiers

Billy Wilson– MAC Board

H. Daniel Wilson– ICA

Ken Wilson– Vineyard

Peter Wilson– Hillsong Speaker, NAR, Latter Rain, Word Faith

Phil Wilthew– New Frontiers

John Wimber– Fullers (Faculty), NAR, Vineyard, TB, Alpha Supporter, Renovare Board, Latter Rain, Word Faith, Prosperity

Lauren Winner– Emerging Church Links

Ralph Winter– MAC member

Sharnael Wolverton– Elijah List

George Wood– LM

Paul Woolley– New Frontiers

N.T. Wright– Emerging Church

Dennis Wrigley– WD

Mark Yaconelli– Emerging Church Links

Mike Yaconelli– Message

Flavil Yeakley, Jr. – ASCG Past President

Barbara and Les Yoder– Elijah List, Vineyard

Paul (David) Yongi Cho – Word Faith, JPT, Latter Rain, Prosperity

Ed Young– Word Faith

Ed Young Jr. – Hillsong Speaker, Latter Rain, NAR, Word Faith, Prosperity

Paul Young– MD

Bill Yount– Elijah List

Michael Youssef– MD

Anthony C. Yu– Fullers (Graduated)

Ravi Zacharias– MAC member

The Organizations listed by me, are ALL ecumenical (or New Age influenced) groups who are uniting with Rome. As Jude told us, we need to be earnestly contending for the TRUE faith once delivered to us and confront these people who are (effectively) working for the Vatican by leading us all to join the ecumenical train.

My list is based on an attempt to awaken us to realize how we are all being seduced by these false guys to become one with Rome and the one world global apostate religion.

Let us RETURN to the Bible for our instructions and no longer be misled by MERE man.
I speak these things out of a heart full of compassion, love and concern for all my true believers in Christ, that they BE NOT DECEIVED by any man or Christian leader who denies the Scriptures as the ONLY standard for our faith. What I have discovered is that ALL those supportive of anything ecumenical associate with Catholics and teach that Catholics are part of the church.

They generally speak well of the pope. They tend to appear and preach at ecumenical meetings and work tirelessly to promote unity with Catholics and the ecumenical movement. Incidentally, I always meant to write up an article on the Elijah List - never got time to do it. The Elijah List is a list of all those who are into the prophetic.

As I understand it, they keep a record of and support all the big public prophetic ministries, advertising them etc. and publishing all the latest prophesies. This list contains many of the names I expose on this blog. They contain mostly those attached to NAR New Apostolic reformation (aka Latter Rain) and the Word of Faith\prosperity preachers. Here is the Elijah List's list of false prophetic ministries.

(**NOTE: Some of the names on his list ARE part of the "Elijah List."   All of the names listed are the product of the Author listed in the website links. They are not mine. Ed.).

You will see the names and faces on these 2 links:

http://www.elijahlist.com/links.html
http://www.elijahlist.com/links2.html

http://watchmanforjesus.blogspot.com/2010/12/l

(**NOTE: This last link is the person who wrote the comments above. Ed.).

_____

"Let Us Reason Ministries:" The New Apostolic Movement: Excellent article on the "who's who" of this deception: http://www.letusreason.org/latrain21.html

Here is just a small list of women to watch out for and avoid:

Jennie Allen
Kay Arthur (Not considered a false teacher, but should approach her stuff with caution).
(** NOTE: Update--Yes, she is a false teacher. See the expose' on her in the main catalogue section. Ed.).

Lisa Bevere
Christine Caine
Nancy Coen
Jennifer Kennedy Dean
Rachel Held Evans
Margaret Feinberg
Charlotte Gambil
Lisa Harper
Jen Hatmaker
Bobbie Houston
Heather Lindsey
Anne Graham Lotz
Rebekah Lyons
Audrey Mack
Joyce Meyer
Kelly Minter
Beth Moore
Rachel Myers
Shauna Niequist
Bianca Olthoff
Victoria Osteen
Sarah Jakes Roberts
Jennifer Rothschild
Susie Shellenberger
Priscilla Shirer
Lysa TerKeurst
Ann Voskamp
Sheila Walsh
Amanda Wells
Paula White
Amanda Bible Williams

Nancy Leigh DeMoss Wolgemuth (Not considered a false teacher, but should approach her stuff with caution. (**NOTE: Her doctrine is questionable. Decide for yourself if she is a false teacher or not. Ed.).

Sarah Young (wrote the book, "Jesus Calling," a blasphemous book; another "Jesus.")
http://bereansdesk.blogspot.com/2017/03/
a-warning-for-christian-women.html

THE EMPOWERED "GLOBAL 21 COUNCIL":

"Is an esteemed group of International Christian leaders, co-chaired by **George O. Wood** and Billy Wilson. These leaders give inspirational oversight to13 Regional Cabinets across the world and seeks to provide resources to address the crucial issues faced by the Spirit-empowered church." So the General Superintendent of the General Council of the Assemblies of God in America is the co-chair of this international coalition. Problem?
 Not until you see who are part of its leadership: **Bill Johnson, Reinhard Bonnke, Lisa Bevere, Kenneth Copeland, Jentezen Franklin, Brian Houston, Cindy "The General" Jacobs, Robert Morris, Phil Pringle** to name a few.
 This is a who's-who of false teachers and wannabe prophets.
 I guess **Osteen, Warren** and **Prince** were just too busy. Seriously. Why in the world would you co-chair this smorgasbord of heresy?
Why would you even want to be on the same website?

 Bill Johnson believes in grave sucking the residual anointing from dead false teachers. He runs his own school for the supernatural where he teaches people the gifts of the spirit - pure blasphemy! **Robert Morris** abuses his sheep and tells them to pay him his tithes before paying their rent or bills or medicine or else God will curse all of their money! **"General" Cindy Jacobs**? Are you serious?
 Kenneth Copeland and **Brian Houston**? The Assemblies should know better.

 Reinhard Bonnke? International charlatan who brags about raising the dead?
The AG threw a banquet in his honor recently. These are not fringe elements in apostasy. These are the leaders beloved.
Then there was the extremely poor decision to get into bed with ex-Catholic mystic **Roma Downey** and her heretical "AD Miniseries." When I say in bed I mean under the covers. The AG actively marketed the "church kit" that **Downey** was selling which turned over your local church to this miniseries for 12 weeks. Each week they would provide you with a video sermon given by a Christian celebrity to match that week's episode. The third lesson was done by none other than **George O. Wood**.

Other notable teachers in the series were the aforementioned **Mark Batterson** and the "Hillsong" false teacher, **Christine Caine**.
The teaching aside, the actual miniseries was a disaster Biblically. It was clear that one of the goals **Downey** had was to overstate the role of women and make any leading male character out to either be a wimp or psychotic. Beloved we are not talking about artistic license. This series simply did not correctly represent the Bible.

I can understand someone who is unsaved not understanding the point but I am talking about the actual story. It was no wonder then that this past year at their annual General Council one of their speakers was **Christine Caine**. Never mind that she is from "Hillsong," the largest international heretical organization on the planet.

Never mind that she is an ardent supporter of someone like **Joyce Meyer**. Never mind that after "shadowing" **Meyer** for a week she tweeted a picture of herself laying hands upon the Bible of **Joyce Meyer** and praying for "an impartation of her "teaching anointing and revelation." The same **Meyer** who teaches Jesus went to hell and had to be born again there. The same **Meyer** who teaches that she never sins. The same **Meyer** who teaches that we are all little gods.

It is no wonder then that the quote that hit the Internet from **Caine** that night which was taken as some deep nugget of wisdom was:

"The size of your ministry is determined by the size of your heart." - **Christine Caine**

Not determined by God. Not determined by the Holy Spirit. Not determined by correct doctrine or preaching the correct Gospel. No beloved. Determined by the size of our wickedly deceptive hearts. Therein sums up the progression of falling away I have witnessed within the Assemblies for the past several years. They bought into the **Warren** theologies of growth and marketing.

They bought into the seeker friendly notions of church growth. They continued to make whatever associations were popular and gained them more exposure with seemingly little concern about doctrine. As a minister for the Assemblies, I am expected to support them and in complete fairness I can no longer do so. There are still some very good AG churches out there beloved. Churches who are trying to do the right thing and preach the whole Gospel.

Eventually they will have to come out from among them if the Assemblies does not stop its free-fall. Locally however, the politics are even worse. The disregard for correct doctrine is widely accepted as long as you can put bodies in the seats each week. Never mind if people leave.

That is a **Warren** principle taught in the Purpose Driven Church called "Blessed Subtraction." This principle teaches pastors that it is OK to let sheep wander away from your flock as long as you replace them. Talk about not understanding the 99 and the one!

But this point is vitally important because Purpose Driven teachings insist that we are no long in the business of reaching the unsaved but rather the unchurched.

That may sound subtle, but it is purely a satanic plot. Instead of focusing on their salvation, pastors now focus on whether they belong to a church. Instead of focusing on their relationship to Jesus they focus on their relationship to ministry.

That is why Blessed Subtraction is so widely accepted theologically even though it violates the entire Bible! As long as you replace the body then the church has not "lost" anything. But what about the sheep that wandered off?

http://www.828ministries.com/articles/2/ (Emphasis Mine).

(**NOTE: The above article is from this website. The "emphasis mine" is also from the writer. Ed.).

THE DECEPTION KNOWN AS <u>SOZO</u>: Inner Healing – Christian or Occult?

Posted on January 31, 2013:

 Having been trained as a <u>SOZO</u> minister I know the dangers it presents first hand. The following is a well written article which relates to <u>SOZO</u> (Christianized inner healing with no basis in Scripture.)   I know there are many of you out there with questions and concerns. I hope this helps shed some light on its origins and why we need to stay away. Christ is sufficient for all our needs. Every one of them.

<u>Inner Healing/Healing of Memories—Christian or Occult?</u>—

<u>Healing of the memories,</u> or <u>inner healing,</u> or healing of the emotions has its roots in the teachings of anti-Christian and <u>occultist</u>, **Agnes Sanford**.

It was carried on after her death by those she influenced, such as lay therapists **Ruth Carter Stapleton** (deceased sister of **Jimmy Carter), Rosalind Rinker**, **John and Paula Sandford** (currently of Elijah House, a demon-deliverance and <u>memory healing center</u> in Port Falls, Idaho), **William Vaswig** (of Renovaré fame), **Rita Bennett,** and others.

John Wimber, David Yonggi Cho, Robert Schuller, and **Norman Vincent Peale** are some of the well-known pop <u>psychological practitioners</u> of <u>inner healing</u>, but it has spread widely in so-called evangelical circles in a more sophistiated form through such "<u>Christian</u>" <u>psychologists</u> as **David Seamands, H. Norman Wright**, and **James G. Friesen**, as well as a number of lay <u>therapists</u> like **Fred** and **Florence Littauer**...

(Two of **David Seamand's** books, "Healing for Damaged Emotions" and "Healing of Memories," are considered the "<u>inner-healer's</u> bibles" in today's psychologically-oriented pulpits.).

 <u>Inner healing therapies are offshoots of Freudian and Jungian theories rooted in the occult. They have destructively impacted secular society for decades and are now taking their devastating toll within the professing Church.</u>
 <u>A variety of "memory-healing" psycho therapies are masquerading under Christian terminology and turning Christians from God to self.</u>

Among the most deadly are "<u>regressive</u>" therapies designed to probe the "unconscious" for buried memories which are allegedly causing everything from depression to fits of anger and sexual misconduct, and must therefore be uncovered and "healed."

– The basic teaching of <u>inner healing</u> is the theory that salvation or healing comes through the uprooting of negative memories or "hurts" caused by others in early childhood that are supposedly buried in the "subconscious" from where they tend to dictate our behavior without us even knowing it. Thus, the blame for one's bad behavior (a.k.a. "emotional problems") in the present is placed upon others (who are perceived to have sinned against us in the past) rather than upon ourselves where it belongs (cf. Ezekiel 18).

In order to "heal" these "diseased memories," the occultic technique of visualization (which is in reality a type of sorcery or divination which has been used by shamans, witch doctors, and sorcerers for thousands of years, and is specifically forbid by the Bible) is frequently used to recreate the distressful childhood scene, "image" Jesus (if one is a professing Christian), bringing Him into the past situation as a "spirit guide"/"healing agent," and then causing Him to sanctify the event, forgive the person who supposedly caused the hurt, and in most cases, even alter the reality of the situation in the subject's mind, all so that the subject might be "delivered" from the "crippling emotional pain" associated with the past negative experience that supposedly "diseased memory" in the first place.

(Charismatic **Roman Catholic** memory-healers employ the same techniques, but generally substitute Mary for Jesus as the "healing agent" whom the subject meets in the fantasy.)

– One of the seemingly attractive forms of inner healing is to have Jesus enter a painful scene from the past. The inner-healer helps the person recreate the memory by having Jesus do or say things that will make the person feel better about the situation.

For instance, if a man's dad had neglected him when he was a boy, an inner-healer may help that man create a new memory of Jesus having played baseball with him when he was a boy. Through verbal encouragement, he would regress him back to his childhood and encourage him to visualize Jesus pitching the ball and praising him for hitting a home run. Some inner-healers regress people back to the womb and lead them through "rebirthing" by guided imagery and imagination.

Thus, through these psychoanalytic/occult techniques, inner-healers should not be surprised at the possibility of actually altering or enhancing the memory in their zeal to replace bad memories with good memories. Inner-healers are always in danger of unwittingly enhancing or engrafting memories through words or actions that mean one thing to the inner-healer, but may communicate something else entirely to the highly vulnerable subject.

– Inner healing is based upon the implication that we clearly need something more than God's love and forgiveness in order to love and forgive others who are perceived to have wronged us in the past. Since the Bible distinctly teaches that Jesus can never be called-up and forced to "perform" at our command, any "Jesus" actually visualized would have to be a demon spirit and not of God.

Of course, that is precisely the danger of the occult technique of visualization — subjects are being taught to experiment with things that God has repeatedly condemned in both the Old and New Testaments alike, not because the phenomena visualized (i.e. "spirit guides") are not real, but rather because they are produced by demons determined to lead one into the worship of other gods and ultimate destruction (Deut. 13 ff.).

The Bible repeatedly warns against becoming involved with the occult on any level, because of what the Bible identifies as "spirits of demons working signs" for the purpose of deceiving the whole world (Rev. 16:14; cf. 13:14).

This exposure to the occult, however unintentional and innocent, could easily lead the undiscerning into far more serious spiritual or "emotional" problems than they ever dreamed possible. Unfortunately, the research is replete with such cases of demonic/occultic influence experienced by first-time dabblers.

– Inner healing practices of regressing into the past, fossicking about in the unconscious for hidden memories, conjuring up images, acting out fantasies and nightmares, and believing lies, all resemble the world of the occult, not the work of the Holy Spirit. An imaginary memory created under a highly suggestible, hypnotic-like state will only bring imaginary healing. It may also plunge people into a living nightmare.

What is being taught as inner healing/healing of memories is nothing but basic **sorcery**, which is an attempt to manipulate reality in the past, present, or future, and denies God's omnipotence by implying that He needs our "creative visualization" in order to apply effectively His forgiveness and healing, while simultaneously sets us up as gods who can, through prescribed rituals, use Him and His power as our tools.

In fact, inner healing/healing of memories is nothing but "Christianized psychoanalysis" that uses the power of suggestion to solve so-called problems, which the technique itself has many times created.

–The Bible has much to say concerning the healing of memories (besides condemning its methodologies).
The Bible clearly teaches that moral choices rather than past traumas determine our current condition and actions, and thereby our responsibility; the Bible has always taught that it is not the act in the past but how one reacts to the act that determines "which soul has sinned" (Ezekiel 18 again).

Since there is no Biblical evidence that any prophet, priest, or apostle ever dealt with anything remotely related to buried or repressed emotions or memories, then shouldn't one question why this is so if inner healing is the big truth that its practitioners say it is?

–If prayer and Bible study and the power of the Holy Spirit are not enough for saints today to deal with life and problems, then the saints of old, including the apostle Paul, must have been greatly lacking.   Despite his many hardships described in Scripture, Paul was able to function and rejoice in the Lord without the help of psychoanalysis. Paul forgot the past and pressed on toward the prize (Phil. 3:13-14) promised to all those who love Christ's appearing (2 Tim 4:7-8).

Likewise, throughout Church history, Christians have managed the same when they should have been at a great disadvantage without the "insights" of modern psychology. It is a dangerous heresy to insist that we must accept this new "revelation" by psychologists or live

deficient lives. The past is of little consequence if Christians truly are new creations for whom "old things are passed away [and] all things are become new" (2 Cor. 5:17).
Searching the past in order to find an "explanation" for one's present behavior conflicts with the entire teaching of Scripture. Though it may seem to help for a time, it actually robs one of the Biblical solution through Christ. What matters is not the past, but one's personal relationship to Christ now.

–The people who are most vulnerable to inner-healers are those who are at a low point in their spiritual walk or who are experiencing difficult circumstances.

The inner-healers entice through all kinds of direct and implied promises for healing damaged emotions, healing roots in the past that prevent personal growth, and enabling a person to have a closer walk with God. They circle about congregations like vultures, waiting for the opportunity to swoop down on those who are near to dropping from "spiritual exhaustion."

They assure their prospective victims of their sincere desire to help and they communicate a Biblical facade' by using butchered Bible verses and Christian-sounding conversation. However, once their talons pierce the person, a penetrating parasitic process begins. And the host/parasite relationship continues as long as the host continues to look to the inner-healer to make him emotionally well and spiritually whole.

–Instead of being healed, there is a very strong possibility that the recipients of inner healing are now living on the basis of a lie from the pit of hell. Inner healing is not based upon truth. It is based upon faulty memory, guided imagery, fantasy, visualization, and hypnotic-like suggestibility.

And while the inner-healers may conjure up a "Jesus" and recite Bible verses, such inner healing is not Biblical. Jesus said, "If ye continue in My Word, then are ye My disciples indeed; and ye shall know the truth, and the truth shall make you free" (Jn. 8:31-32).

Moreover, inner healing is insulting to God when the "healers" attempt to take away His power to bless "emotionally-distressed" people simply in response to their repentance and prayers. It is extra-Biblical, blasphemous, and carnal in its visualization and manipulation of the Son of God. It is dangerous in the way it forces people into childish self-interest, subjectivism, and emotionalism. And it is wickedly presumptuous in its priestly bestowing of forgiveness and assurance.

https://mkayla.wordpress.com/2013/01/31/ (Italics Mine–M'Kayla).

In the "Presenting Jesus" tool, the counselor asks the client to "Picture Jesus and ask for His help." Once again, any such imagined manifestation of Christ in the mind's eye can only be false. Jesus warned of false Christs and false prophets who would arise and show great signs and wonders, using all means possible to deceive the very elect:

"Wherefore, if they shall say unto you, Behold, [Christ] is in the desert, go not forth: [or] behold, he is in the secret chambers; believe it not" (Mt 24:24, 26).

The Greek word for "secret chambers" is tamaon, which means "a secret room" or "inner chamber." Is not the mind such a place? The same word is used figuratively for praying "in your closet" (Mt 6:6), and again in Luke:12:3.

Obviously, we are not only to pray "in closets" because we are elsewhere instructed to "pray without ceasing." We certainly don't live and work in a closet; neither can we pray out loud all day long, in every situation. Clearly, the meaning is that even secret ("closeted") prayers, spoken from our innermost "chambers" of the heart and mind, are heard by our Father in heaven.
However, there is no "secret room" (or secret instruction) in God's Word for visualizing Christ as a means of accessing Him through prayer. In fact, quite the opposite: Scripture repeatedly warns of false Christs who will even appear as "an angel of light" (II Cor:11:14).
Such demons have deceived countless individuals through the ages, many of whom have spawned some of the most widespread cults, based on doctrines of devils (I Tim. 4:1).
Attempting to contact God or Jesus through our "mind's eye," therefore, is a form of divination and necromancy (attempting to communicate with spirits of the dead).
These variations of witchcraft are expressly forbidden in Scripture.

Ironically, "The Sozo User Manual" by Andy Reese explains that if the client is unable to see "Jesus" (which could never be the real Jesus) there is a high likelihood of demonic blockage. In order to probe for the presence of a demon, the counselor is told how to gain access to the client's mind, in much the same way as a hypnotist.

In the example given on page 40, the counselor asks the client to "go to the back seat of your conscience right now—sort of like climbing into the back seat of your car, and we're going to see if there is something that is trying hard to block you from getting freedom [to visualize Christ], Okay?"
Considering just two of the six "tools" found in the Sozo program, it's clear that it is dangerously flawed. Furthermore, its methodology is indistinguishable from forms used by secular psychotherapists, which have their origin in the occult.

Sozo is spiritualized Freudian psychoanalysis that includes psychic determinism and searching out the unconscious through techniques that include various forms of guided imagery.
Anyone involved in Sozo needs to take to heart the admonition given twice in Proverbs: "There is a way which seemeth right unto a man, but the end thereof are the ways of death" (Prv 14:12; 16:25). https://wolvesinthepulpit.blogspot.com/p/sozo-presenting-another-jesus-in.html

(**NOTE: The following pages are additional information that is crucial to your salvation. It is my prayer that should you recognize some of these aberrant teachings in your local church, you would not hesitate to remove yourself immediately—before you become a victim of these teachings. Ed.).

THE TORONTO BLESSING:

In January 1994 at a series of special meetings at the Toronto Airport Vineyard (as the church was then called) there was a dramatic increase in the phenomena **John Wimber** describes, especially laughing and falling over. Believing this was the work of the Holy Spirit, the leaders **John** and **Carol Arnott** continued the meetings.

The dramatic phenomena have continued and, as visitors came and went home, have spread to other places, including Britain. This has come to be known as "The Toronto Blessing." Many people also report dramatic renewal in their Christian lives, inner healing, recovering their first love, being set on fire for Jesus – especially as, having been knocked to the floor by the Holy Spirit, they lie there for as long as seems right.

This was also what **Wimber** had noted about falling over in the Spirit. "Most people are aware of a sense of calm and a sublime indifference to their circumstances. Commonly, no after effects are noted either good or bad. Occasionally this state continues for 12 to 48 hours, in which case profound spiritual changes have been said to follow. The most dramatic falls are those sustained by pastors and ministers...

Toronto Airport Christian Fellowship (TACF): The changes following this experience may also be profound. Their ministry is infused with new power and effectiveness." TACF now have thousands of testimonies to the truth of these words, except that some profound spiritual changes have taken place in much less than twelve hours.

As people at TACF reflected on what was happening, it became clear that the Holy Spirit was not knocking people over because He likes playing skittles, but because He wants people to lie down in an attitude of rest and stillness, so that He can bless and renew them inside.

They think it makes sense then to adopt that resting attitude deliberately, cooperating with the Holy Spirit. This is 'soaking prayer.' Joyce Huggett notes, "a fresh touch of God's Spirit often opens the door to contemplative prayer."

In the middle of prayer ministry at TACF one evening **Carol Arnott** felt tired and decided to have a lie down. After a couple of minutes she was about to pull herself back to her feet when she noticed that there was a slight tingling in the tips of her fingers.
"Lord if this is you, please continue," **Carol** prayed, trying to push away the sense that she really ought to be up and working, praying for others. The tingling moved slowly up her hands. **Carol** stayed lying down as very slowly she felt the Holy Spirit move through the whole of her body. Eventually, she says, all her tiredness was gone, she was "buzzing with the power of God."

She had been on the floor for three hours. "I know, Lord, you could have done that in an instant. Lord why did it take three hours?" **Carol** asked. She thought Jesus replied, "**Carol** it wasn't the empowering, it wasn't the feeling that I was after. I just wanted you to spend time with me. I was lonely for you."

456

Carol explains, "He wants just our presence, not our prayer lists, not our need to's – that's important to Him too, but He just wants us to come into a love affair with Him – what we call soaking in his presence."

PRAYER CENTRES:

TACF are now encouraging people to set up 'Soaking Prayer Centres' in their own churches and homes. Make the room comfortable and inviting. Provide a variety of places for people to sit or lie. Play a CD of quiet worship music. Encourage yourself and others to focus on Jesus. Say 'Come Holy Spirit.'
Then, as **Carol Arnott** teaches, "Wait in a receiving mode, not praying, not speaking in tongues, not helping in any way, just relaxing and waiting and receiving from Him."

It is this expectation of receiving which is the main difference between soaking prayer and classic contemplative prayer, in which 'union with God' is the aim.
John Arnott says: "Soaking is more than just waiting, it is receiving the presence of the Lord."
In soaking prayer, particularly as taught by TACF, there is a strong expectation that people will receive some refreshment, healing, empowering.
The leader does not themselves 'soak' but prays over the 'soakers.'

In Leamington Spa there is a small team moving round, watching over people, praying intently, making, as they see it, a circle of protection over the 'soakers.'

https://wolvesinthepulpit.blogspot.com/p/soaking-prayer-by-roger-harper-in-2000.html

http://www.w3church.org/ChristianMagic.html

Not to be outdone, we also have the "**Elijah List**," which:

The " Elijah List" is a list of all those who are into the prophetic. As I understand it, they keep a record of and support all the big public prophetic ministries, advertising them, etc. and publishing all the latest prophesies. This list contains many of the names I expose on this blog. They contain mostly those attached to NAR New Apostolic reformation (a.k.a. "Latter Rain") and the Word of Faith preachers.

"Here is the "Elijah List's" of false prophetic ministries. You will see the names and faces on these two links": http://www.elijahlist.com/

The author of the above paragraph and his site concerning the list:
http://watchmanforjesus.blogspot.com/2010/03/ list-and-details-on-other-false.html

(**NOTE: As the author of the article states there are two, but they are both the same. Also the extended link doesn't work; it only works this way, however it will still bring you to this list of heretics. Ed.)

We have a surprisingly overlooked "religion" in light of Romans Chapter 1, where the Apostle Paul is writing concerning worshiping **the creature more than the Creator**–the "earth religion" (Rom 1:25):

ENVIRONMENTALISM, CLIMATE CHANGE AND RECYCLING:

In addition to what this verse says, there are also previous verses that speak of changing the glory of God–as to worship–"into corruptible man, and to birds, and four-footed beasts, and creeping things," which are also idols of ancient times as well as today. (Rom. 1:23).
 In this, it is considered by our Lord Jesus Christ that those who ascribe to worshiping other men or animals or inanimate objects are fools, as it is stated in verse 22: "Professing themselves to be wise, they became fools."

Somehow as Christians we have overlooked, or not understood, that these self-serving "religions" are part of the ushering in of the One World government and the One World Religion. The United Nations has an agenda called "UN 2030," which simply stated is a pact among several leaders–including religious leaders–and **Pope Francis** to put in place laws governing the environment, climate change and other humanistic beliefs; a new "religion" of sorts. (See also Rom. Chapter 13).

From Psychology Today–their own humanistic belief system--here is an article that they also find environmentalism to be a "religion":
http://www.independent.org/news/article.asp?id=3309

Also another equally important article, from a nonbelievers thought:
https://www.aei.org/carpe-diem/ michael-chrichton-in-2003-environmentalism-is-a-religion/

https://www.thenewatlantis.com/ publications/environmentalism-as-religion

(**NOTE: Michael Chrichton–deceased-- is the author of "Jurassic Park," and "The Andromeda Strain," among several others. Ed.).

Lastly, here is a comment taken from Yahoo's email regarding Greta Thunberg and her "climate change" accusations about how dire our situation is:
Years of climate lies--

1967: 'Dire famine by 1975.' Salt Lake Tribune
1969: 'Everyone will disappear in a cloud of blue steam by 1989.' New York Times
1970: Ice age by 2000 Boston Globe
1970: 'America subject to water rationing by 1974 and food rationing by 1980.' Redlands Daily Facts
1971: 'New Ice Age Coming' Washington Post
1972: New ice age by 2070 Brown University
1974: 'New Ice Age Coming Fast' The Guardian
1974: 'Another Ice Age?' Time Magazine
1974: Ozone Depletion a 'Great Peril to Life' University of Michigan

1976: 'The Cooling' National Center for Atmospheric Research
1980: 'Acid Rain Kills Life in Lakes' Nobelsville Ledger
1978: 'No End in Sight' to 30-Year Cooling Trend New York Times
1988: James Hansen forecasts increase regional drought in 1990s Miami News
1988: Washington DC days over 90F to from 35 to 85 Gannett
1988: Maldives completely under water in 30 years Canberra Times
1989: Rising seas to 'obliterate' nations by 2000 AP
1989: New York City's West Side Highway underwater by 2019 Salon
1995 to Present: Climate Model Failure CEI.org
2000: 'Children won't know what snow is.' The Independent
2002: Famine in 10 years The Guardian
2004: Britain to have Siberian climate by 2020 The Guardian
2008: Arctic will be ice-free by 2018 Associated Press
2008: Al Gore warns of ice-free Arctic by 2013
2009: Prince Charles says only 8 years to save the planet The Independent
2009: UK prime minister says 50 days to 'save the planet from catastrophe' The Independent
2013: Arctic ice-free by 2015 The Guardian
2013: Arctic ice-free by 2016
2014: Only 500 days before 'climate chaos' Washington Examiner

(**NOTE: Posted by "S" (the author) on November 8, 2019, under the heading "Greta Thunberg shuts down heckler at climate rally" which is a Yahoo storyline. Ed.).

CHURCH OF THE NATIONS:

(COTN) is an "international family of churches relating through love and commitment to see the Kingdom of God extended on earth."

They embrace values such as: "Apostolic alignment... Accountability (being under authority releases authority)...The principle of spiritual Fathers and Sons."
COTN describe their relationship with the body of Christ in part as follows:

"The leaders of COTN will continue to build relationships into the wider body of Christ.

"This will happen through the Apostolic Council relating to apostolic streams, gatherings and other ministries..." (Emphasis Mine: Ed.).

If you happen to be a NAR denialist like **Dr Michael Brown**, then simply ignore the term NAR and compare the statements from COTN in this article to what Scripture teaches. Do the leaders of this movement believe and teach the false doctrines of dominion/kingdom now theology?

 For example, does Scripture instruct us to change culture and transform nations by discipling literal nations?   Has God clearly outlined a "seven mountain mandate" for the church? Does God speak directly to current day apostolic leaders and give them annual words regarding His latest strategy or supernatural moves?

If apostolic leaders claim to have such important words from God, <u>then surely Scripture is insufficient in that it has left ordinary believers in the dark unless current day apostles hear correctly?</u>
Do <u>COTN</u> leaders associate with false <u>prophets</u>? These questions will be answered in this article: "We <u>envision</u> the world learning about, <u>accepting</u> and focusing on <u>Jesus and His Kingdom on earth.</u>"

"We see authentic Christianity as coming under the loving Lordship of Jesus Christ and being joined to a community of believers who are learning to live a <u>new life</u> in a <u>new way.</u>"
"We want each and every person <u>given to us</u> to live a self-governed life while fulfilling their God-given destiny within a community of believers."

"The Great Commission was given by Jesus as <u>an apostolic mandate to disciple nations.</u>" "This was based on God's original purpose stated in Genesis when He gave man <u>a dominion and a domestic mandate.</u> Jesus commanded us to preach the Gospel of the Kingdom, not the Gospel of the church."

"<u>So we see local churches reaching their destiny when aligned to an apostolic vision.</u>
This <u>allows Jesus to fulfill His promise</u> when He said, "I will build my church and the gates of hell will not prevail against it."

Those who are familiar with the aberrant teachings of the <u>New Apostolic Reformation</u> would have to read no further to know that catch phrases in bold \underlined indicate that we are dealing with a movement heavily influenced by the <u>NAR.</u>
The true apostolic vision from God is clear; it's called Scripture. When building a house, an architect is brought in to design the plans. This blueprint for the structure must be implemented by the builder. The builder does not use his <u>imagination, vision,</u> or <u>feelings</u> to decide how the structure should look. In similar fashion, God has given a blueprint to build his church – not only has he supplied the plans, but He is also the builder.

The blueprint is called Scripture, and the foundation is "built on the foundation of the apostles and prophets, Christ Jesus himself being the cornerstone" Eph 2:20.
The prophets wrote most of the Old testament, and the apostles brought us the New Testament – inspired and infallible teachings they heard directly from Christ, as well as the inspiration of the Holy Spirit (John 16:12-14).

This foundation has been laid, it is complete, and the blueprint does not need any corrections. This is why Jude wrote: "I found it necessary to write appealing to you to contend for the faith that was <u>once for all delivered</u> to the saints" Jude 3.

We don't need any <u>new revelations</u> or annual words from God to build a local church:

"All Scripture is breathed out by God and profitable for teaching, for reproof, for correction, and for training in righteousness, that the man of God may be complete, equipped for every good work." 2 Timothy 3:16-17.

EXAMINING WHAT COTN ENVISIONS :

COTN: "international family of churches relating through love and commitment <u>to see the Kingdom of God extended on earth</u>."
On the surface, this sounds Biblical, but when the "kingdom of God" is associated with the "<u>seven mountain mandate</u>"or discipling literal nations, we are dealing with <u>NAR</u> doctrines.
COTN: "We see authentic Christianity as coming under the loving Lordship of Jesus Christ and being joined to a community of believers who are learning to live a <u>new life in a new way.</u>"

Once again, not problematic on the surface; it all depends what they mean by "a <u>new</u> way."

If by "<u>new way</u>" <u>COTN</u> mean the pattern laid out in Scripture, applicable to the church through the ages and relevant today, then I agree.

If by "new way" they mean believers are dependent on <u>new shifts</u> taking place, <u>new methodology</u>, <u>new revelation</u> being given, then I disagree.

COTN: "We want each and every person <u>given to us</u> to live a self-governed life while fulfilling their God-given destiny within a community of believers."
Believers live a life submitted to God, and community does play a role. However, when that community of believers is governed by leaders who hear from God on their behalf, the community are in effect being governed not by God, but by their leaders.

Does this destiny include <u>NAR</u> teachings such as <u>shifting atmospheres</u>, <u>transforming culture</u>, or experiencing God's favor due to God supposedly declaring 2018 is a year of <u>acceleration</u>? We shall find out shortly. When <u>COTN</u> say "disciple nations" they mean literal nations.

 John Scholtz is one of the leaders on the <u>COTN</u> "apostolic council." On 19 February 2017, he delivered a message entitled "Making Disciples of the Nations" in Port Elizabeth (South Africa). In the message, **Scholtz** laments the fact that the <u>Gospel of salvation replaced the gospel of the kingdom</u>.

This false dichotomy of two Gospels is being promulgated by those who teach <u>dominion/kingdom now</u> theology. There is only ONE Gospel, and it includes salvation and discipleship – both possible because of what Christ has done.

Scholtz concedes that the church has not managed to disciple a nation, and for that reason he believes: "the church has never accomplished what it was called to do."
Scholtz therefore believes that the church has been called to <u>disciple</u> literal nations, whereas Scripture teaches the church must preach the gospel in all nations, and that people of all nations will be saved (Revelation 7:9).

Scholtz has fallen for the lies of <u>dominion theology</u> of the <u>NAR</u> and other movements that fall under the <u>NAR</u> – "<u>Manifest Sons of God</u>," "<u>Joel's Army</u>," "<u>Latter Rain</u>," etc.
Scriptures teaches that prior to our Lords return the world will be marked by <u>godlessness not godliness</u> (II Timothy 3) and a falling away, not revival (II Thess 2).

461

On Sunday, May 3rd, 2015, **Scholtz** preached a message entitled "Encounters with God." In the message he said "if we don't disciple the world, the world will disciple the church, somebody's going to win that battle and we are going to win it and....the task of transforming the world takes on an enormity."

We are not called to disciple or transform the world, this is NAR/dominion theology language, and cannot be supported by Scripture.
Unfortunately members of Harvest Christian Church (**John Scholtz** was senior pastor for many years) can access these kinds of teachings from their own library.
Apart from authors which teach false doctrines such as the word of faith heresy and prosperity gospel (**Joyce Meyer, Benny Hinn, Kenneth Copeland, John Bevere**), the Harvest library carries a host of NAR books by none other than the founder of the NAR – the late **Peter Wagner**.

They include: "Territorial spirits: insights on strategic-level spiritual warfare from nineteen Christian leaders" and "Warfare prayer : how to seek God's power and protection in the battle to build his kingdom" – a NAR strategy to take dominion!
One of the leaders on the "apostolic council" is **Tony Fitzgerald**.
Knowing what he teaches, and who he associates with will help us evaluate COTN in terms of being influenced by the NAR.

Tony Fitzgerald is no stranger to the apostolic move. In 2002 **Fitzgerald** attended an ICAL gathering in Dallas, "taking part in the forums and discussions included: **Cindy Jacobs, Bill Hamon, Alan Langstaff**, David Cartledge, **John Eckhart, Ted Haggard** and Bart Pierce."
In 2009 he "had the privilege of participating at the "International Coalition of Apostles."
"I spoke on a panel dealing with "Apostolic Mission to the Nations"...In preparation for the panel, **Peter Wagner** in his report highlighted a prophecy by **Chuck Pierce** given in 1986."
In other words, **Fitzgerald** is more than familiar with the New Apostolic Reformation. The late **Peter Wagner** is the founder of the NAR, and **Chuck Pierce** is one of the false prophets in the movement. In 2013, **Fitzgerald** was at another ICAL conference, which included false NAR prophets **Lance Wallnau** and **Dutch Sheets** – both taught at this conference.

Perhaps you have noticed that the main players in the NAR such as "Bethel " church, refuse to accept reality. The reality is that this world is in a mess, and it's not getting any better. In the light of their beliefs, they are forced to construct their own narrative of reality. Only good news will do, and in many cases facts are exaggerated to suit their agenda.
Contrary to Scripture that teaches of a departure from the faith and increasing wickedness on earth during the last days, the NAR believe in a mass revival (a "billion soul harvest") and growing influence of the church over the world. While the visible church has certainly made their presence felt through the establishment of mega churches and countless meetings in packed out stadiums, the falling away continues at a rate second to none as false doctrines dominate the industrial evangelical complex.

https://fitl.co.za/2018/06/21/
the-acceleration-of-the-new-apostolic-reformations-influence-in-south-africa/

(**NOTE: This article is quite lengthy. I have included a few highlights. The rest can be read on the link provided above. Ed.).

    - **Steve Ashburn** A brilliant author and researcher, his end-times thesis developed while reading Old Testament prophecies, such as Psalm 83, Isaiah 17, Ezekiel 29 and Ezekiel 38-30. He realized other prophetic books in the Old Testament describing future battles against Israel all fit within a 40-year timeline.

Perhaps the most current systematic overview of coming prophetic events can be found in his two books, "The Next Nuclear War: Are We on the Edge of the End Times" and "End Times Dawning: Get Ready!" available at www.endtimesrecord.com. http://www.soundchristian.com/prophecy/who/.

 (**NOTE: He is not among the "wolves" in this book, however his information is worth having here. Ed.).

_____

(**NOTE: The heretical doctrine of "Pleading the Blood" is one of the hallmarks of the Word of Faith (W.O.F.) false preachers and teachers. It is not to be found anywhere in the Scriptures. Ed.).

_____

OCCULT HAND SIGNS:

https://www.olivetjournal.com/ false-ministries-2-occult-hand-signs/

As it has been repeatedly recommended in Olivet Journal articles, the best way to spot false ministries is to find the signs of their affiliation to the Illuminati and Freemasonry, which can be accomplished by recognizing their unconditional praise and support for the current Zionist State of Israel, called the Zionism, the Kabbalah and Masonic symbolism in their logos and designs, and the occult hand signs they exhibit often.

In the first half of this article, we will learn the signs of false ministries and discuss the evidence of all ministries being false. And, you will also see and learn some evidence of "the church," or the entire modern *christianity being false as a whole. As a matter of fact, the *christianity as we know of as a system and a religion is completely Masonic and has been created by the Zionist Illuminati, a.k.a.. "the seed of serpent."

Some strong evidence is presented here.

(*In Olivet Journal articles, TRUE Christianity is spelled with a capital "C," as Christianity; and FALSE christianity with a lower case "c," as christianity). In the last half of the article, we will focus on the "hand signs."

You will see a parade of photos (about 50 individuals) and screen shots of the teachers, preachers, and self-appointed prophets, throughout different orientations, exhibiting the identical hand signs that are known to be Illuminati and Freemasonry related.
I am sure that you are familiar with many of the people you will see in the photos, and may find some of your favorite teachers:

(**NOTE: In order to see the teachers and the hand signs, you need to go to the website; I cannot reproduce it here. Ed.).

MANDALA COLORING BOOKS:

By Lois Putnam
 (**NOTE: Her article can be found on the website listed at the end. Ed.).

Adult coloring has recently become a national passion. In fact, of the top twenty best-selling books on Amazon.com, ten of these were adult color books.   Proof of this can be found in any bookstore where the first thing you'll see upon entering is shelves brimming with every kind of color book imaginable. And congregated around these shelves you'll find enthusiastic colorists who'll be eager to share how enjoyable this current fad can be. Like many others, it may not be long until you'll be picking up a book or two just to try it out.

Now, from your first examination of these color books, you'll note they aren't like the color books of your youth, for at least half of them are distinctly New Age in look and content. And second, you'll note that they almost all purport to help calm, soothe, de-stress, and relax you into a meditative state. Finally, you'll soon discover some of these intriguing books have tantalizing patterns called "mandalas" that will entice you to look at them over and over.

These mesmerizing "sacred circles" are designed to visually take you to their centers to discover "Your Higher Self." And yes, they are deceptive, and no, they aren't Christian!

So be aware that there are many seductive "spiritual" color books out there both for adults and children alike. Thus, if you should decide to try out some coloring or are planning to buy one for someone else, you would do well to heed the admonition in Psalm 101:3 that states: "I will set no wicked thing before mine eyes." And because "mandalas" do have a hidden agenda, this booklet is written to inform colorists and non-colorists exactly what they are, and what their purpose is.

Adult Coloring Adult Coloring Books—A Spiritual Practice?

While there is certainly nothing harmful about adults coloring, in and of itself, much of the contemplative spirituality connection has been propagated by Sybil MacBeth's "Praying in Color" book series.

On MacBeth's website, she gives eight reasons to color while praying:

1) You want to pray but words escape you.
2) Sitting still and staying focused in prayer are a challenge.
3) Your body wants to be part of your prayer.
4) You want to just hang out with God but don't know how.
5) Listening to God feels like an impossible task.
6) Your mind wanders and your body complains.
7) You want a visual, concrete way to pray.
8) You need a new way to pray.

Sybil MacBeth's book, "Praying in Color: Drawing a New Path to God," is endorsed on the back cover by emergent writer **Phyllis Tickle** (who once said **Brian McLaren** could be the next Luther). In MacBeth's book, she speaks frequently about lectio divina, a meditative practice used in contemplative prayer.

With **Tickle's** endorsement and the promotion of contemplative practices, we must question what MacBeth's "new path" to God is. A look at the endnotes in the book may provide an answer to that question.
She cites Thomas Merton (panentheistic contemplative Catholic monk), Parker Palmer (New Age sympathizer), and **Tony Jones** (contemplative emergent leader).

In a 2015 Religious News Service article titled "Coloring Books for Grown-ups: Calming—but a Spiritual Practice?," it states:

Alison Gary used to go to church on Sunday mornings, but lately she's embraced a different ritual: staying home and coloring with her 6-year-old daughter, Emerson. . . "Emerson and I color almost every Sunday morning," Gary said, while her husband, a yoga teacher, cooks and listens to music. "I let my mind let go, and I feel more connected to the world, more centered." . . .Gary is not the only grown-up rediscovering the contemplative joys of what once was considered a childish pastime. . . .

Many books feature circular mandalas and Zen patterns, as well as mystical peacocks. . . .While adult coloring is mostly being marketed as a balm for the stress of modern life, many fans, like Gary, also describe it in spiritual terms. Which raises the obvious question: Can coloring seriously be considered a spiritual practice?
Some may scoff, but "it can become more than just coloring, if you want it to," said Sybil MacBeth, author of the 2007 book "Praying in Color" . . ."
MacBeth shares techniques to "incorporate the intention of prayer into coloring," by doodling names of people or events, and intercessory requests such as healing and peace. MacBeth, a "dancer, doodler and former community college math professor" married to a retired Episcopal priest, believes coloring and doodling can be powerful prayer practices—a revelation she stumbled upon by accident. 1

Sacred Circle Mandalas: Conduits to Meditation

Mandala means "circle" in Sanskrit—a sacred circle or container that uses alluring symbols, dazzling colors, and mystical patterns.

Alberta Hutchinson, in the "Mystical Mandala Color Book," defines mandalas this way: "symmetrical geometric designs which are traditionally used for meditative purposes by drawing our eye to the center of the circle." "Little Mandalas" color book calls them "mystical motifs which symbolize the universe, wholeness, and eternity."

And a kids' color book, "My First Mandalas" by Anna Pomaska maintains mandalas are a Far Eastern tradition with "intriguing centers and fascinating focal points."

In summary, "Mandala" from Religionfacts.com says:

"Simply stated, a mandala is a sacred geometric figure that represents the universe. When completed a mandala becomes a sacred area that serves as a receptacle for deities and a collection point of universal forces. By mentally entering a mandala and proceeding to its center, a person is symbolically guided through the cosmos to the essence of reality." 2

Mandalas are a visual tool to take one into a meditative state just as mantras are a vocal tool to lead one into emptying one's mind. Labyrinths are used in much the same manner. As one repeatedly gazes, contemplates, looks upon, stares at the mandala while following its hypnotic patterns, it can have the effect of relaxing the person into an altered state or even a trance.

Speaking of a "meditative state," on December 12, 2015 the Orlando Sentinel had this front-page article: "Adults Find Meditative State Coloring Away Stresses of Life" by Bethany Rogers.

The accompanying photo showed grandmotherly types coloring "Color Me Calm" pages at the Minneola Schoolhouse Library. This was but one of four "Color Me Calm" sessions where ladies gathered, sipping tea, coloring, and listening to a flute tune titled "Morning Stillness.." 3

Shakti Color Book's Goddesses and Mandalas

A look at Ekabhumi C. Ellik's color book should be an awakening to any who are considering mandala coloring. The cover depicts Bhuvaneshvari, the goddess of spaciousness, regent of manifest creation, and universal earth mother.

On the book's Facebook page, you'll see pictures from the book colored by people who post them to the site. One very disturbing post shows a child posing as a goddess while her mom tells how obsessed with the goddesses her child was.

Ellik's reply to this mother was, "I'm so happy to contribute to helping girls recognize their inner divinity." A comment below reads, "Beautiful little goddess, keep that feeling." Another post photo shows a young girl proudly holding up a goddess in a mandala she'd colored. 4

"Yoga Dork's" article:

"Grab Your Crayon's and Say Om: Coloring Art as a Meditative Practice" has an excerpt from Ellik's book. In it, Ellik speaks of the goddesses depicted in the book by saying: The goddesses who appear in The Shakti Color Book encompass the entire spectrum of cosmic phenomena, mirroring our most expansive Self. . .Their mystic diagrams—their mandalas and yantras —have a powerful influence on our awareness when we mediate upon them and visualize them internally.

"Our energy body is repatterned . . . helping us to recognize behaviors that our of alignment with our most expansive nature, which is the Goddess herself." 5
Ellik has also begun a "Shiva Color Book." And Ellik asks readers: "What images, forms of Shiva, related deities, mandalas or yantras should be included?" Ellik also invites all to join him at an "Embrace Your Shakti: A Yoga Coloring Workshop" where they can begin their New Year with some goddess power.
 In an August 2015 comment, Ellik sums up the purpose of his color book when he says: It's an opportunity to introduce sacred art as an intrinsic part of YOGIC practice to a HUGE number of people who may think it's only stretching and feeling calm.
He also notes, ". . . to have readers introduced to this book is a great way to help shift public opinion away from yoga-is-exercise-to-look-and-feel-good and back toward, well, YOGA."
Ellik gives us a truth many undiscerning Christians are not acknowledging about Yoga and mandalas! Think about it!

Mandalas for Adults

It's clear that coloring pre-printed pages is a pastime many adults enjoy. Whether one finds it relaxing or not is up to the individual. Yet the main thrust of marketing color books to adults seems to be the promise to bring calmness or alleviate stress.
The claims made by the designers of mandala color books, however, go far beyond this and straight into the realm of New Age religious practices, as you will see from these few examples—

Steven Vrancken in "Your Introduction of the Healing Powers of Mandala Color Pages" spells out the powers behind the mandala in this quote that says: I awaken to the power of the mandala, A sacred circle of light and energy, A pathway to center—to my center and to the Universal All, A channel for healing body, mind, and spirit." 6

Presbyterian Jungian psychotherapist and art therapist Susanne F. Fincher is the founder of "Creatingmandalas.com." According to Fincher's website, she has led thousands of people to the "spiritual, psychological, and health enhancing dimensions of creating mandalas." Author of four "Coloring Mandalas" books by Shambhala Publishing, Fincher's book, "Coloring Mandalas 3: Circles of the Sacred Feminine" is completely pagan beginning with "Prayer to the Earth Mother."

Inside notes tell the colorist to consider these sacred images holy and to set aside a sacred space to work on them. Doing this will allow one's "harmonious designs" to kick in just as repeating ancient chants will resonate within one in calming and revitalizing ways. An introductory description of the book explains:

"Coloring the circular designs . . . is a relaxing, meditative activity enjoyed by adults and children alike. . . . The mandalas in this book are . . . designed to provide a creative encounter with the Divine as a feminine presence." 7

"The Mandala Lady," Maureen Frank, is a mandala artist and intuitive reader, who does channeled visualization "Mandala Reading Sessions" for customers via Skype or telephone. Maureen relates that during a Reiki session she was told she wasn't into the creative side of her brain and she should get herself a color book. Maureen did. Later, at a New Age bookstore, she came upon mandalas. First, she colored them, but soon she began to create them and then meditate on them. Soon she had "mandala messages" for others. Now, she creates daily, week, monthly, and yearly mandalas as well as a whole line of "color your own" cards, prints, and color books. 8

Mandalas for Kids of All Ages

Mandala coloring books can be purchased by unsuspecting parents and given to children with the admonishment to "play quietly for a while." This is understandable. But Christian parents should be aware that schools, children's clubs, libraries, and various websites will be luring their young ones to use mandala art in ways that can introduce them to Eastern meditation and the occult.

For example, the "Do You Yoga" website tells kids their whole body is a "mandala" with its center being their "belly button." Kids, in a "child's pose," color mandalas with quiet background music. The site advises when a mandala is finished, hang it up and use it for meditation. It suggests one breathe deeply, gaze at the center of the mandala, and let thoughts and emotions come without following them. Then, "slowly dive deeper into the center of the mandala and into the harmony and love it represents." And "Do You Yoga" says kids from five and up can participate.9

"Everyday Mandala for Children" is a series of activity books designed for ages four and up based on "The Shichida Method" that uses mandalas with youngsters that requires them to mentally capture the image of a mandala within seconds, and apply the colors onto an uncolored mandala. The method boasts even a child of two can do it. Its method includes holding a mandala against a plain wall, asking a child to stare at the mandala focusing on its center, and then visualizing it in their mind. Children are told to hold that image there as long as possible. One article suggests you, as an adult, should join in.10

An article from the "Kids Growing Up Psychic" series by psychic Melissa Leath details how she uses "active meditation" or anything that keeps kids focused and calm while making mandalas.   Afterward, kids softly stare at their mandala while trying not to blink. As they breathe in and out, Leath explains, "a shift" comes while colors in the mandala seem to change and move.

At this point, says Leath, kids will feel energy flowing from the mandala. They are then to close their eyes to see an inner vision, and to feel more energy. And so Leath a medium, mentor, and author leads kids into her psychic world. 11
There are many many children's mandala materials available to the public; the bottom line is that the mandala coloring craze is not just an adult coloring book problem, it is being marketed to children and teens.

 Be watchful! Teach your children what these seducing circles really are about!

http://www.relgionfacts.com/mandala

http://www.usatoday.com/story/life/ 2015/12/13/adult-coloring-books-stress /76916842.
http://www.facebook.com/shakticoloringbook.

http://yogadork.com/?s=grab+your+crayons.

https://mandalacoloringmeditation.com/mandala-coloring/ mandala-articles/ about-mandala-coloring-healing.

http://creatingmandalas.com/susanne-f-fincher.
http://themandalalady.com/bio.

http://www.doyouyoga.com/ mandala-coloring-meditation-for-kids-96460.

http://www.homeeducation.sg

Active Meditation for Kids: Creating Your Own Mandala, by Melissa Leath
https://baptistnews.com/ culture/item/30471-adult-coloring-books-emergingas-popular-spiritual-practice.

http://www.bellyofthewhaleministries.net/directors-welcome.

(**NOTE: There is more to this article, which is found at the link below. Ed.).

https://www.lighthousetrailsresearch.com/blog/?p=19924

"Wandering Stars: Contending for the Faith with the New Apostles and Prophets,"

Authored by Keith Gibson, not only explains the methods of this movement from beginning to end, but it also exposes its satanically inspired contribution to the progressive development of the kingdom and religion of the Antichrist.

Gibson's observations need to be heeded: "The majority of the church has not taken seriously the claims of the modern apostles and prophets [that they are] introducing a new paradigm into the Body of Christ. These claims are far more than idle boasts.
 Indeed the paradigm shifts have already begun in many segments of Christianity.
To say that the movement has grown rapidly would be a gross understatement" (p. 10).
The root fallacy of the movement is the view of how one receives communication from God.
 Most if not all of the leaders subscribe to the teaching that the Greek terms rhema and logos found in the Bible describe different ways of hearing from God.

This has been a fundamental teaching among historic religious movements such as The Latter Rain, Manifest Sons of God, and the prosperity-and-healing-promoting Word/Faith teachers.
They conclude that logos refers to the written word and rhema refers to the spoken word.
Although the Bible uses the terms interchangeably, making no distinction, in practice this false teaching elevates what (supposedly) God has spoken to them as equal to or above what is written in the Scriptures.

It goes far beyond someone stating that he "believes" that the Lord has impressed something upon his heart. Gibson comments: "It is far different to claim an impression than it is to loudly pronounce, 'Thus saith the Lord.' The former is the hesitant expression of a thought, something that may or may not be completely true.
The latter is a claim to divine revelation that by definition cannot contain anything but truth and which carries divine authority and must be obeyed."

 Whether implied or declared, Gibson adds, "The words 'Thus saith the Lord' change everything. A higher level of authority is being claimed. One should be extremely careful before one puts words in the mouth of God" (p. 8).
Many do not realize the dire consequences of being seduced by the "hearing from God" teachings. First of all, they completely undermine the objective nature of the Scriptures.

 In other words, when the Word of God is mixed with what some believe they've heard from God, it is difficult to objectively determine what is truly from God. That fundamentally destroys the value of the Bible in the lives of those who buy into the so-called new prophets of God.
God's written word is no longer relied upon as a determiner of truth, especially regarding the new doctrines presented, which those who are "hearing from God" promote in abundance.
Unfortunately, that's fine with such false teachers because their "new thing that God is doing" cannot then be challenged by the "old written words" found in Scripture.

Gibson notes with great concern: "No doctrine is under more regular assault from within the prophetic community than the doctrines relating to the Scriptures" (pp. 67-68).
He adds, "Today's prophets, and consequently their followers as well, are consistently sloppy in their approach to Scripture, frequently ignoring context, history, and grammar." "They can even be seen redefining words when necessary to force verses to fit their preconceived ideas."
The intent of the author of the text is rarely considered.

"The Bible is left to mean whatever the prophets say it means today" (p. 71).

Gibson spells out the tragic consequences of which few of us are aware: "Because these prophetic teachers do not approach God's Word properly, they reach false conclusions." "These false conclusions then support aberrant doctrines and unbiblical practices."
"These unbiblical practices and false doctrines undermine the historic truths of the church and distract Christians from the pure faith and the true work of the ministry" (p. 80).
https://www.thebereancall.org/content/ they-claim-speak-god-part-one

IS YOGA FOR CHRISTIANS?

A SUBTLE AND DANGEROUS SHIFT IN CHRISTIANITY
POSTED BY MARSHA WEST • OCTOBER 16, 2017 • IN OPINION • DISCERNMENT, WOMEN AND THE CHURCH, YOGA, WEST MARSHA • BOOKMARK PERMALINK

"When I penned this piece in 2010, my aim was to inform professing Christians, who had convinced themselves that it's okay to practice "Christian yoga," that it is not okay at all." "At that point yoga, which has its roots in Hinduism, had taken the Christian community by storm, as you will see in my piece, "Christian Yoga? C'mon!
" But the important thing for readers to understand is that pagan practices such as yoga cannot be Christianized, nor should God's people adopt a pagan practice and attach a Christian title to it acceptable to the Christian community. When God says no, He means No! (II Cor 6:14)."

By Marsha West--

Seems everyone's practicing yoga meditation these days. Physicians recommend it to their patients which means it's beneficial...right? Meditation is said to relieve stress, anxiety, hypertension, acne and post-nasal drip, so go for it! Just tighten those abdominal muscles, inhale deeply and chant Maaaaaaaaa all in one breath and your concerns will drift away like a feather floating on the wind...
But what if you're a Christian? Should you practice the same sorts of things as Buddhist, Hindu's and New Agers? Listen to what the Bible says:

"This book of the law shall not depart out of thy mouth, but thou shalt meditate thereon day and night, that thou mayest observe to do according to all that is written therein: for then thou shalt make thy way prosperous, and then thou shalt have good success (Josh.1:8)."

Firstly, meditating day and night does not mean to stay awake for 24 hours a day.
Secondly, Christian meditation is very different from Eastern meditation.

Followers of Jesus Christ are not to sit in the lotus pose in an altered state of consciousness seeking the "God within" like pagans do. The Bible teaches that when Christians meditate our minds are to be fully engaged.
We are never to go into a trance-state. What does meditation involve? "The word 'meditation' in Hebrew means basically to speak or to mutter. When this is done in the heart it is called musing or meditation.

"So meditating on the Word of God day and night means to speak to yourself the Word of God day and night and to speak to yourself about it."

Before you dive into God's Word take a moment to ask the Holy Spirit to illuminate your mind and to reveal truth to you. As you read, stop to ponder what God has spoken through the words on the page. Always, always, always consider the context. In Charles Spurgeon's sermon "Pray Without Ceasing," he says there are four important questions to be asked:

What do these words imply? Secondly, What do they actually mean? Thirdly, How shall we obey them? And, fourthly, Why should WE especially obey them?

Sometimes you need to read a passage over and over...reflect on it...analyze it...and listen while the Holy Spirit speaks truth to you. A word of warning: Listening to God does not require that you "empty" your mind.

This meditative practice, called <u>Lectio divina</u> a.k.a. <u>spiritual formation</u>...the silence...best known as <u>contemplative (centering) prayer (CP) is a growing trend in evangelical churches despite the fact that this sort of prayer ritual comes from teaching associated with Catholic mystics such as Meister Eckhart, Ignatius of Loyola, St. John of the Cross, and St. Teresa of Avila.</u>

(**NOTE: See pp. 365 and 484 which lists two people who preach this. Ed.).

<u>CP was reintroduced by Thomas Merton, Thomas Keating, Henri Nouwen, William Meninger, Basil Pennington and other mystics.</u>

Many in the <u>Emergent Church movement (ECM)</u> are advancing Roman Catholic <u>mysticism</u> as well. Yet they insist on being seen as mainline evangelicals.

<u>ECM</u> has not only introduced aberrant teaching into our churches, it undermines the authority of Scripture. Gary Gilley laments that there has been a shift from infallible Scriptures to "psychological and sociological experts, opinions of the masses, trends of the moment and the philosophy of pragmatism. This shift has been subtle, which has made it all the more dangerous."

Few have bothered to deny the Bible itself, they just misquote it, abuse its meaning, force their opinion on it, and if necessary mistranslate it to give the appearance that the Scriptures are backing their claims.

<u>The affect of all of this Scriptural manipulation is to both erode the authority of God's Word and to give the appearance that what Scripture has to say isn't really important.</u>

It is only a short step from here to a Christian community that no longer has much use for the Bible." (This is eerily similar to the way liberals/progressives treat the U.S. Constitution.) The Body of Christ needs to know who these apostates are. **Rick Warren** for one. **Warren** has been promoting <u>CP</u> in his books for years.

Other important figures are **Richard Foster, Dallas Willard, Brian McLaren, Leonard Sweet, Frank Viola, Jim Wallis, Tony Campolo, Richard Rohr, Rob Bell, Tony Jones, Doug Pagitt, Dan Kimball** and **Shane Claiborne**.

This is just the tip of the iceberg. Listen to why it can be dangerous:

It has the potential to become, and often does become, a pursuit of mystical experience where the goal is to empty and free the mind and empower oneself.

The Christian... uses the Scriptures to pursue the knowledge of God, wisdom, and holiness through the objective meaning of the text with the aim of transforming the mind according to truth. God said His people are destroyed for lack of knowledge (Hosea 4:6), not for lack of mystical, personal encounters with Him.
One should also consider that emptying or freeing the mind can put a person in contact with demons: [T]he dangers inherent in opening our minds and listening for voices should be obvious.

The contemplative pray-ers are so eager to hear something — anything — that they can lose the objectivity needed to discern between God's voice, their own thoughts, and the infiltration of demons into their minds.

Contemplative prayer is almost identical to how the Zen Buddhists meditate.

Following is part of the meditation process, "Just be still and know":

Sit in the lotus pose (cross legged) keeping your spine straight... put your hands on each other in your lap... Now look at your left hand...just look. Aware of the left part of your body... look at the left hand in an empty manner. Just look. Don't let any thought pop up in your mind...look blankly on your left hand and try to feel the left portion of your body...feel the left part...feel...This very process will activate your right brain.
 When the right brain activates, it results in disappearance of thoughts. Your thought will start disappearing...[Slowly after a few sessions of practicing this meditation, you will be able to instantly achieve this state of disappearance of thoughts]

In Buddhism repeating a single word is known as a mantra. Many Buddhists simply murmur "ommmm" repeatedly. When Christians practice CP, a word or phrase from the Bible is repeated. Many believers, especially young people, have been conned into believing that saying "I love Jesus" over and over will get them in contact with God.

The fact of the matter is this approach to drawing close to God is unbiblical.

 Thus it should be eliminated from the serious Christian's approach to and understanding of meditation and prayer. With these practices and beliefs comes a "virtual encyclopedia of theological error," says Gary Gilley.

Many change agents in the Church are "Progressive Christians" now morphing into "social justice Christians" (SJC). Social justice is doublespeak for socialism.
Spreading the social justice gospel is not the good news the Bible speaks of.
SJCs want to mold America into a socialist saturated nanny state. Their aim is to redistribute the wealth. Before you buy into the SJC hype, check your history books.
In every country socialism has been tried it has failed. Socialism takes away people's freedoms and ultimately leads to tyranny.

So why on earth does America want to copy it? <u>SJCs</u> are bent on reinventing, or as **Dan Kimball** puts it "re-imagining" traditional Christianity. <u>Progressives</u> are pushing <u>pluralism</u>. Because....when the Church becomes <u>ecumenical</u> and includes aspects of other religions <u>it will blend nicely into their perception of how the 21st Century is going to be.</u>

(**NOTE: See the videos listed under **Mark Driscoll**. Most of the underlined sentences above are my emphasis, bringing attention to the subtlety of their deceptions. Ed.).

Authentic Christianity will never blend in! Christianity stands alone. All other religions are based on works righteousness (if you're a good person you will ultimately be rewarded). The Bible is very clear that "there is no one righteous, no not one" (Rom 3:10). We are all sinners in need of a Savior. Sin separates us from a holy God.
Christians believe Christ died for our sins and was raised to life for our justification.
We believe we are saved by grace alone, through faith alone, in Christ's righteousness alone.
True Christians are willing to die for the Truth. Are counterfeit Christians willing to die for their truth?

So, where was I?...Oh yes. <u>Progressive</u> Christians are introducing theological error into the Church faster than a starving cheetah chasing down a gazelle.

In "How to Practice Meditative Prayer" "Acts 29" Pastor Winfield Bevins, explains:

"In Hebrew thought, to meditate upon the Scriptures is to quietly <u>repeat</u> them, giving oneself entirely to God, and abandoning outside distractions. The two main things that we are told to meditate on are God's word and God's goodness."
Paul tells us, "Whatever is true, whatever is honorable, whatever is just, whatever is pure, whatever is lovely, whatever is commendable, if there is any excellence, if there is anything worthy of praise, think about these things" (Philippians 4:8).
 Paul was **not** talking about prayer when he said "think about these things." He was saying that we should let our minds dwell on pure thoughts because what we allow into our minds shapes our actions.
Paul finishes his thought in verse 9: "Whatever you have learned or received or heard from me, or seen in me — put it into practice. And the God of peace will be with you."
Do what you have seen me do, says Paul. This is not about finding a quiet place to sit crossed legged and prayerfully meditate — he was telling them to imitate what they have seen in him!

According to Matthew Henry's "Whole Bible Commentary ":

"In these things he proposes himself to them for an example (v. 9): Those things which you have learned, and received, and heard and seen in me, do. ... What they saw in him was the same thing with what they heard from him. He could propose himself as well as his doctrine to their imitation.
 It gives a great force to what we say to others when we can appeal to what they have seen in us. And this is the way to have the God of peace with us-to keep close to our duty to him. The Lord is with us while we are with Him."

Many Christians lead busy lives so they put off spending time with God. In fact, data shows that most believers spend very little time in their Bibles, even though there's a whole lot of prayin' goin' on! People running hither and yon bombard the Lord with bullet prayers. Now, don't get me wrong. Praying umpteen times a day is what believers should do — we are commanded to pray without ceasing. (1 Thess. 5:17)

We are also commanded to abide in Christ: "I am the vine, ye are the branches: He that abideth in me, and I in him, the same bringeth forth much fruit: for without me ye can do nothing" (John 15:5).

If followers of Jesus Christ are to bring forth good fruit they must stay attached to the Vine. The fruit believers bear when they're not abiding in Christ may look ripe and juicy on the outside. But it is rotten fruit!

There is a story in Luke 10:38-42 of two sisters, Mary and Martha, who thought differently about how to serve their Master. When Jesus came to their home Martha stayed in the kitchen preparing food for their guests. She had her own ideas on how to serve Christ. Martha became vexed that Mary was not helping with the meal. Instead she sat at the feet of Jesus to hear his word.

 Martha actually went to Him to complain. Instead of taking her side, Christ publicly rebuked her: "And Jesus answered and said unto her, Martha, Martha, thou art careful and troubled about many things..."

In his commentary Matthew Henry explains the situation:

"He repeated her name, Martha, Martha; he speaks as one in earnest, and deeply concerned for her welfare. Those that are entangled in the cares of this life are not easily disentangled. To them we must call again and again, O earth, earth, earth, hear the word of the Lord." Jesus continues: "But one thing is needful: and Mary hath chosen that good part, which shall not be taken away from her."

Again, Matthew Henry:

"She had justly given the preference to that which best deserved it; for one thing is needful, this one thing that she has done, to give up herself to the guidance of Christ, and receive the law from his mouth. Note, Serious godliness is a needful thing, it is the one thing needful; for nothing without this will do us any real good in this world, and nothing but this will go with us into another world."

Certainly there is nothing wrong with cooking for guests. But what we need to remember is that we are children of God before we are servants of God. Like Mary, we must sit at our Lord's feet. Martha was so busy serving Jesus that she had no time to spend with Him! Have I hit a nerve?

Prayer is intended as praise, confession, thanksgiving, and asking for others. (Phil. 4:4-7). In prayer we find God's love and we will experience peace. Moreover, through prayer we are conformed to God's will. Prayer is not meant to be an esoteric experience, like the contemplatives would have us believe. The Bible does not teach that God's people are to go into a self-induced altered-state of consciousness to commune with Him.

Again, meditating day and night does not mean we are to look for the "God within," as Eastern mystics and occultist do. For the Christian to be involved in any sort of pagan practice is strictly forbidden by God!
This is because God opposes paganism's polytheism and blatant immorality.
There is no getting around the fact that polytheism and immorality are the pagan way.

The Christian who truly wants to please God will do as the psalmist suggests:
"Let the words of my mouth and the meditation of my heart be acceptable in thy sight, O LORD, my strength and my redeemer" (Psalm 19:14).

https://christianresearchnetwork.org/2017/10/16/ a-subtle-and-dangerous-shift-in-christianity/

http://www.freeworldfilmworks.com/ dov-10danger.htm

(**NOTE: A very thorough list of "Who's Who" in false and demonic teaching and preaching. Ed.).

http://www.so4j.com/ false-teachers#list-of-false-teachers

(**NOTE: A fairly comprehensive list of most of the false preachers\teachers. Ed.).

THE AIM AND DESCRIPTION OF THE NEW AGE TAKEOVER:

We know that one of the hallmarks of the NAR (New Apostolic Reformation) movement is taking dominion over seven spheres of life on Earth, in order to activate the reign of Jesus' Kingdom.
 It's called the "Seven Mountain Mandate," in which Christians are to dominate and fix business, government, media, education, the family, religion, and arts and entertainment—

NAR leaders are very methodical about these takeovers, as you can read about in the extra links below. But what fascinates me is the arts and entertainment sphere.
In doing research I stumbled across, quite by accident, a sub ministry of a highly influential group called the International Coalition of Apostolic Leaders, or ICAL for short.

(**NOTE: Since I included an illustration about this topic, I cannot move the information closer to this page, hence the remainder of this page is blank. Ed.).ICAL was brought to America in 2000 by "Apostle" John P. Kelly, who set up shop in Fort Worth, Texas. Kelly was "directed by the Lord" to ask **C. Peter Wagner** to accept the position of Presiding Apostle over the network of apostles.

New Apostolic Reformation is the term **Wagner** gave to this movement that encompasses hundreds of similar apostolic networks around the world, but not everyone uses **Wagner's** exact terminology.
Another common term for the movement is "apostolic and prophetic."

 The late **Wagner** turned the keys back over to Kelly, whose ICAL mission statement reads: "ICAL is designed to connect apostles' wisdom and resources in order that each member can function more strategically, combine their efforts globally, and effectively accelerate the advancement of the Kingdom of God into every sphere of society." (Mission statement).

GLOBAL HARVEST
MINISTRIES

THE KINGDOM OF GOD

GLOBAL APOSTOLIC NETWORK

7-M COALITION

GOVERNMENT
EAGLES VISION
APOSTOLIC TEAM (EVAT)

INTERNATIONAL COALITION
OF APOSTLES (ICA)

WEALTH
ZION APOSTOLIC COUNCIL

THE HAMILTON GROUP (THG)

WARFARE
APOSTOLIC COUNCIL OF
PROPHETIC ELDERS (ACPE)

INTERNATIONAL SOCIETY OF
DELIVERANCE MINISTERS (ISDM)

UNITED STATES GLOBAL APOSTOLIC
PRAYER NETWORK (USGAPN)

TEACHING
WAGNER LEADERSHIP
INSTITUTE (WLI)

APOSTOLIC COUNCIL
FOR EDUCATIONAL
ACCOUNTABILITY (ACEA)

RELIGION   FAMILY   EDUCATION   MEDIA   ARTS & ENTERTAINMENT   GOVERNMENT   BUSINESS

THE 7 MOUNTAINS = THE 7 BASIC MOLDERS OF CULTURE

On its website, you can find out which leaders have been appointed as modern-day "Apostles," who are to rule over all Christians and bring forth utterances of actual fresh words - oracles if you will - of God Almighty Himself.

http://www.piratechristian.com/berean-examiner/ pureflix-a-strategic-apostolic-alliance

(**NOTE: Excellent websites listed below that gives information about almost all of the New Age "prophets." Ed.).

https://walthope.wordpress.com/2014/05/22/ third-wave-false-revivals/

http://www.sermonindex.net/modules/newbb/ viewtopic.php?topic_id=18960&forum=35

(**NOTE: And finally these names are in the Elijah List, provided by the weblink below. Some of them you may have not heard of, but their list is growing exponentially almost every day. Ed.) Here is the link:

https://churchwatchcentral.com/2015/08/27/
guess-who-elijah-list-challenge-the-culprit-in-the-pulpit/

(**NOTE: Another two excellent websites exposing these charlatans for who they really are. Ed.):

http://www.zedekiahlist.com/cgi-bin/ results.pl?&menuid=V&itemid=X

http://www.deceptioninthechurch.com/ fprophets.html

Note to the reader: It is my sincere prayer that the information contained within this book as a reference to the attack on Christianity has been helpful to you.

This book is in no way exhaustive, for every day there is a new—and deceitful enemy that has risen up to continue the attack on God's Word.

INDEX OF NAMES, WITH PAGE NUMBERS:

Jakes, T.D.	52,109,150,192,194,245,283,300,348, 367,398,422
Jansen, Jeff	194,195,196,197,198
Jenkins, LeRoy	198,199,200
Jeremiah, Dr. David	200,201
"Jesus Culture"	202,209,367,377,378,423,424
Jobes, Kari	166,202,203,304,205
Johnson, Bill	3,15,27,45,46,56,77,87,204,205, 206,207,208,209,211,239,286,348, 362,384,385,387,404, 411,423,424,449
Johnson, Ian	209
Johnson, Jenn	209,210
Jones-Pothier, Kim	210,211
Jones, Robert (Bob)	33,42,49,57,211,212,218,227,356,378
Jones, Tony	106,112,114,212,213,214,215,273, 484,493
Jordan, Bernard	215
Jordan, Manasseh	215
Joshua, T.B.	216,217,315
Joubert, Stephan	217
Joyner, Rick	33,57,87,187,192,211,217,356
Juster, Daniel	48,49,50,217,218,219,364
Kelsey, Morton	219,220,221,251,393,396,397,398
Kenyon, E.W.	67,68,159,160,221
Kerr, Kat	222,223,224

The End

www.ingramcontent.com/pod-product-compliance
Lightning Source LLC
Chambersburg PA
CBHW081425270326

41932CB00019B/3103